Lecture Notes in Computer Science

Lecture Notes in Artificial Intelligence   **15552**

Founding Editor

Jörg Siekmann

Series Editors

Randy Goebel, *University of Alberta, Edmonton, Canada*
Wolfgang Wahlster, *DFKI, Berlin, Germany*
Zhi-Hua Zhou, *Nanjing University, Nanjing, China*

The series Lecture Notes in Artificial Intelligence (LNAI) was established in 1988 as a topical subseries of LNCS devoted to artificial intelligence.

The series publishes state-of-the-art research results at a high level. As with the LNCS mother series, the mission of the series is to serve the international R & D community by providing an invaluable service, mainly focused on the publication of conference and workshop proceedings and postproceedings.

Peng Jin · Qi Su · Jia-Fei Hong

Editors

Chinese Lexical Semantics

25th Workshop, CLSW 2024
Xiamen, China, May 31 – June 2, 2024
Revised Selected Papers, Part I

Springer

Editors
Peng Jin (ID)
Leshan Normal University
Leshan, China

Qi Su (ID)
Peking University
Beijing, China

Jia-Fei Hong
Taiwan Normal University
Taipei, Taiwan

ISSN 0302-9743 ISSN 1611-3349 (electronic)
Lecture Notes in Artificial Intelligence
ISBN 978-981-96-3508-5 ISBN 978-981-96-3509-2 (eBook)
https://doi.org/10.1007/978-981-96-3509-2

LNCS Sublibrary: SL7 – Artificial Intelligence

This Springer imprint is published by the registered company Springer Nature Singapore Pte Ltd.
The registered company address is: 152 Beach Road, #21-01/04 Gateway East, Singapore 189721, Singapore

If disposing of this product, please recycle the paper.

Preface

The 2024 Chinese Lexical Semantics Workshop (CLSW 2024) was the 25th annual meeting and organized by Tan Kah Kee College, Xiamen University (XMU) on 31st May to 2 June. The Chinese Lexical Semantics Workshop (CLSW) is well known for both linguists and computer science academics reporting and discussing their thoughts. Theoretical and applied linguistics, computational linguistics, information processing, and computational lexicography are some of its topics. CLSW serves as one of the most prominent gatherings in Asia for Chinese Lexical Semantics, having a great impact on as well as promoting academic research and application development in those topics.

During this conference, the conference chair Xinchu Su (XMU) invited four keynote speakers: Jianshe Zhou (Capital Normal University), Jia-Fei Hong (National Taiwan Normal University), Chu-Ren Huang (Hong Kong Polytechnic University), and Dahu Baiyila (Inner Mongolia University). These keynote presentations added more academic highlights to the conference. We would like to acknowledge the chairs of the Organization Committee: Jingjing Du (XMU) and Haidao Sun (XMU). Thanks should also be given to the student volunteers of Tan Kah Kee College, Xiamen University for their tremendous contribution to this event.

We received a total of 226 paper submissions for this conference. The review work was done using the Microsoft CMT3 system, with a double-blind review process. Each paper was reviewed by 3 reviewers. Scores were given for three major aspects: (1) the Impact of the work on society and the research domain. (2) The technical correctness of the work, as supported by data and other proof. (3) The clarity of the presentation, meaning whether the paper clearly describes the work.

The review scores were further evaluated by 3 program chairs, and decisions were made based on the review scores and the discussions among program chairs when disputes arose among reviewers. After rigorous evaluation and selection, we arranged 143 paper presentations, including 90 oral presentations and 53 poster presentations, covering a wide range of research topics in Chinese lexical semantics. Furthermore, we re-reviewed the accepted papers and selected 64 to be published in these volumes. We appreciate the time and effort put forth by the entire Program Committee in order to have the submitted papers properly evaluated. We are grateful for the hard work and contributions of all the authors.

December 2024

Peng Jin
Qi Su
Jia-Fei Hong

Organization

Conference Chair

Su, Xinchun   Xiamen University Tan Kah Kee College, China

Advisory Committee Chairs

Cheng, Chin-Chuan   Taiwan Normal University, Taiwan
T'sou, Ka Yin Benjamin   Education University of Hong Kong, China

Program Committee Chairs

Hong, Jia-Fei   Taiwan Normal University, Taiwan
Jin, Peng   Leshan Normal University, China
Su, Qi   Peking University, China

Organizing Chairs

Du, Jingjing   Xiamen University Tan Kah Kee College, China
Sun, Haidao   Xiamen University Tan Kah Kee College, China

Program Committee Members

Baiyila, Dahu   Inner Mongolia University, China
Chang, Yu-Yun   Taiwan Chengchi University, Taiwan
Chen, Sung-Lin   Taiwan Cheng Kung University, Taiwan
Chyu, Shih-Wen   Taiwan Normal University, Taiwan
Dong, Minghui   Institute for Infocomm Research, A*STAR,
                                 Singapore
Dong, Sicong   Harbin Institute of Technology, Shenzhen, China
Du, Jingjing   Xiamen University Tan Kah Kee College, China
Feng, Wenhe   Guangdong University of Foreign Studies, China
Gong, Shu-Ping   Taiwan Chiayi University, Taiwan

Guo, Chunjie	Nanjing University of Aeronautics and Astronautics, China
Han, Yingjie	Zhengzhou University, China
He, Tianqi	Central South University, China
Hou, Renkui	Guangzhou University, China
Hsiao, Huichen S.	Taiwan Normal University, Taiwan
Hsu, Yu-Yin	Hong Kong Polytechnic University, China
Jia, Yuxiang	Zhengzhou University, China
Jiang, Menghan	Shenzhen MSU-BIT University, China
Ke, Yonghong	Beijing Normal University, China
Lee, Lung-Hao	Yang Ming Chiao Tung University, Taiwan
Li, Bin	Nanjing Normal University, China
Li, An	Shandong University, China
Lin, Chih-Kai	Taiwan University of Science and Technology, Taiwan
Lin, Jingxia	Nanyang Technological University, Singapore
Liu, Hongchao	Shandong University, China
Lu, Chiarung	Taiwan University, Taiwan
Lyu, Guoyan	Beijing Information Science and Technology University, China
Peng, Dezhong	Sichuan University, China
Qiu, Bing	Tsinghua University, China
Qu, Weiguang	Nanjing Normal University, China
Teo, Ming Chew	Virginia Tech, USA

Publication Committee

Hong, Jia-Fei	Taiwan Normal University, Taiwan
Su, Qi	Peking University, China
Tang, Xuri	Huazhong University of Science and Technology, China

Contents – Part I

Lexical Semantics

Contents – Part II

Computational Linguistics and Natural Language Processing

Corpus Linguistics and Language Resources

General Linguistics

Lexical Semantics

Exploring Semantic Variations
of Happiness-Denoting Near-Synonyms
with Behavioral Profiles

Zhuo Zhang[(⊠)] [iD] and Meichun Liu[iD]

Department of Linguistics and Translation, City University of Hong Kong, Tat Chee Avenue,
Kowloon, Hong Kong, China
jessy.zh@my.cityu.edu.hk

Abstract. This paper uses a refined behavior profile approach to explore a set of morphologically related Chinese near-synonyms. Most behavior profile studies in lexical semantics rely on manual annotation. We illustrate a modified approach with automatic annotation in a case study differentiating seven Chinese happiness-denoting near-synonyms. Four types of sentential features are analyzed: collocational features, syntactic features, dependency relations, and semantic frames of the logic predicates. Fifty-five contextual variables were annotated automatically by identifying the top n-grams and the results of part-of-speech tagging, dependency parsing, and named-entity recognition. The results show that the seven near-synonyms fall into four clusters of linguistic resemblance, fine-tuning previous research findings in line with linguistic theories. Methodologically, this study modifies the behavioral profile approach by introducing systematic rule-based annotation, position-based collocation variables, and a co-occurrence table of relative frequency and dimension reduction techniques in a less labor-intensive and time-consuming manner that is empirically and applicationally feasible.

Keywords: unsupervised behavioral profiles · Chinese happiness-denoting near-synonyms · dimension reduction

1 Introduction

Happiness-denoting near-synonyms (HNs) share similar syntactic or frame-based constructional behaviors with other emotion predicates expressing various feelings [1, 2]. Chinese HNs express similar feelings pertaining to happiness but display different semantic profiles and usage patterns. Differentiating their subtle semantic distinctions and usage patterns can offer valuable insights into the linguistic inventory of emotion verbs and draw implications on sentiment analysis in natural language processing. Tsai et al. [3] first discussed the grammatical and collocational differences between two Chinese HNs: *gaoxing* and *kuaile*. Chang et al. [1] further extended the study to other categories of emotion verbs based on corpus distributional variances of grammatical features, with a morphological account of verbal compounds. Type-A words represent manner-verb (MV) compounds denoting a change of state, such as *gaoxing* and *kaixin*, while Type-B words represent verb-verb (VV) compounds denoting a homogeneous state, such as *kuaile, yukuai, xiyue, huanle, huanxi*, and *kuaihuo*. This study relied largely on a univariate analysis of grammatical functions and ignored the interaction of variables. Wang and Huang [4] elaborated on the usage variances between *gaoxing* and *yukuai* from a lexicographical perspective and concluded that *gaoxing* is a typical Type-A member, whereas *yukuai* is Type B, similar to *kuaile*. They also pointed out that studies on Chinese HNs are currently far from sufficient, as textbooks and dictionaries fail to differentiate their semantic peculiarities [4]. Along with the underrepresented semantic distinctions, Type-B words exhibit subtle inter-group variance that has largely been ignored by previous works, probably due to the difficulty in analyzing complex distributional data without suitable quantitative approaches.

To address these issues, this study adopts the emerging statistical techniques of multivariate analysis to determine if there is a finer categorization of Chinese HNs and to discover the statistically significant variables (contextual features) that may influence the formation of HN clusters in relation to the semantic and usage variations of the seven HNs. To this end, the behavioral profile (BP) approach [5–8] was fine-tuned to better present the multivariate interactions of variables. The semantics of a word is reflected by its company [9] and associated with lexical collocations and syntactic structures [10, 11]. The idea of a BP approach is to treat these collocational and syntactic features as variables by converting them into a frequency-based occurrence table and to utilize statistical techniques to analyze such distributional profiles. Compared with traditional manual annotation and intuitive analysis, this approach is considered "the most detailed method" for analyzing the distributional preferences of lexical items [12] and has been proven effective in differentiating near-synonyms in various studies [13, 14]. Methodologically, the BP approach is refined to better present the subtle distinctions of HNs by introducing the positions of collocated words into the variable set, adopting rule-based annotations, and generating a co-occurrence table based on relative frequency. Principal component analysis (PCA) was also adopted to reduce the dimensions of interrelated variables and prevent giving too much weight to the interrelated variables. The reduced dimensions were then utilized as the input to the hierarchical clustering on principal components (HCPC), a k-mean consolidated hierarchical clustering algorithm, and this yields HNs' final clustering solutions. The present study can thus fully present the characteristics of HNs as well as boost the methodological advancement of the BP method and facilitate the utilization of automatic annotation.

The remainder of this paper is organized as follows. Section 2 presents the materials and methods used in this study. Section 3 analyzes the principal dimensions, provides cluster solutions with statistically significant variables, and discusses the limitations and implications for future studies. The final section concludes the paper.

2   Materials and Methods

This section presents the methodological design, including materials, variable selection and annotation, the generation of a co-occurrence table, and the statistical models used in this study, namely, PCA and HCPC.

2.1 Materials

The Gigaword 2.0 Mandarin simplified news corpus was accessed on January 26, 2022, via the Sketch Engine, a corpus management tool [15]. HNs that refer to the notion of happiness or joy in a clear sense were identified. Two criteria were applied to the selection: (1) the HN should mainly denote the notion of happiness or joy, not other affective states (e.g., *xingfen* 兴奋 "excited" was excluded.); (2) the HN should be frequently used in the corpus. Seven high-frequency HNs were selected, all of them having over 1000 occurrences in the corpus. Infrequent HNs, such as *huanxi* (欢喜) "merry" (occurrences < 300) were excluded. The seven HNs included in this study are: *kuaile* (快乐) "happy," *yukuai* (愉快) "delightful," *xiyue* (喜悦) "joyful," *huanle* (欢乐) "cheerful," *gaoxing* (高兴) "pleased," *kaixin* (开心) "light-hearted," and *huankuai* (欢快) "joyous." A balanced sample of HNs was obtained by randomly selecting 1000 sentences with each HN for use as the key data for analysis. Below are some simplified examples of the typical uses of the HNs:

(i) as a predicate: *wo hen gaoxing/kuaile* "I am glad/happy."
(ii) as a prenominal modifier: *kaixin de yitian/xiyue de xinqing* "a happy day/joyful mood"
(iii) as a preverbal adverb: *gaoxing/yukuai de chang-ge* "happily/joyfully sing songs"
(iv) as a postverbal adverb: *chang de hen gaoxing/yukuai* "sing happily/joyfully"
(v) nominalized use: *henduo kuaile/xiyue* "a lot of happiness/joy"

2.2 Selection of Variables and Data Annotation

As a preliminary analysis of word collocation, the top bigrams and trigrams were identified to present the words frequently found before and after the HNs. The chosen variables

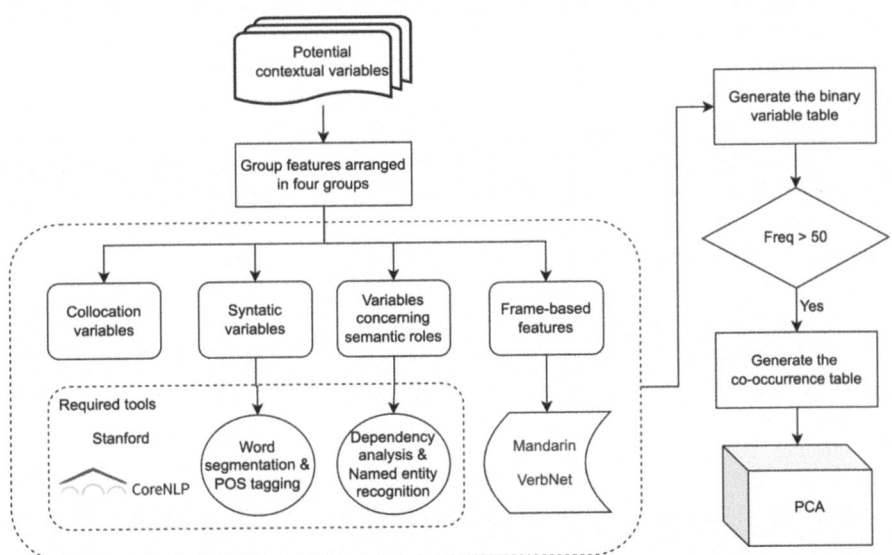

Fig. 1. Data annotation and generation of the co-occurrence table.

were grouped into four categories in terms of collocational behaviors, syntactic features, dependency relations, and semantic frames of the logic predicate.

The annotation steps are summarized in Fig. 1. The first group of variables is concerned with the top-ranked words next to the HNs and the co-occurrence of typical words next to an HN in different contexts. This group also contains grammatical collocations with an HN in a sentence clip, such as aspectual makers and constructional markers of three relevant syntactic forms: exclamations, causative constructions, and juxtapositions in a sentence clip.[1] The second group relies on treebank-specific POS (XPOS) tags via the Stanford CoreNLP toolkit [16]. The third group focuses on a dependency analysis and requires variables of the subject(s) and root of the sentence. A dependency analysis was conducted using a Chinese neural-network dependency parser [17] via the toolkit. Moreover, to differentiate human subjects from others, a refined named-entity recognition (NER) model was added to tag occupations, personal names and collective nouns referring to people. The last group keeps track of the semantic frames of the first verbs after the HNs, with reference to Mandarin VerbNet,[2] a frame-based lexical semantic database.

The annotation of variables is fully rule-based, and we reviewed the tags carefully but did not manually corrected any of the data, because this may bring the problems of consistency and reliability [18]. However, if an excessive number of wrong annotations were generated for a certain variable, it would be abandoned to ensure the quality of the annotation.

2.3 Generation of a Co-occurrence Table

The use of a typical occurrence table was no longer suitable due to the sparsity of a single variable among the 1000 sentences of each HN. As a word can be characterized by its company in a sentence [9], the company it keeps can, in turn, reflect the usage of the word. These relationships are usually shown in a co-occurrence table to measure the associations between words [19]. In the current study, we used a co-occurrence table based on relative frequency (see Table 1). The preference for one HN over another under certain variable conditions can reflect the variances of the HNs. Therefore, the co-occurrence table was generated based on the extent to which a word was preferred over another when a variable condition was met. The total distribution of all individual HNs was generated for each variable. In other words, HNs with similar usages/meanings shared similar frequencies in the variable conditions in the sample.

---

[1] The term "sentence clip" here refers to the section that contains the target HN but can no longer be segmented by punctuation, such as commas and semicolons. The section can be a full sentence, clause, or phrase. Chinese sentences, especially in the news, can be long and complicated, and some parts of a sentence may not be directly connected to the usage patterns of HNs. To better evaluate the performance of the HNs, we examined the co-occurrence features in a sentence clip as a basic unit of measure.

[2] Mandarin VerbNet (2021), semantic frames of the first verb after the HNs, http://ct001.cityu. edu.hk/home (Accessed July 15, 2021).

Table 1. Co-occurrence table based on the relative frequency of variables

HN	Variable A	Variable B
HN1	a1/(a1 + a2 + a3)	b1/(b1 + b2 + a3)
HN2	a2/(a1 + a2 + a3)	b2/(b1 + b2 + a3)
HN3	a3/(a1 + a2 + a3)	b2/(b1 + b2 + a3)

2.4 Hierarchical Clustering on Principal Components

Two related statistical methods, PAC and HCPC, were chosen for the analysis. Linguistic cues in a sentence can be interrelated based on the distribution hypothesis. Therefore, a potential problem is that certain variables can be correlated with each other. When two correlated variables are both used in the cluster analysis, their influence may be over-stressed, thereby affecting the proper interpretations of variable weighting and leading to potentially inaccurate results. Therefore, this study introduces PCA to address the potential problem of collinearity or multicollinearity [20] so that we can include any potential variables, including the position-based variables based on the top bigrams and trigrams. The idea is to reduce the total number of intercorrelated continuous variables while retaining the most distinctive information by transforming correlated variables into fewer uncorrelated components/dimensions. A typical follow-up statistical method for PCA is HCPC, which takes principal components as the input. HCPC combines hierarchical clustering, tree partitioning, and a k-means clustering algorithm. It can be used to cluster high-dimensional data with a more stable and balanced result [21].

The relevant functions were achieved through the R package FactoMineR [22] and Factoextra [23]. The current study retained all dimensions to avoid a potential loss of information. Factor maps of variables for individual HNs were plotted, and statistically significant variables ($p < 0.05$) in the top two dimensions were also provided for reference. Using the PCA dimensions as the input, the HCPC algorithm was conducted with default parameters (distance = Euclidean, method = Ward, nb.clust = −1), automatically suggesting the best cluster solutions by distance.

In sum, this section introduced how a modified BP approach was adopted and applied to a case study on HNs, with a detailed introduction of the corpus, the samples, choice of HNs, variable selection and annotation, generation of a co-occurrence table, and the application of PCA and HCPC as statistical techniques.

3   Results and Discusssion

This section presents the results and interpretations of the results, with discussions of the limitations, significance, applications, and implications of the fine-tuned BP approach adopted in this study.

3.1 Principal Components Analysis

After conducting the PCA, 55 variables were reduced to six principal components characterized in six dimensions with eigenvalues, variance, and cumulative variance (see

Table 2). The eigenvalue indicates the total variance that a component can explain with values that positively correspond to correlations between a dimension and the variables [24]. Components or dimensions with eigenvalues greater than 1 were maintained according to the Kaiser criterion [25]. Therefore, we retained all six dimensions in this study.

Table 2. The eigenvalue and variance of the PCA dimensions

Dimension	Eigenvalue	Variance (%)	(%)
Dim. 1	24.1274	43.8680	43.8680
Dim. 2	13.5475	24.6319	68.4999
Dim. 3	5.9429	10.8053	79.3052
Dim. 4	5.6345	10.2445	89.5497
Dim. 5	3.3013	6.0024	95.5521
Dim. 6	2.4464	4.4479	100.0000

The analysis of features focused on the first two dimensions, with a total variance of approximately 68.50%. The variable factor map (see Fig. 2), displayed in a circle, presents variables as vectors radiating away from the origin. The angles between vectors and the x-axis or y-axis suggest a correlation with the respective dimensions. Vectors pointing in the same or opposite directions indicate a correlation between variables. The length of the vectors (or colors) represents the relative variance of a variable captured in a two-dimensional plane, and a longer length (closer to red) suggests a higher contribution to the variance. Most variables are in yellow and orange, which shows the effectiveness

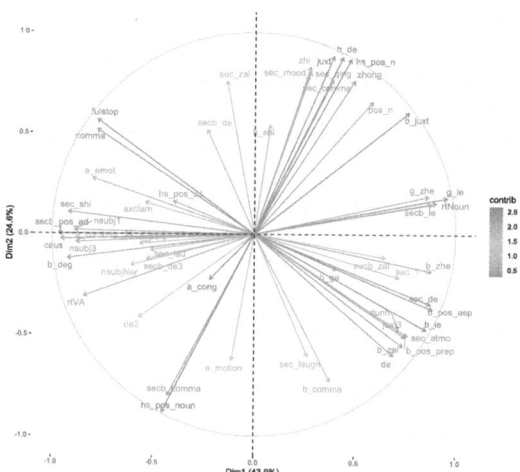

Fig. 2. Variables factor map of the principal component analysis (top two dimensions) (Color figure online).

of the variable set. Some variable arrows are close to or coincide with others, which proves the need to conduct dimension reductions among the variable sets. The underlying mechanisms of how collocations or syntactic patterns may influence HN are still unclear, and interactions among variables are common.

To examine the relative distance of the HNs in the plane, we put the HN individuals (or observations) and variables in a biplot (see Fig. 3). Five out of seven HNs, namely, *xiyue, huankuai, gaoxing, huanle,* and *kaixin,* were better presented in Dimensions 1 and 2 with a higher cosine value than the other two HNs, *yukuai* and *kuaile,* as indicated by the sizes and colors of the individual points. As the top two dimensions occupy almost 70% of the cumulative variance, the biplot may reflect a preliminary formation of four clusters: (1) *gaoxing* and *kaixin,* (2) *kuaile* and *yukuai,* (3) *xiyue,* and (4) *huanle* and *huankuai.* We also found that *kuaile* and *yukuai* in Cluster 2 are underrepresented in Dimensions 1 and 2 when compared with other HNs, as indicated in the first and fourth quadrants (small dots in blue), respectively. Therefore, they are expected to join the same cluster despite being in different quadrants.

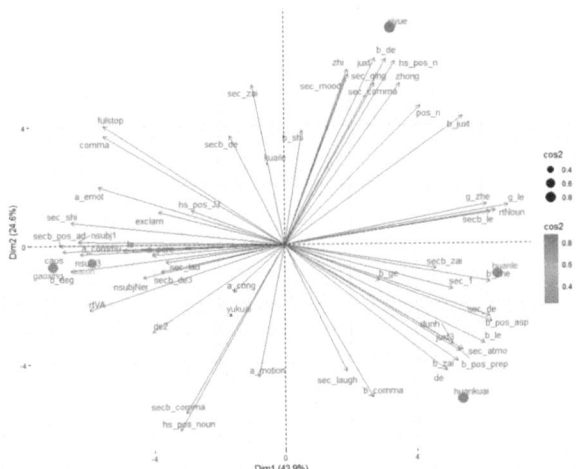

Fig. 3. Biplot of variables and HN individuals (Color figure online).

We then performed dimension descriptions to find the most representative variables. Among all variables, the top two dimensions can represent 29 of 55 with statistical significance. These variables characterize crucial uses of HNs. For example, one of the most represented variables in Dimension 1 is E2 (the uses of causative construction) with a sample instance of *shi laoren kaixin* "to make the elderly happy, to delight the elderly". The causative construction denotes a causative relation, representing a caused effect in the use of Chinese HNs. Cluster 1 HNs, *kaixin* and *gaoxing,* take a dominant lead over other HNs in the causative use. The variables H1 and H2 (the subject as first- or third-person pronoun) also present a similar trend, as distinct features for Cluster 1. Another distinctive variable is G2 rtNoun (root as a noun), which shows a preference for *xiyue, kuaile, and huanle* over other HNs. If the root is a noun, the HN is very likely to be a modifier in a nominative or prepositional phrase as the governor of the phrase, as in *huanle DE yinyue* "joyous music" or *zai yukuai de qifen zhon* "in a joyful atmosphere." These examples show that the fine-grained variables can display a cluster-based trend, which can be attributed to the lexical semantic differences of the HNs.

3.2 Hierarchical Clustering on Principal Components

After conducting HCPC, we obtained four clusters, as shown in Fig. 4(A and B), consistent with the preliminary hypothesis of the biplot in Fig. 3. Figure 4(A) and 4(B) are different versions of representing the same cluster solutions. In Fig. 4(A), the tree-like

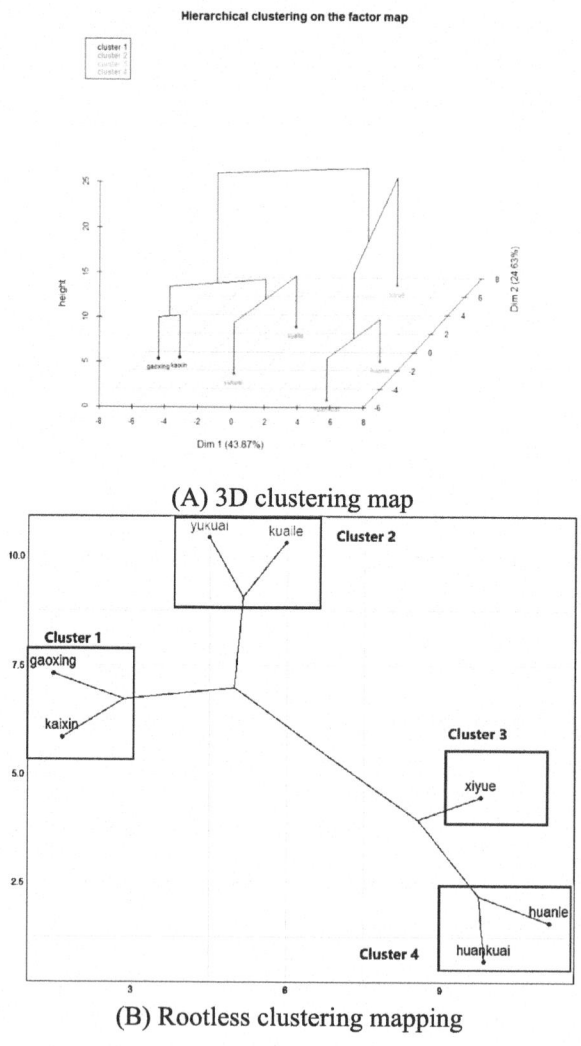

(A) 3D clustering map

(B) Rootless clustering mapping

Fig. 4. Hierarchical clustering on the factor map. (Parameters: distance = Euclidean; method = Ward; nb.clust = − 1.)

chart suggests the sequence of merges of clusters, and the colors represent the consolidated clustering solution of k-means (labeled Clusters 1–4, from left to right). To better present the pairwise distinctions of clusters, a grayscale rootless phylogenetic tree is displayed in Fig. 4(B), in which the four rectangles identify the clustering solutions, as indicated in Fig. 4(A), and the pairwise distance suggests the degree of distinction among different HNs. As illustrated in Fig. 4(B), Cluster 1 (with *gaoxing* and *kaixin*), located at the top, is distinctively different from Cluster 4 (with *kuaikuai* and *huanle*) and Cluster 3 (with *xiyue*) in the bottom right. Located far away from Cluster 1 (*gaoxing* and *kaixin*), *xiyue* in the top-right corner is separated from the other clusters and forms a one-member cluster by itself (Cluster 3).

In general, the clustering results are consistent with findings in previous analytical works, such as Tsai et al. [3] and Chang et al. [1], in that *gaoxing* and *kuaile* are distinctively different in meaning and use. The current study offers more empirical evidence of a finer classification of other HNs based on salient contextual features. This study also supports the finding that *gaoxing* and *yukuai* should belong to different groups with clear statistical justifications [4]. The general distributions of the chosen variables also support the clustering solution associated with different usage patterns. Our analysis of the results shows that among the four clusters, Cluster 1, *gaoxing* and *kaixin*, is characterized by predicative use, frequent collocation with degree markers, and first-person pronouns or human subjects. They also tend to occur as preverbal adverbs with communication verbs in the typical pattern "Experiencer-SBJ + HN + DE_2 + Communication verb + Content." Within the group, *gaoxing*, compared with *kaixin*, is more likely to appear as a postverbal complement in the pattern "Verb + DE_3 + Degree + HN" and collocate with Perception verbs. In contrast, *kaixin* tends to appear more often in exclamatory sentences.

In Cluster 2, *kuaile* and *yukuai* are frequently used as prenominal modifiers to describe nominal states in the typical construction "HN + DE_1 + Noun" (e.g., *kuaile DE rizi* "happy days," *yukuai de jieri* "happy festivals," and *yukai DE hezuo* "happy cooperation"). Between the two HNs, *yukuai* is used more often to modify verbs in the construction of "*yukuai* + DE_2 + VP," with the preferred verbs *jieshou* "accept," *huiyi* "recollect," and *huigu* "retrospect." With the transitive verb *jieshou* "accept," a predominant object is *yaoqing* "invitation," an eventive nominal pertaining to time. However, *kuaile* tends to encode blessings or good wishes associated with festivals or special occasions in the form of "festival name + *kuaile*," such as *chunjie kuaile* "Happy Spring Festival."

The single HN, *xiyue* in Cluster 3, is the most nominalized member among the seven HNs, occurring predominantly in prepositional constructions such as "*zai* + HN + *zhong*/*zhizhong*" "in the midst of" (e.g., *zai xiyue zhong* "in the midst of joy"). It is also used as a noun with a prenominal DE-modifier (e.g., *yangyi zhe fengshou de xiyue* "filled with the happiness of harvest"). When used as a modifier, *xiyue* attracts abstract nouns such as *xinqing* "mood" or *qing* "feeling." It also occurs in conjoined juxtaposition with other abstract nouns, such as *xiyue he zi-hao* "joy and self-pride."

In Cluster 4, *huanle* and *huankuai* are both frequently used with the perfective aspect marker *LE* in a nominative or prepositional phrase that is non-predicative (*zài huānkuài de gēwǔ shēng zhōng* "with a <u>cheerful</u> song and dance") or in a juxtaposed structure marked by "、" (欢快、自信的笑容 "happy and confident laugh."). The two HNs are the least frequent choice to collocate with a first-person pronoun subject. When used as modifiers, they often collocate with the situation-denoting noun *qifen* "atmosphere/situation." Specifically, *huankuai* prefers the modifier use in the form "*huankuai + DE + Noun*," where the noun usually refers to music, sounds, or sounding entities, such as *yuequ* "music," *gewu* "song-dance," *wubu* "dance steps," and *wudao* "dances." In contrast, *huanle* is more flexible in modifying various types of nouns, ranging from natural entities (*haiyang* "ocean" and *qifen* "atmosphere") to holidays (*jieri* "festival"), humans (*renqun* "crowds of people"), and sounds (*xiaosheng* "laughter"). In addition, *huanle* often collocates with another emotion predicate, such as *xianghe* "peaceful," which sets *huanle* apart from other HNs.

It is clear that the four clusters display different usage patterns and collocational associations in relation to their lexical semantic distinctions.

3.3 Further Analysis of the Cluster-Based Form-Meaning Mapping Relations

As emotional predicates, the HNs represent typical emotions that are part of the bodily experiences crucial for human cognitive development [26, 27]. To interpret the clustering solutions from a cognitive perspective, we may further analyze the HN clusters from two perspectives: (1) whether the HN is experiencer-denoting or entity-denoting, and (2) whether the HN presents a rather stable or a changeable state. Figure 5 presents the cluster-based form-meaning mapping relations and the linguistic tendencies revealed by distinct usage-based features.

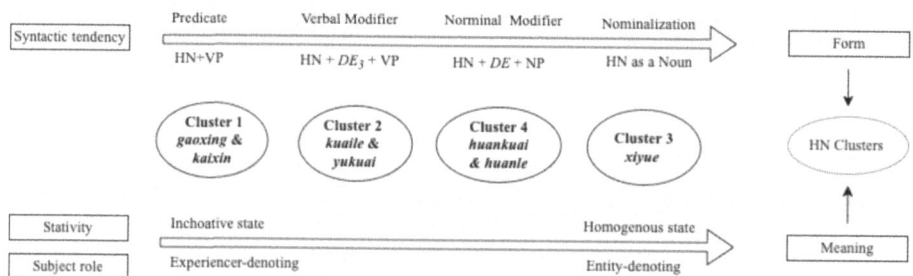

Fig. 5. Form-meaning mapping of the HN clusters

In terms of form-meaning mapping relations, there appears to be a cluster-based cline from verbal to nominal uses, mapped with a semantic cline from experiencer-denoting to entity-denoting. In Fig. 5, the top rows represent usage forms, with arrows indicating frequency-based tendencies. From left to right, the specific values of different features correspond to the clusters in vertical alignment. For example, in the case of HN as a preverbal modifier in the construction of "HN + DE_3 + VP," it is mostly used in Cluster 2, followed by Cluster 1. Based on the syntactic positions and functions of HNs, Cluster 1 is featured by predicative use, Cluster 2 by preverbal adverbial use, Cluster 4 by prenominal modifier use, and Cluster 3 by nominalization. It shows that the cline from verbal predicate to verbal/nominal modifier, and to nominal use is mapped with the cline from Cluster 1 to Clusters 2 and 4, and then to Cluster 3. Another cluster-based variation is observed in the subject types in that Cluster 1 attracts first-person pronouns and human subjects, followed by Cluster 2; Clusters 3 and 4 tend not to take a first-person pronoun as the subject, although it is grammatically acceptable. However, the clusters can be distinguished by the tendency to denote a human experiencer (Clusters 1 and 2) or entity-stimulus (Clusters 3 and 4). Examples (1)–(2) illustrate experiencer-oriented uses of the HNs, whether predicative or adverbial, while examples (3)–(4) illustrate entity-oriented uses, whether predicative or modificational. Experiencer-oriented uses pertain to the emotional state sensed by a human experiencer, while entity-oriented uses pertain to the depiction of a non-human entity as a stimulus.

(1) *kaixin* from Cluster 1: Predicative use with Experiencer-subject

村民	可	开心	了	。
cūn-mín	*kě*	*kāi-xīn*	*le*	.
Villagers	very	Happy	LE	.

"The villagers become very happy."

(2) *yukuai* from Cluster 2: preverbal adverb with Experiencer-subject

细川首相		愉快	地	回忆	了	……
xì-chuān shǒu-xiàng	*hái*	*yúkuài*	*de*	*huí-yì*	*le*	…
Premier Xichuan	also	happily	DE$_2$	recollected	LE	…

"Premier Xichuan happily recollected …."

(3) *huankuai* from Cluster 3: predicative use with Entity-stimulus

整	台	演出	轻松	欢快	。
zhěng	*tái*	*yǎn-chū*	*qīng-sōng*	*huān-kuài*	.
whole	classifier	show	relaxing	joyous	.

"The whole show is relaxing and cheerful."

(4) *xiyue* from Cluster 4: nominal use denoting Entity-stimulus

成功	的	喜悦	鼓舞	了	他	。
chéng-gōng	*de*	*xǐyuè*	*gǔ-wǔ*	*le*	*tā*	.
success	DE	happiness	encourage	LE	him	.

"The joy of success encouraged him."

With regard to stativity, the clusters differ in denoting a relatively changeable or homogeneous state. According to Chang et al. [1], the semantic distinction of emotional predicates is correlated with morphological distinction. Cluster-1 HNs, *kaixin* and *gaoxing*, are morphologically non-VV compounds that tend to denote a change of state, while HNs in Clusters 2 and 3 are mostly VV compounds that tend to denote a homogenous state [1]. Example (3) shows the verbal, inchoative use of *kaixin* compatible with the clause-final aspectual use of LE in marking a change of state. In contrast, example (5) shows the nominal use of *xiyue* (Cluster 3), denoting a homogeneous emotion as a temporally stable entity. Other HNs from Clusters 2 and 3 can also be used as nouns, e.g., following a prepositional marker, as in *chenjin zai kuaile/huanle zhi zhong* "indulged in happiness." The form-function mapping relations do not go against the frequency-based clustering solution but reflect the semantic selection of subject types [26, 27]. It is clear that based on the statistically significant formal and functional distinctions, the four-way clustering solution is not only in line with previous findings, but also strengthens and refines the distinctions with more convincing evidence. The clustering shows a cline of form-meaning mapping relations that are analytically interesting and revealing.

3.4 Significance, Limitations, and Implications

This study achieved its research goals of detecting the semantic clustering of 'happy'-denoting near synonyms in Mandarin by adjusting the BP approach used in previous studies [5, 6, 8, 14]. Specifically, seven happiness-denoting near-synonyms (HNs) are under study and there are four innovative components in this study: we introduced NLP tools to facilitate the implementation of automatic annotation, employed the occurrence table based on relative frequency to fix the problems of variable sparsity, utilized PCA to obtain a finer set of interrelated variables, and provided a consolidated clustering solution via HCPC. The effectiveness of the rule-based annotation serves as a technical foundation for large-scale profiling of near-synonyms and offers methodological insights into similar BP studies on near-synonyms. Given that the variables are interrelated, they were reduced to six dimensions with 100% cumulative variance, manifesting the correlation among variables and the necessity of reducing dimensions. The initial analysis of variable distributions also supports the clustering solutions, which provide a direct reference to HN usages.

Although the study only concerns the set of seven HNs, the proposed modified BP approach can be applied to any number of near-synonyms. As a pilot attempt, this study shows that the integration of NLP tools into a BP approach is rewarding and revealing. It is noted that while the cluster solutions are meaningful and useful based on distributional preferences, the results may be further analyzed to make more 'linguistic sense', if possible. Moreover, to avoid improper selection of variables which may cause unexplainable clusters, we suggest two types of variables may should be utilized as initial variable sets: (1) the linguistic cues that have been discussed in previous studies or observed based on corpus performance, and (2) the features relevant to the top bigrams and trigrams. Because selecting variables can be subjective choices, the suggestions may help facilitate better integration of the NLP-oriented BP approach.

In addition, the auto-annotation replies solely on the accuracy of the utilized NLP tools. The tags generated by NLP models should be reviewed carefully but not manually corrected to ensure consistency and reliability (Newman & Cox, 2020). A common concern about using a tool other than POS tagging is that the overall performance may not be satisfactory. However, no NLP tools are perfect and we should try to find ways to make sensible use of the existent tools. For example, the overall accuracy of dependency parsing may not be adequate, but the identification of subjects was relatively reliable, allowing the conversion of subject types into a variable.

4 Conclusion

This study proposed an unsupervised BP approach to categorize near-synonyms into different groups of linguistic resemblance. The clustering helps to make finer lexical semantic distinctions among the synonym group, thereby providing useful details for linguistic inquiries, language education, and dictionary planning. Methodologically, this work enhances the traditional BP approach to lexical studies by integrating systematic automatic annotation tools, a co-occurrence table of relative frequency, dimension reduction techniques, and a consolidated clustering algorithm. This study also introduces n-grams containing near-synonyms as a preliminary analysis of frequent collocations and includes relative positions to the set of collocation-based variables. The rule-based annotation involves utilizing partial tags produced by the dependency parsing and NER models via the Stanford CoreNLP toolkit that can be easily adapted to corpus-based studies. The proposed co-occurrence tables address the problem of data sparsity, and the effort of dimension reduction allows for a finer collection of potentially interrelated variables. The encouraging results yielded in this study may generate more interest in the multivariate analysis of other sets of words. This study offers new insights into the empirical paradigm of BPs in the investigation of near-synonyms in a more effective and comprehensive way that allows for more refined and generalizable results. Analytically, the clustering results go along with the distinctions of subject type and stativity of emotional expressions. The HNs are distinctly defined to display a conceptual and functional cline from verbal to nominal usage in a cognitively plausible and sensible way [26, 27]. The results not only reinforced the lexical semantic distinctions proposed for Chinese emotional predication [1, 2, 28] with more distributional evidence but they also serve to lay out the detailed form-meaning mapping strategies not fully revealed in previous studies. This study also sheds new light pedagogically and lexicologically by detecting the vital collocational and syntactic patterns, subject tendencies, and semantic attractions of different HN clusters. It ultimately presents a less labor-intensive corpus-based method that is applicable to investigating larger sets of linguistic targets and thus offers useful, empirical resources for language education and applications.

References

1. Chang, L., Chen, K., Huang, C.: Alternation across semantic fields: a study on mandarin verbs of emotion. Computational Linguistics and Chinese Language Processing 5(1), 61–80 (2000)
2. Liu, M.: Emotion in lexicon and grammar: Lexical-constructional interface of Mandarin emotional predicates. Lingua Sinica 2(4), 1–47 (2016)
3. Tsai, M.C., Huang, C.R., Chen, K.J.: The interaction of semantic grammar from the standard of synonym discrimination. In: Yin, Y., Yang, I., Chan, H. (eds.) Chinese Languages and Linguistics: V, Interaction, pp. 439–459. Academia Sinica, Taipei (1999)

4. Wang, S., Huang, C.: Word sketch lexicography: New perspectives on lexicographic studies of Chinese near-synonyms. Lingua Sinica 3(11), 1–22 (2017). https://doi.org/10.1186/s40 655-017-0025-4
5. Divjak, D., Gries, S.: Ways of trying in Russian: Clustering behavioral profiles. Corpus Linguist. Linguist. Theory 2(1), 23–60 (2006). https://doi.org/10.1515/CLLT.2006.002
6. Gries, S.T.: Behavioral profiles: A fine-grained and quantitative approach in corpus-based lexical semantics. The Mental Lexicon 5(3), 323–346 (2010)
7. Gries, S.T.: Corpus-based cognitive semantics: Behavioral profiles for polysemy, synonymy, and antonymy. In: Gries, S.T. (ed.) Ten Lectures on Quantitative Approaches in Cognitive Linguistics, pp. 75–93. Brill, Leiden (2017)
8. Gries, S.T., Divjak, D.: Behavioral profiles: A corpus-based approach to cognitive semantic analysis. In: Evans, V., Pourcel, S.S. (eds.) New Directions in Cognitive Linguistics, pp. 57–75. John Benjamins, Amsterdam (2009)
9. Firth, J.: A synopsis of linguistic theory 1930–1955. In: Palmer, F.R. (ed.) Studies in Linguistic Analysis, Special Volume of Philological Society, pp. 1–32. Basil Blackwell, Oxford (1957)
10. Goldberg, A.E.: Constructions: A Construction Grammar Approach to Argument Structure. University of Chicago Press, Chicago (1995)
11. Levin, B.: English Verb Classes and Alternations: A Preliminary Investigation. University of Chicago Press, Chicago (1993)
12. Lehecka, T.: Collocation and colligation. In: Östman, J-O., Verschueren, J. (eds.) Handbook of Pragmatics Online, pp. 1–20. John Benjamins Publishing Company, Amsterdam (2015). https://doi.org/10.1075/hop.19.col2
13. Gries, S.T., Otani, N.: Behavioral profiles: A corpus-based perspective on synonymy and antonymy. ICAME Journal 34, 121–150 (2010)
14. Liesenfeld, A., Liu, M., Huang, C.R.: Profiling the Chinese causative construction with rang (讓), shi (使) and ling (令) using frame semantic feature. Corpus Linguist. Linguist. Theory 18(2), 263–306 (2022). https://doi.org/10.1515/cllt-2020-0027
15. Kilgarriff, A., et al.: The sketch engine: Ten years on. Lexicography 1(1), 7–36 (2014)
16. Manning, C.D., et al.: The Stanford CoreNLP natural language processing toolkit. In: Proceedings of the 52nd Annual Meeting of the Association for Computational Linguistics: System Demonstrations, pp. 55–60. Association for Computational Linguistics, Baltimore (2014)
17. Chen, D., Manning, C.: A fast and accurate dependency parser using neural networks. In: Proceedings of the 2014 Conference on Empirical Methods in Natural Language Processing, pp. 740–750. Association for Computational Linguistics, Doha (2014)
18. Newman, J., Cox, C.: Corpus annotation. In: Paquot, M., Gries, S.T. (eds.) A Practical Handbook of Corpus Linguistics, pp. 25–48. New Springer, Heidelberg (2020)
19. Gries, S.T.: How to use statistics in quantitative corpus analysis. In: McCarthy, M., O'Keeffe, A. (eds.) The Routledge Handbook of Corpus Linguistics, pp. 168–181. Routledge, New York (2022)
20. Jolliffe, I.T., Cadima, J.: Principal component analysis: A review and recent developments. Philosophical Transactions of the Royal Society A: Mathematical, Physical and Engineering Sciences 374(2065), 20150202 (2016). https://doi.org/10.1098/rsta.2015.0202
21. Husson, F., Josse, J., Pagès, J.: Principal component methods-hierarchical clustering-partitional clustering: Why would we need to choose for visualizing data. Technical Report, September. Applied Mathematics Department, Agrocampus (2010)
22. Lê, S., Josse, J., Husson, F.: FactoMineR: an R package for multivariate analysis. Journal of Statistical Software 25(1), 1–18 (2008). https://doi.org/10.18637/jss.v025.i01
23. Kassambara, A., Mundt, F.: Factoextra: Extract and visualize the results of multivariate data analyses. R package version 1.0.7, https://CRAN.R-project.org/package=factoextra. Last accessed 01 January 2021

24. Levshina, N.: How to Do Linguistics with R: Data Exploration and Statistical Analysis. John Benjamins Publishing Company, Amsterdam (2015)
25. Kaiser, H.F.: The application of electronic computers to factor analysis. Educ. Psychol. Measur. **20**(1), 141–151 (1960). https://doi.org/10.1177/001316446002000116
26. Talmy, L.: Toward a Cognitive Semantics, vol. 1: Concept Structuring Systems. MIT Press, Cambridge (2000a)
27. Talmy, L.: Toward a Cognitive Semantics, vol. 2: Typology and Process in Concept Structuring. MIT Press, Cambridge (2000b)
28. Liu, M.: Morphosyntactic structure and emotion. In: Schiewer, G., Altarriba, J., Ng, B. (eds.) Handbooks of Linguistics and Communication Science, vol. 1, pp. 472–486. De Gruyter Mouton, Berlin (2022). https://doi.org/10.1515/9783110347524-022

Study on Distribution of Single-Item Adjective Attributives and Occurrence and Absence of "*de*"

Rui Song[1] and Ting Zhu[2(✉)]

[1] School of Literature, Shenyang Normal University, Shenyang 110034, China
[2] College of International Business, Shenyang Normal University, Shenyang 110034, China
784576920@qq.com

Abstract. This paper examines 77,845 single-item adjective attributives from articles in "People's Daily" from 2019 to 2021. Distribution characteristics, syllable combination patterns of adhesive attributives and combined attributives, and occurrence and absence tendency of "*de*" are studied from the practical perspective. We find the number of adhesive attributives is significantly less than that of combined attributives, while the frequency of use of the former is 4 - 5 times higher than that of the latter. In the two attributive structures, adjectives and nouns have high proportion of repeated usage, but the proportion of their co-occurrence is relatively small. Besides, occurrence and absence of "*de*" in attributive structures have the characteristic of "polarization", that is for the vast majority of word instances there is a strong tendency to either use "*de*" or not. Presence of "de" has the function of distinguishing meaning and highlighting information while the absence of "*de*" can make the meaning more concise and further solidify the sentence structure. This paper provides a basis and reference for the lexical semantic research of adjective attributive structure.

Keywords: Adjective attributives · Distribution characteristics · Usage tendency

1 Introduction

The single-item adjective attributive structure refers to a modifier-head structure in which the attributive component is only one adjective. According to Zhu Dexi's (1982:148) [1] classification criteria, "adjective + noun" is classified as adhesive attributive structure, while "adjective + *de* + noun" belongs to combined attributive structure. The two forms are similar, but they can express different meanings. For example

(1) Tā fāxiàn zìjǐ bózi hòumiàn zhǎng le yíkuài <u>yìngde gǔtou</u>
'He found <u>a hard bone</u> growing on the back of his neck.'
(2) *Xījí quánxiàn jiāng shàngxià quándòngyuán, fāqǐ zǒnggōngshì, jiānjué kěnxià* <u>*yìnggǔtou*</u>*, dǎyíng tuōpíngōngjiānzhàn*
'All the people in Xi Ji county are mobilized to launch a general offensive. They are determined to resolutely <u>tackle the hard nuts</u> and win the battle against poverty.'

P. Jin et al. (Eds.): CLSW 2024, LNAI 15552, pp. 18–36, 2025.
https://doi.org/10.1007/978-981-96-3509-2_2

In examples (1) and (2), *yìngde gǔtou* 'hard bone' and *yìnggǔtou* 'tackle the hard nuts' represent combined and adhesive single-item attributive structures respectively. Although there is only a single difference of character "*de*", the meanings they express are significantly different. Another example:

---

(3) Yányán xiàrì zhōng, láodòngzhěmen réngrán bǎochí <u>lèguān de xīntài</u>, jiānshǒu zài yīxiàn.

'In the scorching summer, workers still maintain <u>an optimistic attitude</u> and stick to the front line.'

(4) Cánjírén yùndòngyuán de <u>lèguān xīntài</u> ràngrén nánwàng.

'The <u>optimistic mindset</u> of disabled athletes is unforgettable.'

In examples (3) and (4), *lèguān de xīntài* 'optimistic attitude' and *lèguān xīntài* 'optimistic mindset' have a difference in the occurrence of "*de*", but they basically express the same meaning.

In single-item attributive structure, constraints and influences of the occurrence or absence of "de" on the expression of word meanings, as well as the factors and conditions related to the occurrence or absence of "de" need to be explored. The distribution of adhesive and combined single-item attributive structures in large-scale corpora, the number of word instances that can be used interchangeably, and the identification of which word instances are more inclined to appear in adhesive or combined attributive structures are the main contents to be analyzed and discussed in this paper.

Previous scholars have conducted many studies on attributive types, attributive word order and characteristics (Zhu Dexi,1956; Liu Yuehua,1984; Yuan Yulin,1999; Cui Yingxian,2002; Li Xianyin, 2016) [2–6]. There are also studies on the role, occurrence and absence of the word "*de*" in attributive structures (Lü Shuxiang, 1966; Guo Rui, 2000; Zheng Yuanhan, 2004; Wang Guangquan, 2006; Wang Yuanjie, 2008; Xu Yangchun, 2011; Lei Youfang, 2012; Pei Hongbin, 2020; Zhang Junping, 2024) [7–15]. The research findings of previous scholars mainly focused on the theoretical level and the attributive structure itself, lacking evidence of language phenomena and quantitative data analysis. Therefore, from a practical perspective and based on large-scale news text corpora, this paper explores the word instances phenomena of single-item adjective attributive structures. It examines distribution characteristics, combination rules and usage tendencies of these word instances, providing reference for Chinese vocabulary research and teaching.

2   An Investigation on the Distribution Characteristics of Adhesive and Combined Single-Item Attributives

This paper takes the articles in "People's Daily" from 2019 to 2021 as the research corpus, with a total of more than 120 million words. Word segmentation and part-of-speech tagging of these words are completed based on Python and the Language Technology Service Platform (LTP4.0) of Harbin Institute of Technology. All the word instances of adhesive and combined attributive structures are extracted, and then manually proofread and screened. In order to ensure the authenticity, accuracy and objectivity of the extracted word instances, *Modern Chinese Grammatical Information Dictionary*[1] is mainly used as the reference and judgment standard for part-of-speech during screening of word instances.

In data processing, we found some word instances that do not conform to the research scope of this article. For example:

---

(5) Lǐ kèqiáng shuō, jìnqī wǒguó júdì jíduān qiáng jiàngyǔ, zàochéng <u>zhòngdà rényuán shāngwáng</u> hé cái chǎn sǔnshī, lìngrén tòngxīn.

'Li Keqiang said that the recent extremely heavy rainfall in some areas of our country has caused <u>heavy casualties</u> and property losses, which is distressing

(6) Xīnguān fèiyán yìqíng shì dì èrcì shìjiè dàzhàn yǐlái zuì <u>yánzhòng de quánqiú gōnggòng wèishēng tū fā shìjiàn.</u>

' The COVID-19 epidemic is <u>the most serious global public health emergency</u> since the end of World War II.'

In example (5), *zhòngdà rényuán shāngwán* 'heavy casualties' and in example (6), *yánzhòng de quánqiú gōnggòng wèishēng tū fā shìjiàn* 'the most serious global public health emergency', head components are noun phrases or NP structures. Since the head components of the attributive structures defined in this article are all bare nouns, such word instances are removed.

In addition, since *Modern Chinese Grammar Information Dictionary* is relatively old, in the process of counting and screening corpora, we found that some adjectives and nouns are not included, for example, adjectives such as *jīngzhǔn* 'precise' *jīngyàn* 'stunning' *gāoqīng* 'high-definition' *yánkē* 'harsh' *kùxuàn* 'cool', etc., and nouns such as *biànjú* 'change' *zhuāshǒu* 'starting point' *jīngjì tǐ* 'economy' *zhìyuàn zhě* 'volunteer' *hùlián wǎng* 'Internet', etc. After comparison with *Modern Chinese Dictionary (seventh edition)* and *Adjective Classification Dictionary*, a total of 87 uncollected adjectives and 120 uncollected nouns were added. The attributive structures composed of them are classified into the research scope of this article. For example:

Adhesive "adjective + noun" structure: *dà biànjú* 'major changes', *zhòngyào zhuāshǒu* 'important starting points', *gāoqīng píngmù* 'high-definition screens', *gāoduān zhìkù* 'high-end think tanks'... And so on.

Combined "adjective + de + noun" structure: *níngliàn de cíyǔ* 'concise words', *bīzè de zǒuláng* 'narrow corridors', *qīnglì de gēshēng* 'beautiful singing', *shūhuǎn de xuánlù* 'soothing melodies'... And so on.

According to the above screening principles and judgment criteria, after 3 to 4 rounds of manual judgment and screening, we obtained a total of 34,805 instances of adhesive single-item adjective attributives and 43,040 of combined single-item adjective attributives. The overall distribution of the number of word instances and usage frequencies is shown in Fig. 1.

---

[1] *Modern Chinese Grammatical Information Dictionary* is a dictionary suitable for computer classification and processing of natural language, published by Tsinghua University Press in 1998.

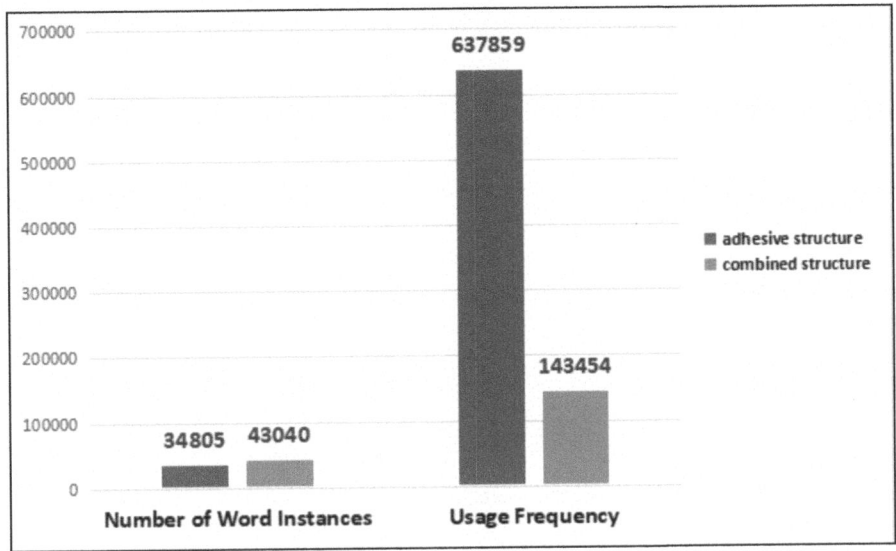

Fig. 1. Comparison of Data Between Adhesive and Combined Word Instances.

We found that the number of word instances of the adhesive structure accounts for about four-fifths of the number of word instances of the combined structure. However, the usage frequency of the former is four to five times that of the latter. The gap is very significant. Why does such a phenomenon occur?

We believe that the adhesive attributive structure is concise in form and condensed in semantics. The connection between the attributive element and the central element is tighter, and the matching relationship between adjectives and nouns in attributive structure is more demanding. The degree of internal restriction on word instances is more pronounced. However, due to the economy principle of language, people are more inclined to use short words and texts for communication. Therefore, the usage frequency of adhesive word instances is much higher than that of combined attributive structures. For example, word instances such as *xīnshídài* 'new era' and *gāozhìliàng* 'high quality' are repeatedly used with very high frequency. In contrast, due to the addition of "*de*", the combined attributive structure weakens the connection between the attributive element and the central element, making the form of it relatively loose. The semantic matching relationship between adjectives and nouns is relatively broad. Therefore, the number of word instances of the combined attributive structure is relatively large and the usage range is relatively wide. However, since the combination mode between various elements within the combined attributive structure is relatively complex, the overall usage number of combined word instances is far lower than that of adhesive attributive structures.

Specifically, the high-frequency word instances (top 10 in ranking) and occurrence probabilities of the adhesive structure and the combined structure are shown in Table 1.

It can be seen that from a practical perspective, the high-frequency word instances and occurrence probabilities of each rank of the adhesive and combined structures are different. For example, the ones ranked first are *xīnshídài* 'new era' and *xīnde lìshǐ* 'new

Table 1. Word Instances of Top 10 Adhesive and Combined Single Attributives

Adhesive Word Instances	Frequency	Combined Word Instances	Frequency
xīn shídài 'new era'	0.338724388	*xīnde lìshǐ* 'new history'	0.027323528
gāo zhìliàng 'high quality'	0.253503757	*xīnde shídài* 'new era'	0.008003083
zhòngyào jiǎnghuà 'important speech'	0.115049136	*xīnde zhēngchéng* 'new journey'	0.00752778
gāojí gōngchéngshī 'senior engineer'	0.083614876	*zhòngyào de zuòyòng* 'important role'	0.006898324
gāo shuǐpíng ' high level'	0.082946882	*zhòngyào de yìyì* 'important significance'	0.005485259
pínkùn rénkǒu 'poor population'	0.07471257	*xīnde qǐdiǎn* 'new starting point'	0.004920033
xīn zhēngchéng 'new journey'	0.074558417	*měilì de shìjiè* 'beautiful world'	0.003918042
tèbié xíngzhèngqū 'special administrative region'	0.073903269	*měilì de shèhuì zhǔyì* 'beautiful socialism'	0.003905196
pínkùn dìqū 'poor area'	0.071462522	*jiānshí de jīchǔ* 'solid foundation'	0.003673967
zhòngyào zuòyòng 'important role'	0.059310168	*xīnde huólì* 'new vitality'	0.003661121

history' respectively. Another example is that *zhòngyào zuòyòng* 'important role' which is only ranked tenth in adhesive word instances rises to the fourth place in the combined word instance *zhòngyàode zuòyòng* 'important role'. The occurrence probabilities of the two are "0.059310168" and "0.006898324" respectively. This shows that although there is only a difference of one character "*de*", in actual corpora, *zhòngyào de zuòyòng* 'important role' is more inclined to be used in the adhesive form. That is, in the two attributive structures, the usage tendencies of word instances are different.

From the perspective of the usage of various elements within the attributive structure, in the adhesive attributive structure, there are a total of 1351 adjective elements in the attributive position, with a usage frequency of 637,859. In the combined attributive structure, there are a total of 1821 adjective elements in the attributive position, with a usage frequency of 143,454. Without considering nouns, there are 1231 adjectives (intersection) in the two attributive structures, accounting for 91.12% of the number of adjectives in the adhesive form and 67.60% of the combined form, as shown in Fig. 2.

The proportion of word instances in the intersection of adjectives is very large, indicating that in the two structures, most adjectives can be used universally. For example:

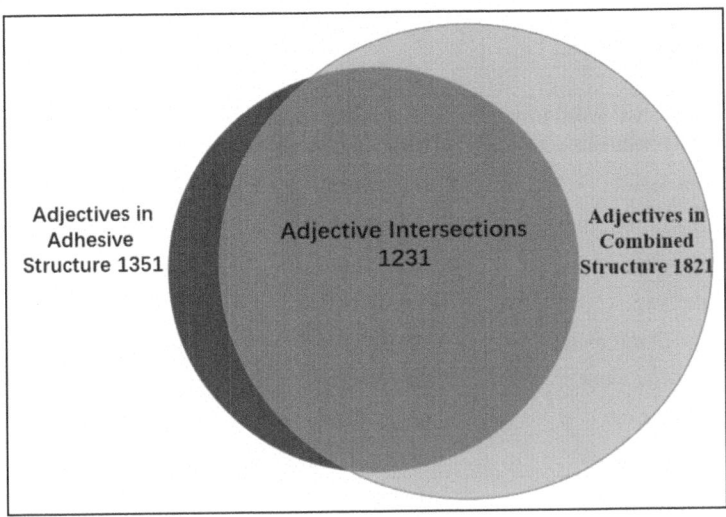

Fig. 2. A Distribution of Adjective Attributive Elements in Adhesive and Combined Structures

Adhesive form: *xīn shídài* 'new era', *xīn zhēngchéng* 'new journey', *xīn jìshù* 'new technology', *xīn néngyuán* 'new energy', *xīn móshì* 'new model', *xīn piānzhāng* 'new chapter'... (the intersection is *xīn* 'new').

Combined form: *xīnde lìshǐ* 'new history', *xīnde shídài* 'new era', *xīnde qǐdiǎn* 'new starting point', *xīnde gòngxiàn* 'new contribution', *xīnde jīyù* 'new opportunity', *xīnde xíngshì* 'new situation'...

The intersection here refers to the same adjectives. Nouns can be the same or different, such as *xīn shídài* 'new era' and *xīnde shídài* 'new era'. The only difference lies in the occurrence or absence of the character "*de*". This situation will be described in detail below.

It can be seen that in the adhesive attributive structure, the vast majority of adjectives (more than 90%) can access the combined attributive structure, while only about 60% of the adjectives in the combined structure can form the adhesive structure. This shows that the adhesive attributive structure has a higher degree of restriction on adjectives. The high-frequency word instances (top 10 in ranking) and occurrence probabilities in the intersection of adjectives are shown in Table 2.

From the comparison of occurrence probabilities, the high-frequency adjectives (top 10) in the intersection have a greater probability of forming the adhesive structure.

The distribution of the central element nouns is as follows. In the adhesive structure, there are 6809 noun word instances, with a usage frequency of 637,859. In the combined structure, there are 7334 word instances of nouns, with a usage frequency of 143,454. Without considering adjectives, there are 4648 nouns (intersection) in two attributive structures, accounting for 68.26% of nouns in the adhesive form and 63.38% in the combined form, as shown in Fig. 3.

In comparison, the proportion of noun intersections is relatively balanced. That is, 65%–70% of the nouns in both attributive structures can be used universally. For example:

Table 2. Word Instances of the Top 10 Adjectives in the Intersection of Adhesive and Combined Attributive Elements.

Ranking	Adjective Word Instances (Intersection)	Probability in Adhesive Structure	Probability in Combined Structure
1	*xīn* 'new'	0.11706448	0.015223092
2	*zhòng yào* 'important'	0.075625262	0.005568831
3	*gāo* 'high'	0.0421662	0.002561073
4	*dà* 'large'	0.035619528	0.008026233
5	*zhòng dà* 'major'	0.036665203	0.00037373
6	*pín kùn* 'poor'	0.026895751	0.00074618
7	*hǎo* 'good'	0.021760805	0.005104228
8	*gāo jí* 'senior'	0.020077741	0.000017919
9	*ān quán* 'safe'	0.016716732	0.002338371
10	*jī běn* 'basic'	0.017412996	0.000430045

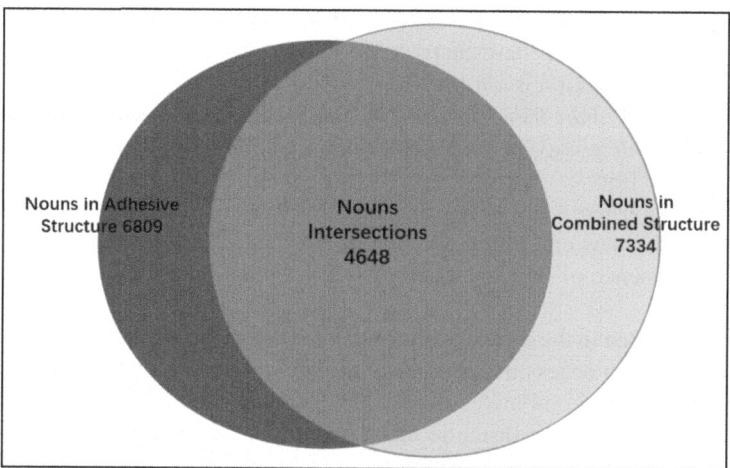

Fig. 3. Distribution of Noun Central Elements in Adhesive and Combined Structures

Adhesive: *xīn shídài* 'new era', *wěidà shídài* 'great era', *jiù shídài* 'old era', *měihǎo shídài* 'beautiful era', *luòhòu shídài* 'backward era'… (the intersection is *shídài* 'era').

Combined: *xīnde shídài* 'new era', *xiānmíng de shídài* 'distinct era', *huīhuáng de shídài* 'glorious era', *yǒuqù de shídài* 'interesting era'…

Here, the intersection means the nouns are the same, while the adjectives can be the same or different. For example, in the case of *xīnshídài* 'new era' and *xīnde shídài* 'new era', the adjectives and nouns are both the same. The only difference lies in the appearance or absence of "*de*". This will be described in detail below.

The high-frequency word instances (top 10 in sorting) and occurrence probabilities in the noun intersection are shown in Table 3.

Table 3. Top 10 Word Instances in the Noun Intersection

Ranking	Noun central elements(intersection)word instances	Occurrence probabilities in adhesive structures	Occurrence probabilities in combined structures
1	*shídài* 'era'	0.034819592	0.001524357
2	*zhìliàng* 'quality'	0.025508343	0.00012287
3	*wèntí* 'problem'	0.017556344	0.001923685
4	*gòngxiàn* 'contribution'	0.011503712	0.000861371
5	*shuǐpíng* 'level'	0.011946557	0.00011903
6	*zuòyòng* 'function'	0.010469556	0.001159586
7	*jiǎnghuà* 'speech'	0.011478114	0.000008959
8	*dìqū* 'area /region'	0.009455877	0.000766658
9	*jìshù* 'technology'	0.008617545	0.001016238
10	*shèhuì* 'society'	0.00719174	0.00173042

Through comparative research, it is found that in the two attributive structures, both adjectives and nouns have positional tendencies. Even in the intersections that can be used universally, the occurrence probabilities of word instances also have obvious high and low distinctions. That is to say, in the actual application of specific word instances, whether they appear in an adhesive structure or a combined structure is not a random collocation and combination, but has a certain degree of distinctiveness and probability tendency.

3   Types of Occurrence and Absence of *"de"* in Single-Item Attributives

The above paper has examined the distribution characteristics and usage tendency of adhesive and combined attributive word instances. In this section we conduct statistics and analysis on the occurrence and absence of *"de"* in single-item attributives. Through sorting through the corpus, we find that the "occurrence" and "absence" of *"de"* in the two attributive structures can be divided into the following four types.

① In single-item attributives, the character *"de"* must be hidden. For example:

---

(7) Zhāxī shì Xīzàng Chāngdū shì dìyī xiǎoxué de <u>gāojí jiàoshī</u>, zhǔjiào kēmù shì zàngyǔwén.

' Zha Xi is <u>a senior teacher</u> at the First Primary School in Changdu City, Tibet. His main teaching subject is Tibetan language.'

(continued)

(continued)

(8) Fāzhǎn shì <u>yìng dàolǐ</u>, shì dǎng zhízhèng xīngguó de dìyī yàowù, yěshì jiějué yīqiè wèntí de guānjiàn
' Development is <u>the absolute principle</u>. It is the top priority for the Party to govern and rejuvenate the country and also the key to solving all problems.'

The above two examples are adhesive attributive structures. In example (7), *gāojí jiàoshī* 'senior teacher' refers to a teacher who has obtained senior professional title qualifications. As a semantic whole, in *gāojí jiàoshī* 'senior teacher', the character *"de"* must be hidden, and cannot be expressed as *gāojí de jiàoshī*. In example (8), *yìng dàolǐ* 'absolute principle' originates from Deng Xiaoping's economic thought "development is the absolute principle", which was put forward during his southern tour in 1992. It belongs to political discourse. And after the accumulation and precipitation of time, the semantics of *yìng dàolǐ* 'absolute principle' has become solidified. Here, *"de"* must be hidden and cannot be said as *yìngde dàolǐ*. At present, there are still differences in the classification of adjectives in the field of Chinese grammar. Some scholars classify adjectives that can only be used as attributives but not as predicates into non-predicative adjectives or distinguishing words such as *gāojí* 'senior' and *dījí* 'junior' (Lü Shuxiang, Rao Changrong 1981) [16]. While some other scholars classify them according to the traditional large category of adjectives. This article, based on the tagging of the word segmentation program and from the perspective of practicality principle, did not make a detailed distinction within adjectives.

② In single-item attributives, the character *"de"* must appear. For example:

(9) Lǎo cūnzhǎng shuō: "Guòqù, wǒmen cónglái méi xiǎngguò huìhē dào zhème <u>gānjìng de shuǐ</u>."
' The old village chief said, "In the past, we never thought that we would drink <u>such clean water</u>".'
(10) Yīwèi gǎnrǎn xīnguān fèiyán de chǎnfù shùnlì chǎnxià yīmíng nányīng, zàichǎng de měi yī gè rén dōu liúxià <u>jīdòng de lèishuǐ</u>.
'A pregnant woman infected with COVID-19 successfully gave birth to a baby boy. Everyone present shed <u>excited tears</u>'

The above two examples are combined attributive structures. In example (9) *gānjìng deshuǐ* 'clean water', *gānjìng* 'clean' serves as a modifying element of *shuǐ* 'water' and has a prominent and emphatic role. It means that the water drunk now is much cleaner than water before. Here, the character *"de"* must appear. Generally speaking, it cannot be said as *hēdào zhème gānjìngshuǐ*, because the sentence meaning is not understandable. In example (10) *jīdòng de lèishuǐ* 'excited tears', the adjective *jīdòng* 'excited' indicates strong inner emotional activities and has a very strong modifying and descriptive nature. Here, the character *"de"* must appear. Generally speaking, it cannot be replaced by *jīdòng lèishuǐ*.

③ The character *"de"* can be hidden or shown, but the meanings are significantly different. For example:

(11) Zuòwéi Xīnjiāpō nǎizhì Dōngméng zuìdà de yínháng, Xīngzhǎn yínháng jiāng jìxù
      tuīdòng zhōngxīn jīnróng hézuò.......

' As the largest bank in Singapore and even in ASEAN, DBS Bank will continue to promote
financial cooperation between China and Singapore...'

(12) Duì quánguó xìng dà yínháng láishuō, zhèkuài yèwù hěnnán zài zhànlüè céngmiàn yǐnqǐ
      zhòngshì.

' For major national banks, this business is difficult to attract attention at strategic level.'

In example (11), *dàde yínháng* 'large bank' refers to the bank with the largest floor
area. For example, *Zhètiáo jiēshàng zuìdà de yínháng shì gōngshāng yínháng.* 'The
largest bank on this street is the Industrial and Commercial Bank of China.' In example
(12), *dà yínháng* 'major bank' means business scope of the bank is national rather than
regional. Although the character "*de*" can be either present or absent, the meanings of the
two are obviously different. For some individual usage of single syllable adjectives such
as *zuìdà* 'biggest' and *zuìyìng* 'hardest', they are often used in conjunction with adverbs.
According to the principle of practicality, this article includes them in the research scope.

④ In single-item attributives, the character "*de*" can be hidden or appear, and the
expressed meanings are similar. For example:

(13) Dǒngshìzhǎng XuēLěi shuō: "Xiànzài chǎnnéng yuǎnyuǎn mǎnzú bùliǎo dìngdān de
      xūqiú, xīn de chǎngfáng zhèngzài jiājǐn jiànshè."

' Chairman Xue Lei said, "Now the production capacity is far from meeting the demand of
orders. A new factory building is under intensified construction".'

(14) Zài chǎngqū yīcè, liǎngdòng xīn chǎngfáng zhèngzài zhuājǐn jiànshè, yùjì jīnnián wǔyuè
      dǐ jiànchéng.

' On one side of the factory area, two new factory buildings are under construction in a hurry
and are expected to be completed by the end of May this year.'

In examples (13) and (14), the attributive structures *xīnde chǎngfáng* and *xīn
chǎngfáng* are different, yet both indicate newly built factory buildings. The character "*de*" in the structure can be hidden or appear, and there is not much difference in
meaning.

Based on the existing corpus size, we have counted the number distributions of word
instances of three types of instances respectively: the character "*de*" must be hidden,
the character "*de*" must be shown, and the character "*de*" can be intersection of being
hidden or shown, as illustrated in Fig. 4.

From the overall distribution, the number of word instances with the character "*de*"
only shown is the largest, while character "de" being intersection is the smallest. They
account for 31.07% of the number of only hidden, and 25.12% of only shown.

We find that the absence and occurrence of the character "de" in real texts have the
characteristic of "polarization". That is, for most word instances, whether to use "*de*"
or not has a strong tendency. For example, for word instances where the character "*de*"
is the intersection such as *xīnde chǎngfáng* and *xīn chǎngfáng* 'a new factory building'
the proportion of such word instances is only between 1/4 to 1/3.

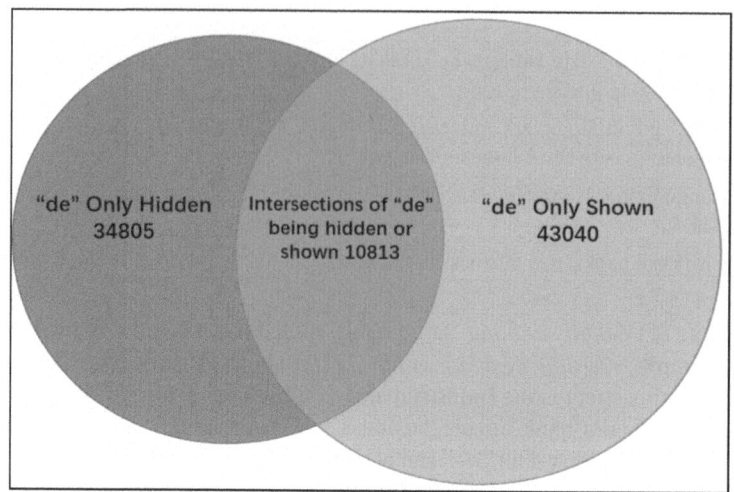

Fig. 4. Distribution of Occurrence and Absence of "*de*"

4   Syllable Combination and the Tendency of Occurrence and Absence of "*de*"

According to statistics, in the two attributive structures, the syllable combination of adjectives as the attributive component and the noun as the central word component is as follows:

For the adhesive "adj. + noun" structure, there are 1351 adjective instances, including 115 monosyllabic instances and 1236 disyllabic instances; there are 6809 noun instances, including 154 monosyllabic instances, 5408 disyllabic instances, and 1247 polysyllabic instances[4]. For the combined "adj. + *de* + noun" structure, there are 821 cases of adjectives, including 136 monosyllabic cases and 1685 disyllabic cases; there are 7334 cases of nouns, including 183 monosyllabic cases, 5602 disyllabic cases, and 1549 polysyllabic cases.

The two attributive structures have common characteristics. That is, the number and proportion of disyllabic adjectives and disyllabic nouns are dominant. In order to examine the syllable combination patterns of various components, we mark word instances according to syllables such as *xiǎolóu* 'small building', *xīnchē* 'new car' as "monosyllabic adjective + monosyllabic noun". Word instances such as *zhòngyào jiǎnghuà* 'important speech' and *yōuxiù chuántǒng* 'excellent tradition' are marked as "disyllabic adjective + disyllabic noun". The specific syllable combination distribution and proportions are shown in Tables 4 and 5.

Through comparison, it is known that in the two attributive structures, the number and proportion of word instances of "disyllabic adj. + disyllabic noun" are both the highest. We believe that this has a great relationship with the genre and expression style of the corpus. As a national key news website, "People's Daily" includes many fields such as important news, comments, economy, politics, culture and society, etc. The language content has the style characteristics of being written, objective, concise,

Table 4. Distribution and Proportions of Syllable Collocation Pattern of Adhesive Structure

Collocation Pattern of Adhesive Structure "adj. + noun"

Collocation pattern	Word instances number	Percentage (100%)	Examples
monosyllabic adj. + monosyllabic n	229	0.66%	xīnchē 'new car'
disyllabic adj. + monosyllabic n	101	0.29%	píngfán rén 'ordinary people'
monosyllabic adj. + disyllabic n	7160	20.57%	xīn shídài 'new era'
disyllabic adj. + disyllabic n	24660	70.85%	zhòngyào jiǎnghuà 'important speech'
monosyllabic adj. + polysyllabic n	707	2.03%	dà bówùguǎn 'big musemu'
disyllabic adj. + polysyllabic n	1948	5.60%	gāojí gōngchéngshī 'senior engineer'

Table 5. Distribution and Proportions of Syllable Collocation Pattern of Combined Structure

Collocation Pattern of Combined Structure "adj. + de + noun"

Collocation pattern	Word instances number	Percentage (100%)	Examples
monosyllabic adj. + monosyllabic n	279	0.65%	gāo de shān 'high mountain'
disyllabic adj. + monosyllabic n	790	1.84%	Kě ài de rén 'lovely person'
monosyllabic adj. + disyllabic n	6330	14.71%	xīn de lìshǐ 'new history'
disyllabic adj. + disyllabic n	31310	72.75%	zhòngyào de yìyì 'important significance'
monosyllabic adj. + polysyllabic n	1044	2.43%	xīn de lǐchéngbēi 'new milestone'
disyllabic adj. + polysyllabic n	3287	7.64%	zhèngquè de jiàzhíguān 'correct values'

and neat. Therefore, the proportion of disyllabic word instances is very high, and the collocation pattern of "disyllabic adj. + disyllabic noun" is most common.

In the collocation pattern of "disyllabic adj. + disyllabic noun", there are 16,889 word instances with the character "de" only hidden, accounting for 30.18%; high-frequency word instances are gāojí jiàoshī 'senior teacher', xiānjìn gèrén 'advanced individual', etc.. There are 23,539 word instances with the character "de" only appearing, accounting for 42.06%; high-frequency word instances include jīdòng de lèishuǐ 'excited tears', *wēnnuǎn de shuāngshǒu* 'warm hands', etc.. There are only 7,771 word instances with the character "*de*" being intersection of being hidden or shown, accounting for 13.89%; high-frequency word instances are *zhòngyào(de)jiǎnghuà* 'important speech', *měilì(de)shìjiè* 'beautiful world', etc..

It is worth noting that when the central word component is a monosyllabic noun, there is a great difference in the syllable collocation pattern of adhesive and combined structures. We find that in the adhesive structure with a monosyllabic noun as the central word, the collocation pattern of "monosyllabic adjective + monosyllabic noun" is dominant. For such structure, the character "*de*" tends to be hidden, as shown in Fig. 5.

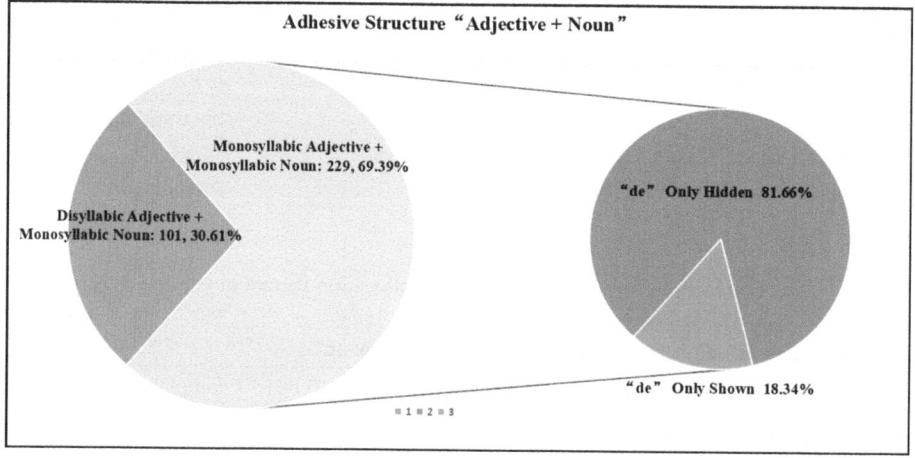

Fig. 5. Syllable Combinations in Adhesive Structures with Monosyllabic Nouns

As can be seen from Fig. 5, the proportion of word instances of "monosyllabic adjective + monosyllabic noun" is close to 70%, and more than 80% of them tend to use the character "*de*" in a way that it is "only hidden". The specific high-frequency word instances (the top 30 cases) are as follows:

dàshěng 'big province'	*xīnlù* 'new road'	*dàbìng* 'serious illness'
xiǎochéng 'small city'	*xiǎolóu* 'small building'	*dàxiàn* 'big county'
xiǎobìng 'minor illness'	*xiǎodiàn* ' small store'	*dàqiú* 'big ball'
xīnchē 'new car'	*dàlèi* ' big category'	*dàshì* 'big city'
xīnjiā 'new home'	*hǎochá* 'good tea'	*dàshān* 'big mountain'
hǎocài 'good dish'	*hǎojiǔ* 'good wine'	*hǎoyào* 'good medicine'
xīngē 'new song'	*hóngxiàn* 'red line'	*lǎochéng* 'old city'
hóngqiáng 'red wall'	*chángjià* 'long vacation'	*lǎowū* 'old house'
xiǎodǎo 'small island'	*xiǎoxiàn* 'small county'	*hǎodiàn* 'good store'
jiǎjiǔ 'fake wine'	*lǎodiàn* 'old store'	*xiǎoshěng* 'small province'

The usage examples are as follows:

(15) Zhōngguó shì nóngyè dàguó, Sìchuān shì nóngyè <u>dàshěng</u>.

'China is a big agricultural country. Sichuan is a <u>big</u> agricultural <u>province</u>.'

(16) Xīwàng tōngguò yǔ Zhōngguó de hézuò, wèi pínkùn dìqū nóngmín zēngshōu xúnzhǎo yītiáo <u>xīnlù</u>.

'It is hoped that through cooperation with China, <u>a new way</u> can be found to increase the income of farmers in poverty-stricken areas.'

In examples (15) and (16), *dàshěng* 'big province'and *xīnlù* 'new road' are both in the combination pattern of "monosyllabic adjective + monosyllabic noun". Generally speaking, the character "*de*" tends to be hidden. However, under some special conditions and contexts, it can also be used as *dà de shěng* 'big province' or *xīn de lù* 'new road', but the types of such word instances are very rare and the number of usage is extremely limited.

In comparison, in the combined structure with monosyllabic nouns as the central word, the combination pattern of "disyllabic adjective + monosyllabic noun" is dominant. And in such structures, the character "*de*" tends to be shown, as shown in Fig. 6.

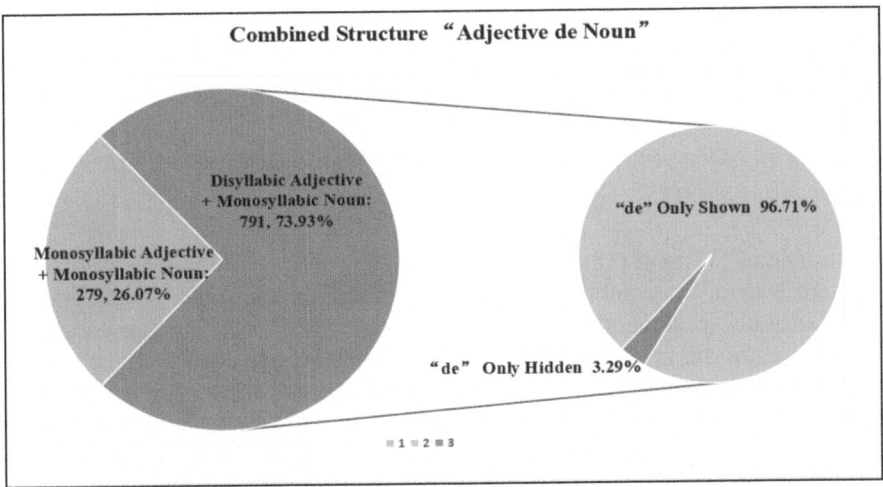

Fig. 6. Syllable Combinations in Combined Structures with Monosyllabic Nouns

In Fig. 6, the proportion of word instances of "disyllabic adjective + monosyllabic noun" reaches more than 73.93%, and most of them, 96.71%, tend to show the character "*de*". The specific high-frequency word instances(the top 30) are as follows:

kěài de rén 'lovely people'	*wēnnuǎn de jiā* 'warm home'
yǒuyòng de rén 'useful people'	*róngyì de shì* 'easy thing'
xìngfú de shì 'happy thing'	*píngfán de rén* 'ordinary people'
pínkùn de xiàn 'poor county'	*kāixīn de shì* 'happy thing'
wěidà de dǎng 'great Party'	*píngfán de shì* 'ordinary thing'
gānjìng de shuǐ 'clean water'	*gāoshàng de rén* 'noble people'
zhòngyào de shì 'important thing'	*xìngfú de jiā* 'happy home'
shànliáng de xīn 'kind heart'	*gāoxìng de shì* 'pleased thing'
wánzhěng de jiā 'complete home'	*kuàilè de shì* 'joyful thing'
kōumén de rén 'stingy people'	*yōuxiù de rén* 'excellent people'
jiǎndān de shì 'simple thing'	*yǒnggǎn de rén* 'brave people'
cūcāo de shǒu 'rough hand'	*wēnnuǎn de guāng* 'warm light'
jiéjìng de shuǐ 'pure water'	*qīngsōng de shì* 'relaxing thing'
guāngmíng de lù 'bright road'	*zhèngquè de shì* 'right thing'
kějìng de rén 'respectable people'	*xìngfú de rén* 'happy people'

The usage examples are as follows:

(17) Yīxiàn de yīwù gōngzuòzhě zuì xīnkǔ, ……, shì xīn shídài zuì kě ài de rén.
'The front-line medical workers are the most laborious…They are the most <u>lovely people</u> in the new era.'
(18) Tā kànzhe kělián de zhízi zhínǚ, ……, yòng róuruò jiānbǎng gěi tāmen yī gè <u>wēnnuǎn de jiā</u>.
'Looking at her poor nephew and niece,…She uses her weak shoulders to give them a <u>warm home</u>.'

In examples (17) and (18), *kěài derén* 'lovely people' and *wēnnuǎn dejiā* 'warm home' are both in the combination pattern of "disyllabic adjective + monosyllabic noun". Generally speaking, the character "*de*" tends to be shown. The "appearance" of the character "*de*" plays a role in highlighting information and deepening the semantic and emotional degree. Here, it generally cannot be said as *kěài rén* or *wēnnuǎn jiā*.

5   Analysis of the Occurrence and Absence Rules of "*de*"

As mentioned above, the two types of single attributive structures have the usage characteristic of "polarization". That is, the number and proportion of word instances where "*de*" can be either present or absent are very small. Then what factors are related to the occurrence and absence of "*de*"? In the word instances where "*de*" can be the intersection of being shown or hidden, is there a tendency? Through sorting out the corpus data and observing language phenomena, the following four features are summarized.

① The appearance of "*de*" has the function of distinguishing word meanings. That is, after omitting "*de*", the adjective and the noun together form a new word or phrase and have a new meaning. For example:

chúnjìng de shuǐ 'pure water' → *chúnjìng shuǐ* 'purified water'
yōuxiù de xuésheng 'excellent students' → *yōuxiù xuésheng* 'merit students'
gāogēn de xié 'shoes with high heels' → *gāogēn xié* 'high-heeled shoes'
xiǎode chéngxù 'small programs' → *xiǎo chéngxù* 'mini programs'

In such word instances, the character "*de*" can be either present or absent, but there is a tendency to omit it. Because the "adjective + noun" structure formed after omitting "*de*" is more concise in form and the meaning scope of the words is narrowed. For example, the semantics of words like *chúnjìng shuǐ* 'purified water' and *gāogēn xié* 'high-heeled shoes' have solidified. People tend to use words that are "concise in form and clear in meaning" for expression and communication. Judging from the specific usage performance of word instances and data, the usage examples with "*de*" omitted account for the vast majority.

② Under specific contexts and conditions, the appearance of "*de*" can play a role in highlighting information and emphasizing emotions. For example:

jīdòng de lèishuǐ 'excited tears' → *jīdòng lèishuǐ
gānjìng de shuǐ 'clean water' → *gānjìng shuǐ
wēnnuǎn de shuāngshǒu 'warm hands' → *wēnnuǎn shuāngshǒu
yōuyì de zhōngyī 'excellent doctor in traditional Chinese medicine' → *yōuyì zhōngyī

In such word instances, the character "*de*" must appear or tend to be shown. For example, *jīdòng de lèishuǐ* 'excited tears' is generally not said as *jīdòng lèishuǐ*. Because the word *jīdòng* 'excited' has a strong descriptive nature and indicates that the speaker's inner emotions are extremely intense. At this time, the addition of "*de*" is needed to highlight the descriptiveness of the adjective. That is, "What kind of tears? They are excited tears." Similarly, "*de*" in *wēnnuǎn de shuāngshǒu* 'warm hands' and *yōuyì de zhōngyī* 'excellent doctor in traditional Chinese medicine' can play a role in highlighting and emphasizing information. If "*de*" is omitted, it is easy to cause incomplete word structures or incomplete semantics.

③ The omission of "*de*" can promote semantic condensation and further solidify sentence structures. When "*de*" is omitted, some word instances formed by adjectives and nouns have metaphorical meanings. Both the literal and the metaphorical meaning can be used, but there is a tendency to use metaphorical meaning. For example:

literal meaning	metaphorical meaning
yìng de gǔtou 'tough bone' → *yìng gǔtou* 'resolute person'	
niú de píqi 'temper of cows' → *niú píqi* 'stubborn temper'	

(*continued*)

(*continued*)

literal meaning	metaphorical meaning
huā de jiàzi 'flower shelf' → *huā jiàzi* 'showy but useless display'	
luòshuǐ de gǒu 'drowned dog' → *luòshuǐ gǒu* 'person in a desperate situation'	

In such word instances, the character "*de*" can be either present or absent. However, the range of word meanings expressed by its presence or absence is different. When "*de*" appears, it expresses the literal meaning and the meaning range is relatively narrow. When "*de*" is omitted, it expresses the metaphorical meaning and the meaning range will be extended. In comparison, the usage examples of metaphorical meaning are more. We believe that metaphor is people's new understanding and cognition generated from existing experience. After omitting "*de*", new and deeper meanings are given to words or phrases. At the same time, after being depicted by metaphor, complex word meanings are expressed in more vivid and intuitive ways, making it easier for people to understand and remember. Therefore, the usage frequency of such word instances that are "simple in structure, easy to understand, and profound in meaning" is higher.

④ The objects referred to by the occurrence and absence of "*de*" are different. After some adjectives with differentiating meanings, the word instances formed by omitting "*de*" have the function of specific reference or refer to a specific type of word instance. For example:

xiǎo de zhànshì 'short soldier' → *xiǎo zhànshì* 'young soldier'	
lǎo de tóngzhì 'old comrade' → *lǎo tóngzhì* 'veteran comrade'	
dà de huòchē 'big truck' → *dà huòchē* 'heavy-duty truck'	
dà de yínháng 'big bank' → *dà yínháng* 'major bank'	

In such word instances, the character "*de*" can be either present or absent. However, its presence or absence expresses different referential functions. For example, *xiǎo de zhànshì* indicates a soldier who is young in age or small in stature. While *xiǎo zhànshì* 'young soldier' has a specific referential function and is often used in expressions like *zhèwèi xiǎo zhànshì* 'this young soldier' and *nàwèi xiǎo zhànshì* 'that young soldier'. Similarly, *dà de huòchē* 'big truck' has a broad meaning and can denote a truck that is large in volume or has a large carrying capacity. After omitting "*de*", *dà huòchē* 'heavy-duty truck' has a narrower meaning and specifically refers to a series type of vehicle like a heavy-duty truck. Judging from the occurrence probability of word instances, there is a tendency to use the form without "*de*". That is, the number of word instances with specific referential functions is dominant.

To sum up, we have summarized four rules and characteristics of the the occurrence and absence of the character "*de*" in single-item attributive structures. However, in the process of distinguishing and using them, for one thing, we can refer to examples in large-scale corpora. For another, we can use the introspective method. Everyone's language sense and judgment criteria are different, and the usage conditions and contexts of words are also not the same. We cannot say that certain words absolutely cannot be used in a certain way. Therefore, the occurrence and absence of the character *"de"* in the attributive structures and the combination rules of various attributive elements discussed in this paper are probabilistic tendencies based on the usage of corpora.

6 Conclusion

We use probabilistic and statistical methods to classify and study the word instances of single-item attributive structures in the articles of "People's Daily" from 2019 to 2021. Through comparative analysis of attributive elements and head components in the two structures, we find that the proportion of repeated use of adjectives and nouns is very high, but the frequency of their common collocation is relatively low. The choice and use of the adhesive or combined structure is not a random collocation, but has a certain degree of distinctiveness and probabilistic tendency.

Through examining and studying the distribution, syllable combination patterns, and occurrence and absence of *"de"* in word instances of adhesive and combined single attributive structures, we find that the number of single attributive word instances in adhesive "adjective + noun" structure is significantly lower than that of the combined "adjective + de + noun" structure, but the usage frequencies of word instances are much higher than those of the combined structure.

Besides, through data analysis, we conclude that the most common and widely used syllable combination pattern is "disyllabic adj. + disyllabic noun". We have also studied the different combination characteristics of the two attributive structures and the tendency of the occurrence and absence of *"de"* when the central word is a monosyllabic noun. In addition, this paper divides the occurrence and absence of the character *"de"* in single-item attributives into three types: "only hidden, only shown, and the intersection of being hidden or shown". What's more, the occurrence and absence of *"de"* in real texts has the characteristic of "polarization". For the vast majority of word instances, there is a strong tendency to use *"de"* or not. The proportion of word instances where the character *"de"* can be both hidden and shown is only about one-third. Moreover, the appearance of *"de"* has the function of distinguishing word meanings and highlighting information. The hiding of *"de"* can make the semantics more concise and further solidify the sentence structure, making certain sentence patterns form specific or metaphorical expressions.

The textual data resources of attributive structures formed in this paper can serve intelligent recognition systems such as newspaper reading and semantic understanding, and provide a basis and reference for the lexical semantic research of adjective attributive structures. In future research, we will continue to expand the corpus scale and incorporate corpus of other stylistic genres such as novels and essays for further analysis and exploration.

References

1. Zhu, D.: *yǔfǎ* jiǎngyì. [Lectures on Grammar], 62–148. The Commercial Press, Beijing (1982)
2. Zhu, D.: xiàndài hànyǔ xín róngcí yánjiū. [A Study on Modern Chinese Adjectives], 14–19. Studies in Language and Linguistics (1956)

3. Liu, Y.: dìngyǔ de fēnlèi hé duōxiàng dìngyǔ de shùnxù.[Classification of Attributes and the Order of Multiple Attributes], 136–157. Anhui Education Press, Hefei (1984)
4. Yuan, Y.: dìngyǔ shùnxù de rènzhī jiěshì jíqí lǐlùn yùnhán. [Cognitive Explanation of the Order of Attributes and Its Theoretical Implications], 185–201. Social Sciences in China (1999)
5. Cui, Y.: xiàndài hànyǔ dìngyǔ de yǔxù rènzhī yánjiū[A Cognitive Study of the Word Order of Modern Chinese Attributes], 294–346. China Social Sciences Press, Beijing (2002)
6. Li, X.: A Study ong the Function of Attribute and the Order of Multiple Attribute in Chinese. Language and Translation, 11–18 (2016)
7. Lü, S.: dānyīn xíngróngcí yòngfǎ yánjiū. [A Study on the Usage of Monosyllabic Adjectives]. Studies of The Chinese Language, 2–11 (1966)
8. Guo, R.: The Conversion of Expressional Functions and an Analysis of Particle *de* in Mandarin Chinese. Contemporary Linguistics, 37–52 (2000)
9. Zheng, Y.: dìngyǔ hòumiàn *"de"* zì de yòng hé bùyòng wèntí. [The Use and Non-use of *"de"* after Attributes]. Contemporary Rhetoric, 9–45 (2004)
10. Wang, G.: Rules of Using *"de"* in Nominal Endocentric Phrases. Jilin University Journal Social Sciences Edition, 115–121 (2006)
11. Wang, Y.: A study on the occurrence of the modifier marker *"de"*. Doctoral Dissertation of Capital Normal University, 9–102 (2008)
12. Xu, Y.: Chunking, Prominence and Usage of *"de"*. Language Teaching and Linguistic Studies, 76–82 (2011)
13. Lei, Y.: A Quantitative Study of Multiple-attributive Phrases and the uses of *"de"* in the Phrases. Master's Thesis of Peking University, 9–88 (2012)
14. Pei, H.: A Review of the Research on the Appearance and Disappearance of *"de"* in Chinese Modifier-head Constructions. Chinese Character Culture, 31–36 (2020)
15. Zhang, J.: Analysis of the Form and Meaning in Collocation of Chinese " V plus Color" Verb-Object Compounds. Chinese Lexical Semantics, CLSW - 22nd Workshop, 415–425 (2023)
16. Lü, S.: shìlùn fēiwèi xíngróngcí. [Study On Non-predicative Adjectives]. Studies of The Chinese Language, 3–45 (1981)

Cognitive Study on Chinese Psychological Noun *"Memory (Jìyì)"*

Peijia Hu(✉) 📷

College of International Education, Southwestern University of Finance and Economics, Chengdu 610074, Sichuan, China
6897493@qq.com

Abstract. Through the research on the conceptual materialization of the Chinese psychological noun *"Memory (Jìyì)"*, we find that, when describing *"Memory (Jìyì)"* in Chinese, there is a basic cognitive tendency, to recognize them as a specific and tangible thing that can be perceived by people's perceptual organs, which is a common cognitive ability of human beings, the ability to materialize concepts. And this cognitive tendency of conceptual materialization is carried out under a basic cognitive strategy: either *"Memory (Jìyì)"* is recognized as a space-like thing or as an entity-like thing, which we call spatialization and substantialization. This differences in cognitive strategies for *"Memory (Jìyì)"* will lead to obvious and complementary differences in Chinese lexical and syntactic expressions. This phenomenon is not only common in Chinese psychological nouns, but also exists in English psychological nouns. We believe that the research on the conceptual reification of Chinese psychological nouns has important research value for expanding our cognition of the abstract concepts of psychological categories.

Keywords: Conceptual Materialization · Cognitive Tendency · Cognitive Strategy · Spatialization · Substantialization

1 Introduction

We have found that in Chinese, there is a basic cognitive tendency when describing psychological nouns such as "memory" - to perceive them as concrete and tangible things that can be perceived by human sensory organs, usually things that we contact in our daily lives, in order to make those abstract concepts easier for us to understand, we can call this the ability to materialize concepts. Ling Zihui and Liu Zhengguang (2008) [1] (Zhengguang, The Explanatory Power of Constraint-guided Conceptual Combination Theory on Abstract N1 + N2in Mandarin Chinese, 2008) referred to this as the concretization function of abstract nouns, and believed that "the concretization function makes the cognitive entities represented by abstract nouns have the properties of 'things', easier to understand and remember, and easier to embed in abstract relationships - in short, easier to manipulate. Moreover, the concretization function also makes abstract concepts more accessible and easier for individuals to consciously recognize, thus becoming an idealized conceptual reference point." Some scholars refer to this phenomenon as conceptual

P. Jin et al. (Eds.): CLSW 2024, LNAI 15552, pp. 37–53, 2025.
https://doi.org/10.1007/978-981-96-3509-2_3

materialization and point out that "the ability of conceptual materialization is the fundamental mechanism of nominalization" [2] (Hang, 2007). The so-called "conceptual materialization ability" is a basic cognitive abilities that has emerged in the long-term survival and evolution of humans, by this abilities human can recognized abstract intangible conceptual categories as concrete tangible conceptual categories for understanding and grasping, and using relevant vocabulary and language forms to describe. According to Lakoff&Johnson, "Human experience of their own body and external physical entities is the foundation for understanding abstract entities. The experience of physical entities enables humans to view various nonphysical entities, such as events, activities, emotions, and thoughts, as physical entities, known as ontological metaphors. Through the mechanism of ontological metaphors, we can refer to, categorize, combine, and quantify abstract entities for reasoning" [3] (Johnson, 2018).

Based on our analysis of the relevant corpora collected, we found that this cognitive tendency towards conceptual objectification is carried out under a basic cognitive strategy, which involves either perceiving abstract concepts as something similar to space or as something similar to an entity, and there are some complementary and compatible attributes between the two:

When "*Memory*" is recognized as a space, its interior is hollow without substance or density, and can accommodate other things within it, with enclosure and storage functions. As a space, it does not have the ability to move in space, but "things" within the space can move in space within or between the interior and exterior. At the same time, the interior of the space can be divided into different levels and parts. And we call this phenomenon the spatialization of "*Memory*".

When "*Memory*" is recognized as a physical entity, it has substance inside, with a certain density, quality, appearance, and can also be endowed with some physical characteristics of natural entities, such as color, smell, temperature, weight, texture, and can be perceived by human sensory organs to produce corresponding perceptions, such as vision, taste, tactile sensation, etc.; There is a possibility to move in space which can be it's own move or moved by external forces. Physical things have discreteness, and their entirety can be composed of different components that have different functions. We call this phenomenon the substantialization of "*Memory*".

We believe that spatialization and substantialization of abstract concepts are two fundamental strategies for conceptual materialization in language. The differences in cognitive strategies for "*Memory*" will lead to different forms in the specific language description of Chinese, resulting in significant differences in lexical and syntactic expression.

2   Differences in the Grammar of "*Memory*" Under Two Cognitive Strategies

2.1   "*Memory*" is "Space"

When the word "*Memory*" is recognized as "Space", its grammatical characteristics are manifested as:

You can Add Directional and Locative Words After it.

Abstract nouns generally cannot be paired with directional words, while *"Memory"* can be paired with directional words such as "in, on, out" to form directional phrases:

(1) in *memory*	(2) on *memory*	(3) out of *memory*

It can also be paired with place words, including various living containers, architectural spaces, and water spaces, such as:

(4) the depths of *memory*	(5) the surface of *memory*
(6) the bottom layer of *memory*	(7) the corners of *memory*
(8) the sea surface of *memory*	(9) the seabed of *memory*
(10) the river surface of *memory*	(11) the riverbed of *memory*

At the same time, *"Memory"* can be further combined with directional words on the basis of collocation with place words, such as:

(12) in the warehouse of *memory*	(13) in the ocean of *memory*
(14) on the sea surface of *memory*	(15) in the corridor of *memory*

Zhang Keding (2021) once pointed out: "The so-called abstract nouns have no spatiality, which actually means that the abstract entities they refer to do not have spatiality. Therefore, if abstract nouns are to be used together with spatial prepositions/postpositions, they need to be given a certain spatiality to the abstract entities they refer to. Specifically speaking...... it is the result of the cognitive subject actively using cognitive imagination to conceptualize abstract entities as entities with spatiality, and using it to describe the abstract spatial orientation relationship between them and a certain material entity." [4] (Keding, 2023)As an abstract concept in psychological consciousness, *"Memory"* does not express the true spatial orientation when paired with directional words. Instead, it metaphorically projects abstract concepts using spatial orientation, a common and easily understandable concrete concept in human cognition. It spatializes psychological consciousness activities and uses vocabulary and language forms that describe spatial orientation to concretize our expression of abstract psychological consciousness activities. At the same time, by adding directional and locative words after *"Memory"*, it has the characteristic of spatial location, which provides a semantic basis for further combining with related prepositions to form adverbial, attributive, complement and other syntactic components, and can play more syntactic roles at the syntactic level. At the same time, by combining with various directional words and place words, *"Memory"* is divided into different dimensions and levels like space, such as "inside and outside, up and down, surface and bottom, deep and shallow", which provides specific coordinates for describing abstract psychological activities.

Acting as an Adverbial

When *"Memory"* acting as an adverbial can indicate the process of virtual movement of things in the virtual space of *"Memory"*, which can be further divided into the following situations:

Firstly, mark the starting point of displacement motion.

---

(16) Campus songs slowly float from *memory* (People's Daily, March 1996)

(17) An old sentence floats from *memory* (Gu Lin's "Green Lanterns Taste Like Childhood")

Secondly, mark the endpoint of displacement motion

---

(18) Carve a faint imprint in my *memory* (Author's Digest, 1997)

(19) This left a strong mark in my childhood *memories* (People's Daily, 1998)

Thirdly, mark the path and trajectory of displacement motion

---

(20) Her childhood past flowed back in her *memory*. (Contradictory Midnight)

(21) There is also a fragrance that lingers in her *memory* all the time (Zhang Xiaoxian's "The Girl Who Sways Starry Nights")

Acting as an Attributive

Mark the position of the modified central phrase in the"Memory"space

---

(22) Let's revisit the indelible imprint in our *memories* together (People's Daily, 2000)

(23) A person cannot easily sell such a precious page in their *memory* (People's Daily, December 1993)

Acting as a Complement

Its main grammatical structure is: "V + P + *Memory* + Directional words".

Firstly, when"*Memory*"acting as a complement is generally used to mark the endpoint of the movement of things in the virtual space of *"Memory"*, and to describe the process of people or things entering the interior of the"*Memory*"space, such as:

---

(24) People inevitably fall into the trap of *memory* at times. (BCC Weibo Corpus)

(25) Let me deeply embed every note into my *memory* (Zhang Haidi's "Dreams in a Wheelchair")

(26) That scene, that time and space have always been written in the *memory* of life. "(People's Daily, 1993)

(27) Last night's events suddenly hit into my *memory* (Sifangyu's "Beautiful Little Evil Star")

Secondly, describe the way relevant *memory* information exists and operates in the"*Memory* space ".

(28) This person has long been dead, but lives in the *memories* of all water people. (Shen Congwen's "Xiangxi")

(29) I am too old to see or hear, too old to expect the future, and can only live in *memory*. (Qiong Yao's "Clothes of Dreams")

One type of situation is to hide or conceal information that one does not want to recall, and place it in the deep layers of the *memory* space where it is not easily discovered. In fact, it is an active and conscious effort to not remember specific information, achieving the goal of forgetting:

(30) It's better to forgotten. It's better to throw it into the depths of *memory*. (BCC Weibo Corpus)

(31) I tried my best to lock everything in a small box, then put on many locks and press them down to the bottom of my *memory*. (Dong Yina's "Unsettled Dust")

Another type of situation is to place the content of *memory* outside the "container" of *"Memory"* to indicate forgetting:

(32) The feelings that flashed past my heart and eyes, I could bear to let them slip out of my *memory* and fade into the vague smoke. (Bingxin, "Complete Works of Bingxin, Volume 5")

(33) At the age of 65, he looked back on the various stages of his life that were connected by women, and the days without women were all out of his *memory*. (Zhang Xianliang's "Habit of Death")

Other Grammatical Attributes
When *"Memory"* is recognized as space, it cannot be modified with quantifiers and does not have the ability of spatial displacement, so it generally cannot serve as a subject or object in syntax.

2.2 *"Memory"* is *"Entity"*

When the word *"Memory"* is recognized as an "Entity", its grammatical characteristics are manifested as:

Can be Modified by Attributive Modifiers to Form a Biased Phrase
Adjectives as attributives
　　Sensory perception adjectives, mainly including visual, tactile, and taste adjectives
　　Firstly, visual adjectives
　　Color adjectives

(34) red *memories*		(35) black *memories*	(36) yellowed *memories*	(37) never fade *memories*

Adjectives describing visual clarity

(38) vague *memories*	(39)elusive *memories*	(40) clear *memories*	(41)hazy *memories*

Adjectives describing spatial distance

(42) distant *memories*	(43) deep m*emories*	(44) shallow *memories*	(45) deep shallow *memories*

Adjectives that describe the spatial shape of things

(46) fragmented *memories*	(47) *memories* broken into ashes

Adjectives describing biological states

(48) fresh *memories*

Adjectives that describe the old and new states of things

(49) outdated *memories*	(50) old *memories*

Secondly, taste adjectives

(51) sweet *memories*	(52) spicy and sour *memories*	(53) bitter *memories*

Thirdly, tactile adjectives
Weight adjectives

(54) heavy *memories*

Pain adjectives

(55) painful *memories*	(56) anguished *memories*

Temperature adjectives

(57) warm *memories*	(58) icy cold *memories*

Adjectives describing liquids

(59) moist *memories*

Fourthly, adjectives from different perceptual domains can be combined across domains to form composite attributive components:

(60) grey and heavy *memories*	(61) heavy and painful *memories*	(62) green and acerb *memories*

Verb as attributive
Firstly, verbs related to biological characteristics are used as attributives

(63) sleeping *memories*	(64) gradually awaken *memories*	(65) awakened *memories*
(66) resurgent *memory*	(67) dead *memory*	(68) moldy *memories*

Secondly, use hand verbs as attributives

(69) *Memories* that cannot be erased	(70) *memories* of youth that cannot be erased indelible *memories*

Thirdly, store preservation verbs as attributives

(71) dust-covered *memories*	(72) sealed *memories*
(73) deeply hidden *memories*	(74) buried *memories*

Can be Modified by Quantifiers
We have found that "*Memory*" in Chinese can be recognized as two-dimensional flat objects, one-dimensional linear objects, as well as liquids, organisms, discrete objects, etc. Therefore, it has the spatial characteristics of these things and can be modified with corresponding quantifiers, such as:
One dimensional quantifier:

(75) a thread of *memory*	(76) a strand of *memory*	(77) a section of *memory*

Two dimensional quantifier:

(78) a page of *memory*	(79) a frame of *memory*	(80) a piece of *memory*

Liquid quantifiers:

(81) drops of *memories*

At the same time, quantifiers can also form compound attributive components with adjectives to modify "*Memory*".

(82) a string of heavy *memories*	(83) a piece of heavy gray *memory*	(84) a section of heavy *memory*

As Long Tao (2011) pointed out, "The cognitive structure of abstract objects is a "mapping" of the cognitive structure of objects in the physical space domain, and the two have isomorphism in terms of cognitive structure. Through metaphorical means, the cognitive structure framework of physical objects is transferred or "mapped" to abstract objects, and the referent becomes the metaphorical form of physical objects, thus obtaining the spatial form characteristics of "size, height, thickness, aggregation, and separation" like physical objects." [5] (Tao, 2011)When Chinese conceptualizes and objectifies "*Memory*", it also assigns various physical attributes of objects in reality to"*Memory*", making them perceptible by visual, tactile, and taste organs. Therefore, "*Memory*" has the language foundation modified by sensory adjectives and various quantifiers mentioned above.

"Memory" Can Serve as the Subject

When "*Memory*"is recognized as a biological, liquid, or discrete entity, it has the possibility of spatial displacement and state change. Under these conditions, "*Memory*" has the basic semantic condition of being the subject:

"*Memory*" can move or change in a way unique to living organisms.

(85) Human *memory* can transcend mountains and rivers (People's Daily, April 4, 2019, 4th edition)

(86) Twenty years of *memories* are running in her mouth (Yan Geling's "The Ninth Widow")

(87) At this moment, *memories* will suddenly jump out (Wei Hui's "Shanghai Baby")

"Memory" Can Serve as an Object

When "*Memory*" is used as the object, it can be the object dominated and influenced by the action, including spatial displacement under external force:

(88) Unknown fonts, unfamiliar names, like a thin and long hook, <u>hook up the long forgotten</u> *memories* from the bottom of my heart. (Dai Houying's "People, People!")

(89) When the door is closed in the afternoon, I will accompany them back to their hometown, go to their alma mater, meet their classmates, and gradually <u>pick up the</u> *memories* <u>that has long been scattered</u>. (Lu Buxuan's "Butcher's View of the World")

Or a change in state under external force:

(90) <u>It awakened my</u> *memory*, like a gust of evening wind blowing through a sleeping flower. (Lao She's "Crescent Moon")

(91) Something suddenly <u>stirred up Hu Guoguang's</u> *memory* (contradiction in "Erosion")

(92) He suddenly <u>captured this</u> *memory* deposited in life (Author's Digest, 1994)

(93) Over three years have <u>washed away many</u> *memories* (People's Daily, 1996)

From the analysis of the corpus, the word *"Memory"* as the object mainly reflects the passive side of the psychological consciousness activity of *"Memory"*, that is, human *memory* is sometimes activated under certain external stimuli. If there is no corresponding stimulus, these *memories* will remain dormant for a long time. Due to the long time, the *memory* subject itself is not aware of the existence of such *memories*. It is not until specific external factors are activated that the *memory* subject becomes aware of it. And this process is in line with the syntactic role of the object in Chinese grammar.

Other Grammatical Attributes

When *"memory"* is recognized as an entity, a complementary difference is formed with *"Memory"* being recognized as a "space", that is, at this time, *"Memory"* cannot carry directional words, place words, or serve as grammatical components such as adverbs and complements.

2.3 Summary

Based on the analysis of the differences in grammatical attributes of the word *"Memory"* after "spatialization" and "substantialization", we found that the fundamental reason for this difference lies in the physiological function of *"Memory"* as a conscious activity. As the main function of *"Memory"* is to record and store external information, and to retrieve and extract it at specific times, this functional characteristic is very similar to the process of humans saving, storing, searching, and extracting items in daily life. When humans store items, they need to put them in specific enclosed spaces. Therefore, when they recognize *"Memory"*, they will "spatialize" it according to the spatial processing in storage activities. Therefore, *"Memory"* possesses the physical properties of space; At the same time, another physiological function of *"Memory"* activity is that it can be sub-consciously activated under specific stimulus conditions, which is often unconscious to the *memory* subject themselves, especially for some older *memories* that the people may think they have forgotten but are activated under specific stimulus conditions. There-fore, when people recognize this type of *memory* activity, they project some biological characteristics onto it, giving it active agency, such as the concepts of "awakening, resurrection, emergence" and the relative concepts as "sleep, death". At the same time, the generation of human *memory* is often closely related to the strong physical stimuli of the external world on human sensory organs, such as visual, tactile, taste, etc. These strong stimuli, when applied to the corresponding sensory organs, produce specific physiological sensations that are packaged and stored together with related *memories*, these specific *memories* may be reactivated when encountering similar physical stimuli, such as childhood *memories* of a particular food taste or smell, or *memories* of something visual or tactile. The strong binding between *memory* activity and physiological perception can be reflected in language by using these perceptual adjectives to modify and describe *memory*, assigning these physical attributes to *memory*. Generally, only entities have such physical attributes, so *memory* has physical attributes.

3 The Dual Characteristics of "Space/Entity" in Chinese Psychological Nouns

Based on our further research, we found that this phenomenon of dual characteristics of "space/entity" also exists in other psychological terms in Chinese, such as (Table 1):

Table 1. The dual characteristics of "space/entity" in Chinese psychological nouns

	Entity	Space
Thought	(94)As this *thought* grew up, I was driven by it and wanted to do some concrete research. (Image Dialogue Techniques in Psychotherapy) (95)A *thought* gradually took shape in Yang's mind: Isn't it easy to explain with waves? (Cao Tianyuan's "Does God Roll Dice? A History of Quantum Physics")	(96)The reason why we emphasize continuing to liberate our minds is because there are still many rules and regulations in our *thoughts* that cannot adapt to the constantly changing objective reality. (People's Daily, March 19, 2012, 7th edition) (97)The Air Force General Hospital emphasizes the purpose of serving the people must take root in everyone's *thoughts* in the hospital (People's Daily, June 14, 1993, 3rd edition)
Idea	(98)Song Ailing's heart became hot, and the *idea* that had been bothering her for days kept rising. (Chen Tingyi's "Complete Biography of the Song Family") (99)Panyun looked at Qianyun and suddenly an *idea* flashed through her mind. What if Qianyun married into the Zhong family? (Qiong Yao's "Gathering and Dispersing Two Yiyi")	(100)In Wong Kar wai's initial *idea*, 'Chongqing Forest' has three stories in total. (Wong Karwai's "Chongqing Forest") (101)In Xia Feng's *idea*, Bai Xue should follow him the opinion of having an abortion(Jia ingwa"Qin Opera")

(*continued*)

Table 1. (*continued*)

	Entity	Space
Concept	(102)Everyone should establish the *concept* that the advantage of Shanxi's coal industry is not mainly based on quantity. "(People's Daily, March 31, 1993, 2nd edition) (103)China is a country with a heavy on the *concept* of 'officials', and both officials and the people are suffocated by this heavy idea in their hearts. (Sun Li and Yu Xiaohui, "Urban Wind and Flow")	(104)When the car crossed the stone road, some familiarity my memories floated into my *concept*. (Lu Yin's "West Lake in Autumn Light") (105)Hope that more cities will come out of the outdated *concept* of registered residence discrimination (People's Daily, April 4, 2006, 13th Edition)
Impression	(106)My first *impression* of Comrade Wang Zhen was that he was upright, outgoing, and easy to approach. (People's Daily, October 24, 1993, 5th edition)	(107)After receiving the notification from the school about studying broad in China, also hesitated because in my *impression*, China is not very developed. (People's Daily, June 6, 2017, 23rd edition)

Based on the above analysis, we found that the dual characteristics of "space/entity" are a common phenomenon in Chinese psychological nouns. Therefore, we can consider this as a fundamental strategy of the Chinese language in recognizing abstract concepts in the category of psychological consciousness, that is, recognizing these psychological consciousness as things that have both spatial and entity attributes, and choosing to highlight their spatial or entity attributes according to different contexts and expression needs, which can be flexibly switched between the two attributes.

We believe that the dual nature of "space/entity" in Chinese psychological nouns can be explained by the "focus background" theory in cognitive linguistics. Talmy (2000) pointed out that "a focus is a moving or conceptually movable entity. Its position, path, or direction is a variable. The specific value of this variable is the relevant problem. The background is a reference entity. Compared to the reference frame, this entity is in a relatively static state. The position, path, or direction of the focus can be determined by this entity." [6] (Leonard Talmy, 2017) The "focus background" theory is based on the "saliency principle" of cognitive linguistics.

Principle of Significance:

Things that protrude from a person's cognitive structure are easily perceived as "bounded individual things" because they are very conspicuous. In terms of grammatical structure, this bounded thing needs to be modified with quantifier attributives and expressed in a "conspicuous form" (i.e. marked form: "quantity name" phrase).

On the contrary, in terms of cognitive structure, "inconspicuous things" are easily seen as boundaryless things, which can be expressed in an "inconspicuous form" (i.e. unmarked light rod form).

According to the "focus background" theory and the "salience principle", when our cognitive attention is projected onto *"Memory"*, *"Memory"* becomes the "focus" and a "bounded individual thing", endowed with physical attributes such as mobility, mass, density, color, temperature, odor, etc., which can be used as a subject or object in grammar and can be modified by adjectives and quantifiers. At this point, our thinking organs such as the mind and brain become the "background" and are recognized as "space". When our cognitive focus is projected onto the object of *"Memory"*, that is, the content of *memory*, such as information about past people, events, objects, etc., these objects become the "focus" and are recognized as "bounded individual things" with physical attributes. And *"memory"* is recognized as "background", seen as an "unbounded thing", [7] endowed with the attribute of "space", and manifested in grammar as being able to be paired with directional words, prepositional phrases, etc. It can be seen from this that the dual attribute of *"Memory"* is due to its cognitive location exactly in the middle between the *memory* object and the thinking organ, although its role constantly switches with changes in the projection point of cognitive attention. We can illustrate this relationship through the following graph (Fig. 1):

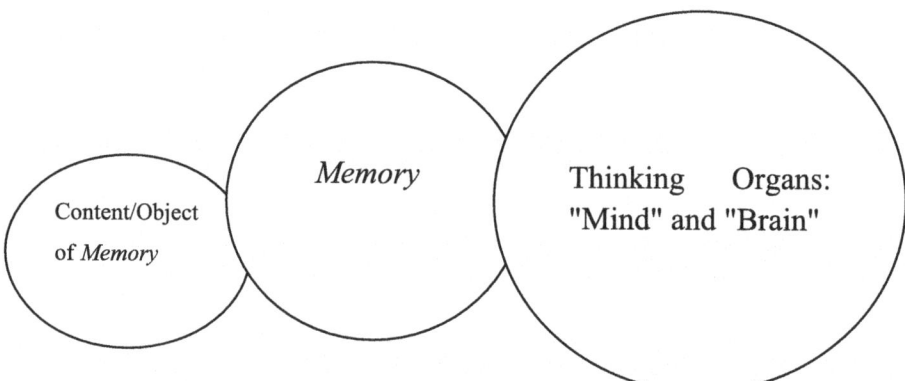

Fig. 1. Focus background relationship between *"Memory"*, *"Memory* Content", and "Thinking Organs"

Talmy (2000) also pointed out in analyzing the concept of "attending" in the category of English psychological consciousness [6] (Leonard Talmy, 2017):

"When the concept of "attending" is conceptualized as an action and expressed through verbs, English grammar provides limited room for expression, almost exclusively limited to "I attended to the music" and "She had me attend to the music". But when this behavior is conceptualized as an entity through the noun attention, we have a lot of options. The entity obtained through concretization can become a static or dynamic focus, serving as the subject of a sentence, such as:

My attention was fixed on the music;
My attention gradually wandered away from the music and on to the events of the day;

It can also serve as a focal point, acting as the direct object of a sentence, such as

The story caught/riveted my attention;
The noise attracted/drew my attention away from the book I was reading;
I directed / redirected my attention toward / away from the statue;
She directed /drew/called my attention to the painting on the far wall;

It can also serve as a background and act as an indirect object of a sentence, such as

The sound was now (squarely/firmly)in (the centre of) my attention;
The matter was (well) out of my attention;
The report eventually came to my attention"

Through the example of "attention" given by Talmy above, we can also see that the cognitive strategy of "spatialization" and "substantialization" of the Chinese psychological nouns we proposed actually exists in English. In the above example, when "attention" is used as the subject and object, this psychological concept is recognized as something similar to an entity, while when "attention" is used as the background and serves as the indirect object of the sentence, we believe that this concept is recognized as a "space/container". Therefore, in the example, "in (the center of) my attention/out of my attention/name to my attention" is used, and "in/out" is used. Mark the difference between the inside and outside of the container.

4　The Significance of Studying the Conceptual Materialization of Psychological Noun

Based on the analysis of the term *"Memory"* in the previous text, we believe that the study of the conceptual materialization phenomenon of psychological nouns in Chinese not only has linguistic research value, but also has cognitive scientific research value.

Firstly, from the perspective of cognitive science:

4.1　The Refinement of the Cognition for Mental Activity

Our study can provide a more comprehensive understanding and classification of abstract psychological activities at different stages.

The conceptual materialization of abstract psychological terms can provide people a clear and comprehensive understanding of the different stages, states, and specific functions of abstract psychological activities, as well as a more precise classification. At the same time, it also enriches and refines people's language to describing them. Taking *"Memory"* as an example, when *"Memory"* is used as a verb, our understanding of *memory* activities is vague and limited. However, when *"Memory"* is conceptualized as an abstract noun, a series of metaphors and concrete descriptions provide us a more detailed and comprehensive understanding of the entire process of *"Memory"* as a psychological activity. According to our analysis of relevant language materials, the process can be divided into the following stages:

The formation and input of *memory*
Memory storage
Retrieval of *memory*
The triggering and activation of *memory*
Retrieval and Reproduction of *memory*
The elimination and disappearance of *memory*

These different stages and functions related to *"Memory"* activities are all summarized and analyzed by us after sorting and analyzing the relevant corpus of materialization of the concept of *"Memory"*. Due to the fact that *"Memory"* is one of the many psychological consciousness activities of human beings and has certain commonalities with each other, the characteristics presented by *"Memory"* can also provide valuable clues and references for us to explore other psychological consciousness activities.

4.2 The Relationship Between Mental Activity and Physical Perception

Our study can provide a further understanding of the connection between human psychological activities and physiological perceptual experiences in the body.

We found that Chinese language often has a close connection with the physiological perception experience of the *memory* subject when describing *"Memory"*: using color, temperature, and taste adjectives to modify *memory* can describe both positive and negative *memory* activities; And weight and pain adjectives can only be used to describe negative and pessimistic *memory* activities. At the same time, these perceptual adjectives can be combined and matched to describe more complex and diverse subjective emotional states.

From a linguistic perspective, it has the following significance:

4.3 Precise and Quantitative Language Expression of Abstract Concepts

The description and expression of psychological consciousness activities in Chinese are often vague and general, and cannot be accurately quantified. However, through the materialization of concepts, we can provide more precise quantitative descriptions of abstract psychological activities

(1) If quantifiers that describe one-dimensional, two-dimensional, liquid, and other things can be used to describe *"Memory"* in different "forms".
(2) After spatializing psychological consciousness activities, spatial orientation can be used to "locate" consciousness activities, to expand the relevant descriptions.

(3) After the spatialization of *"Memory"* which adding directional words or place words after it, the abstract thing of *"Memory"* has spatial orientation divisions such as "high and low, surface/bottom, far and near, inside and outside", which can locate the position of "physical things" located "inside space" or "outside space", and describe the trajectory and direction of their spatial displacement movement.

Based on this setting, many of the concrete descriptions of *"Memory"* activities mentioned above can be further summarized as the position and motion relationship between entities and space, such as:

The storage process of *memory* can be described as the displacement process of entities from the outside to the inside of space;

The operation and continuous process of *memory* can be described as the movement of entities in entangled states or curved trajectories in space, or the state of entities being in a certain space for a long time;

The activation and retrieval process of *memory* can be described as the displacement process of entities in space from bottom to top, from bottom to surface, or from far to near, as well as the contact between entities;

The process of *memory* disappearance and forgetting can be described as the displacement of entities in space from top to bottom, from surface to bottom, or from inside to outside.

4.4   A Detailed Description of an Abstract Concept

Our study can provide more specific and detailed descriptions of the special functions and effects of abstract psychological activities.

Taking *memory* as an example, for conscious humans, its important function is to preserve and reproduce specific information from the past. The length of time for which specific information is preserved, as well as the completeness and accuracy of its reproduction, are extremely important for us. Therefore, it is necessary to describe and evaluate the functional utility of *memory* in language. As can be seen from the relevant analysis earlier in this article, Chinese uses adjectives such as spatial distance and adjectives describing the old and new states of things to describe the timeliness of *memory*; Use visual clarity adjectives to describe the accuracy of *memory*; Use adjectives describing biological states and verbs related to biological characteristics to describe the activation process and activity level of *memory*.

Using different materialization forms to metaphorically describe psychological activities can indicate the intensity of the psychological activity and the magnitude of its impact on the conscious subject. For example, when *"Memory"* appears as a complement in the "V + P + *Memory* + Directional word" structure, the semantic differences expressed by different verbs can reflect the degree of influence of the *"Memory"* on the *memory* subject when it is generated and formed, such as:

Stay in my *memory*
Lingering in my *memory*
Live in my *memory*

(*continued*)

(*continued*)

Cherish it in my *memory*
Imprinted in my *memory*
Engraved in my *memory*
Deeply engraved in my *memory*

From the above examples, we can clearly see that the influence of the psychological activity of *"Memory"* on the *memory* subject gradually increases from top to bottom. "Stay, linger, and live" continue to extend in the duration of time, and from the dimension of time, the influence of *memory* content on the *memory* subject is increasing. "Imprint, engrave" metaphorically refers to the deeper and longer lasting influence of *memory* content on the *memory* subject. At the same time, the adjective "deep" can be used to modify "engraving", further emphasizing the depth of its influence. Moreover, different verbs can also reflect the subjective emotional state of the *memory* subject during *memory* activities. For example, "cherish" can indicate that the *memory* subject actively and consciously wants to preserve *memory* content which has positive value to them, while "engrave" may be a passive *memory* activity and may also be a negative *memory* activity.

5   Conclusion

Based on the above research, we can draw the following conclusions:

The materialization of the concept of *"Memory"* can be mainly divided into two categories: "spatialization" and "substantialization ". Due to the differences in physical attributes between "space" and "entity", there will be differences in grammatical roles, and the essence of these differences lies in people's understanding of the physiological characteristics and functions of the cognitive activity of *"Memory"*.

This dual attribute of "space/entity" is commonly present in the conceptual materialization process of Chinese psychological nouns, as well as in languages like English. It has a certain universal significance and reflects some commonalities in human cognition and language.

According to our research on the phenomenon of conceptual materialization of the term *"Memory"*, it can be seen that conceptual materialization is an important way for people to recognize, understand, and describe abstract concepts, and is also a basic cognitive ability of humans. At the same time, when encoding and describing the same abstract concept, the grammatical roles and functions undertaken by nouns are more diverse and abundant than verbs. This phenomenon should also be taken seriously by relevant researchers. The study of the materialization process of psychological concepts such as *"Memory"* not only has linguistic significance, but also has cognitive scientific significance.

Acknowledgments. All data generated or analyzed during this study are included in this published article. The example sentences quoted in this study are all come from two Chinese corpus:

BCC (BLCU Corpus Center): https://bcc.blcu.edu.cn/.

CCL (Corpus of Center for Chinese Linguistics): http://ccl.pku.edu.cn:8080/ccl_corpus/.

References

1. Ling, Z., Liu, Z.: The Explanatory Power of Constraint-guided Conceptual Combination Theory on Abstract N1+N2in Mandarin Chinese. Foreign Language Research **5**, 20–25 (2008)
2. Gao, H.: Conceptual Reification and Nominalization. Journal of PLA University of Foreign Languages **6**, 16–18 (2007)
3. Lakoff, G., Johnson, M., trans.by Baojia Li.: Philosophy in the Flesh: The Embodied Mind and Its Challenge to Western Thought. Beijing World Publishing Corporation, Beijing (2018)
4. Zhang, K.: Cognitive Research on Metaphorical Spatial Relationship Construction. The Commercial Press, Beijing (2023)
5. Long, T.: Metaphorical "Bounded" Spatial Category Meaning of Abstract Nouns, Wuhan University Journal (Humanity Sciences) **4**, 112—117 (2011)
6. Talmy, L.: trans. by Fuyin Li: Toward a Cognitive Semantics (Volume I): Concept Structuring Systems. Beijing University Press, Beijing (2017)
7. Shen, J.: Bounded and Unbounded. Studies of the Chinese Lauguage **5**, 367–380 (1995)
8. Draaisma, D.: trans. by Xiufeng Qiao: Metaphors of Memory: A History of Ideas about the Mind. Flower City Press, Guangzhou (2009)
9. Lakoff, G.: trans. by Baojia Li, Ting Zhang, Xuezheng Qiu: Women, Fire and Dangerous Things: What Categories Reveal about the Mind. Beijing World Publising Corporation, Beijing (2017)
10. Ning, Y.: trans. by Yi Sun.: The Contemporary Theory of Metaphor: A Perspective from Chinese. The Commercial Press, Beijing (2023)
11. Wang, Z.: Chinese Noun Phrase Metaphor Recognition. Beijing Language and Culture University Press, Beijing (2010)
12. Zhao, Q., Xiong, J., Huang, C.-R.: Linguistic Synaesthesia, Metaphor and Cognition: The Systematicity and Significanceof Linguistic Synaesthesia in Chinese. Studies of the Chinese Lauguage **2**, 240—256 (2019)
13. Zhang, K.: Abstract spatial relation construction of location: its structural property and cognitive motivation. Modern Foreign Languages (Bimonthly) **5**, 360–371 (2021)
14. Wang, W.: The mental structures of spatial metaphorization of "Xin" (Heart) in Chinese. Journal of PLA University of Foreign Languages **1**, 57–60 (2001)
15. Wen, H., Zheng, S.: A study of adding psychological feeling into the model of synaesthesia at the morpheme level in modern chinese. In: Dong, M., Hong, J.F., Lin, J., Jin, P. (eds.) Chinese Lexical Semantics. CLSW 2023. Lecture Notes in Computer Science(), vol 14514. Springer, Singapore (2024). https://doi.org/10.1007/978-981-97-0583-2_31
16. Yi, J., Qiu, B.: A Cognitive Semantic Analysis of the Spatial Dimension Adjective "Deep/Shallow" from the Perspective of Lexical Typology. In: Dong, M., Hong, JF., Lin, J., Jin, P. (eds.) Chinese Lexical Semantics. CLSW 2023. Lecture Notes in Computer Science(), vol 14514. Springer, Singapore (2024). https://doi.org/10.1007/978-981-97-0583-2_24
17. Kim, C.:. An analysis of one-dimensional adjectives from the perspective of lexical semantic typology. In: Dong, M., Hong, J.F., Lin, J., Jin, P. (eds.) Chinese Lexical Semantics. CLSW 2023. Lecture Notes in Computer Science(), vol 14514. Springer, Singapore (2024). https://doi.org/10.1007/978-981-97-0583-2_29

Spatio-Temporal Distribution of Modifying Morphemes in Sinitic Nouns of Foreign Crops

Haoxiang Yang[1] and Sicong Dong[2(✉)]

[1] School of Mechanical Engineering and Automation, Harbin Institute of Technology, Shenzhen, China
220320428@stu.hit.edu.cn
[2] School of Humanities and Social Sciences, Harbin Institute of Technology, Shenzhen, China
dongsicong@hit.edu.cn

Abstract. Crops that were initially introduced as foreign vegetables, such as corn, sweet potato, and potato, have diverse word forms in Sinitic languages. This paper, based on large-scale data, investigates the spatio-temporal distribution of the modifying morphemes in the compound nouns of such crops, including 胡 *hú* 'foreign', 番 *fān* 'foreign', 洋 *yáng* 'oceanic, foreign', 西 *xī* 'Western', 海 *hǎi* 'oceanic', 荷兰 *Hélán* 'Holland', and 倭 *Wō* 'Japan'. These morphemes share one prominent geographical pattern: they take as a core the region where the crop was first introduced. While some show multidirectional distribution, e.g., the 番 *fān* 'foreign' category, some show unidirectional distribution, e.g., the 洋 *yáng* 'oceanic, foreign' category. Diachronically, 胡 *hú* 'foreign' and 番 *fān* 'foreign' precede 洋 *yáng* 'oceanic, foreign' and 西 *xī* 'Western'. Such spatio-temporal distribution can be accounted for by semantic change, sociocultural development, geomorphological environment, and the history of intercultural communication.

Keywords: Sinitic languages · foreign crop · modifying morpheme · geographical distribution · temporal distribution

1 Introduction

Hot and sour shredded potatoes, tomato egg stir-fry… Many of the crops in common dishes in China were originally introduced from abroad. In Sinitic languages, traditionally referred to as Chinese dialects, their names are often compound nouns with a modifier and a nominal head. The head reflects how people categorize the crops and is often based on the taxonomy of indigenous crops. For instance, tomatoes can be categorized as 茄 *qié* 'aubergine' and 柿 *shì* 'persimmon', leading to names such as 番茄 *fānqié* foreign-aubergine and 西红柿 *xīhóngshì* Western-red-persimmon. In contrast, the modifiers of the compound crop names contain more diverse information. They can indicate taste (e.g., 甘薯 *gānshǔ* sweet-potato 'sweet potato'), colour (e.g., 红苕 *hóngsháo* red-potato 'sweet potato'), growing location (e.g., 地瓜 *dìguā* earth-melon 'sweet potato'), and most commonly, the origin of the crop, such as 洋 *yáng* 'oceanic, foreign' and the aforementioned 番 *fān* 'foreign' and 西 *xī* 'Western'. Such information provides ideal data for studying the geographical distribution of words and how these crops spread throughout China.

P. Jin et al. (Eds.): CLSW 2024, LNAI 15552, pp. 54–64, 2025.
https://doi.org/10.1007/978-981-96-3509-2_4

The geographical distribution of nouns for foreign crops has been extensively studied. For example, Suzuki [1] examined the distribution of word forms of nouns 'potato': it is 马铃薯 *mǎlíngshǔ* horse-bell-potato in some places of Guangdong, Guangxi, Hunan, and Jiangxi provinces; while in some places of Guangdong and Fujian, it is called 荷兰薯 *Hélán shǔ* Holland-potato; and in the vast areas concentrated in the lower reaches of the Yangtze River and dispersed in the upper and middle reaches, it is commonly referred to as 洋- *yáng-* 'oceanic, foreign', such as 洋芋 *yángyù* foreign-taro and 洋甘薯 *yánggānshǔ* foreign-sweet-potato. Similarly, distinct distributional patterns can be found in nouns for pumpkins, tomatoes, and chilli peppers [2].

Hence, not only can the modifiers in these nouns reflect the origin of the crop, but they also show clear regional patterns. As noted by Gao and Liu [3] and Yao [4], while 荷兰- *Hélán-* 'Holland' is mainly found in Guangdong, 红毛- *hóngmáo-* 'red hair' is distributed in the southern coastal areas centred around Guangdong; when one crop has two word forms with the widely used 洋- *yáng-* 'oceanic, foreign' and 番- *fān-* 'foreign', the former tends to be used in the north, and the latter in the south.

Previous research has demonstrated that it is feasible and promising to look into the distribution of these modifiers. However, earlier studies only focused on a limited number of crops, lacking a comprehensive examination of foreign crop nouns. Additionally, the number of language points examined in these studies is relatively small, meaning that the distributional patterns need further validation or refinement. Furthermore, few studies observed these patterns from a diachronic perspective, even though the naming of some crops has spread and evolved over time. The above inadequacies highlight a clear direction for our research. We will examine the modifiers in the nouns of nine foreign crops based on large-scale data, and analyse their synchronic distribution and diachronic evolution to explore the underlying mechanism for the spatio-temporal distribution.

2 Method and Data

We first collected word forms of nine foreign crops—corn, sweet potato, potato, peanut, broad bean, radish, chilli pepper, aubergine, and tomato—from 930 data points, based on maps 013 and 015–022 in the *Linguistic Atlas of Chinese Dialects: Lexicon* [5]. Next, we extracted the modifying morphemes in the compound nouns that contain geographical information about the origin of the crop. Such nouns were then categorized into seven types: 番- *fān-* 'foreign', 洋- *yáng-* 'oceanic, foreign', 胡- *hú-* 'foreign', 西- *xī-* 'Western', 海- *hǎi-* 'oceanic', 荷兰- *Hélán-* 'Holland', and 倭- *Wō-* 'Japan'. After calculating the frequency of these modifiers on each map, we obtained a total of 180 occurrences with each modifier being 72, 10, 3, 15, 1, 21, and 58, respectively, as shown in Fig. 1.

Four points are worth noting in data processing:

First, some word forms contain more than one modifying morpheme. For example, 番鬼茄 *fānguǐqié* foreign-ghost-aubergine 'tomato' in Qujiang Yue and 番薯茄 *fānshǔqié* foreign-potato-aubergine 'tomato' in Yueqing Wu have two modifying morphemes, and 番囝芦黍 *fān.jiǎn-lú-shǔ* foreign.NOMINALIZER-reed-millet 'corn' in Tong'an Min has three. In such cases, we classified the word form based on the first morpheme if it is the only morpheme indicating the origin of the crop. Accordingly, the above three examples were all categorized as the 番- *fān-* type.

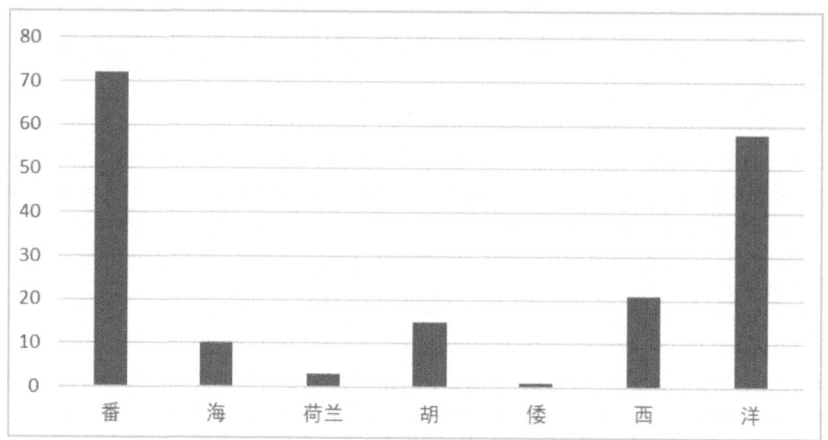

Fig. 1. Number of occurrences of seven modifying morphemes

Second, some word forms have two co-occurring modifiers both indicating the origin. For instance, potatoes are referred to as 洋番芋 *yángfānyù* foreign-foreign-taro in the languages spoken in Haimen and Qidong, Jiangsu Province, where both 洋 *yáng* and 番 *fān* are used. For these word forms, we treated the first morpheme as the primary modifier, following Yao [4]. We again use the case of 洋番芋 *yángfānyù* foreign-foreign-taro 'potato' to illustrate the rationale. Since sweet potatoes were introduced to China earlier than potatoes, it would be natural for the name of the later coming potatoes to be derived from sweet potatoes, which was already locally common. Thus, while 番芋 *fānyù* 'sweet potato' had stronger domestic connotations, the first morpheme 洋 *yáng* 'oceanic, foreign' better represented the foreign origin of potatoes.

Third, some crop nouns have different written forms. For instance, the word 洋芋 *yángyù* foreign-taro 'potato' can also be written as 羊芋 *yángyù* sheep-taro, 阳芋 *yángyù* Yang-taro, and 杨芋 *yángyù* poplar-taro. According to Xiang and Zhou [6], 洋芋 *yángyù* foreign-taro should be the original form, while the others are later homophonous variants. Bearing such caveats in mind, we tried to verify the original forms during data processing and screened out other popular forms.

Fourth, the same word form may refer to different crops at different times. For example, 土豆 *tǔdòu* earth-bean, which means potatoes in Modern Mandarin, indicated hodo, a type of bean, when it was mentioned in *Guest Records of Chang'an* 长安客话 (circa 1600–1610) [7]. Therefore, we tried to ensure that the collected data refer to foreign crops, but not other plants.

To obtain the spatial distribution of the modifiers, we calculated the occurrences of each modifier in each provincial-level division. The results are shown in Table 1, with the divisions listed in alphabetical order. Based on such data, we then plotted their geographical distribution using the 3D mapping feature in Microsoft Excel, as shown in Fig. 2, where the height of the columns represents the number of occurrences and the hollow columns indicate no distribution. Since the data are insufficient from certain regions in the *Linguistic Atlas of Chinese Dialects: Lexicon* [5], our analysis excluded data from Xizang (formerly known as Tibet), Inner Mongolia, Tianjin, Shanghai, Hong Kong, and Macau.

Table 1. Frequency of seven modifiers in provincial-level divisions

Division	番 fān	海 hǎi	荷兰 Hélán	胡 hú	倭 Wō	西 xī	洋 yáng
Anhui	5	0	0	1	0	1	4
Beijing	0	0	0	0	0	1	0
Chongqing	2	1	0	0	0	0	1
Fujian	18	0	0	1	0	2	3
Gansu	2	0	0	0	0	2	2
Guangdong	6	0	2	1	0	1	0
Guangxi	5	1	1	0	0	1	3
Guizhou	1	2	0	1	0	0	3
Hainan	5	0	0	0	0	0	0
Hebei	0	0	0	0	0	1	1
Heilongjiang	0	0	0	0	0	0	0
Henan	1	0	0	1	0	1	2
Hubei	1	1	0	2	0	1	3
Hunan	5	1	0	2	0	1	5
Jiangsu	4	0	0	2	0	0	4
Jiangxi	5	1	0	2	0	2	5
Jilin	0	0	0	0	0	0	1
Liaoning	0	0	0	0	0	0	1
Ningxia	0	0	0	0	0	2	2
Qinghai	0	0	0	0	0	1	1
Shaanxi	0	1	0	1	0	0	3
Shandong	0	0	0	0	0	1	1
Shanxi	0	0	0	0	0	2	2
Sichuan	1	1	0	1	0	0	1
Taiwan	3	0	0	0	0	0	1
Xinjiang	0	0	0	0	0	0	2
Yunnan	1	1	0	0	0	0	2
Zhejiang	7	0	0	0	1	1	5

Several obvious patterns can be found in Fig. 2. The 番- *fān*- and 洋 *yáng*- types, as mentioned earlier, are the most frequently used ones, but distributed in distinct manners.

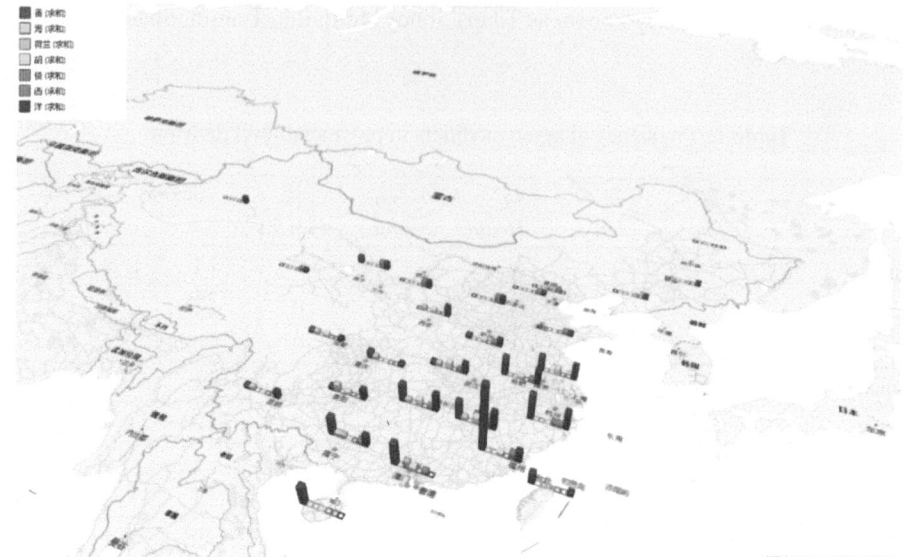

Fig. 2. Geographical distribution of seven modifiers in provincial-level divisions

The use of 番- *fān-* is more concentrated, primarily in the southeastern coastal regions of Jiangsu, Zhejiang, Fujian, Taiwan, Guangdong, Guangxi, Hainan, and neighbouring provinces such as Hunan, Jiangxi, and Anhui. In contrast, the use of 洋 *yáng-* is more widely dispersed in the whole country. Another clear pattern is shown by the 海 *hǎi-* type, which is concentrated in the southwestern provinces and surrounding regions.

Apart from Fig. 2, we also created individual distributional maps for some modifiers, which will be used in the discussion of Sect. 3. The data for these maps are the same as those for Fig. 2, and the maps were generated using the coloured map function in Microsoft Excel. Next, we will analyse in order the spatio-temporal distribution of the seven types of modifiers.

3   Discussion and Analysis

Among the seven modifiers, 胡- *hú-* 'foreign' appeared the earliest to indicate foreign items. During the Western Han dynasty (202 BCE – 9 CE), northern and western ethnic groups were referred to as 胡 *hú*. As the Silk Road increased the communication between China and surrounding countries, crops such as pepper and walnuts were introduced from the Western Regions, roughly present-day Central Asia, and were thus named after 胡 *hú*. The then capital of China, Chang'an, today's Xi'an city of Shaanxi Province, also one end of the Silk Road, was an important entrance for the foreign crops. Therefore, as shown in Fig. 3, the northernmost region where the 胡- *hú-* type is distributed is around Shaanxi Province. The map also indicates that these crops from the Western Regions, after being introduced into China, spread southward and eastward along the borders of the Han Empire. Note that in the maps used in this section, the darker the colour of a provincial-level division, the more frequently the modifier is used.

Fig. 3. Geographical distribution of 胡- *hú-*

However, not all crops introduced during the Han were first cultivated near ancient Chang'an. For instance, according to *Guangya* 广雅 (circa 227 CE), 胡豆 *húdòu* 'broad bean' was first cultivated in today's Sichuan and Yunnan provinces after Zhang Qian brought it to China during his second mission to the Western Regions in 119 BCE. Therefore, the presence of 胡- *hú-* in southwestern China, as shown in Fig. 3, also reflects some of the earliest usages of this modifier.

The modifier of 胡- *hú-* emerged under specific sociocultural conditions, thus often carrying derogatory connotations towards other ethnic groups. A similar case is the later 番- *fān-* modifier. In the dictionary *Shuowen Jiezi* 说文解字 (circa 100 CE), 胡- *hú-* and 番- *fān-* are both defined as body parts of animals: the hanging flesh under a cow's neck and the paws of a beast, respectively. With the connection of their original meanings with animals, the two characters reflected a distinction between "civilized" and "barbarian" peoples when they were used to describe people and cultures.

Such a distinction continued to hold during the Ming dynasty, so when tomatoes and sweet potatoes were first introduced to China after two centuries of maritime isolation in Ming, they were naturally labelled with 番- *fān-*, as in 番茄 *fānqié* 'tomato' and 番薯 *fānshǔ* 'sweet potato'. Evidence can be found in the CCL Corpus [8], where there are 21,349 occurrences of 番- *fān-*, with over 20,000 of which from the Ming dynasty onward, demonstrating a significant shift in naming foreign objects during that period. Since the late Ming government primarily opened its ports in Fujian Province, e.g., the cities of Zhangzhou and Quanzhou, accordingly, the distribution of 番- *fān-* centres around Fujian and radiates towards inland (Fig. 4).

Since the late Ming dynasty, increased trade and ethnic integration have been seen between China and the rest of the world. At the same time, the subsequent dynasty Qing was ruled by non-Han people, the Manchus. Therefore, the old "civilized vs. barbarian"

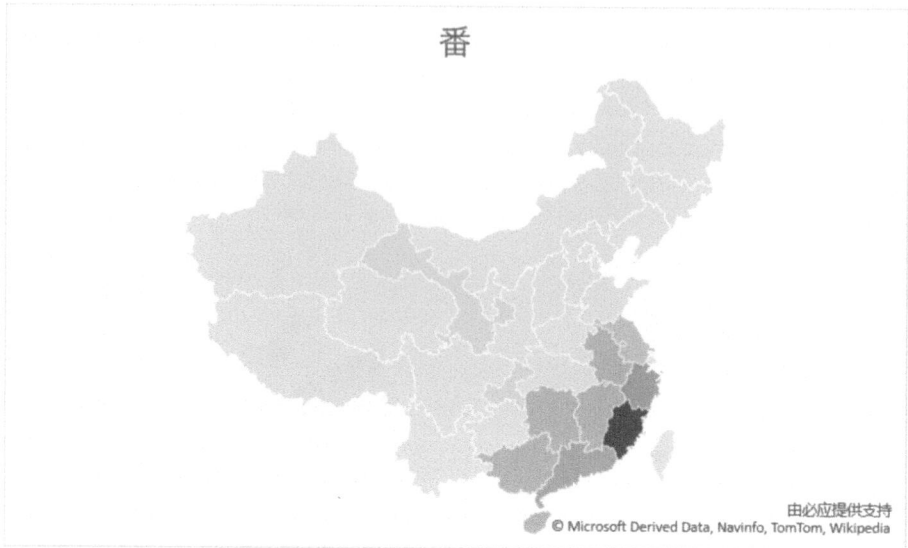

Fig. 4. Geographical distribution of 番- *fān-*

distinction gradually faded. This shift in social thought was reflected linguistically, with foreign crop names gradually being replaced by connotationally neutral modifiers such as 洋 *yáng* 'oceanic, foreign' and 西 *xī* 'Western', e.g., 洋芹 *yángqín* foreign-leaf.celery 'celery', 洋橄榄 *yáng-gǎnlǎn* foreign-Chinese.olive 'olive', 西兰花 *xī-lánhuā* Western-orchid 'broccoli', and 西柚 *xīyòu* Western-pomelo 'grapefruit'. The modifier 洋- *yáng-*, with a primary meaning related to the ocean, also shows an ocean-related distributional pattern.

As previously mentioned, the word form 洋芋 *yángyù* foreign-taro is widely adopted to indicate potatoes, rather uniformly in the inland areas to the west of Hubei and Hunan, centred on the middle and upper reaches of the Yangtze River. However, it is much less frequently seen in the lower reaches, where, on the contrary, a variety of 洋- *yáng-* type can be found: 洋芋头 *yángyùtóu* foreign-taro-head, 洋甘薯 *yánggānshǔ* foreign-sweet-potato, 洋山芋 *yángshānyù* foreign-mountain-yam, etc. This contrast of uniformity and diversity suggests that the former region adopted the word form from the latter via migration or diffusion [9], so the word form 洋芋 *yángyù*, as long as the modifier 洋- *yáng-*, should have originated from the Yangtze Delta and spread inland along the river. This path can be supported by the pattern shown in Fig. 5. Also note that one major group of the treaty ports forced by the Western powers to open during the Qing dynasty is along the Yangtze River, with its delta connected to the world through the ocean, namely, 洋 *yáng*.

The modifier 西 *xī* 'Western' is also widely used, found in the northern, northwestern, central, southern, and southeastern parts of China, as shown in Fig. 6. Our data show that the notable presence of 西 *xī* is due to the widespread use of 西红柿 *xīhóngshì* 'tomato', the "official" name in Standard Mandarin of this common crop. Also, this crop is the reason for the lack of 西 *xī* in Southwestern Mandarin, a Mandarin variety spoken

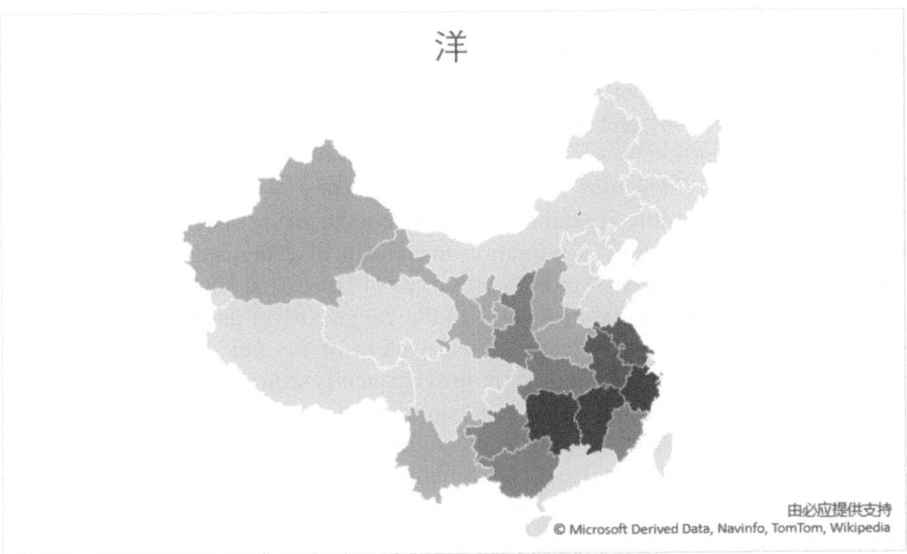

Fig. 5. Geographical distribution of 洋- *yáng-*

in Sichuan, Chongqing, Yunnan, and Guizhou. In this region, tomatoes are commonly called 番茄 *fānqié* foreign-aubergine, as well as other word forms with a regionally distinctive modifier: 海 *hǎi* 'oceanic'.

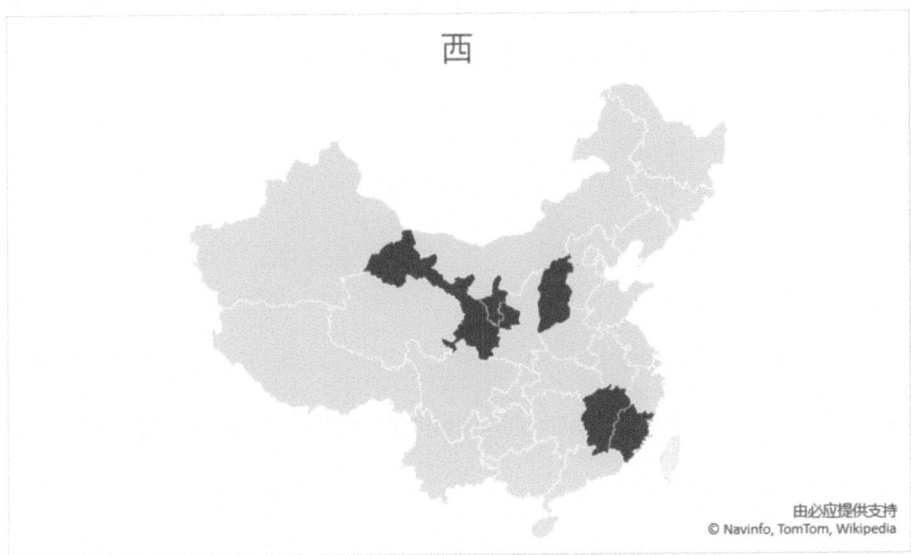

Fig. 6. Geographical distribution 西- *xī-*

The modifier 海 *hǎi* 'oceanic' is primarily used for chilli peppers, namely 海椒 *hǎijiāo* oceanic-pepper, which is a crucial ingredient for local cuisines in southwestern China. One introduction path of chilli peppers to China started in eastern Zhejiang and spread westward [10], and the modifier 海 *hǎi* 'oceanic' clearly reflects its overseas origins. One of the earliest uses of 海椒 *hǎijiāo* 'chilli pepper' can be found in 1684, in *A Gazetteer of Baoqing Prefecture* 宝庆府志 [11] and *A Gazetteer of Shaoyang County* 邵阳县志 [12], both recording vegetable information in the present-day Shaoyang, Hunan Province. During the enormous migration movement of "Huguang Filling Sichuan" (Huguang mainly encompassed today's provinces of Hubei and Hunan), chilli peppers spread along the upper and middle reaches of the Yangtze River into the Sichuan Basin, eventually forming the current distributional pattern of 海- *hǎi-* in the southwestern region, as shown in Fig. 7. This modifier is most frequently seen in Guizhou, the province with the darkest colour in Fig. 7, where it can be used not only for chilli peppers, but also for tomatoes, e.g., 海茄 *hǎiqié* oceanic-aubergine and 海茄瓜 *hǎiqiēguā* oceanic-aubergine-melon. Moreover, since the distribution of 海- *hǎi-* 'oceanic' is restricted to the southwestern region, it has not gained a sense of 'foreign' in Standard Mandarin, unlike the more widely used洋- *yáng-* 'oceanic, foreign' which shares the 'oceanic' sense.

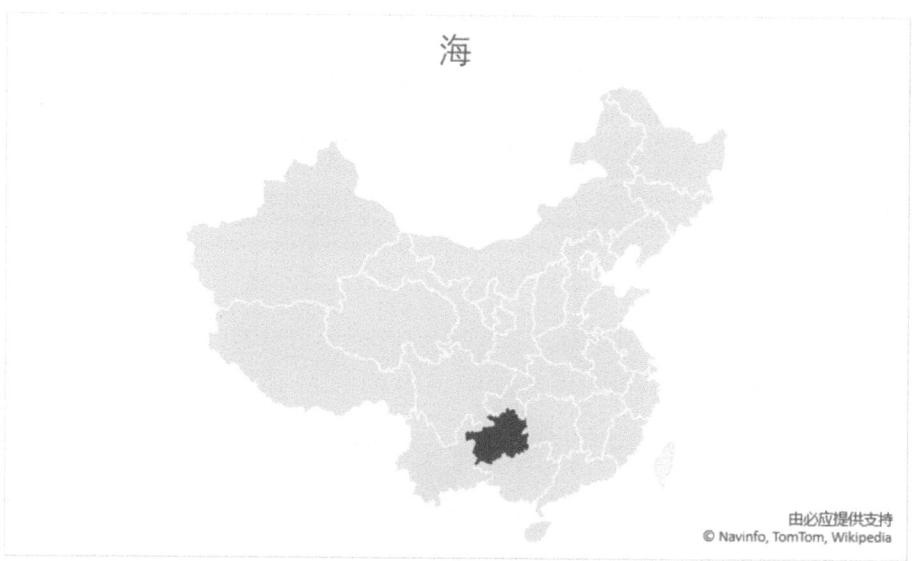

Fig. 7. Geographical distribution of 海 *hǎi-*

The only two modifiers representing specific countries—荷兰 *Hélán* 'Holland' and 倭 *Wō* 'Japan'—are much more limited in distribution. As shown in Fig. 2, while 荷兰 *Hélán* is only found in Guangdong and Guangxi, such as 荷兰薯 *Hélán-shǔ* Holland-potato 'potato', 荷兰薯仔 *Hélán-shǔzǎi* Holland-potato 'potato', and荷兰豆 *Hélán-dòu* Holland-bean 'snow pea'; 倭 *Wō-* is only used in Zhejiang, such as 倭豆 *Wōdòu* Japan-bean 'broad bean'. Such limitation is closely related to the social background. The

Netherlands has established colonies widely in Southeast Asia since the 17th century, where many overseas Chinese who were originally from Guangdong resided. Therefore, imported goods were often labelled 荷兰 *Hélán* in their languages, such as 荷兰水 *Hélán-shuǐ* Holland-water 'soda' and 荷兰牌 Hélán-pái Holland-card 'playing card'. 荷兰薯 *Hélán-shǔ* Holland-potato 'potato' and 荷兰豆 *Hélán-dòu* Holland-bean 'snow pea' followed this pattern. As for the data points of 倭豆 *Wōdòu* Japan-bean 'broad bean', all of them are distributed along the coastline of Zhejiang, which is highly likely a result of the close maritime connections with Japan in ancient times. The modifier 倭 *Wō* has not widely spread due to its derogatory connotation of Japan or the Japanese people.

4   Conclusion

In this paper, we analysed the modifying morphemes in the nouns for foreign crops and mapped out the geographical distribution of these modifiers in Sinitic languages. By using the historical information on crop introduction and sociocultural communication, we successfully accounted for the diverse distributional patterns of languages.

Geographically, these modifiers exhibit a variety of diffusion paths centred on the regions where the crops were first introduced. These patterns include multidirectional spread, as in the case of 番- *fān*- 'foreign', and unidirectional spread influenced by topography, as in the case of 洋- *yáng*- 'oceanic, foreign'. Diachronically, these modifiers follow a clear sequence: 胡- *hú*- 'foreign' and 番- *fān*- 'foreign' were used earlier, often carrying derogatory connotations; 西- *xī*- 'Western' and 洋- *yáng*- 'oceanic, foreign' became more prevalent along the increased communication between China and the rest of the world. We also found that these modifiers are relatively stable once used in a word, and not easily replaced by newer ones, although overlapping cases can be found, such as 洋番芋 *yángfānyù* foreign-foreign-taro 'potato'.

Our study shows that the rich diversity of modifying morphemes in nouns of foreign crops can serve as important data for understanding the change in society, lifestyle, and cross-cultural communications in China, and it is thus promising to investigate the geographical distribution of lexical items and grammatical features from interdisciplinary perspectives. This line of research has also been proved feasible by a series of recent studies on weather expressions in Sinitic and Tibeto-Burman languages [13–22].

References

1. Suzuki, F.: Ditu 24 shulei: malingshu he ganshu [Map 24 tuberous plants: potato and sweet potato]. In: Iwata, R. (ed.) Hanyu Fangyan Jieshi Ditu [Interpretative Maps of Chinese Dialects], pp. 154–161. Hakuteisha Press, Tokyo (2009). (in Chinese)
2. Zhan, B., Zhang, Z.: Hanyu Fangyanxue Da Cidian [The Grand Dictionary of Chinese Dialectology]. Guangdong Education Publishing House, Guangzhou (2017). (in Chinese)
3. Gao, X., Liu, X.: Hanyu miaoxie jieci de dili bianyi–yi shuini feizao xihongshi malingshu deng wei li [The geographical variants of descriptive loans in Chinese]. Chinese Teaching in the World **1**, 68–76 (2008). (in Chinese)

4. Yao, Y.: Cong ganshu malingshu de mingcheng fenbu kan wailai zuowu de mingming fangshi [The naming of exotic plants: based on the study of sweet potato and potato]. Linguistic Sciences **16**(6), 615–627 (2015). (in Chinese)

5. Cao, Z. (ed.): Hanyu Fangyan Ditu Ji (Cihui Juan) [Linguisitc Atlas of Chinese Dialects: Lexicon]. The Commercial Press, Beijing (2008). (in Chinese)

6. Xiang, M., Zhou, Y.: Hanyu fangyan li de malingshu [The names of potatoes in Chinese dialects]. Modern Linguistics **6**(2), 290–322 (2018). (in Chinese)

7. Xiang, M.: Zhongguo malingshu lishi zhaji [Notes on Chinese potato history]. Modern Linguistics **6**(2), 342–377 (2018). (in Chinese)

8. Zhan, W., Guo, R., Chang, B., Chen, Y., Chen, L.: The building of the CCL corpus: its design and implementation. Corpus Linguist. **6**(1), 71–86 (2019). http://ccl.pku.edu.cn:8080/ccl_ corpus. Accessed 7 January 2024 (in Chinese)

9. Hockett, C.F.: A Course in Modern Linguistics. The MacMillan Company, New York (1958)

10. Ding, X., Hu, Y.: Cong fangzhi jizai de lajiao difang mingcheng kan lajiao zai Zhongguo de yinzhong chuanbo [A Study on the spread of chilli peppers in China in terms of their trivial names: focusing on Chinese historical local records]. Journal of Chinese Historical Geography **30**(3), 104–117 (2015). (in Chinese)

11. Huang, Z., Zhang, Z., Deng, X.: Baoqing Fuzhi [A Gazetteer of Baoqing Prefecture]. Hunan Yuelu Publishing House, Changsha (2009). (in Chinese)

12. Compilation Committee of Shaoyang County Gazetteer: Shaoyang Xianzhi [A Gazetteer of Shaoyang County]. Hunan People's Publishing House, Changsha (2008). (in Chinese)

13. Dong, S.: Tianqi biaoda de kuaxueke yanjiu fanshi [Towards an interdisciplinary paradigm for research on weather expressions]. Chinese Journal of Language Policy and Planning **9**(2), 89–96 (2024). (in Chinese)

14. Dong, S., Huang, C.-R.: From falling to hitting: diachronic change and synchronic distribution of frost verbs in Chinese. In: Dong, M., Gu, Y., Hong, J.-F. (eds.) CLSW 2021. LNCS (LNAI), vol. 13249, pp. 22–30. Springer, Cham (2022)

15. Dong, S., Huang, C.-R., Ren, H.: Towards a new typology of meteorological events: a study based on synchronic and diachronic data. Lingua **247**, 102894 (2020)

16. Dong, S., Xu, J., Huang, C.-R.: Angry thunder and vicious frost: remarks on the unaccusativity of Chinese weather verbs. In: Liu, M., Kit, C., Su, Q. (eds.) CLSW 2020. LNCS (LNAI), vol. 12278, pp. 64–73. Springer, Cham (2021)

17. Dong, S., Yang, Y., Huang, C.-R., Ren, H.: Directionality and momentum of water in weather: a morphosemantic study of conceptualisation based on Hantology. In: Hong, J.-F., Zhang, Y., Liu, P. (eds.) CLSW 2019. LNCS (LNAI), vol. 11831, pp. 575–584. Springer, Cham (2020)

18. Dong, S., Yang, Y., Ren, H., Huang, C.-R.: Directionality of atmospheric water in Chinese: a lexical semantic study based on linguistic ontology. SAGE Open **11**(1), 1–13 (2021)

19. Ding, H., Dong, S.: Elevation and fog-cloud similarity in Tibeto-Burman languages. Humanit. Soc. Sci. Comm. **10**, 375 (2023)

20. Ding, H., Dong, S.: Colexification of "thunder" and "dragon" in Sino-Tibetan languages. Asia Pacific Translation and Intercultural Studies (2024)

21. Huang, C.-R., Dong, S.: From lexical semantics to traditional ecological knowledge: on precipitation, condensation and suspension expressions in Chinese. In: Hong, J.-F., Zhang, Y., Liu, P. (eds.) CLSW 2019. LNCS (LNAI), vol. 11831, pp. 255–264. Springer, Cham (2020)

22. Huang, C.-R., Dong, S., Yang, Y., Ren, H.: From language to meteorology: kinesis in weather events and weather verbs across Sinitic languages. Humanit. Soc. Sci. Comm. **8**, 4 (2021)

The Mapping Directionality of Mandarin Synaesthesia: A Study Based on the Self-paced Reading Task

Zhao Wang[1(✉)] and Qingqing Zhao[2]

[1] School of Chinese Language and Literature, Shaanxi Normal University, Shaanxi, China
wangzhao0727@snnu.edu.cn
[2] Institute of Linguistics, Chinese Academy of Social Sciences, Beijing, China
zhaoqq@cass.org.cn

Abstract. This study investigated the mapping directionality of Mandarin synaesthesia, based on a self-paced reading task. We have found that Mandarin synaesthesia also shows mapping directionalities in the language comprehension among native Mandarin Chinese speakers. However, the results of the self-paced reading task do not support the direction of Mandarin synaesthetic mapping from vision to smell found in previous corpus studies. As the reading task makes up for the limited quantity of olfactory words in human languages, synaesthetic mapping directions attested in this study would be the most likely to reflect the actual pattern of Mandarin synaesthesia. In addition, the self-paced reading task demonstrates different characteristics among the linguistic expressions without synaesthetic usages, the expressions following synaesthetic mapping directions, and the expressions incongruent with synaesthetic mapping directions in the reading process. These patterns provide evidence for linguistic synaesthesia as an independent cognitive mechanism, which furthers our understanding of linguistic synaesthesia and metaphor.

Keywords: Synaesthesia · Mapping directionality · Experimental study · Sensory adjectives

1 Introduction

Linguistic synaesthesia is a common linguistic phenomenon in which the concept belonging to one sense is used to describe the perception from another sense [1–3]. For example, the English auditory adjective *loud* can be used to modify the visual color, such as *loud color*, to emphasize the brightness of the color. In Mandarin, linguistic synaesthesia is also systematically employed in the poetic language (e.g., 暗红色的声音 "*dark red sound*", where the visual adjective is used to describe hearing) and in the non-poetic language (e.g., 甜甜的笑容 "*sweet smile*", where the gustatory adjective is used to

---

Z. Wang and Q. Zhao — The two authors contribute equally to the work, which has received the financial support from the NSSFC (NO. 19CYY006).

P. Jin et al. (Eds.): CLSW 2024, LNAI 15552, pp. 65–75, 2025.
https://doi.org/10.1007/978-981-96-3509-2_5

modify vision) [4–6]. Most previous studies on linguistic synaesthesia focused on the synaesthetic directionalities. For example, studies of linguistic synaesthesia in Hebrew, Indonesian, English, Italian, Mandarin, Korean, and Turkish have shown that synaesthetic transfers are not random, but follow certain directionalities, such as generally mapping from touch and taste to vision and hearing, rather than the other way around [7–13]. However, those studies mainly employed the corpus-based method, which might show some inevitable limitations.

Firstly, human senses (e.g., touch, taste, smell, hearing, and vision) are not conceptualized equally in the language. Words dedicated to describing smell are scarce cross-linguistically [14], fewer of which have synaesthetic usages [9, 10]. Zhao et al. summarized the transfer directionality of Mandarin synaesthesia based on synaesthetic usages of sensory adjectives in a large corpus (see Fig. 1) [11]. Specifically, there is an absolute unidirectional transfer from touch to smell in Mandarin synaesthesia. That is, only haptic words can be used to describe smell (such as 冷香 "cold fragrance"), but not the other way around. The transfer from vision to smell is a biased-directional transfer. That is, there are both visual words to describe smell (such as 暗香 "faint fragrance") and olfactory words to describe vision (such as 臭脸 "stinky face") in Mandarin, but the former (from vision to smell) was found to occur more frequently. It should be noted that the model only included four auditory words and two olfactory words with synaesthetic usages. Therefore, it needs to be further tested whether the synaesthetic transfer directionality summarized based on a limited number of sensory adjectives is tenable.

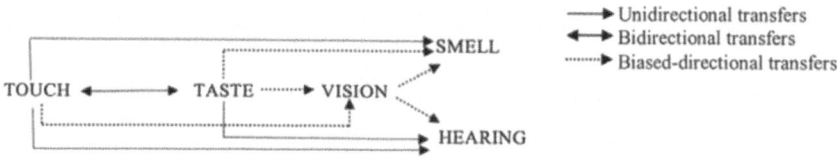

Fig. 1. The transfer directionality of Mandarin synaesthesia [6]

Secondly, corpus-based studies on linguistic synaesthesia mainly employed the earliest sensory meanings or the original meanings of words to determine the synaesthetic directions. For example, Williams referred to the words' earliest recorded sensory meanings in the dictionary to determine the source domains of sensory adjectives in English [3]. Zhao et al. mainly used the original meanings of Chinese words to determine the source domains of synaesthetic transfers [11]. However, the original sensory meanings of words were not always consistent with the usages of the words in the contemporary languages, such as the English adjective *bitter*, which is used in modern English primarily for taste rather than the earliest sensory meaning for touch [15]. Similarly, the most common usage of 美 "*beautiful*" in Mandarin is for vision, rather than its original sensory meaning for taste [16]. Therefore, it can be concluded that the synaesthetic transfer directionality based on the dictionary or the corpus mainly reflects the diachronic change of word meanings. Thus, the synchronically synaesthetic transfer directionality still needs further investigation.

Last but not least, previous experimental studies that have tested the transfer directionality of linguistic synaesthesia obtained inconsistent results. For example, Shen and his colleagues found that synaesthetic expressions in Hebrew that followed the transfer directionality obtained by the corpus-based studies would be easier to understand and remember than those expressions in opposite directions [7, 17–19]. However, Werning et al. found that synaesthetic expressions in German did not support the transfer from touch to hearing obtained by the corpus-based studies [20]. Therefore, it is necessary to test where linguistic synaesthesia in Mandarin shows a transfer directionality during the on-line language comprehension.

This study attempts to test the transfer directionality of Mandarin synaesthesia by using a self-paced reading task. We will focus on the following questions: (1) Does Mandarin synaesthesia follow transfer directionality during the on-line language comprehension? (2) Are the self-paced experimental results of Mandarin synaesthesia consistent with the results obtained by the previous corpus-based studies?

2 Method: A Self-paced Reading Task

The self-paced reading task is a commonly used experimental paradigm for investigating syntactic and semantic processing in psycholinguistics [21, 22]. In the task, sentences are divided into units such as words, word chains, or phrases, and presented on the computer screen in turn. Participants can control their reading speed by pressing specific buttons and reading all of the units. Compared with off-line experimental methods, the self-paced reading task can record more real-time information during the reading process, hence collecting more parameters for language processing research. In addition, by controlling demographic factors (e.g., gender, age, and dialect background) and linguistic variables (e.g., word frequency, syntactic structures, and contexts), the self-paced reading task could reveal the decoding and integration of language processing of human beings.

This study aims to investigate the semantic acceptability and the response time (RT) of Chinese sentences containing different synaesthetic transfers among Chinese native speakers through a self-paced reading task. Specifically, the experiment has employed a 2 (reaction types) × 5 (experimental conditions) design, in which reaction types include the yes-response and the no-response. According to the transfer directionality of Mandarin synaesthesia summarized by Zhao et al., vision can both be the source domain of hearing and smell and the target domain of taste and touch (see Fig. 1) [11]. Therefore, the transfers from vision to hearing and from vision to smell would be common in Mandarin, while the transfers from vision to touch or taste would be rare. In addition, visual adjectives have the most synaesthetic usages in Mandarin [23], which can provide sufficient materials to ensure the stability of the experimental results.

In summary, this study took vision as the source domain and five senses including vision as the target domains, hence setting five experimental conditions, including the [visual-haptic], [visual-gustatory], [visual-olfactory], [visual-auditory], and [visual-visual] conditions. The experimental hypotheses of this study are as follows: (1) As the transfers from vision to hearing and from vision to smell are common in Mandarin, the semantic acceptabilities of [visual-auditory] and [visual-olfactory] sentences might be closer to that of the [visual-visual] sentences, all of which would be higher than those of the [visual-haptic] and [visual-gustatory] sentences; (2) In terms of the reading processing and semantic judgment, the RT of making yes-response may be significantly different from that of making no-response. Specifically, as [visual-haptic] and [visual-gustatory] sentences involve uncommon synaesthetic transfers in Mandarin, the RT to make no-responses for these sentences may be much shorter than that of yes-responses, in contrast to [visual-auditory], [visual-olfactory], and [visual-visual] sentences, where making yes-responses may be faster than making no-responses.

2.1 Participants

All of the participants were right-handed native Mandarin speakers with normal vision or corrected vision. They included 54 undergraduate students (24 males and 30 females). Their average age was 20.28 years old (SD = 1.80). Each participant was paid 50 RMB in cash after completing the reading task.

2.2 Materials

Given the main syntactic function of Mandarin adjectives [24] and the influence of syntactic complexity on sentence processing, subject-predicate sentences constructed by "noun + 很 (*very*) + adjective" were employed in this study. In each experimental sentence, "noun" was mainly used to activate the target domain, including touch, taste, smell, hearing, and vision, while "adjective" was a visual adjective used to activate the source domain. Previous cognitive neuroscience studies have found that during the semantic processing of content words that denote concrete objects, a variety of related sensory representations would be activated at the same time [25–27]. Thus, the constructions formed by sensory verbs and directional verbs were added before the main sentences, including 摸起来 "*it touches like*", 尝起来 "*it tastes like*", 闻起来 "*it smells like*", 听起来 "*it sounds like*", and 看起来 "*it looks like*", to ensure the uniqueness of the target domain activated by the "nouns".

In addition, we manually selected 203 nouns conceptualizing concrete objects and invited 118 native Chinese speakers (mean age = 19.57, SD = 1.95) to evaluate the dominant sensory domains of these nouns. Participants were asked to choose one of the most closely associated senses from touch, taste, smell, hearing, and vision for each noun, and the percentage of each sense selected by the participants was counted. The sense with the highest percentage was taken as the noun's dominant sensory domain. For example, in terms of the word 花香 "*fragrance*", the percentage of its relatedness to touch was 0, to taste was 2.33%, to smell was 90.69%, to hearing was 4.65%, and to vision was 2.33%. Therefore, the dominant sensory domain of 花香 "*fragrance*" was smell. According to the rating results, 203 nouns were divided into five categories: haptic nouns, gustatory nouns, olfactory nouns, auditory nouns, and visual nouns. Given the word frequency and the stroke number, 20 nouns were selected from each category. The analysis of one-way ANOVA showed that there was no significant difference in the word frequency and the stroke number of five noun types (word frequency: $F(4, 95) = 0.348$, $p = 0.845$; stroke number: $F(4, 95) = 0.05$, $p = 0.995)$[1].

---

[1] Word frequency in this study was based on the Mandarin word frequency database [29].

Visual adjectives in the experimental sentences were selected from the Mandarin synaesthetic adjective database built by Zhao [23]. The database contains 67 adjectives with vision as the dominant domain. This study selected 20 visual adjectives, which were disyllable and could co-occur with 很 *"very"* grammatically. Furthermore, all of these words had multi-directional synaesthetic usages, which could describe the haptic, gustatory, olfactory, and auditory senses. The word frequency and the stroke number of the selected adjectives were within the range of plus or minus one standard deviation from the mean of 67 visual synaesthetic adjectives (word frequency: 0–285.27 W/million; stroke number: 9.52–22.74), to ensure that the selected adjectives could reflect the general characteristics of visual synaesthetic adjectives and be understood by participants.

Five types of nouns in different dominant domains were matched with the 20 visual adjectives to form five types of experimental sentences, hence 100 sentences obtained in total. The experimental sentences included four groups of synaesthetic sentences with different mapping directionalities and a group of non-synaesthetic sentences that were treated as the baseline by this study. As linguistic conventionalization would significantly influence reading comprehension [28], all of the experimental sentences in this study were novel, which could not be searched in two commonly used Mandarin corpora (i.e., BCC and CCL). Example (1) – (5) illustrate the experimental sentences used by this study.

(1) 摸起来,材质很宏大。(visual → haptic)

   "The texture is very grand by touching."

(2) 尝起来, 果酱很热烈。(visual → gustatory)

   "The jam is very strong by tasting."

(3) 闻起来, 芳香很明亮。(visual → olfactory)

   "The fragrance is very bright by smelling."

(4) 听起来, 鸟鸣很清纯。(visual → auditory)

   "The birdsong is very pure by hearing."

(5) 看起来, 面容很清白。(visual → visual)

   "The face is very clean by seeing."

We set another 200 sentences as fillers, including 100 non-synaesthetic sentences with grammatical and semantically-acceptable collocations and 100 sentences with ungrammatical and semantically-unacceptable collocations, to ensure that participants could concentrate on the task. After the Latin square processing and pseudo-random arrangement, all of the sentences were formed into four experimental lists, each of which contained 300 sentences in different sequences. Participants selected one of the experimental lists to complete the task randomly.

2.3 Experimental Process

The experimental program was coded by E-prime 2.0 and run on a Windows 7 computer in the lab with a screen resolution of 1024 × 768 pixels. Firstly, a focus point "+" lasting 800 ms was presented in the center of the screen. Then, experimental sentences were presented word by word at the focus point, during which participants controlled their reading speed by pressing the space bar. The window that presented visual adjectives was regarded to be the synaesthetic word window by this study, and the window that presented the full stop was the integration window. After the sentence finished, a series of question marks were presented on the screen as the semantic judgment window, when participants were asked to judge whether they could understand the experimental sentences. They were told that F for yes would be pressed if they could understand it, or they would press J for no.

2.4 Data Collection and Analysis

This study chose the synaesthetic word window, the integration window, and the semantic judgment window as the focused windows with the yes-response ratio and the RT for analyses. That is, the data collected in this experiment included a group of semantic acceptability data, and a total of ten groups of RT data (2 (reaction types) × 5 (experimental conditions)). In terms of semantic acceptability, no extreme values were excluded since semantic judgments depended on participants' acceptability of each experimental sentence. In terms of RT, we eliminated outliers that were more than three times of quartile deviation from the quartile of each group, in order to avoid the mechanical keying or mind-wandering of participants.

One-way ANOVA analysis was used for the semantic acceptability data as they were consistent with normal distribution and homogeneity of variance. After the logarithmic conversion of the original RT data, which made the RT data consistent with normal distribution and homogeneity of variance, the analysis of two-way ANOVA was used for the RT. For the statistical analysis, SPSS 16.0 was used in this study.

3 Results

3.1 Semantic Acceptability

The result of semantic acceptability for five types of experimental sentences is shown in Table 1. A one-way ANOVA analysis revealed that, the difference of semantic acceptability among sentence types was significant ($F_{(4,265)} = 8.890$, $p < 0.001$). Semantic acceptability of [visual-auditory] sentences was significantly higher than those for other four types of sentences ([visual-auditory] vs. [visual-haptic]: 95% CI = (0.203, 0.438), $p < 0.001$; [visual-auditory] vs. [visual-gustatory]: 95% CI = (0.125, 0.360), $p < 0.001$; [visual-auditory] vs. [visual-olfactory]: 95% CI = (0.121, 0.355), $p < 0.001$; [visual-auditory] vs. [visual-visual]: 95% CI = (0.001, 0.236), $p = 0.048$).

Table 1. Mean (M), standard deviation (SD), and confidence interval (95% CI) of semantic acceptability for five experimental sentence types

Experimental sentences types	M	SD	95% CI
Visual-haptic	0.25	0.28	(0.17, 0.33)
Visual-gustatory	0.33	0.35	(0.23, 0.42)
Visual-olfactory	0.33	0.32	(0.24, 0.42)
Visual-auditory	0.57	0.29	(0.49, 0.65)
Visual-visual	0.45	0.30	(0.37, 0.53)

Semantic acceptability of [visual-visual] (no synaesthesia) sentences was significantly higher than those of [visual-haptic], [visual-gustatory] and [visual-olfactory] sentences ([visual-visual] vs. [visual-haptic]: 95% CI = (0.085, 0.319), $p = 0.001$; [visual-visual] vs. [visual-gustatory]: 95% CI = (0.007, 0.241), $p = 0.038$; [visual-visual] vs. [visual-olfactory]: 95% CI = (0.002, 0.237), $p = 0.046$).

Consequently, the semantic acceptability for five types of experimental sentences from high to low is: [visual-auditory] > [visual-visual] > [visual-gustatory], [visual-olfactory], [visual-haptic].

3.2 Response Time (RT)

The mean RT and standard deviation for five types of experimental sentences in all focused windows are shown in Table 2.

In the synaesthetic word window, only the main effect of response types was significant ($F(1,463) = 4.007$, $p = 0.046$). The further pairwise comparative analysis revealed that, only in the [visual-auditory] sentences, the mean RT of the yes-responses was significantly longer than that of the no-responses (95% CI = (0.009, 0.184), $p = 0.03$).

In the integration window, only the main effect of response types was significant ($F(1,463) = 19.014$, $p < 0.001$). The further pairwise comparative analysis showed that the mean RT of yes-responses was significantly longer than those of no-responses in [visual-haptic], [visual-gustatory], and [visual-auditory] sentences ([visual-haptic]: 95% CI = (0.012, 0.152), $p = 0.023$; [visual-gustatory]: 95% CI = (0.032, 0.169), $p = 0.004$; [visual-auditory]: 95% CI = (0.035, 0.164), $p = 0.003$).

In the semantic judgment window, only the main effect of response types was significant ($F(1,468) = 21.525$, $p < 0.001$). The further pairwise comparative analysis showed that the mean RT of yes-responses was significantly longer than those of no-responses in [visual-haptic], [visual-gustatory], and [visual-olfactory] sentences ([visual-haptic]: 95% CI = (0.07, 0.294), $p = 0.001$; [visual-gustatory]: 95% CI = (0.08, 0.301), $p = 0.001$; [visual-olfactory]: 95% CI = (0.008, 0.221), $p = 0.036$).

In summary, no matter in yes-responses or no-responses, there was no significant difference in RT among different sentence types.[2] However, the RT of yes-responses

---

[2] The novel expressions used in this study may lead to shorter RT of no-responses while reading the experimental sentences.

Table 2. The average response time and standard deviation of five experimental sentences types in all focused windows[a]

Experimental sentences types	Synaesthetic word window		Integration window		Semantic judgment window	
	Yes-response	No-response	Yes-response	No-response	Yes-response	No-response
visual-haptic	2.76 (0.19)	2.74 (0.21)	2.87 (0.17)	2.79 (0.16)	3.12 (0.28)	2.94 (0.27)
visual-gustatory	2.79 (0.22)	2.74 (0.21)	2.86 (0.19)	2.76 (0.14)	3.12 (0.31)	2.93 (0.29)
visual-olfactory	2.80 (0.30)	2.74 (0.19)	2.80 (0.20)	2.77 (0.13)	3.03 (0.26)	2.91 (0.24)
visual-auditory	2.80 (0.22)	2.71 (0.22)	2.84 (0.16)	2.74 (0.18)	3.01 (0.23)	2.99 (0.26)
visual-visual	2.75 (0.21)	2.78 (0.24)	2.82 (0.16)	2.80 (0.15)	3.07 (0.23)	3.02 (0.26)

[a] The averaged RT and SD here are logarithmically converted from the original data.

was significantly longer than that of no-responses, which appeared at different focused windows in different types of synaesthetic sentences. Significant differences in the RT between response types appeared and disappeared earliest in the [visual-auditory] sentences, which appeared in the synaesthetic word window and the integration window. The next were [visual-haptic] and [visual-gustatory] sentences, which appeared in the integration window and the semantic judgment window. The last was [visual-olfactory] sentences, which appeared in the semantic judgment window. As the baseline, [visual-visual] sentences totally did not show a significant difference in the RT between response types.

4 Discussion

4.1 Experimental Results

According to the semantic acceptability and the RT of Mandarin native speakers in the self-paced reading task, the experimental sentences could be divided into three types: (1) [visual-auditory] sentences had the highest acceptability and the earliest activation of synaesthetic processing; (2) the acceptability of [visual-visual] sentences was lower than [visual-auditory] sentences but higher than other three types of synaesthetic sentences, and there was no difference of the RT between responses types in all of the focused windows; (3) [visual-haptic], [visual-gustatory] and [visual-olfactory] sentences had the lowest acceptability and relatively later activation of synaesthesia processing. These results partially support our hypotheses. Firstly, the semantic acceptabilities of [visual-auditory] and [visual-visual] sentences were higher than those of [visual-haptic] and [visual-gustatory] sentences. Secondly, the RT of yes-responses in the integration window and the semantic judgment window was slower than that of no-responses in [visual-haptic] and [visual-gustatory] sentences.

For [visual-auditory] and [visual-olfactory] sentences, the RT of yes-responses was higher than that of no-responses, which may be related to the novel expressions we adopted in this study. In addition, the relatively lower semantic acceptability of [visual-olfactory] sentences suggested that it might not be the preferred synaesthetic directionality in Mandarin. Thus, the results reveal that synaesthetic sentences and non-synaesthetic sentences exhibit different cognitive processing modes, and linguistic expressions with different synaesthetic directionalities exhibit different processing characteristics.

Conceptual Metaphor Theory has proposed that mapping from the more concrete and accessible concepts to the more abstract and less accessible concepts conforms to the general cognitive principle [30, 31]. Experimental studies of Ahrens also found that metaphorical expressions conformed to the cognitive principle would get higher acceptability and faster processing speed during language comprehension [28]. Linguistic synaesthesia, as a type of metaphor, is also grounded in the general cognitive principle [32]. Therefore, the significant differences in acceptability and processing speed among the four types of synaesthetic sentences in this study reflect the influence of synaesthetic directionalities on semantic processing. In other words, the results of the self-paced reading task in this study on synaesthetic expressions reveal that the transfer from vision to hearing is consistent with the preferred synaesthetic directionality, but the transfers from vision to touch, vision to taste, and vision to smell are not.

In addition, [visual-visual] and [visual-auditory] sentences have exhibited two different semantic processing modes in this study. Once non-synaesthetic sentences with novel semantic collocation were hard to understand, participants might treat them as semantic mismatched sentences. However, during the comprehension of synaesthetic sentences, participants might try to find more appropriate explanations from multiple perspectives and sensory domains. That might be the reason that sentences conformed to the preferred synaesthetic directionality would get higher acceptability than non-syanesthetic sentences. This assumption could also be supported by the RT results. That is, different from synaesthetic sentences, the processing speed of non-synaesthetic sentences did not exhibit significant differences between response types in each focused window. It indicated that participants might directly make judgments by the semantic collocations of non-synaesthetic sentences, so the overall RT of yes-responses was quite similar to that of no-responses. However, as participants would try to understand the semantic information of synaesthetic sentences from different perspectives by spending more cognitive resources and switching multiple sensory domains, the RT of yes-responses would be significantly longer than that of no-responses.

4.2 Comparisons with Corpus-Based Studies

Both the self-paced reading task and the previous corpus-based studies have shown that synaesthetic transfers in the five senses follow certain directionalities. Moreover, the preferred transfer (vision → hearing) and the non-preferred transfers (vision → touch and vision → taste) of vision have been confirmed in both the online comprehension (the reading task) and the language usages (corpus studies) (see 4.1 and Fig. 1).

However, there are several differences between the self-paced reading task in this study and previous corpus-based studies. On one hand, the results of the reading task do not support the synaesthetic directionality from vision to smell. As mentioned above, the previous corpus-based studies summarized synaesthetic directionalities based on quite a limited number of olfactory words. Our self-paced reading task broke through the limited quantity of olfactory words. Thus, the synaesthetic directionalities found in this study are more consistent with the actual characteristics of Mandarin synaesthesia.

On the other hand, based on the corpus studies, Zhao et al. demonstrated that non-synaesthetic expressions would be used more frequently and be more versatile than synaesthetic expressions [32]. This study further found that there are not only significant differences between non-synaesthetic and synaesthetic expressions, but also between linguistic expressions congruent with synaesthetic directionalities and expressions incongruent with synaesthetic directionalities. Therefore, the self-paced reading task provides evidence for linguistic synaesthesia as an independent cognitive processing mechanism.

5 Conclusion

In this study, we examined the transfer directionalities of Mandarin synaesthesia based on the self-paced reading task. We found that Mandarin synaesthesia also demonstrated directionalities during language comprehension among native Mandarin Chinese speakers. However, the experimental results do not support the synaesthetic directionality from vision to smell, which was summarized by the previous corpus-based studies. In addition, the self-paced reading task found different processing characteristics of non-synaesthetic expressions, synaesthetic expressions congruent with transfer directionalities and synaesthetic expressions incongruent with transfer directionalities. These patterns provide evidence for linguistic synaesthesia as an independent cognitive mechanism, which furthers our understanding of linguistic synaesthesia and metaphor.

References

1. Qian, Z.S.: Seven Subsets, 1st edn. Shanghai Classics Publishing House, Shanghai (1985). (in Chinese)
2. Ullmann, S.: The Principles of Semantics, 2nd edn. Basil Blackwell, Oxford (1957)
3. Williams, J.: Synaesthetic adjectives: a possible law of sematic change. Language 52(2), 461–478 (1976)
4. Yu, N.: Synesthetic metaphors: a cognitive perspective. J. Lit. Semant. 32(1), 19–34 (2003)
5. Zhao, Q.Q., Huang, C.R., Long, Yunfei: Synaesthesia in Chinese: a corpus-based study on gustatory adjectives in Mandarin. Linguistics 56(5), 1167–1194 (2018). https://doi.org/10.1515/ling-2018-0019
6. Zhao, Q., Huang, C.R., Ahrens, K.: Directionality of linguistic synesthesia in Mandarin: a corpus-based study. Lingua 232, 1–15 (2019)
7. Shen, Y.: Cognitive constraints on poetic figures. Cogn. Linguist. 8(1), 33–71 (1997)
8. Shen, Y., Gil, D.: Sweet fragrances from Indonesia: a universal principle governing directionality in synaesthetic metaphors. In: Auracher, J., Peer, W. (eds.) New beginnings in literary studies, pp. 49–71. Cambridge Scholars Publishing, Newcastle (2008)

9. Strik-Lievers, F.: Synaesthesia: a corpus-based study of cross-modal directionality. Funct. Lang. **22**(1), 69–95 (2015)
10. Zhao, Q., Huang, C.R.: Mapping models and underlying mechanisms of synaesthetic metaphors in Mandarin. Language Teach. Linguist. Stud. **01**, 44–55 (2018). (in Chinese)
11. Zhao, Q., Xiong, J., Huang, C.R.: Mapping models and underlying mechanisms of synaesthetic metaphors in Mandarin. Stud. Chinese Lang. **02**, 240–253+256 (2019). (in Chinese)
12. Jo, C.: A corpus-based analysis of synesthetic metaphors in Korean. Linguist. Res. **36**(3), 459–483 (2019)
13. Kumcu, A.: Linguistic synesthesia in Turkish: a corpus-based study of crossmodal directionality. Metaphor. Symb. **36**(4), 241–255 (2021)
14. Levinson, S.C., Majid, A.: Differential ineffability and the senses. Mind Lang. **29**(4), 407–427 (2014)
15. Lynott, D., Connell, L.: Modality exclusivity norms for 423 object properties. Behav. Res. Methods **41**(2), 558–564 (2009)
16. Chen, I.-H., Zhao, Q., Long, Y., Lu, Q., Huang, C.-R.: Mandarin Chinese modality exclusivity norms. PLOS ONE **14**(2), e0211336 (2019)
17. Shen, Y., Cohen, M.: How come silence is sweet but sweetness is not silent: a cognitive account of directionality in poetic synaesthesia. Lang. Lit. **7**(2), 123–140 (1998)
18. Shen, Y., Eisenman, D.: "Heard melodies are sweet, but those unheard are sweeter": synaesthetic metaphors and cognition. Lang. Lit. **17**(2), 101–121 (2008)
19. Shen, Y., Gadir, O.: How to interpret the music of caressing: target and source assignment in synaesthetic genitive constructions. J. Pragmat. **41**(2), 357–371 (2009)
20. Werning, M., Fleischhauer, J., & Beseoglu, H.: The cognitive accessibility of synaesthetic metaphors. In: Sun, R., Miyake, N. (eds.) Proceedings of the 28th Annual Conference of the Cognitive Science Society, pp. 2365–2370. Lawrence Erlbaum Associates, London (2006)
21. Aaronson, D., Scarborough, H.: Performance theories for sentence coding: some quantitative evidence. J. Verbal Learn. Verbal Behav. **16**(3), 277–303 (1977)
22. Mitchell, D.C., Green, D.: The effects of context and content on immediate processing in reading. Q. J. Exp. Psychol. **30**(4), 609–636 (1978)
23. Zhao, Q.: Embodied Conceptualization or Neural Realization: A Corpus-Driven Study of Mandarin Synaesthetic Adjectives, 1st edn. Peking University Press, Beijing (2022)
24. Zhu, D.: The Lecture Notes of Grammar, 1st edn. The Commercial Press, Beijing (1982). (in Chinese)
25. Damasio, A.R.: Concepts in the brain. Mind Lang. **4**(1–2), 24–28 (1989)
26. Gazzaniga, M.S., Ivry, R., Mangun, G.: Cognitive Neuroscience: The Biology of the Mind, 1st edn. Norton, New York (1998)
27. Thompson-Schill, S.L., Kan, I., Oliver, R.: Functional neuroimaging of semantic memory. In: Cabeza, R., Kingstone, A. (eds.) Handbook of Functional Neuroimaging of Cognition, pp. 149–190. MIT Press, Cambridge (2006)
28. Ahrens, K.: Mapping principles for conceptual metaphors. In: Cameron, L., Deignan, A., Low, G., Todd, Z. (eds.) Researching and Applying Metaphor in the Real World, 26, pp. 185–208. John Benjamins Publishing, Amsterdam (2010)
29. Cai, Q., Brysbaert, M.: SUBTLEX-CH: Chinese word and character frequencies based on film subtitles. PLoS ONE **5**(6), e10729 (2010)
30. Lakoff, G., Johnson, M.: Metaphors We Live by, 1st edn. University of Chicago Press, Chicago (1980)
31. Gibbs, R.: Embodiment and Cognitive Science, 1st edn. Cambridge University Press, New York (2005)
32. Zhao, Q., Ahrens, K., Huang, C.-R.: Linguistic synesthesia is metaphorical: a lexical-conceptual account. Cogn. Linguist. **33**(3), 553–583 (2022). https://doi.org/10.1515/cog-2021-0098

Statistical Properties and Community Detection Study of Modern Chinese Synonym Networks

Kexin Yang[1] , Huibin Zhuang[1], and Mu Yang[2](✉)

[1] The School of Culture and Communication, Shandong University, Shandong 264209, China
[2] The School of International Studies, Zhejiang University, Hangzhou 310058, China
yangmufy@163.com

Abstract. This paper constructs a synonym network using the vector representations of 53,946 words listed in the *List of Commonly Used Modern Chinese Words*, with words as nodes and synonym relations as edges, resulting in a network with 26,485 nodes and 71,964 edges. The findings indicate that the network exhibits scale-free, small-world properties. Through community detection, the network can be decomposed into several sub-networks, each representing a distinct synonymous semantic field. Consequently, this study may shed light on the complexity of lexicon networks and the modernization of dictionary compilation.

Keywords: word vector · lexicon network · synonym network · scale-free · small-world · dictionary compilation

1 Introduction

Saussure [1] explicitly introduced the concept of "language as a system of signs", which has garnered widespread acceptance and significant attention [2]. The systematization of language has been examined from multiple perspectives, ranging from symbolic systems to human-driven complex adaptive systems [3]. Hjelmslev [4, 5] examined language systematization through the lens of syntagmatic and paradigmatic relations. Tesnière [6] proposed dependency syntax, which connects linguistic units through dependency relations, thereby facilitating the study of syntactic systematization.

However, these studies often provide only a partial view of the language system due to limited materials. Some people [7, 8] argue that language functions as a complex system, where complex networks are vital tools for quantitatively investigating linguistic structures. Complex networks can be constructed to achieve quantitative analysis of language systems by utilizing the relationships between language symbols. For instance, syntactic dependency relationships can be used to create syntactic dependency networks [9–11], co-occurrence relationships between words can form co-occurrence networks [12–14], and semantic connections among words can lead to semantic networks [15–18].

In contrast to syntactic dependency and co-occurrence, the meanings of words are inherently fuzzy and challenging to formalize. Previous studies on lexicon networks have primarily relied on static resources. For instance, Muller et al. [19] used French dictionaries to assume that words with similar definitions are synonyms, constructing

P. Jin et al. (Eds.): CLSW 2024, LNAI 15552, pp. 76–87, 2025.
https://doi.org/10.1007/978-981-96-3509-2_6

synonym relations based on shared terms within definitions. Similarly, Makaruk and Owczarek [20] examined the Polish synonym network, arguing that it exhibits scale-free properties. Li et al. [18] focused on Chinese lexicons, demonstrating that the Chinese synonym network also displays scale-free properties and a hierarchical structure.

Unlike syntax, which tends to be more stable, words can change rapidly. A significant limitation of constructing lexicon networks in this manner is that static resources do not adapt quickly to semantic shifts, which may lead to a lag. For example, the meanings of words can change due to the emergence of new concepts or shifts in societal attitudes. Due to constraints such as the costs of time and resources, dictionaries often struggle to keep up with these changes on time.

This study employs distributional semantics, utilizing word vectors derived from large-scale corpus data. Focusing on the *List of Commonly Used Modern Chinese Words* [21], we assess the cosine similarity between word vectors to determine whether two words are synonymous. The *List of Commonly Used Modern Chinese Words* is developed based on a corpus of approximately 250 million characters, including 56,008 commonly used terms in modern Chinese. It comprises 3,181 monosyllabic words, 40,351 disyllabic words, 6,459 trisyllabic words, 5,855 tetrasyllabic words, and 162 words with five or more syllables. Using word vectors from the Python package *Synonyms* (https://github. com/chatopera/Synonyms), we calculate the cosine similarity among words from the *List of Commonly Used Modern Chinese Words*. Similarities between words greater than 0.9 are established as edges in our network. With the above efforts, we aim to address the following two questions:

(1) what are the statistical properties of the Chinese synonym network?
(2) how can the synonymous network be utilized to compile synonym dictionaries? Specifically, how can it facilitate the identification of semantic fields?

A semantic field denotes a segment of reality symbolized by a set of related words. The words in a semantic field share a common semantic property [22]. Compiling synonym dictionaries requires the categorization of different words into various semantic fields. When conceptualized, a semantic field can be represented as a complex network, where words are depicted as nodes, and connections between these nodes are established based on shared semantic features. Extracting semantic fields from the synonym network can enhance the practical applications of research in synonym networks.

2 Basic Concepts of the Complex Networks

To begin, we should introduce some basic concepts of complex networks. A complex network can be formalized as a graph $G = (V, E)$, where V denotes a set of nodes and E represents a set of edges. Each edge in E corresponds to a pair of nodes in V. Before analysing, it is important to define the main parameters we will use, which include:

Degree (k): The degree of a node refers to the number of neighbours it has. The degree distribution $P(k)$ represents the probability that a randomly selected node has a degree of k. If the network contains a total of n nodes, and n_k denotes the number of nodes that have a degree of k, the degree distribution can be expressed as Eq. (1).

$$P(k) = \frac{n_k}{n} \tag{1}$$

This formulation allows us to analyze the distribution of connectivity within the network.

If the degree distribution of a network follows a power-law distribution with a degree exponent between 2 and 3, the network is scale-free. This means that there are relatively few nodes with very high degrees and many nodes with very low degrees. Real-world networks typically possess this property.

Average Path Length (L): The average path length quantifies the average shortest path between any two nodes in the network. It reflects the closeness of connections among nodes and provides insight into the overall size of the network. A shorter average path length suggests a more interconnected network, facilitating quicker information flow between nodes.

$$l_G = \frac{1}{n(n-1)} \sum_{i \neq j} d\left(v_i, v_j\right) \tag{2}$$

The total number of node pairs in a network is $n(n-1)$, and $d\left(v_i, v_j\right)$ denotes the shortest path between node i and node j.

Network Diameter (D): The network diameter is defined as the longest of all the shortest paths between any two nodes in a network. In other words, it represents the maximum shortest path length.

Average Clustering Coefficient (C): The average clustering coefficient quantifies the tendency of nodes to cluster together in the network. It is calculated as the average of the local clustering coefficients for all nodes. The formula for the average clustering coefficient is given by:

$$C = \frac{1}{n} \sum_{i=1}^{n} C_i \tag{3}$$

where C_i is the local clustering coefficient of node i. This coefficient provides insight into the degree to which nodes in the network tend to form tightly-knit groups.

Networks displaying small-world properties typically satisfy the conditions $L \approx L_{random}$, $C >> C_{random}$. The small-world property indicates the presence of central nodes within the network that enhance communication efficiency.

In the following sections, these metrics will be used to analyze the Chinese synonym network.

3 Network Analysis of the Chinese Synonym Network

This study extracts words from the *List of Commonly Used Modern Chinese Words* to calculate the cosine similarity between each pair of word vectors. An edge is established between two words if their cosine similarity exceeds 0.9, resulting in a network with 28,475 nodes and 73,291 edges.

However, this network is not fully connected. Using *Gephi*, we identified 771 connected components within our network. With *NetworkX*, we exported each connected component as an independent network. In this section, we focus on the largest connected

Table 1. Main Parameters of the Synonym Network.

Main Parameters	E	N	$\langle k \rangle$	D	C	L
Quantity	71964	26485	5.434	22	0.245	7.212

E: edge; N: nodes; $\langle k \rangle$: average degree; D: network diameter; C: average clustering coefficient; L: average path length.

component, which consists of 26,485 nodes. Additionally, there are 26 networks with nodes ranging from 5 to 16, while the remaining 744 networks consist of only two nodes.

Then, we will further investigate these parameters of the synonym network.

3.1 Degree Distribution of the Synonym Network

If the degree distribution follows power-law, it indicates that the network is scale-free. We fitted the degree distribution of our network to Eq. (1), resulting in the fitted curve shown in Fig. 1.

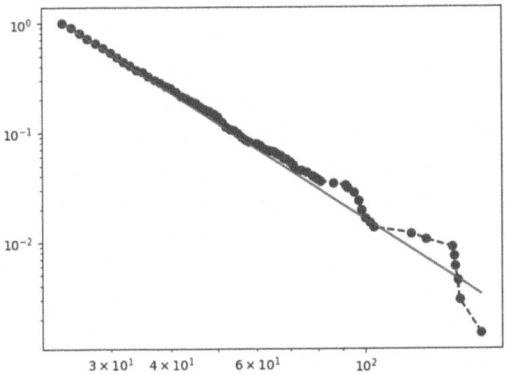

Fig. 1. The degree distribution of the synonym lexicon network.

In Fig. 1, the degree exponent γ is 3.194, with $R^2 = 0.944$. Typically, the degree exponent of a scale-free network will be within the range of 2 to 3 [23]. In our result, the relatively high value of γ suggests a weaker scale-free property. However, as shown in Table 1, the average clustering coefficient is 0.245, indicating that there is still a centralized structure in the network. Thus, the network can be seen as a scale-free network with some key nodes.

3.2 Small-World Properties of the Synonym Network

Watts and Strogatz [24] introduced the concept of small-world properties in social networks, which Solé et al. [25] identified as a statistically universal phenomenon. Furthermore, Steyvers and Tenenbaum [26] analyzed the structures of three semantic networks—word associations, WordNet, and Roget's Thesaurus—and found that they all exhibit small-world properties, characterized by short average path lengths between words, and strong local clustering.

To investigate this property, we generated 100 random networks with 26,485 nodes and 71,964 edges, calculating their average values for average path lengths and clustering coefficients. The results are as follows:

Average Path Length (L_{random}): 6.2073.
Clustering Coefficient (C_{random}): 0.00019628.
Comparing these values to the synonym network:
Average Path Length (L): 7.212.
Clustering Coefficient (C): 0.245.

We observe that $L \approx L_{random}$, $C >> C_{random}$. Therefore, we conclude that the synonym network exhibits small-world characteristics.

3.3 Centrality Analysis of the Synonym Network

To assess the importance of nodes within the synonym network, we compute three centrality parameters: degree centrality, closeness centrality, and betweenness centrality.

Degree Centrality: Degree centrality reflects the extent to which a node is connected to all other nodes in the network. For an undirected graph, the degree centrality of node i can be expressed as:

$$C_D(i) = \frac{deg(i)}{n-1} \tag{4}$$

where $deg(i)$ represents the degree of node i and n is the total number of nodes in the network. We calculate the degree centrality for each node in the synonym network and present the distribution in Fig. 2.

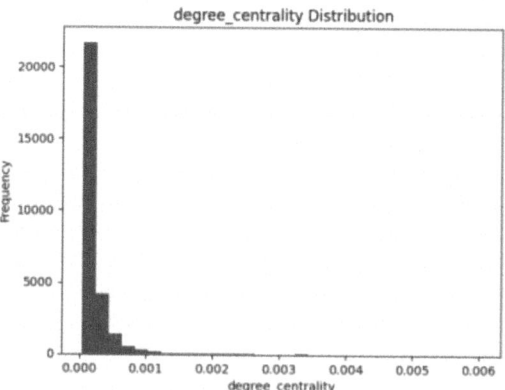

Fig. 2. The degree centrality distribution of the synonym network.

In Fig. 2, it is evident that the degree centrality of the vast majority of nodes is extremely low, with only a small number of nodes exhibiting an extremely higher degree centrality. This phenomenon is a further manifestation of the degree distribution.

Closeness Centrality: Closeness centrality, as defined by Newman [27], quantifies the proximity or accessibility of a node to all other nodes in the network. According to Caldarelli [28], the closeness centrality $C(i)$ of node i is defined as the reciprocal of the average shortest path length from i to all other nodes:

$$C(i) = \frac{1}{\sum_{j=1,n} d_{ij}} \tag{5}$$

where n represents the set of nodes reachable from node i, and d_{ij} denotes the distance between nodes i and j. We compute the closeness centrality for each node in the synonym network and present the results in Fig. 3.

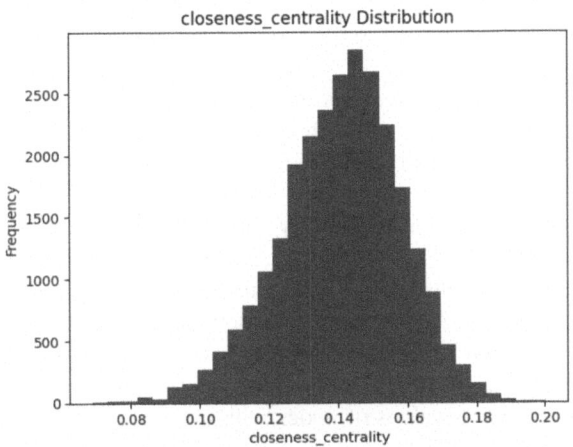

Fig. 3. The closeness centrality distribution of the synonym network.

A higher closeness centrality indicates that a node can more rapidly access other nodes within the network. The graph shows that the closeness centrality of nodes in the synonym network follows a Poisson distribution. Most nodes exhibit relatively concentrated closeness centrality values, with only a few nodes exhibiting exceptionally high or low values. This observation suggests that there are no words that share an extremely high closeness centrality.

Betweenness Centrality: Betweenness centrality measures the importance of a node as an intermediary within a network. A node is considered to have high betweenness centrality if it frequently appears on the shortest paths between other nodes. The betweenness centrality of node i, denoted as $B_C(i)$, can be calculated using the following formula [28]:

$$B_C(i) = \sum_{j \neq k} \frac{b_{jk}(i)}{b_{jk}} \tag{6}$$

where b_{jk} represents the total number of shortest paths between nodes j and k, and $b_{jk}(i)$ represents the number of those shortest paths that include node i. We compute the betweenness centrality for each node in the network, as illustrated in Fig. 4.

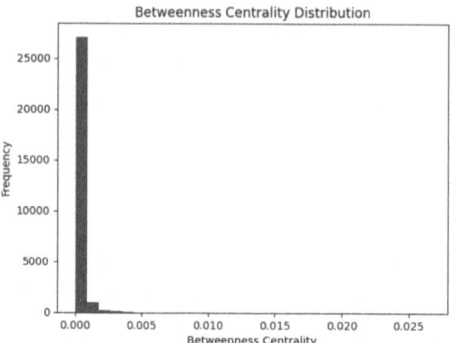

Fig. 4. Betweenness Centrality Distribution.

The results in Fig. 4 reveal that a disproportionately high percentage of nodes exhibit low betweenness centrality, while only a few nodes possess slightly higher values.

We computed the degree centrality, closeness centrality, and betweenness centrality for all nodes in the synonym network. The above results indicate that, despite a lack of significant differences in closeness centrality among nodes, there is a notable differentiation in degree centrality and betweenness centrality. This suggests that central nodes do exist within the network, although they may not be as prominent as those in syntactic and co-occurrence networks. Additionally, we calculated the degree centralization of the network, which reflects the relative strength of central nodes within the network [29]. For the synonym network, the degree centralization was computed to be 0.00586.

Combining the centrality values of nodes with the degree centralization of the network, we argue that synonym networks are not prototypically centralized, implying that not all linguistic networks exhibit a centralized structure. Chen and Liu [30] constructed syntactic dependency networks based on two genres of Chinese treebanks. They selected three Chinese function words as research objects and found that in the syntactic network, the function word 的(de, of) has the highest betweenness centrality and is the most central node in the entire network. Removing this central node resulted in some nodes becoming completely isolated, demonstrating characteristics of a centralized network, where the absence of a central node reduces network connectivity and increases average path lengths. The emergence of central nodes in syntactic networks is attributed to the reliance on function words in languages like Chinese. Without these words, it may become difficult to adhere to the principle of the least effort. However, the relatively weaker centrality in synonym networks suggests that indispensable concepts in semantics are less prevalent compared to function words. Findings from neurolinguistics also lend support, indicating that even when certain brain regions are damaged, patients rarely lose their entire vocabulary but may experience difficulties in word retrieval [31].

The analysis of the network structure suggests that multiple dense community structures may exist within the Chinese synonym network. In the following section, we will identify and analyze these communities, exploring their implications for dictionary compilation.

4 Community Detection in the Chinese Synonym Network

The compilation of synonym dictionaries represents a key application of research on synonym networks. Traditionally, lexicography involves summarizing scattered words into semantic fields, a process that is often time-consuming and labor-intensive, and can be influenced by subjective language intuition. We aim to identify semantic fields within the synonym network by leveraging complex network analysis. Specifically, we seek to discover communities within the complex network and assess whether these communities can be defined as semantic fields. This approach promises a more systematic and efficient method for compiling synonym dictionaries, enhancing both their accuracy and usability in linguistic applications.

4.1 Communities as Independent Components

We computed the cosine similarity among all words in the *List of Commonly Used Modern Chinese Words* and constructed a network. Within this network, we identified 771 independent connected components. In Sect. 3, our analysis focuses on the largest connected components, and other connected components are ignored. In these connected components, 26 share node counts ranging from 5 to 16. We present the subgraph corresponding to 16 nodes in Fig. 5.

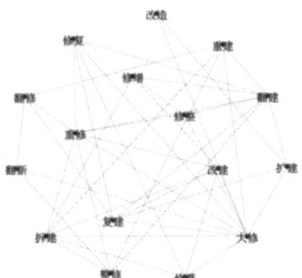

Fig. 5. Subgraph with 16 Nodes.

These nodes are: 修葺 (xiuqi, repair), 大修 (daxiu, major repair), 重建 (chongjian, reconstruction), 修缮 (xiushan, repair), 改造 (gaizao, remold), 重修 (chongxiu, rebuild), 修复 (xiufu, restore), 修整 (xiuzheng, adjust), 复建 (fujian, reconstruct), 整修 (zhengxiu, overhaul), 翻修 (fanxiu, renovate), 翻建 (fanjians, rebuild), 改建 (gaijian, remodel), 拆建 (chaijian, demolition), 扩建 (kuojian, expand), 翻新 (fanxin, refurbish).

By analyzing the meanings of these nodes in Fig. 5, we find that the words can be categorized into a semantic field related to building maintenance. Upon calculating the degree centrality, betweenness centrality, and closeness centrality for all nodes within this semantic field, we identify that the top three nodes in terms of these centralities are "major repair (大修)," "renovation (翻建)," and "reconstruction (重修)." This result indicates that non-largest connected components within synonym networks may be treated as semantic fields, providing a convenient approach to dictionary compilation.

4.2 Community Detection Within the Largest Connected Components

Semantic fields appear in non-largest connected components, which raises the question: do semantic fields exist in the largest one? In this section, we utilize the Louvain algorithm, developed by Blondel et al. [32], which effectively uncovers community structures in the largest connected component.

Applying the Louvain algorithm, we partitioned the synonym network, consisting of 26,485 nodes, into 66 subgraphs. The largest community contains 1,298 nodes, while the smallest has 14 nodes. Larger communities may be subdivided so that smaller networks can be derived through iterative clustering.

To examine the relationship between network scale—quantified by node count—and various parameters, we conduct a Spearman's rho correlation analysis. The result can help us to judge when communities do not require a further split.

The node clustering aims to reveal potential communities, with nodes sharing closely related meanings. Thus, these small-scale communities can also be interpreted as semantic fields in the construction of a synonym dictionary. It is essential to determine the threshold for defining a small community. To this end, we will analyze the correlation between community scale (in terms of nodes and edges) and other network parameters. The results for the 66 subgraphs are presented below (Table 2):

Table 2. The Spearman's rho correlation analysis of parameters of 66 subnetworks.

		$\langle k \rangle$	D	Density	Modularity	C
E	r	0.815	0.164	−0.854	0.277	0.138
	p	0	0.188	0	0.024	0.267
N	r	0.68	0.232	−0.943	0.402	0.024
	p	0	0.061	0	0.001	0.846

The correlation coefficient quantifies the degree of correlation between two variables, ranging from −1 to 1. A value close to 1 indicates a strong positive correlation, while a value near −1 reflects a strong negative correlation. A value of 0 signifies no correlation.

It shows that the number of edges is strongly positively correlated with the average degree ($p < 0.05$) and strongly negatively correlated with graph density ($p < 0.05$). The number of nodes is positively correlated with the average degree ($p < 0.05$) and strongly negatively correlated with graph density ($p < 0.05$). However, the positive correlation between the number of nodes and the average degree is weaker than the correlation between the number of edges and the average degree.

These findings suggest that as the number of edges increases, the average degree of the network also rises, while the graph deity decreases. This indicates that larger networks tend to have more connections per node, but are less densely connected overall. Understanding these relationships will help in determining appropriate thresholds for identifying semantic fields within the largest connected components.

In other words, as the network size gradually decreases, the average degree also decreases, while the graph density increases. This suggests that although the total number of nodes in the network diminishes, the connections among nodes within communities become tighter, leading to a more compact and highly clustered structure.

By analyzing the semantics of words within small-scale subgraphs, we observe that networks with 33 or fewer nodes tend to share a common semantic field. Specifically, for subgraphs with node counts of 33 or less, the average degree is 2.602, and the average graph density is 0.1205. This reinforces the idea that smaller communities are more semantically cohesive, making them suitable for identification as distinct semantic fields in dictionary compilation.

By iteratively applying the Louvain algorim, we generate numerous subgraphs. Spearman's rho correlation analysis indicates that as the network scale decreases, a more compact and highly clustered structure emerges, as evidenced by the changes in average degree and graph density.

Consequently, we propose using the number of nodes, average degree, and graph density as criteria to determine whether further clustering is necessary. Specifically, clustering can stop when the number of nodes is ≤ 33, the average degree is approximately 2.602, and the graph density is around 0.1205.

In summary, the continuous clustering of large synonym networks can be effectively guided by these parameter values, facilitating the identification of meaningful semantic fields. This approach enhances the efficiency of compiling synonym dictionaries by ensuring that only relevant and closely related terms are grouped.

5   Conclusion

Returning to the two questions initially posed in this paper, we address them as follows:
    The synonym network exhibits two key properties:

1. Scale-Free property: The degree distribution of the synonym network follows a power-law distribution, indicating a scale-free property. However, this property is relatively weak when compared with other linguistic networks. This may be due to more pronounced modularity within the conceptual space, where fewer concepts are indispensable, leading to a lesser presence of central nodes.
2. Small-World Property: The synonym network demonstrates small-world properties, suggesting that most nodes can be reached from any other node through a small number of connections.

Synonym networks can be clustered into smaller subgraphs by detecting communities within larger networks. Through parameter analysis, we propose that the number of nodes, average degree, and graph density can serve as criteria for determining the necessity of further clustering. When these parameters approach certain values, the words within subgraphs semantically align with a single semantic field. This insight can be directly applied to the compilation of synonym dictionaries, facilitating the organization of related terms into coherent entries.

In conclusion, our findings provide a framework for utilizing synonym networks in lexicography, enhancing both the efficiency and accuracy of synonym identification and classification.

References

1. de Saussure, F.: Course in General Linguistics. Charles Bally & Albert Sechehaye, New York (1959)
2. Kretzschmar, W.A.: The Linguistics of Speech. Cambridge University Press, Cambridge (2009)
3. Liu, H.: Language as a human-driven complex adaptive system. Phys. Life Rev. **26**(27), 149–151 (2018)
4. Hjelmslev, L.: Prolegomena to a Theory of Language. Transl. by Whitfield, F. J. University of Wisconsin Press, Madison (1969)
5. Hjelmslev, L.: Language, An Introduction. The University of Wisconsin Press, Madison (1970)
6. Lucien, T.: Eléments de syntaxe structurale. Klincksieck, Paris 5 (1959)
7. Cameron, L., Larsen-Freeman, D.: Complex systems and applied linguistics. Int. J. Appl. Linguist. **17**(2), 226–240 (2007)
8. Beckner, C., et al.: Language is a complex adaptive system: Position paper. Lang. Learn. **59**(s1), 1–26 (2009)
9. Cancho, R.F.I., Solé, R.V., Köhler, R.: Patterns in syntactic dependency networks. Phys. Rev. E **69**(5), 051915 (2004)
10. Liu, H.: The complexity of Chinese syntactic dependency networks. Physica A **387**(12), 3048–3058 (2008)
11. Abramov, O., Mehler, A.: Automatic language classification by means of syntactic dependency networks. J. Quant. Linguist. **18**(4), 291–336 (2011)
12. Li, J., Zhou, J.: Chinese character structure analysis based on complex networks. Physica A **380**, 629–638 (2007)
13. Peng, G., Minett, J.W., Wang, W.S.Y.: The networks of syllables and characters in Chinese. J. Quant. Linguist. **15**(3), 243–255 (2008)
14. Shi, Y., Liang, W., Liu, J., Tse, C. K.: Structural equivalence between co-occurrences of characters and words in the Chinese language. In: Proceedings of the International Symposium on Nonlinear Theory and its Applications, pp. 94–97 (2008)
15. Norvig, P.: Building a large lexicon with lexical network theory. In: Proceedings of the IJCAI Workshop on Lexical Acquisition (1989)
16. Polguère, A.: From writing dictionaries to weaving lexical networks. Int. J. Lexicogr. **27**(4), 396–418 (2014)
17. Gilquin, G.: Taking a new look at lexical networks. Lexis: J. English Lexicol. (2008)
18. Li, J., Zhou, J., Luo, X., Yang, Z.: Chinese lexical networks: the structure, function and formation. Physica A **391**(21), 5254–5263 (2012)
19. Muller, P., Hathout, N., Gaume, B.: Synonym extraction using a semantic distance on a dictionary. In: Proceedings of TextGraphs: The first workshop on graph based methods for natural language processing, pp. 65–72 (2006, June)
20. Makaruk, H.E., Owczarek, R.: Hubs in languages: Scale-free networks of synonyms. arXiv preprint arXiv:0802.4112 (2008)
21. Li, X., Su, X.: List of Commonly Used Modern Chinese Words research group: List of Commonly Used Modern Chinese Words. The Commercial Press, Beijing (2008)
22. Brinton, L.J.: The Structure of Modern English: A Linguistic Introduction, vol. 1. John Benjamins Publishing, Amsterdam (2000)
23. Barabási, A.L., Albert, R.: Emergence of scaling in random networks. Science **286**(5439), 509–512 (1999)
24. Watts, D.J., Strogatz, S.H.: Collective dynamics of 'small-world' networks. Nature **393**(6684), 440–442 (1998)

25. Solé, R.V., Corominas-Murtra, B., Valverde, S., Steels, L.: Language networks: their structure, function, and evolution. Complexity **15**(6), 20–26 (2010)
26. Steyvers, M., Tenenbaum, J.B.: The large-scale structure of semantic networks: statistical analyses and a model of semantic growth. Cogn. Sci. **29**(1), 41–78 (2005)
27. Newman, M.E.: A measure of betweenness centrality based on random walks. Soc. Netw. **27**(1), 39–54 (2005)
28. Caldarelli, G.: Scale-Free Networks: Complex Webs in Nature and Technology. Oxford University Press, Oxford (2007). https://doi.org/10.1093/acprof:oso/9780199211517.001.0001
29. Liu, H.: An introduction to Quantitative Linguistics. The Commercial Press, Beijing (2017)
30. Chen, X., Liu, H.: Central nodes of the Chinese syntactic networks. Chin. Sci. Bull. **56**(1), 735–740 (2011)
31. Oldfield, R.C.: Things, words and the brain. Q. J. Exp. Psychol. **18**(4), 340–353 (1966)
32. Blondel, V.D., Guillaume, J.-L., Lambiotte, R., Lefebvre, E.: Fast unfolding of communities in large networks. J. Stat. Mech. **2008**(10), P10008 (2008)

A Study on the Non-parallelism of the Derivative Meanings of Disyllabic Synonyms in Modern Chinese

Ruolin Han[✉]

Beijing Normal University, Beijing, China
`hanruolinn@126.com`

Abstract. This study aims to examine the causative factors which lead to non-parallelism in the derivation process of disyllabic words with the same basic meaning in modern Chinese by comparing the morpheme meanings and the word formations. It is revealed that although lexical derivation occurs in the hierarchy of words, it is still mainly restricted by morphemes, especially the meanings of morphemes. Besides, relations between words, pragmatic contexts and foreign languages influence the derivation as well. Chronologically, synonymous derivative meanings are in a long-term transformation from parallel to non-parallel, which shows the tendency of lexicon evolution.

Keywords: Modern Chinese · Synonyms · Derivative Meaning · Non-parallelism · Semantic Differentiation

1 Introduction

Synonyms, widely existing in languages, are the words which form synonymous relationships in a certain meaning. The related researches on synonyms in modern Chinese focus on the definition of synonyms (Zhang [1]; Liu [2]; Ge [3]; Huang [4], etc.), compilation of synonym dictionaries (such as *Concise Synonym Dictionary* by Zhiyi Zhang, *Modern Chinese Synonym Dictionary* by Shuxin Liu, etc.) and the differences between monosyllabic and disyllabic synonyms in the aspect of style, meaning and interpretation (Cheng, Xu [5]; Liu [6]; Liu [7]; Ding [8]; Li, Li [9], etc.).

Generally speaking, previous studies mainly focus on synonymous meaning of synonyms. However, many synonyms contain more than one meaning. If the basic meanings of synonyms are the same, there may be some relations between their derivative meanings as well, for the derivation is based on the original meaning.

Putting synonyms in the semantic system, we can find that for some synonyms with the same basic meaning, there is a parallel relationship between the derivative meanings, which means the derivative meanings are exactly the same. For example, "引港" (pilot a ship into or out of a harbor; harbor pilot) and "领港" (pilot a ship into or out of a harbor; harbor pilot) have the same meanings. However, for other synonyms, the derivative meanings are not parallel, such as "把脉" (feel the pulse; investigate) and "诊脉" (feel the pulse). They both have the meaning "feel the pulse", while the former has one more metaphorical meaning "investigate".

For words with the same basic meaning, why aren't their derivative meanings parallel? What do they have in common, and what are the peculiarities of each other? Is there a transformation between parallelism and non-parallelism? This study investigates this phenomenon in the derivative meaning system, aiming at revealing the influence of morpheme meaning on lexical meaning, and exploring the commonality within synonyms, as well as the evolution of synonyms.

Given that the disyllabic form is the main form of modern Chinese words, this study focuses on the non-parallel derivative meanings of disyllabic words and selects 394 groups of synonyms with the same basic meaning from *Modern Chinese Dictionary* (7th edition)[1] [10] in total. By referring to the definitions and discriminations of *Modern Chinese Standard Dictionary* (3rd edition) [11], *Great Chinese Dictionary* (2nd edition) [12] and *Great Synonym Dictionary* (2nd edition) [13], 152 groups of non-parallel synonyms are extracted strictly, being used as the corpus basis for quantitative statistics and qualitative analysis.

2 The Characteristics of Disyllabic Synonyms with Non-Parallel Derivative Meanings

The relationships between derivative meanings can be divided into three categories: (1) identical; (2) different; (3) one of the synonyms has derivative meanings, while others don't. The three categories contain 71, 26 and 126 groups of synonyms, respectively. The derivative meanings of the first category are parallel, but those of the other two categories are not, which is the key point this study focuses on. Therefore, we examine the characteristics of the latter two categories separately.

2.1 Synonyms with Different Derivative Meanings

Synonyms in this category can be divided into two subcategories.

In the first subcategory, synonyms have different derivative meanings while sharing similarities in the derivation pattern and direction. 14 groups of synonyms belong to this subcategory. For example, "下游" (lower reaches of a river; backwardness) and "下流" (lower reaches of a river; low inferior position; mean-spirited) are explained in *Xianhan* (7th edition) as follows:

(1) 下游 i) n. lower reaches (of a river);
         ii) n. backwardness
(2) 下流 i) n. same as "下游";
         ii) n. low or inferior position;
         iii) adj. Mean-spirited; obscene; dirty

---

[1] Hereinafter referred to as "*Xianhan*" (7th edition). All the following definitions are quoted from "*Xianhan*" (7th edition).

The derivation of these two words contains similarity: the derivative meanings are both based on orientational metaphor (the same derivative pattern), and have the same cognitive mapping from "nature" to "status" (the same derivative direction). The difference between their derivative meanings is the length of derivation: "下流" (lower reaches of a river; low inferior position; mean-spirited) generates a new meaning in the aspect of moral quality, based on metonymy. This attributes to the morpheme meaning of "流" (river; class), which is "class" or "grade".

In the second subcategory, synonyms have completely different derivative directions. Among them, derivative meanings of 4 groups of synonyms are generated by different cognitive patterns, such as "发声" (pronounce; express opinions publicly) and "发音" (pronounce; sounds):

(3) 发声 v. i) same as "发音";
        ii) express opinions and demands publicly.
(4) 发音 i) v. pronounce; make sounds; enunciate (in a broad sense);
        ii) n. sounds

The derivative meanings of this group of synonyms are generated by the metaphor pattern and metonymy pattern, respectively. As a result, they have different derivative directions.

In addition, derivative meanings of 8 groups of synonyms are generated by the same cognitive pattern, but have different derivative directions. For example:

(5) 接连 i) v. same as "连接";
        ii) adv. in succession; repeatedly; one after the other
(6) 连接 v. i) join; link;
        ii) make sth. Connected

The derivation patterns of these synonyms are both metonymy, but the metonymic mapping of "接连" (link; in succession) is from "action" to "state", and "连接" (link; make sth. Connected) is from "action" to "causative form".

By comparing the derivation of synonyms, we find that, in the meaning generative process, while some synonyms with the same basic meaning vary in derivative meanings, they share commonalities in the cognitive pattern, which is one of the characteristics of synonyms.

2.2 Synonyms with and Without Derivative Meanings

Approximately 80% of the synonyms belong to this category. In a pair of synonyms, only one of them has the derivative meaning, while the other one doesn't. Nearly half of these derivative meanings are the specialization or the generalization of the basic meanings, which is the most prominent characteristic of this category.

In terms of the derivative pattern, most of the derivative meanings are based on metonymy, including the derivation from the non-professional domain to a professional domain or vice versa. For example:

(7) 元素 n. i) same as "要素";
        ii) element; element in algebra; iii) abbr. for chemical element.
(8) 要素 n. essential factor; key element

"元素" (essential factor; element in algebra) was originally a general word, but later it was gradually introduced into mathematics and chemistry, and developed specific meanings in professional domains. However, "要素" (essential factor) remains in the general domain, and doesn't generate a derivative meaning. In fact, it is the original meaning of "元" (initial and basic) that should be responsible for this difference, because the meaning "initial" meets the demand of representing the core feature of mathematical or chemical elements as basic units in the researches.

There are also some metaphor-based derivative meanings. For instance:

(9) 移植 v. i) transplant;
            ii) graft
(10) 移栽 v. same as "移植" (i)

At first, both words are only agricultural terminologies. The original meaning of "植" (plant; grow) is "grow", which is in accordance with the core purpose of organ transplanting, but the original meaning of "栽" is "plant". Therefore, "移植" (transplant; graft) has been generalized to a medical terminology, but "移栽" (transplant) remains in the agricultural domain and has not been generalized.

This kind of difference of derivative meanings is related to the characteristics of terminology. Generally speaking, terminology requires specialty and semantic homogeneity. The national standard also recommends that "The same concept should use the same terminology and avoid using synonyms" (GB/T 1.1-2020) [14]. Therefore, when used from one domain to another, only one of the synonyms tends to have the chance to develop a general or specific meaning, which is the requirement of terminology accuracy.

The results of the classification above are summarized in the following Table 1:

Table 1. Categories of derivative meanings of synonyms

Relationships between derivative meanings	Derivation pattern	Derivation direction	Example	Percentage (%)
Identical	same	same	简称, 略称; 领港, 引港	31.84
Different	same	different	连接, 接连; 下游, 下流	9.87
	different	different	发音, 发声; 道路, 路途	1.79
One has a derivative meaning, while the other doesn't	——	——	元素, 要素; 移植, 移栽	56.50

3   Causative Factors of the Non-Parallel Derivative Meanings

Comparing the derivative meanings synchronically and diachronically, internally and externally, we find that the causative factors of parallelism of derivative meanings are complicated. The specific factors are in the following Table 2.

Table 2. Causative factors of parallelism of derivative meanings

Causative factors	Example	Percentage (%)
Morpheme meanings	昆曲, 昆剧; 闹剧, 笑剧	46.05
Stylistic features of morphemes	满口, 满嘴; 珠子, 珍珠	19.08
Transparency of lexical meanings	脊背, 脊梁; 根基, 根脚	9.21
Relations between words	听力, 耳力; 追叙, 追述	7.24
Structures of words	罗网, 网罗; 结巴, 口吃	6.58
Foreign languages	介绍, 绍介; 移植, 移栽	5.92
Grammatical features of morphemes	复活, 复生; 羞辱, 耻辱	5.26
Pragmatic contexts	妖怪, 妖精	0.66

With the quantitative statistics above, we can conclude that the three major causative factors are: the differences between morpheme meanings, different stylistic features of morphemes and transparency of lexical meanings.

3.1   Differences Between Morpheme Meanings

Synonyms whose differences between derivative meanings are caused by morphemes are mostly in the form of "same morpheme + different morpheme". The relationships between "different morphemes" include four categories: synonymous, near-synonymous, relevant and irrelevant, which constitute a continuum in the similarity of meaning. Generally speaking, the lower the similarity of morpheme meanings, the greater the possibility of having different derivative meanings.

In terms of synonyms with parallel derivative meanings, the meanings of "different morphemes" are highly identical. For instance, among synonyms "难说(not sure; find it hard to say)-难言(not sure; find it hard to say)", "注解(annotate; explanatory)-注释(annotate; explanatory)" and "密报(secretly report; secret report)-密告(secretly report; secret report)" whose basic meanings and derivative meanings are both the same, the "different morphemes" "说(speak)-言(speak)", "解(explain)-释(explain)" and "报(report)-告(report)" have high similarity in meaning. Not only could the synonymous morphemes represent each other since ancient times, but also they can constitute a word with each other. The meaning of the word composed of these synonymous morphemes is identical to each morpheme meaning, such as "言说" (speak), "解释" (explain) and "报告"(report).

In contrast, synonyms whose meanings of "different morphemes" are in low similarity tend to have non-parallel derivative meanings. For example, "昆曲" (opera using *kunqiang* tone; *kunqiang* tone) and "昆剧(opera using *kunqiang* tone)" have the same basic meaning as "opera", but only "昆曲" (opera using *kunqiang* tone; *kunqiang* tone) has the metonymical meaning "*kunqiang* tone". That is because only the morpheme "曲" (song; tone) has a metonymical meaning "tone", the foundation for the word "昆曲" to generate a derivative meaning as "*kunqiang* tone".

Through the phenomenon of having the same basic meaning but different derivative meanings, we can further examine the formation of synonyms from the perspective of morphemes. Among synonyms, there are many words in the form of "same morpheme + synonymous/near-synonymous/relevant morpheme". They become synonymous because the common sememe in morphemes is highlighted. Consequently, they can refer to the same object, action or state from different aspects. However, although the derivative meaning is derived from the basic meaning, it is still restricted by the meaning of morphemes. The different sememes in morpheme meanings will affect the derivative direction and characteristics. Therefore, derivative patterns and directions of synonyms may be different.

3.2 Differences Between Stylistic Features of Morphemes

Among synonyms in the form of "same morpheme + different morpheme", there is a special situation that the "different morphemes" only have a difference in stylistic feature, which means they are respectively the colloquial form and the written language form of the synonymous morphemes. In terms of historical factors, during the development from ancient Chinese to modern Chinese, some words lost their ability to constitute words independently and were degraded to morphemes which conform to written language. In contrast, some synonymous morphemes with colloquial style came into being, and they can be used freely, flexibly and frequently until nowadays.

The stylistic feature of morphemes has an influence on the formation and retention of derivative meanings, which should be analyzed in combination with the sequence between the formation of synonyms and the generation of derivative meanings.

For some synonyms, the derivative meanings appear after they become synonymous. Within these synonyms, words composed of colloquial morphemes are relatively easy to generate derivative meanings and retain, because the colloquial morphemes are more flexible in the context, and more likely to generate temporary new meanings and to be fixed in daily use. In contrast, generally, the written morphemes cannot be used alone at the synchronic stage, which means they have weaker word-formation ability, lower frequency, and less probability of meaning variation in the context. For example, "把脉(feel the pulse; analyze)-诊脉(feel the pulse)" are terminologies in the Chinese medical system. In terms of the "different morpheme", "把" (hold) is more colloquial, more abstract, and more flexible in grammar, which is the reason why "把脉" (feel the pulse; analyze) generates and retains a new metaphorical meaning.

For other synonyms, one of them appears first and generates a derivative meaning, and then forms a synonymous relationship with another word on the basic meaning. The latter word may generate the same derivative meaning or may not. For this kind of synonym, the former word is easier to retain the derivative meaning, which tends to be composed of a written-style morpheme. This is because the former word generates the derivative meaning earlier and the meaning is in continuous use, which helps to keep its position in language. This kind of situation mainly occurs when classical Chinese morphemes are replaced by colloquial morphemes. For example, the derivative meaning of "失足" (slip; go astray) appeared in the Western Han Dynasty and was widely used. Later, "足" (foot) gradually became a classical morpheme that could not be used alone, and its usage was overtaken by "脚" (foot). Appeared in the Northern and Southern Dynasties, "失脚" (slip) generated similar derivative meanings, while its competitiveness was weaker than "失足" (slip; go astray). Finally, "失脚" (slip) had lost its derivative meaning, and was only used as a colloquial form of "失足" (slip; go astray) corresponding to its basic meaning.

3.3 Transparency of Lexical Meanings

Inside the synonyms, there are differences in the transparency of basic meanings: some lexical meanings are composed of morpheme meanings directly, which are relatively transparent; while some are indirectly related to morpheme meanings, namely, their meaning transparency is relatively low [15]. The latter situation, contrastively, is easier to generate derivative meanings.

This phenomenon is most obvious in rhetoric-formatted words. For example:

(11) 脊梁 n. i) same as 脊背;
              ii) spinal column;
              iii) a person who plays a pivotal role in a country, nation,
    or group.
(12) 脊背 n. back.

These words both refer to "back", but their word-formation methods are different. "脊梁" (back; important person) was created through metaphor, while "脊背" (back) wasn't. The basic representation of the vehicle "梁" (bridge) is "桥" (bridge) which has the function of carrying chariots, horses and pedestrians. Therefore, "梁"(bridge) in "脊梁" (back; important person) can bear the meaning "support". The back to the human body is similar to the citizen to the nation. As a result, "脊梁" (back; important person) carries the metaphorical meaning "a useful person for society".

In addition, a small group of non-rhetoric-formatted words may have different transparency in meaning as well. For example:

(13) 队伍 n. i) same as 军队;
              ii) contingent; force;
              iii) ranks; formations.
(14) 军队 n. armed forces; army; troops

Their basic meanings are both "army", but "队伍" (army; contingent; ranks) also has a general meaning, while "军队" (army) continues to be used only in the military domain, because the modified morpheme "军" (military) limits the core meaning of the whole word, enhancing the transparency of the lexical meaning.

3.4 Other Causative Factors

The above three factors can explain most of the non-parallelism phenomenon, in addition, there are some other causative factors as below.

Relations Between Words. One of the synonyms may have semantic relationships with other words and form different semantic fields which restrict the derivative meaning of the word. For example, "听力" (hearing; listening) and "耳力" (hearing) are synonyms on the basic meaning, however, "听" (hear; listen) not only belongs to the semantic field of "sense", but also belongs to the semantic field of "listening-speaking-reading-writing", while "耳" (ear) only belongs to the former one. Therefore, their derivative meanings aren't parallel.

Differences Between the Word Structures. The structure of a word has restrictions on its grammatical function to a certain extent. For instance, verb-object compound words are more likely to be verbs. If synonyms have different structures, the difference may cause different derivative meanings. For example, "消夜" (midnight snack; have a snack at night) is a verb-object word, and "夜宵" (midnight snack) is a modifier-head word. Only the former one generates a verbal meaning based on its structure.

Effects of Foreign Languages. Languages are in connection with each other, and Chinese words are affected by other languages in many aspects [16], especially Japanese and English. For instance, the basic meanings of "遗弃" (abandon; forsake) and "抛弃" (abandon) are both "abandon". In Japanese law, "遗弃" (abandon; forsake) is the crime of "forsaking people in need"[17]. Under the influence of Japanese law, "遗弃" (abandon; forsake) is recognized as a crime in China as well. Subsequently, the word generated the derivate meaning "forsaking one's wife and children", but "抛弃" (abandon) didn't.

Different Grammatical Features of Morphemes. Within the "same morpheme + different morphemes" category of disyllabic synonyms, the words formed by morphemes with richer grammatical properties or more flexible grammatical collocations are relatively easier to generate derivative meanings. For example, "耻辱" (shame n.) and "羞辱" (shame n. & v.) are synonymous when used as nouns. "羞" (shame n. & v.) has grammatical functions as both a noun and a verb, while "耻" (shame n.) is only a noun. Therefore, only "羞辱"(shame n. & v.) gained its derivative meaning as a verb.

The Influence of Pragmatic Contexts. Derivative meanings are easy to be fixed if they are used frequently in pragmatic contexts. In the group of synonyms "妖精" (monster; attractive woman) and "妖怪" (monster), the former is often used in Ming and Qing novels to refer to the women metamorphosed from animals [18], and gradually generated the meaning "physically attractive women".

4 The Transformation of Derivative Meanings from Parallel to Non-Parallel

According to Appearance-Submerging Theory [19], the meanings of words are constantly evolving. Some temporary meanings become fixed meanings due to frequent use, which is the appearance of derivative meanings. Comparatively, some derivative meanings are submerged due to reduced use. In the following part, we investigate the evolution tendency of synonymous derivative meanings diachronically and synchronically.

4.1 Diachronic Evolution of Derivative Meanings

Diachronically, in terms of synonyms with the same basic and derivative meaning in history, some of them remain identical at present, but some have turned to be different in derivative meanings. There are 36 groups of such synonyms in total.

Most of these synonyms are the reverse-ordered words formed with the same morphemes. In history, these words tended to have the same basic meaning and derivative meaning because of their same morphemes and same structures. However, in nearly 78.57% of synonyms, the derivative meaning is assumed by one of the synonyms nowadays, which means the transformation process of derivative meanings from parallel to non-parallel has completed already, such as "负担(carry; burden)-担负(carry)" and "剪裁(cut out a garment; prune)-裁剪(cut out a garment)".

Besides of the reverse-ordered words, there are other kinds of words which also have the same transformation process. For example, in ancient Chinese, "高峻" (high and steep) and "峥嵘" (high and steep; outstanding) have the same basic meaning as well as the same derivative meaning, which are listed in *Great Chinese Dictionary* (2nd d Edition) and the *Ministry of Education's Recompiled Mandarin Dictionary* (Revised Edition). However, in modern Chinese, the derivative meaning "outstanding" is only in the entry of "峥嵘" (high and steep; outstanding), because "高峻" (high and steep) no longer refers to "outstanding" in our day.

4.2 Synchronic Evolution of Derivative Meanings

Synchronically, there are some synonyms with the same basic and derivative meaning, whose frequency of use shows obvious differences. When the difference expands to a certain extent, derivative meanings tend to lead to division of labor. Specifically, it can be divided into two situations.

In one situation, the two words both keep the basic meaning, but the derivative meaning is assumed by only one of them. For example, in *Xianhan* (7th edition), the derivative meanings of "刀口" (blade; crucial point) and "刀刃" (blade; crucial point) are parallel. However, the metaphoric usage of "刀刃" (blade; crucial point) hasn't been seen since 2015 in People's Daily, the most powerful, authoritative and normalized Chinese newspaper. Meanwhile, the metaphoric usage of "刀口" (blade; crucial point) is still in frequent use at present.

Another situation is that one of the synonyms keeps the basic meaning and another word keeps the derivative meaning. For example, "近视" (myopia; short-sighted) and "短视" (myopia; short-sighted) both mean "myopia" and "short-sighted" in the dictionary, but they actually have a clear division of labor in use. "近视" (myopia; short-sighted) only keeps the basic meaning "myopia", and "短视" (myopia; short-sighted) only keeps the derivative meaning "short-sighted". This division of labor is promoted by the Japanese words "近视" (myopia) and "远视" (hyperopia). The separation of medical meaning and metaphoric meaning accords with the professional and unitary requirements of terminology, as well as the economy principle.

In general, all these phenomena above reflect the transformation tendency of derivative meanings from parallel to non-parallel. The main reason for the submergence of derivative meaning is the decrease in the using frequency which puts it at a disadvantage in the competition between synonyms.

5 Conclusion

This study finds that synonyms with the same basic meaning may be non-parallel in derivative meanings. The causative factors are complicated, including morpheme meanings, stylistic features of morphemes, transparency of lexical meanings, relations between words, structures of words, foreign languages, grammatical features of morphemes as well as pragmatic contexts. Among all the causative factors, the first three are the most important ones, which can be used to explain nearly 75% of the phenomenon. It can be concluded that although lexical derivation occurs in the hierarchy of words, it is still mainly restricted by morphemes, especially in the aspect of meaning.

Chronologically, the derivative meanings of synonyms show a transformation tendency from parallel to non-parallel in general, some of which have completed and some of which are still ongoing. It is the reflection of lexical evolution tendency, promoted by the principle of economy in language.

It is necessary that dictionary compilation pay attention to the transformation of synonyms and update the interpretation accordingly. In addition, we also observe that there is another kind of synonyms. These synonyms have different basic meanings but the same derivative meaning, such as "翻车" (a car overturns; suffer a setback midway) and "翻船" (capsize; suffer a setback midway). This special phenomenon also deserves further investigation in the future.

References

1. Zhang, Z.Y.: Several basic viewpoints on the judgements of synonyms. J. Jilin Normal Univ. **15**(1), 62–80 (1965). (in Chinese)
2. Liu, S.X.: A brief discussion on the characteristics of synonyms in modern Chinese. Chinese Lang. Learn. **5**(3), 26–35 (1984). (in Chinese)
3. Ge, B.Y.: Research on Chinese Lexicon. Shandong Education Press, Jinan (1985). (in Chinese)
4. Huang, J.G.: On the similarities of synonyms. J. Zhejiang Univ. (Human. Soc. Sci.) **30**(4), 81–86 (2000). (in Chinese)
5. Cheng, J., Xu, X.H., A study on the synonymous monosyllabic and disyllabic verbs in HSK word list. Chinese Teach. World **18**(4), 43–57+3 (2004). (in Chinese)
6. Liu, C.M.: Differences between the synonymous monosyllabic and disyllabic nouns in Chinese. J. Central China Normal Univ. **52**(1), 128–132 (2006). (in Chinese)
7. Liu, Z.Y.: Contrastive study on the style of the synonymous monosyllabic verb and disyllabic verb with the same morpheme. Appl. Linguis. **16**(2), 96–104 (2007). (in Chinese)
8. Ding, X.W.: A corpus-based comparative study of monosyllabic and disyllabic common words in modern chinese. Lang. Teach. Linguist. Stud. **35**(5), 79–87 (2014). (in Chinese)
9. Li, Q., Li, H.Y.: On the discrimination degree of definition modes between one-syllable and two-syllable verbal synonyms in chinese learner's dictionaries. Chin. Lang. Learn. **43**(5), 92–102 (2002). (in Chinese)
10. Dictionary Editing Office of the Institute of Linguistics, Chinese Academy of Social Sciences: Modern Chinese Dictionary, 7th edn. Commercial Press, Beijing (2016). (in Chinese)
11. Li, X.J.: Modern Chinese Standard Dictionary, 3rd edn. Foreign Language Teaching and Research Press, Beijing (2014). (in Chinese)
12. Luo, R.F.: Great Chinese Dictionary, 2nd edn. Shanghai Lexicographic Publishing House, Shanghai (2011). (in Chinese)

13. Cheng, R.: Great Synonym Dictionary, 2nd edn. Shanghai Lexicographic Publishing House, Shanghai (2017). (in Chinese)
14. Standards Press of China: Guidelines for Standardization Work: Compilation of National Standards, 7th edn. Standards Press of China, Beijing (2020). (in Chinese)
15. Li, J.X., Li, Y.M.: On the Transparency of Lexical Meaning. Stud. Lang. Linguist. **28**(3), 60–65 (2008). (in Chinese)
16. Yang, Y., Ho, H.K.: The Influence of Neologisms from Mainland China on Changes in the Lexical Semantics of Hong Kong Cantonese. In: Dong, M., Hong, J.-F., Lin, J., Jin, P. (eds.) Chinese Lexical Semantics: 24th Workshop, CLSW 2023, Singapore, Singapore, May 19–21, 2023, Revised Selected Papers, Part I, pp. 187–195. Springer Nature Singapore, Singapore (2024). https://doi.org/10.1007/978-981-97-0583-2_15
17. Leng, B.Y.: The magnifying of abandon crime——remove doubts by comparing different legislations. J. Political Sci. Law **22**(5), 40–55 (2006). (in Chinese)
18. An, J.: Fun talk: "fairy" is different from "monster." J. Lit. History **33**(1), 103–104 (2018). (in Chinese)
19. Diao, Y.B.: History of Modern Chinese. Fujian People's Publishing House, Fuzhou (2006). (in Chinese)

Morphology of 'Chilli Pepper' Nouns in Sinitic Languages: A Typological Study

Di Qiu[1] and Sicong Dong[2(✉)]

[1] School of Mechanical Engineering and Automation, Harbin Institute of Technology, Shenzhen, China
210410108@stu.hit.edu.cn
[2] School of Humanities and Social Sciences, Harbin Institute of Technology, Shenzhen, China
dongsicong@hit.edu.cn

Abstract. The nouns that mean chilli pepper have diverse word forms in Sinitic languages after the plant was introduced to China. Based on large-scale field data, this paper generalizes a morphological typology of such nouns and depicts the patterns of their geographical distribution. The distributional patterns can be accounted for by the cultivating history of chilli pepper, the paths of immigration, the local dietary preference, and the features of the plant on which people put the focus. The major findings include: 辣椒 *làjiāo* hot-pepper and 辣子 *là·zi* hot-NMLZ show an east-west distribution, with the latter diachronically preceding the former; while word forms containing 番 *fān* 'foreign' are mainly found in Fujian and Zhejiang, where chilli was introduced to south China, 秦椒 *qínjiāo* Qin-pepper demonstrates the pathway of chilli in the north; Sichuan and Chongqing feature 海椒 *hǎijiāo* oceanic-pepper, which was taken there by immigrants from Hunan.

Keywords: Chilli pepper · Sinitic languages · Morphological variation · Geographical distribution · Lexical typology

1 Introduction

Spiciness or hotness, though physiologically a sense of pain, is commonly recognized in traditional Chinese culinary culture as a basic taste and often juxtaposed with sour, sweet, bitter, and salty [1, 2]. However, the crop that provides this flavour, chilli pepper, was rather recently introduced to China in the late 16th century [3]. It has spread widely in China over four hundred years, a relatively short period for such a large scale of expansion. Yet, alongside this rapid popularization, the nouns denoting chilli pepper in Sinitic languages, or Chinese dialects, did not adopt an identical word form, which should be the most efficient way of naming. On the contrary, such nouns are highly diverse regarding morphological structure and morpheme usage. Their typological complexity is closely associated with non-linguistic factors such as the introduction routes and the cultivation environments of chilli pepper, thus providing valuable data for interdisciplinary research of linguistics, cultural studies, and economic history.

However, the relationship between Sinitic nouns of chilli pepper and its cultivation history has scarcely been examined from a linguistic perspective. Relevant discussions

P. Jin et al. (Eds.): CLSW 2024, LNAI 15552, pp. 99–111, 2025.
https://doi.org/10.1007/978-981-96-3509-2_8

are commonly found in studies of agricultural history and agricultural culture. For example, Hu [4] and Ding & Hu [5] provided detailed analyses based on the local gazetteers from the Ming dynasty to the Republic of China. They claimed there were two centres of the spread of chilli pepper according to the historical distribution of the two word forms 秦椒 *qínjiāo* Qin-pepper and 番椒 *fānjiāo* foreign-pepper, with one in the north of today's Shaanxi, Hebei, and Shandong, and the other in the south covering Fujian, Guangdong, and Taiwan. They also summarized some regional features of the word forms, such as 海椒 *hǎijiāo* oceanic-pepper being common in the southwest, and 番姜 *fānjiāng* foreign-ginger being prevalent in Fujian and Taiwan.

The data used in Hu [4] and Ding & Hu [5] are from local gazetteers, which were compiled by local governments at various levels and possibly revised or recompiled at different times, hence constituting corpora with rich spatiotemporal information [6]. Specifically, their records of local products can reflect the approximate regional distribution and diachronic change of the word forms of chilli pepper. However, such data also have limitations. Firstly, as comprehensive text, the language in gazetteers is not homogeneous and can present a mix of multiple times and locations which are difficult to tell apart. Secondly, the languages/dialects covered in gazetteers are limited, so the data points are insufficient for a complete and precise nationwide distribution of the word forms. Lastly, since they are historical data, gazetteers do not represent the contemporary usage of Sinitic languages.

The above drawbacks are also reflected in some conclusions of Hu [4] and Ding & Hu [5]. For instance, the form 胡椒 *hújiāo* foreign-pepper, which is used for pepper in Standard Mandarin, is commonly used for chilli pepper along the middle and lower reaches of the Yangtze River. But this word form is absent from the list of Hu [4]. Another example is 秦椒 *qínjiāo* Qin-pepper, which is not found to denote chilli pepper in the northeast of China according to the contemporary field data, but is shown to be prevalent there based on the historical data of Ding & Hu [5].

The limitations of gazetteer data and studies based on them highlight the need to integrate historical textual data with contemporary field data. Moreover, the contemporary data of spoken languages are more homogeneous and systematic, more accurately reflecting language usage, and thus should receive greater research emphasis. In light of this, we will analyse the morphology and geographical distribution of 'chilli pepper' nouns based on large-scale Sinitic field data, and explain such typological patterns with the aid of multiple disciplines.

2   Method and Data

We primarily used The Data Collection, Recording, and Display Platform for the Chinese Language Resources Protection Project (hereinafter referred to as the "Language Protection Platform"; accessed at https://zhongguoyuyan.cn/, 7 January 2024) to obtain the word forms of nouns denoting chilli pepper in Sinitic languages. We then created distribution maps for the word forms on this platform. Also, we consulted Fig. 020 in Cao [7] for the word forms and their distribution. The Language Protection Platform includes 1,361 language points with 'chilli pepper' nouns, while Cao [7] contains 930.

We have found over 40 word forms of nouns denoting chilli pepper on the Language Protection Platform, as shown in Fig. 1. The "other" category is automatically generated by the system to group scattered word forms that correspond to only one data point. We checked all these word forms and found that the ones with etymological Chinese characters all fit in the typological system generalized in this section. Therefore, we do not combine the limited data in the "other" category with the others, but only analyse some of its word forms where appropriate.

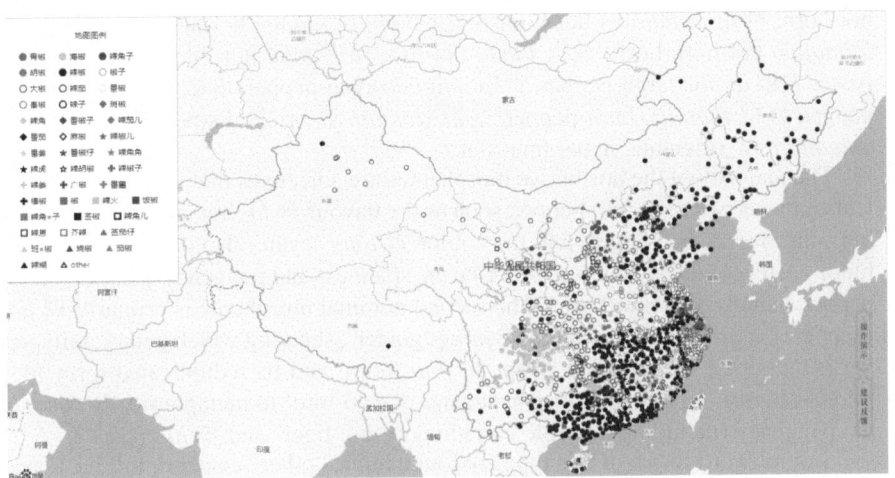

Fig. 1. Distribution of word forms of 'chilli pepper' nouns

Based on the data on the Language Protection Platform, the word forms of 'chilli pepper' nouns in Sinitic languages can be classified into four basic types:

(1) N region + N genus (+ suffix)
      This format consists of a nominal morpheme denoting geographical regions and a following nominal morpheme denoting the genus to which chilli pepper belongs, with some including a nominalizing suffix originally meaning 'son'. The word forms include 番椒 *fānjiāo* foreign-pepper, 番椒子 *fānjiāozi* foreign-pepper-NMLZ, 番椒仔 *fānjiāozǎi* foreign-pepper-NMLZ, 斑椒 *bānjiāo* spot-pepper, 班＝椒 *bānjiāo* ?-pepper (the symbol ＝ indicates homophonous characters), 饭椒 *fànjiāo* meal-pepper, 番茄 *fānqié* foreign-aubergine, 番姜 *fānjiāng* foreign-ginger, 番薑 *fānjiāng* foreign-ginger (薑 is the traditional form of 姜), 海椒 *hǎijiāo* oceanic-pepper, 胡椒 *hújiāo* foreign-pepper, 秦椒 *qínjiāo* Qin-pepper, and 广椒 *guǎngjiāo* Guang-pepper.

      This type of word forms highlights the geographical origin and taxonomical cognition of chilli pepper. Specifically, the initial morphemes mainly include 胡 *hú* 'foreign' and 番 *fān* 'foreign', as well as its possible variations 斑 *bān*, 班 *bān*, and 饭 *fàn*, which were used in ancient Chinese to describe objects with foreign origins, and 海 *hǎi* 'oceanic', which can indicate the foreign origin of objects introduced via the ocean. In addition, morphemes denoting regions inside China, namely, 秦 *qín* 'Qin', a historical region roughly referring to present-day Shaanxi, and 广 *guǎng* 'Guang', roughly referring to the region of Guangdong, Guangxi, and Hainan, are also found in our database. The second nominal morphemes denoting genera are mostly 椒 *jiāo* 'pepper', as well as 茄 *qié* 'aubergine' and 姜/薑 *jiāng* 'ginger'.

(2) ATR + N $_{genus}$ (+ suffix)

This format consists of an attributive carrying non-regional meanings and a nominal morpheme mostly denoting the genus, with some including a nominalizing suffix originally meaning 'son'. These word forms include 辣椒 *làjiāo* hot-pepper, 辣椒儿 *làjiāor* hot-pepper-NMLZ, 辣椒子 *làjiāozi* hot-pepper-NMLZ, 辣茄 *làqié* hot-aubergine, 辣茄儿 *làqiér* hot-aubergine-NMLZ, 辣姜 *làjiāng* hot-ginger, 辣角 *làjiǎo* hot-horn, 辣角子 *làjiǎozi* hot-horn-NMLZ, 辣角儿 *làjiǎor* hot-horn-NMLZ, 辣角角 *làjiǎojiǎo* hot-horn-horn, 辣火 *làhuǒ* hot-fire, 辣虎 *làhǔ* hot-tiger, 辣糊 *làhú* hot-paste, 大椒 *dàjiāo* large-pepper, 青椒 *qīngjiāo* cyan-pepper, 麻椒 *májiāo* numbing-pepper, 烧椒 *shāojiāo* burn-pepper, 签椒 *xiānjiāo* S._orientalis-pepper, and 签茄仔 *xiānqiézǎi* S._orientalis-aubergine-NMLZ.

The majority of the attributive morphemes are adjectives that describe the physical characteristics of chilli pepper, such as the flavour 辣 *là* 'hot' and 麻 *má* 'numbing', the size 大 *dà* 'large', and the colour 青 *qīng* 'cyan (also dark green or light blue)'. A few of the attributives describe the spiciness and pungency caused by chilli pepper, namely 烧 *shāo* 'burn'. The second nominal morpheme is primarily 椒 *jiāo* 'pepper', 茄 *qié* 'aubergine', and 姜 *jiāng* 'ginger', showing which genus chilli pepper is classified. Fewer cases adopt 角 *jiǎo* 'horn' and its reduplicated form 角角 *jiǎojiǎo* horn-horn to depict the shape, and 火 *huǒ* 'fire' to metaphorically describe the pungency (including possible variations 虎 *hǔ* 'tiger' and 糊 *hú* 'paste').

Several word forms of this type are found in the "other" category in Fig. 1, such as 签橄榄 *xiān-gǎnlǎn* S._orientalis-olive in Huilai Min, reflecting the perception of chilli pepper related to olive, and 胡椒鼻 *hújiāobí* foreign-pepper-nose in Yong'an Min, showing the similarity in shape between chilli pepper and nose in people's perception. Additionally, three Hakka islands in Sichuan and Chongqing share a uniform word form with an unknown etymological character: 改椒 *kai³¹tɕiau³⁵* ?-pepper in Panlong Hakka, Chongqing, 该 = 椒 *kai³⁴tɕiau⁴⁴* ?-pepper in Liangshuijing Hakka, Chengdu, and 荄椒 *kai³⁴tɕiau³⁴* ?-pepper in Longquanyi Hakka, Chengdu.

(3) 辣 *là* / 椒 *jiāo* (+ suffix)

This format contains only one content morpheme, 辣 *là* 'hot' or 椒 *jiāo* 'pepper'. While the former highlights the prominent characteristic of chilli pepper, the latter reflects its genus. Most of these word forms include a suffix originally meaning 'son'. The word forms include 辣子 *làzi* hot-NMLZ, 辣崽 *làzǎi* hot-NMLZ, 椒 *jiāo* pepper, and 椒子 *jiāozi* pepper-NMLZ. There is another monosyllabic word form 辣 *là* hot found in Lianping Hakka, Guangdong, in the "other" category in Fig. 1.

(4) Other

Four word forms cannot fit into the aforementioned three categories, namely, 芥辣 *jièlà* mustard-hot, which follows a format of N $_{genus}$ + A, 茄椒 *qiéjiāo* aubergine-pepper and 榛椒 *zhēnjiāo* hazelnut-pepper, both composed of two nominal morphemes indicating genera, and 辣胡椒 *làhújiāo* hot-foreign-pepper, which contains three content morphemes. Furthermore, the word forms 酵母子 *jiàomǔzi* yeast-mother-NMLZ and 酱母子 *jiàngmǔzi* sauce-mother-NMLZ are found in two data points in Hebei in the "other" category of Fig. 1.

In the next section, we will analyse the morphological patterns in detail based on their geographical distribution.

3   Discussion

3.1   辣椒 *làjiāo* hot-pepper and 辣子 *làzi* hot-*NMLZ*

It has been well-documented that many isoglosses in Sinitic languages roughly follow the north vs. south pattern along the line of the Yangtze River or the line of the Qin Mountain and the Huai River; the west vs. east pattern, as a secondary one, also exists, primarily demarcated by the A-Na line, i.e., from Arxan City of Inner Mongolia to Napo County of Guangxi [8]. The west vs. east pattern can be observed in our data.

As shown in Fig. 2, 辣椒 *làjiāo* hot-pepper is centred in the east, while 辣子 *làzi* hot-NMLZ is in the west. The two forms should be competing with each other, as evidenced by their indistinct boundary along the region of Shanxi, Hebei, Hunan, Guangxi, etc., as well as a possible blend of the two, namely, 辣椒子 *làjiāozi* hot-pepper-NMLZ, in this region.

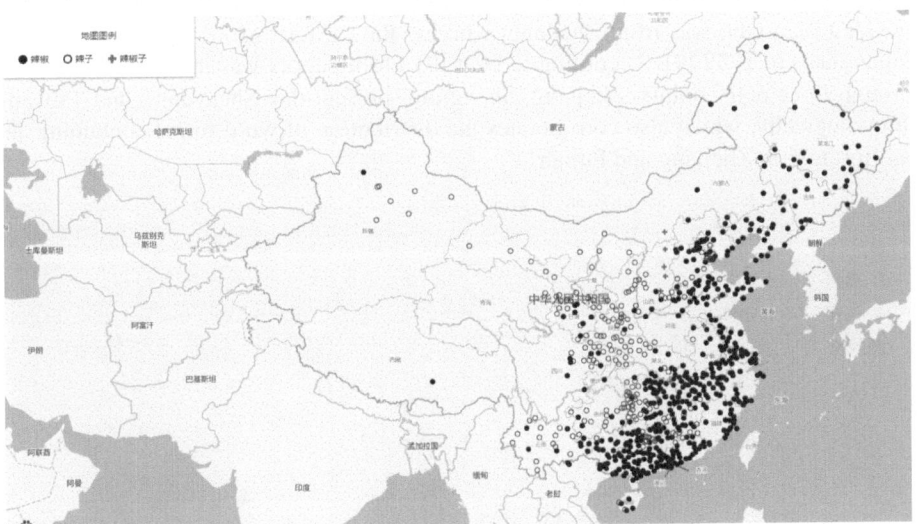

Fig. 2. Distribution of 辣椒 *làjiāo* hot-pepper and 辣子 *làzi* hot-NMLZ

The two forms have different origins. The term 辣子 *làzi* had been used in Chinese before the introduction of chilli pepper, but its meaning was *Zanthoxylum ailanthoides*, a type of prickly-ash [4]. In other words, the chilli pepper sense of 辣子 *làzi* was added to an existing word form. 辣椒 *làjiāo*, by contrast, was created for chilli pepper. It first appeared in 1733 in *Guangxi Tongzhi* (A Comprehensive Gazetteer of Guangxi) and was only used in Guangdong and Guangxi for the next two hundred years [5]. Since it is more economical to add new meanings to existing forms, we speculate that 辣子 *làzi* meaning chilli pepper preceded 辣椒 *làjiāo*; the later form 辣椒 *làjiāo* gradually replaced 辣子 *làzi* in the east, thereby forming the current west vs. east pattern. The widespread adoption of 辣椒 *làjiāo* can be attributed to the fact that it shows more information of both flavour and genus, and later became the official form.

3.2 番 *fān* 'foreign', 胡 *hú* 'foreign', and 海 *hǎi* 'oceanic'

As a foreign crop, the word forms of chilli pepper commonly show its origin, mostly by the morphemes 番 *fān* 'foreign', 胡 *hú* 'foreign', and 海 *hǎi* 'oceanic'. Generally, such morphemes tend to be used where the crop was first introduced or regions it soon reached after the introduction, because its foreign identity will gradually fade once the crop takes root in China. For instance, sweet potato is called 番薯 *fānshǔ* foreign-potato only in the southeastern coastal areas [7], where the crop was first introduced.

The word forms of 'chilli pepper' nouns containing 番 *fān* 'foreign', including its possible variations 斑 *bān*, 班 = *bān*, and 饭 *fàn*, are concentrated in Fujian, Hainan (a prevalently Min speaking region with speakers originally from Fujian), and the areas of Zhejiang adjacent to Fujian, as illustrated in Fig. 3. As mentioned earlier, Ding and Hu [5] indicated that Fujian, Guangdong, and Taiwan served as the south centre of chilli pepper spread. Our findings support the importance of Fujian in the spread of chilli pepper, and suggest that Zhejiang should also hold considerable significance. After all, 番椒 *fānjiāo* first appeared in 1591 in *Zunsheng Ba Jian* (Eight Precepts of Life-Nurturing), authored by GAO Lian who was from Zhejiang; whereas the earliest record of chilli pepper in Fujian dates to 1757 [9]. According to Dott [9], chilli pepper was introduced to China through three entry points: Zhejiang, Shengjing (present-day Shenyang), and Taiwan, chronologically, which also corroborates the distribution of word forms containing 番 *fān* 'foreign' in Zhejiang and Fujian.

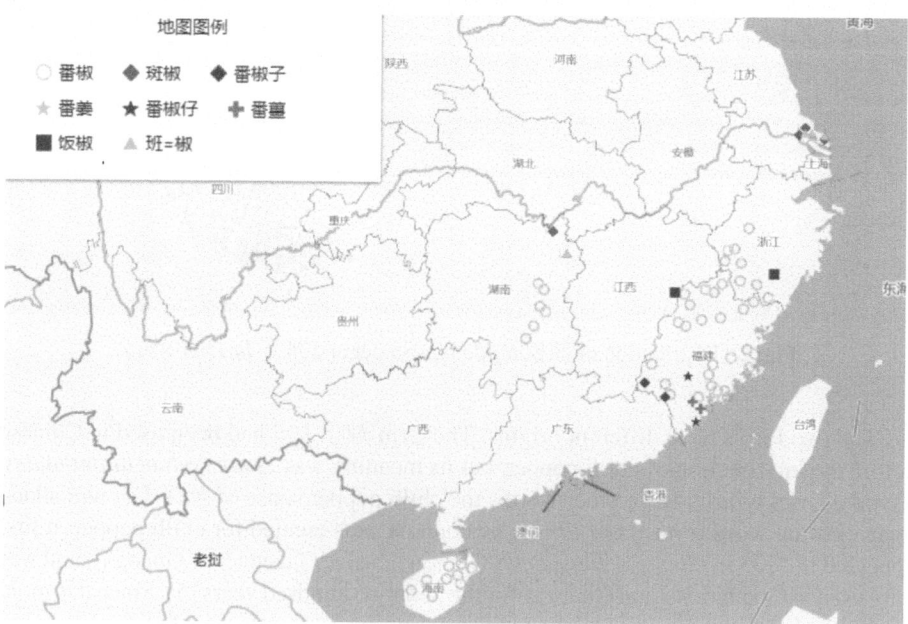

Fig. 3. Distribution of word forms containing 番 *fān* 'foreign'

Now we turn to 胡椒 *hújiāo* foreign-pepper. This word form is used to denote pepper in Standard Mandarin, since 椒 *jiāo* originally referred to Sichuan pepper, a local spice, in Old Chinese, then the morpheme 胡 *hú* 'foreign' was added to form a word for pepper when it was introduced from the Western Regions. However, our data show that 胡椒 *hújiāo* can also be used to mean chilli pepper in many Sinitic languages, chiefly along the Yangtze River in Hubei, Anhui, and Jiangsu, mostly to the north of the river, as shown in Fig. 4.

Fig. 4. Distribution of 胡椒 *hújiāo* foreign-pepper

This distribution may be related to the temporal proximity or overlap between the large-scale cultivation of pepper and the introduction of chilli pepper. It was not until the treasure voyages led by ZHENG He in the Ming dynasty that pepper gradually became a common spice in China, though it entered China during the Han and Jin dynasties and had been regarded as a highly valuable luxury for centuries [10]. Therefore, it is highly likely that ordinary people encountered both pepper and chilli pepper during the Ming dynasty, and the shared pungent properties of the two crops could lead to confusion. This mixed way of perception can also be seen in word forms for chilli pepper such as 辣胡椒 *làhújiāo* hot-foreign-pepper, 麻胡椒 *máhújiāo* numbing-foreign-pepper, and 大胡椒 *dàhújiāo* large-foreign-pepper. Interestingly, they are also distributed in the middle and lower reaches of the Yangtze River. Similar connection between pepper and chilli pepper can too be seen in many European languages, where chilli pepper is referred to as "pepper" because chilli pepper was adopted as a substitute for pepper [11].

The above analysis can be further supported by the yield of chilli pepper. The regions where 胡椒 *hújiāo* is used to mean chilli pepper, i.e., Hubei, Anhui, and Jiangsu, are among the provinces whose pepper yield is at low to medium-low levels [12]. The yield would be even lower during the Ming dynasty. The less frequent contact with pepper could facilitate the confusion between pepper and chilli pepper when the latter spread upstream along the Yangtze River. Similarly, another province with low pepper yield, Jiangxi, also has data points along the Yangtze River using 胡椒 *hújiāo* for chilli pepper according to the data of Cao [7].

The word form 海椒 *hǎijiāo* oceanic-pepper of chilli pepper is an areal feature predominantly found in Sichuan and Chongqing, extending into the northern parts of Guizhou that border these regions, as shown in Fig. 5. It is also found in the border area between Hunan and Guangxi. However, the earliest recorded use of this word form is not in Sichuan or Chongqing, but in Hunan, as evidenced in *Baoqing Fu Zhi* (A Gazetteer of Baoqing Prefecture) and *Shaoyang Xian Zhi* (A Gazetteer of Shaoyang County) [5]. This divergence between earliest usage in Hunan and current prevalence in Sichuan and Chongqing is a result of immigration.

Based on the distribution shown in Fig. 1, with a similar pattern found in Cao [7], the two clusters of 海椒 *hǎijiāo*, namely, one being Sichuan, Chongqing, and northern Guizhou, the other being the Hunan-Guangxi border, are cut apart by a large belt of 辣子 *làzi* and 辣椒 *làjiāo*. This distribution suggests that 海椒 *hǎijiāo* was widely used in the large region of Sichuan, Chongqing, Guizhou, and Hunan earlier than 辣子 *làzi* and 辣椒 *làjiāo*, but later replaced by the latter two in the central part of this region. The widespread of 海椒 *hǎijiāo* is due to the enormous migration movement of "Huguang Filling Sichuan" (Huguang mainly encompassed today's provinces of Hubei and Hunan), during which the immigrants from Hunan, where a spicy cuisine was first developed [13], carried both their dietary habits and the name for chilli pepper to Sichuan and Chongqing. This word form 海椒 *hǎijiāo* is only kept in the current two clusters, because Sichuan and Chongqing are more culturally cohesive, and the Hunan-Guangxi border area is far from political and economic centres in this region, enabling them to retain the older morphological form.

Fig. 5. Distribution of 海椒 *hǎijiāo* oceanic-pepper

3.3 秦 *qín* 'qin' and 广 *guǎng* 'guang'

The morpheme 秦 *qín* 'Qin' representing Shaanxi and 广 *guǎng* 'Guang' representing Guangdong, Guangxi, and Hainan, can be used in nouns meaning chilli pepper, but such word forms are not found in the corresponding provinces. Specifically, 秦椒 *qínjiāo* Qin-pepper is mainly distributed in Henan, also scattered in neighbouring Shandong, Hebei, and Shanxi; 广椒 *guǎngjiāo* Guang-pepper is primarily distributed in southwestern Hubei, and also found in the adjacent Wushan of Chongqing, as shown in Fig. 6. The morphology of 广椒 *guǎngjiāo* is self-evident, indicating that chilli pepper was taken there from the coastal areas of Guangdong, Guangxi, etc., in line with the coast-to-inland direction of chilli pepper spread [14]. Unlike 广椒 *guǎngjiāo*, 秦椒 *qínjiāo* is trickier

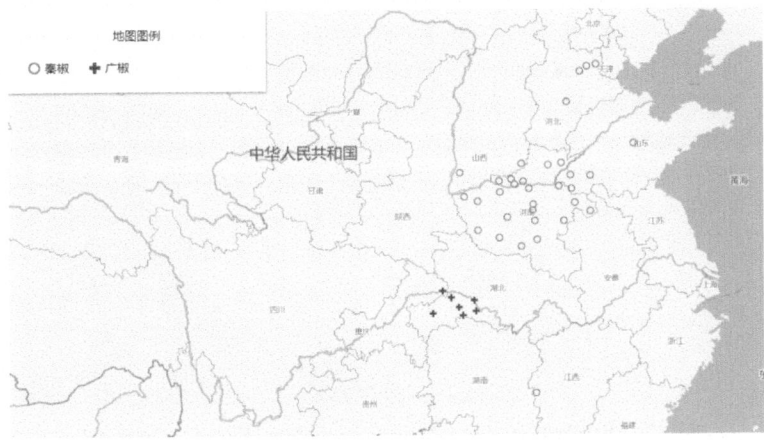

Fig. 6. Distribution of 秦椒 *qínjiāo* Qin-pepper and 广椒 *guǎngjiāo* Guang-pepper

since Shaanxi was not one of the entry points of chilli pepper, and chilli pepper was likely taken to Shaanxi from Zhejiang [15].

Similar to 辣子 *làzi* hot-NMLZ discussed before, 秦椒 *qínjiāo* was also an existing word form when chilli pepper was introduced to China. It originally meant the Sichuan pepper produced in Qin. The newly added sense of 秦椒 *qínjiāo* became prevalent in north China, even in some areas in the southwest [5]. One reason is that there were also entry points of chilli pepper in the north, either Liaoning [4, 9] or Shandong [15], so many Sinitic languages in the north could have a uniform word form during the large-scale spread of chilli pepper. However, 秦椒 *qínjiāo* is ambiguous after all, denoting two common spices, so it was subsequently replaced in the lexical competition, but only primarily kept in the Central Plains.

3.4 茄 *qié* 'aubergine' and 角 *jiǎo* 'horn'

There are two other morphemes with strong areal tendencies: 茄 *qié* 'aubergine', concentrated in Zhejiang and Fujian, and 角 *jiǎo* 'horn', concentrated in Shanxi, as illustrated in Figs. 7 and 8 respectively.

Chilli pepper and aubergine both belong to the Solanaceae family. Aubergine was introduced to China and widely cultivated as early as around the 4th century CE [9]. Hence, when chilli pepper was introduced to Zhejiang, it was named based on the already widely known aubergine which resembles chilli pepper. The word form 辣茄(儿) *làqié(r)* hot-aubergine-NMLZ is rather uniformly adopted in Zhejiang. In contrast, Sinitic languages in Fujian exhibit more diverse forms containing 茄 *qié* 'aubergine', such as 番茄 *fānqié* foreign-aubergine, 茄椒 *qiéjiāo* aubergine-pepper, 签茄仔 *xiānqiézǎi* S._orientalis-aubergine-NMLZ, etc.

When naming chilli pepper, 椒 *jiāo* 'pepper' and 姜 *jiāng* 'ginger' are used to describe its flavour, 茄 *qié* 'aubergine' to describe its shape, while 角 *jiǎo* 'horn' focuses on its darkest red part with most concentrated spiciness [5]. This naming rationale is nearly exclusively seen in data points of Shanxi Province.

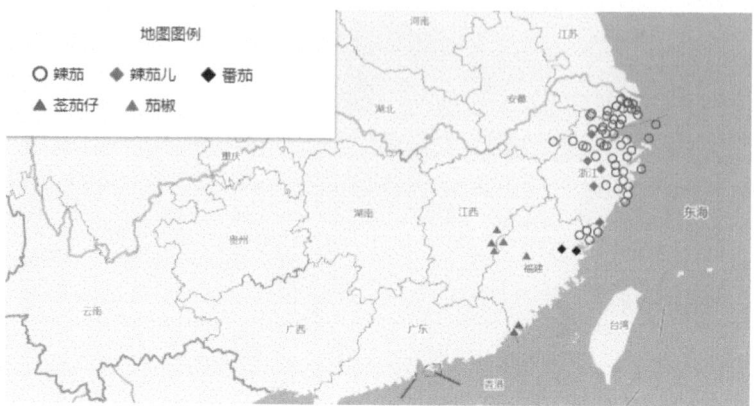

Fig. 7. Distribution of word forms containing 茄 *qié* 'aubergine'

Fig. 8. Distribution of word forms containing 角 *jiǎo* 'horn'

4   Conclusion

We generalized the morphological typology of nouns denoting chilli pepper in Sinitic languages based on over 1,000 data points and successfully accounted for their geographical distribution with interdisciplinary approaches. Three major types of word forms have been identified and analysed in this paper.

The first type consists of a morpheme indicating regions and another indicating genera. Specifically, the word forms beginning with 番 *fān* 'foreign' are distributed in Fujian, Hainan, and Zhejiang, reflecting the southeast coastal region as a significant entry point of chilli pepper; 胡椒 *hújiāo* foreign-pepper is found along the middle and lower reaches of the Yangtze River, possibly related to the confusion between pepper and chilli pepper among local people; 海椒 *hǎijiāo* oceanic-pepper is mainly distributed in Sichuan and Chongqing, associated with large-scale historical immigration from Hunan; 广椒 *guǎngjiāo* Guang-pepper is primarily found in Hubei, reflecting the route of chilli pepper from Guangdong and Guangxi; and 秦椒 *qínjiāo* Qin-pepper is concentrated in the Central Plains, indicating the entry points and spread routes of chilli pepper in the north.

The second type contains an attributive morpheme describing the flavour or appearance of chilli pepper, combined with a nominal morpheme mostly denoting the genus. To be specific, the official word form for chilli pepper, 辣椒 *làjiāo* hot-pepper, is widely distributed in eastern China; word forms containing 茄 *qié* 'aubergine' are concentrated in Zhejiang and Fujian, reflecting the similarity between chilli pepper and aubergine perceived by the people who lived where chilli pepper was first introduced; word forms containing 角 *jiǎo* 'horn' are mainly distributed in Shanxi, named after the spiciest part of chilli pepper.

The third type contains only one content morpheme, 辣 *là* 'hot' or 椒 *jiāo* 'pepper', and almost always ends with a suffix. One common word form 辣子 *làzi* hot-NMLZ originally referred to a type of prickly-ash, and later acquired the meaning of chilli pepper and became widely distributed in western China, forming a west vs. east pattern with 辣椒 *làjiāo* hot-pepper.

This paper demonstrates that the field linguistic data, though synchronic, can be useful for diachronic studies because the distributional patterns shown today are the results of historical development. With the help of geolinguistic analysis and historical data such as gazetteer texts, it is feasible to reveal the developmental details. Such diachronic findings, furthermore, can provide evidence from the linguistic perspective for other disciplines such as cultural studies and economic history.

Our research also shows that it is promising to conduct interdisciplinary studies of Sinitic languages based on the Geographic Information Systems (GIS), in addition to recent studies of weather expressions [6, 16–24]. Typological features of languages are geographically distributed, and so is the non-linguistic information such as crop cultivation, immigration, dietary preference, weather, etc. By plotting multi-layered maps incorporating various information, we can detect prominent patterns and provide convincing explanations.

References

1. Dong, S., Zhong, Y., Huang, C.-R.: How do non-tastes taste? A corpus-based study on Chinese people's perception of spicy and numbing food. In: Proceedings of the 32nd Pacific Asia Conference on Language, Information and Computation: 25th Joint Workshop on Linguistics and Language Processing, pp. 858–866. Association for Computational Linguistics, Stroudsburg (2018)
2. Zhong, Y., Huang, C.-R., Dong, S.: Bodily sensation and embodiment: a corpus-based study of gustatory vocabulary in Mandarin Chinese. J. Chin. Linguist. **50**(1), 196–230 (2022). https://doi.org/10.1353/jcl.2022.0008
3. Zhu, D., Wang, D., Li, X.: Zhongguo Zuowu Ji Qi Yesheng Jinyuan Zhiwu: Shucai Zuowu Juan [Crops and their wild relatives in China: Vol. vegetable crops]. China Agriculture Press, Beijing (2008). (in Chinese)
4. Hu, Y.: Lajiao Mingcheng Kaoshi [Interpretation of the name of pepper]. Ancient Mod. Agric. **4**, 67–75 (2013). (in Chinese)
5. Ding, X., Hu, Y.: Cong Fangzhi Jizai De Lajiao Difang Mingcheng Kan Lajiao Zai Zhongguo De Yinzhong Chuanbo [A study on the spread of chili peppers in China in terms of their trivial names ――― focusing on Chinese historical local records]. J. Chin. Hist. Geog. **30**(3), 104–117 (2015). (in Chinese)

6. Dong, S., Yang, Y., Ren, H., Huang, C.-R.: Directionality of atmospheric water in Chinese: a lexical semantic study based on linguistic ontology. SAGE Open **11**(1), 1–13 (2021). https://doi.org/10.1177/2158244020988293

7. Cao, Z.: Hanyu Fangyan Dituji (Cihui Juan) [Linguistic Atlas of Chinese Dialects (Lexicon)]. The Commercial Press, Beijing (2008). (in Chinese)

8. Cao, Z.: Hanyu Fangyan De Dili Fenbu Leixing [The geographical distribution types of Chinese dialects]. Lang. Teach. Linguist. Stud. **5**, 11–19 (2011). (in Chinese)

9. Dott, B.R.: The Chile pepper in china: a cultural biography. Columbia University Press, New York (2020)

10. T'ien, J.-K.: Chêng Ho's voyages and the distribution of pepper in China. J. R. Asiat. Soc. G.B. Irel. **113**(2), 186–197 (1981). https://doi.org/10.1017/S0035869X00157910

11. Jin, G., Ye, N.: "Putaoyaren Da Chuanbo": Lajiao Ru Yin Ji Ru Hua Shi Kaolue — Ouzhou Shiliao Shijiao Xia De Xinlun [Great Portuguese Propagation: the research of the history of hot pepper's different in India and China in the view of the European materials]. Acad. Res. **10**, 117–131 (2022). (in Chinese)

12. Zou, Z., Zou, X.: Geographical and ecological differences in pepper cultivation and consumption in China. Front. Nutr. **8**, 718517 (2021). https://doi.org/10.3389/fnut.2021.718517

13. Yang, X.: Lajiao Zai Hunan De Chuanbo Ji Qi Yingxiang [The spread and influence of chili in Hunan Province]. J. Mudanjiang Univ. **22**(12), 109–112 (2013). (in Chinese)

14. Zou, X., Ma, Y., Dai, X., Li, X., Yang, S.: Lajiao Zai Zhongguo De Chuanbo Yu Chanye Fazhan [Spread and industry development of pepper in China]. Acta Horticulturae Sinica **47**(9), 1715–1726 (2020). (in Chinese)

15. Zou, X., Zhu, F.: Lajiao Chuanru Zhongguo De Tujing Yu Chuanbo Lujing [The path of pepper introduction into China and its spreading route in China]. J. Hunan Agric. Univ. (Nat. Sci.) **46**(6), 629–640 (2020)

16. Dong, S., Yang, Y., Huang, C.-R., Ren, H.: Directionality and momentum of water in weather: a morphosemantic study of conceptualisation based on Hantology. In: Hong, J.-F., Zhang, Y., Liu, P. (eds.) CLSW 2019. LNCS (LNAI), vol. 11831, pp. 575–584. Springer, Cham (2020). https://doi.org/10.1007/978-3-030-38189-9_59

17. Huang, C.-R., Dong, S.: From lexical semantics to traditional ecological knowledge: on precipitation, condensation and suspension expressions in Chinese. In: Hong, J.-F., Zhang, Y., Liu, P. (eds.) CLSW 2019. LNCS (LNAI), vol. 11831, pp. 255–264. Springer, Cham (2020). https://doi.org/10.1007/978-3-030-38189-9_27

18. Dong, S., Huang, C.-R., Ren, H.: Towards a new typology of meteorological events: a study based on synchronic and diachronic data. Lingua **247**, 102894 (2020)

19. Dong, S., Xu, J., Huang, C.-R.: Angry thunder and vicious frost: remarks on the unaccusativity of Chinese weather verbs. In: Liu, M., Kit, C., Su, Q. (eds.) CLSW 2020. LNCS (LNAI), vol. 12278, pp. 64–73. Springer, Cham (2021)

20. Huang, C.-R., Dong, S., Yang, Y., Ren, H.: From language to meteorology: kinesis in weather events and weather verbs across Sinitic languages. Humanit. Soc. Sci. Commun. **8**, 4 (2021). https://doi.org/10.1057/s41599-020-00682-w

21. Dong, S., Huang, C.-R.: From falling to hitting: diachronic change and synchronic distribution of frost verbs in Chinese. In: Dong, M., Gu, Y., Hong, J.-F. (eds.) CLSW 2021. LNCS (LNAI), vol. 13249, pp. 22–30. Springer, Cham (2022). https://doi.org/10.1007/978-3-031-06703-7_2

22. Ding, H., Dong, S.: Elevation and fog-cloud similarity in Tibeto-Burman languages. Humanit. Soc. Sci. Commun. **10**, 375 (2023). https://doi.org/10.1057/s41599-023-01877-7

23. Ding, H., Dong, S.: Colexification of "thunder" and "dragon" in Sino-Tibetan languages. Asia Pacific Translation and Intercultural Studies (2024)
24. Dong, S.: Tianqi biaoda de kuaxueke yanjiu fanshi [Towards an interdisciplinary paradigm for research on weather expressions]. Chin. J. Lang. Policy Plan. **9**(2), 89–96 (2024). (in Chinese)

A Study on the Lexical Meanings of Monosyllabic Nouns, Verbs and Adjectives in International Chinese Education

Huizhou Zhao[✉], Yu Zhao, and Siting Chen

Beijing Language and Culture University, Beijing, China
zhaohuizhou@blcu.edu.cn, zhaoyu000513@163.com,
202111680714@stu.blcu.edu.cn

Abstract. The diverse grading glossaries utilized in international Chinese Education provide the "form" and "pronunciation" of words, with limited entries also indicating their "part of speech". However, in actual teaching practice, students primarily focus on learning the "meaning" of these words. This paper delves into the meanings of elementary level monosyllabic nouns, verbs, and adjectives in the *Chinese Proficiency Grading Standards for International Chinese Language Education*, aiming to identify those meanings that constitute the fundamental "word meaning" of these terms. Firstly, the "form" and "pronunciation" of the monosyllabic words under examination are carefully selected from the elementary glossaries outlined in the C*hinese Proficiency Grading Standards for International Chinese Language Education*. Secondly, the interpretations of these "forms" and "pronunciations" in six different sets of international Chinese elementary comprehensive textbooks are annotated with the corresponding meanings of Chinese characters as referenced in the *Modern Chinese Dictionary (7th Edition)*. Finally, this paper introduces an ordering model that sequences "elementary teaching meanings" based on commonality and difficulty. This research can facilitate various applications, including textbook compilation and the realm of international Chinese education, text grading through meaning analysis, and decision-making regarding the significance of meanings in compiling dictionaries tailored for foreign learners of Chinese.

Keywords: Elementary Word Meaning · Teaching Meanings · *Chinese Proficiency Grading Standards for International Chinese Language Education* · International Chinese Education

1 Preface

Vocabulary is an important language element in language education. In the field of international Chinese education, multiple standardized word lists have played an important role in textbook development, classroom teaching, and language assessment. For example, in 1992, the Examination Center of the Office of the National HSK Committee developed the "Graded Syllabus of Chinese Vocabulary and Character". In 2010, the

P. Jin et al. (Eds.): CLSW 2024, LNAI 15552, pp. 112–126, 2025.
https://doi.org/10.1007/978-981-96-3509-2_9

China National Office for Teaching Chinese as Foreign Language and Confucius Institute Headquarters developed the "New HSK Test Syllabus Level 1" to "New HSK Test Syllabus Level 6". In the same year, the China National Office for Teaching Chinese as Foreign Language and the Social Sciences Department of the Ministry of Education developed the "The Graded Chinese Syllables, Characters and Words for Application of Teaching Chinese to the Speakers of Other Languages" (GF0025-2010). In 2021, the Ministry of Education and State Language Affairs Commission released the "Chinese Proficiency Grading Standards for International Chinese Language Education" (GF0025-2021) (hereinafter referred to as "Grading Standards"). These standardized word lists are all graded word lists, with each word having "form" and "pronunciation", and a small number of words labeled with "part of speech". Therefore, comparative research [1, 2] and teaching application research [3–6] based on word lists mostly use the combination of "form" and "pronunciation" of words as the minimum level of detail.

But in teaching practice, students learn "word meanings". The characteristic of Chinese is that words with the same form and pronunciation have multiple meanings. In the teaching of Chinese as a second language, particularly during the elementary stage, guiding students to learn "word meanings" in a controlled manner is essential to reducing their learning burden and facilitating a gradual acquisition of the language. We believe that based on the standardized graded word list of "form" and "pronunciation" combinations, researching the ordered word list of "form", "pronunciation" and "meaning" combinations will better play the guiding role of the standardized word list in teaching practice. Yilan [7] constructed a database of all morphemes and morpheme items involved in the elementary vocabulary of the "Grading Standards". Based on the first occurrence grade of morphemes and morpheme items, the ability of word formation and the average degree of meaning, morphemes and morpheme items were classified into levels, resulting in the "Level 1–3 Morphemes Grades Table" and "Level 1–3 Morpheme Items Rating Table ". Xuelian [8] defined words with the same writing form and pronunciation but no meaning connection as perfect homonyms. She examined the quantity and level of perfect homonyms in the vocabulary list of the "Grading Standards" included in the comprehensive textbook "Developing Chinese", and proposed suggestions and example designs for the teaching of perfect homonyms. The studies of the combination of "form", "pronunciation", and "meaning" in a small number of graded morphemes and graded words brings us the following experience: (1) monosyllabic words in the vocabulary of the "Grading Standards" have strong polysemy; (2) The statistical analysis combining the vocabulary of the "Grading Standards" with the textbook corpus has more guiding significance for teaching practice based on textbooks. These experiences provide good references for the research design of this article.

In terms of the ordering of meanings, the classification of morpheme levels in [7] relies on the graded word list and morpheme analysis in the "Grading Standards", and there has been no research on meanings ordering based on large-scale corpora. However, there have been relevant achievements in the research of vocabulary and grammar order in academia. Modern Chinese frequency dictionary [9] was the first reference book to use the frequency and distribution of words as a measure of word usage. Xinchun [10] proposed a frequency level calculation method suitable for the use of multiple corpora, which converts frequency into frequency levels and can compare the generality of corpora of different sizes. Zhimin, W. and Shiwen [11] successfully implemented the functionality of updating both new and outdated vocabulary within a large-scale corpus framework by establishing a standard for the continuous distribution of statistical time points. Zhimin et al. [12] and Jinghua et al. [13] used coverage and positional interval information of the ordered objects in their research on basic vocabulary ordering and grammar item ordering, respectively. The sequencing method of the above language elements provides a good idea for the research in this article.

This article will take the meanings of elementary monosyllabic nouns, verbs, and adjectives in the "Grading Standards" as the research object. Based on the text corpus of multiple comprehensive textbooks, the "elementary teaching meanings" of these words will be counted; that is, the meanings that appear in international Chinese education practice at the elementary level; and design a ranking model based on the frequency and difficulty of the meaning items, to sort the "elementary teaching meaning items".

2 Investigation of Elementary Monosyllabic Words in the "Grading Standards"

This section examines the proportion and distribution of meanings of elementary mono-syllabic words in the "Grading Standards", and then determines the meanings of elementary monosyllabic nouns, verbs, and adjectives as the research objects.

2.1 Proportion of Elementary Monosyllabic Words in the "Grading Standards"

The "Grading Standards" adopts a "three levels and nine bands" framework, where the elementary level refers to band one to three, with a total of 2,245 elementary vocabulary items, including 500 vocabulary items from the first band, 772 vocabulary items from the second band, and 973 vocabulary items from the third band [14]. But some items contain "I" or "()", belonging to the category of "multiple words in one item" [2], such as "爸爸|爸 (dad | dad)", "零|〇(zero | 0)", "有时候|有时 (sometimes | sometimes)", "好玩 (儿) (fun)", "哪 (儿) (where)", "有 (一) 些 (there are)", etc. in the first band word list. Each of these items actually refers to two words. This article breaks down the example of "multiple words, one item" in the elementary level vocabulary of the "Grading Standards" and adjusts it to "one word, one item". After the splitting, the monosyllabic words, polysyllabic words, total number of words, and proportion of monosyllabic words in bands 1–3 are shown in Table 1.

Table 1 shows that the proportion of low-band monosyllabic words is significantly higher than that of high-band monosyllabic words. According to the statistics in [1], the proportion of monosyllabic words in the first six bands of the "Grading Standards" is 19.8%. It can be inferred that among the newly added words in bands 4–6, monosyllabic words account for less than the average proportion of words in bands 1–3, which is 26.18%. This confirms the viewpoint that "monosyllabic words in Chinese are often commonly used words" [15].

Table 1. The proportion of syllables and polysyllabic words in the elementary level in the "Grading Standards" ("one word, one item" form).

Band	Monosyllabic words	Polysyllabic words	Total number of words	Proportion of monosyllabic words
1	220	303	523	42.07%
2	200	582	782	25.58%
3	177	798	975	18.15%
Total and average proportion	597	1683	2280	26.18%

2.2 Distribution of the Number of Elementary Monosyllabic Word Meanings in the "Grading Standards"

Multisyllabic words have significantly reduced polysemy to monosyllabic words due to the greater number of Chinese characters compared. In the Modern Chinese Dictionary (7th edition) (hereinafter referred to as "Modern Chinese v7"), it is manifested that the number of meaning items in single-character entries far exceeds that in multi-character entries. This article only examines the number of meanings of monosyllabic words in "Modern Chinese v7".

Determine the Elementary Monosyllabic Words in the "Grading Standards". The "Grading Standards" adopts a "four-dimension benchmarks" consisting of syllables, Chinese characters, vocabulary, and grammar. Hongbin [16] examined the internal effective interaction between the grammar and vocabulary of the "four-dimension benchmarks". The correspondence between the "grammar" and the "vocabulary" at band 1 shows that many monosyllabic words are grammatical items, such as personal pronouns "我(I)", "你(you)", and "他(he)". The majority of grammatical words are words other than nouns, verbs, and adjectives. Grammar words are a closed system, and although their members are high-frequency, their meanings may not be rich. Non-grammatical words (i.e. lexical words) are open systems with rich meanings. Therefore, when examining the distribution of word meanings in monosyllabic words, this article divides words into two categories: "nouns, verbs, and adjectives" and "words other than nouns, verbs, and adjectives". Considering the phenomenon of multi-category words and the fact that a small number of words in the "Grading Standards" have part of speech tagging, this study determines the following rules for the part of speech of elementary level monosyllabic words:

(1) Determine word items based on the combination granularity of "form" and "pronunciation", for example, the 3-band monosyllabic words "调(diao4)"(Transfer. Assign. Assignment. Investigation. Swap. Tone. Argument.) and "调(tiao2)" (Make harmony and uniformity appropriate. Make peace. Mix and match. Mocking, teasing. Smooth and well matched.) are two word items.

(2) If monosyllabic words with the same "form" and "pronunciation" at different bands are labeled with different parts of speech, these word items will be merged into

one, and the part of speech of each band will be combined into the part of speech label of the new word item. For example, the first band monosyllabic word "花(名(noun))(hua1)" (Flowers. Ornamental plants. Something shaped like a flower. A type of fireworks made from black gunpowder and other chemicals, set off at night and capable of producing many sparks for human viewing. Pattern.) and the second band monosyllabic word "花(动(verb))(hua1)"(Use. Cost.) are merged into "花(名(noun)、动(verb))(hua1)", with the second band.

(3) Monosyllabic words with the same "form" and "pronunciation", if some items are tagged with part of speech and some items are not tagged with part of speech, these word items will be merged into one without tagging part of speech. For example, the second band monosyllabic words "背(动(verb))(bei4)"(Memorize. Violate. In the opposite direction. Back facing (opposite to "facing"). Departure. Avoiding; Concealing.), the third band monosyllabic words "背(名(noun))(bei4)"(A part of the torso that is opposite to the chest and abdomen.) and "背(bei4)"(Memorize. Violate. In the opposite direction. Back facing (opposite to "facing"). Departure. Avoiding; Concealing. A part of the torso that is opposite to the chest and abdomen. Hearing impairment. Bad luck. Remote.) are merged into "背(bei4)", with the third band.

(4) The affix items don't merge with the same "form" and "pronunciation" non-affix items. For example, the first band monosyllabic word "小(xiao3)" (Refers to the area, volume, capacity, quantity, strength, and power that are not as good as the average or compared object, as opposed to "large". Narrow scope, shallow degree, and unimportant nature. Short time. Young and youngest, ranked last.) and the second band monosyllabic word "小(小王)(xiao3(Xiao3 Wang2))"(The prefix used when addressing younger individuals.) are listed as two separate items.

After merging the 1–3 band monosyllabic words based on the above four rules, the "Grade Standard" elementary level monosyllabic word list was obtained, with a total of 560 items. There are four additional word items: "小(小王)(xiao3(Xiao3 Wang2))" (The prefix used when addressing younger individuals.), "老(老王)(lao3(Lao3 Wang2))"(The prefix used when addressing older individuals.), "头(里头)(tou2(li3 tou0))"(The suffix appended to directional terms.), and "一下(儿)(yi2xiar4)"(All at once.). The meanings of these four word items will not be examined in the following text. Among the 556 word items to be examined, 470 items without part of speech tagging or with one of "noun", "verb", and "adjective" part of speech tagging are classified as monosyllabic "nouns, verbs, and adjectives" words, and there are no duplicate combinations of "form" and "sound" in these 470 items. There are a total of 86 monosyllabic "words other than nouns, verbs, and adjectives".

Statistics on the Distribution of Elementary Level Monosyllabic Word Meanings in the "Grading Standards". Considering the authority of "Modern Chinese v7" in the definition of modern Chinese words, this article uses the number of meaning items of single-character entries in "Modern Chinese v7" for statistical analysis. There are two explanations regarding the calculation of the number of meaning items:

(1) Items that have the same "form" and "pronunciation" but need to be processed separately in meaning, separate into single-character entries in "Modern Chinese v7",

which are marked with Arabic numerals in the upper right corner of the character. For example, "白 (bai2) " has four single-character entries: "白1", "白2", "白3", and "白4". The sum of all the meaning items of these 4 single-character entries is the meaning items of "白 (bai2) ". This is because in the international Chinese education practice, the distinction between different meanings of perfect homophones is not given enough attention [8], and regardless of the meaning of any individual entry, it is a manifestation of polysemy for learners.

(2) In "Modern Chinese v7", the single-character entry meanings are divided into single-character meanings, single-character morpheme meanings, and single-character specific meanings (such as surname meanings). When calculating the number of monosyllabic word meanings, all three-type meanings mentioned above are counted.

Figure 1 is a distribution diagram of the number of elementary level monosyllabic word meanings in the "Grading Standards" based on the single-character entry meanings in "Modern Chinese v7". The blue curve represents monosyllabic "nouns, verbs, and adjectives", while the orange curve represents monosyllabic "words other than nouns, verbs, and adjectives". The horizontal axis represents the number of meanings, and the vertical axis represents the relative number of monosyllabic words with that number of meanings. The relative number calculation method is shown in formula (1).

$$y_i(x) = \frac{c_i(x)}{\max_x c_i(x)}, \quad i = 1, 2, \quad x = 1, 2, \ldots, 28 \tag{1}$$

In formula (1), $i = 1$ represents monosyllabic "nouns, verbs, and adjectives", $i = 2$ represents monosyllabic "words other than nouns, verbs, and adjectives", and $c_i(x)$ is the number of monosyllabic words in the series i with a meaning count of x number.

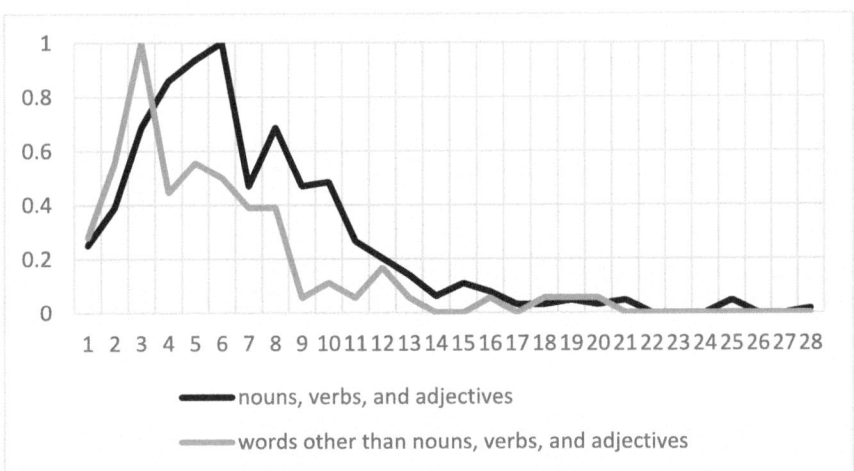

Fig. 1. Distribution of elementary level monosyllabic word meanings in the "Grading Standards" (based on single-character entry meanings in "Modern Chinese v7").

From Fig. 1, it can be seen that the "nouns, verbs, and adjectives" series has the highest number of monosyllabic word meanings with 6, while the "words other than nouns, verbs, and adjectives" series has the highest number of monosyllabic word meanings with 3. From the peak envelopes of the two series, it can be seen that "words other than nouns, verbs, and adjectives" curve is on the left side of "nouns, verbs, and adjectives" curve, which indicates that a higher proportion of "words other than nouns, verbs, and adjectives" monosyllabic words have fewer meanings. The average number of meanings number of "nouns, verbs, and adjectives" is 6.97, while the average number of meanings number of "words other than nouns, verbs, and adjectives" is 5.6. It can be seen that in the elementary level monosyllabic words of the "Grading Standards", the "nouns, verbs, and adjectives" series has richer meanings than the "words other than nouns, verbs, and adjectives" series.

In summary, based on the principles of "more commonly used words" and "richer meanings", this article selects elementary level monosyllabic nouns, verbs, and adjectives from the "Grading Standards" for teaching meaning annotation and sequencing research.

3   Construction of Meaning Annotation Corpus

3.1   Textbook Selection and Corpus Extraction

The meaning annotation corpus of this study is based on six sets of international Chinese education elementary comprehensive textbooks, which are listed in Table 2.

Table 2. Elementary comprehensive textbook selected for the meaning annotation corpus.

Textbook name	Volume name	Number of volumes
New Practical Chinese Textbook (Second Edition)	1, 2, 3, 4	4
Traveling Across China (Student Book)	1, 2, 3, 4	4
Happy Chinese	1, 2, 3	3
HSK Standard Tutorial	1, 2, 3, 4(Part 1, Part 2)	5
The Road to Success "Elementary Chinese Comprehensive"	Starting Sect. (1, 2), smooth Sect. (1, 2), progress Sect. (1, 2, 3)	7
Elementary Comprehensive of Erya Chinese	Part 1(1,2), Part2(1,2)	4
Total	–	27

These 6 sets of textbooks are widely used international Chinese education comprehensive textbooks both domestically and internationally, among which "HSK Standard Tutorial" is a test textbook and "Happy Chinese" is a textbook for child learners. The selection of volumes for all textbook sets refer to the applicable vocabulary for learners in the instructions of the textbooks. After completing the textbook, the learners' vocabulary should not exceed the range of 2000–3000, and this textbook level is compatible with the elementary level of the "Grade Standards".

After segmenting the texts of the six sets of textbooks into whole sentences, this study extracted whole sentences containing 470 monosyllabic nouns, verbs, and adjectives processed in Sect. 2.2.1 from the text corpus as meaning annotation items. If there are multiple instances of word forms in a sentence, then the sentence has multiple copies. For example, for the monosyllabic word "爱", the entire sentence in the text "林娜爱穿旗袍, 爱吃中国菜, 还喜欢看越剧、听中国民乐, 好像也有点儿中国化了。(Linna loves to wear cheongsams, loves to eat Chinese food, and also likes to watch Yue opera and listen to Chinese folk music, which seems a bit Sinicized.)" requires two copies, and when annotating the meaning of these two "爱" in the subsequent two examples of the entire sentence. This is to annotate only one meaning for each instance of "single character - whole sentence" when annotating the meaning.

When extracting whole sentences, this study only considers the "form" matching of monosyllabic words and does not consider the matching of "form" and "pronunciation" combinations. This is because automatic "phonetic conversion" of the text corpus may result in errors, while "character shape" matching is exactly right. When annotating the meaning in the later stage, the "pronunciation" can be determined at the same time. Therefore, this article follows the principle of "should be extracted as much as possible" to extract whole sentence instances that match the "shape" of monosyllabic words. The potential problem with this research design is that the extracted monosyllabic words have a "pronunciation" or "the part of speech" that exceeds the scope of the elementary level monosyllabic word list in the "Grading Standards", or the meaning of the extracted monosyllabic words is not a word meaning but morpheme meaning. But this does not affect the goal of this study, which is to explore the meanings of monosyllabic words that actually appear in the teaching practice.

After extracting the corpus according to the above rules, there are a total of 68,042 instances of "single character - whole sentence" for meaning annotation.

3.2 Annotation of Monosyllabic Word Meanings

For the 68,042 instances to be annotated obtained from the processing in Sect. 3.1, we use the following meaning annotation rules:

(1) If it belongs to the meanings of the single-character entries in the "Modern Chinese v7", it should be annotated according to the meanings of the single-character entries in the "Modern Chinese v7". There are 63,474 instances in this category.

(2) The target words in proper nouns are marked as the category of "words in proper nouns". For example, "西(Xi1)" in "西晋(Xi1 Jin4)"(A dynasty name.), "花(Hua1)" in "花木兰(Hua1 Mu4lan2)"(A person's name.), "上(Shang4)" in "上海(Shang4hai3)"(Shanghai city.), "中(Zhong1)" in "中国(Zhong1 Guo4)"(China.), "Jia" in "家美租房公司(Jia1mei3 Zu1Fang2 Gong1Si1)"(Jiamei Rental Company), "人(Ren2)" in "人民币(Ren1min2bi4)"(RMB.), "红(Hong2)" in "红楼梦(Hong1lou2meng4)"(*Dream of the Red Chamber.*), etc. There are a total of 3,474 examples in this category.

(3) The target word in the transliterated word is marked as the category of "word in the transliterated word". For example, "比(bi3)" in "比萨饼(Bi3sa4bing3)" (pizza) and "对(dui4)" in "派对(Pai4dui4)"(party), etc., there are 16 instances in this category;

(4) Target words in Chinese characters or dialect words are marked as "language element words". For example, "回(Hui2)" in the word "'回'字有几种写法(How many ways of writing of '回')", "子(Zi3)" in the word "木子李(Mu4 Zi3 Li3)"(The character "Li" is formed by combining the radicals "wood" and "zi".), and "拉(La1)" in "阿拉(A1la1)"(Shanghai dialect.). There are three examples in this category.

(5) Target words in multi-syllable words whose meaning items are not included in the meaning items of the single-character entries in the "Modern Chinese v7" are marked as the category of "uncovered word meaning items". For example, "水(Shui3) " in "水平"(level), "东(Dong1)" and "西(Xi1)" in "东西"(things), etc. There are a total of 1075 instances in this category.

Among the 63,474 instances that can be covered by the meaning entries of the single-character entries in the "Modern Chinese v7", there are a total of 1,516 meanings (i.e., the combination of "form, pronunciation, and meaning" of a single-character), involving 502 single-character "form and pronunciation", and 456 a single-character "form".

The number of textbook sets for each of the 1,516 meanings (i.e., the number of senses covered in textbook sets) is listed in Table 3. There are 202 meanings that appear in all six sets of textbooks.

Table 3. The number of meanings covered in different number of textbook sets.

Number of textbook sets	Number of meanings
1	413
2	224
3	226
4	248
5	203
6	202
Total	1516

The frequency distribution of the number of meanings and the number of meanings for the 502 single-character "form and pronunciation", are listed in Table 4. Among them, 260 items have a number of meanings of 1 and 2, which exceeds 50% of the number of single-character "form and pronunciation", accounting for 24.9% of the total meanings. About 10% of the single-character words have 6 or more meanings of "form and pronunciation", accounting for 28.6% of the meanings. The two "form and pronunciation" words with the most meanings are "下(Xia4) "with 18 meanings and "打(Da3)" with 16 meanings.

Table 4. The number of meanings of a single-character (distinguished by "form and pronunciation").

Number of meanings of a single-character	Single-characters count	Accumulated number of single-characters	Percentage of single-characters accumulation	Number of meanings	Accumulated number of meanings	Percentage of meanings accumulation (%)
1	142	142	28.3%	142	142	9.4%
2	118	260	51.8%	236	378	24.9%
3	99	359	71.5%	297	675	44.5%
4	52	411	81.9%	208	883	58.2%
5	40	451	89.8%	200	1083	71.4%
6	17	468	93.2%	102	1185	78.2%
7	5	473	94.2%	35	1220	80.5%
8	11	484	96.4%	88	1308	86.3%
9	4	488	97.2%	36	1344	88.7%
10	3	491	97.8%	30	1374	90.6%
11	3	494	98.4%	33	1407	92.8%
12	3	497	99%	36	1443	95.2%
13	3	500	99.6%	39	1482	97.8%
16	1	501	99.8%	16	1498	98.8%
18	1	502	100%	18	1516	100%

4 A Model for Ordering the Meanings of Monosyllabic "Nouns, Verbs, and Adjectives" in Elementary International Chinese Textbooks

This section will study the importance of the 1,516 monosyllabic meanings annotated in Sect. 3, and design a meaning ordering model based on the two dimensions of commonness and difficulty of meanings. Regarding the frequency of use of meaning items, it is essential to consider their coverage in textbooks and texts. The greater the number of textbooks and texts that incorporate a particular meaning the higher its frequency of use is deemed to be. Regarding difficulty level, one should consider the initial occurrence of the meaning in the textbook. The earlier it appears in the textbook, the lower its difficulty level. The meaning ordering model is formula (2), and the larger the U value, the more important the meaning.

$$U = \frac{BF * TF}{Avg(FirstPosRel)} \tag{2}$$

In formula (2), BF is the number of textbooks in which the meaning appears, TF is the number of texts in which the meaning appears, and Avg(FirstPosRel) is the average position of the first occurrence of the meaning in the textbooks in which it appears.

Due to the different number of texts in each set of textbooks, the text position PosRel is the relative position of the text in the textbook, and its calculation method is shown in formula (3). Where TSN is the natural number numbering of the text in a textbook set,

TSNMax is the total number of texts in a textbook set (i.e., the largest text number), and PosRel has a value range of (0,1].

$$PosRel = \frac{TSN}{TSNMax} \tag{3}$$

The 1516 meanings are sorted according to the meaning ordering model shown in formula (2), based on the definitions in the "Modern Chinese v7". The monosyllabic noun, verb, and adjective meanings that rank in the top 20 are selected, and the results are shown in Table 5.

Table 5. List of the top 20 monosyllabic nouns, verbs, and adjectives.

Monosyllabic word	Meaning	Part of speech	Textbook sets frequency	Text frequency	Mean value of the first appearance of the textbook	U
在 (zai4)	Indicating the location of people or things	verb	6	550	0.028203	117010.310683
人 (ren2)	Higher animals that can make tools and use them for labor	noun	6	386	0.031918	72560.277756
是 (shi4)	Linking two things to indicate that they are the same or that the latter explains the type attributes of the former	verb	6	346	0.034402	60346.190046
好 (hao3)	(physical) Health; (disease) Recover	adj	6	102	0.010874	56279.693401
是 (shi4)	Connecting two things means that the object of the statement belongs to the situation described after "is"	verb	6	505	0.071923	42128.530518
有 (you3)	Indicate existence	verb	6	432	0.082942	31250.762205
去 (qu4)	From one's current location to another (as opposed to "coming")	verb	6	322	0.062788	30770.001367
学 (xue2)	Study	verb	6	225	0.045355	29765.091363
看 (kan4)	Make eye contact with people or objects	verb	6	315	0.068225	27702.641082

(continued)

Table 5. (*continued*)

Monosyllabic word	Meaning	Part of speech	Textbook sets frequency	Text frequency	Mean value of the first appearance of the textbook	U
天 (tian1)	The 24-h period of a day, sometimes specifically referring to the daytime	noun	6	248	0.058659	25366.932191
家 (jia1)	Family	noun	6	177	0.042938	24733.389817
大 (da4)	Exceeding the average or the compared object in terms of volume, area, quantity, strength, intensity, etc. (opposite to "small")	adj	6	261	0.074397	21049.266837
叫 (jiao4)	(Name) Is; Be called	verb	6	85	0.028410	17951.7299102
有 (you3)	To indicate possession (as opposed to "none, not having")	verb	6	184	0.063532	17377.103511
想 (xiang3)	Hope; Plan	verb	6	218	0.083552	15654.957554
说 (shuo1)	Expressing meaning with words	verb	6	329	0.143214	13783.583676
多 (duo1)	Large quantity (as opposed to "few, small")	adj	6	278	0.123648	13489.883867
问 (wen4)	If you have any questions or do not understand something, please ask someone to explain	verb	6	193	0.086366	13407.991583
好 (hao3)	Having many advantages; Satisfactory (as opposed to bad)	adj	6	237	0.109087	13035.469634
吃 (chi1)	Put food and other things into the mouth and swallow them after chewing (including sucking and drinking)	verb	6	180	0.090726	11903.921247

From the results of the ordering of the meanings of monosyllabic nouns, verbs, and adjectives listed in Table 5, it can be seen that:

(1) The top 20 meanings are all covered by all six sets of textbooks, indicating that these meanings are considered essential by textbook writers for elementary international Chinese textbooks.

(2) Observing the "mean value of the first appearance of the textbook" for the top 20 meanings, it can be found that all values are below 0.15, with 17 meanings below 0.1. For a set of textbooks with 4 volumes and 60 lessons, a value of less than 0.1 for the first occurrence of a meaning in the textbook means that the meaning appears no later than lesson 6, and a value of less than 0.15 for the first occurrence of a meaning in the textbook means that the meaning appears no later than lesson 9, showing that the meaning appears in the first 2/3 of the textbooks' first volume. It can be seen that this is a particularly simple monosyllabic word recognized by textbook writers.

(3) There are 13 verbs, 3 nouns, and 4 adjectives. This is related to the high proportion of verbs and nouns in elementary communication expressions, but the diversity of noun meanings is stronger than that of verb meanings. The four adjectives have two meanings of "good", one meaning of "big" and one meaning of "many", all of which are commonly used positive adjectives. This is related to the priority given to expressing positive emotions in elementary communication.

Based on the above analysis, the results of the elementary international Chinese education meanings ordering based on the meaning ordering model proposed in this article are consistent with both the experience of textbook writing experts and the distribution characteristics of the part of speech of elementary communication expressions.

5 Conclusion

Vocabulary, as one of the important elements of language learning, has always been an important target of grading and standardization in the field of international Chinese education. In view of the problem that existing normative word lists are standardized in terms of "form" and "pronunciation" with insufficient attention paid to the standardization of "meaning", this article, based on the "Grade Standard", uses six sets of widely used elementary comprehensive textbooks as the corpus, and the meaning items of the single characters in "Current Chinese v7" as the standard for meaning items, to study the meaning items of elementary vocabulary in international Chinese teaching practice.

A statistical analysis of the elementary vocabulary in the "Grade Standard" shows that monosyllabic words account for 26.18% of the elementary vocabulary, with a higher proportion of monosyllabic words in the first-band vocabulary, accounting for 42.07%. The statistics of elementary monosyllabic word meanings based on the "Current Chinese v7" show that the richness of meanings for monosyllabic nouns, verbs, and adjectives is higher than that for other parts of speech. Therefore, this article chooses to study the teaching meanings of monosyllabic nouns, verbs, and adjectives with a high proportion of entries and rich meanings.

Based on the meaning tagging of the corpus, this article obtained the distribution of monosyllabic nouns, verbs, and adjectives in six sets of textbooks, and proposed a meaning ordering model based on commonality and difficulty. The results of the top 20 monosyllabic nouns, verbs, and adjectives based on the model show that the model comprehensively considers the frequency of coverage in textbooks, the frequency of coverage in texts, and the position of the first occurrence of the meanings, which can reflect the consistency with the textbook writers' views on important meanings.

The research results of this article can be used to guide the compilation of international Chinese textbooks, the grading of elementary international Chinese education texts based on meaning analysis, and the decision-making of important meanings in the compilation of the foreign oriented Chinese dictionaries.

Acknowledgments. The research is supported by Science Foundation of Beijing Language and Culture University (supported by "the Fundamental Research Funds for the Central Universities")(22YJ080013); Major Program of National Social Science Foundation of China (18ZDA295); 2020 Beijing Higher Education Undergraduate Teaching Reform and Innovation Project "Reform and Practice of the Training Mode of Language Knowledge Engineering Innovative Talents Based on Emerging Engineering Education".

References

1. Zun, L.: Analysis of changes in the vocabulary list of Chinese Proficiency Grading Standards for International Chinese Language Education: taking elementary vocabulary as an example. Sinogram Cult. **5**, 167–171 (2023). (in Chinese)
2. Hua, L.: Improvement of the word list of CPGS2021: an analysis based on the comparison with GCSCW. Lang. Teach. Linguist. Stud. **2**, 34–41 (2023). (in Chinese)
3. Ziheng, Z.: Comparative analysis of vocabulary between the examination syllabus of the new HSK and the actual test questions: taking the published CET-5 exam questions as an example. Kaoshi Zhoukan **57**, 3 (2012). (in Chinese)
4. Jun, W.: Docking and adjustment: vocabulary teaching strategies based on Chinese Proficiency Grading Standards for International Chinese Language Education. J. Int. Chin. Teach. **4**, 10–19 (2022). (in Chinese)
5. Gang, C., Zheng, D., Juan, X.: Construction of vocabulary knowledge map and vocabulary adaptive learning platform based on Chinese Proficiency Grading Standards for International Chinese Language Education. J. Int. Chin. Teach. **1**, 21–30 (2023). (in Chinese)
6. Jie, Y.: Rethinking the words beyond Chinese Proficiency Grading Standards for International Chinese Language Education in Chinese news textbooks: a perspective from the new standard system. TCSOL Stud. **3**, 87–94 (2023). (in Chinese)
7. Yilan, Z.: Research on the grading of morphology and morphological items of elementary vocabulary in Chinese Proficiency Grading Standards for International Chinese Language Education. Master's thesis, Central China Normal University (2023). (in Chinese)
8. Xuelian, L.: Study on the teaching of perfect homonyms based on Chinese Proficiency Grading Standards for International Chinese Language Education. Master's thesis, Jiangxi Normal University (2023). (in Chinese)
9. Institute of Language Teaching: Beijing language and culture university: modern Chinese frequency dictionary. Beijing Language and Culture University Press, Beijing (1986). (in Chinese)
10. Xinchun, S.: The role of quantitative methods in vocabulary research and frequency level statistical methods. Yangtze River Acad. **2**, 118–124 (2007). (in Chinese)

11. Zhimin, W., Shiwen, Y.: New updates on teaching Chinese vocabulary based on large-scale corpus a case of "nouns" in Graded Chinese syllables, characters and words (GCSC). Lexicogr. Stud. **5**, 64–74+122 (2019). (in Chinese)
12. Zhimin, W., Huizhou Z., Junping Z., Caihong C.: Research on basic vocabulary extraction based on chinese language learners. In: Chinese lexical semantics - 19th workshop, CLSW 2018, pp. 126–135. Springer, Chiayi, Taiwan (2018)
13. Jinghua L., Zhimin W.: Sequencing of grammatical items in textbooks oriented towards international Chinese language education. In: Chinese lexical semantics - 21st workshop, CLSW 2020, pp. 148–160. Springer, Hong Kong, China (2020)
14. Yinglin, L.: Development and application of Chinese Proficiency Grading Standards for International Chinese Language Education. J. Int. Chin. Teach. **1**, 6–8 (2021). (in Chinese)
15. Zerun, P.: Chinese Pinyin orthography and the "word-style writing" of Chinese. Lang. Plan. **4**, 19–23 (1998). (in Chinese)
16. Hongbin, W.: An interactive study on the four-dimensional benchmark of Chinese Proficiency Grading Standards for International Chinese Language Education. J. Tianjin Normal Univ. (Soc. Sci.) **3**, 1–9 (2023). (in Chinese)

Research on the Network-Based Construction of Chinese Psychological Lexicon for International Students in China from the Perspective of Systems Theory

Wen Yang[✉]

Guangzhou University, Guangzhou, Guangdong, China
yangwen000@bfsu.edu.cn

Abstract. Starting from the network nature of the Chinese vocabulary system, we can construct various vocabulary networks. Teaching through the activation relationships between each node can help students restructure their mental lexicon and master more vocabulary within the same class time. The network-based construction teaching of Chinese psychological lexicon for international students based on the perspective of systems theory, represents an optimized teaching model within the existing curriculum framework. This approach emphasizes the increase of the proportion of vocabulary teaching in Chinese language classes. By integrating vocabulary network construction closely with skilled-based course teaching through centralized vocabulary instruction, it seamlessly blends into various stages of classroom introduction, lectures, practice, review, and assessment.

Keywords: Systems theory · Chinese psychological lexicon for international students in China · Lexicon network construction · Teaching model

1   Introduction

As Li, R. [1] pointed out, "An adequate vocabulary is essential for training in listening, speaking, reading, and writing. However, due to the specific instruction goals of these skills and influence of incidental learning theory, organized and planned vocabulary instruction has not received sufficient attention in skill-based classes." Traditionally, under the paradigm of a "grammar-centric" teaching approach, teachers have been accustomed to "explaining words in context" and employing a "fragmented" teaching method where vocabulary is taught as it appears in texts. However, this scattered approach to vocabulary instruction disrupts the systematic nature of Chinese vocabulary, relying solely on key vocabulary from textbooks which is not conducive to the construction of a Chinese psychological lexicon for second language learners. Consequently, there is limited improvement in vocabulary size. Zhang, J. [2] compared the productive vocabulary sizes of Chinese second language learners and native speakers and revealed that at various stages of learning Chinese as a second language, learners' vocabulary sizes did not meet the requirements outlined in the vocabulary curriculum.

P. Jin et al. (Eds.): CLSW 2024, LNAI 15552, pp. 127–140, 2025.
https://doi.org/10.1007/978-981-96-3509-2_10

Considering the current limitations preventing the immediate implementation of reforms in the Chinese language teaching model for a large number of international students studying in China in the short term, such as adjustments in course types and curriculum restructuring, we propose the concept of "Constructing a Networked Chinese Psychological Lexicon for International Students in China from a Systems Theory Perspective" (referred to as "Lexical Network Construction" hereafter). This approach represents an optimized instructional model guided by systems theory, emphasizing the enhancement of vocabulary teaching in Chinese language proficiency courses. By closely integrating lexical network construction with skills-based course instruction, the objective is to reorganize and refine students' psychological lexicons within the context of various course types, ultimately increasing the efficiency of vocabulary acquisition for international students.

2 The Construction Model of Psychological Lexicon in Second Language Learners

The term "psychological lexicon" refers to a vast dictionary-like system stored in the human brain, encompassing all vocabulary and related information, including phonetic, spelling, semantic, syntactic, and collocational aspects. [3]. Unlike conventional dictionaries, the psychological lexicon has its unique organizational and construction methods, carrying a wealth of information. It is not merely a linear arrangement of entries in alphabetical order but a three-dimensional, network-like distribution. "The mental lexicon of second language learners is a non-semantic network of lexical entries formed by phonetic, morphological, and more non-native-like heterogeneous responses." [4]. Various models exist regarding the matching of word forms and concepts [5]:

Parallel Representation Model (Fig. 1)

A. Lexical Connection Model: posits that in the mental lexicon of second language learners, word forms convey semantics through the mediation of the native language, applicable to low-proficiency second language learners.
B. Conceptual Mediation Model: suggests that the mental lexicons of the native language and second language are two independent language systems but can share the same conceptual representation, suitable for high-proficiency learners.

Asymmetric Model (Fig. 2)

This model, proposed by Dong, Y. [6], is a hierarchical adjustment model. She suggests that the connection between vocabulary and concepts in the mental lexicon of second language learners is a dynamic process, with shared conceptual representations. As proficiency in the second language increases, the linkage between vocabulary representations and concepts becomes stronger, enhancing the independence of the second language mental lexicon. This model entails a multi-level, interactive activation process where the strength of the connection between two linked units increases with their frequency of use.

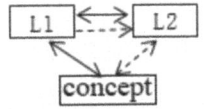

Fig. 1. Parallel Representation Model A B. (Cited from Liu, S., Chen, J.: Psychological Lexicon Theory and Teaching of Chinese Vocabulary for Foreigners. Modern Chinese Language, 05 (2013).)

Fig. 2. Asymmetric Model. (Cited from Liu, S., Chen, J.: Psychological Lexicon Theory and Teaching of Chinese Vocabulary for Foreigners. Modern Chinese Language, 05 (2013).)

Based on the literature reviewed, scholars have not yet reached a consensus on issues such as the storage methods of vocabulary in the mental lexicon of second language learners, the matching patterns between word forms and concepts, and the impact of the native language on the construction of the second language mental lexicon. Is the storage of the second language mental lexicon independent of the learner's native language mental lexicon or mixed with it? We agree with Zhang P. who asserts, "the manner in which the second language lexicon is stored may be related to specific differences in words, parts of speech, and the learner's language development level...It may not be simply categorized into a single pattern" [7]. For international students in China immersed in the target language environment, focusing on individual learner differences, helping them clarify relationships between word meanings, derivations, and collocations based on their learning progress and proficiency, and frequently reinforcing connections between new and old words as well as related vocabulary, will aid in cultivating their thinking in the target language and improving the efficiency of vocabulary retention.

3   Multi-perspective Construction of the Chinese Psychological Lexicon Network from the Perspective of Systems Theory

The term "xitong (system)" originates from the transliteration of the English word "system", referring to an organized whole formed by orderly arrangement and compilation of scattered elements. According to Ma, L. [8], system theory emerged in the field of natural sciences as a new universal theory rapidly developing in the 20th century. It views the objects of study as "systems", delineating the boundaries of systems and internal elements from the environment, identifying the laws of connection and constraints between internal and external components, and seeking possibilities for optimizing objectives within these constraints. The network-based construction of a Chinese psychological lexicon for international students in China treats Chinese vocabulary as a system, dividing the boundaries of vocabulary connections based on specific course types, teaching subjects, and instructional materials, determining the various node vocabularies and related knowledge that constitute the vocabulary system, while also specifying the connections between vocabulary nodes. Through the redesign of architecture and the integration of existing knowledge graphs, Li, Y. et al. have constructed a universal Lexical Semantic Knowledge Graph (GLSKG), providing a comprehensive overview of lexical definitions, parts of speech, and examples, while detailing the semantic dependency relationships between vocabularies, such as dependency, hyponymy, and synonymy. [9]. This inspires us to construct visual lexical networks based on four fundamental clues—pronunciation, character form, semantics, and structure—to represent collocational blocks, synonyms, antonyms, hypernyms, and other lexical relationships, using lines to connect node vocabularies and indicate their relationships, supplemented with examples, illustrations, and other information based on textbooks and teaching styles. Each specific lexical network serves a local function, influenced by specific classroom conditions like teaching styles, student levels, and textbook difficulties.

It is important to note that the following examples only demonstrate methods for vocabulary linking and lexical network construction, which may be useful during learners' vocabulary review stages. In the practical process of teaching Chinese, it is essential to base lexical network construction on specific teaching styles, integrate textbook content, consider learner proficiency levels, and vocabulary linking directions, among other factors. The four clues of pronunciation, character form, semantics, and structure are not isolated but can be flexibly utilized in actual teaching to build comprehensive lexical networks. To this end, we also provide a teaching design based on authentic texts for reference.

3.1 Phonological Aspect

Polyphones sharing the same written form, having similar pronunciation, and bearing semantic relevance can be effectively studied together to leverage their interconnections. However, when constructing a network of polyphonic words, attention should be paid to the relationships between the derivations of each syllable, with general phonetics typically preceding and extended meanings following. For instance, for the character " 和" (hé), at the intermediate and advanced stages, it can be initially introduced as the conjunction and preposition "hé" (and), then extended to the verbs "hè" (echo) and "hú" (complete a set in mahjong), further extended to "huó" (mix (powder) with water, etc.), and finally introduce "huò" (mix).

In Standard Mandarin phonology, approximately 400 meaningful syllables can be formed by combining initials and finals. As a result, nearly every syllable is associated with a plethora of homophones, many of which share common radicals in their character composition, exhibiting both phonetic similarity and visual resemblance, making them well-suited for concentrated study. For example (Fig. 3), 龙 (lóng) (dragon/loong), 聋 (lóng) (deaf), 笼 (lóng) (cage), 珑 (lóng) (exquisite/delicate), and 胧 (lóng) (dim/hazy) share a common phonetic element. Some variations may arise in terms of tones or initials, resulting in near-homophones, such as 龙 (lóng) (dragon/loong), 垄 (lǒng) (monopoly), 陇 (lǒng) (another name for Gansu Province), and 拢 (lǒng) (gather together). When constructing networks for homophonic and near-homophonic characters, it is crucial to emphasize the differing components within homophones, encouraging students to uncover the principle of character formation and enhancing their awareness of distinguishing these varying components.

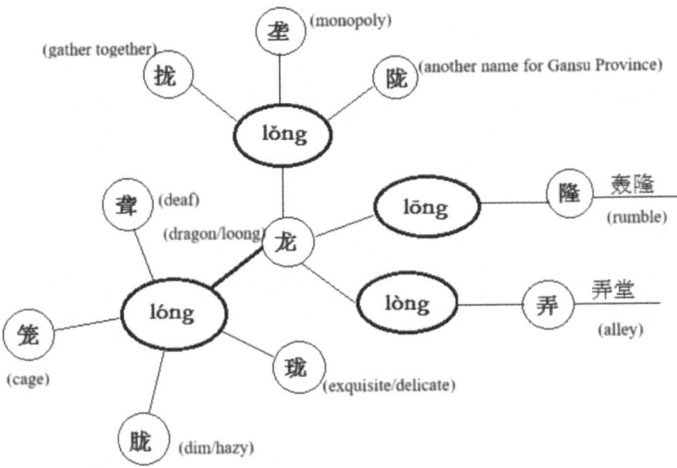

Fig. 3. Lexical Network of the Near-Homophonic Characters for "龙" (lóng)

3.2 Graphical Aspect

In a morphology-based character network, emphasis is placed on the shared components (radicals) of characters, which can cultivate students' ability to generalize the meanings of specific components. When necessary, it is essential to conduct etymological analyses. For example, "忄" is a variant form of the radical "心" (xīn) (heart/mind), indicating that characters with the "忄" radical are generally related to emotions or feelings, such as 惊 (jīng) (to startle), 悚 (sǒng) (fightened), 悯 (mǐn) (to sympathize), 惭 (cán) (ashamed), 怜 (lián) (to pity), and so forth.

Furthermore, characters that share similar outlines, exhibit subtle variations, and possess high visual resemblance are suitable for concentrated teaching. For instance (Fig. 4), 己 (jǐ) (oneself) - 已 (yǐ) (already) - 巳 (sì) (the period of the day from 9 a.m. to 11 a.m.), 外 (wài) (outside) - 处 (chù) (location/dispose), 审 (shěn) (judge) - 宙 (zhòu) (universe), and so on fall into this category. By constructing networks of visually similar characters for comparative teaching, students' ability to distinguish the shapes of Chinese characters and their cognitive skills in recognizing the relationships between form, sound, and meaning can be effectively enhanced.

3.3 Semantic Aspect

Within a given topic domain, vocabulary exhibits semantic interrelatedness. Constructing a word network that strings together words based on topics can significantly support situational teaching, aiding in the enhancement of communicative abilities while also reinforcing the learned vocabulary during usage. When building topic-based word networks, it is essential to select and supplement words according to the difficulty level of the textbook. The vocabulary list provided in the textbook should be adjusted in sequence based on the word network.

Additionally, a group of words with similar or closely related meanings can form a network of synonyms. Words within this network mutually assist in providing definitions,

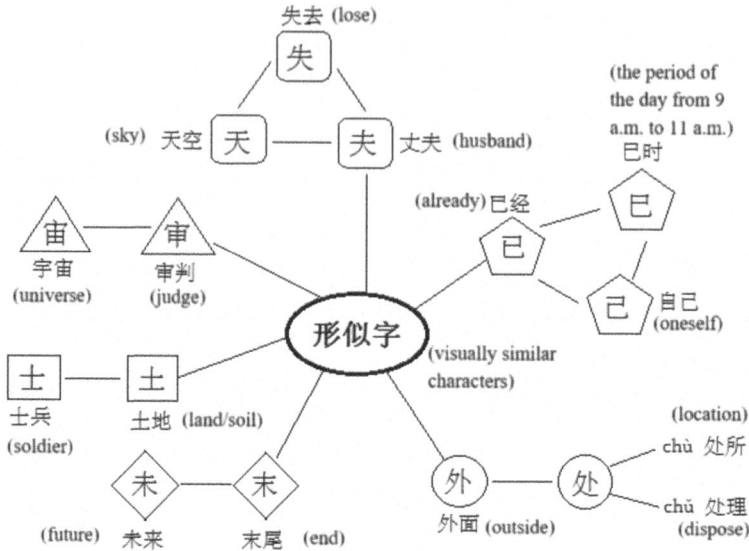

Fig. 4. Lexical Network of Visually Similar Characters

facilitating the differentiation of subtle nuances between synonyms for more precise usage. Correspondingly, antonym networks can also be constructed. Learning through antonyms serves as an effective method for acquiring new vocabulary while reinforcing existing terms.

Furthermore, presenting hyponyms and hypernyms in the form of mind maps can stimulate students' associative thinking, leading to a better understanding of the relationships between vocabularies. For instance, at the elementary level, when discussing vocabulary related to "clothing", using a tree diagram can assist students in distinguishing various clothing items.

3.4 Structural Aspect

A significant characteristic of Chinese lexical generation is the phenomenon of words with the same morpheme. These common morphemes possess strong derivational capabilities, easily combining with other morphemes to create new vocabulary. Teaching through the construction of vocabulary networks with same morpheme is advantageous for students to grasp the classifying features of Chinese vocabulary. For instance, at the elementary level, employing a word network centered around the common morpheme "车" (chē) (vehicle) (Fig. 5) serves as an illustrative teaching method.

Similarly, the phenomena of affixes and pseudo-affixes can also form systematic lexical networks. Generally, the positions and meanings of affixes and pseudo-affixes are relatively fixed, emphasizing both formal and structural meanings. Once these are integrated into a word network, students can more easily discern patterns and thereby generalize their knowledge. For example, through a word network, students may deduce that terms like "模仿秀" (mófǎng xiù) (imitation show), "时装秀" (shízhuāng xiù) (fashion show), and "脱口秀" (tuōkǒu xiù) (talk show) all ending with "～秀" indicate a type

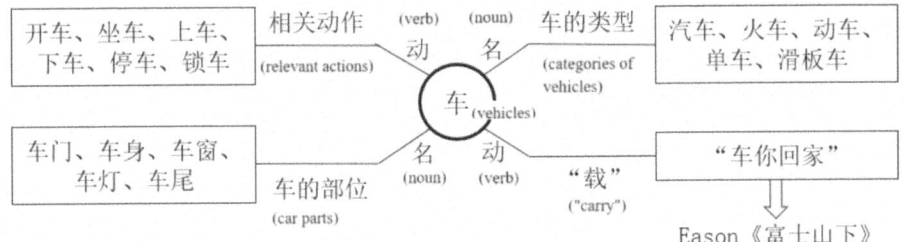

Fig. 5. Lexical Network with the Same Morpheme "车" (chē) (Vehicle)

of performance. Consequently, encountering a word like "达人秀" (dárén xiù) (talent show), students can infer that it relates to a performance involving individuals.

Furthermore, in language, there exist relatively stable collocations where components tend to appear in fixed sequences, enabling the formation of structural networks that facilitate students' holistic extraction for efficient use. These fixed sequences are known as "chunks". For instance, in the context of "经济" (jīngjì) (economy), common collocations include "经济繁荣" (jīngjì fánróng) (prosperous economy), "发展经济" (fāzhǎn jīngjì) (develop economy), "经济发展" (jīngjì fāzhǎn) (economic development), "经济利益" (jīngjì lìyì) (economic benefit), and so forth. Moreover, phrases resembling fixed collocations can also contribute to such structural networks, like "因为……所以" (yīnwèi… suǒyǐ) (because… Therefore), "……就好了" (jiù hǎole) (…then it's fine), offering the advantage of swift and efficient usage.

3.5 Comprehensive Aspect

A comprehensive word network is constructed from the perspectives of phonetics, orthography, semantics, and structure. Its hallmark lies in utilizing associative divergent thinking to interconnect related vocabularies from various angles. Networks from different viewpoints can intertwine, but they must adhere to the same principle: starting from the most easily associated term, each linkage point simultaneously radiates outward to expand the network. For instance, using "旅行" (lǚxíng) (travel) as a core vocabulary, associations could lead to terms like "沙滩" (shātān) (beach) and "海边" (hǎibiān) (seaside). From the radicals of "沙" (shā) (sand), "滩" (tān) (beach), and "海" (hǎi) (sea), one might think of words like "江" (jiāng) (river), "河" (hé) (river), "湖" (hú) (lake), and "瀑布" (pùbù) (waterfall), with each node triggering numerous related terms. The network itself possesses spatial extensibility and openness. As learning progresses, students can continually supplement new vocabulary into the network and continuously integrate and reorganize their mental lexicon based on the word network.

4 Pedagogical Design: A Case Study of Vocabulary Teaching Using "I Go to the Post Office to Pick Up a Package"

In international Chinese language teaching, the teaching at the elementary stage has always been the most crucial. As noted by Lu J. [10] "Vocabulary teaching should be a focal point, especially at the elementary stage. For a foreign student to excel in Chinese, it is crucial to master a large amount of vocabulary, to possess an adequate vocabulary size". Hence, we have chosen to design a vocabulary teaching module using a typical elementary Chinese integrated course as an example. The lesson selected is Lesson 13 from the "Boya Chinese - Elementary · Initiation I", the new generation Chinese language Textbook series published by Peking University Press. This textbook series is widely used domestically as a comprehensive Chinese course material and holds a certain level of representativeness.

4.1 Course Basic Information

(1) Course Type: Comprehensive Chinese Language Course
(2) Target Learners: Second language learners of Chinese with elementary proficiency who have completed the previous 12 lessons of the textbook.
(3) Teaching Objectives:
   ① Cognitive Objectives:
     A. Mastering relevant and extended vocabulary related to the topic of "post office": 寄信 (mail letters), 寄包裹 (send parcels), 寄东西 (send things), 信封 (envelope), 邮票 (stamp), 邮编 (postal code), 电话号码 (phone number), 地址 (address), 寄信人 (sender), 收信人 (recipient), 取 (pick up), 发 (send), etc.;
     B. Reinforcing related existing words: 学校 (school), 校园 (campus), 大学 (university), 教室 (classroom), 教学楼 (teaching building), 宿舍楼 (dormitory building), 同屋 (roommate), 图书馆 (library), 房间 (room), 卫生间 (restroom), 家 (home), 酒吧 (bar), 啤酒 (beer), 咖啡 (coffee), 电影院 (cinema), etc.;
     C. Understanding structures through vocabulary networks: V不V (V not V), A不A (A not A), S + VP1 + VP2, etc.;
     D. Mastering relevant vocabulary and phrases related to the topic of "go shopping": 商店 (store), 购物中心 (shopping center), 星期天 (Sunday), 周末 (weekend), 关门 (closed), 开门 (open), 打算 (plan), 咱们 (we), 一起 (together), 衣服 (clothes), 书 (book), 怎么样 (how about), 贵 (expensive), 质量 (quality), 还可以 (okay), 不错 (not bad), 先……然后……最后 (first...then...finally), etc. Extended vocabulary and phrases: 逛街 (shopping), 便宜 (cheap), 有点儿 (a bit), 太……了 (too much), etc.
   ② Skills Objectives:
     A. Learning to construct topic-based vocabulary networks, being able to construct vocabulary networks in class, and organizing related paragraphs through these networks;
     B. Mastering the method of vocabulary networks learning, consciously categorizing and organizing new words, gradually improving the mental lexicon, and enhancing the Chinese vocabulary.
   ③ Affective Objectives:
   Inspiring students' interest in "drawing" vocabulary networks and cultivating the concept of vocabulary network learning.
(4) Teaching Focus:

① Vocabulary teaching centered on the topics of "邮局"(post office) and "逛街" (go shopping).

② Grammar points involved in vocabulary network teaching: V不V (V not V), A 不A (A not A), S + VP1 + VP2, 先……然后……最后 (first…then…finally), 有点儿 (a bit) vs 一点儿 (a bit).

(5) Teaching Tools: PowerPoint slides, A4 paper, pictures, real objects, etc.

(6) Teaching Duration: 50 min for the entire class, with 25 min dedicated to vocabulary network construction.

(7) Teaching Methods: By means of enlightening and guiding, we help students to master new words, grammar and text content through the construction of vocabulary network.

4.2 Design of Specific Teaching Steps

(1) Classroom Organization (2 min)

Divide the class into small groups, each consisting of 4 to 5 students. Provide each student with three A4 sheets of paper for use. Inform students that today they will be creating three vocabulary networks. Similar to before, they need to create radial connections based on the central vocabulary determined by the teacher. They should continuously refine their networks during the teacher's explanation and instruction, forming a piece of work to be submitted to the teacher before the end of the class.

(2) Teaching Introduction (3 min)

Introduction through pictures, displaying slides or prepared pictures to the students.

Teacher: Look at this picture, guess where this is? What do Li Jun and David want to do? Try to answer in Chinese, and use English vocabulary for words you don't know.

Students: They are on the road. I think they want to go somewhere. They discuss how to get there.

Teacher: A very good answer, thank you. Let's see together where they want to go and what they are talking about. (At the same time, write "去哪儿" (Where to go) in the center of the chalkboard as the central topic for the subsequent network, prompting students to start building the network.)

(3) Vocabulary Network Construction Teaching (25 min)

We adopt a dual-track approach of network construction and teaching. The teacher provides continuous prompts to the students during vocabulary teaching, and the students continuously construct and refine the networks based on the teacher's explanations and guidance.

Teacher: Look at the vocabulary list. Who can tell me what we can do at the post office?

Students: Mail letters, send parcels.

Based on the students' responses, the teacher connects the first branch "邮局" (post office) to the center "去哪儿" (Where to go) on the blackboard. Then connects "信" (letters) and "包裹" (parcels), writes the verb "寄" (send) on the connecting line. The teacher inform the students that we commonly say "寄东西" (send things) and connects "东西" (things) to the network.

Teacher: According to the vocabulary list, what do we need to mail a letter?

Students: Envelope, stamp.

Teacher: What needs to be written on the envelope? (Shows a slide: Format of an envelope).

Students: Sender, recipient, phone number, address, postal code.

The teacher adds these key words to the vocabulary network on the blackboard and then explains the format of writing an envelope in detail. Students can mark this format on their own lexical networks.

Teacher: Besides sending things, what else can we do at the post office?

Students: Pick up things.

Teacher: Yes, we can also pick up parcels and letters.

Another branch "取"(pick up) is added to the word "邮局" (post office) on the blackboard, with the vocabulary "信" (letter) and "包裹" (parcel) written. Using the vocabulary network on the board as an example, students enrich their own lexical networks.

Teacher: Now, please answer the first question I asked earlier with a complete sentence: What are David and Li Jun doing at the post office?

Students: David and Li Jun are sending parcels at the post office.

Teacher: (Pointing to a picture) What do you do at the post office?

Students: I mail letters at the post office.

Teacher: (Pointing to another picture) What is he doing at the post office?

Students: He is picking up parcels at the post office.

After several practice rounds, the teacher displays the answers on the slides, allowing students to summarize the sentence pattern S + VP1 + VP2 and mark it on their own lexical networks.

Teacher: David is going to pick up parcels at the post office. What is Li Jun going to do?

Students: (Referring to the text) He will first go to the store to buy something, and then go to the library to send an email.

Teacher: Very good, first do…, then do…

Subsequently, the teacher displays three to four sets of pictures, asking students to form sentences using "先…然后" (first…then) and adding the vocabulary "最后" (finally).

Teacher: Li Jun is going to the library to send an email, and David also wants to send an email, so they can go to the library together. (Prompting students to mark "一起" (together) on their lexical network.)

Teacher: How does David say it?

Students: "I also want to send an email. Let's go together."

Teacher: (Distinguishing between "咱们" (zánmen) (we) and "我们" (wǒmen) (we)) "咱们" includes the speaker and the person being spoken to, while "我们"can include the person being spoken to or not.

Afterwards, practice with a few examples: Choose between "咱们"and "我们"to fill in the blanks.

_____家有三口人, 你们家呢? (There are three members in our family, how about you?).

你明晚有空吗, _____去逛街吧? (Do you have time tomorrow night? Let's go shopping.)

At this point, the lexical network branches based on the topic "邮局" (post office) are mostly completed, as shown in the diagram in Fig. 6. The teacher then proceeds to lecture on the text.

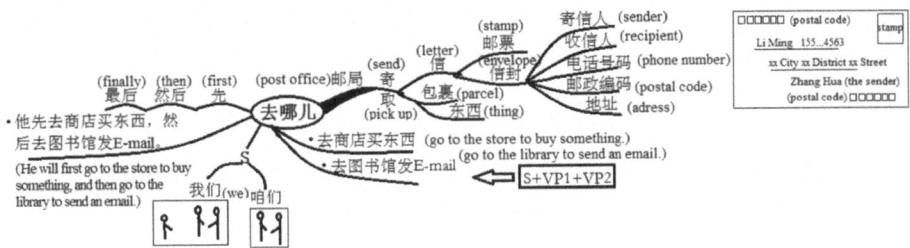

Fig. 6. The Branching Lexical Network of "Post Office" within the Semantic Topic of "Where to Go"

Then transitioning naturally to the review of location-related vocabulary.

Teacher: (Pointing to pictures) Where are you going?

Students: I am going to school.

At this point, with "去哪儿" (Where to go) as the central phrase, another branch can be created for "学校" (school), promoting students to associate vocabulary related to school and construct this branch network themselves. See Fig. 7 for reference.

Fig. 7. The Lexical Network of Other Branches within the Semantic Topic of "Where to Go"

Teacher: (Pointing and asking) Are you going to school?

Student: I'm going to school.

Teacher: (Pointing and asking) Are you going to the cinema?

Student: I am not going to the cinema.

Teacher: (Showing a slide) "V…吗?" We can also use the structure "V不V" to express. So we can also ask "你去不去学校?" (Are you going to school or not?) "你去不去电影院?" (Are you going to the cinema or not?) (Students connect this structure to the vocabulary network).

Teacher: (Writing down the central vocabulary "逛街" (shopping) and explaining, students start constructing a lexical network centered around "逛街" (shopping).) Are you going shopping or not?

Student: I am going shopping.

Teacher: (Showing pictures from the Text 2, where the word "购物中心" (shopping mall) is labeled along with pinyin.) Look at the pictures, where are they going shopping?

Student: They are going shopping at the shopping center.

Teacher: Look at the vocabulary list, where else can you go shopping?

Student: Store.

Teacher: What time do stores open? When can you go to the store? ("Expressions for telling time" belong to the review content).

Student: Stores open at 8 o'clock.

Teacher: The opposite of "开门" (open) is "关门" (close). (Showing a slide with the vocabulary "周末" (weekend) and "星期一" (Monday) to "星期天" (Sunday)) Do stores open on Sunday?

Student: Stores are closed on Sunday.

Teacher: (Pointing and asking) When do you go to the shopping center?

Student: I go to the shopping center on weekends.

Teacher: What do you buy at the shopping center?

Student: Clothes, things.

Teacher: (Showing a slide with pictures of clothes) This piece of clothing is 450 yuan, that one is 100 yuan. We say "这件衣服太贵了" (This piece of clothing is too expensive), "那件衣服很便宜" (That one is very cheap).

Teacher: (Showing a slide with picture of clothes, which is 300 yuan and then comparing it with former two.) We say, "这件衣服有点儿贵" (This piece of clothing is a bit expensive.). Using "有点儿 < 很 < 太…了" to express the degree of intensity.

Then comparing "有点儿" and "一点儿". At the elementary stage, we only need students to grasp one situation: 有点儿 + adj.; adj. + 一点儿.

Teacher: (Showing a slide with vocabulary "质量" (quality) and words "好" (good), "不好" (not good), "差" (poor), "还可以" (okay), "不错" (not bad)) What do you think of this piece of clothing?

Student: Good.

Teacher: The quality of this piece of clothing is very good. (Hinting to students to respond with complete sentences).

Teacher: Is the quality of this piece of clothing good or not?

Student: The quality of this piece of clothing is good.

Teacher: Is this item expensive or not?

Student: This item is not expensive.

Teacher guides students to summarize: A不A = A…吗. At this point, the vocabulary network is built based on the topic of "买东西" (buying things) and the central vocabulary "逛街" (go shopping). Refer to Fig. 8. Finally, the teacher proceeds to lecture on the text.

Fig. 8. The Lexical Network within the Semantic Topic of "Go Shopping"

(4) Consolidation Practice (10 min)

In addition to the exercises conducted during lexical network teaching, we allocate a few minutes to focus on student practice. Specifically, the teacher can first guide students in orally retelling the text based on the lexical network on the blackboard. Then, students can role-play in pairs, with the teacher moving around the classroom to observe students' practice and the construction of their lexical networks. After the practice session, a few groups of students can be selected to present and showcase their lexical network creations.

(5) Summary and Feedback (5 min)

Based on student presentations, the teacher provides feedback and rewards, focusing on both the construction of the lexical network and the effectiveness of dialogue practice. Finally, students submit their works, which are assessed and returned to them for future revision purposes.

5   Conclusion

The network-based construction teaching of Chinese psychological lexicon for international students in China is an optimized vocabulary teaching model under existing curriculum conditions, suitable for second language learners at various stages and Chinese proficiency courses. However, specific teaching should adhere to the following principles:

(1) Depending on the targeted course type, the proportion of network-based teaching should vary; vocabulary-intensive teaching is more suitable for intensive reading classes, followed by listening and speaking classes, and writing classes;

(2) For multiple meanings or parts of speech of content words, their meanings and usage in the text should be highlighted. By grasping the core features of vocabulary and integrating textbooks, the construction of the lexical network should differentiate between common basic meanings and those acquired through contextual understanding;

(3) Emphasis should be placed on the direction of word connections during teaching. In the beginner stage, connections should focus on pronunciation and character forms, guiding students to promptly summarize common radicals and nurturing the concept of phonetic-semantic characters. In the intermediate and advanced stages, emphasis should shift towards connecting vocabulary structures and meanings, summarizing networks of homophones, synonyms, and affixes. In the advanced stage, networks

of polysemous words, synonyms, and topic-related terms should be constructed to meet the natural language expression needs of international students;

(4) Teaching methods should align closely with the type of lexical network. For instance, teaching synonym networks should emphasize comparison and contrast, while teaching networks of homophones should emphasize analogical reasoning, and topic-based networks should encourage extended expression on specific topics;

(5) When constructing lexical networks, students should be at the center, with teachers determining the core of the networks and the direction of connections based on the text, guiding and inspiring students to independently organize their mental lexicon in a balanced manner.

The network-based construction teaching of Chinese psychological lexicon for international students from a systemic perspective is proposed based on the inherent network characteristics of the Chinese lexical system. This approach advocates increasing the emphasis on vocabulary teaching in Chinese classrooms and expanding learners' vocabulary efficiently through constructing vocabulary networks and teaching through these networks. This method also holds significance for vocabulary arrangement in textbooks and the development of reference materials. The author previously applied the network construction teaching method in practice, which effectively stimulated international students' interest in drawing and associative abilities, demonstrating a certain level of feasibility. However, due to the limitations of the author's academic capacity and experimental conditions, further empirical research is needed to verify the effectiveness of lexical network construction teaching in different types of courses.

References

1. Li, R.: An overview of research on chinese vocabulary teaching in recent years. Chin. Lang. Teach. Res. **02** (2017). (in Chinese)
2. Zhang, J.: A comparative study of productive vocabulary size between Chinese L2 learners and native speakers. Lang. Linguist. Appl. **02** (2019). (in Chinese)
3. Yin, Q.: Thinking about vocabulary teaching from the perspective of psychological lexicon theory. J. Kunming Univ. Sci. Technol. (Soc. Sci.) **02** (2002). (in Chinese)
4. Chen, S. et al.: A comparative study of the structure of mental lexicons of Chinese English learners in L1 and L2. J. Shandong Univ. Sci. Technol. (Soc. Sci.) **02** (2015). (in Chinese)
5. Liu, S., Chen, J.: Psychological lexicon theory and teaching of Chinese vocabulary for foreigners. Mod. Chin. Lang. **05** (2013). (in Chinese)
6. Dong, Y.: Shared (distributed) asymmetric model of bilingual mental lexicons. Mod. Foreign Lang. **03** (1998). (in Chinese)
7. Zhang, P.: Vocabulary association and mental lexicon: research status of in-depth vocabulary knowledge. Theory Pract. Foreign Lang. Teach. **03** (2009). (in Chinese)
8. Ma, L.: Popular talks on the system information theory and cybernetics. Hebei People's Publishing House, Shijiazhuang (1987). (In Chinese)
9. Li, Y., Shao, Y., Zhao, Y.: Construction of a general lexical-semantic knowledge graph. In: Liu, M., et al. (eds.) Chinese lexical semantics, CLSW 2020. Lecture notes in artificial intelligence, vol. 12278, pp. 464–472. Springer, Cham (2021)
10. Lu, J.: Grammar teaching in "teaching Chinese as a foreign language". Lang. Teach. Res. **03** (2000). (in Chinese)

The Semantic Logicality of Terminology Formation in Chinese Industry

Miao Wang[✉] and Daoxin Zhang

College of International Education, Liaoning Normal University, Dalian, China
dalianwangmiao@163.com

Abstract. Through the statistics of 10 national standards, it is found that the selection of semantic features based on the semantic structure of the object. The terminology formation in Chinese industry takes semantic structure of terms as the meaningful material. In the selection of lexical morphemes, there are two situations where lexical morphemes directly and indirectly reflect the internal form. However, the terminology formation in Chinese industry all follows the semantic logic rules of "Principle of Identity" as well as the mechanisms of "Naming by Attribute" and "Focus Selection". This study reveals the semantic logic mechanism of terminology formation in Chinese industry and explores its semantic tendency. It is found that most lexical morphemes are selected based on the categories of [STATE][STRUCTURE][FUNCTION] and [GENUS]. It hopes to improve the rational level and scientific design of teaching methods of vocabulary in teaching Chinese as a foreign language. It also hopes to provide academic references for the standardization and internationalization of Chinese industry terminology.

Keywords: Semantic Logicality · Terminology Formation · Chinese Industry

1 Introduction

Terminology refers to the specialized vocabulary used in a particular discipline. Industry generally refers to the categories of occupation. Terminology in industry refers to the special terms used in a certain occupation. In 1985, the National Committee for Terminology in Natural Sciences[1] was established, marking a new phase in the review and unification of terminology in natural sciences in China. By the end of 1996, the Committee was renamed as the "National Committee for Terminology in Science and Technology", formulating the working principles of "comprehensive planning, reliance on experts, unified coordination, scientific review, and official publication" to guide the smooth implementation of terminology standardization efforts. Subsequently, the National Terminology Committee gradually incorporated the review of terminology in humanities and social sciences, as well as military science, into its scope of work. So far, the National Terminology Committee has established over a hundred subcommittees, covering various scientific and technological fields such as science, engineering,

---

[1] Hereinafter referred to as the National Terminology Committee.

P. Jin et al. (Eds.): CLSW 2024, LNAI 15552, pp. 141–153, 2025.
https://doi.org/10.1007/978-981-96-3509-2_11

agriculture, medicine, humanities and social sciences, and military, forming a comprehensive system for scientific and technological terminology work. In March 2020, the National Standardization Administration Committee issued the "Key Points of National Standardization Work in 2020", emphasizing that "focusing on the modernization of national governance system and governance capacity, vigorously promoting the implementation of standardization strategy", and raising standardization to a national strategic level [1].

Yeqisong [2] believes that terms have conceptual attributes, and their conceptual attributes are the foundation for formulating principles and methods of term standardization. At the same time, terms also have features such as univocality and motivation. This article focuses on the standardization of terminology formation, using the theory of Lexical Semantic Logic Analysis to reveal the semantic logic mechanism, and explore the semantic tendency of terminology formation. It hopes to provide academic references for the internationalization and standardization of Chinese industry terms. Industry terminology can be categorized into various scopes based on different criteria. However, due to the limitations of space, this article will solely delve into the naming issues of object terminology within the realm of industry terminology. The semantic logicality of other scope terminologies will be addressed in separate articles.

The example terms and definitions used in this article are quoted from the national standards issued by the General Administration of Quality Supervision, Inspection and Quarantine of the People's Republic of China and the Standardization Administration of China. Meanwhile, to ensure the comprehensiveness of the standard selection as much as possible, two standards are selected from each category: those issued within the past three months, those issued within the past year, those issued within the past two years, those issued within the past three years, and those issued more than three years ago, which include "Standard Terminology Relating to Apparel" (GB/T 15557-2008), "Coffee and Coffee Products—Vocabulary" (GB/T 18007-2011), "Ski—Vocabulary" (GB/T 40931-2021), "Digital Camera—Vocabulary" (GB/T 20733-2022), "Freight Container Vocabulary" (GB/T 1992-2023), "Bicycle Parts Classification, Name and Main Terms" (GB/T 3564-2023), "Natural Rubber—Vocabulary" (GB/T 14795-2023), "Pallets for Materials Handling—Vocabulary" (GB/T3716-2023), "Smart Garments—Technology and Definitions" (GB/T 43830-2024) and "Wood Floor and Parquet—Vocabulary" (GB/T 43649-2024)[2]. At the same time, the definitions in the "Modern Chinese Dictionary" (7th Edition)[3] are also referred to.

2 Semantic Structure of Industry Terms

2.1 What is "Semantic Structure"?

In terms of formation, the meaning of a word is the conceptual content associated with its phonetic form, and this conceptual content reflects objective things [3]. The essence of word meaning is a knowledge system about specific objects, which is the conceptual

---

[2] Hereinafter referred to as "Apparel" "Coffee" "Ski" "Digital Camera" "Freight Container" "Bicycle" "Rubber" "Pallets" "Smart Garments" and "Wood floor" respectively.

[3] Hereinafter referred to as "Modern Chinese".

content. The superficial aspect of word-formation is the construction of phonetic and written forms, while the deep aspect is the selection of semantic features based on the semantic structure of the object. The semantic structure of the object and the semantic features it contains reflect the object. Therefore, to investigate the semantic mechanism of word-formation, it is necessary to start by establishing a semantic structure of a specific object. The semantic structure of the object refers to the composition of various semantic features that are suitable for language communication based on the understanding of specific objects.

There are numerous attributes in a specific object. The ancient Greek philosopher Aristotle believed that the result of human's understanding of objects are categorized, and various attributes belong to categories such as "substance, quantity, quality, relation, place, time, position, state, action, or affection". Aristotle's category theory systematically reveals the logicality of human's understanding of objects, which is categorized and systematic, rather than being chaotic and disordered [4]. Drawing on Aristotle's category theory and using theoretical and methodological approaches in Lexical Semantic Logic Analysis, we can create a logical schema for the semantic structure of a specific object [5]:

Word   =   {[SUBJECT][TIME][SPACE][QUANTITY][MOTION] [STATE][PROPERTY][OBJECT][RELATION][FUNCTION] [METHOD][STRUCTURE][GENUS][EVALUATION][GRAMMAR]   [PRAGMATICS]...}

This schema demonstrates the specificity, knowledgeability, collectiveness, categorical nature, structurality, infinity, and associativity of the semantic structure of words. Specificity is reflected in the fact that the semantic structure of a word corresponds to only one specific object, meaning that each sense (or sense entry) corresponds to a single object rather than multiple objects. Knowledgeability is the evidence of the object. Collectiveness manifests as the meaning of a word is a collective of numerous semantic features. Categorical nature is reflected in the fact that each semantic feature belongs to a certain attribute category. Structurality is demonstrated by the fact that the semantic structure of a word is composed of semantic features from various categories, rather than being a "holistic whole" [6]. Infinity is seen in the fact that the semantic structure of words is an open system, with semantic features constantly in flux. Associativity is expressed in the fact that the word form and semantic structure are solidified into a single meaningful entity, where the word form can refer to the entire content of the semantic structure of a specific object, or it can represent a particular semantic feature within it.

This schema also shows that the semantic structure of a specific object is a collection of semantic features of several categories which are infinite, and each category contains several sub-categories. In terms of industry terms, the basic meaning of each category is: [SUBJECT] represents the subject category of the object, including sub-categories such as producer, utilizer, discoverer and etc.; [TIME] represents the time category of the object, including sub-categories such as moment, duration, sequence and etc.; [SPACE] represents the spatial category of the object, including sub-categories such as location, direction and etc.; [QUANTITY] represents the quantity category of the object, including sub-categories such as number, length, proportion, degree and etc.; [MOTION] represents the motion category of the object, including sub-categories such as production, action, expression and etc.; [STATE] represents the state category of the object, including sub-categories such as physical state, state of affairs, and mental state; [PROPERTY] represents the property category of the object, including sub-categories such as naturalness, sociality, materiality, spirituality and etc.; [RELATION] includes the quantity and action relationships between the object and other things, such as cause, effect, whole, part etc.; [OBJECT] represents the object category of the object, including sub-categories such as objects that are acted upon and objects that are produced by motion; [FUNCTION] represents the function category of the object, where function attributes are the actions of objects on other objects, including sub-categories such as physical, psychological function and etc.; [METHOD] represents the method category of the object, including sub-categories such as strategy, instrument, material and etc.; [STRUCTURE] represents the structure category of the object, including sub-categories such as element, component, ingredient and etc.; [GENUS] represents the knowledge classification of the object, including sub-categories such as clothing, human, zone and etc.; [EVALUATION] represents the value judgment about the object, including sub-categories such as positive, negative and neutral; [GRAMMAR] represents the grammatical category of referring to the grammatical meaning of words including sub-categories such as noun, verb and etc.; [PRAGMATICS] represents the pragmatic category of referring to the pragmatic meaning of words, including sub-categories such as style, context and etc.

2.2 A Subsection Sample

We use the definition of "electronic still-picture camera" as an example to illustrate the establishment of semantic structure for industry terms. According to "Digital Camera", "electronic still-picture camera" refers to "camera incorporating an image sensor that outputs an analogue or digital signal representing a still picture". Based on the definition and relevant knowledge, the following semantic structure can be established:

> Electronic still-picture camera = {[SUBJECT: PRODUCER: PERSON | USER:PERSON][QUANTITY: LENGTH; WIDTH][SPACE:ORIGIN PLACE; USE PLACE][MOTION: PRODUCTION; USE; PURCHASE][STRUCTURE: BODY][NATURE: ARTIFICIALITY; MATERIALITY;][FUNCTION: PHOTOGRAPHING][METHOD: STRATEGY:PROCESSING | MATERIAL: PLASTIC; METAL][GENUS:CAMERA][GRAMMAR: NOUN][PRAGMATICS: ORAL; WRITTEN]…}

Evidently, the semantic structure analyzed through schema can visually present what specific objects are recognized, how they are evaluated, and what the linguistic application rules of words are. This allows the semantics of "electronic still-picture camera" to exhibit the structural and categorical thinking characteristics. In the process of word formation, these categories play different roles. Categories such as subject, time, space, quantity, motion, manner, relation, function, nature, state, structure, and object pertain to the ontology of the object. The relevant semantic components represent an objective understanding of attributes, while evaluation belongs to a non-ontological category, representing additional subjective judgments. Grammar and pragmatics fall into the category of linguistic rules and are unrelated to the object's ontology. In Chinese, the word formation for objects of things primarily relies on semantic components from the ontological and evaluative categories as the main semantic materials. Although semantic components of grammatical categories can be displayed as grammatical function markers in morphological languages, they are not necessarily conditions in Chinese. Only by using noun suffixes such as "子 (zi in pinyin)" "儿(er in pinyin)" and "头(tou in pinyin)" can the grammatical meaning be explicitly expressed. The semantic components of the pragmatic category play a role in selecting the color meaning of morphological morphemes.

Therefore, the semantic structure of an industry term is established based on the attributes of the object, and a set of various semantic features originate from these attributes and become the backup materials for terminology formation and the basis for definition.

3 Semantic Logic Rule of Terminology Formation: Principle of Identity

3.1 Two Aspects on Principle of Identity

The Principle of Identity in terminology formation refers to the identity between the form of a specific object and the semantic structure, that is to say the word forms, as the phonetic and written forms reflecting objects, except for slangs and code words, originate from the semantic structures of objects. Specifically, there are two basic aspects. First, the internal form and the semantic structure have identity. Second, the choice of lexical morphemes and the internal form have identity. The Principle of Identity is the logical prerequisite to ensure the correlation between word forms and object attributes.

The Internal Form and the Semantic Structure Have Identity. The internal form was proposed by German linguist Wilhelm von Humboldt. He believes that "the internal form of language" refers to the "inner, intellectual part of language" that is opposed to "language form". It refers to "the concept formation" and "the laws of speech combination" in the process of language formation [7]. The internal form reflects the relationship between the linguistic symbol and the object it refers to. It is the unseen force that guides how we conceptualize the world and communicate our thoughts and feelings through language. For word formation, the internal form originates from semantic structures, which means it is extracted from numerous semantic features, rather than selecting components that are irrelevant to the object.

The Choice of Lexical Morphemes and the Internal Form Have Identity. The choice of lexical morphemes refers to the process of selecting appropriate morphemes when constructing words or expressing specific meanings. This involves an understanding of the available morphemes in the language and selecting them based on the internal form of a word. Words are used to represent objects or communicate ideas in language. The internal form is the semantic condition for word formation. The morphemes that make up a word should convey or reflect the internal form. If they do not, it would result in a disconnect between the morphemes and the attributes or semantic features of the object they are intended to represent.

3.2 Direct and Indirect Expressions[4]

As mentioned above, the choice of lexical morphemes is based on internal form. There are two approaches. One is that lexical morphemes directly reflect internal forms, and the other is that lexical morphemes indirectly reflect internal forms.

The Direct Expressions. The lexical morphemes that directly reflect semantic features usually express internal form in basic meanings. For example, "智能环境监测服装(intelligent environment monitoring garments)" in "Smart Garments", is defined as "clothing that can perform intelligent detection of the environment.". The semantic structure can be:{[SUBJECT: PRODUCER: PERSON | USER: MAN; WOMAN][SPACE: ORIGIN PLACE; USE PLACE][QUANTITY: LENGTH; WIDTH][MOTION: PRODUCTION; USE][OBJECT: ENVIRONMENT][NATURE: MATERIALITY; ARTIFICIALITY; INTELLIGENCE][STRUCTURE: TOP; PANTS][FUNCTION: MONITORING; COVERING][METHOD: PROCESSING; WEARING | MATERIAL: CLOTH; THREAD; CHEMICAL MATERIAL][GENUS: GARMENT: CLOTHES]…}.

For communication purposes, according to the semantic structure of the object, people mainly extracted [NATURE: 智能(INTELLIGENCE))][OBJECT: 环境(ENVIRONMENT))][FUNCTION: 监测(MONITORING)] and [GENUS: 服装(GARMENT)] to construct the internal from. Therefore, corresponding lexical morphemes were selected to create word forms, materializing internal forms. The mechanism can be demonstrated by the following diagram:

X= {[NATURE: 智能 (INTELLIGENCE))][OBJECT: 环境 (ENVIRONMENT))][FUNCTION: 监测 (MONITORING)][GENUS: 服装 (GARMENT)] … }

| ↓ | ↓ | ↓ | ↓ |
| 智能 | 环境 | 监测 | 服装 |

It can be seen that the conceptual object "a kind of clothing which can monitor the environment" constructs the word form "智能环境监测服装(intelligent environment monitoring garments)". From the internal form to the word form, it follows the Principle of Identity, and the word form can directly associate with the signified object.

"三点式游泳衣(three-point swimming suit)" is defined as "a women's swimming suit made up of very small pants and a bra". The semantic structure can be: {[SUBJECT: PRODUCER: PERSON | USER: WOMAN][STATE: THREE-POINT][SPACE: ORIGIN PLACE; USE PLACE][NATURE: MATERIALITY; ARTIFICIALITY][STRUCTURE: BRA; PANTS][QUANTITY: LENGTH: SHORT | AREA: SMALL][MOTION: PRODUCTION; EFFECT][RELATION: RESULT: ATTENTION: HIGH][FUNCTION: SWIMMING; COVERING][METHOD: STRATEGY:

---

[4] In order to show how morphemes are selected for term formation, in the following parts we put Chinese expressions of the terms together with English to demonstrate.

PROCESSING; WEARING | MATERIAL: CLOTH; THREAD][GENUS: CLOTHING: CLOTHES]…}.

For communication purposes, according to the semantic structure of the object, people mainly extracted [STATE: 三点式 (THREE-POINT)][FUNCTION: 游泳 (SWIMMING)] and [GENUS: 服装 (CLOTHING): 衣(CLOTHES)] to construct the internal from. Therefore, corresponding lexical morphemes were selected to create word forms, materializing internal forms. The mechanism can be demonstrated by the following diagram:

$$X= \{ [STATE: 三点式(THREE\text{-}POINT)][FUNCTION: 游泳$$
$$(SWIMMING)][GENUS: 服装(CLOTHING): 衣(CLOTHES)] \cdots \}$$

↓	↓	↓
三点式	游泳	衣

It can be seen that the conceptual object "a women's swimming suit made up of very small pants and a bra" constructs the word form "三点式游泳衣(three-point swimming suit)". From the internal form to the word form, it follows the Principle of Identity, and the word form can directly associate with the signified object.

Besides Direct Expressions, There are Indirect Expressions. The lexical morphemes that indirectly reflect semantic features usually are metaphorical morphemes based on identical semantic features. No matter how they are expressed, they all follow the Principle of Identity. A synonymy for "three-point swimming suit" is "比基尼(bikini/bikini)". "Bikini/bikini" is a simple word, although its word form is different from that of the compound word "three-point swimming suit", they both originate from the same concept, so their semantic structures are the same. "Bikini Island/Bikini" is a small island in the Pacific Ocean in the United States. Before the three-point swimming suit came out, an atomic bomb was exploded on this island, which shocked the world and attracted worldwide attention. In order to attract customers' attention, the designer of this swimsuit, Louis Reard, gave it (X) an explosive name and created the word form "bikini", as shown in the following diagram:

$$X= \{ [RELATION: RESULT: ATTENTION: HIGH] \}$$
The atomic bomb explosion on the island of Bikini= { [RELATION: RESULT: ATTENTION: HIGH] }
$$\downarrow$$
X=Bikini

This approach of word formation utilizes the consistent semantic features of "Bikini" and X [RELATION: RESULT: ATTENTION: HIGH], creating the word form of X as "bikini/bikini". Unlike the direct expression of "三点式游泳衣(three-point swimming suit)", this is an indirect expression, and the selected lexical morphemes are metaphorical morphemes with consistent semantic features as in Bikini.

The above demonstrates how lexical morphemes reflect internal forms in both direct and indirect ways. For another example, "周底托盘(perimeter-base pallet)" in "Pallets" is defined as "flat pallet which in the bottom deck has the outer bottom components arranged as a complete frame with one or two centre bottom components". The simplified semantic structure can be: [SPACE: 周(PERIMETER); 底部 (BASE)] [GENUS: 托盘(PALLET)]. Lexical morphemes "周 (PERIMETER)" " 底部 (BASE)" and "托盘(PALLET)" are selected to directly reflect the semantic features of the internal form, [SPACE] and [GENUS]. A synonymy for "周底托盘(perimeter-base pallet)" is "窗式托盘 (window pallet)". It is clear that this kind of word-formation approach utilizes the consistent semantic features [STATE: 窗户状(WINDOW-STYLE)] as in "窗户(window)", which is defined as "an opening in the wall or roof of a building, car, etc., usually covered with glass, that allows light and air to come in and people to see out" to create another word form that "周底托盘(perimeter-base pallet)"refers to. In this case, the lexical morphemes with metaphorical meanings are selected to indirectly reflect internal forms and create word forms.

"人字式拼花地板(herringbone parquet flooring)" in "Wood Floor" is defined as "parquet made up of stripes of the same dimensions, having the ends cut at a right angle, laid perpendicularly one to another at an angle of 45°relative to the directions of the walls and/or of battens". This kind of word-formation approach utilizes the consistent semantic features [STATE: 人字形(REN-SHAPED)] as in "人(Ren)" together with other essential features [MOTION: PARQUET][STATE: PATTERN] and [GENUS: FLOORING] to create a word from that the definition refers to. In this case, the lexical morphemes with metaphorical meanings are selected to indirectly reflect the internal form and create a word form.

From this, it is not difficult to see that whether it is a direct or indirect reflection, the selection of lexical morphemes are fundamentally based on the semantic structure of the object. Therefore, under the Principle of Identity, the process of terminology formation can be summarized as a logical chain: The semantic structure of the referent of the new word comes from the understanding of the object, the internal form comes from the semantic structure, and the lexical morphemes come from the internal form.

4 Semantic Logic Mechanism: Naming by Attribute

4.1 What is "Naming by Attribute"?

As mentioned above, there are two approaches of terminology formation: direct expressions and indirect expressions. However, no matter which approach is used, the mechanism of "Naming by Attribute" is adopted [8], which refers to the use of attributes or semantic features to denote objects. Additionally, people follow the principle of economy in speaking, intending to use elliptical structures, leaving out unnecessary words or phrases to save time and effort. This principle implies that the word form should be as concise as possible. Therefore, when constructing word forms, the expression of word meaning can only be "brief", rather than "elaborate". Consequently, in the practical application of the mechanism of "Naming by Attribute", partial attributes or semantic features are selected to name objects. Not all features are equally important. For practical purposes, the essential features of the intension shall be the focus of terminology formation.

The essential features of a concept shall be identified. The absence of an essential feature in the course of terminology formation leads to poor or even erroneous understanding of the concept. On the other hand, if a feature is removed, the concept is not altered. This feature is not indispensable to understand the concept and thus it is a non-essential feature. When the concept in question is highly complex, it can be necessary to categorize features explicitly as essential features and non-essential features.

The essential semantic features are selected from the semantic structure of objects to provide direct semantic materials for internal forms and word forms. In other words, the meaning reflected by the lexical morphemes that constitute a compound word only reflects some rather than all semantic features of the object.

4.2 "Naming by Attribute" and "Focus Selection"

In the actual process of terminology formation, the construction of compound words is a complex process. In the following part, we will delve into the word-formation mechanism of "Naming by Attribute" and "Focus Selection" of terminology formation in Chinese industry.

How does "Naming by Attribute" actually work? The following examples will be used to demonstrate. "肼-甲醛胶乳 (hydrazine-formaldehyde latex)" is defined in "Rubber" as "the latex obtained by graft copolymerization of methyl methacrylate and natural rubber molecules". The word form is created by selecting only the essential semantic features of [STRUCTURE: 肼(HYDRAZNE); 甲醛(FORMALDEHYDE)] and [GENUS: 乳胶(LATEX)]. If the feature "肼(hydrazne)" and "甲醛 (formaldehyde)" are removed, the concept represents a different concept corresponding to a different object or cannot be distinguished from other concepts, such as "天甲乳胶(heveaplus MG latex)" with the essential semantic features of [STRUCTURE:天然乳胶(NATURAL LATEX); 甲基丙烯酸甲酯(HYDRAZNE)] and [GENUS: 乳胶(LATEX)].

"立柱式托盘(post pallet)" is defined in "Pallets" as "pallet having posts to permit stacking, and fitted with either removable rails or gates". The word form is created by selecting only the essential semantic features of [STATE: 柱状(POST-SHAPED)], [MOTION: 立(STAND)] and [GENUS: 托盘(PALLET)]. If the feature "柱状 (post-shaped)" is removed, the concept represents a different concept corresponding to a different object or cannot be distinguished from other concepts, such as "罐式托盘(tank pallet)" with the essential semantic features of [STATE: 罐式(TANK-SHAPED)] and [GENUS: 托盘(PALLET)] and "嵌套托盘(nestable pallet)" with the essential semantic features of [MOTION: 嵌(EMBED); 套(NEST)] and [GENUS: 托盘(PALLET)].

Another interesting example is "高飞滑雪板(goofy)" in "Ski", which is defined as "snowboard riding with the right foot forward". It comes from Goofy, the mythical Disney character, who, in an old cartoon called "Hawaiian Holiday", went out on the waves with his right foot forwards, when almost all surfers were Regulars, who put their left feet forward while surfing. Since then, the expression Goofy to describe the position right foot forwards on snowboard has entered all sideways board sports, particularly surfing, skating and snowboarding. Therefore, based on the definition and relevant knowledge, the following semantic structure can be established:

goofy   =   {[SUBJECT:
PRODUCER: PERSON I USER: GOOFY; MAN; WOMAN][SPACE: ORIGIN;
USE PLACE][QUANTITY: LENGTH; WIDTH][NATURE: MATERIALITY;
ARTIFICIALITY]][STRUCTURE: BOARD][METHOD: STRATEGY: PRO-
CESSING; SKIING I MATERIAL: PLASTIC; METAL; WOOD][FUNCTION:
SKIING[MOTION: PRODUCTION; USE; PURCHASE][GENUS:SKIS]…}

Consequently, we can see that the naming of the "高飞滑雪板(goofy)" also originates from its semantic structure, and the establishment of this semantic structure stems
from the understanding of this object.

At this point, it is necessary to explain another way of terminology formation
that exists in Chinese industry. For example, when creating a word form for an
object "a skirt with side seams open on both sides", the basic semantic structure can
be: X = {[SUBJECT: USER: WOMAN][STATE: FORKED][MOTION: PRODUC-
TION; ACTION][METHOD: STRATEGY: PRODUCTION; WEARING][SPACE:
LEFT; RIGHT; SIDE SEAM][QUANTITY: LENGTH: LONG; SHORT][PROPERTY:
MATERIALITY; ARTIFICIALITY][CATEGORY: CLOTHING: SKIRT]…}. People
did not directly select the semantic features of X for word-formation, but found
that another object similar to X, which is "旗袍 (Qipao)" (Qipao is a traditional
Chinese female robe with a standing collar, a right large lapel, a tight waist, and
an open fork at the hem.) Its semantic structure can be {[SUBJECT: QI PEOPLE:
FEMALE][STRUCTURE: STANDING COLLAR; RIGHT LARGE LAPEL; HEM;
…][STATE: FORKED][GENUS: CLOTHES: ROBE]…}, which has similar attributes
to X. Therefore, according to the principle of economy, "旗袍(Qipao)" is used to represent the state of [FORKED] as in X to create a word form, which is supplemented
by [GENUS: 裙(SKIRT)], creating a word form "旗袍裙(Qipao style skirt)". This approach of creating word forms still belongs to "Naming by Attribute", which means using
"旗袍(Qipao)" to represent the attribute of [STATE: FORKED].

How does "Naming by Attribute" interact with "Focus Selection"? From the
examples above, we can see that "Naming by Attribute" is the mechanism of Chinese
industry formation. Meanwhile, when the "Naming by Attribute" is in process, it also
interacts with the mechanism of "Focus Selection".

"纵梁 (stringer)" and "支承梁 (bearer)" are synonyms in "Pallets", and both
are defined as "continuous longitudinal component underneath the top or between
the top deck and bottom deck, which provides space for the entry of forklift
forks and pallet-truck fingers". As the references of these two words are identical, it is feasible to establish an identical semantic structure for them as follows:{[SUBJECT: PRODUCER; USER][SPACE: UNDERNEATH][FUNCTION: 支
承(SUPPORT)][STATE: 纵向 (LONGITUDINAL); 梁状 (STRINGER-SHAPED] and
[RELATION: WHOLE; PART]…}. Under the mechanism of "Naming by Attribute",
the essential semantic features are selected to create the word form. For "纵
梁(stringer)", [STATE: 纵向(LONGITUDINAL); 梁状(STRINGER-SHAPED] are
selected. For "支承梁(bearer)", [FUNCTION: 支承(SUPPORT)]and [STATE: 纵
向(LONGITUDINAL)] are selected.

Another example is "中粒种咖啡(robusta coffee)" and "罗巴斯塔种咖啡(robusta coffee)" in "Coffee", which are also synonyms and defined as "coffee of the botanical species Coffea canephora Pierre ex A. Froehner, with some varieties and cultivars of these species". It is not difficult to see that "中粒种咖啡(robusta coffee)" is created by selecting the essential semantic features of [QUANTITY:DEGREE: 中(MEDIUM)][STATE: 颗粒状(GRANULAR)] and [GENUS: 咖啡(COFFEE)], while "罗巴斯塔种咖啡(robusta coffee)" is created by selecting the essential semantic features of [SPACE: ORIGIN PLACE: 罗巴斯塔(ROBUSTA)] and [GENUS: 咖啡(COFFEE)]. No matter what features chosen by "中粒种咖啡 (robusta coffee)" or "罗巴斯塔种咖啡(robusta coffee)", they all come from the semantic structure of this kind of coffee itself.

It is apparently shown that guided by the mechanism of "Naming by Attribute", people focus on different semantic features and select those features to name things, a process known as "Focus Selection". The variations in focal point selection are influenced by various factors such as nationality, regionality, and domain-specificity, which will be discussed in separate articles.

From the analysis above, it can be seen that there is a mechanism in Chinese industry terminology formation that focuses on selecting essential semantic features to construct word forms based on semantic structures.

5 Statistical and Analytical Results

We sorted out all the entries in the ten national standards of industry terms mentioned above with a total of 896 entries. It was found that as for the semantic tendency of terminology formation, there are similarities and differences in various industries. Generally speaking, in "Apparel"and "Pallets" most lexical morphemes are selected based on the basic categories of [STATE][RELATION] and [GENUS]. In "Bicycle" "Wood floor" and "Coffee", [SPACE][RELATION] and [MOTION] are the basic categories. In "Rubber" [STRUCTURE] and [GENUS] are basic categories. In "Smart Garments""Ski" and "Freight Container" [FUNCTION] and [GENUS] are basic categories. In "Digital Camera", [NATURE][RELATION] and [GENUS] are basic categories.

However, most semantic features are extracted not from a single category, but from compound categories. Statistics shows that extraction of semantic features and selection of lexical morphemes based on [STATE] and [GENUS] have the largest proportion, reaching 22%. The second largest proportion is 20%, which is based on [FUNCTION] and [GENUS].

Through the statistics and analysis, it can be found that there are both semantic logic commonalities and individual differences in the creation of Chinese industry terminology. Specifically, there are two aspects:

First, Chinese language emphasizes on the whole and integration. It usually uses an upper-level term to refer to all or most of the objects of the same category, highlights the shared features of objects in the same category, and supplements the upper-level term with differential morphemes, which can be taken as distinctive features, to reflect differences and distinguish the object from others within the category. For example, "特种货物集装箱(specific cargo container)" as in "Freight Container" defined as "general cargo container that has constructional features either for the 'specific purpose' of facilitating packing and emptying other than by means of doors atone end of the container,or for other specific purposes such as ventilation" supplements with "加热(heated)" [METHOD: STRATEGY: HEATED], "罐式(tank)" [STRUCTURE: TANK], "干散货(dry bulk)" [OBJECT: BULK][STATE: 干(DRY)] as differential morphemes to construct the lower-level terms,"加热集装箱 (heated container)""罐式集装箱(tank container)" and "干散货集装箱(dry bulk container)".

Second, as for the terminology formation in various industries, there are cases where the choice of lexical morphemes directly or indirectly reflects the internal form. Of course, due to different focuses, different internal forms are formed when selecting semantic features for the same object, which are then converted into lexical morphemes to create different word forms for the same object, such as the aforementioned "周底托盘 (perimeter-base pallet)" and "窗式托盘 (window pallet)". However, the prerequisite for using lexical morphemes that indirectly reflect semantic features to form words is that the selected morphemes share consistent semantic features with the object to be named. Take the naming of "海绵乳胶 (sponge latex)" as an example. The semantic features of "海绵(sponge)" include [QUANTITY: MANY] and [STATE: POROUS(多孔的)], which share consistent semantic features with the latex to be named. Consequently, "海绵" is used to name this type of latex. But, it is necessary to emphasize that from the statistical results, it can be seen that the cases of direct reflection account for a larger proportion.

Despite the semantic mechanism in industry terminology formation, through statistics, it is found that there is no unified standard in Chinese industry terminology formation or the selection of semantic focus. Eugen Wüster believes that "all term processing starts with the concept" [9]. According to the International Standard, "Terminology Work-Principles and Methods" (ISO 704-2022), as for terminology formation, each feature of the concept under study shall be analyzed with regard to other relevant concepts. Similarities between concepts should be indicated by shared features; differences that set a concept apart should be signaled by distinctive features.

These views essentially advocate that the selection of internal form construction should choose generic and distinctive semantic features, and the choice of lexical morphemes should reflect these two types of semantic features, which is to form a framework of "specific distinctive semantic features + generic shared features" in internal form, and a framework of "specific delimiting lexical morphemes + generic shared lexical morphemes" in lexical form [10]. This will help to analyze the similarities and differences between concepts and therefore, results in identifying the unique set of features that make up a given concept.

6   Conclusion

This paper uses the theory and method of Lexical Semantic Logic Analysis to investigate the phenomenon of terminology formation in Chinese industry. It is found that the mechanism of "Naming by Attribute" is the semantic logical basis for constructing internal forms and creating term forms. However, through statistics, it is found that there is no unified standard in Chinese industry terminology formation or the selection of semantic focus. To explore the mechanism of Chinese industry terminology formation not only helps to reveal the motivation for terminology formation, but also contributes to the scientific design of teaching methods of vocabulary in teaching Chinese as a foreign language[11], as well as to the standardization and internationalization of terminology formation.

Acknowledgments. This study has received support from various funding sources, including: Special Project of the Research Center for Teachers' Ethics and Styles Construction of Liaoning Normal University (Research on the Promotion of Professional Development of International Chinese Language Teachers through the Construction of Teachers' Ethics in Colleges and Universities, 206010132407); Basic Scientific Research Project of Liaoning Provincial Department of Education in 2023 (A Comparative Study on the Semantic Logic of Chinese-English Industry Terminology under the Background of "Chinese + Vocational Skills", JYTMS20231084); Project Approval of Liaoning Education Science Planning in 2022 (Research on Strategies for Improving the Ideological and Political Literacy of Teachers of Chinese as a Foreign Language from the Perspective of Niche Expansion, JG22DB415); Undergraduate Teaching Reform Research Projects of Liaoning Normal University in 2024 (Research and Practice on the Application of the "Understanding Contemporary China" International Chinese Series of Textbooks in the Construction of Advanced Chinese Writing Courses, lsbkjg202430).

References

1. Xu, Y., et al.: Development of a Chinese tourism technical word list based on corpus analysis. In: Dong, M., et al. (eds.) CLSW 2023, LNAI, vol. 14514, pp. 406–422. Springer, Heidelberg (2023)
2. Ye, Q.-S.: Terminology: turn from method to methodology. China Terminol. **17**(2), 10–14 (2015). (in Chinese)
3. Fu, H.-Q.: Modern Chinese vocabulary. Peking University Press, Beijing (2003). (in Chinese)
4. Aristotle: Categories and de interpretatione. Translated by Fang Shuchun. The Commercial Press, Beijing (2003). (in Chinese)
5. Zhang, D.-X., Dong, H.: The theory of modern chinese lexical category. China Social Sciences Press, Beijing (2014). (in Chinese)
6. Jia, Y.-D.: Chinese semantics. Peking University Press, Beijing (1999). (in Chinese)
7. Von Humboldt, W.: On the diversity of human language structure and its influence on the development of human thought. Translated by Yao Xiaoping. The Commercial Press, Beijing (1997). (in Chinese)
8. Wang, M., Zhang, D.-X.: A tentative discussion on the similarities and differences of semantic derivation phenomena of somatosensory adjectives in Chinese and English. J. Liaoning Norm. Univ. (Soc. Sci. Ed.) **47**(02), 50–57 (2022). (in Chinese)
9. Qiu, B.-H.: The father of terminology: Eugen Wieder. J. Sci. Tech. Terminol. **3**(3), 30–34 (2001). (in Chinese)
10. Cao, R., Zhang, D.-X.: On the semantic-grammatical mechanism of standardization of Chinese item names. Appl. Lang. Writ. **2021**(1), 100–109 (2021). (in Chinese)
11. Zhu, S., et al.: Text readability assessment for Chinese second language teaching. In: Hong, J.-F., et al. (eds.) CLSW 2019, LNAI, vol. 11831, pp. 393–405. Springer, Heidelberg (2020)

The Grammaticalization and Evolution Motivation of *Shēngshēng*

Yulin Huang[(✉)]

Department of Chinese Language and Literature, Xiamen University, Xiamen, China
emailhuangyulin@qq.com

Abstract. *Shēngshēng* 生生 functions both as an adverb acting as the adverbial modifier and as a suffix indicating degree. Context expansion and subjectivity are important factors contributing to its semantic evolution. The predicative components modified by *shēngshēng* have the meaning of damage, which are categorized into damage to life and damage to interests, and *shēngshēng* absorbs the contextual meaning due to its frequent occurrence in damage-related contexts. The predicative components expand from disyllabic verbs to the verb-resultative construction and verb-degree construction, and the damaged object expands from animate to the inanimate. The semantic function of *shēngshēng* is weakened and the expressive function is strengthened under the effect of subjectivity. The semantics of *shēngshēng* are reduced from 'alive' to 'cruelly' and 'miserably' and other subjective evaluation meanings. *Shēngshēng* as an adverb combines with *yìng* 硬 and *huó* 活 to form *yìngshēngshēng* 硬生生 and *huóshēngshēng* 活生生, while *shēngshēng* as a suffix gives rise to a series of X + *shēngshēng* X生生. Both uses exhibit similar word formation.

Keywords: *shēngshēng* 生生 · grammaticalization · diachronic evolution · subjectivity

1 Introduction

The term *shēngshēng* 生生 has three meanings according to the Modern Chinese Dictionary (7th edition) [1]: (1) Adverb: *huóhuó* 活活. It refers to something in a living state, often implying that a living entity has been harmed. (2) Adverb: It indicates something being done forcefully or rigidly. (3) Suffix: Used after nominal or adjectival morphemes, it often indicates a high degree or vitality. What are the semantic connections between these meanings? Is there a sequential relationship in this historical development? These questions pertain to the semantic evolution—grammaticalization—of the word *shēngshēng*.

So far, only two studies by Min [2] and Zhang [3] have examined the diachronic evolution of *shēngshēng*. Min argued that *shēngshēng* evolved from a phrase structure to a reduplicative adverb, focusing on changes in syntactic position and the trend of disyllabification. However, she did not research the evolution of the suffix *shēngshēng*. Zhang pointed out that *shēngshēng* underwent a process of lexicalization, subjectification, and

P. Jin et al. (Eds.): CLSW 2024, LNAI 15552, pp. 154–170, 2025.
https://doi.org/10.1007/978-981-96-3509-2_12

suffixation. The co-occurrence with synonymous adverbs facilitated its grammaticalization from an adverb into a suffix. However, the corpus shows that when *shēngshēng* evolved into an adverb, it had already begun to be used as a suffix.

This paper will explore the grammaticalization of *shēngshēng* from a diachronic perspective. It describes its collocational patterns and semantic expressions and analyzes the expansion of its related predicative components, argument and contexts. Additionally, this paper outlines two relatively independent developmental paths of *shēngshēng* as an adverb and a suffix. It will illustrate the evolution from a syntactic reduplication to an evaluative adverb, as well as from depicting objective situations to expressing subjective emotions. Finally, the paper will investigate the underlying mechanisms driving these changes.

2 The Grammaticalization of *Shēngshēng*

The term *shēngshēng* appeared as early as the Pre-Qin period (approximately 21st century BCE – 221 BCE). Although its form is identical to the one discussed in this paper, its meanings during that time were 'reproduction and nurturing of life', 'all living beings' and 'eternal life' (cf. [2]), which differ from the usage of *shēngshēng* meaning 'in a living state'. Additionally, the disyllabification process from the degree adverb *shēng* 生 expressing 'extremely' or 'most' to the morphological reduplication *shēngshēng* is beyond the scope of this study. Min [2] traced the grammaticalization and pointed out that monosyllabic verb *shēng*, acting as an adverbial modifier, had already appeared in the Pre-Qin period. During the Yuan dynasty, *shēngshēng* absorbed the function of *shēng* and became a reduplicative form. Over time, *shēng* was gradually replaced by *shēngshēng*. Zhang [3] suggested that after the Song and Yuan dynasties, the trend toward disyllabification in ancient colloquial Chinese intensified, and the reduplicative form *shēngshēng* was used to harmonize the metrical foot. Since both researchers identified the emergence of *shēngshēng* in the Yuan dynasty, this study uses this period as a turning point to explore the evolution of *shēngshēng*.

2.1 Yuan Dynasty

Shēngshēng first appeared as an adverbial modifier in Yuan zaju (a form of Yuan drama). It was later marked by the adverbial marker *de* 地 indicating 'in a living state':

(1) 凤北鸾南, 生生地镜剖与钗分

    fèng   bĕi luán nán, shēngshēng de   jìng pōu   yŭ chāi   fēn
    phoenix north luan south *shēngshēng* DE mirror shatter and hairpin divide

    'The phoenix flies north, the luan flies south, we were separated in life like a shattered mirror and a divided hairpin. (*You Gui Ji*)'

Interestingly, in the Yuan zaju, *shēngshēng* also appeared as a suffix, as in:

(2) 白生生面皮, 软溶溶肚皮

> *bái   shēngshēng miànpí,   ruǎn róngróng dùpí*
> fair   *shēngshēng* complexion soft *róngróng* belly

'A very fair complexion and a very soft belly. (*The Complete Yuan Qu*)'

(3) 支生生头发似人揪

> *zhī   shēngshēng tóufà shì rén   jiū*
> stand-upright *shēngshēng* hair as-if someone pull

'My hair stands on end, as if someone were pulling it. (*The Complete Yuan Qu*)'

Chu [4] conducted a study on ABB-type adjectives with suffixes in Yuan drama. She pointed out that when A is an adjectival morpheme, it conveys the basic meaning of the word, while BB functions as a suffix that adds extra meaning, supplementing the degree, state, or emotional connotation of A. When A is a verbal morpheme, BB describes the state of A by depicting the physiological or psychological actions of a person, and sometimes emphasizing the degree of A. For example, in case (2), *bái* 白 which means 'fair' is an adjectival morpheme, and *shēngshēng* serves to indicate a deep degree, meaning 'very fair'. In case (3), *zhī* 支 meaning 'to extend' or 'to stand upright' is a verbal morpheme, and *shēngshēng* depicts the scene of cold wind causing hair to stand upright. Referring to the partially grammaticalized examples listed by Chu, such as *xūpiāopiāo* 虚飘飘, *xiūqièqiè* 羞怯怯, *bìlínlín* 碧粼粼 and *gāowēiwēi* 高巍巍, the A and B elements in these ABB formations are semantically compatible. However, there is no clear semantic connection between *bái* 白 and *shēng* 生, or between *zhī* 支 and *shēng* 生, which indicates that *shēngshēng* has already undergone grammaticalization. Upon consulting relevant dictionaries, such as the Dictionary of Song-Yuan Language [5], the following definitions were found: *báishēngshēng* 白生生 is also rendered as *báisēnsēn* 白森森, meaning 'very fair'. *Zhīshēngshēng* 支生生 refers to hair standing upright. In the Dictionary of Theatrical Terms [6], *zhīshēngshēng* 支生生 is explained as 'one by one', and in the Dictionary of Early-Modern Chinese [7], it is defined as 'upright in appearance'. These dictionary entries point to the primary word A, without reflecting any independent lexical meaning for *shēngshēng*. Therefore, we conclude that in the Yuan dynasty, *shēngshēng* functioned as a morphemic suffix, having undergone semantic bleaching, and its pragmatic function of indicating degree became more prominent.

2.2 Ming Dynasty

During the Ming Dynasty, on the one hand, *shēngshēng* continued to serve as an adverbial modifier, and the morphological reduplication gradually transformed into syntactic reduplication. *Shēngshēng* evolved into a disyllabic adverb, still influenced by the original meaning of the verb *shēng,* which depicted objective situations. For example:

(4) ......成夜只是哭, 生生忧虑出病儿来了

> *chéngyè   zhǐshì kū, shēngshēng yōulù chū   bìnger   lái le*
> all-night just cry *shēngshēng* worry COMP illness COMP LE

'They cried all night, worried themselves into an illness while still alive. (*The Golden Lotus, Chapter 62*)'

This example describes how the protagonist, still alive, became ill due to excessive worry, and the argument is animate. *Shēngshēng* has the meaning of 'in a living state', which is consistent with the meaning of the monosyllabic verb *shēng*.

On the other hand, the predicative components modified by *shēngshēng* expanded from disyllabic verbs to the verb-resultative construction, emphasizing the result of actions. For example:

(5) 一个丫头生生的逼杀了

> *yī   gè   yātóu shēngshēng de   bī   shā   le*
> one CL maid *shēngshēng* DE force death LE

'A maid was forced to death while still alive. (*The Awakening of the World, Volume 2*)'

(6) 我一个......女儿, 生生的打杀了

> *wǒ yī gè   nǚ'ér   shēngshēng de   dǎ   shā   le*
> my one CL daughter *shēngshēng* DE beat death LE

'My daughter was beaten to death while still alive. (*The Awakening of the World, Volume 2*)'

In these examples, the predicative components convey the meaning of damage, with the damaged objects being animate. Notably, *shēngshēng* is paired with a verb-resultative construction, which often describes lethal actions. This is evident in examples (5) and (6), where the complement *shā* 杀 denotes 'death', indicating that the patient transitions from life to death. In these cases, if *shēngshēng* were interpreted simply as 'in a living state', it would seem redundant. In other words, when *shēngshēng* is used with verbs that imply death, the speaker emphasizes that the affected party experienced death while still alive, highlighting their focus on the suffering of the harmed subject. Hence, while *shēngshēng* continues to depict objective circumstances, it also, to some extent, expresses the speaker's subjective perspective on the affected individual.

At the same time, this period inherited the use of *shēngshēng* as a suffix in Yuan dynasty, maintaining the symmetrical structure in Yuan drama.

2.3 Qing Dynasty

During the Qing Dynasty, the frequency of *shēngshēng* combined with disyllabic verbs and verb-resultative constructions increased significantly.

During this period, *shēngshēng* frequently appeared in contexts where damage occurred, with the predicative components conveying fatal consequences. This usage primarily emphasizes the harm to the patient's life during the action, which we term 'life damage'. While describing objective circumstances, the speaker's subjective stance and emotional attitude are also activated. When the speaker's perspective shifts, *shēngshēng* can be extended to express different meanings.

First, when the speaker's focus is on the agent and the action, *shēngshēng* can be extended to mean 'forcibly', 'brutally' or 'ruthlessly', as in:

(7) 生生儿的要了你的女儿命了

> *shēngshēnger de yàole nǐde nǚ'ér   mìng le*
> *shēngshēng* DE take your daughter life LE

'You have ruthlessly taken your daughter's life. (*The Seven Heroes and Five Gallants, Volume 1*)'

(8) ......生生儿将他两个爱妾的性命断送

> *shēngshēnger jiāng tā liǎng gè ài   qiè   de xìngmìng duànsong*
> *shēngshēng* BA his two CL beloved concubine DE life   end

'The righteous hero had no choice but to brutally end the lives of his two beloved concubines. (*The Seven Heroes and Five Gallants, Volume 1*)'

In the above examples, the speaker describes the event from the perspective of the agent, *shēngshēng* emphasizes that the agents harmed the affected parties while they were alive, highlighting the speaker's subjective stance and attitude toward the agent's harsh and cruel actions.

Second, when the speaker's focus is on the affected subject and the result, the tragic fate of the subject is highlighted, and *shēngshēng* can be extended to mean 'pitifully', 'tragically', 'miserably' or 'helplessly', as in:

(9) 看着你女儿一条性命生生丢在水中

> *kànzhe nǐ   nǚ'ér   yī tiáo xìngmìng shēngshēng diū zài shuǐzhōng*
> watch your daughter one CL life   *shēngshēng* lose in river

'How could I just watch your daughter drown helplessly in the river? (*The Nine-Tailed Turtle, Volume 2*)'

(10) 嫁我十年......生生的饿死了

> *jià   wǒ shí nián shēngshēng de è   sǐ   le*
> marry me ten year *shēngshēng* DE starve death LE

'Having been married to me for ten years, she starved to death miserably! (*The Old Man's Exposed Words*)'

In the example, the patient is the starting point of the narration. The speaker identifies with the affected party, using *shēngshēng* to emphasize that their lives were taken while in a living state, conveying a personal attitude toward the pitiable and tragic fate of the patient.

From the examples, it is evident that the predicative components inflict harm on the life of the affected party. By using *shēngshēng*, the speaker further emphasizes that the harm occurred while the affected party was still alive, highlighting either the agent's action or the outcome for the patient. As the speaker's involvement in the discourse increases, the expressive function of *shēngshēng* also gradually intensifies. Furthermore, during this period, some predicative components did not directly cause fatal harm but resulted in negative consequences for the patient. We term this 'interest damage', as in:

(11) ......竟要生生的吃亏六百块钱

> *jìng   yào   shēngshēng de chīkuī   liù bǎi   kuài qián*
> actually will   *shēngshēng* DE suffer-losses six hundred CL   money

'He is actually going to suffer a loss of six hundred yuan. (*The Nine-Tailed Turtle, Volume 4*)'

(12) ......被人生生的一口咬死是他

> *bèi   rén   shēngshēng de yī kǒu yǎosǐ shì tā*
> BEI people *shēngshēng* DE one CL blame be he

'He was wrongly blamed for the crime (*A Dream in Red Mansions, Chapter 34*)'

Just as life is inextricably linked to a person, so are personal interests. This similarity facilitated the expansion of the predicative components from 'life damage' to 'interest damage'. In the examples, behaviors such as suffering losses and being wrongfully blamed are not directly connected to life, but they violate the will of the patient. In these cases, interpreting *shēngshēng* as related to 'life' would be inappropriate. This suggests that its objective meaning was suppressed, while the context of damage is retained, with the speaker's subjective emotions regarding the affected party's unfortunate situation becoming more prominent.

Additionally, during this period, certain verb-resultative constructions differed from previous ones. In these constructions, *shēngshēng* can be used in the form of '*shēngshēng* + psychological verb + *sǐ* 死' where the resultative complement *sǐ* 死 undergoes semantic generalization. Some of its semanteme were lost, and its scope of application broadened, with the meaning of 'death' generalized to indicate degree. We refer to this as the verb-degree construction, as in:

(13) ......这就生生闷死我了

> *zhè jiù shēngshēng mèn sǐ   wǒ le*
> this will *shēngshēng* bore death me LE

'This is going to bore me. (*The Awakening of the World, Volume 2*)'

(14) ……岂不将你母生生吓死

> *qǐ   bù   jiāng   nǐ   mǔ   shēngshēng   xià   sǐ*
> will NEG BA your mother *shēngshēng* scare death

'Won't your mother be scared? (*The Three Heroes of the Sword, Volume 1*)'

Tang and Chen [8] argued that the process from birth to death is temporal, and death, as the ultimate point in the life process, reflects the extremity of the concept of time. The notions of 'ultimate' and 'extremity' inherently carry the meaning of degree, and through metaphorical mechanisms, *sǐ* 死 has acquired this degree-related meaning. In the examples, *mēnsǐ* 闷死 indicates extreme discomfort and frustration, while *xiàsǐ* 吓死 refers to being excessively frightened, with no real loss of life. Tang and Chen argued that the V-*sǐ* 死-O (Verb-*sǐ* 死-Object) construction, expressing degree, appeared no later than the Song Dynasty. Therefore, in these examples, *sǐ* 死 functions as a degree complement, both semantically and historically, and can be extended to mean 'reaching an extreme'. Here, the speaker uses the degree of harm to metaphorically convey the intensity of his subjective evaluation. *Shēngshēng* further amplifies the speaker's exaggerated exclamation, leading to additional semantic bleaching.

In further developments, *shēngshēng* began to express counter-expectation information in discourse:

(15) 生生是你下了毒手……为何反来问我呢?

> *shēngshēng shì nǐ   xiàle   dúshǒu   wèihé fǎnlái   wèn wǒ   ne*
> *shēngshēng* be you deliver fatal-blow why   instead ask me SFP

'It was clearly you who delivered the fatal blow… Why are you asking me about it instead? (*The Seven Heroes and Five Gallants, Volume 1*)'

(16) 你这好人生生多事, 为何将我救活?

> *nǐ   zhè   hǎorén   shēngshēng duōshì,   wèihé jiāng wǒ   jiù   huó*
> you this do-gooder *shēngshēng* meddlesome why BA   me save alive

'You meddlesome do-gooder, why did you save me? (*The Seven Heroes and Five Gallants, Volume 1*)'

In these examples, *shēngshēng* conveys information that is contrary to the speaker's expectations, meaning that the objective event conflicts with the speaker's anticipated outcome. (cf. [9]) In example (15), speaker believed that the listener had caused someone's death. However, the listener unexpectedly inquired about the cause of death. In example (16), The person who had drowned believed that no one would save him, but instead, a young man rescued him. In these cases, *shēngshēng* indicates that the actual situation is contrary to the speaker's expectations and serves an emphatic function. The meaning of *shēngshēng* in these contexts is close to terms like *míngmíng* 明明, *piānyào* 偏要, *piānpiān* 偏偏, *lèngshì* 愣是 and it no longer carries its original meaning related to life.

Simultaneously, the affected objects modified by *shēngshēng* shifted from animate to inanimate entities:

(17) 我们中国生生就坏在这条辫子上

wǒmen	*zhōngguó*	*shēngshēng*	*jiù*	*huài*	*zài*	*zhè*	*tiáo*	*biànzi*	*shàng*
our	China	*shēngshēng*	exactly	downfall	in	this	CL	queue	COMP

'It is precisely this queue that has led to our downfall in China. (*A Brief History of Civilization, Chapter 1*)'

In this example, the affected object is inanimate entities *zhōngguó* 中国. The speaker positions himself as inanimate object, expressing his anger or regret. The reason the affected objects can be inanimate is that non-living entities undergo change from intact to damaged, similar to how living entities change from alive to dead. This metaphorical mechanism allows *shēngshēng* originally used for living beings, to also apply to inanimate objects.

During the same period, the quantity of the suffix *shēngshēng* also rose sharply, and its types became more diverse, such as *zhǎishēngshēng* 窄生生, *tiěshēngshēng* 铁生生, *lánshēngshēng* 蓝生生, *tiánshēngshēng* 甜生生, the lexical meanings of A and B are incompatible. This shows that *shēngshēng* continued to serve as a morphological suffix during this period, carrying an emphatic meaning that highlights its degree. Interestingly, we found the following examples:

(18) 两口子含着两肚皮的眼泪硬生生分手而别

liǎngkǒuzi	*hánzhe*	*liǎng*	*dùpí*	*de*	*yǎnlèi*	*yìngshēngshēng*	*fēnshǒuérbié*
couple	with	two	belly	DE	tear	*yìngshēngshēng*	part-ways

'The couple parted ways forcefully, with tears streaming down like a river. (*The Eight Immortals Achieve Dao, Volume 1*)'

(19) ……活生生将奴夫身陷禁监

huóshēnshēng	*jiāng*	*núfū*	*shēnxiàn*	*jìnjiān*
huóshēnshēng	BA	servant	trap-in	imprison

'They forcefully imprisoned the servant alive. (*Ascending the Spring Terrace*)'

In these examples, *yìngshēngshēng* 硬生生 and *huóshēngshēng* 活生生 fit the structure of 'adjective + *shēngshēng*'. Yet, in the sentences, they function as adverbial modifiers. Here, *shēngshēng* retains a strong lexical meaning of 'forcefully' or 'in a living state', and removing *yìng* 硬 and *huó* 活 does not affect the semantic expression. Zhang

[3] argues that *yìng* and *huó* function as synonymous adverbs. When the speaker focuses on the agent and the action, they use *yìng*. In contrast, when they focus on the patient and the result, they use *huó*.

2.4 Republican Era

During the Republican era, the usage of *shēngshēng* in combination with synonymous adverbs *yìng* and *huó* continued. And the use of *shēngshēng* as a suffix also became increasingly diverse, like *cuìshēngshēng* 脆生生, *qièshēngshēng* 怯生生. However, the following example is somewhat different:

(20) 子爵夫人至今还是活生生的

zǐjuéfūrén zhìjīn		*háishì huóshēngshēng de*
countess	to-this-day still	*huóshēngshēng* DE

'The countess is still very lively and vivid. (*Continued History of the East*)'

Zhang [3] argues that *yìngshēngshēng* or *huóshēngshēng* were initially synonymous adverbs used together. However, *shēngshēng* weakened to become a suffix due to the clarity and redundancy of language expression. With the expanded usage of *yìngshēngshēng* and *huóshēngshēng*, a series of derived words in the form of 'X + *Shengsheng*' gradually emerged. We argue, however, that while synonymous adverbs co-occurred, *shēngshēng* did not lose its semantic function completely. Instead, *shēngshēng* simultaneously carries the meanings of both 'forcefully' and 'life', with the synonymous combinations of *yìng* + *shēngshēng* and *huó* + *shēngshēng* serving to highlight the speaker's focus. Both combinations can still be replaced by *shēngshēng* alone. Moreover, the series of 'X + *shēngshēng*', which became common during the Republican era, actually trace their roots back to the Yuan, Ming, and Qing dynasties.

Therefore, *yìngshēngshēng, huóshēngshēng* and the series of 'X + *shēngshēng*' share similarities only in word formation, but are not derivationally related. The Modern Chinese Dictionary (7th edition) includes the word *huóshēngshēng* with the following definitions: (1) Adjective. It refers to something real or something that is happening right in front of you; (2) Adverb. *huóhuó* 活活. In example (20), *huóshēngshēng* means existing in reality, functioning as an adjective with a suffix. In this context, *huóshēngshēng* further illustrates the countess's vivid existence, and *shēngshēng* is used to intensify the degree, belonging to the 'X + *shēngshēng*'.

2.5 Contemporary Era

In the contemporary period, the usage of the suffixal adjective *huóshēngshēng* 活生生 has increased, primarily modifying animate subjects or parts of animate beings. For example:

(21) 他也该高兴看到……活生生的扫墓者吧!

> *tā yě gāi   gāoxìng kàndào huóshēngshēng de   sǎomùzhě   ba*
> he also should happy   see   *huóshēngshēng* DE tomb-sweeper SFP

'He should be happy to see the real tomb sweeper as well!' (*The Swallows at the Tip of the Branches*)'

(22) 这一张张活生生的脸孔

> *zhè yī   zhāng zhāng huóshēngshēng de   liǎnkǒng*
> this one CL   CL   *huóshēngshēng* DE face

'These lively and vivid faces. (*Crying Camels*)'

In addition, the head nouns modified by the adjective *huóshēngshēng* can also be inanimate. The similarity between the real existence of inanimate objects and the survival of animate beings allows *huóshēngshēng*, through a metaphorical mechanism, to also modify inanimate entities. For example:

(23) 这不是活生生的证据嘛

> *zhè bù   shì huóshēngshēng de   zhèngjù ma*
> this NEG be *huóshēngshēng* DE evidence SPF

'Isn't this vivid evidence? (*I Love My Family*)'

The Modern Chinese Dictionary (7th edition) only includes the word *huóshēngshēng* and does not include *yìngshēngshēng*. In the diachronic corpus, we did not find instances of *yìngshēngshēng* used as an adjective. A search of the Contemporary Chinese Corpus in the Center for Chinese Linguistics Peking University yielded only one example:

(24) 那硬生生的黑脊梁……令人难忘

> *nà yìngshēngshēng de   hēi   jǐliáng lìng rén   nánwàng*
> that *yìngshēngshēng* DE black spine   make people unforgettable

'The rigid black spine is unforgettable. (*People's Daily, 1996*)'

In example (24), *yìngshēngshēng* expresses 'particularly rigid'. Removing *shēngshēng* does not change the meaning, indicating that it belongs to the 'X + *shēngshēng*'. Its meaning differs from the adverbial *yìngshēngshēng*. In most corpus instances, *yìngshēngshēng* continues to function primarily as an adverb, synonymous with *shēngshēng* in the sense of 'forcefully'. On the other hand, both uses of *huóshēngshēng* are still widely used today, and the suffixal adjective *huóshēngshēng* is even more common than the synonymous adverb *huóshēngshēng*. We speculate that this may be one of the reasons why *huóshēngshēng* is included in the dictionary.

To summarize, we outline the diachronic evolution of *shēngshēng* as follows: Since the Yuan Dynasty, *shēngshēng* has had two uses, functioning both as an adverbial modifier and as a suffix. The reduplicative form *shēngshēng* inherited the meaning of the monosyllabic verb *shēng*, expressing the objective meaning of life, and was employed to describe the conditions of things. The predicative components indicate fatal consequences, and their basic usage was closely related to the damage inflicted on the patient's life during an action. As the predicative components expanded from disyllabic verbs to verb-resultative constructions, the objective life-related meaning became increasingly redundant. While it continued to describe objective phenomena, it gradually incorporated the speaker's subjective evaluation. When the speaker's perspective is focused on the agent and the action, *shēngshēng* conveys meanings such as 'forcibly' or 'cruelly'. When the focus shifts to the patient and the result, *shēngshēng* expresses meanings like 'pitifully' or 'tragically'. As damage-related contexts gradually increased, *shēngshēng* absorbed the meaning of damage. Through a metaphorical mechanism, the scope of damage extended from life damage to interest damage, and the objective meaning of 'life' in *shēngshēng* became suppressed. When the resultative complement in verb-resultative constructions underwent semantic bleaching and expanded into verb-degree constructions, *shēngshēng* developed to express the speaker's exaggerated exclamation. As the speaker became more engaged in the discourse meaning, the propositions containing *shēngshēng* could convey counter-expectation information. In terms of arguments, the affected objects expanded from animate to inanimate objects, with the speaker adopting the perspective of inanimate objects, furthering the semantic bleaching of *shēngshēng*. By the Republican era, *shēngshēng* could be used in combination with synonymous adverbs like *yìng* and *huó* to emphasize the speaker's focus. Meanwhile, the suffix *shēngshēng* was steadily inherited across periods, with increasing frequency and diversity, leading to the formation of numerous 'X + *shēngshēng*' derivatives. Among these, the suffixal adjective *huóshēngshēng* and the synonymous adverb *huóshēngshēng* share similarities in word formation. We have represented the diachronic evolution of *shēngshēng* in Fig. 1.

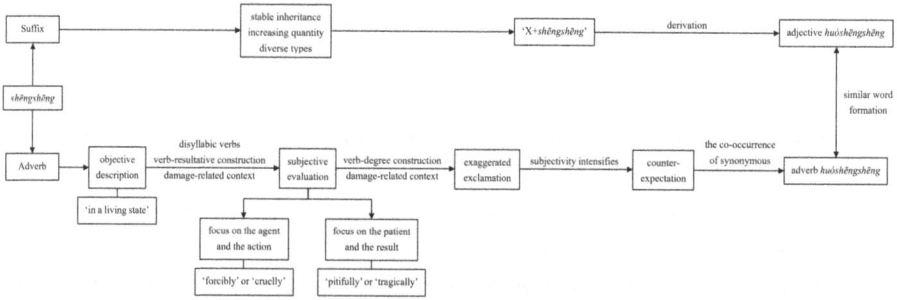

Fig. 1. The diachronic evolution of *shēngshēng*

3 Analysis of the Motivation Behind the Evolution of *Shēngshēng*

The evolution of *shēngshēng* from describing objective circumstances to expressing subjective evaluation was influenced by various factors. Among these, the interaction between context expansion and subjectivity played a key role.

In everyday communication, speakers not only express propositional meanings but also convey speaker-oriented meanings, the latter reflecting the subjectivity of language. Subjectivity refers to the way in which natural languages, in their structure and their normal manner of operation, provide for the locutionary agent's expression of himself and of his own attitudes and beliefs. (cf. [10–12]). When subjectivity is encoded with a clear construction, or when a linguistic form acquires the function of expressing subjectivity, this is referred to as subjectivization. Traugott [13] incorporated subjectivization into grammaticalization studies, proposing it as a process of semantic and pragmatic change in which meaning increasingly reflects the speaker's beliefs and attitudes toward the propositional content. Throughout this process, a word's meaning tends to shift from conveying propositional content to conveying expressive meaning. This grammaticalization process increasingly relates to the speaker's stance, attitude, and emotions.

As for *shēngshēng*, the reduplicative form initially inherited the meaning of the monosyllabic verb *shēng*, primarily expressing the meaning of life and depicting the circumstances of things. The lexical items forming syntactic relationships with *shēngshēng* expanded, with the predicative components extending from disyllabic verbs to verb-resultative constructions that conveyed fatal consequences. This shift indicated a transformation in the state of life of the affected object, rendering the objective meaning of life in *shēngshēng* redundant. Thus, while *shēngshēng* continued to express objective phenomena, it increasingly incorporated the speaker's subjective evaluation to varying degrees. For example:

(25) ......被母夜叉赛无盐给打死

> *bèi mǔyèchā Sài Wúyán   gěi   dǎ   sǐ*
> BEI hag   Sai Wuyan PREP beat death

'She was killed by the hag Sai Wuyan.'

(26) ......被母夜叉赛无盐给生生打死

> *bèi mǔyèchā Sài Wúyán   gěi   shēngshēng dǎ   sǐ*
> BEI hag   Sai Wuyan PREP *shēngshēng* beat death

'She was killed by the hag Sai Wuyan while she was still alive.' (*The Case of Peng Gong (Volume 1)*)

In example (25), the verb-resultative construction *dǎsǐ* 打死 reflects the transformation of the affected object from life to death, and the proposition merely expresses a fact. However, in example (26), the speaker uses *shēngshēng* to emphasize that the affected object was still alive when it was killed, highlighting the speaker's focus on the participants in the event.

Zhang [14] argues that when a speaker expresses an objective phenomenon, there is always a degree of subjective evaluation involved. When the speaker aims to emphasize an emotion, or to fulfill a specific pragmatic need, the implicit subjective elements are brought to the forefront. The subjectivization of the adverb *shēngshēng* occurs precisely because the predicative components already carry the meaning of life. By using *shēngshēng* again, the speaker emphasizes their subjective understanding, thereby revealing the implicit subjectivity.

Throughout its evolution, the predicative components consistently conveyed the meaning of damage. With its frequent use in damage-related contexts, *shēngshēng* absorbed the meaning of damage from the context. In some cases, although *shēngshēng* still appeared in damage-related contexts, the predicative components only harmed the interests of the affected object and were not directly related to life. The semantic focus of *shēngshēng* shifted from objective life to subjective emphasis, leading to a gradual weakening of its function in depicting objective reality, while its subjective function correspondingly increased. At this stage, since *shēngshēng* was often used to express the speaker's subjective understanding, it gradually acquired a subjective meaning, paving the way for the development of stronger subjective functions. In the process of emphasizing the speaker's subjective evaluation, the combinatory elements of *shēngshēng* underwent further expansion. The resultative complement in the verb-resultative construction became generalized, shifting from a meaning of death to one of degree. The speaker used the degree of harm suffered by the affected party to metaphorically express the degree of the subjectivity, resulting in further semantic bleaching of *shēngshēng*.

Furthermore, the subjectivity expressed by *shēngshēng* can be reflected through specific perspectives and emotions. Perspective means the speaker's point of view when observing or narrating an objective situation, while emotion denotes the subjective feelings added to that perspective (cf. [12] and [15]). Kuno [16] pointed out that the speaker can choose different perspectives to describe an event or state. In some cases, the speaker can completely identify with one of the participants, describing the event or state from that participant's viewpoint. Regarding *shēngshēng*, when the speaker's focus is on the agent and the action, *shēngshēng* can extend to mean 'forcefully', 'rigidly', 'cruelly' or 'brutally'. When the speaker's focus is on the patient and the result, *shēngshēng* can extend to mean 'pitifully', 'tragically', 'painfully' or 'helplessly'. For example:

(27) 你生生的断送了我的官

> *nǐ   shēngshēng de duànsòng le   wǒde guān*
> you *shēngshēng* DE take-away   LE   my   official-position

'You have forcefully taken away my official position. (*The Awakening of the World, Volume 2*)'

(28) 可惜令兄这样好人，与妾亡姊姊……生生的阻隔两处

> *kěxī lìng xiōng zhèyàng hǎo rén,   yǔ   qiè wáng zǐzǐ*
> pity your brother such   good people and my   late sister
> *shēngshēng de zǔgé   liǎng chù*
> *shēngshēng* DE separate two   place

'It's a pity that such a good person as your brother is tragically separated from my late sister in two places. (*The First Collection of Startling Cases, Volume 2*)'

In example (27), the speaker is clearly viewing the action from the perspective of *nǐ* 你, subjectively perceiving the act as rigid and cruel. In example (28), the perspective shifts, the speaker is expressing sympathy from the standpoint of *lìngxiōng* 令兄 and *zǐzǐ* 姊姊, lamenting the fact that they were separated from one another. This also carries a strong sense of subjectivity. *Shēngshēng* reflects the speaker's subjective involvement and extends to convey different meanings, which clearly depends on the perspective the speaker adopts when observing the world.

Comrie [17] considers animacy as a parameter related to language evolution. When the patient described by *shēngshēng* expands from animate to inanimate entities, the objective meaning of life in *shēngshēng* is entirely suppressed, yet the agent's action still conveys a sense of damage. *Shēngshēng* remains within a damage-related context, with the speaker placing themselves in the position of the inanimate object, expressing their subjective understanding of the perceived object.

As subjectivity further intensifies, the proposition containing *shēngshēng* is used to express discourse that conveys information contrary to expectations. The occurrence of an event, whether intentionally or unintentionally, deviates from the speaker's expectations. The speaker uses *shēngshēng* to express their subjective attitude toward this situation, which is also a manifestation of subjectivity. For example:

(29) 是你下了毒手……为何反来问我呢？

> *shì nǐ xiàle dúshǒu wèihé fǎnlái wèn wǒ ne*
> be you deliver fatal-blow why instead ask me SFP

'It was you who delivered the fatal blow… Why are you asking me about it instead?'

(30) 生生是你下了毒手……为何反来问我呢？

> *shēngshēng shì nǐ xiàle dúshǒu wèihé fǎnlái wèn wǒ ne*
> *shēngshēng* be you deliver fatal-blow why instead ask me SFP

'It was clearly you who delivered the fatal blow… Why are you asking me about it instead? (*The Seven Heroes and Five Gallants, Volume 1*)'

(31) 是你生生下了毒手……为何反来问我呢？

> *shì nǐ shēngshēng xiàle dúshǒu wèihé fǎnlái wèn wǒ ne*
> be you *shēngshēng* deliver fatal-blow why instead ask me SFP

'It was you who delivered the fatal blow cruelly… Why are you asking me about it instead?'s

Comparing the above three examples, in example (29), the speaker just asks the listener a question without obvious emotion. However, in example (30), it is clear that the speaker initially held certain expectations about the agent's reaction (such as calmly admitting to the crime) but later found that the situation was contrary to his expectations. Thus, *shēngshēng* is used to express this counter-expectation, conveying a sense of surprise along with the inquiry. It is important to note that here, *shēngshēng* appears before the copular verb *shì* 是, occupying a syntactic position outside the proposition and becoming a super-propositional element. It does not contribute to the propositional content but instead expresses the speaker's affirmative inference regarding the truth value of the proposition, that is, modality. This further enhances its subjectivity. This function differs from previous one. For example, in case (31), *shēngshēng* is located within the proposition, participating in the expression of propositional content. The speaker, from the agent's perspective, subjectively perceives the harshness and cruelty of the imposed action.

At this stage, *shēngshēng* underwent complete semantic bleaching, and its function became quite distant from its usage in damage-related contexts. As a result, the adverb *shēngshēng*, used for subjective evaluation, gradually formed.

In summary, *shēngshēng* initially expressed a concrete, objective meaning related to life, but later it adopted the speaker's subjective evaluation reflecting its self-awareness. The key to the development of the subjective function of *shēngshēng* was the emergence of damage-related contexts. As the types of lexical items that entered into syntactic relationships with *shēngshēng* expanded—whether referring to life-related or non-life-related damage, as well as animate or inanimate patient—*shēngshēng* consistently appeared in damage-related contexts. It is a natural human reaction to develop subjective emotions when witnessing a subject suffer harm. Thus, semantic bleaching in *shēngshēng* can be seen as a gradual increase in the speaker's subjectivity. As the speaker's involvement in the meaning of the discourse increased, the meaning of *shēngshēng* became increasingly dependent on the speaker's beliefs and attitudes toward the propositional content.

Additionally, regarding the relationship between the adverb *shēngshēng* and the suffix *shēngshēng*, we consider the use of *shēngshēng* in damage-related contexts as the primary usage of the adverb, comparing it with the suffix *shēngshēng*. Their usage patterns are illustrated in Fig. 2. From the Ming to the Qing dynasties, the usage of *shēngshēng* as both an adverb and as a suffix experienced a significant increase, with minimal differences in frequency among the later periods. Therefore, the two usages largely followed relatively parallel developmental paths. Whether there is a semantic connection between them remains to be further explored.

4 Conclusion

Zhang [18] categorized adverbs based on their degree of semantic bleaching into descriptive adverbs, restrictive adverbs and evaluative adverbs. These three types form a continuum from concrete to abstract. Zhang suggests that *shēngshēng* has further bleached from a descriptive adverb depicting circumstances into an evaluative adverb expressing modality. In the diachronic corpus, we have also confirmed that the adverb *shēngshēng* has transitioned from a descriptive adverb to an evaluative adverb through ongoing semantic bleaching and subjectivization.

In the dictionary, the adverb *shēngshēng* is used to depict objective circumstances, while 'forcefully' or 'rigidly' conveys subjective evaluations. Zhang [3] posits that under

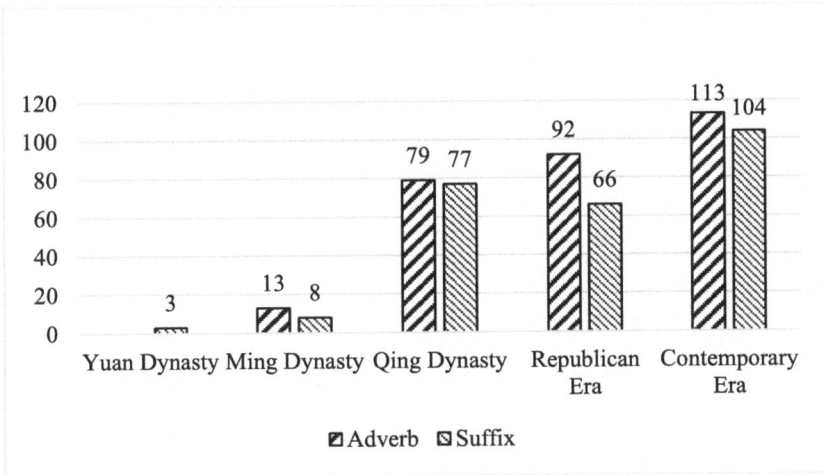

Fig. 2. The quantity of the adverb *shēngshēng* and the suffix *shēngshēng* in different dynasties

the overarching trend of subjectivization, each adverb retains its unique characteristics based on the semantic accumulation from its inception, including syntactic functions and semantic tendencies. Under the influence of subjectivity, *shēngshēng* has evolved into an evaluative adverb, reflecting the speaker's subjective attitudes or emotional awareness while stating an objective proposition. As the contexts of use vary, if this evaluative meaning can be successfully understood and accepted by the listeners, it may become conventionalized through repeated use, transforming into a conventional meaning.

References

1. Institute of Linguistics, CASS: Modern Chinese dictionary, 7th edn. The Commercial Press, Beijing (2016)
2. Min, J.: A Multi-Perspective Examination of the Adverbs 'Sheng' and 'Shengsheng', Master thesis, Shanghai Normal University, Shanghai (2011)
3. Zhang, Y.S.: From the describing situation to the expressing modal: on re-grammaticalizational analysis of adverb Shengsheng(生生). Stud. Lang. Linguist. **35**(3), 38–47 (2015)
4. Chu, F.X.: A study on the affixes in YuanQu. Doctor thesis, Shandong University, Shandong (2007)
5. Long, Q.X.: Dictionary of Song-Yuan language. Shanghai Lexicographical Publishing House, Shanghai (1985)
6. Lu, D.A.: Dictionary of theatrical terms. Shanghai Classics Publishing House, Shanghai (1981)
7. Bai, W.G.: Dictionary of early-modern Chinese. Shanghai Education Publishing House, Shanghai (2015)
8. Tang, X.Q., Chen, L.: The diachronic development and cross-linguistical investigation of 'death' as the function of degree complement. Stud. Lang. Linguist. **31**(3), 79–85 (2011)
9. Wu, F.X.: On the pragmatic function of the construction "X bu-bi Y·X." Stud. Chin. Lang. **3**, 222–231+287 (2004)

10. Lyons, J.: Semantics, vol. 2. Cambridge University Press, Cambridge (1977)
11. Lyons, J.: Deixis and subjectivity: Loquor, ergo sum? In: Jarvella, R.J., Klein, W. (eds.) Speech, place and action: studies in deixis and related topics. John Wiley and Sons Inc, Chichester and New York (1982)
12. Shen, J.X.: A survey of studies on subjectivity and subjectivisation. Foreign Lang. Teach. Res. **4**, 268–275+320 (2001)
13. Traugott, E.C.: On the rise of epistemic meanings in English: an example of subjectification in semantic change. Language **64**, 31–55 (1989)
14. Zhang, Y.S.: On the grammaticalization and subjectivisation of the adverb Dou(都). J. Xuzhou Norm. Univ. **1**, 56–62 (2005)
15. Shao, J.M.: On the types of subjectivity and paths of subjectivization. Chin. Linguist. **4**, 2–9+95 (2017)
16. Kuno, S.: Functional syntax: anaphora. Discourse and Empathy. University of Chicago Press, Chicago (1987)
17. Comrie, B.: Language universals and linguistic typology: syntax and morphology. University Of Chicago Press, Chicago (1989)
18. Zhang, Y.S.: A study of adverbs in modern Chinese. Xuelin Publishing House, Shanghai (2000)

A Contrastive Collostructional Analysis of "X + Shuāng + N" and "X + Pair of + N": on the Definition of the Classifier "Shuāng" in Chinese-English Learner's Dictionaries

Li Zeng[✉]

School of English Studies, Sichuan International Studies University, No. 33, Zhuangzhi Road, Shapingba District, Chongqing 400031, China
zengli2020@foxmail.com

Abstract. A contrastive collostructional analysis of "X + shuāng + N" and "X + pair of + N" offers insight into the differences between Chinese and English languages in constructing collective classifier constructions. The study, grounded in construction grammar and employing collostructional analysis, conducts a contrastive analysis of the two constructions. The findings reveal that: 1) there are more differences than similarities in collostructional nouns associated with "X + shuāng + N" and "X + pair of + N"; 2) the two constructions exhibit distinct collostructional categorization mechanisms; and 3) the prototypical meaning of "X + shuāng + N" is to measure binary and homogeneous body parts or objects related to the body, while "X + pair of + N" typically measures both binary and homogeneous body-related and non-body-related objects. Variations in etymological features, cognitive patterns, and grammatical roles account for the collostructional differences between these two constructions. Based on these contrastive findings, this paper suggests improvements to the definition of the classifier "shuāng" in Chinese-English learner's dictionaries.

Keywords: "X + shuāng + N" · "X + pair of + N" · collostructional strength · dictionary definition

1 Introduction

The cognitive ability to quantify objects or people is a fundamental skill of human beings, which is reflected in linguistic systems and gives rise to various methods for expressing quantity across different languages. These linguistic mechanisms for expressing quantity can be broadly categorized into two types: singular-plural and classifier systems. English belongs to the former category, while Chinese belongs to the latter [1]. Classifiers represent a distinctive word class in Sino-Tibetan languages, setting them apart from Indo-European languages. Modern Chinese classifiers are particularly abundant, as evidenced by the number of entries in specialized dictionaries. For example, *Dictionary of Common Modern Chinese Classifiers* [2] lists 789 classifiers, while *Handbook of*

P. Jin et al. (Eds.): CLSW 2024, LNAI 15552, pp. 171–184, 2025.
https://doi.org/10.1007/978-981-96-3509-2_13

Modern Chinese Classifiers [3] includes 558 classifiers, and *Standardized Dictionary of Modern Chinese Classifiers* [4] features 663 classifiers. Modern Chinese classifiers can be generally categorized into three types: noun classifiers, verbal classifiers, and time classifiers. Noun classifiers can be further divided into individual classifiers, collective classifiers, measure words, and temporary classifiers [5]. The most common classifier construction in modern Chinese is "X + classifier + noun".

While English does not possess a grammatical category equivalent to the Chinese classifier, there are comparable constructions in English, especially in terms of constructions resembling "X + classifier + noun". These typically take two forms: 1) "article/numeral + countable noun"; 2) "article/numeral + N1 + of + material nouns/plural noun". In the second construction, N1 functions similarly to a Chinese classifier, referred to here as an English classifier[1], and the construction itself is termed an "English classifier construction". Approximately 100 collective classifiers exist in English [6], including words such as "pair", "couple", "group", "bundle", "band" and "crowd".

Given the prominent role that collective classifiers play in both Chinese and English classifier systems, it is valuable to explore the correspondences between Chinese collective classifiers and their English equivalents. The classifier "shuāng" in Chinese, which follows the construction "X + shuāng + N", indicates a definite number of quantified objects. After searching for the construction "X + shuāng + N" in three Chinese-English bilingual parallel corpora (including the CCL Chinese-English bilingual corpus, the Chinese-English parallel corpus of the Four Great Classical Novels, and the Chinese-English bilingual parallel corpus of Lu Xun's novels), 147 pairs of Chinese-English correspondences were identified [7]. Among these, 61 pairs show that "X + shuāng + N" corresponds to "X + pair of + N" in English, as demonstrated in the following sentence examples.

(1) "shuāng guài yǎn sì míng xīng, liǎng ěr guò jiān chá yòu yìng."
   His devil eyes shone like stars. His ears were long and hard. (Chapter 4 of *Journey to the West*).

(2) "Zhèng shuō zhe, zhī jiàn yī gè xiǎo yā tóu duān le yī gè chá pán ér, yī gè wǎn, yī shuāng yá zhù, dì gěi shè yuè dào: "zhè shì gāng cái huā gū niáng yào de, chú fáng lǐ lǎo pó zǐ sòng le lái le."
   While they were talking a young maid had brought in a saucer, bowl and pair of chopsticks, which she handed to Sheyue saying: "Just now Miss Xiren asked for these, and the old woman from the kitchen has brought them." (Chapter 89 of *A Dream of Red Mansions*).

(3) "Sān cáng děng huí tóu guān kàn, jiàn nà dà xiān, yáo yáo bǎi bǎi, hòu dài zhe yī shuāng yā jì péng tóu de xiǎo tóng ér, wǎng lǐ zhí jìn."
   Sanzang and his disciples turned round to look and saw the three Great Immortals come majestically in, followed by a pair of page boys with their hair in bunches. They walked straight in. (Chapter 45 of *Journey to the West*).

In addition, after reviewing six Chinese-English Learner's Dictionaries (hereafter referred to as CELDs) for non-native speakers, it was observed that all dictionaries define

---

[1] The term "classifier" is used here for ease of exposition, with the awareness that it does not really function like typical Chinese classifiers, an issue not at the center of this paper.

the classifier "shuāng" using "pair" or "pair of" (see Sect. 5 for details). While data from both bilingual corpora and CELDs suggest that "shuāng" generally corresponds to the English classifier "pair," the degree of equivalence between these two terms remains uncertain. Is the use of "pair" or "pair of" in CELDs truly supported by empirical linguistic evidence? Addressing this question requires a focused contrastive analysis, which has yet to be thoroughly explored.

To fill this gap, the present study draws on linguistic data from Modern Chinese Corpus of Chinese Language Commission and Corpus of Global Web-based English (hereafter referred to as GloWbE). Drawing on construction grammar and collostructional analysis, this study compares the semantic distributions, collostructional categorization mechanisms, and constructional meanings of "X + shuāng + N" and "X + pair of + N. Based on these findings, the study offers targeted recommendations to refine the definition of the classifier "shuāng" in CELDs.

2 Research Design

2.1 Research Questions

This study addresses the following key questions:

1) What are the similarities and differences in the semantic distributions of nouns between "X + shuāng + N" and "X + pair of + N"?
2) How do the collostructional categorization mechanisms of "X + shuāng + N" differ from those of "X + pair of + N"?
3) What are the prototypical meanings of "X + shuāng + N" and "X + pair of + N," and in what ways do these meanings align or diverge?
4) What are the implications of these findings for refining the definition of the classifier "shuāng" in CELDs?

2.2 Theoretical Foundation

The primary function of a classifier is to quantify objects, which is determined not by the classifier in isolation but by its co-occurrence with other lexical units at the syntagmatic level. In Chinese, the most common classifier construction is "X + classifier + noun," whereas in English, it is typically structured as "article/numeral + N1 + of + material nouns/plural nouns". Understanding the use of classifiers in both languages requires an exploration of their constructions and collocations. Hence, this contrastive study employs construction grammar as its theoretical foundation.

Construction Grammar, one of the core theories in cognitive linguistics, emerged in the late 1980s through the seminal work of scholars like Kay and Fillmore [8]. These scholars investigated idiomatic expressions and developed Construction Grammar in response to critiques of generative grammar and its limitations in explaining non-compositional language phenomena. According to Goldberg[9, 10], constructions are the fundamental units of language, defined as form-meaning pairings that can range from fully idiomatic and non-compositional patterns to more schematic and compositional ones. While Construction Grammar often emphasizes non-transparent constructions, it also accommodates compositional patterns that occur frequently and exhibit systematic associations between form and meaning. Importantly, the lexical slots of constructions are partially open, allowing certain qualified lexical items to fill them.

2.3 Research Method

This study adopts the collostructional analysis method, introduced by Stefanowitsch & Gries [11], which is rooted in construction grammar and follows a bottom-up approach. By calculating collostructional strengths between the lexical items in the open slot of the construction and the construction, the semantic distributions and categorization mechanisms can be investigated. This process facilitates a detailed analysis of each construction. For example, in "X + shuāng + N," the lexical items in the N-slot that exhibit significant collostructional strength with the construction suggest semantic congruity. When these lexical items display semantic clustering, the categorization mechanisms and meanings of the construction can be explored.

Three specific approaches are encompassed within collostructional analysis: collexeme analysis, multiple distinctive collexeme analysis, and co-varying collexeme analysis [11]. The collexeme analysis examines the relationship between lexical items and their construction to uncover semantic features. The multiple distinctive collexeme analysis compares collostructional patterns across near-synonymous constructions, while the co-varying collexeme analysis investigates correlations between lexical items across different slots within a single construction. This study focuses on the collexeme analysis, as it provides a clear contrast between "X + shuāng + N" and "X + pair of + N" in relation to nouns. The other approaches are not used because they either filter out similarities or focus on different slots within the same construction, which is outside the scope of this research.

2.4 Data Collection and Treatment

The linguistic data for this study were sourced from Modern Chinese Corpus of Chinese Language Commission and GloWbE. The Modern Chinese Corpus contains approximately 100 million characters and is representative of a wide variety of text types. The GloWbE includes around 1.9 billion words from English texts across 20 countries.

By searching "X + shuāng + N" and "X + pair of + N" within these corpora, 485 lexical items were identified for "X + shuāng + N" and 9,879 for "X + pair of + N". To ensure consistency and reliability, the 50 most frequent nouns in each construction were selected for analysis. These were input into the R software program, and the script Coll.analysis 3.2 [14] was used to compute collostructional strength values. These values reveal whether a noun is significantly attracted to or repelled by a given construction. The relationships between collostructional strengths and statistical p-values are classified as follows:

Coll.strength > 1.30103 ≥ p < 0.05: significant;
Coll.strength > 2 ≥ p < 0.01: very significant;
Coll.strength > 3 ≥ p < 0.001: highly significant.

When the collostructional strength exceeds 1.30103, a significant correlation exists between a lexical item and its construction. Higher collostructional strength values indicate stronger correlations (Table 1).

Table 1. Contingency table for the collostructional analysis of "X + shuāng + N" and "yǎn jīng"

Constructions	yǎn jīng	¬ yǎn jīng	Total
"X + shuāng + N"	139	346	485
¬"X + shuāng + N"	2777	12838854	12841631
Total	2916	12839200	12842116

3 The Contrastive Collostructional Study of "X + Shuāng + N" and "X + Pair of + N"

3.1 Results of the Collostructional Analysis

Following the calculation of the top 50 nouns in "X + shuāng + N" and "X + pair of + N," it was found that 35 nouns showed significant attraction correlations with "X + shuāng + N," and 50 nouns were significantly attracted to "X + pair of + N". Table 2 presents the top 10 words in each construction, ranked by collostructional strengths.

Table 2. Top 10 collostructional nouns in "X + shuāng + N" and "X + pair of + N"

No	"X + shuāng + N"		"X + pair of + N"	
	Words	Coll.strength	Words	Coll.strength
1	yǎn jīng (eyes)	Inf	shoes	Inf
2	xié (shoes)	Inf	tickets	Inf
3	shǒu (hands)	118.992643	jeans	Inf
4	dà yǎn (big eyes)	35.255328	scissors	Inf
5	wà zǐ (socks)	34.757288	boots	Inf
6	kuài zǐ (chopsticks)	33.164025	glasses	Inf
7	jiǎo (feet)	29.977468	socks	Inf
8	ér nǚ (children)	23.697525	binoculars	Inf
9	xiǎo jiǎo (small feet)	15.502246	shorts	Inf
10	yǎn guāng (vision)	13.379327	pants	Inf

The collostructional analysis revealed more differences than similarities between the nouns in "X + shuāng + N" and "X + pair of + N". As shown in Table 2, only "xié" (shoes) and "wà zǐ" (socks) appear in both lists.

According to the principle of semantic congruity, the nouns most strongly associated with a construction are considered the most representative of that construction's meaning [6]. The semantic features of the collostructional nouns in these constructions were analyzed to investigate the semantic distributions, categorization mechanisms, and constructional meanings of "X + shuāng + N" and "X + pair of + N". Following the methodology of the study "X + shuāng/duì/fù + N" [15], the semantic features of nouns were divided into four categories: biological features (body parts, persons, animals, and body-related objects), quantitative features (oneness, binary, and pluralism), aggregate features (discreteness and aggregate), and equivalent features (homogeneity and heterogeneity).

Both Chinese and English collective classifiers quantify objects by distinguishing between oneness (treated as a whole), binary (two members), and pluralism (multiple members). They also differentiate homogeneous and heterogeneous members within the quantified scope. While discreteness and aggregate differences exist in this scope, their influence on this study's results is minimal.

In the collostructional analysis of "X + shuāng + N," nouns were categorized based on biological features into four groups: body parts, body-related objects, persons, and non-body-related objects. These biological features formed the basis for the contrastive study, which was further supplemented by analyses of quantitative and equivalent features. Table 3 summarizes the semantic features and distributions of nouns in both constructions.

Table 3. Semantic features and distributions of nouns in "X + shuāng + N" and "X + pair of + N"

Constructions		"X + shuāng + N"	"X + pair of + N"
Biological Features	Body Parts (%)	51.43%	8.00%
	Body-Related Objects (%)	31.43%	60.00%
	Persons (%)	14.29%	8.00%
	Non-Body-Related Objects (%)	2.86%	24.00%
Quantitative Features	Oneness (%)	0	32.00%
	Binary (%)	100.00%	68.00%
	Pluralism (%)	0	0
Equivalent Features	Homogeneity (%)	94.29%	100.00%
	Heterogeneity (%)	5.71%	0

According to Table 3, the collostructional nouns in "X + shuāng + N" and "X + pair of + N" exhibit general similarities in quantitative and equivalent features, but they differ markedly in biological features. Specifically, the category of body parts (51.43%) plays the most prominent role in "X + shuāng + N" nouns (e.g., "yī shuāng yǎn jīng" [a pair of eyes]). Additionally, "X + shuāng + N" frequently collocates with body-related objects (31.43%) (e.g., "yī shuāng xié" [a pair of shoes]), but it rarely co-occurs with persons (14.29%) (e.g., "yī shuāng ér nǚ" [a pair of children]) or non-body-related objects (2.86%) (e.g., "yī shuāng máo wū" [a pair of huts]).

Most of the nouns in "X + shuāng + N" are binary (100%) entities (e.g., "yī shuāng kuài zǐ" [a pair of chopsticks]), and the homogeneity feature (94.29%) (e.g., "yī shuāng wà zǐ" [a pair of socks]) is far more dominant than the heterogeneity feature (5.71%) (e.g., "yī shuāng ér nǚ" [a pair of children]). In the similar sense, "X + pair of + N" similarly collocates with binary (68.00%) and homogeneous (100.00%) entities (e.g., "a pair of shoes"). In terms of biological features, "X + pair of + N" most often collocates with body-related objects (60.0%) (e.g., "a pair of boots"), and frequently with non-body-related objects (24.0%) (e.g., "a pair of tickets"). Fewer instances are found with body parts (8.00%) (e.g., "a pair of eyes") or persons (8.00%) (e.g., "a pair of brothers").

3.2 Collostructional Categorization Mechanism of "X + Shuāng + N"

The grammatical meaning of many Chinese classifiers is closely linked to their original verbal or nominal forms [17]. Thus, it is essential to trace their etymological roots when studying classifiers. The simplified form of "shuāng" (双) is derived from the traditional character (雙), which is ideographic. According to *Shuowen Jiezi*, "shuāng" originally referred to "two birds" [18], combining the components for "bird" (zhuī) and "hand" (yòu). As a result, "shuāng" was initially associated with binary and homogeneous biological organisms.

As shown in Table 3, the nouns in "X + shuāng + N" fall into the following categories in descending order: body parts > body-related objects > persons > non-body-related objects. Body parts rank first, realized through metonymy and metaphor based on the etymological meaning of "two birds". For instance, the extension from "two birds" to "yī shuāng yǎn jīng" (a pair of eyes) involves whole-for-part metonymy and metaphorical mapping in terms of quantity and homogeneity. Similarly, body-related objects are extended in the same way. For example, the shift from "yī shuāng shǒu" (a pair of hands)

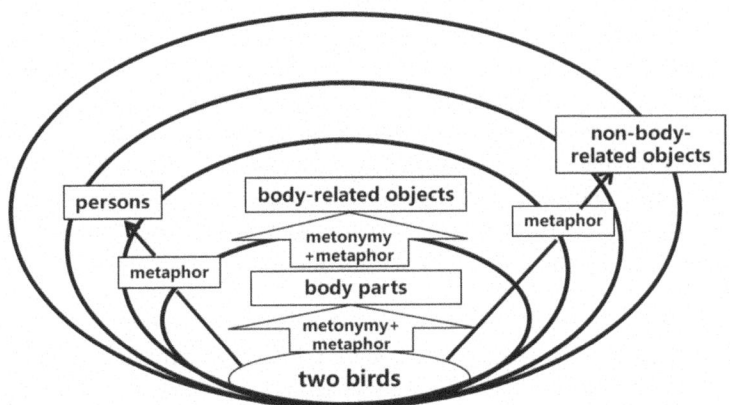

Fig. 1. Collostructional categorization mechanism of "X + shuāng + N"

to "yī shuāng shǒu tào" (a pair of gloves) is not only based on whole-for-part metonymy but also metaphorical mapping in quantity and homogeneity. The next category includes personal nouns, extended through metaphorical mapping in quantity. It is important to note that this category introduces some variability in homogeneity. For instance, in "yī shuāng ér nǚ" (a pair of children), the words "ér" (son) and "nǚ" (daughter) are heterogeneous in a conceptual sense. The lowest frequency occurs in non-body-related objects, with only one instance, "máo wū". Here, the extension is purely metaphorical, based on quantity. According to the principle of semantic congruity, the prototypical meaning of "X + shuāng + N" is to measure binary and homogeneous body parts or body-related objects. See Fig. 1 for the collostructional categorization mechanism of "X + shuāng + N".

3.3   Collostructional Categorization Mechanism of "X + Pair of + N"

According to the Online Etymology Dictionary [18], the word "pair" first appeared in the mid-13th century, originally meaning "a set of two, two of a pair, or a couple in use." It derives from the Old French word "pair", directly coming from the Medieval Latin word "paria" which means "equals". "Paria" is the neutral plural form of "par", which means "a pair, counterpart, equal" and is the noun usage of the adjective "par" ("equal, equal-sized, well-matched"). "Pair" is originally associated with two homogeneous or paired objects, with binary, homogeneity, and abiotic features.

According to Table 3, categories of nouns in "X + pair of + N" are in the order of body-related objects > non-body-related objects > persons = body parts. Body-related objects rank first. The extension is realized owing to the metaphorical mechanism based on the etymological meaning of "a set of two". Taking "a pair of shoes" as an example, the mapping from "a set of two" to "a pair of shoes" is based on the metaphorical mapping in quantity between the two. It is worth noting that the etymological meaning of "pair" has no direct connection with body parts, but body-related objects rank as the category with the highest frequency. The extension is realized without the metonymy (body parts → body-related objects). In fact, it is because body-related objects, which are closely related with body parts, often show homogeneous and binary features of the latter, which are just in accordance with the abiotic, binary and homogeneity features of the etymological meaning of "pair". What follow are non-body-related objects, to which are extended from body-related objects by means of the metaphorical mechanism. Taking "a pair of tickets" as an example, the extension from "a pair of shoes" to "a pair of tickets" is owing to the metaphorical mapping in abiotic, binary and homogeneity features. The nouns with lower frequency are persons, which are realized by means of the metaphorical mapping in quantity and homogeneity, such as "a pair of twins". The nouns with the lowest frequency are body parts, which are realized on the basis of persons by the means of the mechanisms of metonymy and metaphor. Taking "a pair of hands" as an example, the extension from "a pair of twins" to "a pair of hands" is not only owing to the whole-for-part metonymy, but also to the metaphorical mapping in quantity and homogeneity. According to the principle of semantic congruity, the prototypical meaning of "X + pair of + N" is to measure binary and homogeneous body-related or non-body-related objects. See Fig. 2 for the collostructional categorization mechanism of "X + pair of + N".

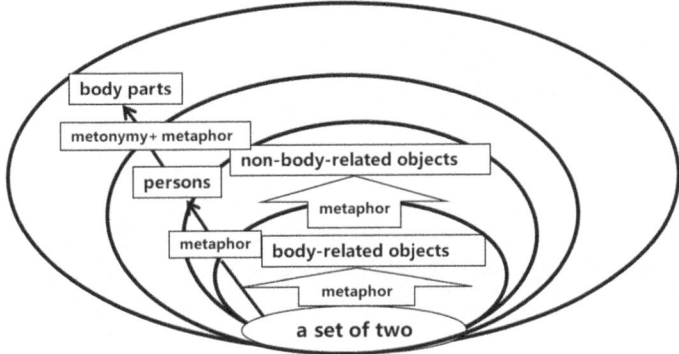

Fig. 2. Collostructional categorization mechanism of "X + pair of + N"

4   Discussion

Based on the above findings, the nouns in "X + shuāng + N" and "X + pair of + N" exhibit more differences than similarities. In terms of collostructional strengths, the categorization of nouns follows the sequence: body parts > body-related objects > persons > non-body-related objects in "X + shuāng + N", while in "X + pair of + N", the order is body-related objects > non-body-related objects > persons = body parts. The two constructions employ distinct cognitive mechanisms for collostructional categorization. The categorization mechanism for "X + shuāng + N" involves metonymy + metaphor, metonymy + metaphor, metaphor, and metaphor, whereas for "X + pair of + N", the pattern includes metaphor, metaphor, metaphor, and metonymy + metaphor. The prototypical meaning of "X + shuāng + N" is primarily concerned with quantifying binary and homogeneous body parts or body-related objects, while the prototypical meaning of "X + pair of + N" is focused on quantifying binary and homogeneous body-related or non-body-related objects. The following analysis delves into the underlying reasons for these differences.

1) Difference in etymological features
   The etymological difference between the classifiers "shuāng" and "pair" regarding their biological attributes contributes to their distinctions in collostructional nouns. The etymology of "shuāng" emphasizes biological characteristics, leading to its frequent collocations with nouns for body parts. In contrast, "pair" lacks this biological attribute and is more often collocated with body-related objects or non-body-related objects. This etymological difference gives rise to different prototypical meanings between "X + shuāng + N" and "X + pair of + N". Therefore, etymological features play a crucial role in shaping the semantic categories of classifiers.

2) Difference in cognitive patterns
   Differences in cognitive patterns between Chinese and English speakers shape distinct categorization mechanisms in "X + shuāng + N" and "X + pair of + N". Chinese pattern tends to rely more on metonymy, favoring concrete imagery, while English pattern rarely employs metonymy, instead favoring a single metaphorical model and

abstract concepts. These cognitive differences highlight the unique ways in which the two languages conceptualize the world.

3) Difference in grammatical roles

Through the contrastive collostructional analysis, it is found that the collocations of "X + shuāng + N" is typically limited to specific, tangible and paired body-related objects, such as "yǎn jīng"(eyes) and "shǒu"(hands), emphasizing symmetry and uniformity. On the other hand, "X + pair of + N" is more semantically flexible, its collocations covering both body-related and non-body-related objects. This difference may stem from the core grammatical role that classifiers play in Chinese compared to their auxiliary function in English. In Chinese, classifiers are a central grammatical component, and their collocation with nouns is integral to sentence meaning. In English, although classifiers are important, they mainly serve an auxiliary role, providing additional information rather than the core meaning of the sentence. The grammatical role difference leads to different patterns of classifier usage between the two languages.

Through the above analysis, it is explored that differences in etymological features, cognitive patterns, and grammatical roles contribute to the differences in classifier usage, shaping the collostructional differences between "X + shuāng + N" and "X + pair of + N". Both "shuāng" and "pair" originally denotes two identical objects, and through lexical evolution, both have come to quantify multiple objects as a collection. Thus, the similarities between "X + shuāng + N" and "X + pair of + N" lie in their shared etymological roots of expressing quantity, accommodating duality and homogeneity. The differences, however, emerge in the specific collostructional nouns, categorization mechanisms, and prototypical meanings, which are rooted in the differences in etymological features, cognitive patterns, and grammatical roles. These differences also have implications for the definitions of classifiers in dictionaries, which will be explored in the following section.

5 Implications for the Definition of the Classifier "Shuāng" in CELDs

In essence, any bilingual dictionary is an exercise in contrastive lexicology [20]. As the core of any dictionary, the definition forms the foundation of an entry. Based on the contrastive findings, this section examines the definition of the classifier "shuāng" in CELDs for non-native speakers. First, the definitions of "shuāng" in six CELDs published in the 21st century are summarized in Table 4. These dictionaries include CCED (*A Concise Chinese-English Dictionary [Revised Edition]*) [21], ABC (*ABC Chinese-English Comprehensive Dictionary*) [22], CED (*A Chinese-English Dictionary*) [23], CEDFL (*A Chinese-English Dictionary for Foreign Learners*) [24], CED (C-E) (*Chinese Essential Dictionary [Chinese-English]*) [25], and the mobile APP *PLECO*.

All six CELDs provide "pair" as the English equivalent for the classifier "shuāng". Specifically, CED includes a Chinese description of the quantified objects, while CED (C-E) specifies that "shuāng" is a unit word for shoes. PLECO offers more detailed

Table 4. Definitions of the classifier "shuāng" in CELDs

词典	表征模式
CCED	[量]❶pair
ABC	M. pair
CED	< 量 > 用于左右对称的或成对的东西 pair
CEDFL	< 量 > pair
CED (C-E)	unit word for shoes pair of
PLECO	MEASURE WORD [for shoes, socks, chopsticks, etc.] pair

descriptions, specifying the objects involved ("for shoes, socks, chopsticks, etc."). However, CCED, ABC, and CEDFL simply use the English equivalent "pair" without further explanation of the quantified objects, which might lead dictionary users to equate "shuāng" with "pair" in an overly simplistic way. As demonstrated by the contrastive study, significant differences exist between nouns in "X + shuāng + N" and "X + pair of + N". Therefore, three suggestions are made to optimize the definition of "shuāng" in CELDs:

1) Given the differences in the semantic categories of nouns between "X + shuāng + N" and "X + pair of + N," CELDs should not merely provide the English equivalent "pair," but also make clear the collostructional categories associated with the classifier "shuāng."
2) The collostructional information for "shuāng" should be organized according to cognitive mechanisms, which will assist dictionary users in better understanding the connection between semantic categories and enable them to grasp the collostructional features of "shuāng" more effectively.
3) The meaning of "shuāng" should be placed within its construction. The constructional form and prototypical meaning should guide the entry to convey comprehensive usage information to dictionary users. The definition of "shuāng" is re-written according to these three recommendations (no dictionary examples are provided here as they were not discussed in the study) (Fig. 3).

In this revised entry, the constructional form and prototypical meaning of "shuāng" serve as a guide to help dictionary users understand the usage of the construction. The senses are organized and listed according to collostructional categories and cognitive mechanisms, establishing connections between categories for the users. Each sense is accompanied by its corresponding semantic categories and frequent collocations.

 <量 meas.> pair

（X+双+N）对二元、同质性身体部位或体关联物进行表量

to measure binary and homogeneous body parts or body-related objects

<1> 用于身体部位（眼睛/手/脚/翅膀等）for body parts

<2> 用于体关联物（鞋/袜子/筷子等）for body-related objects

Fig. 3. The re-written entry for the classifier "shuāng" in CELDs

6   Conclusion

The contrastive study between Chinese and English classifiers provides valuable insights into the differences in how each language conceptualizes the quantification of objects. By utilizing construction grammar as the theoretical foundation and employing collostructional analysis as the method, this study examines the collostructional features of "X + shuāng + N" and "X + pair of + N". The findings reveal that, while the collostructional nouns of "X + shuāng + N" and "X + pair of + N" share similarities in quantitative and equivalent features, they differ significantly in terms of biological features. For "X + shuāng + N", the order of collostructional strength is body parts > body-related objects > persons > non-body-related objects, whereas for "X + pair of + N", it is body-related objects > non-body-related objects > persons = body parts. There are distinct differences in the collostructional categorization mechanisms between "X + shuāng + N" and "X + pair of + N". The categorization mechanism for "X + shuāng + N" involves metonymy + metaphor, metonymy + metaphor, metaphor, metaphor, while "X + pair of + N" follows a different pattern, involving metaphor, metaphor, metaphor, metonymy + metaphor. The prototypical meaning of "X + shuāng + N" is to quantify binary and homogeneous body parts or body-related objects, whereas for "X + pair of + N" it is to quantify binary and homogeneous body-related or non-body-related objects. The need to quantify objects drives the functions of both "shuāng" and "pair". However, the differences in etymological features, cognitive patterns, and grammatical roles are the primary factors responsible for the divergence in their collostructional features. Based on the contrastive findings, finally, three suggestions are put forward to optimize the definition of the classifier "shuāng" in CELDs for non-natives.

Acknowledgements. This work is supported by Chongqing Municipal Education Commission (Grant No. CYB23273).

References

1. Yuzhi, S.: The cognitive foundations of the shape based classifiers in modern Chinese. Lang. Teach. Res. **01**, 34–41 (2001)
2. Huanxian, Y., Ping, H.: The dictionary of common modern Chinese classifiers. Shandong University Press, Jinan (1991)
3. Xianzhen, G.: Handbook of modern Chinese classifiers. China Peace Publishing House, Beijing (1987)
4. Xingjian, L.: Standardized dictionary of modern Chinese classifiers. Hebei Education Press, Shijiazhuang (2010)
5. Shengshu, D., Shuxiang, L., Rong, L., et al.: Grammatical Speech of Modern Chinese, 2nd edn. Commercial Press, Beijing (2009)
6. Shiyou, W., Xiuyun, M.: Chinese and Chinese teaching. Chinese Language Teaching Press, Beijing (2012)
7. Zeng, L.: The collostruction-based definition model of chinese collective classifiers "Bǎ" and "Shuāng" in language-specific Chinese-English learner's dictionaries. [Master's thesis, Southwest University of Science and Technology] (2021)
8. Kay, P., Fillmore, C.J.: Grammatical constructions and linguistic generalizations: The what's X Doing Y? Construction. Language **75**(1), 1–33 (1999)
9. Goldberg, A.: Constructions: a construction approach to argument structure. University of Chicago Press, Chicago (1995)
10. Goldberg, A.: Construction at work. The nature of generalization in language. Oxford University Press, New York (2006)
11. Stefanowitsch, A., Gries, S.: Collostructions: investigating the interaction between words and constructions. Int. J. Corpus Linguist. **8**(2), 209–243 (2003)
12. Gries, S.T., Stefanowitsch, A.: Extending collostructional analysis: a corpus-based perspective on "alternations." Int. J. Corpus Linguist. **9**(1), 97–129 (2004)
13. Gries, S.T., Stefanowitsch, A.: Co-varying collexemes in the into-causativ. In: Michel, A., Kemmer, S. (eds.) Language, culture, and mind, pp. 225–236. CSLI, Stanford (2004)
14. Gries, S.: Coll. analysis 3.2a. A Program for R for Windows 2.x (2007)
15. Gries, S., Hampe, B., Schönefeld, D.: Converging evidence II: more on the association of verbs and constructions. In: Rice, S., Newman, J. (eds.) Empirical and experimental methods in cognitive functional research, pp. 59–72. CSLI, Stanford (2010)
16. Jinhai, W., Xiugui, Q., Xiaoli, Y.: An empirical comparative study of the intricate categorization of "X shuang/dui/fu N" classifer constructions. J. Foreign Lang. Inst. PLA **45**(04), 43–51 (2022)
17. Wang, L.: Historical manuscript of Chinese (part II). Zhonghua Book Company, Beijing (1980)
18. Xu, S.: Shuowen Jiezi. Zhonghua Book Company, Beijing (1963)
19. Online Etymology Dictionary. (n.d.). Pair. Retrieved November 23, 2023, from https://www.etymonline.com/word/pair
20. Tomaszczyk, J.: On bilingual dictionaries: the case for bilingual dictionaries for foreign language learners. In: Hartmann, R.R.K. (ed.) Lexicography: principles and practice. Academic Press, London (1983)
21. Compiling Group of A Concise Chinese-English Dictionary: A concise Chinese-English dictionary. Commercial Press, Beijing (2002)
22. DeFrancis, J.: ABC Chinese-English comprehensive dictionary. Chinese Dictionary Press, Shanghai (2003)
23. Wang, X., Yao, N.: A Chinese-English bilingual dictionary. Foreign Languages Press, Beijing (2007)

24. Compilation Group of Chinese-English Dictionary for Foreign Learners: Chinese-English dictionary for foreign learners. Shanghai Translation Publishing House Press, Shanghai (2008)
25. Dingou, Z.: Chinese essential dictionary (Chinese-English). Beijing Language and Culture University Press, Beijing (2017)

Comparative Analysis of Cross-Linguistic Semantic Elements and Lexicalization Patterns: A Case Study of Chinese and English *Lāchě* Verbs

Jia Yi[⊠]

Department of Chinese Language and Literature, School of Humanities and Social Sciences, Tsinghua University, Beijing100084, China
Yij21@mails.tsinghua.edu.cn

Abstract. Different languages often employ distinct strategies to encode the same concept, leading to variations in lexicalization patterns based on which semantic elements are combined. The semantic elements of "*lāchě*" verbs include actions, tools, directions, manners and degrees. Chinese and English display different lexicalization strategies for expressing the concept of "pulling". This paper focuses on verbs that convey the meaning of "pulling" in both Chinese and English, using "semantic component patterns" as the analytical framework. By referencing dictionary definitions, examining language use in context, refining definitions, and identifying semantic elements, this study compares the semantic components and lexicalization patterns between the two languages. It further investigates the similarities and differences in word meanings and lexicalization strategies within verb clusters that express the same semantic field in both languages.

Keywords: Semantic Elements · Lexicalization Patterns · *lāchě* · Verbs

1 Introduction

Different languages often employ distinct methods to encode the same concept, and there are varying choices regarding which semantic elements to package into a word, resulting in different lexicalization patterns. Talmy [1] decomposes displacement events into six semantic elements; however, other semantic categories beyond displacement events can also be broken down into distinct semantic components. The action of pulling or tugging, for instance, can be divided into several semantic elements, such as tool, direction, force, manner and object. In English, specific relational objects involved in pulling actions are often encapsulated in single words, such as "tow". However, in modern Chinese, there is no equivalent single word to express this concept. Instead, phrases like "*yòng shéngsuǒ huò liàntiáo tuōlā chē huò chuán*(用绳索或链条拖拉车或船, to tow a cart or boat with a rope or chain)" must be used to convey it.

The comparative analysis of cross-linguistic word meanings is a significant aspect of lexicology, with word-meaning comparisons primarily grounded in semantic analysis. Various approaches have been explored in academia for analyzing word meanings, among which the componential analysis method is particularly prominent. Recent developments in lexical typology focus on the unique ways different languages package semantic material into words. In the 1990s, Fu H.Q. introduced the "Semantic Component–Semantic Structure Pattern" analysis method (hereafter referred to as "Semantic Component Pattern") [2]. Although this method was inspired by componential analysis, it differs in key aspects. The "Semantic Component Pattern" approach posits that word meanings are ultimately expressed through expansive lexical items (commonly known as explanatory statements). Semantic analysis can use a specific meaning pattern as a basic framework to identify semantic components and patterns from the explanatory lexical items that interpret the meaning of a word.

"Lāchě(拉扯,pull)" Verbs are a subcategory of hand-related verbs in Modern Chinese, referring to verbs in which the agent applies a certain horizontal force to an object, causing the object to move. The actions of pulling or tugging constitute a crucial aspect of commonly used verbs, and many of these actions are challenging for learners due to their similar meanings and minimal differences. Previous research on "lāchě" verbs has yielded some findings, though most studies have focused on them within the broader category of hand-related verbs [3, 4]. Research specifically on "lāchě" verbs as a distinct category is less common, with a few notable exceptions [5, 6]. Additionally, there have been analyses of individual cases of "lāchě" verbs [7, 8]. Overall, these studies encompass diachronic research on the semantic evolution of "lāchě" verbs in Chinese, as well as synchronic analyses of the distributional shift of "lāchě" verbs from hand actions to mouth actions. However, studies focusing on "lāchě" verbs from the perspective of cross-linguistic semantic comparison and lexicalization pattern analysis have not yet been explored.

Therefore, this paper focuses on Chinese and English "lāchě" verbs and employs the "Semantic Component Pattern" method to conduct a comparative analysis of word meanings. By examining dictionary definitions and actual language usage, the study aims to identify semantic components. It further compares these semantic components and lexicalization patterns, analyzing the similarities and differences in the meanings of word clusters that express the semantic theme of "lāchě" in both languages.

2   Key Points in the Cross-Linguistic Comparative Analysis of Action-Related Verbs

Fu [9] identifies three key points for analyzing verbs that denote actions: (1) using the "semantic component pattern" of action verbs as an analytical framework; (2) comparing definitions from various dictionaries and examining language use to determine semantic components; and (3) selecting appropriate methods of definition to construct a semantic component model. Following the above steps, the final stage involves comparing the semantic component patterns of different languages, exploring the similarities and differences between word clusters that express the same semantic theme in various languages.

The "Semantic Component Pattern" method uses expanded word definitions (i.e., explanatory statements) as the object of study. However, many action-related verbs exhibit considerable complexity and often convey multiple meanings. Thus, both Chinese and English dictionaries tend to prioritize simplicity and clarity in their definitions, often only escribing a portion of the characteristics denoted by the verb. Because dictionaries aim for brevity, some implicit details are naturally omitted. As a result, dictionary definitions often fail to reach the level of precision required for in-depth semantic analysis. Fu [10] suggests that "comparing the definitions from different dictionaries, identifying their commonalities and distinctions, is beneficial for research in both definition theory and semantics." Therefore, we selected *The Contemporary Chinese Dictionary* (7th edition) (hereafter "*Xianhan*") [11], *The Grand Chinese Dictionary* (hereafter "*Dacidian*") [12], *The Learner's Dictionary of Modern Chinese* (hereafter "*Xuexi*") [13], *Collins Dictionary* (hereafter "*Collins*") [14], *Oxford Advanced Learner's English-Chinese Dictionary* (hereafter "*Oxford*") [15], and *Longman Dictionary of English Language & Culture* (hereafter "*Longman*") [16] as the basis for our research. By comparing definitions across dictionaries and analyzing actual language usage, we aim to determine the semantic content of these verbs and explain their meanings according to the semantic structure patterns of action verbs. It is important to note that, for the sake of comparison, we have standardized the metalanguage for definitions, using Chinese as the metalanguage for both Chinese and English terms.

The following sections will illustrate this analytical method by using specific examples, such as the Chinese verbs "*lā*(拉,pull)" and "*tuō*(拖,drag)":

lā 用力使朝自己所在的方向或跟着自己移动。*(Xianhan).*

To force something to move toward oneself or follow one's movement.

牵挽;牵引。*(Dacidian) Lead; pull.*

用力使物体朝着自己所在的方向或跟着自己移动。*(Xuexi).*

To force an object to move towards oneself or follow one's movement.

tuō 拉着物体使挨着地面或另一物体的表面移动。*(Xianhan).*

To pull an object so that it moves along the surface of the ground or another object.

曳引;拉。*(Dacidian) Tow; pull.*

牵引;拉;拽。*(Xuexi) Pull; drag; tug.*

The definitions provided by the dictionaries above for both verbs are relatively concise. Based on these definitions and actual language use, the following analysis is presented: (1) Action and Result of Action: Most dictionaries describe the action as "*lā*", with *Xianhan* explaining that the result of both actions is "causing movement." Although the wording differs slightly between dictionaries, the result of the actions described by both verbs can be interpreted as "*shǐ yídòng*(使移动, cause to move)".(2) Objects of Action: The dictionary definitions do not provide detailed descriptions of the objects involved in the actions of "*lā*" and "*tuō*". However , based on actual language use, the object of both verbs in various texts can refer to either people or things, as in "*lāzhētā*(拉着他, pulling him)" "*lāchuānglián*(拉窗帘, pull the curtain)"or "*tuōyǐzi*(拖椅子, drag the chair)". However, "*tuō*" rarely appears with a person as the object in texts, and there is a subtle difference in the types of objects each verb applies to.(3) Action Restrictions for *lā*: The definitions explicitly state that "*lā*" involves applying force to move something toward oneself, meaning that direction of force is also a semantic feature of "*lā*".(4) Action Restrictions for "*tuō*": Xianhan clarifies that the action involves movement "*yánzhē dìmiàn huò wùtǐ biǎomiàn*(沿着地面或物体表面,along the ground or the surface of another object)", indicating this as a characteristic of "*tuō*". Based on this analysis, the meanings and lexicalization patterns of these two verbs can be summarized as follows:

lā: yònglì   cháo zìjǐ suǒzài de fāngxiàng   lā   rén/wù,   shǐ yídòng.
用力   朝自己所在的方向   拉   人/物,   使移动。
exert force   towards oneself   pull   sb/sth   cause to move
[Force + Direction + Action]

tuō: yánzhe dìmiàn huò lìng yī wùtǐ de biǎomiàn   lā   rén/wù,   shǐ yídòng.
沿着地面或另一物体的表面   拉   (人)/物,   使移动。
along the ground or the surface of another object   pull   (sb)/sth   cause to move
[Manner + Action]

Similarly, the Chinese "*tuō*" and the English "drag" can be compared as follows:
tuō As defined above.
drag To pull sb/sth along with effort and difficulty.*(Oxford)*.
If you drag sth, you pull it along the ground, often with difficulty.*(Collins)*.
To pull (something heavy) along with great effort.*(Longman)*.

The definitions of "drag" in English dictionaries are generally consistent, indicating that the core action is "pull", and the manner involves moving "along the ground" with significant effort. The usage contexts for "drag" in English closely resemble those for "*tuō*" in Chinese, as both can be used with objects like "chair", "table", or "branch". Thus, the meanings and lexicalization patterns of these two verbs can be summarized as follows:

tuō: As analyzed above: **[Manner + Action]**

drag: yánzhe dìmiàn huò lìng yī wùtǐ de biǎomiàn   yònglì   lā   rén/wù,   shǐ yídòng.
沿着地面或另一物体的表面   用力   拉   人/物,   使移动
along the ground or the surface of another object   with force   pull (sb)/sth
cause to move
[Manner + Force + Action]

The semantic components of words that express the same semantic theme in Chinese and English fluctuate within certain parameters. Different words for the same theme in the two languages contain different semantic components and form distinct lexicalization patterns, which share similarities as well as differences.

3   Analysis of Semantic Components and Lexicalization Patterns of *"Lāchě"* Verbs in Chinese and English

Typical *"lāchě"* verbs refer to those in which the agent applies a certain amount of force to the patient, causing the patient to undergo displacement or a change in state. This study identifies the research subjects based on *A Thesaurus of Modern Chinese* [17] and *the Oxford Study Thesaurus* [18].The common verbs expressing *"lāchě"* in Chinese include: *lā*(拉,pull), *chě*(扯, tear, pull), *tuō*(拖, drag), *zhuài* (拽, tug), *jiū*(揪, grab, pull tightly), *qiān* (牵, lead), *yǐn* (引,draw), *bá*(拔, pluck), *tuī*(推, push), *chōu* (抽, pull out), *bēng* (绷, stretch), *zhé*(折,break), *bāi* (掰, break), *cǎi* (采, pick), *zhāi* (摘, pick), *bāo* (剥, peel), *jiē*(揭, lift, uncover), *sī*(撕, tear, rip). In English, the relevant verbs include: *pull, drag, haul, tow, tug, draw, lug, pluck, push, thrust, stretch, break, pick, peel, shell, tear, rip*. The analysis focuses on individual meanings (semantic units) of these verbs. For polysemous words, only their meanings and usages related to *"lāchě"* are selected. There are 18 common Chinese verbs and 17 common English verbs representing this meaning. In the following discussion, the term "word meaning" specifically refers to the meaning of a semantic unit. Based on the above method, we grouped and analyzed their meanings, revealing that Chinese and English *"lāchě"* verbs can be categorized into the following groups.

3.1   Direction + Action

This category of verbs includes the Chinese words *"lā"*, *"chě"*, *"tuī"* and the English words "pull", "haul", "push", "thrust". These verbs are fundamental members of the semantic field of *"lāchě"*, where the directional aspect of the action is a necessary semantic component. The core characteristic of these verbs is the emphasis on direction, making "direction" the key semantic element that differentiates this group. The lexicalization pattern for these words can be summarized as [Direction + Action]. Through corpus analysis, it becomes clear that both force and direction are crucial elements in distinguishing among these verbs, allowing further division into two subgroups: [Force + Direction + Action] and [Direction + Action]. The lexicalization patterns of these words are analyzed as follows:

"*lā*" and "pull" follow the same pattern:

yònglì	*cháo zìjǐ suǒzài de fāngxiàng*	*lā*	*rén/wù,*	*shǐ yídòng.*
用力	朝自己所在的方向	拉	人/物，	使移动。
exert force	towards oneself	pull	sb/sth	cause to move

[Force + Direction + Action]

"*tuī*" and "push" follow the same pattern:

yònglì	*xiàng wài*	*tuī*	*rén/wù,*	*shǐ yídòng.*
用力	向外	推	人/物，	使移动。
exert force	outward	push	sb/sth	cause to move

[Force + Direction + Action]

haul:	*yìzhí yònglì*	*cháo qián huò xiàng shàng*	*lā*	*rén/wù,*	*shǐ yídòng.*
	一直用力	朝前或向上	拉	人/物，	使移动。
	exert force continuously	forward or upward	pull	sb/sth	cause to move

[Force + Direction + Action]

thrust:	*túrán*	*yònglì*	*xiàng wài*	*tuī*	*rén/wù,*	*shǐ yídòng.*
	突然	用力	向外	推	人/物，	使移动。
	suddenly	exert force	outward	push	sb/sth	cause to move

[Time + Force + Direction + Action]

chě:	*cháo zìjǐ/xiàng shàng/láihuí*	*lā*	*rén/wù.*
	朝自己/向上/来回	拉	人/物。
	towards oneself/ upward/ back and forth	pull	sb/sth

[Direction + Action]

yǐn: cháo zìjǐ suǒzài de fāngxiàng	*lā*	*rén/wù,*	*shǐ yídòng.*
朝自己所在的方向	拉	人/物，	使移动。
towards oneself	pull	sb/sth	cause to move

[Direction + Action]

Although the lexicalization patterns of "*lā*", "*tuī*", "pull", "haul", "push" are identical, their meanings differ. The verbs "*lā*" and "pull" versus "*tuī*" and "push" form antonymic pairs: "*lā*" and "pull" express the feature of pulling toward oneself, with the force directed toward the agent, while "*tuī*" and "push" represent the force moving outward, away from the agent.

The lexicalization patterns of "*lā*" and "pull", as well as "*tuī*" and "push", are completely aligned and can be directly translated between Chinese and English. While these verbs can involve the use of tools (e.g., "*lā*" with vehicles, ropes, sledges, etc., or "*tuī*" with carts), tools are not essential components of their meanings. The consistency of these patterns reflects a close relationship between the two languages in terms of meaning representation.

"Haul" emphasizes the force and direction of the action. Typically, "haul" refers to pulling large or heavy objects forward or upward, such as luggage or furniture, which requires significant effort. Other "*lāchě*" verbs can be applied to various contexts but may not necessitate the sustained force that "haul" implies. This indicates that "haul" has more specific semantic restrictions related to force and direction, whereas Chinese lacks a single word for this meaning, instead relying on a phrase like "*yìzhí yònglì wǎngqián/wǎngshàng lā*(一直用力往前/向上拉, continuously exert force to pull forward/upward)", indicating a lexical gap. "Thrust" differs from "*tuī*" and "push" due to its additional temporal constraint, emphasizing suddenness as a semantic feature. English uses a distinct word to convey this meaning, while Chinese expresses it through the phrase "*tūrán tuī*(突然推,suddenly push)", again pointing to a lexical gap.

Finally, the pattern [Direction + Action] is exclusive to the Chinese words "*chě*" and "*yǐn*". "*Chě*" incorporates additional elements like speed and force, but "direction" remains the distinguishing semantic component. For example, the direction in "*chě*" is not fixed but can vary. "*Chě*" most commonly refers to pulling toward oneself, as in phrases like "*chěyīfu*(扯衣服,pulling clothes)", "*chěgēbo*(扯胳膊,pulling an arm)", or "*chěyūwǎng*(扯渔网,pulling a fishing net)". The upward motion of "*chě*" is akin to pulling out, as in "*chěxiǎomài*(扯小麦,pulling wheat)" or "*chědàcōng*(扯大葱,pulling green onions)". Additionally, in certain contexts, "*chě*" signifies back-and-forth motion, as in playing instruments like the èrhú (a Chinese stringed instrument), e.g., "*chě èrhú*(扯二胡,playing the èrhú)", where the motion involves oscillation rather than a unidirectional pull.

"*Yǐn*", in contrast to "*lā*", typically focuses less on the physical application of force and more on guidance or control. While "*lā*" emphasizes physical pulling or dragging, "*yǐn*" often connotes leading or directing, highlighting a conceptual rather than a physical distinction in force.

3.2　Manner + Action

This group of verbs includes Chinese words "*tuō*", "*qiān*", and the English verb "drag". These verbs are essential members of the "*lāchě*" conceptual domain, where the manner of action is a critical semantic component. The action manner is the primary semantic element distinguishing this group, and their lexicalization pattern can be summarized as [Manner + Action]. However, despite their common emphasis on manner, the specific meanings of these verbs differ. The lexicalization patterns of these words are analyzed as follows:

tuō: As analyzed above: **[Manner + Action]**
drag: As analyzed above:**[Manner + Force + Action]**

qiān: (yòng shéngzi děng)	*liánjiē zài yīqǐ*	*lā*	*rén/wù,*	*shǐ yídòng.*
（用绳子等）	连接在一起	拉	人/物，	使移动。
using a rope or similar object	linked together	pull	sb/sth	cause to move

[(Tool) + Manner + Action]

The meanings of the Chinese word "*tuō*" and the English word "drag" emphasize both the force exerted and the manner of movement, specifically pulling an object along the ground or the surface of another object. In these cases, "manner" serves as the key semantic element that distinguishes these verbs. The lexicalization pattern of these verbs can be summarized as [Action + Force + Manner]. The semantic components of both "*tuō*" and "drag" include force and manner because they are often used to describe the act of dragging heavy or large objects, which typically requires significant force. In Chinese, "*tuō*" is less commonly used with human objects, highlighting a subtle difference in the relational objects of the two verbs. The meaning of "*tuō*" is to cause the object being acted upon to move from its original position, typically while remaining in close contact with the ground or the surface of another object. For example:

(1)看　大门　　的　　福顺　　扯　　起　　她　　的　　胳膊，
Kàn dàmén de Fúshùn chě qǐ tā de gēbo,
Watch gate DE Fushun pull up 3SG DE arm
像　　拖　　一　　条　　狗，　溜　　地　　拉　　去。
Xiàng tuō yī tiáo gǒu, liū de lā qù.
Like drag one CL dog slide DE pull away
Fushun, the gatekeeper, grabbed her arm and dragged her like a dog, pulling her away.

The meaning of the Chinese word "*qiān*" emphasizes the manner of the action, specifically the connection between two entities followed by pulling or guiding. Compared to other "*lāchě*" verbs like "*lā*" and "*chě*", which focus more on direct pulling without stressing the connection between objects, "*qiān*" highlights the idea of linking the agent and the object, causing the object (often a person or an animal) to move in the same direction as the agent. In Chinese, "*qiān*" is typically associated with animate objects, such as "horses, cattle, or dogs", where pulling is used to guide or control the movement of the animal, like leading a horse or cattle. This is a specific usage that differs from other general "*lāchě*" verbs. For example:

(2) 一　个　老头　　牵　　着　　一　　条　　大　　狗　向　　这　边　　走　　来。
Yī gè lǎotóu qiān zhe yī tiáo dà gǒu xiàng zhè biān zǒu lái.
one CL oldman lead ZHE one CL big dog towards this side walk come
An old man is walking this way, leading a big dog.

(3) Lǎonǎinai qiān zhe tā de sūnnǚ qù shàngxué.
老奶奶　牵　着　她　的　孙女　去　上学。
Grandma lead ZHE 3SG DE granddaughter go to school
Grandma is leading her granddaughter to school.

The action of "*qiān*" involves hands, or alternatively, tools such as ropes or chains. In a sentence, the object of "*qiān*" can refer to the entity being led, the part being held, or even the tool used, as in:

(4)琪琪　牵　　着　　爸爸　的　手，　跳　　着　　走。
Qíqí qiān zhe bàba de shǒu, tiào zhe zǒu.
Qiqi lead ZHE father DE hand jump ZHE walk
Qiqi is holding her father's hand, jumping as she walks.

(5)他们　牵　起　羊　颈　上　　的　绳子，
Tāmen qiān qǐ yáng jǐng shàng de shéngzi,
they lead up sheep neck on DE rope
拴　　在　一　棵　小　　树　上。
shuān zài yī kē xiǎo shù shàng.
tie LOC one CL small tree on

They led the rope around the sheep's neck and tied it to a small tree.

3.3 Force + Action

This category includes the Chinese verb "*zhuài*" and the English verbs "draw", "lug", and "tug". These words are core members of the semantic domain of "*lāchě*", where the concept of "force" is an essential element of the meaning, characterizing the action. In other words, "force" is the primary semantic feature that distinguishes these words. The lexical pattern of these words can be summarized as [force + action]. Due to differences in specific meanings, they can be subdivided into three categories, with their respective lexical patterns analyzed as follows:

draw: *qīngqīng* *lā*   *rén/wù,*   *shǐ yídòng.*
  轻轻 拉 人/物， 使移动。
  gently pull sb/sth cause to move
  [force + action]
lug: *yònglì* *lā* *zhòngwù,* *shǐ yídòng.*
  用力 拉 重物， 使移动。
  with force pull heavy object cause to move
  [force + action + specific object]
"*zhuài*" and "tug" follow the same pattern:
  túrán *yònglì* *lā* *rén/wù,* *shǐ yídòng.*
  突然 用力 拉 人/物， 使移动。
  suddenly with force pull sb/sth cause to move
  [speed + force + action]

In this group of words, "draw" emphasizes a light force and a relatively gentle action. English uses a specific word to express this meaning, while Chinese can only convey it through the phrase "*qīngqīngdelā*(轻轻地拉,gently pull)", indicating a lexical gap in Chinese.

Similarly, "lug" involves significant force, and the object being pulled is often something heavy, such as luggage or large furniture, which typically requires considerable strength to move. English has a specific term for this meaning, whereas Chinese relies on phrases like "*yònglì lā*(用力拉,pull with force)" or "*yònglì tuō*(用力拖,drag with force)", reflecting a lexical gap in Chinese.

The Chinese verb "*zhuài*" and the English verb "tug" both emphasize the speed and force of the action, with "force" being the primary distinguishing factor. "*Zhuài*" and "tug" typically refer to pulling something quickly and forcefully, often with a sense of urgency or suddenness.

3.4 Action + Specific Object

This category includes the Chinese verbs "*chōu*" "*bá*" "*cǎi*" "*zhāi*" "*bāo*", and the English verbs "tow" and "pluck". These words are core members of the semantic domain of "*lāchě*", where "specific object" is an essential element of the meaning, showing the characteristics of the action. In other words, "specific object" is the primary semantic feature that distinguishes these words. The lexical pattern of these words can be summarized as [action + specific object]. Due to differences in meaning, there are also distinctions in the tools used and the direction of the action. The lexical patterns of these words are analyzed as follows:

tow: *yòng shéngsuǒ huò liàntiáo   lā   qìchē, chuán huò qīngxíng fēijī,   shǐ yídòng.*
用绳索或链条   拉   汽车、船或轻型飞机，   使移动。
using a rope or chain   pull   car, boat, or light aircraft   cause to move
[Tool + Action + Specific Object]

chōu: *qǔchū   jiā zài zhōngjiān de dōngxi,   shǐ tuōlí yuán fùzhuódiǎn.*
取出   夹在中间的东西，   使脱离原附着点。
take out   the thing trapped in the middle   detach from the original attachment point
[Action + Specific Object]

"*bá*" and "pluck" follow the same pattern:
wǎngwài lā gùdìnghuòyǐncángzàiqítāwùtǐlǐdedōngxi, shǐ tuōlí yuán fùzhuódiǎn.
往外   拉 固定或隐藏在其他物体里的东西，   使脱离原附着点。
outward   pull   the thing fixed or hidden inside another object
detach from the original attachment point
[Direction + Action + Specific Object]

"*cǎi*" and "pick" follow the same pattern:
yòng shǒu   lāchě   zhíwù de huā, guǒ, yè,   shǐ tuōlí yuán fùzhuódiǎn.
用手   拉扯   植物的花、果、叶，   使脱离原附着点。
with hands   pull   the flowers, fruits, or leaves of a plant
detach from the original attachment point
[Action + Specific Object + Result]

zhāi: *yòng shǒu lāchě zhíwù de huā, guǒ, yè huò dài zhe, guà zhe de dōngxi, shǐ tuōlí yuán fùzhuódiǎn.*
用手 拉扯 植物的花、果、叶或戴着、挂着的东西，使脱离原附着点。
with hands   pull   the flowers, fruits, or leaves of a plant or things worn or hung
detach from the original attachment point
[Action + Specific Object + Result]

bāo: *yòng shǒu   lāchě   wùtǐ wàimiàn de pí huò ké,   shǐ líkāi fùzhuóchù.*
用手   拉扯   物体外面的皮或壳，   使离开附着处。
with hands   pull   the outer skin or shell of an object
detach from the original attachment point
[Action + Specific Object + Result]

peel: *yòng dāo děng   lāchě   shuǐguǒ, shūcài děng de pí,   shǐ líkāi fùzhuóchù.*
用刀等   拉扯   水果、蔬菜等的皮，   使离开附着处。
using a knife or similar object   pull   the skin of fruits, vegetables, etc
detach from the original attachment point
[Action + Specific Object + Result]

shell: *yòng shǒu lāchě jiānguǒ, wāndòu děng de wàiké huò fùgàiwù, shǐ líkāi fùzhuóchù.*
用手   拉扯   坚果、豌豆等的外壳或覆盖物，   使离开附着处。
with hands   pull   the shell or covering of nuts, peas, etc
detach from the original attachment point
[Action + Specific Object + Result]

The English verb "tow" refers to pulling or towing a car, boat, or light aircraft using a rope or chain. This word emphasizes not only the tool, such as a rope, but also the specific object, namely a car, boat, or light aircraft. The primary semantic features distinguishing this word are [specific tool + action + specific object]. Compared to "pull", "tow" adds restrictions on both the tool and object. English uses a specific word to express this meaning, while Chinese can only use the phrase "*yòng shéngsuǒ huò liàntiáo tuō/lā/qiānyǐn qìchē, chuán huò qīngxíng fēijī*" to convey it, reflecting a lexical gap.

The meaning of "*chōu*" is to pull out something wedged between other objects, with a focus on the specific object being pulled. Chinese uses a specific word to express this meaning, while English can only use the phrase "take out (from in between)", indicating a lexical gap in English. Both "*bá*" and "pluck" emphasize the specific object and direction, where the object is fixed or hidden within other objects, and the pulling direction is outward.

In Chinese, "*cǎi*" is usually paired with flowers, fruits, or leaves from plants, while "*zhāi*" has a broader range of objects. English combines both into the word "pick". On the other hand, "*bāo*" in Chinese covers a wider range of objects, whereas English uses two different words depending on the object: "peel" (for fruits and vegetables) and "shell" (for nuts, peas, etc.). Although the lexicalization patterns are similar, there are differences in their application to specific objects.

3.5 Action + Result

This category includes the Chinese verbs "*bēng*" "*zhé*" "*bāi*" "*jiē*" "*sī*" and the English verbs "tear" "rip" "break", and "stretch". These words are also core members of the "*lāchě*" semantic domain, where "specific result" is an essential element of the meaning, highlighting the characteristic of the action. In other words, "specific result" is the primary semantic feature distinguishing these words. The lexical pattern of these words can be summarized as [action + specific result]. Due to differences in meaning, there are also distinctions in the tools used and the direction of the action. The lexical patterns of these words are analyzed as follows:

"*bēng*" and "stretch" follow the same pattern:

    yònglì   *lāchě*   *wù,*   ***shǐ jǐn.***

    用力   拉扯   物，   使紧。

    with force   pull   sth   make tight

    [force + action + result]

"*zhé*" and "break" follow the same pattern:

    yònglì   *lāchě*   *wù,*   ***shǐ duàn.***

    用力   拉扯   物，   使断。

    with force   pull   sth   cause to break

    [force + action + result]

bāi: yòngshǒu   *lāchě*   *wù,*   ***shǐ fēnkāi huò zhédiàn.***

    用手   拉扯   物，   使分开或折断。

    with hands   pull   sth   cause to separate or break

    [action + result]

jiē: yòngshǒu lāchě fùzhuó zài wùtǐ shàng de piànzhuàng wù chéng piàn, shǐ líkāi fùzhuóchù.

    用手 拉扯 附着在物体上的片状物成片，使离开附着处。

with hands pull the attached flat piece on the object   detach from the attachment point

    [action + specific object + result]

sī: yòngshǒu lāchě báo piànzhuàng de wùtǐ, shǐ lièkāi huò líkāi fùzhuóchù.

    用手   拉扯 薄片状的物体，   使裂开或离开附着处。

with hands pull the thin, flat object   cause to crack or detach from the attachment point

    [action + specific object + result]

tear: *lāchě*   *báopiànzhuàng de wùtǐ,*   ***shǐ suìliè huò líkāi fùzhuóchù.***

    拉扯   薄片状的物体，   使碎裂或离开附着处。

    pull   the thin, flat object   cause to shatter or detach from the attachment point

    [action + specific object + result]

rip: *túrán*   *yónglì*   *lāchě*   *báo piànzhuàng de wùtǐ,*   ***shǐ suìliè.***

    突然   用力   拉扯   薄片状的物体，   使碎裂。

    suddenly   with force   pull   the thin, flat object   cause to shatter

    [speed + force + action + specific object + result]

The Chinese verbs "*jiē*" and "*sī*" both involve specific objects, such as sheet-like materials. However, the English verb "rip" places additional emphasis on speed and force, which in Chinese would require a phrase like "*túrán yònglì sī*(突然用力撕, suddenly tear with force)" to express, indicating a lexical gap in Chinese.

3.6 Action + Degree

This category includes only the Chinese verb "*jiū*". "*Jiū*" means tightly grabbing, seizing, and pulling. In this verb, "degree" is the primary distinguishing semantic feature, meaning that "degree" is the key element separating it from other verbs. The lexical pattern of this verb can be summarized as [action + degree]. The semantic components of "*jiū*" also include aspects of speed and duration, but these elements do not play a significant role in distinguishing its meaning and are not the main features. Chinese uses a specific word to express this meaning, whereas in English, the phrase "hold tight" is used, indicating a lexical gap in English.

Chinese and English "*lāchě*" verbs can be divided into different categories based on the characteristics of the action. Overall, there are six categories, each with distinct key semantic features.

4 Analysis of Semantic Components and Lexicalization Patterns in Chinese and English "*Lāchě*" Verbs

Below, Tables 1 and 2 respectively summarize the semantic elements and lexical patterns of "*lāchě*" verbs in Chinese and English.

Table 1. Frequency of Key Semantic Elements in Chinese and English "*lāchě*" Verbs

	Tools	Action Restriction					Specific Object	Specific Result
		Speed	Force	Direction	Manner	Degree		
Chinese	(1)	1	6	5	2	1	7	8
English	1	2	11	5	1		8	7

From the above analysis, we can draw the following conclusions:

(1) Pulling actions involve the agent applying a certain level of force to the patient, causing displacement or a change in state. Typically, these actions involve several aspects, including the agent, the action, the result, and action restriction. Action restriction encompass factors such as the speed, force, manner, and direction of the force. For example, compared with the Chinese verb "*tuī*" and the English verb "thrust", the verb "thrust" emphasizes the speed and suddenness of the action, and its meaning includes a restriction on the speed of the action. This results in differences in the semantic components and lexical patterns of the two verbs. While the lexical patterns of "*lāchě*" verbs in Chinese and English are not identical, the semantic elements consistently fit within the following framework: [Agent] + [Tool] + [(Speed, Force, Direction, Manner, Degree) Action Restriction] + [Action] + [Object] + [Result].

(2) The agent, action, and result are the necessary semantic components of "*lāchě*" verbs. Force, direction, object, and result exert the greatest influence on the meaning of these verbs and are the primary elements for their analysis. Both Chinese and English distinguish pulling actions primarily based on these semantic components. Below is a more detailed analysis:

(a) Tools: Pulling actions involve the agent applying force to the patient, often using tools such as vehicles or materials like ropes and chains. Vehicles, such as trucks or tractors, serve as powered tools that enable objects to move (e.g., "*chē lā huòwù*[车拉货物,a car pulls cargo]", where "*lā*" implies transporting). Material tools assist in applying force, as seen in actions like "tow". Chinese does not emphasize the semantic element of "tool" as much as English, where it is highlighted once.

(b) Action Restriction: The action restrictions of "*lāchě*" verbs involve various aspects, including speed, force, manner, and the direction of the applied force.

Table 2. Lexicalization Patterns of "*lāchě*" Verbs in Chinese and English

Lexical Pattern		Chinese	English
Direction + Action	Direction + Action	2	
	Force + Direction + Action	2	3
	Time + Force + Direction + Action		1
Manner + Action	(Tool) + Manner + Action	1	
	Force + Manner + Action	1	1
Force + Action	Force + Action		1
	Force + Action + Specific Object		1
	Speed + Force + Action	1	1
Action + Specific Object	Action + Specific Object	1	
	Tool + Action + Specific Object		1
	Direction + Action + Specific Object	1	1
	Action + Specific Object + Result	5	4
Action + Result	Action + Result	1	
	Force + Action + Result	2	2
	Speed + Force + Action + Specific Object + Result		1
Action + Degree	Action + Degree	1	

Speed: Speed is a crucial semantic element for distinguishing "*lāchě*" verbs in both Chinese and English. There is a relationship between speed, force, and the object being pulled. For example, "*tuō*" and "*drag*" imply slow movement because the object is typically heavy or large, while "*zhuài*" and "*tug*" emphasize sudden, quick actions.

Force: Speed and force are often interconnected—faster pulling actions are often accompanied by greater force, while slower pulling actions may suggest a more relaxed or cautious application of force. Different pulling actions can be distinguished based on the degree of force applied. For instance, in English, verbs like "*haul*" and "*tug*" imply forceful pulling, while "*draw*" suggests gentle pulling, and verbs like "*pull*" and "*pluck*" do not emphasize the magnitude of force. The semantic element of force is highlighted 6 times in Chinese, compared to 11 times in English, where force is emphasized more frequently.

Direction: Direction influences the result of the action. For instance, "*lā*" and "*pull*" usually indicate pulling toward oneself, while "*tuī*" and "*push*" indicate pushing away from the agent. However, the direction of "*chě*" is not fixed; it can be toward oneself, upward, or back and forth, as seen in the phrase "*chě èrhú*", where "*chě*" implies playing a musical instrument. Both Chinese and English highlight the direction of force 5 times.

Manner: The manner of action is also an important semantic feature for distinguishing "*lāchě*" verbs. For instance, "drag" and "*tuō*" characterized by pulling along a surface, while the Chinese verb "*qiān*" emphasizes using tools like ropes or chains to guide or control animate objects.

Degree: Degree is another important semantic feature in Chinese, distinguishing verbs like "*jiū*" which implies tightly grabbing and pulling. English lacks a specific verb that conveys this exact meaning.

(c) Object: Both Chinese and English place significant emphasis on the object being acted upon, often using different verbs to express actions involving different objects. The relationship between the object and factors like force and speed is closely interconnected.

(3) While Chinese and English "*lāchě*" verbs share many semantic elements, the relative importance of each element differs between the two languages. In Chinese, the frequency of highlighted semantic elements follows this order: Specific Result > Specific Object > Force > Direction > Manner > Speed/Degree/Tool. In English, the order is: Force > Specific Object > Specific Result > Direction > Speed > Tool/Manner. This indicates that, in Chinese, specific results are the most important semantic element in the lexicalization of "*lāchě*" verbs, while in English, force takes precedence. Additionally, "degree" is a unique semantic feature in Chinese "*lāchě*" verbs, which is not emphasized in English.

(4) The differences in lexicalization patterns between the two languages reflect varying preferences for packaging certain semantic components into single words. Both Chinese and English exhibit diverse lexical patterns, with both tending to incorporate specific objects into verbs. However, English places greater emphasis on force, as evidenced by the presence of multiple verbs indicating "forceful pulling/pushing" (e.g., haul, thrust, lug, tug).

5 Conclusion

Regarding cross-linguistic semantic comparison, this paper explores the feasibility of using Chinese as a metalanguage and applying the "semantic component-pattern" analysis method. By taking Chinese and English "*lāchě*" verbs as the research object, this study employs the "semantic component pattern" method to conduct a comparative analysis of the verbs' meanings. Through comparing lexical patterns and semantic elements, the analysis identifies the similarities and differences in how the two languages express the semantic theme of "pulling".

The comparison reveals that the two languages make different choices in packaging semantic components. Some concepts are integrated into single words in English, such as "tow", whereas in Chinese, they are expressed through phrases, such as the equivalent phrase for "tow" in Chinese: "*yòng shéngsuǒ huò liàntiáo tuō/lā/qiānyǐn qìchē, chuán huò qīngxíng fēijī*", highlighting a lexical gap.

Furthermore, both languages exhibit diverse lexical patterns. "*Lāchě*" verbs involve restrictions on various aspects, including speed, force, manner, and direction. While both Chinese and English tend to incorporate specific objects into verbs, their choice of prominent semantic elements differs. English places more emphasis on force, but aside from this key distinction, the overall order of importance of semantic elements in both languages is largely consistent, with elements like speed, manner, and tools being of relatively lower importance.

Acknowledgments. This work was supported by the National Social Science Foundation of China (Grant No.23VJXG058 and 23&ZD311).

References

1. Talmy, L.: Lexicalization patterns: semantic structure in lexical forms. In: Shopen, T. (ed.) Language typology and syntactic description, vol. 3, pp. 57–149. Cambridge University Press, New York (1985)
2. Fu, H.Q.: Analysis and description of word meanings. Foreign Language Teaching and Research Press, Beijing (2006). (in Chinese)
3. Lv, Y.H.: Study on the Chinese verbs that indicate the motion of hands based on corpus. Doctoral dissertation, Shandong University (2008). (in Chinese)
4. Dong, Z.C.: The transition from hand actions to mouth actions in the evolution of word meanings. Stud. Chin. Lang. **2**, 180–183 (2009). (in Chinese)
5. Zhang, Y.H.: Semantic evolution of pulling type monosyllable verbs based on the corpus. Doctoral dissertation, Xiangtan University (2017). (in Chinese)
6. Guo, X.N.: Study on the development of lexical systems in conceptual fields of displacement of objects in ancient Chinese language. Doctoral dissertation, Zhejiang University (2010). (in Chinese)
7. Liu, C.Y.: An Exploratory analysis of the causes of negative AABB reduplicated verbs: a case study of "lālāchěchě" and "tiāotiāojiǎnjiǎn." Lexicogr. Stud. **2**, 61–68 (2020). (in Chinese)
8. Yin, C.L.: Exploration of the Semantic Differences of Motion Verbs from the Perspective of Image Schemas——Taking the Verbs "lā", "zhuài" and "tuō" as Examples. In: Q. Su et al. (Eds.):CLSW 2022, LNAI 13495, pp. 506–520 (2023)
9. Fu, H.Q.: Semantic component-pattern analysis (for action-related verbs). Chin. Lang. Learn. **5**, 3–9 (1996). (in Chinese)
10. Fu, H.Q.: Comparison of dictionary definitions. Lexicogr. Stud. **1**, 1–4 (1990). (in Chinese)
11. Edited by the Dictionary Editing Office, Institute of Linguistics, Chinese Academy of Social Sciences: The contemporary Chinese dictionary, 7th edn. The Commercial Press, Beijing (2016). (in Chinese)
12. Edited by the Compilation Committee of Grand Chinese Dictionary: The Grand Chinese Dictionary. Shanghai Dictionary Publishing House, Shanghai (2011). (in Chinese)
13. Liu, Z.L.: The learner's dictionary of modern Chinese. Beijing Education Press, Beijing (2011). (in Chinese)
14. Collins, U.K. (ed.): Collins COBUILD advanced learner's English-Chinese dictionary, 9th edn. Foreign Language Teaching and Research Press, Beijing (2023). (in Chinese)
15. Hornby, A.S. (ed.): Yu Haijiang (Trans.). oxford advanced learner's English-Chinese dictionary, 10th edn. The Commercial Press, Beijing (2023). (in Chinese)
16. Pearson Education Ltd.: Longman dictionary of English language & culture. Foreign Language Teaching and Research Press, Beijing (2023). (in Chinese)
17. Su, X.C.: A thesaurus of modern Chinese. The Commercial Press, Beijing (2013). (in Chinese)
18. Spooner, A.: The Oxford study thesaurus. Foreign Language Teaching and Research Press, Beijing (2014). (in Chinese)

Evidence for Semantic-Based Association in Chinese Learners' Mental Lexicon: A Word Association Test Study

Hanbo Yan[1] (ID), Ting Ma[2], and Dawei Jin[3](✉) (ID)

[1] Shanghai International Studies University, 550 W Dalian Road, Shanghai, China
[2] Suzhou High School Affiliated to Nanjing University of Aeronautics and Astronautics, 501 W Jinling Road, Suzhou, China
[3] School of Humanities, Shanghai Jiao Tong University, 800 Dongchuan Road, Shanghai 200030, China
daweijin@sjtu.edu.cn

Abstract. The current paper performed word association tests on 10 native Mandarin Chinese speakers and 30 English-speaking Mandarin Chinese learners. The aim of the experimental study was to understand the way lexical association is achieved in L1 and L2 learners of Mandarin Chinese. Several major findings followed from our experiment. First, predominantly syntagmatic responses were recorded in the word association patterns of L1 speakers, followed by paradigmatic responses and non-semantic responses. Second, L2 speakers whose native language is English resembled the pattern of responses by L1 speakers, with the main difference being that a higher percentage of non-semantic responses were recorded for L2 speakers with lower lexical proficiency. Third, the word association pattern of L2 speakers tended towards that of L1 speakers as language proficiency progressed. It is further found that the extent to which lexical proficiency progresses is a function of the duration of residence in the country of target language.

Keywords: Word association · Psycholinguistics · Second language acquisition · Chinese · English

1 Introduction

The mental lexicon, also known as the internal lexicon, is the organization of words stored in the long-term memory [1], including the phonological, phonetic, and semantic knowledge of the lexicon. There are different ways to study the mental lexicon [2], among which the Word Association Test (WAT) is an important paradigm in investigating how words are stored in the lexicon (e.g., [3]). In the test, participants are asked to say or write a response word as soon as they hear or read a certain word. The response word should be the first word that comes to their mind. Researchers could then observe the storage of the mental lexicon based on the association between the stimulus and the response word.

P. Jin et al. (Eds.): CLSW 2024, LNAI 15552, pp. 201–215, 2025.
https://doi.org/10.1007/978-981-96-3509-2_15

WATs have been used to examine the relationship between native speakers' and second language (L2) learners' mental lexicon. Although the mental lexicon can be studied via a number of phenomena such as the tip of the tongue, the slip of the tongue and speech disorders, it is challenging to obtain such data from L2 learners. Hence, results from WATs not only allow us to understand the storage pattern of the mental lexicon, but also shed light on lexical development and second language acquisition ([4–6]; among others).

1.1 Types of Word Association

Word association can be categorized into two types, semantic response and non-semantic (form-based) response. Semantic response refers to a syntagmatic or paradigmatic association between the stimulus and the response word in terms of semantics ([3, 4, 7]).

A syntagmatic association indicates a linear syntactic relationship, whereby the stimulus and the response word can form a phrase or a simple sentence, such as *white-dress*, *beautiful-woman*. A paradigmatic association means that the stimulus and the response word belong to the same word class, and can appear at the same syntactic position, for example, *black-white, beautiful-handsome*. McCarthy [8] mentioned a third category of semantic response, namely encyclopedic association. Under such association, the response word relates to the stimulus in a specific context or based on personal experience in the real world, such as *bank-money*. On the other hand, non-semantic responses, *viz.* Form-based association, pertain to cases where the stimulus and the response word are phonologically or orthographically (but not semantically) related, for example, *black-slack, communicate-confiscate*.

Psycholinguistic studies of speech errors have further identified fine-grained subclasses within the semantic relation in question. Hotopf [9] analyzed English semantic speech errors in both paradigmatic and syntagmatic word substitution. The most common speech errors were found to involve word associates, such as co-hyponyms (words sharing the same superordinate category, e.g. *dog-cat*) and complementary antonyms (words in a converse relationship, e.g. *hot-cold*). Levelt [10] and Arnaud [11] corroborated the finding by Hotopf, noting the prevalence of antonyms, co-hyponyms, and other word associates in lexical substitution errors in English and French, respectively, as well as a general lack of synonyms (*begin-start*) or superordinates/subordinates in the errors. Harley & MacAndrew [12] expanded on this line of research by examining 784 paradigmatic substitution errors in English. According to them, the most common errors were synonyms, superordinates and coordinates, followed by antonyms and associates. Jaeger [13] examined 133 speech errors in adult English. Her study revealed that the majority of paradigmatic substitution errors were coordinates and associates, with subsumatives, synonyms, and contrastives accounting for a smaller percentage. Wan & Ting [14] investigated 616 semantically related lexical errors. The most frequent type of target-error relationship was found to be coordinates (*jiaoshi-bangongshi*, 'classroom'-'office'), followed by associates (*zhaodao-jiuchu*, 'find'-'rescue'), and finally contrastives (*jieshou-jujue*, 'accept'-'reject'). These findings align with those from studies in other languages, suggesting that certain semantic relationships are more likely to occur in speech errors.

1.2   Previous Studies

WATs are first used among children, adults, and participants with speech disorders to investigate the mental lexicon of native speakers, and how it might be influenced by demographic factors such as age. Entwisle [3] indicated that paradigmatic association was the predominant pattern of native English speakers, followed by syntagmatic association. Brown & Berko [15] and Ervin [16] showed that phonetic-based responses of native English speakers decreased with age, whereas semantic responses increased. Targeted at data from children, their studies identified a change from syntagmatic association to paradigmatic association, indicating a gradual organization of vocabulary. An additional finding involved the variation of word association patterns across languages. For instance, Nissen & Henriksen [17] pointed out that unlike native English speakers, the predominant association was syntagmatic for native Danish speakers, followed by paradigmatic association.

Research on the word association patterns of native Mandarin Chinese speakers has been limited. They converged on the finding that the primary type of word association is semantic association, yet they reached different conclusions regarding the primacy among the subtypes within semantic association. Zhong [18] and Li & Jiang [19] found paradigmatic association to be the predominant pattern, whereas Li & Wang [20] and Zhang & Chen [21] suggested syntagmatic association. This disagreement may be attributed to their different methodologies, including the number of stimuli and participants, the background of the participants and response word calculation.

Meara [4] applied WATs to second language acquisition, testing 76 English-speaking French learners. The results showed that these learners' mental lexicon was significantly different from that of native French speakers. Native speakers organized their mental lexicon in terms of semantic association, while learners exhibited a form-based organization. Subsequent research has formed differing hypotheses about whether the L2 mental lexicon of learners is constructed similarly to the L1 mental lexicon of native speakers. A series of studies found that the L2 mental lexicon was also based on semantic association, which would be regulated by L2 proficiency ([22–26]; among others).

Unlike the L2 mental lexicon of alphabet-based languages like English, character-based languages have received considerably less attention. Zhong [18] conducted a WAT on 20 Chinese learners with various language backgrounds, and found that intermediate-level learners exhibited both syntagmatic and paradigmatic association, while high-level learners demonstrated a predominantly paradigmatic association similar to native Chinese speakers. Li & Jiang [19] tested 50 English-speaking Chinese learners from Australia and obtained consistent results with Zhong [18].

1.3   Current Study

Given the inconsistencies in previous research regarding how the mental lexicon is constructed across native Chinese speakers, we aim to investigate whether the L2 mental lexicon of learners is constructed the same as the L1 mental lexicon of native speakers. In this paper, we examined word association patterns of native Chinese speakers and English-speaking Chinese learners, and further tested how length of residence and vocabulary knowledge would influence learners' word association pattern. Considering that L2 learners may have yet to develop a pattern of paradigmatic association with suffi-cient complexity, and also in order to make the current research comparable with earlier Chinese word association studies, we opted to stick with the basic categories of word association alluded to above ([4, 18, 19]; among others), rather than adopting a more fine-grained semantic taxonomy as advocated in [13, 14]. Based on the different results of previous research, various predictions can be made, the corroborations of which may lead to different theoretical implications.

First, if the construction of L2 learners' mental lexicon is mainly based on form, then English-speaking Chinese learners should exhibit a form-based word association pattern, regardless of the word association pattern of native Chinese speakers. Meanwhile, length of residence and vocabulary knowledge should not have an effect on their patterns of Chinese word association.

Second, if the mental lexicon of L2 learners is regulated by their L2 vocabulary knowledge, then length of residence and vocabulary knowledge should impact their word association patterns. That is to say, L2 learners should initially exhibit a form-based word association pattern with a shorter period of residence and a smaller vocabulary. As their vocabulary and length of stay increase, their mental lexicons should transition to meaning-based associations.

Third, while both Chinese and English native speakers exhibit meaning-based lexical association patterns, paradigmatic association is the predominant pattern among English native speakers, whereas studies on native Chinese speakers' association pattern are inconclusive. If native Chinese speakers also demonstrate a paradigmatic association pattern, then under the assumption that learners' lexicon transition to meaning-based with extended periods of learning, English-speaking Chinses learners with longer residence and larger vocabularies should pattern similarly to native Chinese speakers. However, if native Chinese speakers exhibit a syntagmatic association pattern, then depending on whether L1 transfer occurs, the learners may either show a paradigmatic association pattern like their native language, or associate Chinese words in a syntagmatic way.

2   Methodology

2.1   Participants

Participants were divided into a native Chinese speaker group and a group of learners of Chinese with English as their native language. The former group served as a baseline, which comprised 10 persons, all enrolled in a graduate program at a public university in Shanghai at the time of recruitment. The mean vocabulary of the baseline group numbered at 9,080. None of the participants had previous experience in similar tasks prior to their recruitment into our experiment. The target group consisted of 30 learners of Chinese, with a mean vocabulary of 3,710.[1] The mean period of learning for the learners that were based in their home country was 32 months, and the mean for those with residence in China was 19 months. On average the duration of Chinese language learning was 25.5 months.

---

[1] We used a vocabulary competence test adapted from the Chinese Vocabulary Self-Adaptation Test Platform of Beijing Normal University (see Sect. 2.3 for details).

2.2 Stimuli

Previous studies have shown a considerable impact of the word class and lexical frequency of the stimuli on word association. To guarantee the reliability of our results, we chose a total of 72 lexical stimuli. As a first step, the disyllabic words culled were shared across three widely used glossaries for teaching Chinese as a foreign language: Levels I-III of the 2012 HSK vocabulary, the glossary from the 2008 edition of *Xiandai Hanyu Changyong Cibiao* (A List of Frequently Used Words in Modern Chinese) and the glossary from *Chenggong Zhi Lu* (Path to Success), Levels 1–3 (5 volumes *in toto*). We next controlled for the word class consistency of our culled words by excluding words cross-classified with multiple word classes and only retaining those words that were singularly classified, based on the annotation of word categories in *Xiandai Hanyu Cidian* (Modern Chinese Dictionary, 7th edition). As a final step, we extracted 72 high-frequency lexical items from our list of culled words (evenly spread out across nouns, adjectives and verbs, 24 items apiece) using bigram frequency list and individual mutual information scores (MIS) provided at the Da Jun Chinese Text Computing website (https://lingua. mtsu.edu/chinese-computing/) [27]. A complete list of our test stimuli is provided in the Appendix.

2.3 Procedures

The current experiment included a Chinese word association test (WAT), a questionnaire investigating familiarity with Chinese vocabulary, a language learning background questionnaire, and a Chinese vocabulary competence test. The WAT and familiarity questionnaire were implemented on Paradigm [28].

Participants were instructed to fill in the language background questionnaire first. Upon starting the experiment, participants read an introduction to the experiment. In the case a participant failed to understand the written description, the experimenter would offer an explanation in English. To ensure that participants fully understand the process, three practice sessions preceded the formal experiment.

The 72 lexical stimuli in the formal experiment were divided into two lists of 36 items at random. Participants could choose to rest between lists. However, all participants completed tasks from both lists without a pause. After the WAT, they completed the vocabulary familiarity questionnaire and the vocabulary competence test. More details on the four parts of the experiment are provided below.

The Language Background Questionnaire for Chinese Learners. The language background questionnaire was designed to better gauge the specifics of language use for the participants. The survey comprised three parts. The first part covers basic information, including gender, place of birth, current occupation, major/specialty field, as well as vision impairments or other disabilities. The second part covers the languages spoken by the participants, including their first language(s), the language(s) of their parents, the languages primarily used at each age level and their competence. The third part inquires after the background about the participants' Chinese language learning, including the age when learning started, duration of learning (differentiated by the duration while residing in the home country vs. residing in China), current HSK level and HSK test scores.[2]

Chinese Word Association Test. The lexical stimuli in the current experiment were presented simultaneously in a visual and an auditory manner. Participants were instructed to name the associated word immediately after seeing and hearing each stimulus, before proceeding to the next stimulus with the associated word recorded. The experimenter would interrupt when confusion arose and ask for further clarification about the way the association was established. Only the initial associated word from the participants' response was recorded to prevent a chain reaction.

Chinese Vocabulary Familiarity Questionnaire. The current experiment also investigated the extent of vocabulary familiarity among the participants who were learners of Chinese, to make sure that the lexical stimuli encountered during the WAT were all familiar to them. We administered a modified version of the five-point lexical knowledge scale from Wesche & Paribakht [29]. Specifically, we presented a four-point scale to force participants to make a more definitive judgment. Among the four points to be chosen from,

1 stands for: I've never seen/learned this word
2 stands for: I've seen/learned this word, but I've forgotten what it means
3 stands for: I've seen/learned this word and I know what it means
4 stands for: I've seen/learned this word, I know what it means, and I can use it in a sentence

Chinese learners completed the vocabulary familiarity questionnaire immediately following the WAT. All words in the questionnaire came from the lexical stimuli within the WAT. We would remove the responses to those lexical stimuli that registered a low familiarity score based on the questionnaire results, specifically the lexical items that received a score of 0 or 1 in the questionnaire and their associated words. However, all stimuli received a score of at least 2.

Chinese Vocabulary Competence Test. The current study employed the Chinese vocabulary self-adaptation test platform developed by Beijing Normal University (http://hanyu.ironpy.cn/) to assess L2 learners' Chinese vocabulary competence. Upon logging in to the platform and registering via email, participants were instructed to fill in background information such as name, gender, nationality, whether or not they were of Chinese descent, mother tongue, learning duration, HSK level/scores, etc. The self-adaptation test was administered after registration and completion of the relevant information.

The platform employed dynamic adjustments, such that the test questions each participant encountered were customized according to the language background information provided and the way the preceding questions were completed. Consequently, the number of test questions and the duration of the test differed by participant. As a general rule, participants with a longer period of Chinese learning and higher proficiency faced

---

[2] We did not use HSK levels/scores in determining the learners' proficiency level in our experiment, because some of the participants had not taken an HSK test by the time of the experiment.

longer tests and a larger number of questions in order to achieve an assessment of their overall vocabulary, whereas those with shorter Chinese learning experience and lower proficiency completed shorter tests with fewer questions.

2.4 Data Analysis

The current experiment followed a response word categorization that synthesized the criteria in previous studies ([17, 20, 21, 26, 30, 31]). The response words were first categorized into semantic associations, form-based associations and other associations. Semantic associations were further categorized as syntagmatic association (*jieshu* 'end'-*bisai* 'match'), paradigmatic association (*pingguo* 'apple'-*li* 'pear'), and encyclopedic association (*yinhang* 'bank'-*qian* 'money'). Form-based associations were mainly expressed as phonological association (*pingguo* 'apple'-*pingheng* 'balance') and orthographical association (*jingcai* 'spectacular'-*jingli* 'energy'). Other responses than semantic and form-based responses were categorized as other associations, including no responses, repeated responses (repetition of the test stimuli), and unrelated responses.

3 Results

The response words from the WAT were examined. According to the familiarity judgement, all stimuli were rated as highly familiar by both native speakers and L2 learners (received a 2 or 3 rating in the judgement task). All native speakers' responses were included in the analysis (720 trials, 72 stimuli per participant * 10 participants). 93% of the learners' responses were categorized as either meaning-based or form-based association (2013/2160 trials, 72 stimuli per participant * 30 participants), and the rest were categorized as other.

Table 1 shows the frequencies and percentages of association type for both native speakers and L2 learners. We can see that both groups predominantly used syntagmatic associations, followed by paradigmatic, encyclopedic, and form-based. The first three types of word association, which were all meaning-based, were each more frequent among native speakers than L2 learners. Moreover, L2 learners more frequently produced form-based (8.75% *versus* 1.39%) and other (9.03% *versus* 3.06%) response words than native speakers. A chi-squared test of independence between Speaker Type and Response Type confirmed a significant correlation between the two factors ($\chi^2(4, N = 2,880) = 88.84, p < 0.001$).

Numerically, the word association patterns are similar for both native speakers and learners. To test whether the pattern is the same, a multinomial logistic regression model was conducted with Speaker Type as the predictor variable, and Response Type as the dependent variable, using the R package nnet [32]. The results are listed in Table 2.

Results from our statistical analysis revealed that compared with the syntagmatic association of native Chinese speakers, the log odds of producing an Encyclopedic association decrease by 0.36 for L2 learners. Conversely, the log odds of producing a Form-based and Other association increase by 1.92 and 1.16, respectively, when moving from native speakers to L2 learners.

Table 1. Description of the word association test

Association Type	native speakers		learners	
	Frequency	Percentage	Frequency	Percentage
Syntagmatic	349	48.47%	969	44.86%
Paradigmatic	204	28.33%	546	25.28%
Encyclopedic	135	18.75%	261	12.08%
Form-based	10	1.39%	189	8.75%
Other	22	3.06%	195	9.03%

Table 2. Multinomial logistic regression model results of the word association test (syntagmatic association and native Chinese speakers as the baseline)

	Speaker Type: Learners			
	β	SE	z	p
Paradigmatic	−0.04	0.10	−0.36	0.72
Encyclopedic	−0.36	0.12	−2.94	**0.003**
Form-based	1.92	0.33	5.80	**6.46e-09**
Other	1.16	0.23	4.97	**6.59e-07**

$p \leq 0.1 * p \leq 0.05 ** p \leq 0.01 *** p \leq 0.001$.

To further investigate how Word Class, Length of Residence and Vocabulary Size influence Chinese word association for native speakers and L2 learners, we ran multinomial logistic regression models with each group of speakers separately. For the data of native Chinese speakers, the dependent variable was Response Type, and the independent variables were Word Class (adjective, noun, and verb) and Vocabulary Size. For the data of English-speaking Chinese learners, Length of Residence was also included as an independent variable.

Native Chinese Speakers. Our likelihood ratio test revealed that Vocabulary Size did not have an effect on native speakers' word association pattern ($\chi^2(4)$ 5.16, $p = 0.27$). The multinomial regression model with Word Class as the independent variable was the best model. Results of the model are listed in Table 3.

As shown in Table 3, compared with Syntagmatic word association, the log odds of an Encyclopedic word association increase significantly (by 0.51) if the Word Class changes from Adjective to Noun, and the log odds of the response words being Paradigmatic-associated versus Syntagmatic-associated decrease significantly (by 0.76) if the Word Class changes from Adjective to Verb. The results indicate that nouns tended to elicit encyclopedic associations more often than adjectives did, and verbs were less likely to be paradigmatically associated than adjectives.

Table 3. Multinomial logistic regression model results of the word association test of native Chinese speakers (syntagmatic association and adjective as the baseline)

	Word Class: Noun				Word Class: Verb			
	β	SE	z	p	β	SE	z	p
Paradigmatic	−0.36	0.21	−1.70	0.09	−0.76	0.22	−3.48	**0.0005**
Encyclopedic	0.51	0.25	2.01	**0.04**	−0.07	0.27	−0.28	0.78
Form-based	−0.46	0.92	−0.50	0.62	0.25	0.74	0.34	0.74
Other	−1.15	0.59	−1.95	0.05	−0.95	0.52	−1.85	0.06

$p \leq 0.1 * p \leq 0.05 ** p \leq 0.01 *** p \leq 0.001.$

Three coefficients are marginal: The log odds of producing a Paradigmatic word association and Other versus Syntagmatic word association decrease by 0.36 and 1.15 if changing from Adjective to Noun, and the log odds of producing Other versus Syntagmatic word association decrease by 0.95 if changing from Adjective to Verb. All the other coefficients are not significant.

English-Speaking Chinese Learners. For L2 learners, we first calculated the Pearson correlation coefficient between Length of Residence and Vocabulary Size. Our calculation showed that Vocabulary Size was significantly correlated with Length of Residence (t (2158) = 33.34, $p < 0.001$), indicating that the longer the learners live in China, the larger their vocabularies grow.

A likelihood ratio test revealed that Word Class, Vocabulary Size, and Length of Residence all influenced learners' word association pattern. The best model was the one with all three predictors. Results of the model are listed in Table 4.

Several key takeaways can be derived from these results. First, if Word Class changes from Adjective to Noun, compared with being syntagmatic association, the log odds of being Paradigmatic, Form-based, and Other decrease significantly, by 0.35, 0.98 and 1.26 respectively, and the log odds of being Encyclopedic association increase significantly, by 1.09. When Word Class changes from Adjective to Verb, the log odds of being Paradigmatic, Encyclopedic, Form-based, and Other versus being Syntagmatic association all decrease significantly, by 0.38, 0.04, 1.13, and 1.49 respectively. This means that compared with Adjectives, Nouns were less likely to have paradigmatic, form-based and other associations than syntagmatic associations, but more likely to have encyclopedic associations. Verbs were also less likely to be paradigmatic, encyclopedic, form-based, or other compared to syntagmatic associations.

Second, a one-unit increase in the variable Vocabulary Size was associated with significant decreases in the log odds of learners producing response words of Paradigmatic, Encyclopedic, Form-based, and Other associations versus producing those of Syntagmatic associations. Third, a one-unit increase in Length of Residence was associated with lower log odds of Form-based associations (log odds decrease by 0.02) and marginally lower odds of encyclopedic and other associations.

Table 4. Multinomial logistic regression model results of the word association test of English-speaking Chinese learners (syntagmatic association and adjective as the baseline)

	Word Class: Noun				Word Class: Verb			
	β	SE	z	p	β	SE	z	p
Paradigmatic	−0.35	0.05	−6.51	**7.39e-11**	−0.38	0.06	−6.71	**1.90e-11**
Encyclopedic	1.09	0.02	48.03	**<2e-16**	−0.04	0.02	−2.48	**0.001**
Form-based	−0.98	0.004	−227.46	**<2e-16**	−1.13	0.01	−204.83	**<2e-16**
Other	−1.26	0.003	−363.05	**<2e-16**	−1.49	0.004	−334.03	**<2e-16**

	Vocabulary Size			
	β	SE	z	p
Paradigmatic	−6.61e-05	1.76e-05	−3.76	**0.0002**
Encyclopedic	−5.31e-05	2.34e-05	−2.27	**0.02**
Form-based	−3.96e-04	2.85e-05	−13.89	**<2e-16**
Other	−3.49e-04	2.77e-05	−12.61	**<2e-16**

	Length of Residence			
	β	SE	z	p
Paradigmatic	−0.0002	0.002	−0.10	0.92
Encyclopedic	−0.004	0.002	−1.80	0.07
Form-based	−0.02	0.005	−2.97	**0.003**
Other	−0.01	0.004	−1.74	0.08

$p \le 0.1 * p \le 0.05 ** p \le 0.01 *** p \le 0.001$.

4   Discussion

In the current study, a word association test was used to investigate the mental lexicon of native Chinese speakers and English-speaking Chinese learners. Our results showed that overall, syntagmatic association was the dominant category for both groups, followed by paradigmatic and encyclopedic associations. Form-based associations, including orthographical and phonological association, were limited. In addition, vocabulary size did not have an effect on native speakers' association pattern, but word class did. For L2 learners, word class, vocabulary size, and length of residence all influenced their associations. These results have the following implications.

First, the current results help us to further understand the mental lexicon of native Chinese speakers. Our findings support the notion that Chinese speakers primarily associate words semantically, consistent with recent research, such as the latest finding in Allassonnière-Tang, Wan, & Lee's [33] that the semantic distance is shorter than the phonological distance for the target and the response word. To be more specific, adjectives, nouns and verbs all elicit more syntagmatic association responses. The result where syntagmatic association is the dominant pattern is consistent with the findings by Li & Wang [20] and Zhang & Chen [21] while contrasting with the findings in Zhong [18] and Li & Jiang [19]. Such discrepancies might be attributed to differences in stimuli and methodologies that were employed in these individual studies. Although all four studies employed a pencil and paper paradigm, Li & Wang [20] and Zhang & Chen [21] collected a larger sample size than Zhong [18], that is, 1,872 responses in Li & Wang [20] and 3,600 in Zhang & Chen [21], compared to 360 in Zhong [18], raising the possibility that the lack of convergence among these results arises from sample size differences. While the study in Li & Jiang [19] also had a large sample size (i.e. 1,114), their data were collected in Australia, a non-Chinese environment. It is possible that native Chinese speakers living in Australia might be influenced by English to some extent.

Second, in terms of word association pattern, L2 learners have a similar mental lexicon to that of native speakers in that syntagmatic association is the major pattern of association. In terms of L2 and L1 mental lexicon comparison, the result provides support for a large number of previous studies ([18–23, 26]; among others) that L2 learners are capable of building semantic relationship among lexical words. In terms of the L2 mental lexicon of Chinese learners, however, the result is inconsistent with Zhong [18] or Li & Jiang [19]. The inconsistency is possibly due to the fact that the learners from Zhong [18] have multiple language backgrounds, while the current study only focused on native English speakers. Also, as mentioned above, Li & Jiang [19] recruited learners in a non-target language environment (Australia), while learners of the current study were all studying in China at the time of the experiment. They additionally possessed a relatively large vocabulary, averaging 3,710.

Another interesting finding is that despite paradigmatic associations being common in English, English-speaking Chinese learners exhibited a preference for syntagmatic associations in their Chinese WAT. This suggests a lack of L1 transfer, possibly due to these learners' intermediate-advanced proficiency, which limits L1 influence. Another possible explanation is that certain linguistic features in Chinese, such as compounds and limited morphological marking, result in more syntagmatic association, which exert an influence on the learners during acquisition. Compounding is extraordinarily productive in Chinese, which frequently involves syntagmatic relationships, e.g., *fei-ji* 'plane (lit. Fly-machine)' or *bi-ye* 'graduate (lit. Finish-instruction)'. These word structures may lead to more syntagmatic associations as the interpretation of their meaning is often achieved compositionally, via the combination of each of the (mutually related) component parts. Furthermore, Chinese lacks morphological markers, and relies on word order in marking grammatical relations. These features encourage focusing on word relationships and sequences, as exemplified by *kuaile* 'happy' eliciting syntagmatic responses like *shenghuo* 'life', or *zhoumo* 'weekend', rather than a paradigmatic response (such as a synonym *kaixin* or *yukuai*). Moreover, the reduction in inflectional morphology and the decrease in syllable numbers per word over the course of history of the Chinese language have given rise to an overabundance of homophones ([34–36]; among others). One consequence is the reliance on context for lexical disambiguation, which further promotes syntagmatic associations, where word meanings are understood within their syntactic context.

Finally, as the length of residence grows, learners acquire a larger vocabulary. The results showed that when vocabulary increases, paradigmatic, encyclopedic, form-based and other associations all decrease. That is to say, learners would have more syntagmatic responses as their language proficiency improves. When length of residence increases, form-based responses will also decrease significantly, indicating a growing similarity between their mental lexicon and that of native speakers with a longer stay in the target language environment.

To conclude, the present study demonstrates that it is possible for learners to construct a mental lexicon that is similar to that of native speakers, even though the mental lexicon of their native language is constructed in a different way. Both native Chinese speakers and learners exhibit a meaning-based association pattern for their mental lexicon. Furthermore, it is necessary to point out that our findings show that all experimental stimuli in the current study are highly familiar to both groups.

5 Conclusion

The current study examined the mental lexicon of native Chinese speakers as well as how English-speaking Chinese learners associate Chinese disyllabic words. A Word Association Test revealed that both L1 and L2 speakers store words into their Chinese mental lexicon semantically, with the predominant pattern being syntagmatic association. These findings are consistent with the assumptions that L1 and L2 mental lexicons are structurally similar, despite differences in the construction of individual, native language lexicons. It is further found that word class, length of residence and vocabulary size influence word storage in the mental lexicon.

Acknowledgments. We gratefully acknowledge two anonymous reviewers for the 2024 CLSW meeting for their valuable feedback, and all the participants recruited during our study who contributed to the data reported here. This work is supported in part by the Philosophy and Social Sciences Office of the Government of Shanghai (Grant No. 2021BYY007). All the remaining errors are ours.

Disclosure of Interests. The authors have no competing interests to declare.

Appendix Stimuli

名词 Noun	动词 Verb	形容词 Adjective
汉语 Chinese	谢谢 to thank	新鲜 fresh
饭店 restaurant	跳舞 to dance	快乐 happy
老师 teacher	介绍 to introduce	困难 difficult
苹果 apple	吃饭 to eat meals	不错 not bad
音乐 music	觉得 to think	有名 famous
手机 cell phone	欢迎 to welcome	漂亮 beautiful
超市 supermarket	拍照 to take a picture	安静 quiet

(continued)

(continued)

名词 Noun	动词 Verb	形容词 Adjective
名字 name	认识 to get to know	干净 clean
周末 weekend	学习 to learn	开心 blissful
同学 classmate	知道 to know	可爱 cute
汉字 Chinese character	帮助 to help	年轻 young
啤酒 beer	出发 to depart	容易 easy
英文 English	再见 to bid farewell	聪明 intelligent
现金 cash	迟到 to not arrive on time	活泼 vivacious
朋友 friend	告诉 to tell	无聊 boring
银行 bank	复习 to review	顺利 smooth
教室 classroom	旅行 to travel	重要 important
食堂 canteen	听说 to hear about	精彩 spectacular
商店 shop	安排 to arrange	厉害 impressive
味道 flavor	参加 to participate	普通 normal
书法calligraphy	提高 to improve	积极 positive
地铁 metro	休息 to rest	合适 proper
蛋糕 cake	结束 to end	简单 simple
大学 university	看见 to see	健康 healthy

References

1. Carroll, D.W.: Psychology of language, 5th edn. The Thomson Corporation, Belmont (2008)
2. Aitchison, J.: Words in the mind: An introduction to the mental lexicon. Blackwell, Oxford (2012)
3. Entwisle, D.R.: Word associations of young children. The Johns Hopkins Press, Baltimore (1966)
4. Meara, P.: Word association in a foreign language: A report on the Birkbeck Vocabulary Project. Nottingham Linguistic Circular **11**, 29–37 (1982)
5. Peppard, J.: Exploring the relationship between word-association and learners' lexical development. University of Birmingham, Center for English Language Studies (2007)
6. Roux, P.W.: Words in the Mind: Exploring the relationship between word association and lexical development. Polyglossia. **24**, 80–91 (2013)
7. Cruse, D.A.: Meaning in language: An introduction to semantics and pragmatics, 2nd edn. Oxford University Press, Oxford (2004)
8. McCarthy, M.: Vocabulary. Oxford University Press, Oxford (1990)
9. Hotopf, W.: Semantic similarity as a factor in whole-word slips of the tongue. In: Fromkin, V. (ed.) Errors in Linguistic Performance: Slips of the Tongue, Ear, Pen, and Hand, pp. 97–109. Academic Press, New York (1980)
10. Levelt, W.J.: Speaking: From Intention to Articulation. Mil Press, Cambridge, MA (1989)
11. Arnaud, P.J.: Target-error resemblance in French word substitution speech errors and the mental lexicon. Appl. Psycholinguist. **20**(2), 269–287 (1999)

12. Harley, T., MacAndrew, S.: Constraints upon word substitution speech errors. J. Psycholinguists Res. **30**, 395–418 (2001)
13. Jaeger, J.J.: Kids' Slips: What Young Children's Slips of the Tongue Reveal about Language Development. Lawrence Erlbaum Associates, Mahwah, NJ (2005)
14. Wan, I.-P., Ting, J.: Semantic relationships in Mandarin speech errors. Taiwan Journal of Linguistics. **17**(2), 33–66 (2019)
15. Brown, R., Berko, J.: Word association and the acquisition of grammar. Child Dev. **31**(1), 1–14 (1960)
16. Ervin, S.: Changes with age in the verbal determinants of word association. Am. J. Psychol. **74**, 361–372 (1961)
17. Nissen, H.B., Henriksen, B.: Word class influence on word association test results. Int. J. Appl. Linguist. **16**, 389–408 (2006)
18. Zhong, Q.: An experiment study of Chinese word association in intermediate and advanced international students. Papers of the Seventh Beijing Postgraduate Forum for Teaching Chinese as a Foreign Language. **11**, 21–39 (2014)
19. Li, G., Jiang, W.: A study of the correlative features in the vocabulary network of L2 learners of Chinese: A case study of Australian learners of Chinese of the beginner and the intermediate level. Huawen Jiaoxue yu Yanjiu [Chinese Language Teaching and Research]. **15**(4), 22–29 (2015)
20. Li, X., Wang, W.: A comparative study of mental lexical association pattern and specificity effect in English and Chinese. Waiyu Jie [Foreign Language Circle]. **5**, 70–78 (2016)
21. Zhang, J., Chen, D.: A study of the mental lexicon in Chinese university students. Yuyan Wenzi Yingyong [Language and Character Application]. **4**, 75–84 (2018)
22. Söderman, T.: Word associations of foreign language learners and native speakers: The phenomenon of a shift in response type and its relevance for lexical development. In: Ringbom, H. (ed.) Near-native proficiency in English, pp. 91–182. Abo Akademi, Abo, Finland (1993)
23. Singleton, D.: Exploring the second language mental lexicon. Cambridge University Press, New York (1999)
24. Wolter, B.: Comparing the L1 and L2 mental lexicon: A depth of individual word knowledge model. Stud. Second. Lang. Acquis. **23**(1), 41–69 (2001)
25. Zareva, A.: Structure of the second language mental lexicon: How does it compare to native speakers' lexical or organization. Second. Lang. Res. **23**(2), 123–153 (2007)
26. Zhang, P.: A comparative study of the mental lexicon association pattern in Chinese learners of English. Waiyu Jiaoxue yu Yanjiu [Foreign Language Teaching and Research]. **42**(1), 9–16 (2010)
27. Da, J.: Chinese text computing. https://lingua.mtsu.edu/chinese-computing (2004)
28. Tagliaferri, B.: Perception research systems Inc. (Paradigm). Retrieved from http://www.paradigmexperiments.com/ (2015)
29. Wesche, M., Paribakht, T. M.: Assessing vocabulary knowledge: Depth vs. breadth. Canadian Modern Language Review. **53**, 13–40 (1996)
30. Fitzpatrick, T.: Word association patterns: Unpacking the assumptions. Int. J. Appl. Linguist. **17**, 319–331 (2007)
31. Fitzpatrick, T.: Word Association profiles in a first and second Language: Puzzles and problems. In: Fitzpatrick, T., Barfield, A. (eds.) Lexical Processing in Second Language Learners: Papers and Perspectives in Honor of Paul Meara, pp. 38–52. Cambridge University Press, New York (2009)
32. Ripley, B., Venables, W.: Feed-forward neural networks and multinomial log-linear models. R package version **7**, 3–17 (2022)
33. Allassonnière-Tang, M., Wan, I.-P., Lee, C.: Semantic and phonological distances in free word association tasks. In: Dong, M., Hong, J.F., Lin, J., Jin, P. (eds.) Chinese Lexical Semantics. CLSW 2023. LNCS, vol 14515, pp. 91–100. Springer, Singapore (2024)

34. Li, C.N., Thompson, S.A.: Mandarin Chinese: A functional reference grammar. University of California Press, Oakland (1989)
35. Duanmu, S.: Wordhood in Chinese. In: Packard, J. (ed.) New Approaches to Chinese Word Formation: Morphology, Phonology and the Lexicon in Modern and Ancient Chinese, pp. 135–196. Mouton de Gruyter, Berlin (2011)
36. Duanmu, S.L.: Word-length preferences in Chinese: a corpus study. Journal of East Asian Linguistics **21**(1), 89–114 (2012)

Research on the Paraphrasing of Mental Verbs in the Outward-Oriented Chinese Learner's Dictionary from the Perspective of Frame Semantics

Weili Wang[1,2(✉)], Jianshe Zhou[1,2], and Kai Zhang[1,2]

[1] Chinese Department, Capital Normal University, Beijing, China
wangweili100@cnu.edu.cn
[2] Research Center for Language Intelligence of China, Beijing, China

Abstract. Based on Charles Fillmore's Frame Semantics Theory, we summarize and categorize a series of paraphrasing models for mental verbs. By comparing two outward-oriented Chinese learner's dictionaries, *Commercial Press Learner's Chinese Dictionary* and *Contemporary Chinese Learner's Dictionary*, with the inward-oriented *Modern Chinese Dictionary (7th edition)*, we propose the following suggestions for paraphrasing mental verbs: (1) Placing verbs within a "scenario" for paraphrasing aligns with the cognitive characteristics of second language learners; (2) Accurately and comprehensively reflecting frame elements which differentiate meanings can enhance the precision of paraphrasing; (3) Using the most frequent syntactic representations as references for syntactic realizations in paraphrasing helps learners in both understanding the meanings and mastering the usages of the words; (4) The quantity and quality of frame elements can be used as criteria to evaluate the quality of dictionary paraphrasing.

Keywords: Frame Semantics Theory · Mental Verbs · Paraphrasing · Outward-Oriented Chinese Learner's Dictionary

1 Introduction

1.1 Problems in the Paraphrasing of Current Outward-Oriented Chinese Learner's Dictionary

With the development of international Chinese education, the demands for Chinese learner's dictionaries have significantly increased. Zhang [1] pointed out that the five major English learner's dictionaries (*Oxford Dictionary*, *Longman Dictionary*, *Collins Dictionary*, *Cambridge Dictionary*, and *Macmillan Dictionary*) have achieved remarkable success domestically and occupied 93.19% of the market share for learner's dictionaries. While Chinese learner's dictionaries published in China are not well accepted by non-native Chinese learners, and only 6.8% of users purchase them. This situation compels us to reflect on the underlying reasons for this discrepancy.

© The Author(s), under exclusive license to Springer Nature Singapore Pte Ltd. 2025
P. Jin et al. (Eds.): CLSW 2024, LNAI 15552, pp. 216–230, 2025.
https://doi.org/10.1007/978-981-96-3509-2_16

Compared to inward-oriented Chinese dictionaries which focus on providing the most comprehensive paraphrasing, learner's dictionaries are more inclined to give detailed descriptions of word meanings to facilitate better understanding for second language learners. However, many Chinese learner's dictionaries still follow the paraphrasing models, and even the content, of authoritative inward-oriented Chinese dictionaries, neglecting both the semantic features of the words being defined and the cognitive characteristics of second language learners. A common issue in many learner's dictionaries is the use of synonymous explanations. For example,

(1) Kàndài: 【dòng】Duìdài。(《XiànDài HànYǔ XuéXí Cí Diǎn》)
     看待: 【动】对待。(《现代汉语学习词典》) [2]
     'Treat: 【Verb】To treat or deal with. (*Modern Chinese Learner's Dictionary*)'
(2) Duìdài: 【dòng】Yòng mǒuzhǒng tàidù huò xíngwéi lái yìngfù rén huò shì。
     (《XiànDài HànYǔ XuéXí Cí Diǎn》)
     对待: 【动】用某种态度或行为来应付人或事。(《现代汉语学习词典》) [2]
     'Treat: 【Verb】To handle or deal with people or matters using a certain attitude
or behavior.(*Modern Chinese Learner's Dictionary*) '

"kàndài 看待" and "duìdài 对待" are not completely synonymous and are often not interchangeable. For instance, in the sentence "Zīxúnzhě yǐ bù réndào de fāngshì qù duìdài tāmén。咨询者以不人道的方式去对待他们。'The consultants treat them in an inhumane manner.'", the phrase "bù réndào de fāngshì qù duìdài tāmén 不人道的方式去对待他们 'treat them in an inhumane manner'" cannot be replaced with"bù réndào de fāngshì qù kàndài tāmén 不人道的方式去看待他们 'view them in an inhumane manner'". Similarly, in the sentence "Pǔbiàn de guāndiǎn shì kèguān de kàndài zìjǐ de zhuàngkuàng cái shì jiànkāng de。普遍的观点是客观地看待自己的状况才是健康的。'The prevailing opinion is that it is healthier to view one's situation objectively.'", the phrase "kèguān de kàndài zìjǐ de zhuàngkuàng 客观地看待自己的状况 'view one's situation objectively'" cannot be replaced with "kèguān de duìdài zìjǐ de zhuàngkuàng 客观地对待自己的状况 'treat one's situation objectively'". The distinction between "kàndài 看待" and "duìdài 对待" lies in their nuanced features: "kàndài 看待" emphasizes the perspective or attitude, while "duìdài 对待" focuses more on action or behavior.

Furthermore, many learner's dictionaries exhibit issues of cross-paraphrasing and circular-paraphrasing. Cross-paraphrasing refers to explaining one word using two or more words whose meanings partially overlap, or using synonyms where the meanings of the explained terms and the explanation overlap. Circular-paraphrasing occurs when term A is defined as term B, and term B is then defined as term A. For example,

(1) Lǐjiě: 【dòng】Dǒng, liǎojiě。（《Xué HànYǔ YòngLì CíDiǎn》）

理解:【动】懂，了解。（《学汉语用例词典》）[3]

'Understand: 【Verb】To understand, to comprehend.（*Chinese Dictionary of Usage for Learners*）'

(2) Rènshi: 【dòng】Fēnbiàn shíbié; liǎojiě, dǒngdé。（《Xué HànYǔ YòngLì CíDiǎn》）

认识:【动】分辨识别；了解，懂得。（《学汉语用例词典》）[3]

'Recognize: 【Verb】To distinguish and recognize; to understand, to comprehend.（*Chinese Dictionary of Usage for Learners*）'

This phenomenon of cross-paraphrasing also reflects the issue of synonymous explanations which can lead to the accumulation of words and to create an ambiguous feeling. So cross-paraphrasing makes learners to grasp the meanings of the words more difficultly. These two paraphrasing methods prevent second language learners from both understanding the specific usages of the defined words and distinguishing the defined words from its synonyms. Zhang [1] pointed out that such paraphrasing may be somewhat helpful for general reference and reading comprehension for native speakers. However, this approach is not necessarily suitable for outward-oriented learner's dictionaries. The reason is that completely synonymous words are rare in any language, and synonymy often only exists in a particular meaning or context. These words often have subtle distinguishing features which second language learners, who lack linguistic knowledge and native intuition, discern very difficultly. Since second language learners lack the linguistic intuition and cultural knowledge possessed by native speakers, dictionary compilers must avoid omitting the information from the perspective of native speakers. And they should instead consider the cognitive characteristics of second language learners when paraphrasing.

1.2 Problems in the Paraphrasing of Current Outward-Oriented Chinese Learner's Dictionary

This research adopts Frame Semantics as the theoretical foundation because it approaches language from the cognitive perspective of second language learners. The theory builds cognitive commonalities between the target language and the learner's native language, which facilitates better comprehension of word meanings. Additionally, Frame Semantics tends to refine word meanings, allowing for the categorization of different meanings through various frames and enriching meaning through the detailed description of frame elements.

By displaying both core frame elements and noncore frame elements, Frame Semantics can comprehensively analyze the rational meaning and characteristic usage of words, while also can highlight the semantic features that differentiate them. Using Frame Semantics for paraphrasing words allows for a thorough analysis of both the rational meanings and the distinctive usage models of words. Many definitions in learner's dictionaries are incomplete, sometimes they even omit crucial information. For instance, the definitions of the word "tǎolùn 讨论 'discuss'" in various dictionaries.

(1) Tǎolùn: 【dòng】Jiù mǒu yī wèntí jiāohuàn yìjiàn jìnxíng biànlùn. (《Xué HànYǔ YòngLì CíDiǎn》)

讨论:【动】就某一问题交换意见进行辩论。(《学汉语用例词典》) [3]

'Discuss: 【Verb】To exchange opinions and debate on a particular issue.(*Chinese Dictionary of Usage for Learners*)'

(2) Tǎolùn: 【dòng】Liǎng rén yǐshàng jiù mǒu yī wèntí shuō chū yìjiàn huò jìnxíng biànlùn. (《HSK HànYǔ ShuǐPíng KǎoShì CíDiǎn》)

讨论:【动】两人以上就某一问题说出意见或进行辩论。(《HSK 汉语水平考试词典》) [4]

'Discuss: 【Verb】Two or more people express opinions or debate on a specific issue. (*HSK Chinese Proficiency Examination Dictionary*)'

(3) Tǎolùn: 【dòng】Jiù mǒu yī gè wèntí jiāohuàn yìjiàn huò gòngtóng fēnxī, yánjiū. (《HànYǔ Jiāo Yǔ Xué CíDiǎn》)

讨论:【动】就某一个问题交换意见或共同分析、研究。(《汉语教与学词典》) [5]

'Discuss: 【Verb】To exchange opinions or jointly analyze and study a specific issue. (*Dictionary of Chinese Teaching and Learning*)'

From the definitions of the word "tǎolùn 讨论 'discuss'" in the three dictionaries above, it is evident that their forms and content are quite similar, employing either paraphrasing methods or synonymous explanations. In the context of "tǎolùn 讨论 'discuss'", the participants may not necessarily be discussing problems. And they might also be addressing a particular person or event, which can be encapsulated by the theme. Moreover, "tǎolùn 讨论 'discuss'" is inherently purposeful, either aiming to reach a consensus or to resolve a specific issue. Using Frame Semantics, the frame elements of "tǎolùn 讨论 'discuss'" include the speaker, listener, topic, and purpose. The three dictionaries mentioned above only identify two of these frame elements. The primary distinction between "tǎolùn 讨论 'discuss'" and "liáotiān 聊天 'chat'" is that "tǎolùn 讨论 'discuss'" is characterized by having a topic and a purpose. Without specifying these two frame elements, it becomes easy to confuse the two terms.

Utilizing Frame Semantics for paraphrasing can also highlight the different semantic characteristics of words. For example, the word "yǐncáng 隐藏 'hide'" can evoke two frames based on the hidden object "hide_object" and "subject_hide". The frame elements for "hide_object" include the hider, the hidden item and the location. Whereas the frame elements for "subject_hide" include the hiding subject and the location. Examples are as follows:

(1) Tā zǒngshì xiǎng yào yǐncáng mǒuzhǒng cuìruò. (yǐncáng _ wù)

她总是想要隐藏某种脆弱。(隐藏_物)

'She always to try to hide some kind of vulnerability. (Hide_Object)'

(2) Tā lǐng le shí míng jǐnyīwèi, zài jiéshíshān xià shùlín lǐ yǐ yǐncáng liǎng tiān liǎng yè le. (zhǔtǐ _ yǐncáng)

他领了十名锦衣卫,在碣石山下树林里已隐藏两天两夜了。(主体_隐藏)

'He led ten imperial guards and hid in the woods at the foot of Jieshi Mountain for two days and two nights. (Subject_Hide)'

Many learner's dictionaries merge these two meanings together. For instance,

(1) Yĭncáng: 【dòng】 Cáng qĭlái bù ràng rén fāxiàn. (《ShāngWùGuǎn XuéHànYǔ CíDiǎn》)

隐藏:【动】藏起来不让人发现。(《商务馆学汉语词典》) [6]

'Hide: 【Verb】 To conceal or hide something so that it cannot be discovered. (*The Commercial Press Learner's Chinese Dictionary*)'

(2) Yĭncáng: 【dòng】 Cáng qĭlái bù shĭ rén fāxiàn. (《HSK ZhōngGuó HànYǔ ShuĭPíng KǎoShì CíHuì DàGāng HànYǔ 8000 Cí CíDiǎn》

隐藏:【动】藏起来不使人发现。(《HSK 中国汉语水平考试词汇大纲汉语 8000 词词典》) [7]

'Hide: 【Verb】 To hide something to prevent it from being discovered. (*HSK Chinese Vocabulary Outline 8000 Words Dictionary*)'

(3) Yĭncáng: 【dòng】 Cáng qĭlái bù ràng fāxiàn. (《Xué HànYǔ YòngLì CíDiǎn》)

隐藏:【动】藏起来不让发现。(《学汉语用例词典》) [3]

'Hide: 【Verb】 To conceal something so that it cannot be found. (*Chinese Dictionary of Usage for Learners*)'

The paraphrasing methods employed by learner's dictionaries do not adequately reflect the two meanings of "yĭncáng 隐藏 'hide'" nor do they illustrate the hidden objects it collocates with.

In the light of the above circumstances, this research focuses on the issues related to the paraphrasing of verbs in Chinese learner's dictionaries, specifically examining a sub-category of verbs—mental verbs. Utilizing the theoretical framework of Frame Semantics, this research aims to provide a perspective and suggestions for the compilation of paraphrasing in Chinese learner's dictionaries.

2 Theory About Frame Semantics

Frame Semantics is a branch of cognitive linguistics, proposed by American linguist Charles Fillmore in the late 1970s. It is a theory for describing and explaining lexical semantics. The fundamental idea is that the meaning of a word is associated with its corresponding "semantic frame". To adequately describe a word, it must be placed within the relevant frame. Fillmore noted that a frame is a system of related concepts that people establish in their minds. To understand any one of these concepts, one must grasp the entire conceptual structure of which it is a part. When a concept within this structure is introduced into text or dialogue, other concepts are automatically activated. [8].

Fillmore emphasized the significance of Frame Semantics for the study of words and meanings. He argued that words represent categories of experience, where each category is based on a scenario activated within a cognitive and experiential context. Frame Semantics can be seen as an effort to understand why a speech community creates a particular category of words and to explain the meanings of the words by proposing and clarifying the reasons behind them [9].

The development of frame networks has practical significance in many fields such as natural language processing, semantic researches and lexicography. Researchers from Shanxi University and Shanghai Normal University have drawn on FrameNet to construct a Chinese FrameNet database (Chinese FrameNet, CFN) and an automatic semantic annotation tool. You [10], Ma [11] and Zhou [12] have explored the guiding principles and operational methods for constructing frame networks. Li [13] elaborated on the main content of frame networks, noting that they can serve as multifunctional lexical databases and as online comprehensive dictionaries. Liu and Wan [14] pointed out the issue of frame semantic networks which focus solely on frame semantic roles while neglecting syntactic expressions. They proposed a research method called "frame-based, construction-oriented" to address this issue. And basing on this approach, they constructed a Chinese lexical semantic network to paraphrase verbs attributes through "frame elements" and "paraphrasing constructions". In her analysis of the semantic distinctions of Mandarin physical contact verbs, Liu [15] proposed a comprehensive framework based on lexical construction criteria. This framework represents a significant task in the construction of the Mandarin verb network and plays an important role in the study of verb semantics.

The annotations of frame elements, grammatical functions, and phrase types in FrameNet provide new and effective research avenues for analyzing word meanings. Domestic scholars have leveraged the achievements of frame semantic networks in some fields such as natural language processing, demonstrating the rationality and effectiveness of this annotation method. Therefore, this research intends to analyze word meanings using this annotation methods.

Drawing from the framework of Generative Lexicon Theory, this research aims to elucidate patterns within the varied collocations of mental verbs with the objective of establishing scientifically interpretable models for these collocations.

3 Establishment of the Research Objects

This research is based on Charles Fillmore's Frame Semantics and aims to verify whether the paraphrasing of verbs in Chinese learner's dictionaries adequately present the scenarios expressed by the words, specifically whether they completely describe the frames and frame elements. There are numerous verbs in the Chinese language, and this research focuses on psychological activity verbs, which are mental verbs frequently used by international students. The classification of psychological activity verbs reference the work of Mei and others, that is 《TóngYìCí CíLín》《同义词词林》 'Synonym Forest' [17].

According to the classifications provided by Mei et al. in *Synonym Forest*, there is a vast number of psychological activity verbs, many of which are infrequently used and therefore not suitable for international students. This research compared three dictionaries: 《XiànDài HànYǔ CíDiǎn》《现代汉语词典》 'Modern Chinese Dictionary' (7th edition) [18], the representative Chinese learner's dictionary 《ShāngWùGuǎn XuéHànYǔ CíDiǎn》《商务馆学汉语词典》 'Commercial Press Learner's Chinese Dictionary' [6], and the relatively newer 《DāngDài HànYǔ XuéXí CíDiǎn》《当代汉语学习词典》 'Contemporary Chinese Learner's Dictionary' [19]. From these, 14 verbs were selected: chóngbài 崇拜 'worship', zūnjìng 尊敬 'respect', chóngjìng 崇敬 'revere', zūnzhòng 尊重 'honor', xīnshǎng 欣赏 'appreciate', rèài 热爱 'love ardently', téngài

疼爱 'cherish', xīnténg 心疼 'love dearly', huíyì 回忆 'recall', huígù 回顾 'review', xiǎngniàn 想念 'miss', huáiniàn 怀念 'long for', tǐliàng 体谅 'understand' and zhǎngwò 掌握 'grasp'.

Subsequently, a corpus query was conducted in the Center for Chinese Linguistics PKU corpus, extracting 10% of the data for each verb. The extracted data were analyzed to filter out instances that met the criteria for parts of speech and meanings. Each scene evokes a frame, and each scene corresponds to a lexical item in frame semantic networks. Therefore, the analysis of the corpus was used to determine the lexical items from the verbs. The analysis results of the frame semantic network for the lexical items include the associated frame, entry report, and example interpretations. The frame section encompasses the frame evoked by the lexical item, the types and meanings of the frame elements, relationships with other frames, and other lexical items which trigger the frames.

Based on the relevant frames of Frame Semantics, we adjusted the paraphrasing frames. The adjusted frames classify the psychological activity verbs into the following categories: "Respect Frame", "Like Frame", "Love dearly Frame", "Miss Frame", "Recall Frame", "Empathy Frame" and "Grasp Frame". The core frame elements for the "Respect Frame" include "Cognizer", "Object of respect" and "Content of respect". The core frame elements for the "Like Frame" include "Cognizer" and "Object of affection". The core frame elements for the "Love dearly Frame" include "Cognizer" and "Object of hurt". The core frame elements for the "Miss Frame" include "Cognizer" and "Object of missing". The core frame elements for the "Recall Frame" include "Cognizer" and "Content of recall". The core frame elements for the "Empathy Frame" include "Cognizer", "Object of empathy" and "Content of empathy". Finally, the core frame elements for the "Grasp Frame" include "Cognizer" and "Content being grasped".

Since core frame elements determine the fundamental characteristics of a frame, it is crucial to identify which frame elements are core frame elements. According to Frame Semantics, core frame elements are the essential components and distinguishing features of a frame. When distinguishing core frame elements from non-core frame elements, we can refer to the following criteria:

(1) Core frame elements are essential components that are indispensable to the frame.
(2) The core frame elements of a particular frame have distinctive characteristics compared to those of other frames.
(3) Core frame elements are frequently instantiated.

During the corpus analysis, we found that not all core frame elements fully meet these three criteria. For example, the "Cognizer" elements are presented in all the frames studied in this paper. The "Cognizer" elements are essential components of the mental verb frames and are frequently instantiated, but they do not exhibit distinguishing features across different frames. Similarly, the "Degree" elements are instantiated frequently in some frames, but they are not indispensable components of the frames and does not distinguish themselves from other frames. Therefore, the determination of core frame elements must first satisfy the first criterion, following the second and third criteria in succession.

Since the classification and determination of frames cannot rely solely on personal experience, they must be inductively analyzed from a large corpus. We can refer to the methods proposed by Fillmore for identifying semantic frames in Frame Semantics researches:

(1) Browse relevant examples of a target word.
(2) Focus on the semantic types of phrases that co-occur with the target word (i.e., frame elements) and look for other words with similar meanings that can also co-occur with similar phrases.
(3) Pay attention to the types of phrases which share the same meanings with this group of words.
(4) Assume that there are two categories of phrases which can co-occur with the target word: one category frequently co-occurs with a specific group of words, while the other category frequently co-occurs with another group. This can serve as strong evidences for (frame-based) categorizing meanings.

After identifying the core frame elements, lexical items with the same core frame elements are grouped into the same frames, while words that co-occur with different frame elements are split into multiple lexical items, which lead to the classification of different frames. Following adjustments, the original 14 lexical items increased to 18, and the 7 frames were adjusted to 11. The frame elements were also described in more specific and detailed terms. Due to the limitations of the text length, we selected "zūnjìng 尊敬 'Respect' Frame" from the 11 frames for illustrative analysis.

The "zūnjìng 尊敬 'Respect' Frame" is derived from the original "Holding Respect Frame". And some adjustments are made to these lexical items. The situation depicted by the "zūnjìng 尊敬 'Respect' Frame" is as follows: someone holds respect for another person. Its core frame elements include the "Cognizer" (cog) and the "Object of Respect" (dx). While non-core frame elements may include "Degree" (degr) among others. The lexical items associated with this frame are "zūnjìng 尊敬 'respect'" and "chóngjìng 崇敬 'revere'".

4   Statistical Analysis of Frame Elements

Frame Semantics posits that each component on the surface of a sentence activates a frame element. Analyzing the syntactic realization of frame elements can intuitively distinguish between core and non-core frame elements, as well as clarify how different frame elements are syntactically realized on the surface of sentences.

The syntactic realization of frame elements refers to the syntactic components which express the phrase types of these frame elements. As noted earlier, the syntactic components of frame elements for psychological activity verbs primarily include subjects, objects, adverbials, complements and modifiers. The expressed phrase types may include noun phrases and prepositional phrases among others.

This research will conduct a specific statistical analysis of the syntactic realization of frame elements. The analysis will reference the Chinese Frame Semantics Network and will categorize the statistical content into eight parts: "Frame Elements", "Phrase Types", "Syntactic Components", "Annotation Quantity", "Proportion of Syntactic Realization", "Proportion of Each Frame Element", "Distinction Degree" and "Element Type". The "Frame Elements" column will indicate the names of the frame elements. "Phrase Types" and "Syntactic Components" will be denoted using abbreviations. The "Annotation Quantity" represents the number of syntactic realizations of the particular frame elements within example sentences. The "Proportion of Syntactic Realization" indicates the ratio of the number of syntactic realizations to the total number of extracted corpora. The "Proportion of Each Frame Element" reflects the proportion of each frame element in the total corpus. The "Distinction Degree" denotes whether the elements possess distinct characteristics that differentiate them from other frames, which are represented as "high" or "low". The "Element Type" includes "Core Frame Element" or "Non-Core Frame Element". In the case of non-core frame elements, those with low frequency of occurrence and minimal impact on the frames will not be included in the statistics. In the "zūnjìng 尊敬 'respect' Frame", core frame elements include "cognizer" (cog) and "object of respect" (dx). And the non-core frame element is "degree" (degr). The followings are the statistical analysis table of the syntactic realizations for 19 lexical items (Table 1).

Table 1. Syntactic Realization of the Lexical Item "zūnjìng 尊敬 'respect'" in the "Respect Frame"

Frame Element	Phrase Type	Syntactic Function	Number of Annotations	Syntactic Realization Proportion	Proportion of Each Frame Element	Distinctiveness	Number of Annotations
Cognizer (cog)	np	subj	113	0.4520	0.7480	Low	Core
		atta	74	0.2960			
Object of Respect (dx)	np	obj	36	0.1440	0.6320	High	Core
		subj	86	0.3440			
	pp	adva	26	0.1040			
		atta	10	0.0400			
Degree (degr)	d	adva	28	0.1220	0.1220	Low	Non-core

Based on the statistics from the table, it can be observed that the "Cognizer" element primarily appears in the sentence as a noun phrase functioning serving as the subject. Similarly, the "Object of Respect" element also frequently presents itself as a noun phrase serving as the subject. When the "Object of Respect" is a noun phrase used as the subject, it often requires supporting words such as "shòudào 受到 'receive'" or "yíngdé 赢得 'earn'".

5 Paraphrasing Models of Mental Verbs and Comparison with Dictionary Paraphrasing

5.1 Summary of Paraphrasing Models

Paraphrasing models refer to the standardized and formulaic descriptions of word meanings. Previous scholars have analyzed dictionary paraphrasing models from various perspectives including paraphrasing metalanguage (Fu [20], An [21], Hu [22], Weng [23]), metaphorical meanings (Zhong [24]), and cognitive structures (Zhang [25]). This research approaches the paraphrasing of mental verbs from the perspective of cognitive frameworks, focusing on 18 lexical items related to psychological activity verbs. The summarized paraphrasing models in this research consist of "core framework elements" + "paraphrasing keywords" + "distinctive features" + "syntactic realizations".

Through the framework analyses and researches on frame elements, we have concluded that lexical items within the same frameworks share fundamental characteristics inherent to that frameworks. For example, in the "Respect Frame", both lexical items "zūnjìng 尊敬 'respect'" and "chóngjìng 崇敬1 'revere'" possess the feature of "treatment" which we refer to as the "paraphrasing keywords". Core frame elements can be used to fill in the paraphrasing frame, distinguishing them from other frames. For instance, within the "Miss Frame", the frame elements "Object of Missing" generally refers to people, countries, hometowns as well as past events.

Moreover, lexical items within the same frames exhibit distinctive features which enable their differentiation. For instance, in the "Miss Frame", the objects of the lexical item "xiǎngniàn 想念 'miss'" can only be people or environments, whereas the objects of the lexical item "huáiniàn 怀念 'long for'" can also include "past events" and "people" often being those who cannot be seen again.

The syntactic realizations of word meanings in dictionary paraphrasing should align as closely as possible with the syntactic forms which appear most frequently in the corpus analyses. For example, the frame elements "Object of Empathy" and "Content of Empathy" in the "Empathy Frame" predominantly appear as noun phrases serving as objects in the corpus. Thus, this should be reflected in the object position of dictionary paraphrasing. Additionally, this research employs generic referential terms such as "mǒurén 某人 'someone'" or "tārén 他人 'others'" to denote core frame elements which lack distinctive features.

In the "zūnjìng 尊敬 'Respect' Frame", the frame element "Cognizer" typically appears in the form of noun phrases as the subject in sentences, lacking distinctive features. And the element "Cognizer" can be represented by the generic referential term "mǒu rén 某人 'someone'". The distinctive features of the "Object of Respect" element for the lexical item "zūnjìng 尊敬 'Respect'" lean towards individuals who are elders, those in higher positions or those who have made significant contributions. And it also predominantly appears as noun phrases functioning serving as subjects in sentences. The paraphrasing keyword for the "Respect Frame" is "treat" in the paraphrasing to be expressed as "to hold in esteem and treat with great politeness" (Table 2).

Table 2. Lexical Item Paraphrasing Models in the "zūnjìng 尊敬 'Respect' Frame"

Lexical Item	Core Framework Element	Distinctive Features	Paraphrasing Language	Paraphrasing Pattern
Respect	(cog) Cognitive Agent (cog)	None	Someone	Someone shows respect and treats elders, people of higher status, or those who have made significant contributions with great politeness
	Object of Respect (dx)	Elders, people of higher status, or those who have made significant contributions	Elders, people of higher status, or those who have made significant contributions	
Reverence	(cog) Cognitive Agent (cog)	None	Someone	Someone shows great respect for those of high status or who have made significant contributions and treats them with great politeness
	Object of Respect (dx)	People of high status or those who have made significant contributions	People of high status or those who have made significant contributions	

5.2 Comparison of Dictionary Paraphrasing

This study analyzes the *Modern Chinese Dictionary (7th Edition)*, along with two Chinese dictionaries for foreign learners, namely the *Commercial Press Learner's Chinese Dictionary* and the *Contemporary Chinese Learner's Dictionary*. Given that each learner's dictionary presents different frameworks and frame elements for the same term, this research first conducts a horizontal analysis of the frame classifications and descriptions of frame elements in the *Commercial Press Learner's Chinese Dictionary* and the *Contemporary Chinese Learner's Dictionary*.

Many outward-oriented learner's dictionaries often reference the *Modern Chinese Dictionary*, so this analysis will also include a vertical comparison between outward-oriented and inward-oriented dictionaries in their representation of frameworks and frame elements. Finally, suggestions will be provided from the perspective of Frame Semantics for improving verb paraphrasing in Chinese learner's dictionaries (Table 3).

For the term "zūnjìng 尊敬 'respect'", the "Cognitive Agent" element does not possess distinguishing features and can be omitted from the paraphrasing. The "Object of Respect" element does have distinguishing features which both outward-oriented Chinese learner's dictionaries reflect. However, the generalization of the frame elements are not comprehensive enough. The "Object of Respect" element encompasses "elders, individuals of higher status, or those who have made significant contributions."

Regarding the frame elements, the "Cognizer" element lacks distinguishing features and can be omitted from the paraphrasing. However, the "Object of Respect" element possesses distinguishing characteristics and can be represented by the paraphrasing "others" and "abstract concepts". The *Contemporary Chinese Learner's Dictionary* presents the

Table 3. Comparison of Paraphrasing for the "zūnjìng 尊敬 'respect' Frame"

Term	Modern Chinese Dictionary	Commercial Press Learner's Chinese Dictionary	Contemporary Chinese Learner's Dictionary
Respect	To treat with importance and respect	The object of respect is often teachers and elders	To treat with respect and politeness in speech and attitude, mainly used for older or higher-status individuals. To treat with importance and respect
Reverence	To highly esteem and respec	(From the heart) Worship and respect	To place great importance on respect

"Object of Respect" frame element in details, while the *Commercial Press Learner's Chinese Dictionary* does not specify these frame elements.

6   Recommendations for Verb Paraphrasing in Outward-Oriented Chinese Learner's Dictionaries

This research analyzes authentic corpora from the perspective of Frame Semantics, aiming to identify suitable paraphrasing models and provide recommendations for verb paraphrasing in Chinese learner's dictionaries.

(1) **Paraphrasing verbs should be defined within a "context".**

Frame Semantics posits that understanding a term necessitates awareness of the context it activates. Paraphrasing verbs within a "context" is vivid and aligns with the cognitive commonalities of both the target and native languages, facilitating understanding and learning of word meanings for second language learners. Each frame represents a context corresponding to a distinct meaning, which aids dictionary compilers in delineating meanings. Analyses of two outward-oriented Chinese learner's dictionaries reveal that some words fail to present varying contexts, which restricts second language learners in using these terms in certain situations.

(2) **Distinct frame elements should be reflected in the paraphrasing.**

Frame elements are the participants in constructing frames and are the fundamental units supporting them. The comprehensive presentation of frame elements, especially those with distinguishing features, determines the completeness of context descriptions, which thereby affects the accuracy of paraphrasing. Analyses of two outward-oriented dictionaries, including the representative *Commercial Press Learner's Chinese Dictionary* and the latest *Contemporary Chinese Learner's Dictionary*, show that they lack core frame elements with distinguishing features. Some outward-oriented Chinese learner's dictionaries exhibit significant influence from their source texts, aligning completely with the *Modern Chinese Dictionary* in their selection of frame elements. They even exhibit issues of paraphrasing with words whose meanings partially overlap. And these paraphrasing words may be synonymous explanations, which is detrimental to second language learners' understanding of word meanings.

Additionally, frame elements are synthesized and distilled from frames containing different lexical items. And they possess a generalizing nature which cannot precisely describe every term. Thus, it is crucial to use paraphrasing words which second language learners can comprehend. Therefore, the research and summarization of paraphrasing words in outward-oriented Chinese learner's dictionaries are also necessary.

(3) **Frame elements should be summarized with distinguishing features accurately and comprehensively.**

The accurate and comprehensive presentation of frame elements also influences the precision of paraphrasing. Analyses of the two outward-oriented dictionaries show that many lexical items exhibit frame elements, but some of these elements are too broad or not comprehensive enough. This affects second language learner's ability to accurately understand and use these terms. To accurately and comprehensively summarize frame elements with distinguishing features, extensive analyses of authentic corpora are required to extract thorough and precise frame elements.

(4) **The syntactic representations of frame elements should be used as references for the syntactic realizations of paraphrasing.**

When analyzing dictionaries, it is observed that the syntactic forms of the same verb's paraphrasing vary across different dictionaries. Even within the same dictionary, different verbs may have different syntactic forms. For instance, some frame elements are represented in prepositional phrases like "duì 对 'to'……", while others are expressed in verb-object structures. How should the syntactic forms of verb paraphrasing be determined? The syntactic representations of frame elements can serve as reference criteria. Paraphrasing words based on the syntactic forms of the most frequently occurring core frame elements are beneficial for second language learners, which helps them to understand word meanings while mastering their usages.

If the syntactic forms of paraphrasing cannot align with the syntactic representation of frame elements, the examples can still reflect the syntactic representations of frame elements, especially those with high usage frequency.

(5) **The quantity and quality of frame elements should be used as criteria for evaluating the quality of dictionary paraphrasing.**

With the increasing number of outward-oriented Chinese learner's dictionaries, discerning the quality of different dictionaries has become a significant issue. Under the theoretical framework of Frame Semantics, frame elements serving as the basic units of contexts and meanings play decisive roles in the quality of paraphrasing. Therefore, studying the quantity and quality of frame elements can be reference points for evaluating the quality of dictionary paraphrasing. The paraphrasing of mental words based on Frame Semantics is also beneficial for the semantic understanding of polysemous words in affective computing for artificial intelligence, as well as for the construction of emotion lexicons [26, 27].

Acknowledgments. This paper has received support from various funding sources, including: The Na-tional Language Commission's key project: Research on the Construction of a Chi-nese

Mental Lexicon Corpus Based on Intelligent Computing (ZDI145-17); Beijing Municipal Social Science Foundation Key Project: Research on the Historical and Current Lexicon in Beijing Dialect Over the Past Century in the Context of Lan-guage Contact(22YYA002); The phased achieve-ments of the following major pro-jects: the National Language Commission's 14th Five-Year Research Plan for 2023 Provincial and Ministerial-Level Major Projects: Research on Language Talent De-velopment in the Context of Collaborative Development of Education, Science, and Talent (ZDA145-12); the Key Project: Research on the Theory and Key Technolo-gies of Intelli-gent Assessment of Chinese Expression Ability (ZDI145-92); the China Educational Technology Association's major project: Development of Chinese Expression Ability (CEA) Standards and Innovation in Their Intelligent Assessment Application" (XJJ202205003).We are grateful for the support provided by these funding sources, which has enabled us to carry out this research.

References

1. Zhang, Y.: Cognitive Semantics and Multidimensional Definitions in the New Generation of Bilingual/Bilingual Dictionaries. Foreign Language Teaching and Research (1) (2011)
2. The Dictionary Research Center of the Commercial Press: Modern Chinese Learning Dictionary. Commercial Press, Beijing (2010)
3. Liu, C.: Dictionary of Example Sentences for Learning Chinese. Beijing Language and Culture University Press, Beijing (2005)
4. Shao, J., Wang J., Wu Y., Xu Z.: HSK Chinese Proficiency Examination Dictionary. East China Normal University Press, Shanghai (2000)
5. Shi, G.: Dictionary of Teaching and Learning Chinese. Commercial Press, Beijing (2010)
6. Lu, J.: Commercial Press Chinese Dictionary. Commercial Press, Beijing (2007)
7. The HSK Center of Beijing Language and Culture University: The HSK Vocabulary Outline Chinese 8000 Word Dictionary. Beijing Language and Culture University Press, Beijing (2000)
8. Fillmore, C.J.: Frame Semantics. In Linguistics in the Morning Calm, edited by the Linguistic Society of Korea, pp. 111–112. Hanshan Publishing Co., Seoul (1982)
9. Fillmore, C.J.: Some Problems for Case Grammar. Report of the Twenty-Second Annual Round Table Meeting on Linguistics and Language Studies. Georgetown University Press, Washington, D.C.
10. You, L.: Research on the Construction of Modern Chinese Frame Semantic Knowledge Base. PhD Dissertation. Shanghai Normal University, Shanghai (2006)
11. Ma, H.: Research on the Frame Semantic System of Chinese Transaction Domain. PhD Dissertation. Shanghai Normal University, Shanghai (2008)
12. Zhou, L.: A Comparative Study of Chinese and English Semantic Frame Networks. Chinese as a Foreign Language (4) (2009)
13. Li, Q.: Frame Net: A Lexical Project Based on Frame Semantics. Chinese Science and Technology Information (16) (2005)
14. Liu, M., Wan, M.: Research on Chinese Verbs and Classification: Construction and Appli-cation of the Semantic Network of Chinese Verbs. Dictionary Research (02), 42–60 (2019)
15. Liu, M., He, T., He H., and Cao Y.: Mandarin Physical Contact Verbs: A Frame-Based Constructional Approach. In: Chinese Lexical Semantics, 22nd Workshop, CLSW 2021, pp. 187–205 (2021)
16. Zhang, Y.: Cognitive Semantics and Multidimensional Definitions in the New Generation of Bilingual/Bilingual Dictionaries. Foreign Language Teaching and Research **42**(05), 374–379+401 (2010)

17. Mei, J.: Synonym Forest. Shanghai Lexicographical Publishing House, Shanghai (1983)
18. Dictionary Institute of Linguistics, Chinese Academy of Social Sciences. Modern Chinese Dictionary. Commercial Press, Beijing (2016)
19. Zhang, Z.: Contemporary Chinese Learning Dictionary. Commercial Press, Beijing (2020)
20. Fu, H.: The Division of Semantic Units and Meaning Items. Dictionary Research (3) (1995)
21. An, H.: Research on the Theory and Application of Meta-Language in Chinese Definition. Xuelin Publishing House (2009)
22. Hu, W., Zhang, Y.: The impact of definition patterns in Chinese-English dictionaries on Chinese EFL Learners' English Production Ability. Foreign Languages (5) (2011)
23. Weng, X., Chao, Z.: Research on definition patterns in foreign language Chinese Learning dictionaries based on meta-language. Language and Character Studies (4) (2011)
24. Zhong, Z.h.: Metaphor definitions and their definition patterns. Foreign Languages (Journal of Shanghai International Studies University) 35(02) (2012)
25. Zhang, Y.: Constructing cognitive semantic structures and meaning-driven definition patterns: a discussion on the nature and structure of definitions in bilingual chinese dictionaries. Modern Foreign Languages (04) (2006)
26. Wang, W., Zhou, J., Zhang, K.: Research on the semantic collocations of mental verbs and the generative mechanisms of polysemy: the generative lexicon. In: Chinese Lexical Semantics, 24st Workshop, CLSW 2023, pp. 196–210 (2023)
27. Rosa, R.L., Schwartz, G.M., Ruggiero, W.V., Rodríguez, D.Z.: A knowledge-based recom mendation system that includes sentiment analysis and deep learning. IEEE Trans. Industr. Inf. 15(4), 2124–2135 (2018)

Semantic System and Configuration Mechanism of Individual Classifier in Yue Dialect Along Yulin Route

Yuanhao Bi[1]($\boxtimes$), Fengyu Qin[2], and Yonglin He[3]

[1] Department of Chinese Language and Literature, Sun Yat-sen University, Guangzhou 510275, Guangdong, China
yh.bi@foxmail.com
[2] School of Liberal Arts, Guangxi University, Nanning 530004, Guangxi, China
[3] School of International Culture, South China Normal University, Guangzhou 510630, Guangdong, China

Abstract. The individual classifier forms in the Yulin area of Guangxi are particularly diverse. The Yulin urban has three forms: *kœ32, khœ54*, and *nap1*; Xingye has four forms: *kau22, kœ22, khœ35* and *nap1*; Beiliu also has three forms: *kau11, khœ42* and *nap1*; while Rong has four forms: *kau24, kœ21/khœ45* and *nap1*. The classifier semantic system of the Yulin Yue dialect is a result of grammatical replication due to contact with Kra-Dai languages. In the process of lexical diffusion of new forms, the individual classifier systems in various regions have adopted similar rearrangement patterns, constrained by cognitive system limitations on available pathways. However, differences remain due to variations in subsequent omissions and adjustments.

Keywords: Classifier · Yulin Yue dialect · Semantic system · Language contact · Degree semantic

1 Introduction

In Yulin City and its subordinate counties—Xingye, Beiliu, and Rongxian (collectively referred to as the *Yulin route* in this paper, as they are situated along an east-west axis)— there exists a distinctive system of individual classifiers in the Yue dialect. In Yulin urban, there are three forms of individual classifiers:: *kœ32, khœ54 and nap1*; in Xingye, there are four forms of individual classifiers: *kau22, kœ22, khœ35* and *nap1*; in Beiliu, there are three forms of individual classifiers: *kau11, khœ42*, and *nap1*; and Rongxian's individual classifiers has four forms: *kau24, kœ21/khœ45*[1] and *nap1*.

The four regions along the Yulin area are bordered by Cenxi to the east, Hengzhou to the west, Guigang to the north, and Luchuan and Bobai to the south. The maximum span,

---

[1] Here is separated by a *slash* / to indicate a free variant relationship, which will be discussed in detail later.

P. Jin et al. (Eds.): CLSW 2024, LNAI 15552, pp. 231–240, 2025.
https://doi.org/10.1007/978-981-96-3509-2_17

from east to west and north to south, is approximately one degree of latitude and longitude ($22°14'$N–$23°12'$N, $109°66'$E–$110°90'$E). Within this relatively small geographic area, the encoding of classifiers is highly complex and variable, demonstrating strong markedness. Despite some tonal differences, most localities exhibit a classifier *kœ* with the unaspirated consonant /k/ and a classifier *khœ* with the aspirated consonant /kh/, which can likely be considered cognate derivations. This paper will provide a detailed description of the semantic features of individual classifiers in the Yue dialect spoken along Yulin, and explore the potential configuration mechanisms.

2 Semantic Features

2.1 Basic Semantic Features

Languages typically employ either classifiers or number markers to indicate the category of number (cf. Qiu [1]). Thus, individual classifiers are used exclusively to encode countable entities, excluding uncountable ones and abstract concepts. For example, consider Yulin urban dialect:[2]

(1) a. individual[2]:

jat5   **kœ32/khœ54/nap1** sek2tau21

one   CL   stone

a piece of stone

b. uncountable:

*jat5   **kœ32/khœ54/nap1** sœi33

one   CL   water

*a drop of water

c. abstract:

*jat5   **kœ32/khœ54/nap1** nam21fat5

one   CL   thought

*a piece of thought

Individual classifiers in each of the four regions (Yulin urban area, Xingye, Beiliu, and Rongxian) form a paradigm, with differences in size manifested in the syntagmatic relation. Given the variations in the number of individual classifiers across the four regions and the differences in their phonological forms, it is essential to examine the situation in each region individually to determine the semantic patterns encoded by the different classifiers.

Here we propose the *Polarity Scale Test* and the *Non-Polarity Scale Test*, which provide a feasible experimental approach for determining multilevel classifier sequences. The former is conducted by directly adding the modifier adjectives *big/small* and observing their acceptability, while the latter involves comparing the classifiers to establish their size relationships, addressing situations that cannot be resolved by the former.

---

[2] The following abbreviations are used: CL = classifier, LOC = locative, CMP = comparative.

Yulin Urban. There are three forms of individual classifier collections in Yulin urban area: *kœ32, khœ54* and *nap1*.

The first is the Polarity Scale Test:

(2) kɔ52   pɔng24   jau33   **kœ32**   tɔi52/*ɬai54   sek2tau32

     this   LOC   exist   CL   big/*small   stone

     There is a big/*small stone.

(3) kɔ52   pɔng24   jau33   **khœ54**   ɬai54/*tɔi52   sek2tau32

     this   LOC   exist   CL   small/*big   stone

     There is a small/*big stone.

(4) kɔ52   pɔng24   jau33   **nap1**   ɬai54/*tɔi52   sek2tau32

     this   LOC   exist   CL   small/*big   stone

     There is a small/*big stone.

The results of the Polarity Scale Test show that *kœ32* can only accept the adjective *big* modification but not *small* modification; both *khœ54* and *nap1* can only accept the adjective *small* modification but not *big* modification. Thus, it can be concluded that *kœ32* is bigger than *khœ54* and *nap1*, while the relationship between *khœ54* and *nap1* remains to be determined by the Non-Polarity Scale Test.

Non-Polarity Scale Test:

(5) *khœ54* VS. *nap1*:

     kɔ52   **khœ54**   tau52fu33 tɔi52/*nai54   kɔ52   a54 **nap1**

     this   CL   toufu   big/*small   CMP   that CL

     tau52fu42

     toufu

     This toufu is bigger/*smaller than that toufu.

The results of the Non-Polarity Scale Test show that when *khœ54* and *nap1* are compared in terms of size, the former can only be used for cases bigger than the latter, so *khœ54* is bigger than *nap1*.

Combining the above results of the Polar Scale Test and the Non-Polarity Scale Test, the size relationship between the different forms of coding for the individual classifiers in the Yulin urban area can be determined as follows:

I. *kœ32* > *khœ54* > *nap1*

Xingye. There are four forms of individual classifiers in Xingye: *kau22, kœ22, khœ35* and *nap1*.

The first is the Polarity Scale Test:

(6) kɔ52   tu33   jau24   **kau22**   tɔi52/*nɯɪ33   sek3thau22
     this   LOC   exist   CL   big/*small   stone

There is a big/*small stone.

(7) kɔ52   tu33   jau24   **kœ22**   tɔi52/*nɯɪ33   sek3thau22
     this   LOC   exist   CL   big/*small   stone

There is a big/*small stone.

(8) kɔ52   tu33   jau24   **khœ35**   nɯɪ33/*tɔi52   sek3thau22
     this   LOC   exist   CL   small/*big   stone

There is a small/*big stone.

(9) kɔ52   tu33   jau24   **nap1**   nɯɪ33/*tɔi52   sek3thau22
     this   LOC   exist   CL   small/*big   stone

There is a small/*big stone.

The results of the Polarity Scale Test show that both *kau22* and *kœ22* can only be modified by the adjective *big*, whereas both *khœ35* and *nap1* can only be modified by the adjective *small*, which makes it possible to determine that *kau22* and *kœ22* are bigger than *khœ35* and *nap1*, but it is not possible to determine the magnitude relationship between *kau22* and *kœ22*, as well as *khœ35* and *nap1*, and thus the Non-Polarity Scale Test is still needed.

Non-Polarity Scale Test:

(10) a. *kau22* VS. *kœ22*:

         kɔ52   **kau22**   tau31fu52   tɔi52/*nɯɪ33   kɔ52   a52
         this   CL   toufu   big/*small   CMP   that

         kœ22 tau31fu52
         CL   toufu

This toufu is bigger/*smaller than that toufu.

     b. *khœ35* VS. *nap1*:

         kɔ52   **khœ35**   tau31fu52   tɔi52/*nɯɪ33   kɔ52   a52
         this   CL   toufu   big/*small   CMP   that

         nap1 tau31fu52
         CL   toufu

This toufu is bigger/*smaller than that toufu.

The results of the Non-Polarity Scale Test show that when *kau22* is compared with *kœ22* and *khœ35* with *nap1* in terms of size, the former can only be used for cases bigger than the latter as well, thus *kau22* is bigger than *kœ22* and *khœ35* is bigger than *nap1*.

Combining the results of the Polarity Scale Test and the Non-Polarity Scale Test mentioned above, the size relationship between the different forms of coding for the Xingye individual classifiers can be determined as follows:

II. *kau22 > kœ22 > khœ35 > nap1*

Beiliu. There are three forms of individual classifiers in Beiliu: *kau11, khœ42* and *nap1*.

The Polarity Scale Test:

(11) kɔ52   tu11   jau33   **kau11**   tai11/*łai33   sek1 thau33

      this   LOC   exist   CL   big/*small   stone

    There is a big/*small stone.

(12) kɔ52   tu11   jau33   **khœ42**   tai11/łai33   sek1 thau33

      this   LOC   exist   CL   big/small   stone

    There is a big/small stone.

(13) kɔ52   tu11   jau33   **nap1**   łai33/*tai11   sek1 thau33

      this   LOC   exist   CL   small/*big   stone

    There is a small/*big stone.

The results of the Polarity Scale Test show that *kau11* can only be modified by the adjective *big*, *khœ42* can be modified by both adjectives *big* and *small*, and *nap1* can only be modified by the adjective *small*. As a result, without resorting to the Non-Polarity Scale Test, the size relationships of the different forms of the individual classifiers encoded in the Beiliu can be determined as follows:

III. *kau11 > khœ42 > nap1*

Rongxian. There are four forms of individual classifiers in Rongxian: *kau24, kœ21/khœ45* and *nap1*.

The Polarity Scale Test:

(14) kɔ52   tau52   jau33   **kau24**   tai31/*sai52   sek1 tau31

      this   LOC   exist   CL   big/*small   stone

    There is a big/*small stone.

(15) kɔ52   tau52   jau33   **kœ21/khœ45**   tai31/sai52   sek1 tau31

      this   LOC   exist   CL   big/small   stone

    There is a big/small stone.

(16) kɔ52   tau52   jau33   **nap1**   sai52/*tai31   sek1 tau31

      this   LOC   exist   CL   small/*big   stone

    There is a small/*big stone.

The results of the Polarity Scale Test show that *kau24* can only be modified by the adjective *big*, *kœ21/khœ45* can be modified by both adjectives *big* and *small*, and *nap1* can only be modified by the adjective *small*. Again, without resorting to the Non-Polarity Scale Test, the size relationships of the different forms of the individual classifiers can be determined as follows:

IV. *kau24 > kœ21/khœ45 > nap1*

2.2 Summary

Through the Polarity Scale Test and the Non-Polarity Scale Test, the hierarchical relationships of individual classifiers in the four regions along Yulin are now clear. Their semantic
encoding of dimensions can be categorized into four levels: *big*, *sub-big*, *sub-small*, and
smallest, as shown in the following table (Table 1):

Table 1. Individual classifier semantic system of Yue Dialect along Yulin.

	Yulin Urban	Xingye	Beiliu	Rongxian
Big	*kœ32*	*kau22*	*kau11*	*kœ21/khœ45*
Sub-Big		*kœ22*	*khœ42*	*kau24*
Sub-Small	*khœ54*	*khœ35*		
Smallest	*nap1*	*nap1*	*nap1*	*nap1*

Among these, the Xingye dialect exhibits all four semantic levels (*kau22 > kœ22 >
khœ35 > nap1*), while the other three do not. In Yulin urban area, *kau* is not used,
Beiliu does not use *kœ*, and Rongxian does not distinguish between *kœ* and *khœ*. All four
regions share the classifiers *nap1* and *khœ*, with the former encoding the smallest form,
and the latter (except in Rongxian) primarily occurring in non-extreme positions. It is
noteworthy that the semantic hierarchies of the *kœ* and *khœ* classifiers fluctuate across
the four regions, although they are clearly cognate. The configuration mechanism behind
this phenomenon warrants further investigation.

2.3 Markedness of Semantic Features

Aikhenvald [2] summarizes the basic referential categories for encoding various types
of nominal and quantitative classifiers. Among these, she argues that the *size* category
should follow a binary classification pattern, corresponding to *big* and *small* respectively.
Therefore, the binary categorization of size in a given dimension is very common in
classifier languages and is, in fact, the most frequent pattern, as it aligns closely with the
basic dualistic model through which humans perceive the world. For other Yue dialects
in Guangxi, with the exception of a few regions where the new generation has gradually
introduced the general classifier from Standard Mandarin, all exhibit a bifurcated pattern,
i.e. *kau* and *nap*, which aligns with Aikhenvald's [2] commonality of human languages.
Although the area covered by the Yue dialect across the four regions along the Yulin route
is not extensive, the individual classifiers within this area exhibit strong markedness, as
shown below:
Firstly, it differs from typologically common patterns. Instead of the typical dichotomous
pattern, a tripartite and quartal pattern is observed. This tripartite and quartal pattern does
not extend to the Yulin route and is not found in Hengzhou, the western neighbor, or
Cenxi, the eastern neighbor.

Secondly, it is a different pattern than common in the same region. The Yue dialect of the region is dichotomized as *kau* and *nap*[3], but along the Yulin route, there are generally *kœ* and *khœ* in sizes bigger than *nap*, and there is no *kau* in Yulin urban area.

3 Configuration Mechanisms

It is worth exploring the configuration mechanism behind such a marked phenomenon in the small geographical area of the four regions along the Yulin route.

3.1 Motivation: Language Contact

Although individual classifiers with semantics beyond bifurcation are rare in Chinese, among the individual classifiers of Zhuang, a Kra-Dai language, instances of Aikhenvald's [2] bifurcation pattern being surpassed occur periodically. For instance:

(17) Wuming Zhuang (cf. Zhang [3]): *ŋa:u5> ŋeu5/kai5> ŋi5*

(18) Naan Zhuang (cf. Nong [4]): *khaaŋ22> nau22> met55> nek21*

(19) Guigang Zhuang (field work): *me6/nan1> ʔdak7> nat1> ŋve:i6*

As can be seen from the above examples, it is common for individual classifiers in Zhuang to exhibit a four-part division. This is linked to the development of classifiers across the Kra-Dai language family. Not only individual classifiers, but also other types of classifiers, including referent classifiers, show multi-level distinctions [5]. The Yue dialect in Guangxi, due to its long history of coexistence with Zhuang, has been deeply influenced by various grammatical features of Zhuang, and grammaticalization triggered by this contact is also very common.

Hilário [6] demonstrated through a series of parametric statistical analyses that far-southern Chinese languages, such as Cantonese, are much closer to the non-Chinese typological features of the mainland Southeast Asian language area (MSEA). Qin [7] previously examined several grammatical features shared by the Guangxi region as a linguistic area, and Huang & Wu [8] explicitly suggested that south-central Guangxi can be considered a micro-grammaticalization area within the mainland Southeast Asian linguistic area, which consists of Kra-Dai and Sinitic languages. The Yue dialects along the Yulin route discussed in this paper are also included in this area.

While most individual classifiers in the Yue dialect of Guangxi exhibit a binary size distinction, characterized by the forms of *kau* and *nap*, the Zhuang language has a more complex, multilevel size encoding system, which goes beyond a simple dichotomy. In this respect, Zhuang provides a model for the Yue dialect, which can then adopt or replicate this system. In this process, Zhuang is the model language and Yue dialect is the replica language, and the process by which the replica language copies a category in the model language is grammatical replication [9]. Since *kœ* and *khœ* are clearly a pair of cognate forms and have the same consonantal form with *kau52*, we determine that they are both derived from *kau52*.

---

[3] This pronunciation may not be the case for all Yue dialects, but since they all correspond to 嘥 and 粒 in Chinese, and for ease of presentation we also standardize here with *kau* and *nap*.

3.2 Mechanisms for Semantic Matching

It is noteworthy that *kœ* and *khœ*, as cognate derivatives, exhibit different patterns of behavior across the four regions of the Yue dialect. Specifically, new constituents are created and subsequently merged to varying degrees in these regions, a phenomenon that can be explained within the framework of Degree Semantics.

Cresswell's [10] study is often considered the foundation of of Degree Semantics, which was initially applied primarily to address the comparative problems of adjectives. He introduced the concept of *scale* in Degree Semantics, and argued that *When we make comparisons, there are points of various scales in our brains.* As a result, Cresswell [10] proposed that the meaning of a hierarchical adjective includes a degree-theoretic component, e.g., the meaning of ⟨tall, man⟩ can be roughly expressed as *x is a man who is tall to degree y.* In this paper, we argue that the same framework of Degree Semantics can be applied to the analysis of individual classifiers. Specifically, we suggest that < *kau*, stone > = *x is a stone which is big to degree y, y = kau.*

Kennedy [11] further conceptualized the abstraction of magnitude as an infinitely long (or infinite) measuring scale and provided a quantitative representation of objects with gradable properties. We combine the illustrations from Kennedy [11] and Yuan [12] and present them as Fig. 1, as shown below:

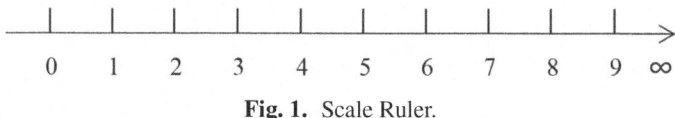

Fig. 1. Scale Ruler.

Yuan [12] argued that the positive interval along this axis is [N-p, ∞], while the negative interval is [0, N-n], with a middle ground between the two represented as [N-n, N-p][4]. We can thus see that at the small size end of the spectrum is a closed jurisdiction (i.e., as small as 0) and at the large size end of the spectrum is an open jurisdiction (i.e., all the way to infinity ∞).

If we now set $p = kau$ and $n = nap$, the traditional *kau-nap* pattern can be roughly represented as in the following diagram (Fig. 2):

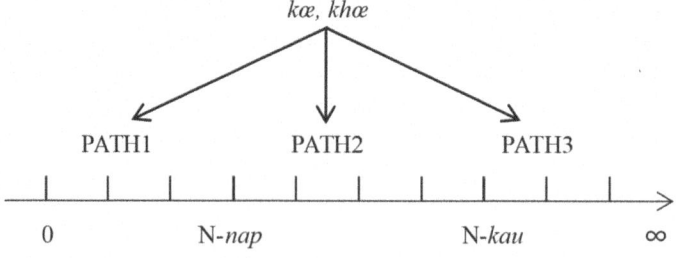

Fig. 2. Match Mechanism.

---

[4] -*N* and -*p* represent subscript values, respectively, and $n < p$. (Author's note).

A. [0, N-nap]: narrow closed domain, narrow cognitive space, difficult to insert new components;
B. [N-nap, N-kau]: fuzzy gray middle ground, fluid cognitive space, most likely to insert new components;
C. [N-kau,∞]: open domain with wide cognitive space, also with the possibility of inserting new components.

These three sections at the same time correspond to PATH1, PATH2 and PATH3 respectively, where new constituents may be introduced (see above). In Yue dialect along Yulin, the adoption of PATH1 does not occur due to the difficulty of inserting new constituents into the closed and narrow cognitive domain, so the minimal encoding form of individual quantifiers is fixed as *nap* in all places. PATH2 is used most often, with Yulin urban, Xingye and Beiliu matching it, because the value between *kau--nap* is not very clear, making it difficult to judge to what extent it is big and to what extent it is small. Therefore, it is difficult to define the value of *kau--nap* in between, and it even varies from person to person, which makes it an ideal space for the introduction of new components. PATH3 is used only in Rongxian, where both *kœ* and *khœ* are coded as larger than *kau*, which is not the best location for the addition of new constituents, but the open cognitive domain provides a possibility for it.

4   Conclusion

This paper focuses on the semantic features of the individual classifier system in the Yue dialect along the Yulin route, and examines the internal composition and semantic encoding of the individual classifier system in each place along the route. We identify the four semantic quantitative forms in the region are *kau, kœ, khœ* and *nap*. The specific conclusions can be summarized in the following three points:

I. The individual quantifiers *kau, kœ, khœ* and *nap* in the four areas along Yulin exhibit a semantic pattern with three and four points in terms of dimensions, a pattern that is rare in the Yue dialect and is influenced by contact with Zhuang.
II. II. The original pattern in Yue dialect is *kau--nap*, and *kœ/khœ* are newly added lexical items to align with Zhuang's multi-component pattern.
III. III. On the basis of the *kau--nap* dichotomy, the four regions incorporated the newly added *kœ/khœ* into the scale to form a three/four-point pattern like Zhuang. Different semantic matching mechanisms were employed by each region during the insertion process, leading to adjustments in their internal systems and resulting in the semantic drift of *kœ/khœ* across the regions.

References

1. Qiu, B.: A Study on the Evolution of Post-nominal Plural Expressions in Chinese Based on Tagged Corpora. In: Liu, M., Kit, C., Su, Q. (eds.) CLSW 2020. LNAI, vol. 12278, pp. 268–275. Springer, Cham (2021)
2. Aikhenvald, A.Y.: Classifiers: a typology of noun categorization devices. Oxford University Press, Oxford (2001)

3. Zhang, Y.-S.: A new exploration of nominal classifiers in Wuming Zhuang. J. Minzu Univ. of China **4**, 77–86 (1993). (in Chinese)
4. Nong, C.-S.: A study of Classifiers in Naan Zhuang. Master Dissertation. Minzu University of China, Beijing (2012). (in Chinese)
5. Wei, Q-.W.: A study of Zhuang Grammar. Guangxi Nationalities Publshing House, Nanning (1985). (in Chinese)
6. Hilário, D.S.: The far southern Sinitic languages as part of mainland southeast Asia. In: Enfield, N.J., Comrie, B. (eds.) Languages of Mainland Southeast Asia: The State of the Art, pp. 356–442. Mouton de Gruyter, Berlin (2015)
7. Qin, D.-S.: On Three Areal Grammatical Features in Guangxi. Doctor Dissertation, Hebei Normal University, Shijiazhuang (2013). (in Chinese)
8. Huang, Y., Wu, F.: Central southern guangxi as a grammaticalization area. In: Hancil, S., Berban. T., José, V.L. (eds.) New Trends on Grammaticalization and Language Change, pp. 105–134. John Benjamins Publishing Company, Amsterdam and Philadelphia (2018)
9. Heine, B., Kuteva, T.: On Contact-induced Grammaticalization. Stud. Lang. **27**(3), 529–572 (2003)
10. Cresswell, M.J.: The Semantic of Degree. In: Partee, B.H. (eds.) Mantague Grammar. Academic Press. London (1976)
11. Kennedy, C.: Comparison and Polar Opposition. In: Aaron, L. (eds.) Proceedings of SALT. vol.VII, pp. 240–257. Cornell University, New York (1997)
12. Yuan, Y.-L.: The polar degree of adjectives and their sentence-completing restrictions. Studies of the Chinese Language **2**, 131–144 (2022). (in Chinese)

The Sensorimotor Norms for the Chinese Classifiers

Yimei Shao[(⊠)], Yu-Yin Hsu, and Chu-Ren Huang

Department of Chinese and Bilingual Studies, The Hong Kong Polytechnic University, Hong Kong SAR, China
yimei.shao@polyu.edu.hk

Abstract. Sensorimotor norms have been developed in different languages for research on the relationship between perceptual and conceptual systems. This paper sets up the first sensorimotor norms for 192 Chinese classifiers. For each word, we report values for the following 11 dimensions: vision, hearing, taste, smell, touch, interoception and foot/leg, hand/arm, head excluding mouth, mouth/throat, and torso. The results indicate that the cognitive encoding implicit in Chinese classifiers is largely related to external visual feature and internal feeling. These norms will aid in further exploring the semantic relationship between classifiers and nouns and contribute to studying the influence of perceptual information on word processing and grounded cognition.

Keywords: Sensorimotor Norms · Embodied Cognition · Chinese Classifier

1 Introduction

In Mandarin Chinese, noun is typically preceded by a classifier, for example, '一条蛇 (one + classifier + snake)'. The rule that governs the pairing of classifiers and nouns in Chinese is not completely clear, but the association can often be predicted to some extent based on factors such as animacy, shape and size [1–4]. In other words, the classification is closely linked to the salient perceptual properties of the named entity [5]. In the example of '一条蛇', the classifier '条 tiáo' indicates that it will be followed by a reference to an object that is long and slender [6].

Various studies of classifiers have provided detailed descriptions of the attribute associations between classifiers and the nouns that follow them. For example, Shi regarded the ratio between the dimensions of objects as the preferred cognitive basis for determining shape classifiers [7]. Similarly, Ahrens and Huang showed different sortal classifiers reflect the different meanings of a noun, thus emphasizing the salient properties of the noun's referent [8]. Shao also discussed that the use of a classifier preceding a noun largely depended on semantic properties, particularly the context. For example, the feature of a small quantity expressed by '滴 dī' and '点 diǎn' is aligned with '水 tiao' in contexts in which water is scarce [9].

The link between the semantic encoding and the properties of objects in the classifiers is emphasized by the empirical studies as well. By comparing incongruent classifier-noun pairs with the congruent ones, researchers [10–12] found that the classifier-noun mismatches induced an N400 effect, supporting the view that the comprehension of Chinese classifiers includes the semantic process.

Many studies have operationalized cognitive knowledge in words or concepts, including perceptual and motor-related dimensions [13]. For example, perceptual strength norms, also known as modality exclusivity norms, are typically obtained by assessing how strongly individuals experience a concept through sensorimotor dimensions. It goes without saying that semantic knowledge is highly dependent on sensory input. Sensorimotor norms could provide a multidimensional perspective on how people experience concepts through various sensory (e.g., visual, auditory and tactile) and motor (e.g., hand, foot, head) dimensions, allowing for a comprehensive view of cognitive and semantic associations. For example, Zhong and colleagues conducted a study of sensorimotor strength norms for 664 disyllabic nouns in Chinese, providing evidence of the strengths of sensory modalities and action effectors in Chinese nouns [14].

Although the introspective analysis and empirical studies have showed certain semantic features of classifiers, such as visual property, it is still not clear the general picture of the interaction between the sensorimotor dimension and classifier. Thus, this study provides an overview of classifiers in Mandarin and to assess the extent to which each classifier can be perceived through sensorimotor dimensions.

2   Method

2.1   Participant

30 native speakers of Chinese participated in the experiment. The participants were recruited in university and reported no sensory or reading disabilities. The average age of participants was 24.43 years old ($SD = 0.79$, range $= 24$–26 years). All participants claimed cities in mainland China as their current places of residence and said Mandarin was their first language (inclusive of Chinese dialects). They spent an average of 85.05 min on the survey. Each participant has received certain compensation after the experiment.

2.2   Procedure

Criteria for Selecting Classifiers   The classifiers were selected based on the following criteria. First, we reviewed popular Chinese classifier dictionaries available so far and chose the most recent one [15], which also contained the largest number of classifiers. Next, the classifiers that are used only in the Ancient Chinese, as well as those directly translated from English (e.g., '打 dá dozen' and '听 tīng tin') were excluded. Finally, we removed classifiers that can only be paired with the numeral '一 one' and those that are exclusively used in idioms and colloquial expressions. Ultimately, 192 classifiers were retained.

Experiment Procedure   This study primarily followed the design of the sensorimotor norms study conducted on Chinese nouns [14]. Participants were required to rate their level of sensory experience for each of the 192 classifiers across six perceptual senses (vision, hearing, taste, smell, touch, and interoception) and five distinct action effectors corresponding to different parts of the body (foot/leg, hand/arm, head excluding mouth, mouth/throat, and torso). Ratings were provided on a scale from 0 (indicating no sensory experience) to 5 (indicating very strong sensory experience).

The questionnaire was created and sent through an online survey platform (https://wj.qq.com/) in Mainland China. All classifiers were presented in Simplified Chinese. Demographic information, including gender, age, highest level of education, language background, and place of residence, was collected from the participants at the beginning of the survey. Participants were also asked to disclose any cognitive disorders that might affect their ability to perceive stimuli through sensory organs.

Additionally, participants were presented with four simple Chinese language knowledge questions, which included tasks such as transcribing pinyin to words, identifying radicals within characters, selecting the correct word composed of accurate character forms, and determining the correct semantic meaning of a word. These questions were used as criteria to assess the participants' basic Chinese language comprehension skills and to ensure the quality of the results.

In the questionnaire, if a classifier has multiple pronunciations, we retain these classifiers and indicate the different pronunciations in the questionnaire, for example, '卷 juǎn' in 一卷纸 (a roll of paper) and '卷 juàn' in 一卷画轴 (a painting scroll).

Data Processing We collected and calculated several metrics as follows. First, we assessed the strength of perceptual and motor experiences in 11 dimensions, namely vision, hearing, taste, smell, touch, interoception, leg/foot, hand/arm, mouth/throat, head, and torso. Second, we calculated the mean value for each classifier across these 11 dimensions. The mean value was utilized to determine the dominant dimension associated with each classifier. Lastly, we counted the number of classifiers from each dominant dimension and ranked them to give a general picture of the sensorimotor association with Chinese classifiers.

3 Results

After assigning the dominant perception and effector to the 192 classifiers, we analyzed the distribution of mean ratings in each dominant sensorimotor dimension. Table 1 indicates the overall mean ratings across the 11 sensorimotor dimensions, along with standard derivations and standard errors.

Among the six perceptual dimensions illustrated in Fig. 1, the majority of the classifiers are primarily linked to the visual sense, with the interoceptive dimension coming next in terms of association [14]. A total of 132 classifiers scored higher in the visual dimension than in other dimensions. The interoceptive dimension followed with 48 classifiers scoring the highest in this dimension. Three classifiers, namely '曲 qǔ', '声 shēng', and '首 shǒu', scored the highest in the auditory dimension. Gustatory and tactile senses shared the last two places, having the lowest number of ratings as the dominant sense. '口 kǒu' scored the highest in the gustatory dimension, and '针 zhēn' scored the highest in the tactile dimension. It is worth noting that there are three classifiers that scored the same in both the visual and interoceptive dimensions, namely '名 míng', '篇 piān', and '胎 tāi'.

Table 1. Mean ratings (0–5) across 11 sensorimotor dimensions.

Sensorimotor Dimension	Mean	*SD*	*SE*
Visual	2.22	1.94	0.05
Auditory	0.17	0.73	0.01
Gustatory	0.20	0.81	0.02
Olfactory	0.20	0.81	0.02
Tactile	0.26	1.05	0.02
Interoceptive	0.71	1.55	0.04
Leg/Foot	0.10	0.56	0.01
Hand/Arm	0.40	1.08	0.02
Mouth/Throat	0.15	0.71	0.01
Head	0.05	0.38	0.01
Torso	0.11	0.59	0.01

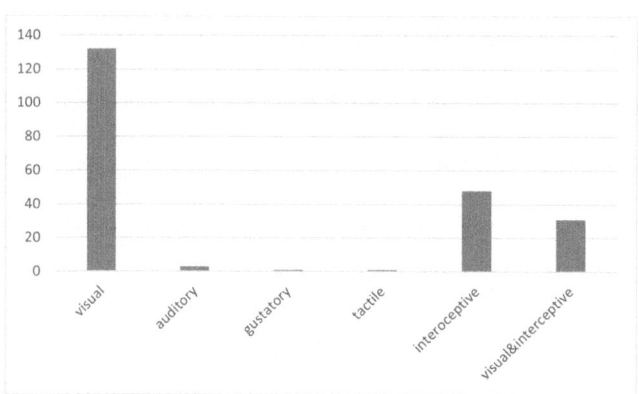

Fig. 1. The number of classifiers in dominant perceptual dimensions.

Figure 2 illustrates the number of classifiers with different dominant body parts. Hand/arm is perceived as being associated with most of the classifiers. There are 70 classifiers that score the highest in the hand/arm dimension, followed by mouth/throat with 23 classifiers and torso with 19 classifiers. In the leg/foot dimension, there are 13 classifiers, and in the head dimension, the fewest with 8 classifiers. An unexpected finding is that 51 classifiers score 0 in all five body-related dimensions.

When considering both perceptual and body-related dimensions together, most classifiers are closely connected to the visual sense, and the interoceptive dimension follows as the next significant factor. A total of 117 classifiers scores the highest in the visual dimension, followed by the interoceptive dimension with 52 classifiers. The classifiers in these two dimensions together account for 88 percent of the total. The auditory dimension still has '曲 qǔ', '声 shēng', and '首 shǒu' as the top classifiers. In the gustatory

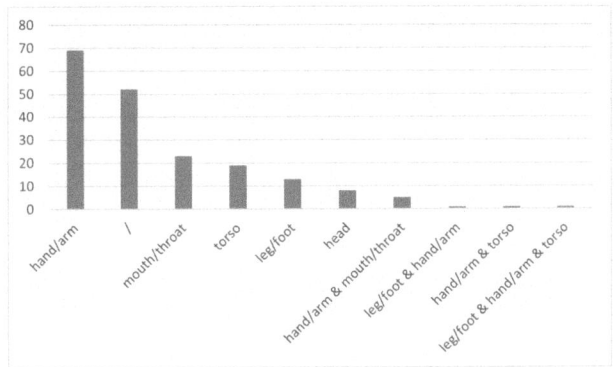

Fig. 2. The number of classifiers in dominant motor dimensions.

dimension, '餐 cān' and '顿 dùn' score the highest, while '针 zhēn' takes the top spot in the tactile dimension. In the leg/foot dimension, '步 bù', '脚 jiǎo', '趟 tàng' are the highest-scoring classifiers, while '把 bǎ', '手 shǒu', '抔 póu', '拳 quán' and '屉 tì' top the hand/arm dimension. '口 kǒu' scores the highest in the mouth/throat dimension. Additionally, there are 5 classifiers that score the highest in both the visual and interoceptive dimensions, namely '册 cè', '撮 cuō', '伙 huǒ', '名 míng', and '胎 tāi', '站 zhàn' scores the highest in both the visual and leg/foot dimensions (Fig. 3).

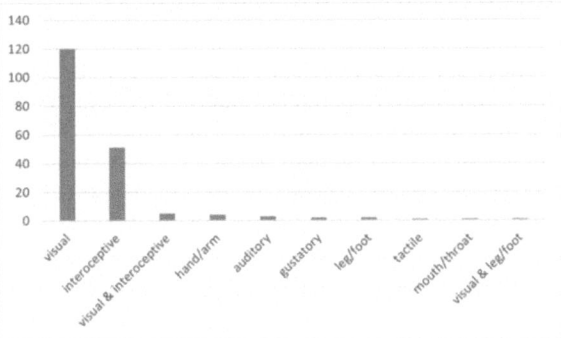

Fig. 3. The number of classifiers in dominant sensorimotor dimensions.

To explain the effectiveness of the sensorimotor ratings, we selected the synonym classifiers '条 tiáo' and '根 gēn'. The ratings of the two classifiers were shown in Fig. 4. The left chart for '条 tiáo' primarily showed a concentration in the visual dimension, indicating that nouns associated with '条 tiáo' typically possess strong visual characteristics, which aligns with its use for long, thin objects that are visually prominent, as mentioned in the Introduction section. The right chart for '根 gēn' also demonstrated a visual component but with a relatively higher distribution in the tactile dimension. This suggests that nouns associated with '根 gēn' are not only visually identifiable but also have some tactile attributes. Combined with its usage, '根 gēn' can be used for describing the long, solid and thick objects. The texture of the object may be notable, for example, '一根木棍 (a wooden stick)'.

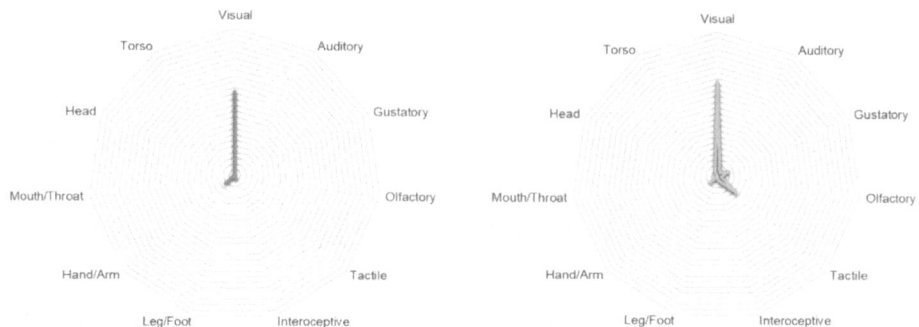

Fig. 4. The sensorimotor distribution for classifiers '条 tiáo' (left) and '根 gēn' (right).

4 Discussion

By collecting the sensorimotor ratings for Chinese classifiers, this study drew a general picture of the sensorimotor dimensions and the Chinese classifiers. In general, the results showed that the external visual scene and interoceptive accounts for a major part of Chinese classifiers.

This study confirms that visual modality is the most dominant sense [14, 16]. Vision provides a rich source of information about the external world. It allows us to perceive a wide range of details, shapes, colors, distances, and movements, which can be crucial for survival and interaction with the environment. Zong pointed out that the primary semantic function of classifiers is to categorize various nouns into groups [17]. Visual perception, being the most readily accessible sensory modality, naturally finds its way into classifiers as part of the semantic encoding. However, there are numerous subcategories within the visual dimension, including but not limited to shape, quantity, and more. Our study did not delve into detailed distinctions within these sub-dimensions. Scoring for the visual sub-dimension may help us achieve a clearer delineation within classifiers.

Interoception ranks the second dominant dimension after the visual modality. Interoception is often associated with abstract matters [18], indicating that a considerable portion of semantic features in Chinese classifiers may be relatively abstract. For instance, compared to '片 piàn' which is used to describe flat and thin objects, '只 zhī' is hard to express the external features of the objects it represents. After careful consideration, we think that the concept of 'Interoceptive' may have misled participants when translated as '内在感觉 internal sensation' in the questionnaire. Although the instructions clarified that '内在感觉 internal sensation' refers to sensations within the body, such as hunger, nausea, or fatigue, participants might gradually interpret '内在感觉 internal sensation' as related to abstract concept during the evaluation process. This is also reflected in the results, where nouns following highly grammaticalized classifiers were more challenging to associate with sensorimotor features, yet their interoceptive ratings were relatively high. However, this study did not rate the variable of abstractness. Future study can include the variable of abstractness in the Chinese classifiers, thus it might be able to investigate the relationship between abstract classifiers and their dominant dimensions.

It's worth noting that in the classifier ratings, there are very few classifiers related to the body, with only 9 classifiers having a dominant dimension related to the body. Classifiers distinguish between nominal and verbal. We identified high-frequency verbal classifiers in the database, namely '次 cì', '下 xià', '遍 biàn', '回 huí', and '场 chǎng'. The results showed that the dominant dimension for all five of these verbal classifiers is interoception, indicating that verbal classifiers may no longer be directly associated with the body but rather with the action in events [8]. Therefore, it is worth considering how to classify classifiers from the perspective of action-related events.

5 Conclusion

It is widely recognized that Chinese is a classifier language [16]. The choice of a classifier for a noun in Chinese is influenced by the noun's semantic properties [18, 19]. This study presents the first and relatively comprehensive sensorimotor norms for the Chinese classifiers. With sensorimotor ratings for Chinese classifiers, we explored the complex interplay between sensorimotor strength and semantic encoding in the classifiers. Our findings reveal that a significant portion of classifiers is intimately linked with external visual experiences and interoceptive sensations, underscoring the dominance of the visual modality in previous studies [14, 16].

Furthermore, the secondary dominance of interoceptive dimensions highlights the role of abstract semantic features in classifier usage, particularly in verbal classifiers where the body-related dimensions are less directly involved, as indicated in previous study [8].

This work may also have certain limitations. First, given that the dimension 'interoceptive' may mislead the participants to rate based on the abstractness of the classifier, which may not reflect the dimension of the internal body feeing. Second, though visual is a dominant dimension for most classifiers, there are sub-dimensions under the visual domain, such as size, shape and color. Future study can investigate the detailed distinctions within the visual sub-dimensions. Additionally, assessing classifiers' concreteness or abstractness should also be considered in the future study which could provide deeper understanding of how these attributes influence classifier choice and noun categorization in Mandarin.

Availability of Data. The data for the experiment is available at https://osf.io/wn74e/.

Appendix

Classifier	Interpretation	Example
把	handful of	一把米 (a handful of rice)
版	edition	一版书 (an edition of a book)
半	half	半个苹果 (half an apple)
瓣	petal	一瓣蒜 (a clove of garlic)
帮	group of people	一帮朋友 (a group of friends)
包	package	一包糖 (a package of sugar)
杯	cup	一杯茶 (a cup of tea)
辈	generation	三辈人 (three generations)
本	book	一本书 (a book)
笔	sum of money	一笔钱 (an amount of money)
遍	time (throughout)	读一遍 (read once)
柄	handle of	一柄伞 (a handle of an umbrella)
步	step	走一步 (walk one step)
部	part	一部电影 (a movie)
餐	meal	一餐饭 (a meal)
册	volume	一册书 (a volume of a book)
层	layer	一层楼 (a floor of a building)
茬	crop	一茬庄稼 (a crop of grain)
场	session	一场比赛 (a match)
车	vehicle	一车人 (a car full of people)
出	performance	一出戏 (a performance)
串	bunch	一串葡萄 (a bunch of grapes)
次	time (frequency)	一次机会 (an opportunity)
丛	cluster	一丛草 (a cluster of grass)
簇	bunch	一簇花 (a bunch of flowers)
撮 cuō	pinch	一撮盐 (a pinch of salt)
沓	stack	一沓纸 (a stack of paper)
代	generation	一代人 (a generation)
袋	bag	一袋米 (a bag of rice)
单	piece	一单生意 (a business deal)
档	file	一档节目 (a program)
道	road	一道菜 (a dish of food)
滴	drop	一滴水 (a drop of water)
点	bit	一点糖 (a bit of sugar)
顶	top	一顶帽子 (a hat)

(continued)

(*continued*)

Classifier	Interpretation	Example
栋	building	一栋楼 (a building)
度	degree	一度 (a degree)
段	section	一段话 (a section of speech)
堆	pile	一堆沙 (a pile of sand)
队	team	一队人 (a team of people)
对	pair	一对情侣 (a couple)
顿	meal	一顿饭 (a meal)
朵	flower	一朵花 (a flower)
垛	pile	一垛稻草 (a pile of straw)
番	time	一番话 (a speech)
份	portion	一份礼物 (a gift)
封	letter	一封信 (a letter)
幅	piece of cloth	一幅画 (a painting)
副	pair	一副眼镜 (a pair of glasses)
格	cell	一格抽屉 (a drawer compartment)
个	general classifier	一个人 (a person)
根	root	一根绳子 (a rope)
管	tube	一管牙膏 (a tube of toothpaste)
罐	jar	一罐蜂蜜 (a jar of honey)
锅	pot	一锅汤 (a pot of soup)
行	row	一行字 (a line of text)
盒	box	一盒巧克力 (a box of chocolates)
壶	pot	一壶茶 (a pot of tea)
户	household	一户人家 (a household)
环	ring	打一环 (a ring)
回	time	打一回 (one time)
伙	group	一伙人 (a group of people)
级	level	一级台阶 (a level of stair)
集	set	一集电视剧 (an episode of a TV series)
季	season	一季比赛 (a season of competition)
剂	dose	一剂药 (a dose of medicine)
家	family	一家人 (a family)
架	rack	一架飞机 (an airplane)
间	room	一间房 (a room)
件	piece	一件衣服 (a piece of clothing)

(*continued*)

(*continued*)

Classifier	Interpretation	Example
脚	kick	踢一脚 (kick it once)
觉	sense	睡一觉 (have some sleep)
节	section	一节课 (a class period)
截	section	一截木头 (a section of wood)
届	session	一届会议 (a session of a conference)
局	game	一局棋 (a game of chess)
句	sentence	一句话 (a sentence)
具	piece	一具骨架 (a skeleton)
卷 juǎn	roll	一卷纸 (a roll of paper)
卷 juàn	volume	一卷书 (a volume of a book)
棵	tree	一棵树 (a tree)
颗	grain	一颗珠子 (a bead)
刻	moment	一刻钟 (a quarter of an hour)
课	class	上一课 (have a class/lesson)
口	mouthful	一口水 (a mouthful of water)
块	piece	一块石头 (a piece of stone)
款	model	一款手机 (a model of phone)
筐	basket	一筐水果 (a basket of fruit)
捆	bundle	一捆柴火 (a bundle of firewood)
栏	column	一栏表格 (a column of a table)
类	kind	一类人 (a type of person)
例	instance	一例 (an example)
粒	grain	一粒米 (a grain of rice)
辆	vehicle	一辆车 (a car)
列	row	一列火车 (a train)
绺	wisp	一绺头发 (a wisp of hair)
笼	cage	一笼鸡 (a cage of chickens)
楼	floor	一楼杂物 (a whole floor of stuff)
缕	strand	一缕阳光 (a ray of sunlight)
轮	round	一轮比赛 (a round of a competition)
摞	stack	一摞书 (a stack of books)
枚	piece	一枚硬币 (a coin)
门	subject	一门课 (a course)
名	person	一名学生 (a student)
抹	smear	一抹微笑 (a hint of a smile)

(*continued*)

(*continued*)

Classifier	Interpretation	Example
幕	curtain	一幕戏 (a scene)
排	row	一排椅子 (a row of chairs)
盘	plate	一盘菜 (a plate of food)
泡	soak	一泡茶 (a brew of tea)
盆	basin	一盆花 (a pot of flowers)
捧	handful	一捧土 (a handful of soil)
批	batch	一批货 (a batch of goods)
匹	horse/match	一匹马 (a horse)
篇	piece/article	一篇文章 (an article)
片	slice/piece	一片面包 (a slice of bread)
票	ticket	一张票 (a ticket)
瓶	bottle	一瓶水 (a bottle of water)
抔	handful	一抔土 (a handful of soil)
期	period	一期杂志 (an issue of a magazine)
畦	plot/ridge	一畦菜地 (a plot of vegetable land)
起	instance	一起事件 (an incident)
腔	cavity	一腔热血 (a passion)
曲	song/tune	一曲歌 (a song)
圈	circle	一圈朋友 (a circle of friends)
拳	punch	打一拳 (beat a punch)
群	group	一群鸟 (a group of birds)
勺	spoonful	一勺糖 (a spoonful of sugar)
身	body	一身衣服 (an outfit)
声	sound/voice	一声叫喊 (a shout)
手	hand	一手好字 (a fine handwriting)
首	head/first	一首歌 (a song)
束	bundle	一束花 (a bouquet of flowers)
树	tree	一树梨花 (a pear tree)
双	pair	一双鞋 (a pair of shoes)
丝	thread	一丝头发 (a strand of hair)
艘	ship	一艘船 (a ship)
所	place	一所学校 (a school)
胎	birth/child	生一胎 (give birth to one baby)
台	platform/stage	一台电脑 (a computer)
摊	spread	一摊水 (a puddle of water)

(*continued*)

(*continued*)

Classifier	Interpretation	Example
滩	beach	一滩水 (a puddle)
坛	jar	一坛酒 (a jar of wine)
堂	hall/class	一堂课 (a class)
趟	trip	一趟旅程 (a journey)
套	set	一套衣服 (a set of clothes)
提	lift/raise	一提包 (a carrying bag)
屉	drawer	一屉糕点 (a drawer of pastries)
条	strip/item	一条鱼 (a fish)
贴	sticker	一贴广告 (an advertisement)
帖	post	一帖留言 (a post)
桶	bucket	一桶水 (a bucket of water)
筒	tube	一筒牙膏 (a tube of toothpaste)
通	notice/message	一通电话 (a phone call)
头	head	一头牛 (a cow)
团	group	一团人 (a group of people)
坨	lump	一坨泥 (a lump of mud)
袭	attack	一袭衣服 (a set of clothing)
下	time/instance	打一下 (beat once)
箱	box	一箱书 (a box of books)
项	item	一项任务 (a task)
些	some	一些人 (some people)
眼	glance	看一眼 (a glance)
样	kind	一样东西 (a kind of thing)
页	page	一页纸 (a page of paper)
夜	night	待一夜 (stay for one night)
员	member	一名队员 (a team member)
扎	bundle	一扎鲜花 (a bundle of flowers)
遭	incident	走一遭 (experience once)
则	rule	一则消息 (a piece of news)
扎	a bundle of/ a bouquet of	一扎啤机 (a pitcher of beer)
盏	lamp	一盏灯 (a lamp)
站	station	一站 (a station)
张	sheet	一张纸 (a sheet of paper)
章	chapter	一章 (a chapter)
招	recruit	耍一招 (paly a move)

(*continued*)

(*continued*)

Classifier	Interpretation	Example
针	needle	扎一针 (stick a needle)
帧	frame	一帧照片 (a frame of a photo)
阵	wave/burst	一阵风 (a gust of wind)
支	branch/stick	一支笔 (a pen)
只	individual animal	一只猫 (a cat)
枝	branch	一枝花 (a branch of a flower)
种	type/kind	一种植物 (a type of plant)
周	week	一周 (a week)
株	plant	一株树 (a tree)
桩	pile	一桩生意 (a business deal)
幢	building	一幢楼 (a building)
桌	table	一桌菜 (a table of food)
宗	case/religion	一宗罪行 (a crime)
组	group/set	一组数据 (a set of data)
撮 zuǒ	pinch	一撮盐 (a pinch of salt)
座	building/mountain	一座山 (a mountain)

References

1. Allan, K.: Classifiers. Language **53**, 285–311 (1977)
2. Croft, W.: Semantic universals in classifier systems. Word **45**, 145–171 (1994)
3. Lakoff, G.: Classifiers as a reflection of mind. Noun Classes Categorization **7**, 13–51 (1986)
4. Tien, Y.M., Tzeng, O.J., Hung, D.L.: Semantic and cognitive basis of Chinese classifiers: a functional approach. Langu. Linguist. **3**, 101–132 (2002)
5. Tai, J. H.: Chinese classifier systems and human categorization. In: M. Chen., O. Tzeng. (eds.) honor of William S.-Y. Wang: Interdisciplinary Studies on Language and Language Change, Pyramid Publishing Co, pp. 479–494 (1994)
6. Chao, Y.R.: A grammar of spoken Chinese, 2nd edn. University of California Press, Berkeley and Los Angeles (1968)
7. Shi, Y.Z.: The cognitive foundations of the shape based classifiers in modern Chinese [biao wuti xingzhuang liangci de renzhi jichu]. Lang. Teach. Linguist. Stud. [yuyan jiaoxue yu yanjiu] **01**, 34–41 (2001)
8. Ahrens, K., Huang, C.-R.: Classifiers. In: Huang, C.-R., Shi, D. X. (eds.) A Reference Grammar of Chinese, Cambridge University Press, UK pp.169–198 (2016)
9. Shao, J.M.: Semantic analysis of classifiers and their bidirectional selection with nouns [liangci de yuyi fenxi ji qi yu mingci de shuangxiang xuanze]. Stud. Chin. Lang. [zhongguo yuwen] **03**, 181–188 (1993)
10. Hsu, C.-C., Tsai, S.-H., Yang, C.-L., Chen, J.-Y.: Processing classifier-noun agreement in a long distance: An ERP study on Mandarin Chinese. Brain Lang. **137**, 14–28 (2014)

11. Qian, Z., Garnsey, S.: An ERP study of the processing of Mandarin classifiers. In: H. Tao (Ed.) Integrating Chinese Linguistic Research and Language Teaching and Learning, J. Benjamins, Amsterdam Philadelphia pp. 59–80 (2016)

12. Chan, S.-H.: An elephant needs a head but a horse does not: an ERP study of classifier-noun agreement in Mandarin. J. Neurolinguistics **52**, 1–16 (2019)

13. Barsalou, L.W.: Grounded cognition. Annu. Rev. Psychol. **59**(1), 617–645 (2008)

14. Zhong, Y., Wan, M., Ahrens, K., Huang, C.-R.: Sensorimotor norms for Chinese nouns and their relationship with orthographic and semantic variables. Lang. Cogn. Neurosci. **37**(8), 1000–1022 (2022)

15. Liu, Z. P.: Chinese classifier dictionary [Hanyu liangci da cidian]. Shanghai Lexicographical Publishing Company [shanghai cishu chubanshe], Shanghai, China (2013)

16. Lynott, D., Connell, L.: Modality exclusivity norms for 400 nouns: the relationship between perceptual experience and surface word form. Behav. Res. Methods **45**(2), 516–526 (2013)

17. Zong, S. Y.: The path and motivation of classifiers' categorization [liangci fanchouhua de tujing he dongyin]. Journal of Shanghai Normal University (Philosophy and Social Sciences Edition) [shanghai shifan daxue xuebao (zhexue shehui kexue ban)] **03**, 109–116 (2011)

18. Zhong, Y., Huang, C.-R., Ahrens, K.: Embodied grounding of concreteness/abstractness: a sensory-perceptual account of concrete and abstract concepts in Mandarin Chinese. In: 22nd Chinese lexical semantic workshop (CLSW 2021), Nanjing Normal University, China, 15–16 May 2021. Revised Selected Papers, pp. 72–83. Springer, Hidelberg (2021)

19. Wang, S., Huang, C.-R.: Towards an event-based classification system for non-natural kind nouns. In: 13th Chinese lexical semantic workshop (CLSW 2012), Wuhan, China, 6–8 July 2012. Revised Selected Papers, pp. 381–395. Springer, Hidelberg (2013)

The Synchronic and Diachronic Study of the Degree Adverb *hěn*

Fei Gu[✉]

Literature College of Shaanxi Normal University, Shaanxi, China
gufei@snnu.edu.cn

Abstract. The use of *hěn*(很) in Chinese dialects and Mandarin shows a comple-mentary distribution. The relationship between *hěn*(很) and *hěn*(狠) and *hěn*(哏) is i-ntricate. The modern Chinese adverb of degree *hěn*(很) was shaped through a ble-nd of internal development and external contact with the Mongolian lan-guage. Du-ring the Tang and Song dynasties, the meanings of *hěn*(很) and *hěn*(狠) began to intertwine. The incorporation of the adverb *hěn*(哏) in the Yuan Dynasty advanc-ed the reshaping of the semantic patterns of *hěn*(很) and *hěn*(狠). The adverb *hěn*(哏) inherited the adjective meaning of *hěn*(狠), while *hěn*(很) inherited the adver-bial meaning. The unique use of *hěn*(很) in the dialect is actually the retention of the adjective meaning of *hěn*(哏).

Keywords: Chinese dialects · adverbs of degree · *hěn*(很)

1 Introduction

The use of *hěn*(很) as an adverb was very common in the Ming and Qing dynasties. However, there is no evidence of *hěn*(很) was used directly as an adverbial modifying the central element in a sentence. Different views exist on its origin and nature: (1) Wang Li believes that the adverb *hěn*(很) was about to be changed from the adjective *hěn*(狠) [1]. (2) Wang Guoshuan, Ning Yanhong, [2] and Wang Jing [3] think that the adverb *hěn*(很) originated in the Yuan Dynasty, possibly related to the contact with the Mongolian language. (3) Rao Jiting divided the adverb *hěn*(很) into the adverb of degree *hěn*(很) and the adverb of quantity *hěn*(很) based on its functional distribution. [4] (4) Nie Zhiping believes, from the perspectives of system and origin, that *hěn*(很) in the complement position is an adjective, while *hěn*(很) in the adverbial position is an adverbial [5].

Wang Hang and Ge Pingping have explored the origin and evolution of *hěn*(很) from a historical perspective [6], and this paper explores the concurrent distribution of *hěn*(很) and its dynamic development in dialect based on previous studies.

2 The Situation in the Dialect Corpus

According to the *Modern Chinese Dialect Dictionary* edited by Li Rong [7], the use of the degree adverb *hěn*(很) is found in Xuzhou, Nanjing, Chengdu, Luoyang, Yinchuan, Nanchang, and so on, indicating that it is mostly used in prestigious dialects. Other

P. Jin et al. (Eds.): CLSW 2024, LNAI 15552, pp. 255–273, 2025.
https://doi.org/10.1007/978-981-96-3509-2_19

dialects often do not use *hěn*(很), but employ words like *zéi*(贼), *kě*(可), *sǐ*(死), *tuī*(忒), *jǐ*(几), *tōng*(通), *xiā*(瞎), *xuě*(血), *mán*(蛮), and so on to indicate the degree. The use of *hěn*(很) as a complement is more widespread, and it always requires the conjunction *de*(得) before it. It is found in Ji'nan, Xuzhou, Luoyang, Harbin, Nanjing, Wuhan, Guiyang, Liuzhou, Xi'an, Changsha, Lichuan, Jian'ou, Danyang, Xinzhou, and Urumqi.

The use of *hěn*(很) in Chinese dialects differs from its use as the modern Chinese degree adverb. In the structure of *hěn*(很) + X, "X" can be an action verb, and when "X" is an adjective, *hěn*(很) is usually not used. The structure of X + *hěn*(很) does not require the complement conjunction *de*(得). Based on the field surveys and the search of dialect materials, the specific distribution of the use of *hěn*(很) + X and X + *hěn*(很) is as follows (according to geographical distribution):

Table 1. Distribution of *hěn*(很) in Chinese dialects

Geographic Distribution	hěn + X	X + hěn	Example	source of material
Harbin	+	+	哏叨(scold too much); 热得很(very hot)	*Dictionary of Modern Chinese Dialects*
Urumqi	-	+	好底很(very good)	*Dictionary of Modern Chinese Dialects*
Yinchuan	-	+	美气得很(very nice)	*Dictionary of Modern Chinese Dialects*
Anhui	-	+	热得很(very hot)	*Compendium of Hebei Dialect Words*
Beijing	+	+	很聪明的孩子(This kid is very clever.); 这孩子机灵得很(This kid is very clever.)	*CCL corpus*
Lanzhou	-	+	这个娃娃烦人得很(This kid is very annoyed.)	*Studies on the Grammar of the Lanzhou Dialect*
Xinzhou	-	+	天气凉哩很(The weather is very cool.)	*Dictionary of Modern Chinese Dialects*
Xi'an	-	+	这娃乖 (得) 很(This kid is very cute.)	*A Grammatical Survey of the Xi'an Dialect*
Ji'nan	-	+	累的很(very tired.)	*Dictionary of Modern Chinese Dialects*
Tai'an	+	-	你俩很打呗(You two just fight hard.)	*A Study of the Degree Adverbs of the hěn*(很) *Category in Tai'an Dialect*
Luoyang	+	+	很好(very good); 累得很(very tired)	*Dictionary of Modern Chinese Dialects*

(continued)

Table 1. (*continued*)

Geographic Distribution	hěn + X	X + hěn	Example	source of material
Qinyang	+	-	别很打孩儿(Don't be too harsh on the child.)	investigation by the author
Qixian	+	+	坚持下去, 很跑(Stick to it, run with force.); 美哩很 (very nice)	*hěn(很)VP in Qixian dialect of henan*
Xuzhou	+	+	很甜的吃多了不好(Eating too much of sweet is not good for you.); 街上车很 了(There are so many cars on the road.)	*Dictionary of Modern Chinese Dialects*
Lian yungang	+	+	河里很鱼了(There are so many fish in the river.); 他 (长) 高很了(He is growing taller and taller.)	*Special Use of hěn(很) in the Northern Jiangsu Dialect*
Suzhou	+	-	很学, 才能考上好大学(To get into a good university, one must study very hard.)	*hěn(很) + VP in Northern Anhui colloquialisms*
Fuyang	-	+	做菜少口[za]些盐, 多很了, 会苦的(Cooking with a bit of salt is good, but too much can make it bitter.)	*Grammar of Chinese Dialects*
Yangzhou	-	+	今天天气好得很(Today's weather is extremely good)	*The adverbs of degree man(蛮) and xi(稀) in the Yangzhou dialect*
Nanjing	+	+	他跑起来很快(He runs very fast.); 他嘴巴子会讲 得很(He is very good at speaking.)	*Dictionary of Modern Chinese Dialects*
Danyang	-	+	好则很(very good)	*Dictionary of Modern Chinese Dialects*
Nantong	-	+	你对她好很叻(You are too good to her.)	*A Study of Degree Adverbs in Nantong Dialect*
Sichuan	+	+	这间屋很大(This room is too big.); 走很了(Walked too much)	*A Study of Degree Adverbs in Sichuan Dialect*
Chengdu	+	+	哭很了眼睛遭不住(Cried too much, my eyes can't take it anymore.); 你很是 吃[a] (You ate too much.)	*AP/VP + hěn in Chengdu Dialect*

(*continued*)

Table 1. (*continued*)

Geographic Distribution	hěn + X	X + hěn	Example	source of material
Changsha	+	+	那个妹子很白净(That girl is so beautiful.); 好得很(Very good)	*Adverbs of Degree in Changsha Dialect*
Wuhan	-	+	好得很(very good)	*Dictionary of Modern Chinese Dialects*
Hukou	-	+	其个嗬才动身嗒, 也晏很了些嗬是啊(He's only leaving now, isn't it a bit too late?)	*hěn(很) in the Hukou dialect of Jiangxi*
Nanchang	-	+	好得很(very good)	*Dictionary of Modern Chinese Dialects*
Lichuan	-	+	好得很(very good)	*Dictionary of Modern Chinese Dialects*
Guiyang	-	+	好得很(very good)	*Dictionary of Modern Chinese Dialects*
Liuzhou	-	+	好得很(very good)	*Dictionary of Modern Chinese Dialects*
Jian'ou	-	+	好得很(very good)	*Dictionary of Modern Chinese Dialects*
Fuzhou	-	+	这一批货有趁 饣僧 狠赚了但不多(This batch of goods made a good profit, but not much.)	*Dictionary of Modern Chinese Dialects*
Yunnan	-	+	我的文章被老师批评很(My article was heavily criticized by the teacher.)	*Ruminations on the Complement of the Degree Adverb hěn(很) in Yunnan Dialect*
Qiandongnan	+	+	她很骂人(She scolds others a lot); 他今天哭很(Today he cried a lot)	*Research on the Grammar of Qiandongnan Dialect*

[a]This part of the corpus was obtained through the author's field survey.

According to Table 1, we can observe the geographical distribution of *hěn*(很): *hěn*(很) + X is mainly distributed at the two ends and the middle in whole China. The North Pole is Harbin, and the South Pole is Qiandongnan, with a concentration in the Jin dialects in northern Henan, the Central Plains official language area in northern Jiangsu, the Jianghuai official language area in the center, including regions like Anhui, Sichuan and Qiandongnan, forming a diamond shape.

Chinese has a well-developed complementary structure, so X + *hěn*(很) is found in almost all of the Qin and Jin dialects, the Guanhua dialects, and the southeastern dialects.[1] However, in most dialects, the structures *hěn*(很) + X and X + *hěn*(很) do not coexist. According to Table 1, in Yinchuan, Hebei, Lanzhou, Xinzhou, Xi'an, Fuyang, Yangzhou, Danyang, Nantong, Wuhan, Hukou, Nanchang, Lichuan, Guiyang, Liuzhou, Jian'ou, Fuzhou, Yunnan, etc., only X + *hěn*(很) is found, but not *hěn*(很) + X, and the structure of X + *hěn*(很) is not present in most of Chinese dialects. In some Chinese dialects, the usage of X + *hěn*(很) is richer than in Mandarin. For example, in Lanzhou dialect, X + *hěn*(很) is more common than in Mandarin [8].

The object of this paper is to trace the nature and origin of the modern Chinese adverb *hěn*(很) through its special usage in Chinese dialects. We will analyze the special usage of *hěn*(很) in terms of its syntactic function, meaning, and origin.

2.1   hěn(很) + X

As for the special usage of *hěn*(很) + X in Chinese dialects, "X" can be an action verb, a noun, etc. However, *hěn*(很) is often not used to modify adjectives, mental verbs, etc. The specific usage is illustrated in the table below (Table 2).

Table 2. Distribution of forms and meanings of *hěn*(很) + X in Chinese dialects

Geographic distribution	Structure	Function	Meaning	Example
Beijing	hěn(很) + adjective	adverbial	degree	这句话实在是说得很模糊(The words you said are really vague);情况实在是很紧急啊(The situation is really urgent!)
	hěn(很) + mental verb			我很喜欢这件衣服(I love this dress.);他很感激你做的这些事(He appreciates too much what you have done.)
Harbin	hěn(很) + action verb	adverbial	excessive	恨叨(scold too much)
Tai'an				这孩子忒不听话了, 给我很揍(He's so disobedient, beat this child hard.);别剩下饭了, 很吃(Don't leave any rice left over, eat hard.)
Suzhou				很学, 才能考上好大学(Study hard to get into a good university!)他很买书(He buys books with great enthusiasm.)
Chengdu				你很 (是)吃(You eat a lot.)

(*continued*)

---

[1] The classification of Chinese dialects here refers to Liu Xunning. Revisiting the classification of northern Chinese dialects[J]. Chinese Language, 1995, (6): 447–454.

Table 2. (*continued*)

Geographic distribution	Structure	Function	Meaning	Example
Qiandongnan				莫看他个子小, 还很跑(Don't judge by his small stature, he runs so fast.)他书没读多少, 但很讲(He doesn't read a lot, but he's a great speaker.)
Qinyang				你都很打咧你(You've been hitting so hard)天天都光知个外头很耍, 不知学习(Always out there playing hard, never thinking about studying.)
Qixian				马上到终点了, 坚持下去, 很跑(You're almost at the finish line, hang in there, run with force.)
Hukou	hěn(很) + noun	attributive	vicious	世上冇既个很人, 是么嗝不让我用(There's no one in the world who's so vicious that won't let me use anything.)
Lianyungang	hěn(很) + noun + le(了)	predicate	large number	河里很鱼了(The river is full of fish.)他家很钱了(His family has a lot of money.)

Compare the dialectal use of *hěn(很)*, which is different from the modern Chinese adverb of degree *hěn(很)*:

(1) Structurally, in addition to *hěn(很)* + X, in some Chinese dialects, *le(了)* must follow *hěn(很)* to complete the sentence, such as Lianyungang dialects. The type of "X" is primarily based on action verbs, which constitutes the biggest difference from the modern Chinese adverb of degree *hěn(很)*, which in Mandarin can only co-occur with adjectives, mental verbs, verb phrases, etc.

(2) Functionally, *hěn(很)* is in the adverbial position, indicating a deep degree. However, in Chinese dialects of Hukou in Jiangxi Province and Lianyungang in Jiangsu Province, *hěn(很)* can also serve as a determiner and a predicate, which is relatively rare in other Chinese dialects.

(3) In terms of meaning, *hěn(很)* not only indicates degree but also carries the connotation of "excessive". In Chinese dialects, it can also be written as *hěn(狠)*, *hěn(哏)*, and so on. Rao Jiting pointed out that this type of *hěn(很)* does not signify "degree" but rather "much", and he considered this use of *hěn(很)* not to be an adverb of degree [4].

According to Table 1, in most Chinese dialects, adverbs of degree tend not to use *hěn(很)*, with the exception of Beijing, Luoyang, Yangzhou, and other areas, where *hěn(很)* can be both prepositional and postpositional forms. For example, in the Qiandongnan dialect, *hěn(很)* corresponds to *man(蛮)* in Mandarin, and *man(蛮)* is also used in Jianghuai dialects and Wu dialects. Previously, some scholars believed that *hěn(很)* was the result of further deflation based on *hěn(狠)*. However, later on, scholars like Rao and

Nie made corrections to this statement. The difference between the dialectal usage of *hěn*(很) and its Mandarin usage lies in the inherent nature of the two.

2.2   X + *hěn*(很)

Compared to the specific usage of *hěn*(很) in the *hěn*(很) + X construction, the X + *hěn*(很) structure is more widely employed and exhibits greater variation across Chinese dialects. This is closely related to the well-developed complementary structure of the Chinese. As illustrated in the following table (Table 3).

Table 3. Forms and meanings of X + *hěn*(很) distribution in Chinese dialects

Region of Distribution	Structure			Function	Meaning	Example
Beijing	Adjective + hěn(很)			complement	degree	这孩子可怜得很(This kid is so poor.);你小子机灵得很啊(You're so smart.)
	Mental verb + hěn(很)					这件衣服我喜欢得很(I like this dress very much.);他总是让人担心得很(He always makes people too worried.)
Hukou	action verb	+ hěn(很) + le(了)		complement	Excessive, degree	其姆妈肯定是又打很了(His mother must have beaten him too harshly.)
Xuzhou						钱花很了(Spent too much money.)
Lianyungang						我午饭吃很了(I ate too much for lunch.)
Chengdu						哭很了眼睛遭不住(Cried too much, my eyes can't take it anymore.)
Qiandongnan		+ hěn(很)				我妹哭很, 你先走嘛(My sister is crying hard, you go first.)
Fuzhou						这一批货有趁 艁 狠赚了但不多(This batch of goods made a good profit, but not much.)

(*continued*)

Table 3. (*continued*)

Region of Distribution	Structure		Function	Meaning	Example
Yunnan					我的文章被老师批评很(My article was heavily criticized by the teacher.)
	adjective	+ hěn(很)			他家离昆明远很(His family is far away from Kunming)
Xuzhou		+ hěn(很) + le(了)			天冷很了(It's getting more and more cold.)
Lianyungang					他高很了(He is growing taller and taller.)
Fuyang					做菜少口 [za]些盐, 多很了, 苦(Cooking with a bit of salt is good, but too much can make it bitter.)
Chengdu					你硬是能干很了(You're very capable.)
Hukou					其个嗬现在才动身出发嗒, 也晏晚很了些嗬(He's only leaving now, isn't it a bit too late.)
Yancheng		le(了) + hěn(很) + le(了)			菜烧了甜了很了(The food is too sweet.)
Nantong		+ hěn(很) + dao(叨)			你对她好很叨(You are too good to her.)
Lianyungang	noun	+ hěn(很) + le(了)	predicate	large number	家里苹果很了(There are lots of apples at home)
Xuzhou					街上车很了(There's a lot of cars on the street.)

(1) Structurally, there are many variations of the *X* + *hěn*(很) construction, including *X* + *h-ěn*(很) + *le*(了), *X* + *le*(了) + *hěn*(很) + *le*(了), *X* + *hěn*(很) + *dao*(叨), among others. "X" can be an act-ion verb, an adjective, a noun, etc. In the northern part of Jiangsu Province, Xuzhou and Lia-nyungang have the most diverse types of "X". Otherwise, the specific usage of "X" tends to be monosyllabic, while bisyllabic forms predominate in the Beijing dialect.

(2) Functionally, most instances are similar to the Beijing dialect in their use as compl-ements. However, in some dialects of northern Jiangsu, *hěn(*很*)* can also be used as a predica-te. Some argue that *hěn(*很*)* may be the complement of the light verb *yǒu(*有*)*, rather than a predicate [9].

(3) Meaningfully, *hěn(*很*)* exhibits varying degrees of grammaticalization across differentChinese dialects. In the Beijing dialect, *hěn(*很*)* is highly grammaticalized and is used exclusi-vely to indicate a high degree. In the Central Plains Mandarin - Xuhuai dialects, Jianghuai M-andarin, and Southwestern Mandarin, *hěn(*很*)* not only signi-fies "a high degree" but also impli-es "excessive" when paired with an action verb. When used with nouns, *hěn(*很*)* denotes "a l-arge number" of specific items. *hěn(*很*)* can also highlight changes in a character's mood or t-he dynamics of something, suggesting a "the more… The more…" meaning. For example, *lěng hěn le(*冷很了*)* means that the weather is getting colder and colder compared to before. In m-odern Chinese, *hěn(*很*)* is an absolute adverb of degree, lacking comparative usage, and servesas a general term for degree [10], but the special usage of *hěn(*很*)* in Chinese dialects implies comparative meaning.

Record the modern Chinese adverb of degree *hěn(*很*)* as *hěn(*很*)* ₁ and the Chinese dialects as *hěn(*很*)*₂. Compare the collocations of *hěn(*很*)*₁, *hěn(*很*)*₂ and *hěn(*狠*)* (Table 4).

Table 4. Syntactic combinatorial functions of *hěn(*很*)* ₁ *hěn(*很*)* ₂ and *hěn(*狠*)*

	verbal component			adjectival component	morphological component	conjunction "de(得)"
	psychological verb	action verb	verb phrase	adjective	noun	
*hěn(*很*)* ₁	+	-	+	+	-	+
*hěn(*很*)* ₂	-	+	-	±	+	-
*hěn(*狠*)*	-	+	-	+	+	-

From the perspective of syntactic combination functions, the co-occurring compo-nents of *hěn(*很*)*₂ and *hěn(*狠*)* show greater consistency, and they can be combined with action verbs, adjectives and nouns. Additionally, there is no complement marker when used as a compleme-nt, which is the main difference between *hěn(*很*)*₁ and *hěn(*狠*)*. Semantically, *hěn(*狠*)* has the most concrete meaning, such as "vicious" or "ruthless" [11]. *hěn(*很*)*₁ serves as an absolute adv-erb of degree, expressing "a high degree". *hěn(*很*)*₂ is intermediate, capable of expressing both "degree" and "excessive". The key dif-ference between *hěn(*很*)*₁ and *hěn(*很*)*₂ lies in *hěn(*很*)*₂'s implication of a comparison with the previous situation when expressing degree. Considering the similarity in the collocation between *hěn(*很*)*₂ and *hěn(*狠*)*, is the specific of *hěn(*很*)* in dialects related to *hěn(*狠*)*?

3   Situation in the Ephemeral Corpus

The relationship between *hěn(*很*)* and *hěn(*狠*)*, as well as the nature of *hěn(*很*)*, has long beena topic of discussed. According to Lü Shuxiang, he has examined *hěn(*很*)* and *hěn(*狠*)* from three perspectives: character shape, character sound, and word meaning. He argued that the twoare not derived from one another, but that they were distinct in character shape, sound, and meaning in early times. With the evolution of the language, they gradually overlapped,and in the early days, the two were different in form and sound [12]. Tatsuo Ota pointed out that *hěn(*很*)* originally meant "against" and "disobedience", but later it was used as "angry", "vicious" and "cruel". Examples of *hěn(*很*)* being used as an adverb did not appear until the Yuan Dyn-asty, which might have be a variation resulting from contact with the Mongols [13]. It is kno-wn that *hěn(*很*)$_2$ is closely related to *hěn(*狠*)*.

3.1   Semantic Development of *hěn(*很*)* and *hěn(*狠*)*

In the *Shuowen Jiezizhu*[2] by Duan Yucai, it is noted that *hěn(*很*)* means "not listen" and "difficult to walk", while *hěn(*狠*)* means "barking sounds". Duan Yucai comments on *hěn(*狠*)*: "barking sounds. Nowadays, it is very common to use *hěn(*狠*)* as *hěn(*很*)*, but the meanings of *hěn(*很*)* and *hěn(*狠*)* were different in the Xu Shen's era." This shows that there was a difference between the Xu Shen period and the Duan Yucai period. Zhu Junsheng's *Shuowen Tongxun Dingsheng*[3] states: "Nowadays, *hěn(*狠*)* is borrowed from *hěn(*很*)*." Zhu believed that the two characters were in a borrowed relationship.

Semantic Development of hěn(很**).** In the Literature Collected so Far, the Earlier Occurrence is *hěn(*很*)*[4]:

---

(1) 今王将很天而伐齐 (《国语·吴语》)

Now the king will *disobey* God and conquer Qi. (*Guoyu-Wuyu*).

(2) 见过不更,闻谏愈甚,谓之很 (《庄子》)

Seeing or hearing others' remonstrance not only fails to correct one's ways but instead makes one even more *stubborn*, which is called as hěn.(*Zhuang Zi*)

(3) 重刑而连其罪,则褊急之民不斗,很刚之民不讼,怠惰之民不游。(《商君书》)

If the punishment is severe and the offense involves the relatives, then people with narrow minds will not engage in fights, *stubborn* individuals will not litigate lawsuits, and lazy individuals will not travel long distances. (*Shang Jun Shu*)

(continued)

---

[2] Duan, Y.: *Shuowen jiezi zhu* (说文解字注), Shanghai Ancient Books Publishing House photocopy of the Jingyunlou engraving: 2 vols.

[3] Referring to Zhu, J.: *Shuowen tongxun dingsheng*(说文通训定声), Wuhan Ancient Bookstore photocopies the Linxiaoge text: 15 vols., pp. 807.

[4] The following corpus is from the CCL corpus of the Centre for Chinese Language Studies, Peking University, unless otherwise specified.

(continued)

(1) 今王将很天而伐齐 (《国语·吴语》)

(4) 慢弃刑法,倍奸齐盟,傲很威仪,矫诬先王。(《左传》)

Neglect and discard the criminal law, breaching others and forming alliances of their own, arrogant and *stubborn* in dignity, falsely accusing the former king. (*Zuo Zhuan*)

(5) 兄弟阋于墙,外御其务。(《诗经·小雅·常棣》)

Brothers may *quarrel* at home, but they will unite to defend against external threats. (*Shijing-Xiaoya-Changdi*)

hěn(很) is used as a predicate and can be followed by an object, as in the example (1), where *hěn*(很) means "against, disobey", which is the original meaning of *hěn*(很). Based on.

this verb meaning, *hěn*(很) further derives the meaning of "fierce, overbearing, stubborn", as s-een in examples(2), (3),and (4). In "hěn gāng(很刚)" and "àu hěn(傲很)", *hěn*(很), àu (傲), gāng(刚) are parallel adjectives, all meaning "fierce, overbearing". Additionally, *hěn*(很) also c-arries the meaning of "litigious, quarrel", as in the following example (5). *Mao Zhuan* notes: "*xì*(阋) means *hěn*(很)", and Kong Yingda comments: "Here *hěn*(很) is equal to quarrel".

Semantic Development of hěn(狠). The original meaning of *hěn*(狠) is the sound of a barking dog, from which *hěn*(狠) derives the meaning of "vicious", as seen in the following examples (6)and (7). However, *hěn*(狠) has also acquired some meanings similar to *hěn*(很).

For instance, in examples (8)and (9), *hěn*(狠) means "stubborn", which can be confused with the meaning of *hěn*(很).

(6) 不思忘爱曰刺,愎狠遂过曰刺。(《逸周书》)

Refusing to reflect and forgetting others help is referred to as *ci*, being headstrong and *vicious*, and continuing to make mistakes is also referred to as *ci* . (*Yi Zhoushu*)

(7) 好勇斗狠,以危父母,五不孝也 (《孟子》)

Fierce and *vicious*, risking the safety of one's parents, is considered the fifth act of unfilial behavior. (*Meng Zi*)

(8) 昔者县宗之君,狠而无听,执事不从 (《逸周书》)

In the past, the ruler of Xianzong, who was contentious and *stubborn*, refused to heed advice. (*Yi Zhoushu*)

(9) 故狠者类知而非知,愚者类仁而非仁。(《淮南子》)

Stubborn individuals may seem wise on the surface, but it is not the true wisdom, foolish individuals may appear compassionate, but it is not true compassion. (*Huai Nan Zi*)

Semantic Intersection of hĕn(很) and hĕn(狠). *Hĕn(很)* and *hĕn(狠)* are semantically similar, and there was a period of competitive symbiosis between the two, but there are still distinctions, e.g.:

---

(10) 以夷多刚很,旧各本作狠,廖本改。(《华阳国志》)

The southern ethnic minorities are mostly *stubborn* and disobedient. The old version of the book referred to *hĕn(狠)*, but the Liao's version changed it to *hĕn(很)*. (*Huayang Guozhi*)

---

(11) 白羊性很,不得独留。(《齐民要术》)

The character of sheep is very *stubborn* and must not be left alone. (*Qimin Yaoshu*)

Example (10) the original text reads: "The southern ethnic minorities are very stubborn a-nd do not obey the rich and powerful people (以夷多刚很,不宾大姓富豪)". Here, *hĕn(很)* means "disobedient and stubborn". Liao Yin changed *hĕn(狠)* to *hĕn(很)*. It can be seen that.

during the Wei and Jin Dynasties, the meanings of *hĕn(很)* and *hĕn(狠)* were still different; *h-ĕn(狠)* had a more singular, pejorative connotation. However, *hĕn(很)* not only had the meanin-g of "vicious", but also included the meaning of "disobedient and stubborn", as in example(11),where *hĕn(很)* had a more neutral meanings.

By the Tang and Song Dynasties, the contexts in which the two *hĕn(很)* and *hĕn(狠)* ap-peared gradually overlapped, for example:

---

(12) 安帝下诏曰: 刘毅傲很凶戾。(《晋书》)

Emperor An issued an edict stating: Liu Yi is proud and *vicious*. (*Jin Shu*)

---

(13) 傲狠反常,横辱无畏。(《旧唐书》)

People who are arrogant and *vicious*, always capricious, and horizontally insulting without fear. (*Jiu Tang shu*)

---

(14) 则有性既严酷,貌复凶很。(《册府元龟》)

The nature is harsh, and the appearance is *vicious*. (*Cefu Yuangui*)

---

(15) 李宗奭本于凶狠,自抵诛夷。(《册府元龟》)

Li Zongshi's nature is harsh and *vicious*; he resists and exterminates the barbarians on his own. (*Cefu Yuangui*)

---

(16) 绍凶很无赖。(《资治通鉴》)

Shao is a cruel, *vicious*, and rascally person. (*Zizhi Tongjian*)

---

(17) 如人很戾,固是暴。(《朱子语类》)

If a person's personality is *vicious* and harsh, their behavior will inevitably be fierce. (*Zhuzi Yulei*)

(*continued*)

(continued)

(18) 很,很戾也,俗作狠。(《广韵》)
hěn(很) means *vicious* and cruel, commonly known as *hěn*(狠). (*Guang Yun*)

(19) 牛很不从引也。(《广韵》)
Cattle are *stubborn* and do not obey the lead. (*Guang Yun*)

hěn(狠) and *hěn*(很) have become completely intertwined in the literature, often being ind-istinguishable within the same book, as seen in examples (14) (15). The co-occurring contexts of *hěn*(很) overlap with those of *hěn*(狠), such as "fierce/vicious" and "proud/vicious". It is al-so evident in the rhyme books that *hěn*(很) and *hěn*(狠) were common words in that time.

However, when expressing the meaning of "disobedience", *hěn*(很) is used instead of *hěn*(狠), as demonstrated in the following example (19). The meaning of the word *hěn*(很) differs from *hěn*(狠). The meanings of *hěn*(很) include "disobedience, difficult to walk, vicious, stubborn,

quarrel". From the perspective of linguistic economy, the common use of *hěn*(很) and *hěn*(狠) leads to a redistribution of lexical meanings and the formation of a new semantic pattern.

3.2 Phonological Development of *hěn*(很) and *hěn*(狠)

In addition to the difference in meaning, there is also a difference in sound between *hěn*(很) and *hěn*(狠). The two ancient pronunciations are shown in the table below:

From the semantic relationship between *hěn*(很) and *hěn*(狠), it may be concluded that *hěn*(狠) is differentiated from *hěn*(很). However, there is a significant difference between the two phonetically. Before the Ming Dynasty, *hěn*(很) and *hěn*(狠) had different vowels and tones. As shown in Table 5, the initial of *hěn*(很) is "ɣ", and the initial of *hěn*(狠) is "ŋ".

Futhermore, their tones also differ. After the Ming Dynasty, under the influence of "devo-icing of the fully voiced initials", both sounds devoiced into voiceless initials, becoming phone-tically closer to each other. Combined with the overlapping of semantic meanings, the two gr-adually converged in form, sound, and meaning. Zhang Yongquan believes that *hěn*(很) and *h-ěn*(狠) belong to the borrowing relationship [14]. Previously, *hěn*(很) and *hěn*(狠) were different.

in form and sound. By the Tang and Song Dynasties, *hěn*(狠) was borrowed as *hěn*(很), and.

after the Ming Dynasty, they became closer to each other in form, sound and meaning.

4 Relationship Between *hěn*(哏), *hěn*(狠) and *hěn*(很)

From the view of grammaticalization, it's common to create new function words from content words. However, there are no examples in the literature of *hěn*(很) and *hěn*(狠) being gramma-ticalized, and some believe this phenomenon belongs to language

Table 5. Ancient sounds of *hěn(*很*)* and *hěn(*狠*)*

Title	hěn(很)				hěn(狠)			
	Fanqie	IPA[a]	tone	initial	Fanqie	IPA	tone	initial
Shuōwén JiěZì[b] 说文解字	胡墾切	/	shǎng(上)	ɣ	五还切	/	píng(平)	/
Guǎng Yùn[c] 广韵	胡墾切	ɣən	shǎng(上)	ɣ	五闲切	yan	píng(平)	Ø
Jí Yùn[d] 集韵	下墾切	ɣən	shǎng(上)	ɣ	鱼巾切	ŋiən	píng(平)	ŋ
	尸袞切	ɣuən						
Hóngwǔ Zhèngyùn[e] 洪武正韵	下墾切	ɣən	shǎng(上)	ɣ	/	/	/	/

[a]For phonetic references, see Wang, L., Li, Z., Zhou, C., The Chinese Characters Ancient and Modern Tone List (Revised Edition), Zhonghua Shuju Press, Beijing(1999).
[b]Referring to Xu, S. and Xu X., *Shuowen Jiezi* (说文解字), photocopied by the Zhonghua Shuju Press, engraved by Chen, Ch.: 2 vols.
[c]Reference (Song) by Chen, P. Qing Guangxu eight to ten years Zunyi Lishi Japan Tokyo make carve ancient Yi series over Song carving: Guangyun 5 vols: Volume 3, pp. 120, 274.
[d] Referring to (Song) Ding, D., Qing Kangxi 45th year Cao, Y. Yangzhou engraved and repaired: 10 volumes of Jiyun: Volume 5, pp. 265, 628, 767.
[e] Reference (Ming) Le, S., Engraved by Liu Yijie in the 40th year of the Jiajing reign of Ming dynasty: Hongwu Zhengyun 16 vols: vol. 8, pp. 446.

contact. Wang Jing believes that it is impossible to directly determine whether *hěn(*很*)* and *hěn(*狠*)* are the result of a gra-dual grammaticalization of adjective meaning [3]. Examples of *hěn(*很*)* or *hěn(*狠*)* directly modi-fying adjectives have appeared in the literature after the Yuan and Ming dynasties, which has attracted attention from the academic community.

4.1 Origin of the *hěn(*哏*)*

It is worth noting that some new linguistic phenomena have emerged in Yuan Dynasty. Until.

the emergence of *hěn(*哏*)* in *Nogeoldae* of the Yuan Dynasty. According to Tatsuo Ota, *hěn(*哏*)* is the modern Chinese adverb of degree *hěn(*很*)*, which was used in the Yuan dynasty a-mong the northern people who had more contact with Mongolia. The following material is fro-m the *Nogeoldae*[5] (原刊老乞大).

---

(20) 那里就便投马市里去哏近。

It's *very* close to the horse market from there.

---

(21) 这桥便是我夜来说的桥比在右哏好有。

This bridge, the one I mentioned at night, is *much* better than the one on the right.

(continued)

[5] For the different versions of *Nogeoldae*, we refer to Wang Weihui's *The Compendium of Ten Textbooks of Chinese Language in the Joseon Era*. Shanghai Education Press, Shanghai(2022).

(continued)

(20) 那里就便投马市里去哏近。

(22) 主人家哥说的哏是。

The master of the family said it *very* correctly.

In the Yuan dynasty, the adverb *hěn*(哏) indicating degree of meaning was newly created, and the character used when this word was first created was indeterminate, as shown in the following table of the adverbs of degree in the different editions of *Nogeoldae* in different eras (Table 6).

Table 6. Usage of the adverb of degree *hěn*(哏) in different versions of *Nogeoldae*

Title	Examples
Nogeoldae	哏好价钱。The price is good
Nogeoldae eonhae	最好价钱。The price is good
Junggan Nogeoldae eonhae	所以价钱狠好。So the price is good
Cheong-eo Nogeoldae	所以价钱狠好。So the price is good

In addition, in the translation and writing version, it is written as and *hěn*(狠), but it is al-so written as *hěn*(很) in the photocopying version.[6] It can be seen that in the literature, there are writings of *hěn*(哏), *hěn*(很) or *hěn*(狠), and the earliest writing is *hěn*(哏). The followi-ng table is a summary of the origin of *hěn*(哏):

The origin of the word *hěn*(哏) is closely related to the contact between the Mongolian an-d Chinese languages, as it is mainly found in specific documents [6]. In the Yuan Dynasty, *hěn*(哏) has both adjective and adverb functions. In literature involving direct translation and directspeech, it mostly expresses the meaning of degree. However, in vernacular texts of *pure Chin-ese*, such as *Yuan zaju* (元杂剧), it mostly expresses the meaning of vicious.

4.2 *hěn*(哏) and *hěn*(狠)

In the literature, the structures of *hěn*(哏) + X and X + *hěn*(哏) are used, for example:

(23) 军户每根底使气力哏骚扰有。(《通制条格》卷十六)

The military is going to cause *too much* harassment. (*Tongzhi Tiaoge,* Volume 16)

(24) 哏损着田禾。(元·任仁发《水利集》卷一)

(continued)

---

[6] Wang, W.: The Compendium of Ten Textbooks of Chinese language in the Joseon Era (II) (in Chinese). Shanghai Education Press, Shanghai, 1, pp. 8b,10b(2022).

(*continued*)

It damages the fields *too much*. (Yuan - Ren Renfa, *Shuili Ji*, Volume 1)

(25) 你没事哏。(元·孙仲章《堪头巾》)

You are making *too much* trouble. (Yuan - Sun Zhongzhang, *Kan Toujin*)

"X" can represent action verbs such as "harass", "damage" and "say". The phrases "没事哏" and "没事狠" convey "excessive", with *hěn*(哏) also written as *hěn*(狠) [15]. The collection *Quan yuanqu* contains 44 instances of *hěn*(哏) and 38 of *è hěn hěn*(恶哏哏), a usage equivalent to *è hěn hěn*(恶狠狠). Though the CCL corpus search, we discovered that the colloquial forms *è hěn hěn*(恶哏哏) and *è hěn hěn*(恶狠狠) emerged simultaneously and first appeared in Yuan Dynasty and subsequent literature. This suggests that the specific use of *hěn*(很) in dialects may preserve the historical usage of *hěn*(哏) due to language contact over time.

4.3 hěn(哏) and hěn(很)

The interlocking relationship between *hěn*(哏), *hěn*(很), and *hěn*(狠) can be further sorted out with the help of the phonetic situation. The photocopy of *Ten Types of Chinese Textbooks in the Joseon Dynasty* preserves the phonetic notation of that time:

In the photocopied version, there are two kinds of notation for *hěn*(很). On the left side, t-here is the "current sounds" represented by voiced consonants, which was developed by Shen- Shuzhou[7] based on the spoken language of that time [16]. On the right side, there is the "class-ical sounds" represented by voiceless vowels, which Shen created according to the method ofwriting characters in *Hongwu Zhengyun* (洪武正韵). About half a century later, Shen's "currentsounds" were transformed into "classical sounds" by Cui Shizhen[8], and the right annotation e-volved into the "current sounds".

In the early days, *hěn*(哏) was pronounced as indicated by the left annotation with a voice-d vowel, which was recorded as [ɣ], the same as *hěn*(很). From Table 5, *hěn*(很) is also rec-orded as [ɣ]. Combining the meanings, consonants, and tones, *hěn*(哏) and *hěn*(很) have the s-ame consonants and tones, while *hěn*(哏) *and hěn*(狠) also share the same vowel. After the Ming Dynasty, due to the devoicing of fully voiced initials, the two sounds of *hěn*(很) and h-*ěn*(狠) gradually merged. The sound and meaning of *hěn*(很) and *hěn*(狠) became identical. T-he attachment of *hěn*(哏) occurred before the intersection of the two. According to the princip-le of economy, the phonetically similar *hěn*(很) was chosen to attach to it, and the degree of the adverbial meaning of *hěn*(哏) was correspondingly added to *hěn*(很), while the adjective meaning was added to *hěn*(狠).

hěn(哏) comes from contact with the Mongolian language, and with the change in languag-e policy and the redistribution of the semantic pattern of *hěn*(很) and *hěn*(

---

[7] Shen Shuzhou (1417–1475) wrote *Si Sheng Tong kao*(四声通考), A Comprehensive Study of the Four Tones.

[8] Cui Shizhen (1478–1534) wrote *Si Sheng Tong jie*(四声通解), the Four Tones of the General Explanation.

Table 7. Historical development of the word *hěn*(哏)[a]

Date	Word class	Sound	Semantic	Sxample	文献释证
Liao dynasty (907–1125)	/	亡版反	/	/	*Longkan shoujing* 龙龛手镜
Jin dynasty (1115–1234)	/	亡版切	/	/	*Sisheng Pianhai* 四声篇海
Yuan dynasty (1279–1368)	adverb	㕯匣母	high degree	哏好、哏坏事有	*Nogeoldae*老乞大, *Sisheng tongjie*四声通解, *Danzijie*单字解
Yuan dynasty (1279–1368)	adjective	同"狠"	vicious	这婆娘寸心毒哏千般计	*Yuan zaju*元杂剧
Yuan,Ming and Qing dynasties	Onomatopoeia	真文韵阴平调	Fierce look, angry voice	哏地一声道、哏哏	*Zhongyuan Yinyun*中原音韵, *Zhongzhou Yinyun*中州音韵, *Yunlü Yitong*韵略易通
Yuan,Ming and Qing dynasties	affix	狠平声	fierce and vicious look	恶哏哏、气哏哏	*Yuanqu xuan*元曲选
Now	adjectives	gén	Funny, amusing	逗哏	*Modern Chinese Dic-tionary* 现代汉语词典
	noun		Funny, interesting language or gestures		

[a]Cited from Wang, H., Ge,P.: The Origin and Evolution of the Degree Adverb *Hen*(很) in Modern Chinese (in Chinese). Studies in Language and Linguistics, 44,03, pp. 38–50(2024).

Table 8. Pronunciation of the word *hěn*(很) in the *Junggan Nogeoldae eonhae*

	left annotation 혼 [ɣən]	right annotation 흔 [xən]
Sìshēng Tōngkǎo 四声通考	current sounds	classical sounds
Sìshēng Tōngjiě 四声通解	classical sounds	current sounds

狠), *hěn*(哏) becameestablished as the character for degree, while *hěn*(狠) continued to be used as the character for"vicious". The character *hěn*(很) was established as the character of "degree", while *hěn*(狠) c-ontinued to be the character of "vicious" (Fig. 1 and Table 8).

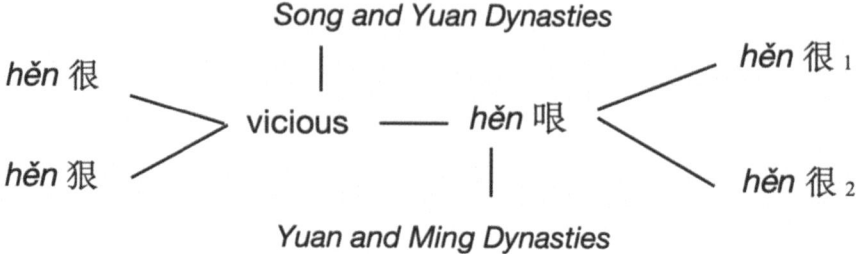

Fig. 1. Evolution of *hěn*(哏), *hěn*(狠) and *hěn*(很)

5 Conclusion

Combined with the linguistic phenomenon of co-occurrence in the dialect, it is found that there is a special usage of *hěn*(很) in the dialect that is different from that of the modern Chinese adverb of degree *hěn*(很). In the structure of *hěn*(很) + X and X + *hěn*(很), "X" can be an action verb, and *hěn*(很) not only means "degree" but also has the meaning of "vicious", and in the complementary structure, X + *hěn*(很) does not need conjunctions. Combining the dialectal phenomena with the historical corpus, it is actually the retention of *hěn*(哏) in the dialect. In modern Chinese dialects, the character for *hěn*(哏) is hardly used anymore, but in Harbin dialect, it is still recorded as "hěn dāu(哏叨)" or "hěn chì(哏斥)".

In the early period, *hěn*(很) and *hěn*(狠) were distinct in sound and meaning. By the Tang and Song Dynasties, they both could express "vicious" and were used interchangeably. *hěn*(很) had a broad semantic scope, encompassing "disobey, difficult to walk, vicious, stubborn, quarrel," among others, and it was used synonymously with *hěn*(狠) when referring to "vicious". Originally, *hěn*(很) and *hěn*(狠) developed in parallel, but their semantic boundaries gradually blurred. The intervention of *hěn*(哏) further reshaped their semantic patterns. During the Yuan Dynasty, as shown in Table 7, *hěn*(哏) included both adjective and adverb uses. Although *hěn*(哏) phased out in written form, its usage persisted. The adjective meaning merged with *hěn*(狠), and the adverbial meaning with *hěn*(很). Consequently, *hěn*(很) and *hěn*(狠) were semantically redistributed. The unique usage of *hěn*(很) in the dialect, seemingly without origin, can actually be traced back to *hěn*(哏), a relic of language contact in the dialect.

References

1. Wang, L.: Zhongguo yuwen jianghua(Chinese Language Speeches)(in Chinese). China Youth Publishing Group, Beijing (1954)
2. Wang, G., Ning, Y.: The origin of the adverb *hěn*(很) and the grammatical format *A de hěn*(得很) (in Chinese). Journal of Hebei Normal University (Philosophy and Social Sciences) (2002). https://doi.org/10.13763/j.cnki.jhebnu.psse.2002.01.013
3. Wang, J.: The grammaticalization process of *hěn*(很) (in Chinese). Journal of Huaiyin Teachers College(Social and Sciences Edition) (2003)
4. Hu, Y.: xiandai hanyu cankao ziliao (Modern Chinese Reference Materials) (in Chinese). Shanghai Education Press, Shanghai. **5**, 627 (1982)

5. Nie, Z.: On the nature of *hěn*(很) in the structure *X hěn*(很) (in Chinese). Studies of the Chinese Language, 1 (2005)
6. Wang, H., Ge, P.: The Origin and Evolution of the Degree Adverb *Hen*(很) in Modern Chinese (in Chinese). Studies in Language and Linguistics **44**(3) (2024)
7. Li, R.: Xiandan hanyu fangyan dacidian(Dictionary of Modern Chinese Dialects) (in Chinese). Jiangsu Education Press, Nanjing (2012)
8. Huang, B., Shi, G., Sun, L., Qi, X., Wang, H.: hanyu yufa leibian (Grammar of Chinese Dialects) (in Chinese), p. 392. Qingdao Publishing House, Qingdao (1996)
9. Ge, P.: Clausal Structures with *Hen*(很) and Their Formation in Donghai Dialect in Jiangsu Province (in Chinese). Dialect **3** (2021)
10. Wang, L.: zhongguo xiandai yufa (Modern Chinese grammar) (in Chinese), 1, pp. 141. Beijing United Publishing Co., Ltd., Beijing (2019)
11. Institute of Linguistic in Chinese Academy of Social Sciences. Modern Chinese Dictionary, 7th ed (in Chinese), p. 534. The Commercial Press, Beijing (2016)
12. Lü, S.: On *hěn*(很) and *hěn*(狠), zhongguo yuwen jiaoxue (Chinese Language Teaching) (in Chinese), No. 4 (1986)
13. Ota, T.: trans by Jiang S., Xu Ch.: Historical Grammar of the Chinese Language(in Chinese), p. 251. Peking University Press, Beijing (2003)
14. Zhang, Y.: Research on Chinese vulgar characters (in Chinese), p. 106. The Commercial Press, Beijing (2010)
15. Zhang, X.: The Rhetorical Interpretation of Poetry and Song (in Chinese), p. 463. Shanghai Classics Publishing House, Shanghai (2009)
16. Yuchi, Z.: Phonetic basis for the phonetic interpretation of Chinese character sounds in the *Nogeoldae* and *Piao Tongshi Yanjie* (in Chinese). Studies in Language and Linguistics, 1 (1990)

Lexical-Pragmatic Change in Social Media Platform: A Case Study of Gratitude Verb Constructions

Tianqi He[1]([✉]) [iD], Meitong Chen[2] [iD], and Qian Zhong[3] [iD]

[1] School of Humanities, Central South University, Changsha, China
tianqihe@csu.edu.cn
[2] Department of Linguistics, The University of Hong Kong, Pok Fu Lam, Hong Kong
[3] School of Foreign Languages, Wuhan Institute of Technology, Wuhan, China
qzhong5-c@my.cityu.edu.hk

Abstract. This paper explores the lexical-pragmatic changes of gratitude verb constructions on social media platforms. Gratitude constructions display a wide range of formal innovations on social media platforms, encompassing both novel lexical and phrasal constructions. These constructions have become highly conventionalized and are now used as fixed idioms. Two kinds of pragmatic changes are observed: positive and negative implicatures. The former category conveys positive emotions such as appreciation, delight, and teasing, which are mainly motivated by the causal chain of thanking events. The latter subtype denotes negative feelings like speechlessness, unhappiness, and anger, which are motivated by the pragmatic shift of *xiè-xiè* 谢谢 'thanks' in daily communication and reinforced by the online keyword censorship. Driven by the context collapse in social media, the pragmatic functions of gratitude constructions have shifted from positive to negative. This paper aims to shed light on lexical-pragmatic studies and Internet language changes.

Keywords: Pragmatic Change · Gratitude Verb Construction · Context Collapse

1 Introduction

Gratitude is considered a positive emotional reaction towards a perceived benefactor [1]. It is an integral part of social interaction. Utterances of gratitude have been researched extensively as an important speech act of thanking, categorized as illocutionary acts where speakers perform the act by uttering the sentence [2–4]. Expressions of gratitude in English can occur in many forms, including functional lexical chunks such as *thank you* [1], verbs such as *appreciate* and *acknowledge* [5], nouns such as *appreciation* and *indebtedness* [5], and adjectives such as *grateful* [5], nominalized expressions [6], and passive constructions [6]. Gratitude verbs and constructions like these have drawn scholarly attention over the past few decades to their formulaic sequences in corpora [1], generic structures and linguistic structures [6], differences in expressing gratitude among speakers from various language and cultural backgrounds [7], gratitude across context

P. Jin et al. (Eds.): CLSW 2024, LNAI 15552, pp. 274–286, 2025.
https://doi.org/10.1007/978-981-96-3509-2_20

variations [8]. However, expressing gratitude in Mandarin is intrinsically different from that of English, involving less direct speech act of thanking and using different syntactic structures and compliment response strategies [9]. This paper uses empirical data from Sina Weibo to study the lexical-pragmatic change of gratitude verb constructions on social media platforms to research their usage and the shift of pragmatic functions. Such gratitude verb constructions include both lexical constructions like *xiè-xiè* 谢谢 'thanks' and phrasal constructions like *tīng wǒ shuō xiè-xiè nǐ* 听我说谢谢你 'listen to me say thank you'.

1.1 Previous Studies on Gratitude Verbs and Constructions

A large body of existing literature on gratitude verbs and constructions has researched compliment responses and thanking strategies [9–14]. Lang found that Mainland Chinese students may perceive appearance compliments as being more socially polite than performance compliments and that their perceptions of the utterances are highly dependent on the friendliness and refinement of the speakers' utterances [11]. Similarly, Chuang & Hsieh investigated the syntactic and semantic features of gratitude verbs in Mandarin Chinese and English [9]. The Mandarin expression *xiè-xiè* 谢谢 'thanks' serves a dual role in compliment responses, extending beyond mere gratitude to encompass both rejection and appreciation, whereas *gǎn-xiè* 感谢 'appreciate' is predominantly used for thanking. Conversely, the English phrases *thank you* and *thanks* predominantly align with acceptance and the act of thanking within compliment responses. Syntactically, *xiè-xiè* 谢谢 'thanks' often appears in the middle or at the sentence-final positions, in contrast to the English counterparts which are typically found at the beginning or middle of the sentence. Tang & Zhang found that Chinese participants were less likely to use *Acceptance* strategies and more inclined towards *Evasion* and *Rejection* strategies compared to their Australian peers while expressing a compliment [15]. Wong and Liu examined other variations of Chinese, namely, Hong Kong Cantonese, and compared the two ways of saying '*thank you*' in Hong Kong Cantonese: *m-goi* 唔該 'thank you' vs. *do-ze* 多謝 'thank you' 16]. They concluded that the major difference between the two terms is the perceived level of gratitude: *m-goi* expresses a lower degree of thanks for what the addressee has done, while *do-ze* conveys a higher level of appreciation.

Additionally, thanking verbs have also been extensively studied as an important type of speech act [2, 3]. Cheng identified six primary categories of the speech act of thanking: thanking, appreciation, non-gratitude, combinations, thanking a third party, and formal speech [17]. Among these, the speech act of thanking can be used both to express gratitude and as non-gratitude, serving various illocutionary functions like relief, offer rejection, politeness, greetings, and concluding conversations [17].

In sum, previous studies on gratitude verbs and constructions have mainly focused on compliment responses, thanking strategies, and the speech act of thanking verbs.

1.2 Previous Studies on Pragmatic Change

Pragmatic change in language refers to the evolution of the ways in which language is used for communication, including changes in meaning, context, and function of words or expressions over time. Speech act theory [3] is essential for understanding pragmatic change as it explains the intention and function of language use over time. Brown and Levinson's politeness theory has been instrumental in studying pragmatic change, particularly how strategies for expressing politeness and managing face needs have evolved [18]. Linguistic relativity theory examines how changes in cultural and social norms influence language use and how shifts in societal values and beliefs are reflected in the pragmatic functions of language [19]. Conceptual metaphor theory offers another lens for viewing the development of new pragmatic meanings in metaphorical and metonymic expressions as a cognitive process [20].

Linguistic borrowing is a typical form of pragmatic change, sometimes termed pragmatic borrowing [21]. Typically, one language may borrow the discourse functions of a particular syntactic form from another language. More specifically, speakers might find two syntactic forms in two different languages analogous to each other, and then borrow the form from another language. This kind of pragmatic borrowing occurs frequently on social media platforms, giving rise to novel usages of language.

Traugott views pragmatic shifts as either primarily logical or interactional, highlighting that pragmatic implicatures are context sensitive [22]. Context is particularly important for the newly emerging usage of language on social media platforms. Novel lexical changes on social media platforms are affected by context collapse in social media [23, 24]. Context collapse refers to the breakdown of traditional boundaries of social and contextual settings, giving rise to the dynamic features that shape online communication [23, 24]. Social media, unlike traditional communication, inherently involves multiple audiences, as individuals can broadcast messages to diverse and massive online communities, each of which may vary in sociolinguistic norms and perspectives. Moreover, the absence of nonverbal contextual cues in digital communication can lead to various misunderstandings, as well as diverse interpretations of a message, due to the lack of context and exposure to a broad audience [25]. Context collapse therefore has a profound impact on the emergence of polysemous words in internet communication, given the diverse audiences with diverse backgrounds, whereby a single term can be interpreted very differently. The amplification and repetition of content on the internet also contribute to the rise of polysemy as new usages are recurrent in numerous contexts and experiential domains.

In sum, previous studies on pragmatic change have used various linguistics theories to construe pragmatic change. However, pragmatic change on social media platforms requires particular attention due to the context collapse phenomenon, which might give rise to polysemous words and novel lexical uses.

1.3 Data Collection from Sina Weibo

The present study used empirical data and a self-constructed corpus to study the usages of thanking verbs on social media platforms in order to research the pragmatic change of gratitude verb constructions. The data were retrieved automatically from Sina Weibo using Python by searching key gratitude words or constructions. For every gratitude verb or construction such as *xiè-xiè* 谢谢 'thanks' and phrasal constructions *tīng wǒ shuō xiè-xiè nǐ* 听我说谢谢你 'listen to me say thank you', 500 sentences were randomly selected from Sina Weibo on 11 May, 2023 for the current study, according to the following selection criteria:

1. The meaning of the sentence is clear. The pragmatic function of the utterance is explicit, without any grammatical errors, misspellings, or impolite expressions.
2. The sentence is easy to understand. The sentence uses everyday language and does not include niche community language.
3. The sentence consists solely of text and does not include any images or videos.

After all the data were properly retrieved, the researcher with linguistic expertise double-checked the sentences to ensure that any incomplete or ungrammatical ones were excluded from the self-constructed corpus used in the current study. The researcher then used the corpus to observe the pragmatic shift of each gratitude verb or construction, with a specific focus on the phrasal constructions *tīng wǒ shuō xiè-xiè nǐ* 听我说谢谢你 'listen to me say thank you'.

In sum, the current study adopts a corpus-driven approach to observe empirical data from Sina Weibo to examine the lexical-pragmatic change of gratitude verb constructions and explore their shifting pragmatic functions. Section 1 provides the introduction. Section 2 thoroughly reviews the gratitude constructions and variations in Weibo, as well as the preliminary observations of pragmatic implicatures changes. Section 3 focuses on the newly emerged pragmatic functions of gratitude constructions. Distribution data of the pragmatic implicatures of representative constructions will also be provided. Section 4 presents the conclusion.

2 Gratitude Verb Constructions in Sina Weibo

Thanking is an important communicative act in which an individual expresses gratitude or appreciation toward another person or entity for a favor, assistance, gift, or any other form of help or kindness received [26]. Constrained by traditional Chinese culture, gratitude expressions, especially direct speech acts of thanking, are not commonly used in Mandarin [9]. However, it has been found that people tend to use more straightforward and emotional expressions in social media, to counteract the social distance caused by online communication [27]. Thanking expressions are more frequently used in social media contexts, which are commonly realized via gratitude verb constructions [17, 28].

Based on preliminary observations of our Weibo corpus, the usage of gratitude-related verb constructions appears to be more dynamic, exhibiting features distinct from traditional spoken and written language. On the one hand, there are more variations in form. Except for the conventional expression *xiè-xiè* 谢谢 'thanks', there are also homophones (e.g., *xuē-xuē* 靴靴 'thanks', *shuān-Q* 栓Q 'thank you') and gratitude-related constructions (e.g., *wǒ zhēn-de huì xiè* 我真的会谢 'I really appreciate', *tīng wǒ shuō xiè-xiè nǐ* 听我说谢谢你 'listen to me say thank you'). On the other hand, gratitude-related constructions in the Weibo context display more diverse pragmatic functions. Besides denoting gratitude, they may also convey appreciation, delight, teasing, speechlessness, unhappiness, and even anger.

Following this vein, this chapter will systematically examine the gratitude-related verb constructions found on Weibo and briefly discuss the variation in their pragmatic functions.

Two types of constructions that may denote gratitude have been identified in Sina Weibo: lexical constructions and phrasal constructions. Details are listed in Table 1.

Table 1. Gratitude Constructions in Sina Weibo.

Type	Subtype	Examples
Lexical constructions	Spoken language derived	*xiè-xiè* 谢谢 'thanks' *gǎn-xiè* 感谢 'appreciate'
	Written language derived	*qiān-ēn-wàn-xiè* 千恩万谢 'a thousand thanks' *bú-shèng-gǎn-jī* 不胜感激 'deeply grateful' *gǎn-jī-tì-líng* 感激涕零 'overcome with gratitude' *gǎn-ēn-dài-dé* 感恩戴德 'deeply appreciative'
	Homophonic expression	*xiè-xiè* 蟹蟹 'thanks', *xuē-xuē* 靴靴 'thanks' *sān-Q* 3Q 'thank you', *shuān-Q* 拴Q 'thank you' *ā-lǐ-gā-duō* 阿里嘎多 'thanks' *kāng-sāng-hā-mì-dá* 康桑哈密达 'thanks'
Phrasal constructions	Gratitude verb related constructions	*wǒ zhēn-de XX* 我真的XX 'I really XX' *tīng wǒ shuō xiè-xiè nǐ* 听我说谢谢你 'listen to me say thank you' *gǎn-ēn de xīn, gǎn-xiè yǒu nǐ* 感恩的心, 感谢有你 'a heart of gratitude, thank you for being there'

As illustrated in the above table, three subtypes of lexical constructions are found in Weibo. The first category originates from spoken language, such as *xiè-xiè* 谢谢 'thanks' and *gǎn-xiè* 感谢 'appreciate'. The second type consists of idioms derived from ancient Chinese. For example, *gǎn-jī-tì-líng* 感激涕零 'overcome with gratitude' and *bú-shèng-gǎn-jī* 不胜感激 'deeply grateful' are originated from Zhu Geliang's <Chu Shi Biao>, and are reactivated in the social media context to express strong gratitude. The third type includes homophonic expressions of '*thank you*' in various languages. For instance, *xiè-xiè* 蟹蟹 'thanks' and *xuē-xuē* 靴靴 'thanks' are homophonic words of *xiè-xiè* 谢谢 'thanks', *sān-Q* 3Q 'thank you' and *shuān-Q* 拴Q 'thank you' are homophonic lexical items of *thank you*, *ā-lǐ-gā-duō* 阿里嘎多 'thanks' is the transliteration of *thanks* in Japanese, and the pronunciation of *kāng-sāng-hā-mì-dá* 康桑哈密达 'thanks' is similar to *thanks* in Korean. All these words can be used as typical gratitude verbs in contexts, as shown in Example (1).

(1) a. 今天　　也是　蹭到　　　　　车　的　一天，　　感恩戴德。
　　　Jīn-tiān yě-shì cèng-dào　　　chē de yī-tiān　gǎn-ēn-dài-dé
　　　Today　also　get a ride-DAO car　DE one day　thanks
　　　'Thanks a lot! Today I got a ride.'

　　b. 感谢　　张总　　　大老远　　　从　苏格兰　给　我　带　　的
　　　gǎn-xiè zhāng-zǒng dà-lǎo-yuǎn cóng sū-gé-lán gěi wǒ dài　de
　　　thanks Mr. Zhang　far away　　from Scotland give I　bring DE
　　　羊毛　　　　围巾，　栓Q！
　　　Yang-máo wéi-jīn shuān Q !
　　　wool　　　scarf　　thank you
　　　'Thank Mr. Zhang for the wool scarf he brought me all the way from
　　　Scotland. Thank you!'

　　c. 阿里嘎多，　真是　　一段　难忘　　　的　旅程。
　　　Ā-lǐ-gā-duō zhēn-shì yī-duàn nán-wàng　de　lǚ-chéng
　　　Thank you　really　a　　　unforgettable DE journey
　　　'Thanks! What a unforgettable journey!'

On the other hand, there are also some popular phrasal constructions denoting gratitude, which are mainly thanking verb related constructions that are generated from buzzwords. For instance, *tīng wǒ shuō xiè-xiè nǐ* 听我说谢谢你 'listen to me say thank you' and *gǎn-ēn de xīn, gǎn-xiè yǒu nǐ* 感恩的心，感谢有你 'a heart of gratitude, thank you for being there' are actually lyrics from popular songs, which have been adopted by netizens to express gratitude in a rhetorical way. *Wǒ zhēn-de XX* 我真的XX 'I really XX' is a semi-opened construction that has a range of variants, including different gratitude verbs, such as *wǒ zhēn-de huì xiè* 我真的会谢, *wǒ zhēn-de shuān-Q* 我真的栓Q *and wǒ zhēnde xuē-xuē* 我真的靴靴 'I really appreciate'. This kind of phrasal construction is highly fixed due to frequent usage in social media and can be used separately as gratitude idioms in contexts, as shown in Example (2).

(2) a. 我们　　导师　　真的　　好好　　呀！感恩　的　心，　　感谢　有　　你！
　　　Wǒ-men dǎo-shī zhēn-de hǎo-hǎo ya gǎn-ēn de xīn gǎn-xiè yǒu nǐ
　　　Our　　tutor　really-DE great　YA　　thanks DE heart thanks have you
　　　'Our tutor is really great! Thanks a lot!'

　　b. 我　真的　　栓Q，　一　　回家　　就　赶上　　　百年不遇
　　　wǒ zhēn-de shuān-Q yī huí-jiā jiù gǎn-shàng bǎi-nián-bú-yù
　　　I　really-DE thank you once go home then meet　　once in a century
　　　的　查寝，　　　　服了。
　　　de chá-qǐn　　　fú le
　　　DE check dormitory you got me
　　　'I'm depressed. As soon as I got home, I caught up with the once-a-century
　　　dormitory inspection. You got me!'

As illustrated in (2a), *găn-ēn de xīn, găn-xiè yŏu nĭ* 感恩的心, 感谢有你 'a heart of gratitude, thank you for being there' is used in a separate sentence to express gratitude. In (2b), the pragmatic function of *wŏ zhēn-de shuān-Q* 我真的拴Q 'I really appreciate' has changed. It does not refer to gratitude but denotes the negative emotion 'unhappy or depressed'.

In sum, the gratitude verb constructions on Weibo are more active and diverse than ever, which has also resulted in the change of semantic and pragmatic functions.

3 Pragmatic Change of Gratitude Verb Constructions

As illustrated by Example (2), gratitude constructions may serve various pragmatic functions in social media contexts. Based on corpus data from Sina Weibo, two subtypes of emerging pragmatic implicatures of gratitude constructions are observed, which will be further discussed with examples in this section.

3.1 Emerging Positive Pragmatic Implicatures

Gratitude is a speech act that involves a series of positive emotions, such as appreciation towards people or entities that offer assistance, and delight and thankfulness from those who receive help. Thus, gratitude constructions in social media may shift towards related positive implicatures. As shown in our corpus data, three positive implicatures have recently emerged in social media: appreciation, delight, and teasing.

Appreciation. As suggested by Manela [29], gratitude includes two sub-categories: i) Y is grateful *to* R for Ø-ing (Y is the beneficiary, R is the benefactor, and Ø is something that R has done), and ii) Y is grateful *that* p (Y is the beneficiary, and p is some proposition that Y finds beneficial). The latter type, 'gratitude *that*', is actually a special kind of appreciation focused on acknowledging and expressing thanks for something received [30]. Therefore, gratitude words may easily express appreciation in social media. When someone uses words like *xiè-xiè* 谢谢 'thanks' and *shuān-Q* 拴Q 'thank you', they are expressing appreciation for a kind gesture, action, or gift. These words convey a sense of acknowledgment, recognition, and thankfulness towards the person who has done something for them. As shown in Example (3), gratitude constructions serve as a means of expressing appreciation for the actions or contributions of others.

(3) 我 真的   谢谢! 爱奇艺 视频   的 清晰度   太 高 了!
     Wŏ zhēn-de xiè-xiè ài-qí-yì shì-pín de qīng-xī-dù tài gāo le
     I   really thanks IQiYi video DE resolution too high LE
     'I really appreciate the high resolution of IQiYi.'

As suggested in the above example, *wŏ zhēn-de xiè-xiè* 我真的谢谢 'I really appreciate' is a separate interjection that indicates compliment and recognition for IQiYi, for its high resolution. Unlike 'gratitude to', the benefactor R and the beneficial action Ø-ing have been compressed into an integrated p (i.e., *ài-qí-yì shì-pín de qīng-xī-dù tài gāo le* 爱奇艺视频的清晰度太高了 'the resolution of IQiYi video is too high'), which the beneficiary *wŏ* 我 'I' finds valuable.

Delight. Both gratitude and delight are positive emotions closely linked to appreciation [31]. In particular, expressing gratitude may indirectly contribute to feelings of joy or delight, especially if the act of kindness is acknowledged as bringing happiness or satisfaction. Specifically, gratitude may involve beneficial consequences and ultimately lead to happiness [32, 33]. Therefore, thanking constructions may not only merely convey delight or joy, but also contribute to positive emotions in specific contexts, as illustrated in Example (4).

(4) 天哪! 我 真的 会 谢! 一天 两次 中奖,
Tiān-na wǒ zhēn-de huì xiè yī-tiān liǎng-cì zhōng-jiǎng
OMG I really-DE will thanks one day two times win a prize
太 快乐 了!
tài kuài-lè le
too happy LE
'OMG! Thank you! I won two prizes in a day. It is really delightful!'

As suggested in Example (4), the gratitude construction *wǒ zhēn-de huì xiè* 我真的会谢 collocates with other emotional interjections that express surprise, such as *tiān-na* 天哪 'oh my god', or delight, such as *tài kuài-lè le* 太快乐了 'so happy'. In Example (4), the benefactor does not appear; rather, the gratitude construction is used to emphasize the delight and joy of winning two prizes in one day, rather than 'thanking someone for something'.

Teasing. Teasing involves playful or mocking behavior intended to provoke laughter or amusement, with the speaker aiming to establish a close relationship with the listener by uttering statements that are obviously untrue in a literal sense and may be disadvantageous to the speaker [34, 35]. Previous works indicate that the user's attitude towards teasing is positive [36]. While gratitude words are not typically used to express teasing, they can be used in a teasing context if the intention is to playfully exaggerate gratitude or to mockingly express thanks in a humorous or ironic manner. This would be considered a playful or sarcastic use of gratitude words rather than a genuine expression of appreciation, as shown in Example (5).

(5) 妈妈 说 我 吃 的 东西 像 屎, 妈妈 蟹蟹 您。
Mā-mā shuō wǒ chī de dōng-xī xiàng shǐ mā-mā xiè-xiè nín
Mom say I eat DE things like shit mon thank you
'Mom says that my food likes shit. Thank you a lot!'

As illustrated in Example (5), the relationship between *wǒ* 我 'I' and *mā-mā* 妈妈 'mom' is close enough to allow for jokes. Mom playfully teases me about the unappealing appearance of the food I am eating. In response, I humorously reply with the gratitude construction *mā-mā xiè-xiè nín* 妈妈蟹蟹您 'thank you, mom'. However, this does not indicate gratitude but instead implies teasing in context.

3.2 Emerging Negative Pragmatic Implicatures

Except for the above-mentioned positive implicatures, it has been found that gratitude constructions in social media may also indicate negative emotions. According to corpus data, gratitude constructions may denote speechlessness, unhappiness, and anger. These implicatures are mainly evoked by the pragmatic shift of *xiè-xiè* 谢谢 'thanks'. Some crosstalk programs, especially Beijing crosstalk performers, tend to use expressions such as *wǒ kě tài xiè-xiè nín le* 我可太谢谢您了 'thank you very much' in an ironic way to express dissatisfaction or condemnation of certain behaviors. On the other hand, due to the strict censorship mechanism, uncivil language cannot be displayed on social platforms. Users are more inclined to use linguistic devices such as irony and orthographical play to express negative emotions [37, 38]. As a result, gratitude constructions may be used to convey negative feelings in online contexts.

Speechlessness. Speechlessness refers to the helpless or confused state that occurs when people are unable to comprehend a certain event or the behavior of a particular individual. Gratitude constructions are also used in this context, usually to express the speechless feeling towards a certain patient. Similar to the benefactor in conventional thanking expressions, this patient is the one who should be blamed directly, as illustrated in Example (6).

(6) 送　我 25 块　话费,　　　　　分　25 个　月,　每个　　　月
　　Sòng wǒ 25 kuài huà-fèi　　　fèn　25 gè　yuè　měi-gè　yuè
　　Give I　25 buck telephone charge divide 25 GE month every-GE month
　　送　我 一块。　中国　　移动,　听　我 说　谢谢　你。
　　sòng wǒ yī kuài　zhōng-guó yí-dòng　tīng wǒ shuō xiè-xiè nǐ
　　give I　one buck China　　Mobile　listen I say　thank　you
　　'Give me 25 bucks for my phone charge and divide into 25 months. One buck for each month. China Mobile, listen to me say thank you.'

As shown in Example (6), the patient of *tīng wǒ shuō xiè-xiè nǐ* 听我说谢谢你 'listen to me say thank you' is the company *zhōng-guó yí-dòng* 中国移动 'Chine Mobile', which should be condemned for something it has done (i.e., *Sòng wǒ 25 kuài huà-fèi, fèn 25 gè yuè, měi-gè yuè sòng wǒ yī kuài* 送我25块话费, 分25个月, 每个月送我一块 'Give me 25 bucks for my phone charge and divide into 25 months. One buck for each month'). Thus, the gratitude construction here does not imply gratitude, but denotes the helpless, confused, and frustrated emotions evoked by the event.

Unhappiness. Unhappiness refers to the annoyed, frustrated, and depressed feelings caused by certain people, behaviors, or events. Compared to speechlessness, it has a more negative implicature. In specific contexts, gratitude constructions may be adopted to express unhappiness, by collocating with the reason that may cause this feeling, as listed in Example (7).

(7) 清明节　　　　　上班,　　我 真的　　谢谢。
　　Qīng-míng-jiē　shàng-bān wǒ zhēn-de　xiè-xiè
　　Qingming Festival work　　I　really-DE appreciate
　　'I have to work on Qingming Festival. I really appreciate!'

As shown in the sentence above, *wǒ zhēn-de xiè-xiè* 我真的谢谢 'I really appreciate' is used as an interjection to express dissatisfaction with overwork (i.e., *Qīng-míng-jiē shàng-bān* 清明节上班 'work in Qingming Festival').

Anger. Following the same vein, gratitude constructions may be used to imply anger in specific contexts. This shift is usually realized by collocating with anger-related emotion words, as suggested by Example (8).

(8) 发霉 了，幸好   我 吃 之前   看 了 一眼，也 没有   过
    Fā-méi le   xìng-hǎo wǒ chī zhī-qián kàn le yī-yǎn yě méi-yǒu guò
    Moldy LE   lucky   I eat before look LE once also not   past
    保质期。   真的   会 生气   蟹蟹。
    bǎo-zhì-qī zhēn-de huì shēng-qì xiè-xiè
    sell-by date really-DE will angry   thanks
    'It's moldy. Luckily that I looked at the date before I ate it, and it hasn't past the sell-by date. I am really angry. Thanks.'

As shown in Example (8), *xiè-xiè* 蟹蟹 'thanks' is used after the angry-denoting verb *shēng-qì* 生气 'angry', to express anger towards the above event (i.e., *fā-méi le* 发霉了 'It's moldy').

3.3 Distribution of the Newly Emerged Pragmatic Functions

To provide a complete picture of the pragmatic functions of gratitude constructions in Sina Weibo, we randomly selected 500 posts containing the representative thanking expression *tīng wǒ shuō xiè-xiè nǐ* 听我说谢谢你 'listen to me say thank you' and manually calculated the distribution of its pragmatic implicatures. Details are listed in Table 2.

Table 2. Distribution of the pragmatic functions of 听我说谢谢你.

Types	Subtype	Frequency
Positive implicatures	Appreciation	12/500 (2.4%)
	Delight	11/500 (2.2%)
	Teasing	49/500 (9.8%)
Negative implicatures	Speechlessness	**123/500 (24.6%)**
	Unhappiness	**284/500 (56.8%)**
	Anger	22/500 (4.4%)

As presented in Table 2, the overall negative implicatures of *tīng wǒ shuō xiè-xiè nǐ* 听我说谢谢你 'listen to me say thank you' are significantly higher (85.6%) than the positive implicatures (14.4%). Among the negative implicatures, unhappiness occupies the largest proportion (56.8%), while speechlessness is slightly less frequent, accounting for

24.6% in total. Among all the positive implicatures, teasing occupies the largest percentage (9.8%). This indicates that the pragmatic functions of gratitude constructions have not only increased and changed but have also shifted towards a certain direction: from positive to negative, which corresponds to the recreational nature and the polarization trend in social media.

In sum, gratitude constructions display various pragmatic implicatures in the Sina Weibo context, including conveying positive emotions like appreciation, delight, and teasing, as well as denoting negative feelings in an ironic way, including speechlessness, unhappiness, and anger. This pragmatic shift is mainly motivated by the context collapse in social media. Considering the audience for each post is uncertain and diverse, the context in social media is actually a highly compressed space allowing for various possibilities. As a result, speakers are encouraged to create more innovative expressions and usages, while hearers are allowed to have diverse interpretations of a single post. Therefore, the semantic and pragmatic changes in social media are more active than ever. Specifically, the negative implicatures of gratitude constructions are mainly motivated by the functional shift of *xiè-xiè* 谢谢 'thanks' in conventional communication and are enhanced by the online censorship mechanism.

4   Conclusion

This paper systematically examines gratitude constructions in social media and discusses their newly emerged pragmatic implicatures. It has been found that gratitude constructions display a more diverse form on Sina Weibo, in terms of both lexical constructions and phrasal constructions. These novel usages are now highly conventionalized and can be used as fixed idioms. Based on the corpus data from Sina Weibo, two kinds of newly emerged pragmatic changes are observed: positive and negative implicatures. The former category includes appreciation, delight, and teasing, which are motivated by the causal chain of the thanking event. Specifically, gratitude is a form of appreciation when people express recognition or compliments for a certain event or entity, rather than a personalized benefactor, while delight refers to the joyful mood caused by the gratitude event. Besides, teasing is primarily used as a rhetorical device to indicate the close relationship between the benefactor and beneficiary. The negative implicatures are mainly evoked by the functional change of *xiè-xiè* 谢谢 'thanks' in daily communication, which has been further encouraged by Sina Weibo's keyword censorship. The distributional data presented in Sect. 3.3 indicate that the pragmatic functions of gratitude constructions have shifted from positive to negative in recent times. The pragmatic shift of gratitude constructions is likely caused by the context collapse in social media.

References

1. Schauer, G.A., Adolphs, S.: Expressions of gratitude in corpus and DCT data: Vocabulary, formulaic sequences, and pedagogy. System **34**, 119–134 (2006)
2. Austin, J.L.: How to do Things with Words, 2nd edn. Clarendon Press, Oxford, Eng (1975)
3. Searle, J.R., Kiefer, F., Bierwisch, M. (eds.): Speech act theory and pragmatics, Vol. 10.D. Reidel Publishing Company, Dordrecht/Boston/London (1980)

4. Allan, K.: Speech act theory: Overview. In: Lamarque, P. (ed.) Concise Encyclopedia of Philosophy of Language, pp. 454–466. Pergamon, Exeter U.K. (1997)
5. Afful, J.B.A.: A genre study of undergraduate dissertation acknowledgements in a Ghanaian university. ESP Today. 4(2), 202–224 (2016)
6. Nguyen, T.T.L.: Generic structures and linguistic features of TESOL master's thesis acknowledgements written by Vietnamese postgraduates. 3L, Language, Linguistics, Literature, Vol. 23, pp. 27–40. Bangi Selangor, Malaysia (2017)
7. Cui, X.B.: A cross-linguistic study on expressions of gratitude by native and non-native english speakers. J. Lang. Teach. Res. 3(4), 753–760 (2012)
8. Yang, W.: Comparison of gratitude across context variations: a generic analysis of dissertation acknowledgements written by Taiwanese authors in EFL and ESL contexts. Int. J. App. Linguist. Eng. Literat. 1(5), 130–146 (2012)
9. Chuang, K.T., Hsieh, S.C.Y.: Ways of thanking in mandarin Chinese and English. US-China Foreign Language 11(2), 120–128 (2013)
10. Chen, R.: Responding to compliments A contrastive study of politeness strategies between American English and Chinese speakers. J. Pragmat. 20, 49–75 (1993)
11. Lang, Y.: "Thank you" and" no, no": Communicative context and Chinese perceptions of and responses to American English compliments. Doctoral dissertation. The University of Tennessee, Tennessee (1998)
12. Chen, S.E.: Compliment response strategies in Mandarin Chinese: Politeness phenomenon revisited. Concentric: Studies in Linguistics 29(2) 157–184 (2003)
13. Al Falasi, H.: Just say thank you: A study of compliment responses. The Linguistics Journal 2(1), 28–42 (2007)
14. Sudarwati, E.: Thank you, it really makes my day: compliment responses revisited. Language Literacy: Journal of Linguistics, Literature, and Language Teaching 5(2), 321–331 (2021)
15. Tang, C.H., Zhang, G.Q.: A contrastive study of compliment responses among australian english and mandarin Chinese speakers. J. Pragmat. 41(2), 325–345 (2009)
16. Wong, J., Liu, C.: Two ways of saying 'thank you' in Hong Kong Cantonese: m-goi vs. do-ze. Further advances in pragmatics and philosophy: Part 2 theories and applications, 20, 435–447 (2019)
17. Cheng, S.W.: A corpus-based approach to the study of speech act of thanking. Concentric: Studies in Linguistics 36(2), 257–274 (2010)
18. Brown, P., Levinson, S.: Universals in Language usage: Politeness phenomena. In: Goody, E.N. (ed.) Questions and politeness: Strategies in social interaction, vol. 8, pp. 56–289. Cambridge University Press, Cambridge (1978)
19. Lucy, J.A.: Linguistic relativity. Annual Review of Anthropology 26(1), 291–312 (1997)
20. Lakoff, G., Johnson, M.: The metaphorical structure of the human conceptual system. Cogn. Sci. 4(2), 195–208 (1980)
21. Prince, E.F.: On pragmatic change: the borrowing of discourse functions. J. Pragmat. 12(5–6), 505–518 (1988)
22. Traugott, E.C.: Pragmatics and language change. In: Allan, K., Jaszczolt. K. (eds.) The Cambridge handbook of pragmatics, pp. 549–566. Cambridge University Press, Cambridge (2012)
23. Scott, K.: Pragmatics Online. Routledge, New York (2022)
24. Scott, K.: The pragmatics of rebroadcasting content on twitter: how is retweeting relevant? J. Pragmat. 184, 52–60 (2021)
25. Sweetser, E.: Role and individual interpretations of change predicates. In: Nuyts. J. Pederson. E (eds.) Language and conceptualization, pp. 116–136. Cambridge University Press, Cambridge (1997)
26. Eisenstein, M., Bodman, J.: Expressing gratitude in American English. Interlanguage pragmatics, 6481 (1993)

27. Buder, J., Rabl, L., Feiks, M., Badermann, M., Zurstiege, G.: Does negatively toned language use on social media lead to attitude polarization? Comput. Hum. Behav. **116**, 106663 (2021)
28. Tunçel, R.: Speech act realizations of Turkish EFL learners: a study on apologizing and thanking. Doctoral dissertation. Anadolu University, Turkey (2014)
29. Manela, T.: Gratitude and appreciation. Am. Philos. Q. **53**, 281–294 (2016)
30. Watkins, P.C.: Gratitude and the good life: toward a psychology of appreciation. Springer Science & Business Media, Dordrecht/Heidelberg/New York/London (2013)
31. Roberts, R.C.: The blessings of gratitude: A conceptual analysis. In: Emmons, R.A., McCullough, M.E. (eds.) The psychology of gratitude, Vol. 1. pp. 58–78. Oxford University Press, Oxford (2004)
32. Emmons, R.A.: Thanks!: how the new science of gratitude can make you happier. Houghton Mifflin Harcourt, Boston/New York (2007)
33. Watkins, P.C., Woodward, K., Stone, T., Kolts, R.L.: Gratitude and happiness: development of a measure of gratitude, and relationships with subjective well-being. Soc. Behav. Personal. Int. J. **31**(5), 431–451 (2003)
34. Tu, J.: Cognitive research on irony. Journal of foreign Languages **02**, 7–9+73 (2004)
35. Bansal, S., Garg, N., Singh, J.: Exploring the psychometric properties of the Cyberbullying Attitude Scale (CBAS) and its relation with teasing and gratitude in Indian collegiates. Int. J. Educ. Manag. **37**(1), 225–239 (2023)
36. Hao, Y.: Analysis of the variation of network language. Yuwen Jianshe. **24**, 75–76 (2017)
37. Allan, K., Burridge, K.: Forbidden words: Taboo and the censoring of language. Cambridge University Press, Cambridge (2006)
38. Battistella, E.: Bad language: are some words better than others? Oxford University Press, Oxford (2005)

The Construction Tendency and Cognitive Motivation of [X+PLACE] Compounds from the Perspective of Qualia Structure

Mengli Wu and Jiapan Li[✉]

Teachers College of Beijing Language and Culture University, Beijing, China
lijiapan@blcu.edu.cn

Abstract. This paper examines the interaction of semantics, grammatical class, and prosody in Chinese [X+PLACE] compounds, specifically from the perspective of Qualia Structure. It focuses on construction tendencies between constituents of [X+PLACE] compounds and explores the underlying cognitive motivations. The findings reveal that the construction tendency of the internal semantics in [X+PLACE] compounds is as follows: [FORMAL+PLACE] > [TELIC+PLACE] > [AGENTIVE+PLACE] > [CONSTITUTIVE+PLACE] > [HANDLE+PLACE]. In terms of grammatical class, the tendency is NN > VN > AN. Furthermore, the prosodic models demonstrate a construction tendency of [1+1] > [2+1] > [1+2]. Due to principles of formal economy and semantic accuracy, the grammatical class and prosodic models of [X+PLACE] compounds exhibit different construction tendencies from the perspective of qualia models. Moreover, the natural or artificial attributes of PLACE significantly influence compound construction: head constituents of artificial places tend to form [TELIC+PLACE], while those of natural places tend to form [FORMAL+PLACE].

Keywords: Qualia Structure · [X+PLACE] compounds · Construction tendency · Cognitive motivation

1 Introduction

In modern Chinese, there exists a group of compounds, such as "海塘(*hǎi-táng, seawall*)" - "海滩(*hǎi-tān, beach*)", "月台(*yuè-tái, moon viewing platform*)" - "月宫(*yuè-gōng, moon palace*)", "水库(*shuǐ-kù, reservoir*)" - "水榭(*shuǐ-xiè, water pavilion*)", etc. In these compounds, the head constituents refer to "place" and the structure can be formalized as [X+PLACE]. The semantic relationships between the modifier X and the head PLACE varies subtly, with X defining PLACE from different perspectives. For example, "海塘(*hǎi-táng, seawall*)" emphasizes the protective function against the sea, while "海滩(*hǎi-tān, beach*)" refers to a specific geographical location by the sea; "月台(*yuè-tái, moon viewing platform*)" suggests a purpose or activity associated with the moon, while "月宫(*yuè-gōng, moon palace*)" refers to a mythical or spatial concept; "水库(*shuǐ-kù, reservoir*)" highlights the function of water storage, whereas "水

P. Jin et al. (Eds.): CLSW 2024, LNAI 15552, pp. 287–300, 2025.
https://doi.org/10.1007/978-981-96-3509-2_21

榭(*shuǐ-xiè, water pavilion*)" indicates the structure situated by water. In words like "海塘(*hǎi-táng, seawall*), 月台(*yuè-tái, moon viewing platform*), 水库(*shuǐ-kù, reservoir*)", X emphasizes the function of PLACE, whereas in words like "海滩(*hǎi-tān, beach*), 月宫(*yuè-gōng, moon palace*), 水榭(*shuǐ-xiè, water pavilion*)", X emphasizes the position of PLACE.

Previous studies have primarily analyzed [X+PLACE] compounds from two perspectives. The first perspective generalizes compounds from a semantic category standpoint as "person/animal/thing+place" [1], e.g., 皇宫(*huáng-gōng, imperial palace*), 虎穴(*hǔ-xué, tiger's den*), 银行(*yín-háng, bank*)". However, the internal semantic relationships in these compounds are complex, and labeling the modifiers simply as "person/animal/thing" fail to capture the place's function. Additionally, the grammatical class models can also be "V/A+place", e.g., "游泳馆(*yóuyǒng-guǎn, swimming pool*), 大厅(*dà-tīng, hall*)". The second perspective frames compounds within a "thing-action/relation-place" structure based on case roles [2], e.g., "林区(*lín-qū, forest area*), 景点(*jǐng-diǎn, tourist attraction*), 花园(*huā-yuan, garden*)". However, the case relationships centered on verbs do not fully account for noun-centered modifier-head structures [3, 4]. At times, classification based on case relationships fails to explain the commonalities and differences in the semantics of modifier-head compounds. For instance, "道场(*dào-chǎng, temple*)", a place where Taoist priests perform rituals, is categorized as [AGENT+PLACE], while "菜场(*cài-chǎng, vegetable market*)", a type of marketplace where fresh vegetables are sold, falls under [PATIENT+PLACE], even though both describe the place's function. Similarly, "免税区(*miǎnshuì-qū, tax-free zone*), 洪泛区(*hóngfàn-qū, floodplain*)" are both classified as [ACTION+PLACE], but their heads describe different aspects of place's function and formation.

Qualia structure of Generative Lexicon Theory, which centers on nouns, provides a systematic and objective framework for describing noun semantics, effectively unifying form and meaning. In recent years, it has been widely used in the study of Chinese compound nouns. This paper examines [X+PLACE] compounds through lens of Qualia Structure, using Modern Chinese Dictionary (7th edition) [5] as the basis. It offers a detailed analysis of the conduction rules governing the qualia, the grammatical class of constituents, and the prosody of these compounds. The study seeks to answer the following questions: What semantic relationships are encoded in [X+PLACE] compounds? How does the semantic category of PLACE constrain the selection of X semantics? How do the qualia, grammatical class, and prosody of [X+PLACE] compounds match? By elucidating the specific semantic relationships within [X+PLACE] compounds, this paper also explores the underlying cognitive motivations.

2   Definition of [X+PLACE] Compounds

This study focuses on modifier-head [X+PLACE] compounds, such as "学校(*xué-xiào, school*), 公园(*gōng-yuán, park*), 邮局(*yóu-jú, post office*)", which exhibit locative characteristics when denoting a place and object-related characteristics when referring to an institution or entity. Due to their dual semantic functions and distinct distribution features, these compounds have attracted considerable attention in Chinese linguistics. Previous researches have primarily addressed their categorization, classification, and scope, with a central debate regarding whether location words represent a subclass of nouns or an independent word category [6–11]. This paper also explores the relationship between [X+PLACE] compound and ordinary nouns or location words, as it is key to defining the scope of this study, delineating research objects, and ensuring corpus purity. According to [7], we treat terms like "教室(*jiào-shì, classroom*), 工厂(*gōng-chǎng, factory*), 操场(*cāo-chǎng, playground*)" as "nouns with locative functions". Therefore, [X+PLA-CE] compounds are classified as locative nouns, distinct from general location words. The challenge, however, lies in distinguishing locative nouns from location words and differentiating them from ordinary nouns. Given that these compounds lie at the boundaries of these categories, it is essential to integrate both formal and semantic evidences in the research methodology.

First, based on distributional criteria, we can differentiate between ordinary nouns, locative nouns, and location words. The distinction between locative nouns and location words is that locative nouns can directly serve as the objects of the prepositions "在(*zài, at/in/on*)" and "到(*dào, to/arrive at*)". Ordinary nouns, however, must be accompanied by directional words to serve as the objects of these prepositions. For example, with "操场(*cāo-chǎng, playground*)", can stand alone as "在操场(*zài cāochǎng, at the playground*)", but "桌子(*zhuōzi, table*)" cannot: "在桌子(*zài zhuōzi, on the table*)" is incorrect, whereas "在桌子上(*zài zhuōzi shàng, on the table*)" is acceptable. Locative nouns can take localizers, but location words cannot. For example, "教室(*jiào-shì, classroom*)" becomes "教室里(*jiàoshì lǐ, in the classroom*)", while "野外(*yě-wài, outdoors*)" cannot be used as "野外上(*yěwài shàng, on the outdoors*)". Furthermore, Chinese location words can function directly as adverbials, which is a key criterion. For example, location words like "中国(*zhōngguó, China*)" in "咱们中国见(*zánmen zhōngguó jiàn, see you in China*)" are used adverbially. Even less typical location words or locative nouns, such as "江北(*jiāng-běi, Jiangbei*)" or "学校(*xué-xiào, school*)" can also be used as adverbials, as in "咱们江北见(*zánmen Jiangbei jiàn, see you indoors*)" or "咱们学校见(*zánmen xuéxiào jiàn, see you in the school*)". In contrast, ordinary nouns generally cannot function directly as adverbials.

Second, at the semantic level, this study applies prototype theory to suggest that word meanings exhibit prototypicality. Specifically, each word class has a prototypical meaning: nouns typically denote things, while verbs denote actions. Prototypical nouns refer to three-dimensional entities. Thus, typical nouns function semantically to indicate entities, typical location words indicate positions, and locative nouns combine both entity and position. Examples include institution nouns like "邮局(*yóu-jú, post office*), 医院(*yī-yuàn, hospital*), 教育部(*jiàoyù-bù, Ministry of Education*)", and location nouns such as "教室(*jiào-shì, classroom*), 操场(*cāo-chǎng, playground*), 山脚(*shān-jiǎo, foothill*)". The distinction between entity and position functions exists on a continuum, with varying degrees of differentiation among typical nouns, locative nouns, and typical location words. Table 1 compares typical location words, non-typical location words, and ordinary nouns.

In this study, we rely on formal criteria and semantic interpretation to identify 1,415 [X+PLACE] compounds as our research subjects.

Table 1. Comparison of Typical Location Words, Non-Typical Location Words, and Typical Nouns.

		Typical Location Words	Location Words/Nouns		Typical Nouns
		Toponymy	[X+LOCALIZER] compounds	[X+PLACE] compounds	Entity Nouns
Semantics		Position		Entity-Position	Entity
Formal criteria	Acts as Preposition's Object	+	+	+	-
	Carries Localizer	-	-	+	+
	Acts as Adverbial Modifier	+	+	+	-
Example		中国(China) 北京(Beijing)	野外(outdoors) 江北(Jiangbei)	学校(school) 公园(park)	桌子(table) 笔筒(brush pot)

3 Types of Qualia Relationships and Construction Tendencies Between Constituents in [X+PLACE] Compounds

3.1 Types of Qualia Relationships Between Constituents in [X+PLACE] Compounds

Qualia Structure expresses the meaning of lexical items and mainly involves four levels of semantic knowledge: what kind the item is, what it includes, how it is brought about, and what it is used for. These levels correspond to formal, constitutive, agentive, and telic roles respectively [12, 13]. [14] expanded this framework to include ten types. This study adopts the following qualia relationship types.

Formal role describes the attributes that distinguish an object within a cognitive domain, such as position, size, shape, dimension, or color. For example, in "内陆湖(nèilù-hú, inland lake)", "内陆(nèilù, inland)" highlights the lake's position, while "拱桥(hong-qiáo, arched bridge)", "拱(hong, arched)" emphasizes the bridge's shape. In "大田(dà-tián, large field)", "大(dà, large)" underscores the field's area.

Telic role refers to an object's function or purpose. For instance, in "盐湖(yán-hú, salt lake)", "盐(yán, salt)" highlights the lake's purpose, and in "住房(zhù-fáng, house)", "住(zhù, living)" emphasizes the house's function (to provide accommodation). In "凉台(liáng-tái, cooling platform)", "凉(liáng, cooling)" highlights the platform's purpose (to cool down).

Agentive role describes how an object is formed or produced, encompassing creation or causal relationships. For example, in "沙荒(shā-huāng, sand wasteland)", "

沙(shā, sand)" indicates the cause of the wasteland (desertification). In "堰塞湖(yànsè-hú, barrier lake)", "堰塞(yànsè, barrier)" underscores the cause of the lake's formation (blocked by a landslide or volcanic lava flow).

Constitutive role illustrates the material or component that make up an object. For example, "咸水湖(xiánshuǐ-hú, saline lake)" refers to the lake with a high salt content, where "咸水(xiánshuǐ, saline water)" emphasizes the composition of the lake.

Handle role describes habitual actions or behaviors related to an object, especially how it is interacted with. For example, "辖区(xiá-qū, administrative area)" refers to an area under management, where "辖(xiá, administering)" highlighting how the "区(qū, area)" is governed.

3.2 Construction Tendencies Between Constituents in [X+PLACE] Compounds

In this study, we annotate and classify 1,415 [X+PLACE] compounds based on the semantic, grammatical, and prosodic relationships between their constituents. The statistical results are presented in Table 2.

Table 2. Semantic, Grammatical Class, and Prosodic Construction Models in [X+PLACE] Compounds.

		1+1	2+1	1+2	Total
[FORMAL+PLCAE]	NN	278	45	14	337
	VN	45	17	——	62
	AN	223	24	16	263
[TELIC+PLACE]	NN	264	55	——	319
	VN	160	91	——	251
	AN	15	9	2	26
[AGENTIVE+PLACE]	NN	51	7	1	59
	VN	6	18	——	24
[CONSTITUTIVE+PLACE]	NN	31	6	1	38
[HANDLE+PLACE]	VN	22	14	——	36
Total		1095	286	34	1415

As shown in Table 2, the semantic, grammatical class, and prosodic models in [X+PLACE] compounds exhibit the following construction tendencies:

(1) Tendency in semantic construction models: [FORMAL+PLACE] > [TELIC+PLA-CE] > [AGENTIVE+PLACE] > [CONSTITUTIVE+PLACE] > [HAN-DLE+PLACE]. [FORMAL+PLACE] compounds account for 46.8%, e.g., "丁字街(dīngzì-jiē, T-junction street), 环路(huán-lù, ring road), 大厅(dà-tīng, hall)". [TELIC+PLACE] compounds make up 42.1%, e.g., "盐湖(yán-hú, salt lake), 住房(zhù-fáng, house), 凉台(liáng-tái, cooling platform)". These two categories dominate the semantic models. In contrast, [AGENTIVE+PLACE] compounds account for

5.9%, e.g., "沙荒(shā-huāng, sand wasteland), 堰塞湖(yànsè-hú, barrier lake), 房改房(fánggǎi-fáng, reform housing)". This category exclusively contains "N/V agentive+PLACE" compounds. [CONSTITUTIVE+PLACE] compounds make up 2.7%, e.g., "咸水湖(xiánshuǐ-hú, saline lake), 茅屋(máo-wū, thatch house), 沙坑(shā-kēng, sand pit)". This category includes only "N constitutive+PLACE" compounds. Lastly, [HANDLE+PLACE] compounds account for 2.5%, e.g., "包房❷(bāo-fáng, private room), 禁地(jìn-dì, restricted area), 辖区(xiá-qū, administrative area)". This category consists solely of "V handle+PLACE" compounds. Overall, the last three categories represent weaker semantic models.

(2) Tendency in grammatical class construction models: NN > VN > AN. NN is the dominant grammatical class model, accounting for 53.2%, such as "皇宫(huáng-gōng, imperial palace), 银行(yín-háng, bank), 菜园(cài-yuán, vegetable garden)". VN constructions make up 26.4%, such as "学校(xué-xiào, school), 邮局(yóu-jú, post office), 看守所(kānshǒu-suǒ, detention center)", significantly fewer than NN compounds. AN constructions, such as "大厅(dà-tīng, hall), 凉台(liáng-tái, cooling platform), 小卖部(xiǎo-màibù, convenience store)", account for the smallest proportion at 20.4%. NN compounds dominate modern Chinese lexical, with NN modifier-head compounds serving as the prototype formation model. Using nominal constituents as modifiers is a conventional approach in modifier-head word formation [15]. VN modifier-head compounds are less productive, and AN constructions typically emerge only under semantic motivation, indicating they are not a productive model for word formation [4].

(3) Tendency in prosodic construction models: [1+1] > [2+1] > [1+2]. The [1+1] model is the most prevalent, accounting for 77.4%, such as "菜园(cài-yuán, vegetable garden), 学校(xué-xiào, school), 大厅(dà-tīng, hall)". The [2+1] model accounts for 20.2%, such as "图书馆 (túshū-guǎn, library), 电影院(diànyǐng-yuàn, cinema), 看守所(kānshǒu-suǒ, detention center)". The [1+2] model is the least frequent, accounting for only 2.4%, such as "彩牌楼(cǎi-páilóu, decorative archway), 小卖部(xiǎo-màibù, convenience store), 活火山(huó-huǒshān, active volcano)". The [1+1] model aligns with the standard prosodic words, reflecting a tendency toward disyllabification in Chinese. The [2+1] model represents super-prosodic words [16], while the [1+2] model reflects a prosodic shift due to syntactic or semantic coercions. Consequently, [N+N] compounds with [1+2] structure are either nonexistent or extremely rare [17].

How do semantics, grammatical class, and prosody models align in [X+PLACE] compounds? The next section will analyze the construction characteristics and cognitive motivations of [X+PLACE] compounds from the perspective of Qualia Structure.

4 Construction Characteristics and Cognitive Motivations of Semantics, Grammatical Class, and Prosody in [X+PLACE] Compounds

The construction of [X+PLACE] compounds is determined by mutual selection and constraints across three dimensions: semantics (qualia), grammatical class, and prosody. This section focuses on the semantic level, anchored by the qualia models, while simultaneously considering grammatical class and prosody models. The study analyzes the cognitive motivations behind the construction of the form and meaning in [X+PLACE] compounds from two perspectives: qualia-prosody and qualia- grammatical class.

4.1 The Semantic Attributes of PLACE and the Construction Characteristics of the Qualia Models in [X+PLACE] Compounds

Based on Qualia Structure, Generative Lexicon Theory distinguishes between natural kinds, artifacts, and synthetic nouns [18, 19]. The key distinction between natural kinds and artifacts is that artifacts embody human intention and purpose [20]. In [X+PLACE] compounds, the head can be classified as either an artificial or natural place, depending on whether human intention is involved. Artificial places are designed for specific purposes and possess human-made attributes, while natural places exist independently in nature and have inherent characteristics. Previous studies have shown that the artificial/natural distinction is pivotal in word construction [21]. Additionally, the artificial/natural distinction in Chinese compounds shapes their overall meaning [22]. Therefore, the artificial/natural nature of PLACE affects and constrains the semantic compatibility between the head and modifier. Table 3 illustrates the semantic classes of PLACE and construction tendencies of the qualia models in compounds.

When PLACE is artificial, the qualia model in [X+PLACE] compounds tends to align with [TELIC+ARTIFICIAL PLACE]. Artificial places are human-made to serve specific functions, with the telic role being the most appropriate for their definition. The cognitive prototype of artificial places consists of spatial entities and institutions. When the artificial place is a spatial entity, it provides space for specific activities, as exemplified by the term "房(*fáng, house*)", a typical representation of an artificial place. In compounds like "药房(*yào-fáng, pharmacy*), 产房(*chǎn-fáng, maternity ward*), 健身房(*jiànshēn-fáng, gym*)", modifiers emphasize the specific telic role of "房(*fáng, house*)". Conversely, when the artificial place is an institution, it is designed for specific functions, as in "博物院(*bówù-yuàn, museum*), 检察院(*jiǎnchá-yuàn, procurator ate*), 医院(*yī-yuàn, hospital*)", where "院(*yuàn, institution*)" represents a typical artificial place. Here, modifiers underscore the institution's specific function. Moreover, the modifier X can highlight the natural attributes of artificial places, as seen in "耳房(*ěr-fáng, side room*), 平房(*píng-fáng, bungalow*), 楼房(*lóu-fáng, building*)", where the semantic model tends to reflect [FORMAL+ARTIFICIAL PLACE]. Artificial places are primarily physical entities, and their natural attributes are essential for human recognition, often based on sensory experiences like shape, size, or position. Regardless of being artificial or natural, places undergo a formation process linked to their existence. Thus, head constituents may be modified by agentive and constitutive roles. The extent of human intervention in this formation process significantly influences the place's semantic attributes, as seen in "人工湖(*réngōng-hú, artificial lake*), 自然村(*zìrán-cūn, natural village*)", which straddle the boundary between artificial and natural places. These terms represent non-prototypical artificial or natural places. Artificial places are closely associated with human activities. Humans not only utilize these space but may also manage them, as in "包房❷ (*bāo-fáng, private room*), 围城❷ (*wéi-chéng, besieged city*), 直辖市(*zhíxiá-shì, direct-controlled municipality*)", where the handle role is implied.

When PLACE is natural, the qualia model in [X+PLACE] compounds tends to adhere to [FORMAL+NATURAL PLACE]. This tendency arises because humans often emphasize the perceptible natural attributes when referring to natural objects. Sensory experiences capture the primary characteristics of these objects, making the formal role particularly suitable for defining natural places. Whether the natural place refers to regions, such as "海区(hǎi-qū, maritime area), 极地(jí-dì, polar region), 老区(lǎo-qū, old area)", or to terrains, such as "海滩(hǎi-tān, beach), 鱼鳞坑(yúlín-kēng, fish scale pit), 荒山(huāng-shān, barren mountain)", or even to constituents, like "岬角(jiǎ-jiǎo, cape), 沙嘴(shā-zuǐ, sandbar), 山顶(shān-dǐng, mountaintop)", the semantic model typically align with [FORMAL+NATURAL PLACE]. However, many compounds follow the [TELIC+NATURAL PLACE] model. Even natural places lacking inherent telic roles—such as "山(shān, mountain)" and "湖(hú, lake)"—can acquire additional telic meanings through human experiences and cultural influences. This leads to compounds like "矿山(kuàng-shān, mining mountain)" and "盐湖(yán-hú, salt lake)". In these cases, X_{telic} can highlight the natural telic function of the place, as in "分界线(fēnjiè-xiàn, boundary line)" and "分水岭(fēnshuǐ-lǐng, watershed)". Nevertheless, X_{telic} in most cases emphasizes human-induced telic roles, as seen in "米粮川(mǐliáng-chuān, rich grain-producing area)" and "漕河(cáo-hé, a river channel for transporting grain)", where modifiers reflect various aspects of human utilization of natural place.

Table 3. Semantic Classes of PLACE and Qualia Model Construction Tendency in [X+PLACE] compounds.

Semantic Class of PLACE	Qualia Model Construction Tendency in [X+PLACE] compounds
ARTIFICIAL PLACE	[TELIC+PLACE] > [FORMAL+PLACE] > [AGENTIVE+PLACE] > [HANDLE+PLACE] > [CONSTITUTIVE+PLACE]
NATURAL PLACE	[FORMAL+PLACE] > [TELIC+PLACE] > [AGENTIVE+PLACE] > [CONSTITUTIVE+PLACE]

In summary, when PLACE is artificial, the modifier tends to select a telic role, emphasizing specific or unique functions. Conversely, when PLACE is natural, the modifier tends to adopt a formal role, highlighting inherent attributes. Consequently, influenced by the semantic attributes of PLACE, the [FORMAL+PLACE] and [TELIC+PLACE] represent stronger qualia models, while the [AGENTIVE+PLACE], [CONSTITU-TIVE+PLACE], and [HANDLE+PLACE] represent weaker qualia models. The following section will further explore the cognitive motivations behind the qualia, grammatical class, and prosody models in [X+PLACE] compounds.

4.2 Cognitive Motivations of Semantics, Grammatical Class, and Prosody Construction in [X+PLACE] Compounds

(i) [FORMAL+PLACE] Compounds. The prosodic construction models follow the sequence [1+1] > [2+1] > [1+2]. Disyllabic models are concise, featuring less semantic content and fewer restrictions, thereby adhering to the principle of formal economy. In contrast, trisyllabic models convey more semantic content and impose clearer restrictions on the attributes of places, aligning with the principle of semantic accuracy, as seen in examples like "坡路(pō-lù, slope road) -下坡路(xiàpō-lù, downhill road) -上坡路(shàngpō-lù, uphill road)". For formal attributes, the principle of formal economy generally takes precedence over semantic accuracy. The tendency sequence of grammatical class construction is NN > AN > VN, with NN showing a clear advantage, while AN is more frequent than VN.

When the grammatical class construction is NN, N $_{fomal}$ highlights perceptible attributes of PLACE, such as size, shape, time, and position. N $_{fomal}$ can emphasize the shape of PLACE, as seen in examples like "丁字街(*dīngzì-jiē, T-junction street*), 云崖(*yún-yá, cloud cliff*), 鱼鳞坑(*yúlín-kēng, fish-scale pit*)". It also highlights spatiotemporal attributes, such as "地宫(*dì-gōng, underground palace*), 早市❶ (*zǎo-shì, morning market*)". Additionally, N $_{fomal}$ can emphasize possession attributes, which are divided into ownership of property and spatial possession. Ownership refers to possession between entities, such as "婆婆家(*pópo-jiā, mother-in-law's house*)" and "夫妻店(*fūqī-diàn, husband and wife shop*)". Spatial possession reflects the relationship between the whole and its parts, as in "市郊(*shì-jiāo, suburb*), 海面(*hǎi-miàn, sea surface*)". The [FORMAL+BODY CONSTITUENT] construction generates numerous place-denoting compounds. In these cases, metaphor emphasizes perceptible or possessive attributes. For instance, the similarity between "丁字(*dīngzì, T-shape*)" and the shape of "街(*jiē, street*)" in "丁字街(*dīngzì-jiē, T-junction street*)" illustrates this, as does the metaphorical use of "心(*xīn, heart*)", "头(*tóu, head*)", and "面(*miàn, surface*)" in "街心(*jiē-xīn, heart of the street*)", "埠头(*bù-tóu, wharf*)", and "海面(*hǎi-miàn, sea surface*)", indicating "中间(*zhōng-jiān, middle*), 一端(*yī-duān, end*), 表层(*biǎo-céng, surface*)" respectively. Concrete bodily concepts provide the internal logic for abstract spatial concepts. The rich array of attributes in the "N $_{formal}$+PLACE" model ensures semantic accuracy. The metaphorical model, while more indirect, fulfills the need for vivid imagery.

When the grammatical class construction is VN, the [1+2] model is not observed. The [1+2] "V+PLACE" usually corresponds to a verb-object structure that is unlikely to form the compound. Examples include "吃食堂(*chī shítáng, eat at canteen*), 闯关东(*chuǎng guāndōng, venture into Northeast China*)". Even when extended, this structure usually refers to actions rather than places. V $_{formal}$ highlights the perceptible attributes of PLACE dynamically, particularly its shape, as in "回廊(*huí-láng, winding corridor*), 悬河(*xuán-hé, suspended river*)". It can also underscore the properties of PLACE, such as "不冻港(*bùdòng-gǎng, non-freezing port*), 冻原(*dòng-yuán, tundra*)". Observations reveal that the semantic class of PLACE affects the features highlighted by V $_{formal}$. When PLACE denotes a natural setting, V $_{formal}$ emphasizes its inherent attributes, as in "悬崖(*xuán-yá, cliff*), 内流河(*nèiliú-hé, endorheic river*)". Conversely, when PLACE refers to an artificial setting, V $_{formal}$ highlights design attributes, as in "环路(*huán-lù, ring road*), 拱棚(*gong-péng, arched shed*)". The dynamic presentation of attributes in the "V $_{formal}$+PLACE" model creates vivid imagery.

When the grammatical class construction is AN, A $_{formal}$ highlights the perceptible attributes of PLACE, such as volume or shape, as in "高地(*gāo-dì, highland*), 大街 (*dà-jiē, avenue*)", as well as spatiotemporal aspects like "旧居(*jiù-jū, former residence*), 外地(*wài-dì, foreign place*)". A $_{formal}$ can also emphasize the inherent properties of PLACE, such as in "公海(*gōng-hǎi, high seas*), 宝地(*bǎo-dì, treasured land*)". Unlike the VN construction, AN highlights static morphological characteristics. Additionally, while NN often involves metaphorical expressions, AN tends to assign attributes more directly. Adjectives typically express these attributes—for example, "大(*dà, large*)" directly measures spatial entities like "面积(*miàn-jī, area*), 体积(*tǐ-jī, volume*)". The direct and precise presentation of attributes in the "A $_{formal}$+PLACE" model ensures semantic accuracy and efficiency.

(ii) [TELIC+PLACE] Compounds. The prosodic construction models follow the sequence [1+1] > [2+1] > [1+2]. Disyllabic models prioritize formal economy, often leading to ambiguous meanings. For example, in different contexts, "酒吧(*jiǔ-bā, bar*)" can imply various activities, such as "buying alcohol", "selling alcohol" or "drinking alcohol". Similarly, "跳台(*tiào-tái, diving platform*)" requires encyclopedic knowledge to specify its functional meaning. In contrast, trisyllabic models convey their functional meanings more clearly, adhering to the principle of semantic accuracy. Examples include "电站(*diàn-zhàn, power station*) - 核电站(*hédiàn-zhàn, nuclear power station*) - 变电站(*biàndiàn-zhàn, substation*)" and "走道(*zǒu-dào, path for walking*) - 车行道(*chēxíng-dào, road for vehicles*) - 人行道(*rénxíng-dào, sidewalk*)". The tendency sequence of grammatical class construction is NN > VN > AN.

When the grammatical class construction is NN, the [1+2] model is absent. N $_{telic}$ can be either referential, like "瓷窑(*cí-yáo, ceramic kiln*)" or descriptive, such as in "样板房(*yàngbǎn-fáng, model home*)". The semantic structure typically follows [AGENT+PLACE], as in "道场(*dào-chǎng, temple*)", or [PATIENT+PLACE], as in " 粮仓(*liáng-cāng, granary*)". Agents and patients, as core argument roles closely linked to predicates, exhibit higher activation probabilities. Implied functional predicates can be activated solely by N $_{telic}$, such as "靶场(*bǎ-chǎng, shooting range*)", where "shooting" serves as the telic role of "靶(*bǎ*, target)". Alternatively, PLACE can also activate implied functional predicates, as in "币市❶(*bì-shì, coin market*)", where "buying and selling" is the functional role of "市(*shì, market*)". Most implied functional predicates are activated by PLACE, since places often represent spaces for various activities. Thus, the "N $_{telic}$+PLACE" model effectively captures rich semantic relationships, aligning with the principle of semantic accuracy.

When the grammatical class construction is AN, A does not directly modify PLACE; instead, it modifies the function of PLACE. In semantic construction, functional predicates must be introduced to complete the meaning. Relevant modifiers include "冷(*lěng, cold*), 暖(*nuǎn, warm*), 温(*wēn, mild*)", as in "冷库(*lěng-kù, cold storage*), 暖阁(*nuǎn-gé, warm pavilion*), 温室(*wēn-shì, greenhouse*)". In "冷库(*lěng-kù, cold storage*)", " 冷(*lěng, cold*)" modifies the functional predicate associated with "库(*kù, storage*)", which is "藏(*cáng, store*)", rather than directly modifying "库(*kù, storage*)". A $_{telic}$ represents the effect PLACE can achieve, which is the functional result of artificial places. Therefore, the semantic construction in the "A $_{telic}$+PLACE" model is relatively indirect.

When the grammatical class construction is VN, the [1+2] model is not observed. The distinction between VN and NN or AN lies in the direct presentation of functional predicates within VN compounds. This can be further divided into regular and special uses. Typically, V rarely represents the regular use of PLACE, as redundancy contradicts the principle of economy. For example, "住房(*zhù-fáng, house*)" and "房(*fáng, house*)" convey the same meaning; the primary function of "房(*fáng, house*)" is to provide a living place, as seen in "监狱(*jiān-yù, prison*), 学校(*xué-xiào, school*)". Conversely, V usually signifies a special function of PLACE. Special uses derived from PLACE need specification and are not represented in NN construction, which highlights the object, such as "客房(kè-fáng, guest room), 客厅(kè-tīng, living room)". Instead, VN more directly expresses the function of PLACE, as in "捕房(bǔ-fáng, police station), 舞厅(wǔ-tīng, dance hall)". Disyllabic constructions of V telic are more specific, as in "巡捕房(xúnbǔ-fáng, patrol office), 歌舞厅(gēwǔ-tīng, song and dance hall)". The "V telic+PLACE" model directly presents semantic relationships, aligning with the principles of semantic accuracy and economy.

(iii) [AGENTIVE+PLACE] Compounds. The prosodic construction models follow the sequence [1+1] > [2+1] > [1+2]. Disyllabic models align with the principle of formal economy and tend to have relatively vague meanings, while trisyllabic models convey more explicit and refined meanings, such as "灾区(zāi-qū, disaster area) - 重灾区(zhòngzāi-qū, severely affected area)". The tendency sequence of grammatical class construction is NN > VN > AN.

When the grammatical class construction is NN, N agentive highlights the involvement in formation processes of PLACE, often involving specific events or causes, following a causal or sequential relationship. PLACE can refer to both artificial and natural settings. When PLACE refer to natural settings, N agentive often relate to the formation cause. These words typically imply predicates of "occurring", which refer to events beyond human control, thus expressing a natural agentive relationship. For example, "火场(huǒ-chǎng, fire site)" denotes a site where a fire has occurred, where N agentive represents a natural disaster or calamity that has "occurred" at the indicated PLACE. Conversely, when PLACE refer to artificial settings, N agentive relate to the creator or the tool used in its formation. The words typically imply predicates of "creating". The semantic model of such words is generally [CREATOR+UNIT], as in "民族乡(mínzú-xiāng, ethnic township)" or [TOOL+ENTITY], as in "机井(jī-jǐng, mechanical well)".

When the grammatical class construction is VN, V agentive highlights how PLACE is created. Accompanied by occurrence of the action V, PLACE comes into existence from nothing. For example, "溶洞(róng-dòng, karst cave)" refers to a natural cave formed by the dissolution of rocks by flowing water. PLACE can refer to artificial or natural settings. When PLACE refer to artificial sites, V agentive highlights the method of human intervention in its formation, such as in "高架路(gāojià-lù, elevated road), 分店(fēndiàn, branch store)". Conversely, when PLACE refers to naturally formed settings, V agentive highlights the natural process of its formation, as in "堰塞湖(yànsèi-hú, barrier lake), 洪泛区(hóngfàn-qū, floodplain)".

In conclusion, the complex presentation of semantic relationships in [AGENTIVE+PLACE] model satisfies the need for accurate semantic construction in compounds.

(iv) [CONSTITUTIVE+PLACE] Compounds. The prosodic construction models follow the sequence [1+1] > [2+1] > [1+2]. Disyllabic models align with the principle of formal economy, but their meanings are relatively vague. In contrast, trisyllabic models convey clearer, more refined meanings. For example, in "索道(suǒ-dào, cableway)", the material "索(suǒ, cable)" is not immediately apparent from the surface meaning; it becomes clear only when defining "道(dào, way)" as "钢索(gāng-suǒ, steel cable)". Conversely, "铁索桥(tiěsuǒ-qiáo, iron cable bridge)" explicitly indicates that the bridge is made of "铁索(tiěsuǒ, iron cables)". The grammatical class construction model favors NN. PLACE can refer to both artificial and natural places, though artificial places are more prevalent. N _{constitutive} can represent constituent elements, as in "茅棚(*máo-péng, thatch hut*)", where "茅(*máo, thatch*)" highlights the material of the "棚(*péng, hut*)". Additionally, N _{constitutive} can signify a state of composition, such as "盐碱地 (*yánjiǎn-dì, alkali soil*)", where "盐碱(*yánjiǎn, salt and alkali*)" emphasizes the saline content of "地(*dì, soil*)". Thus, the diverse semantic relationships in [CONSTITUTIVE+PLACE] model fulfill the requirement for semantic accuracy.

(v) [HANDLE+PLACE] Compounds. The prosodic construction models follow the sequence [1+1] > [2+1], with the grammatical class construction model favoring VN. Disyllabic models are concise, effectively conveying meaning, though the semantic construction can be complex, typically arising from metonymy within the VN structure. For example, "围城❶ (*wéi-chéng, to besiege the city*)" transforms into "围城❷ (*wéi-chéng, besieged city*)", shifting from an action to its patient. The [2+1] model expresses meaning more explicitly, combining individual morpheme meanings, as in "廉租房(*liánzū-fáng, low-rent housing*), 自留地(*zìliú-dì, private plot*)". The [1+2] VN model generally follows a verb-object structure and does not easily form compounds. V expresses how PLACE is processed, altering its nature or state of PLACE, typically following the [HANDLE METHOD+PLACE] model. Changes to PLACE occur in several ways:

(1) [POSESSION/TRANSFER+PLACE]. For example, "领土(*lǐng-tǔ, territory*), 失地❷ (*shī-dì, lost land*), 封地(*fēng-dì, feudal land*)". Here, in "领土(*lǐng-tǔ, territory*)", "领(*lǐng, to possess*)" highlights how "土 (*tǔ, land*)" is obtained.

(2) [DAMAGE+PLACE]. Examples include "围城❷ (*wéi-chéng, besieged city*), 包围圈(*bāowéi-quān, encirclement*), 殖民地(*zhímín-dì, colony*)". Here, the model suggests "PLACE that is acted upon by V", indicating that V affects N, leading to the inference that "N is acted upon by V".

(3) [DETERMINING/DEFINING+PLACE]. In "选址(*xuǎn-zhǐ, site selection*)", PLACE, initially indefinite, becomes fixed through "选 (*xuǎn, selection*)". Additionally, PLACE can be managed, with V highlighting managing method, as in "辖区(*xiá-qū, jurisdiction*), 自治州(*zìzhì-zhōu, autonomous prefecture*), 直辖市(*zhíxiá-shì, direct-controlled municipality*)".

(4) [PROHIBITION+PLACE]. Examples include "禁区(*jìn-qū, restricted zone*), 禁地(*jìn-dì, forbidden land*)", where the result of the action is that PLACE becomes prohibited.

In conclusion, the [HANDLE+PLACE] model not only involves complex semantic relationships but also highlights intricate semantics construction.

5 Conclusion

The construction of [X+PLACE] compounds is determined by mutual selection and constraints across three dimensions: semantics (qualia), grammatical class, and prosody. The semantic model of [X+PLACE] compounds can be classified into five types of qualia models. The findings show that the semantic construction tendency sequence is [FORMAL+PLACE] > [TELIC+PLACE] > [AGENTIVE+PLACE] > [CONSTITUTIVE+PL-ACE] > [HANDLE+PLACE]. The grammatical class construction tendency sequence is NN > VN > AN. The prosodic construction tendency sequence is [1+1] > [2+1] > [1+2]. Under the influence of the artificial/natural semantic attributes of PLACE, [FORMAL+PLACE] and [TELIC+PLACE] emerge as strong qualia models, while [AGENTIVE+PLACE], [CONSTITUTIVE+PLACE] and [HANDLE+PLACE] are relatively weaker qualia models. Guided by the principles of formal economy and semantic accuracy, different qualia models have varying construction tendencies.

The complex and intricate interaction among prosody, grammatical class, and semantics in compounds warrant further exploration. The interactions at prosody-grammatical class, prosody-semantics, and grammatical class -semantics in [X+PLACE] compounds remain areas for further investigation.

Acknowledgments. This paper was supported by the Science Foundation of Beijing Language and Culture University (supported by "the Fundamental Research Funds for the Central Universities") (24YCX034).

References

1. Zhou, J.: A Study of Chinese Lexical Structure, 1st edn. Shanghai Lexicographical Publishing House, Shanghai (1991)
2. Zhu, Y.: Semantic Word Formation of Chinese Compound Word, 1st edn. Beijing University Press, Beijing (2016)
3. Song, Z.Y.: A study of modifier-head compounds based on construction theory and qualia structure-from the perspective of verbs to nouns. Chinese Teaching in the World **01**, 33–48 (2022)
4. Zhao, Q.: Theories of Motivation and the Semantic Structure of Chinese Compounds, 1st edn. The Commercial Press, Beijing (2023)
5. The Dictionary Editing Room of Institute of Linguistics, CASS, Modern Chinese Dictionary. 7th edn., The Commercial Press, Beijing (2016)
6. Chu, Z.X.: The categorical status of chinese place words and its typological significance. Chinese Language **03**, 31–224 (2006)
7. Guo, R.: Research on Word Classes in Modern Chinese, Revised The Commercial Press, Beijing (2018)
8. Lu, J.M., Shen, Y.: Fifteen Lectures on Chinese Language and Chinese Studies, 1st edn. Peking University Press, Beijing (2004)
9. Lü, S.X.: An Outline of Chinese Grammar, 1st edn. The Commercial Press, Beijing (1956)
10. Zhao, Y.R.: A Grammar of Spoken Chinese, 1st edn. The Commercial Press, Beijing (1979)
11. Zhu, D.X.: Lectures on Grammar, 1st edn. The Commercial Press, Beijing (1982)
12. Pustejovsky, J.: The Generative Lexicon, 1st edn. MIT Press, Cambridge, MA (1995)
13. Pustejovsky, J.: The generative lexicon. Comput. Linguist. **04**, 409–441 (1991)
14. Yuan, Y.L.: A Study of the Semantic Knowledge System Based on Generative Lexicon Theory and Argument Structure Theory. Journal of Chinese Information Processing **06**, 23–30 (2013)
15. Dong, X.F.: The Lexicon and Morphology of Chinese, 1st edn. Peking University Press, Beijing (2004)
16. Feng, S.L.: On Chinese "Natural Foot." Chinese Language **01**, 40–47 (1998)
17. Feng, S.L.: On Chinese "Prosodic Words." Social Sciences in China **01**, 11–176 (1996)
18. Pustejovsky, J.: Type construction and the logic of concepts, 1st edn. Cambridge University Press, The Language of Word Meaning, Cambridge (2001)
19. Pustejovsky, J.: Type theory and lexical decomposition. Journal of Cognitive Science **06**, 39–76 (2006)

20. Song, Z.Y.: The role of telic features in the lexical meaning and word formation of nouns: From the perspective of language values and linguistic values. Studies of the Chinese Language **1**, 44–57 (2016)
21. Levin, B., Lelia G., Dan J.: Systematicity in the semantics of noun compounds: The role of artifacts vs. natural kinds, Linguistics 57(3): 1–43 (2019)
22. Du, T.T., Li, J.P.: A Study on the Combination of the "Artificial/Natural" Semantics in the Chinese NN Attribute-head Compounds. In: Dong, M., Hong, J.-F., Lin, J., Jin, P. (eds.) Chinese Lexical Semantics: 24th Workshop, CLSW 2023, Singapore, Singapore, May 19–21, 2023, Revised Selected Papers, pp. 495–510. Springer, Cham (2024)

Quantitative Study on the Moral Tendency and Moral Types of Chinese Adverbs

Shaqi Huang[1(✉)], Dong Yu[1], Hongrui Wang[2], Pengyuan Liu[3], and Jiaqi Liu[1]

[1] College of Information Science, Beijing Language and Culture University, Beijing, China
514490724@qq.com
[2] College of International Education, Minzu University of China, Beijing, China
[3] National Language Resources Monitoring and Research Center for Print Media, Beijing, China
liupengyuan@pku.edu.cn

Abstract. Current research on the semantics of adverbs primarily focuses on emotional and stylistic meaning. However, adverbs also have distinct moral semantics, reflecting their moral tendencies and correlation with moral type. To explore this, we developed a framework for moral semantics and compiled a corpus of 10,313 adverbial phrases from the BCC (Beijing Language and Culture University Corpus Center). Our quantitative analysis revealed that 73 adverbs exhibit clear moral inclinations, with 12 showing particularly strong tendencies. Additionally, we identified 37 adverbs closely linked to specific moral types. These findings deepen our understanding of adverb semantics and highlight the significance of moral dimensions in their usage.

Keywords: Adverbs · Moral Semantics · Analytical Framework

1 Introduction

Natural language reflects extensive human moral knowledge, combining rational meanings with moral evaluations, known as moral semantics[1].

Research on adverbial semantics primarily focuses on emotional or stylistic meaning, with limited attention to morality. This is reflected in adverbs' distinct moral tendencies, closely linked to specific moral types. Previous studies, such as Graham et al.'s English Moral Foundation Dictionary (MFD) [1], Wang Hongrui's Chinese Moral Dictionary [2], and Peng et al.'s dataset of 100,000 labeled moral sentences [3], have advanced moral analysis in texts. However, the moral semantics of adverbs remains underexplored. Some words, like the verb "to kill," have clear moral meaning, while others, such as "随手(*sui shǒu*, casually)" paired with "丢(*diū*, to throw)", reveal negative connotations only in specific contexts.

To fill this gap, this paper develops a framework for analyzing moral semantics and compiles a corpus of 10,313 adverbial phrases from the BCC. This study aims to quantify the moral semantics of adverbs, enriching semantics and providing innovative methods for analyzing lexical moral meaning.

---

[1] https://bcc.blcu.edu.cn/.

P. Jin et al. (Eds.): CLSW 2024, LNAI 15552, pp. 301–315, 2025.
https://doi.org/10.1007/978-981-96-3509-2_22

2 Related work

2.1 Moral Semantics Research and Application

Moral semantics refers to the moral evaluations and attitudes associated with linguistic units. Shen Jiaxuan defines "moral words" as those reflecting societal moral norms [4]. Current research has noticed the moral meaning in words and apply it to the moral computation tasks. Analyses of moral semantics vary across studies due to differing social contexts and objectives. For example, Graham et al. [1] developed the Moral Foundation Dictionary (MFD) in English, based on Moral Framework Theory, categorizing moral into five universal foundations: caring/harming, fairness/deceit, loyalty/betrayal, authority/subversion, and sanctity/degradation, to quantify moral foundations in texts. In the Chinese context, Hongrui Wang [2] created a large-scale moral lexicon for moral computation in Chinese texts, analyzing lexical moral meaning through dimensions such as moral polarity (i.e., morally positive, neutral, and negative) and types. Additionally, Peng Shiya et al. [5] focused on identifying the moral semantics of sentences, creating a dataset of 100,000 labeled Chinese moral sentences and analyzing the moral meaning based on the presence or absence of morality, as well as positive and negative moral aspects. However, a significant gap remains in assessing the moral semantics of phrases. Furthermore, existing studies often rely on intuitive judgments of lexical morality without considering the combinations of lexical moral meaning.

2.2 An Analysis of Semantics Variation in Adverbial Combinations

Compound structures go beyond merely combining component meanings, involving qualitative transformations [5]. Certain word combinations can trigger semantics shifts, such as prominence, enhancement, and transformation [6]. Scholars like Zou Shaohua [7], Zhang Zhi [15], and Chen Wei [9] have noted that neutral words acquire new connotations in semi-fixed structures. For example, "问题 (wèn tí, problem)" often takes on a derogatory meaning in the structure "有 (yǒu, have) + N." Similarly, Hou Min et al. [10] found that a non-emotive word combined with a negative term can express emotional nuances.

While most studies on semantics shifts in combinations focus on emotional and evaluative changes, transformations in moral meaning remain underexplored. In adverbial phrases, adverbs act as adjuncts and complements, modifying various elements within combinations [11].The same adverb can express different positive or negative meanings depending on its collocations [12], and its subjective quantity may vary with context [13, 14].Given the ambiguous definition of adverbs, they are often seen as a heterogeneous group of linguistic elements. Therefore, studying their moral semantics necessitates analyzing them within broader linguistic units. This paper analyzes adverbial moral semantics through annotated adverbial phrases.

3   Framework for Moral Semantics Analysis and Corpus Construction

A valid moral evaluation relies on a comprehensive process, requiring the evaluator to have factual judgments of the subject and the affective cognition, such as evaluative judgment, and attitudes [15]. Thus, this study delineates the framework for analyzing moral semantics into two principal dimensions: moral tendency and moral type.

3.1   Moral Tendency Analysis Framework

Research indicates that adverbs can express evaluative polarity, influencing the agent of verbs. For example, "悉心 (*xī xīn*, meticulously)" conveys a positive connotation, "悍然 (*hàn rán*, recklessly)" a negative one, and "徒步 (*tú bù*, on foot)" remains neutral [16]. In sentiment analysis, adverbs' impact on emotional polarity is classified as positive, negative, neutral, or irrelevant [17]. To construct a moral semantics knowledge base, Wang Hongrui developed four moral labels: positive, negative, neutral, and passive [2]. Additionally, word collocation frequency significantly shapes meaning and structure [7], with context influencing emotional intensification [7, 17].

Building on these findings, we developed the moral tendency analysis framework, as illustrated in Fig. 1.

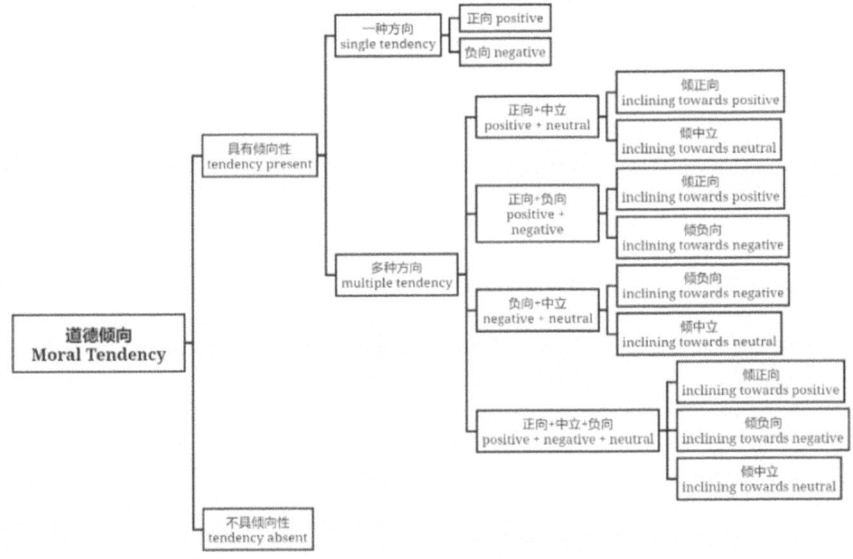

Fig. 1. Moral Tendency Analysis Framework

3.2   Moral Type Analysis Framework

Factual judgments of evaluated subjects align with the moral type dimension in the moral tendency framework. Emotional semantics classifications encompass not only positive and negative aspects but also nuanced dimensions such as joy, anger, sorrow, and happiness. Certain adverbs are inherently linked to moral concepts; for instance, "按时 (*àn shí*, on time)" and "按期 (àn qī, on schedule)" reflect "诚实守信 (*chéng shí shǒu xìn*, integrity)."

The moral type analysis framework is based on Wang Hongrui's system [18], which draws on the 2009 Implementation Outline for Citizen Moral Construction in the New Era. This framework includes four moral scenarios and 24 distinct moral types, as shown in Fig. 2.

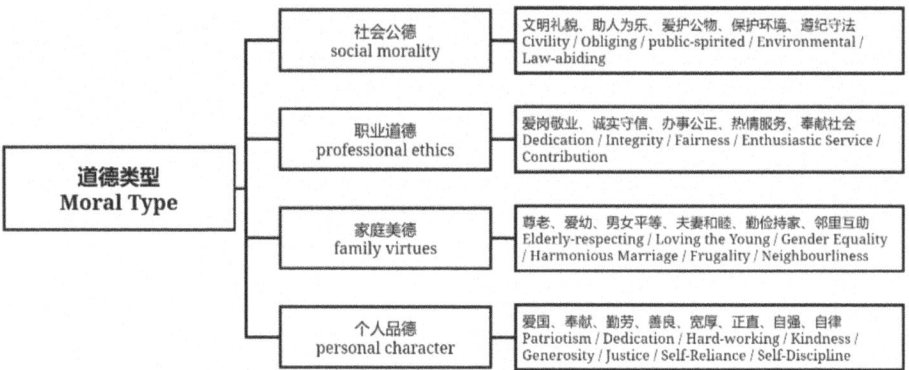

Fig. 2. Moral Type Analysis Framework

3.3   Calculation of Moral features

Langacker's "extraction and activation" model [19] suggests that word order influences cognitive attention, guiding the interpretation of meaning. In adverbial phrases, the sequence of adverbs significantly shapes the phrase's moral semantics. Thus, we constrained the verb to be neutral, then evaluated the moral semantics of adverbs within these phrases. In accordance with the established framework, we manually annotated the pre-processed corpus based on moral tendency and moral type.

The first step involves assessing moral tendency. With neutral verbs, the phrase's moral tendency reflects that of the adverb. For instance, in "并肩+前行 (*bìng jiān* + *qián xíng*, marching side by side)," classified as positive, the adverb "并肩" is similarly positive.

Next, we quantify the internal moral tendency of each adverb by calculating the ratio of its inclinations across different directions, as shown in Formula (1).

$$pt(x) = n(x)/n * 100\%. \tag{1}$$

In this context, *pt(x)* denotes the ratio of moral tendency for adverb *t* towards type *x* (positive, negative, or neutral). *n(x)* represents the number of phrases containing *t* annotated as type *x*, and *n* is the total occurrences of *t* in the corpus. For example, the phrase "任意+V" (*rèn yì* + verb, casually + verb) appears 121 times, with 47 instances labeled as negative and 74 as neutral. The formula for calculating the moral tendency ratio is given in Formula (2).

$$p任意, casually(_{负向, negative}) = 47/121 * 100\% = 38.84\%.$$

$$p任意, casually(_{中立, neutral}) = 74/121 * 100\% = 61.16\%.$$

(2)

A higher ratio of a specific moral tendency for an adverb reflects a stronger predisposition toward that tendency.

To explore the moral types of adverbs, we assign moral labels to phrases which are labeled with positive or negative connotations. The moral type of an adverb is determined by its co-occurrence with specific moral categories. For example, the phrase "高声+V (gāo shēng + verb, speaking loudly + verb)" is associated with the moral type "文明礼貌 (wén míng lǐ mào, civility)", indicating that "高声" is consistently linked to this moral type. Additionally, we construct a co-occurrence heatmap of adverbs and their moral types, providing insights into the internal moral tendencies.

3.4 Corpus Construction and Annotation

This study developed a corpus of adverbial phrases as the basis for the research. The flowchart and detailed steps for constructing this corpus are depicted in Fig. 3.

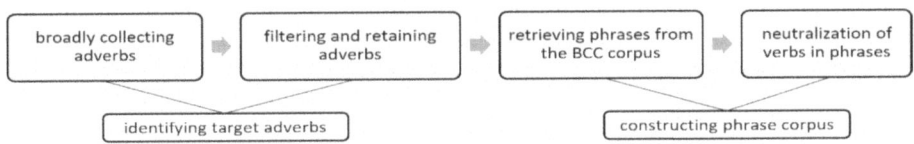

Fig. 3. Corpus Construction Flowchart

We utilize the adverb list compiled by Zhang Yisheng [20] alongside a three-year corpus of People's Daily. After summarizing and deduplicating, a final list of 1,526 adverbs was compiled, ensuring comprehensive coverage of various adverb types. Researchers then evaluated the moral relevance of these adverbs, ultimately narrowing the list to 220 adverbs linked to moral content.

Subsequently, these 220 adverbs were entered into the search pattern "adverb + V" within the BCC corpus. Phrases with a frequency of 10 or more were extracted, yielding 10,313 adverbial phrases. To ensure neutrality of the verbs, we applied the Chinese moral dictionary [2] and processed the data using Python, retaining only phrases with neutral verbs. This resulted in 9,111 adverbial phrases, reducing the relevant adverbs to 207.

The study manually annotated the moral tendency of 9,111 adverbial phrases, excluding incomplete semantics phrases (e.g., "不屑理 (bù xiè lǐ, disdain to care)"). Phrases were classified into three categories: 1 (positive), 2 (negative), and 3 (neutral), those could not be categorized which labeled as "unknown." Additionally, phrases were classified according to the moral behavior classification system [18], with those that could not be categorized marked as "unknown." In summary, we established a moral annotation system, with examples provided in Table 1.

Table 1. Example data for annotation

Adv+v	Moral Relevance	Moral Behavior Classification	Labels (1/2/3)
按时+缴纳 pay on time	Relevant	诚实守信 Integrity	1
暗中+操作 operate in secret	Irrelevant	未知 unknown	3
久久+回荡 linger for a long time	Relevant	遵纪守法 Law-abiding	2

After screening, two researchers annotated 9,111 phrases, achieving a consistency rate of 90.39% (8,236 cases). Discrepancies were resolved through verification. The final corpus, excluding 438 incomplete phrases, consisted of 8,673 phrases with 106 adverbs: 938 with a positive tendency, 1,074 with a negative tendency, and 6,661 with a neutral tendency.

Among the 2,012 phrases with positive or negative moral meaning, those with identifiable moral types were labeled accordingly, while phrases without determinable moral types were marked as "unknown." The detailed results of the moral type annotations are shown in Fig. 4.

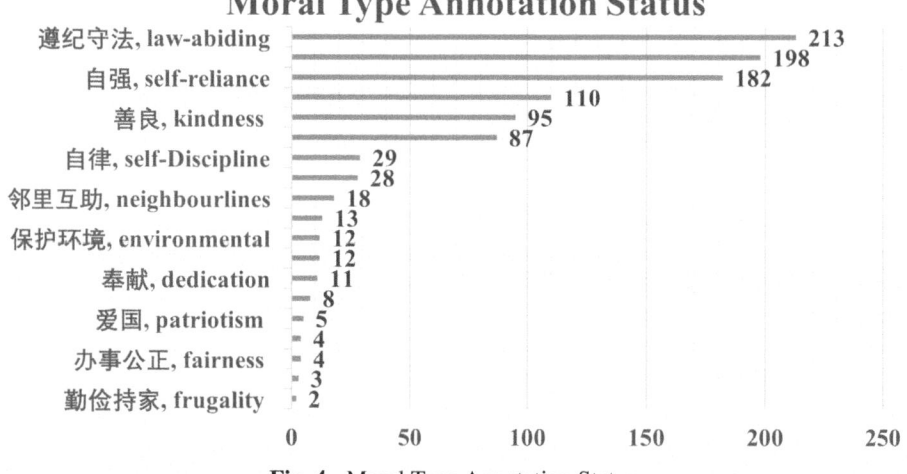

Fig. 4. Moral Type Annotation Status

4   Quantitative Analysis of the Moral Tendency of adverbs

Based on the annotation results, this section provides a quantitative analysis of the moral tendencies of adverbs, which reveals distinct characteristics in these tendencies. The statistical results are presented in Table 2.

Table 2. Statistics of Adverb Moral Tendency Results

Type	Specific Category	Moral Tendency	Number of Adverbs
With Moral Tendency	Single Tendency (2.83%)	Positive	1 (0.94%)
		Negative	2 (1.89%)
	Multiple Tendencies (66.04%)	Positive + Neutral	43 (41.90%)
		Negative + Neutral	13 (12.26%)
		Positive + Negative + Neutral	14 (13.21%)
Without Moral Tendency	No Moral Tendency (31.13%)	Neutral	33 (31.13%)

4.1 Adverbs with a Single Moral Tendency

The analysis shows that three adverbs exhibit a single moral tendency. Specifically, "舍命(shě mìng, to risk one's life)"has a positive connotation, while "悍然(hàn rán, recklessly)" and "过分(guò fèn, excessively)"are negative. These adverbs are semanticsally clear and exhibit distinct moral characteristics. For example, "舍命" is used as follows:

（1）　廖凯波在防汛中脚骨裂伤，绑着绷带夹板仍坚持上堤指挥，群众深
　　　受感动，纷纷[**舍命**]护提。
Liao Kaibo, despite a foot fracture, continued to command the embankment with his foot bandaged, inspiring the public to protect it at all costs.

In the *Contemporary Chinese Dictionary* (7th ed.), "舍命" is defined as "to risk one's life." In sentence (1), the verb "护" (hù, to protect) is neutral, while the adverb "舍命" conveys a positive moral tendency, embodying the value of self-sacrifice.

4.2 Adverbs with Multiple Moral Tendencies

The findings indicate that 70 adverbs display multiple moral tendencies.

(1)Analysis of Adverbs with positive + neutral tendencies

Within this group, 43 adverbs exhibit a "positive + neutral" tendency. The adverbs displaying a positive inclination are as follows: "大力 (dà lì, vigorously), 悉心 (xī xīn, meticulously), 如实 (rú shí, truthfully), 苦心 (kǔ xīn, painstakingly), 如数 (rú shù, in full), 奋力 (fèn lì, strenuously)". "悉心" is taken as an example:

（2）　白云生率领镇政府一班人跑遍了全镇16个村，他[**悉心**]听取各方意
　　　见，认真研究建校方案。
Bai Yunsheng led the town government to visit all 16 villages, carefully listening to feedback and studying the school construction plan.

"悉心"means "to use all one's energy." When paired with verbs in (2) that convey the semantics characteristics of [dedicating time, energy, and subjective initiative], it expresses positive qualities such as dedication or enthusiasm for helping others.

(2)Analysis of Adverbs with negative + neutral tendencies

13 adverbs exhibit a "negative + neutral" tendency. Among these, "过于"(guò yú, excessively) and "肆意"(sì yì, wantonly) display a predominantly negative tone, with "肆意"showing a 52.94% negative tendency:

（3）　有的工厂[**肆意**]排放废气、废液和粉尘，超标造成严重环境污染。
Some factories recklessly discharge waste, causing severe pollution.

（4）　媒体把此事当八卦兼黄色笑料进行传播，还把当事人照片、视频[**肆意**]传播，是对受害人的再伤害！
The media spread this as gossip and crude humor, further victimizing the individual.

The term "肆意" implies that the actor acts without restraint, consciously generating a negative impact and carrying a strong negative evaluative tone, often central to the phrase's meaning. In sentences (3) and (4), it pairs with the neutral verbs "排放 (pái fàng, emit)" and "传播 (chuán bō, spread)," respectively, reflecting a disregard for environmental protection and professional ethics.

(3)Analysis of Adverbs with positive + negative+ neutral tendencies

There are 14 adverbs exhibit a "positive + negative + neutral" tendency. Excluding "大举(dà jǔ, on a large scale)", which shows a negative tendency of 51.06%, most of these adverbs lean toward neutrality. These adverbs are generally restrictive and abstract, conveying elements such as time, space, or degree. Examples include "当众(dāng zhòng, in public)", "硬是(yìng shì, forcefully)", and "日夜(rì yè, day and night)". For instance, the adverb "当众" often refers to actions or behaviors performed in front of others, implying a neutral stance:

（5）　女子竟然在派出所内[**当众**]小便。
The woman urinated in the police station in public.

（6）　他[**当众**]发言说：这把学术和政治硬扯在一起，岂不是陷罪于人。

According to moral standards, the action of "小便" (urinating) in sentence (7) requires the semantics feature of [open space -], while "当众" introduces the semantics feature of [open space +], which violates social ethics. Consequently, the adverb itself conveys a negative meaning in this context. In contrast, the phrase "当众发言" (dāng zhòng fā yán, speaking in public) in sentence (8) has fewer spatial restrictions and does not conflict with moral standards.

(4) Analysis of Adverbs with a Neutral Tendency

In addition, some tend toward neutrality, though some may convey positive or negative nuances in specific contexts. These can be categorized into two groups:

The first group comprises descriptive adverbs with distinct moral tendencies, including 9 adverbs such as "纵情(zòng qíng, indulging), 按期 (àn qī, on schedule), 成心 (chéng xīn, intentionally), 豁然 (huò rán, suddenly enlightened)." For example, "如期(rú qī, as scheduled)" demonstrates a neutral tendency.

（7） 又因为贷款利率低，有些企业甚至不考虑[**如期**]归还贷款。
Due to low loan rates, some businesses neglect timely repayment.

（8） 按照国家规定现行建设程序，这4个项目可在年前[**如期**]开工。
These 4 projects will start on time, as per national regulations.

"如期" signifies the completion of a task by an agreed-upon date. When paired with verbs that convey [+ outwardness] and [+ interaction], it tends to display a positive tone. For instance, in sentence (7), if a company fails to return a loan as scheduled, it reflects a negative moral tendency associated with dishonesty. However, in practice, it is predominantly used in contexts like that in sentence (8).

The other group includes adverbs with ambiguous semantics, such as "不断(*bù duàn*, continuously), 猛然 (*měng rán*, suddenly)," totaling 49 adverbs. For example, the adverb "依次" (*yī cì*, in order) has a neutral tendency rate of 84.21%, totaling 49 adverbs. For example, the adverb "依次" has a neutral tendency:

（9） 在食堂门口，大家分别在西、南两侧出入口自觉排队[**依次**]进入。
At the canteen entrance, people lined up on the west and south sides to enter in order.

Among the 19 combinations of "依次 + V," only 3 are morally relevant. For instance, in sentence (9), "依次进入(*yī cì jìn rù*, entering in order)" reflects an orderly and civilized social demeanor. The remaining 16 phrases are morally neutral, with the adverb exhibiting a neutral tone.

Additionally, there are 2 adverbs—"并肩(*bìng jiān*, side by side)" and "鼎力(*dǐng lì*, strongly)"—that display equal ratios of positive and neutral tone, while "悄声(*qiāo sheng*, in a whisper)", shows equal ratios of negative and neutral tone. These three adverbs lack prominent tendencies. Although they do not exhibit strong semantics, their contextual usage can emphasize different meaning characteristics.

4.3 Adverbs Without Moral Tendency

Among the analyzed adverbs, 33 exhibit no distinct moral tendencies, instead describing the explicit state or manner of actions, as with "分头(*fēn tóu*, separately), 暗里(*àn lǐ*, in secret), 当场(*dāng chǎng*, on the spot)". For example:

（10） 他们天不明就起床，[**分头**]出发，翻山越岭。
They woke at dawn, setting off separately across mountains.

"出发(*chū fā*, to depart)" typically falls outside the scope of moral evaluation. In sentence (10), "分头" merely describes the manner of "出发," meaning "分头出发" (*fēn tóu chū fā*, departing separately) carries no moral semantics.

Additionally, among the 33 adverbs, some, like "正色(*zhèng sè*, seriously)"and "按理(*àn lǐ*, according to reason)", carry specific semantics but often pair with auxiliary verbs that lack moral alignment, yielding no clear moral tendency. For instance, with "按理":

（11）　农民工[**按理**]可以从社保机构得到包括企业缴纳的大部分保险金。
Migrant workers should receive most insurance, including employer contributions.

"按理" conveys a positive connotation but, when paired with non-action verbs like "来说(*lái shuō*, speaking of)" or "可以(*kě yǐ*, can)", often lacks moral semantics, instead signaling pragmatic meanings like "should have been done but wasn't."

5   Quantitative Analysis of the Moral Type of Adverbs

5.1   Criteria for Determining Adverb Moral Types

We compiled the co-occurrence of each adverb with specific moral types, using the number of co-occurring types as a criterion. The results are presented in Fig. 5. Furthermore, A heatmap was created using JS to illustrate these co-occurrences, and the example is shown in Fig. 6.

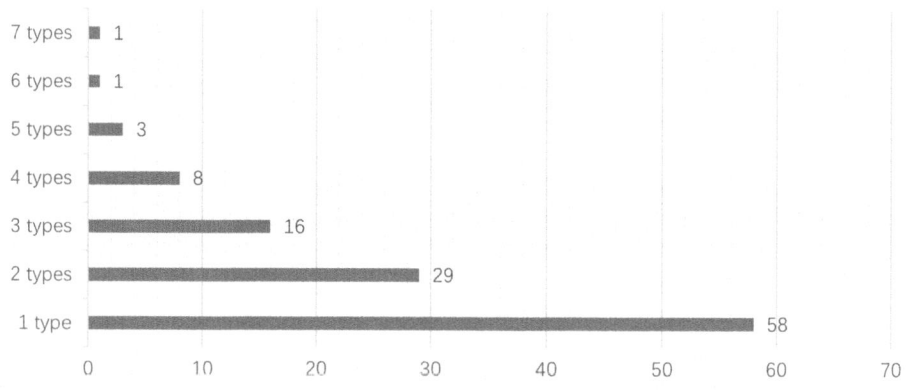

Fig. 5. Number of Moral Types Co-occurring with Adverbs

The heatmap shows adverbs on the vertical axis and moral types on the horizontal axis, with darker blocks indicating more frequent co-occurrences. For example, "擅自(*shàn zì*, without authorization)" pairs 65 times with "遵纪守法(*zūn jì shǒu fǎ*, law-abiding)", while "按时" (*àn shí*, on time) has no co-occurrence with "宽厚" (*kuān hòu*, generosity), shown by a white block.

Figures 5 and 6 reveal that adverbs with fewer moral type pairings tend to show stronger associations. However, "擅自", though it co-occurs with five types, is strongly aligned with "遵纪守法". Therefore, we analyze adverb moral types from three perspectives: co-occurring types, internal tendencies, and co-occurrence frequency, as shown in Fig. 7.

Based on this, we retained 58 adverbs with a frequency greater than 5, most of them are correlated with a specific moral type, and some did not. Below is the analysis of their moral type relevance.

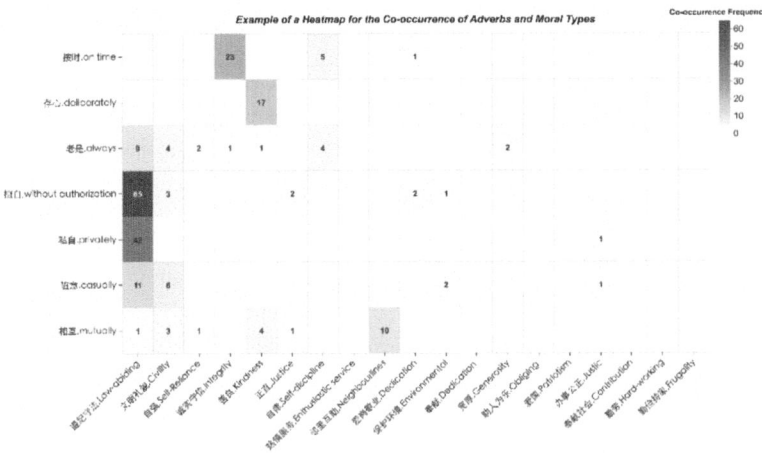

Fig. 6. Heatmap of Co-occurring Moral Types for Selected Adverbs

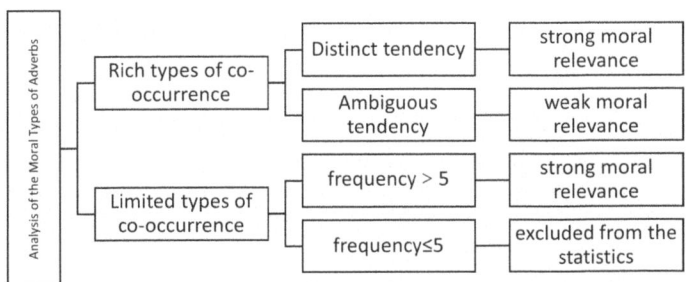

Fig. 7. Flowchart for Analyzing the Moral Types of Adverbs

5.2 Analysis of Adverbs Strongly Correlated with Moral Types

After verification, 37 adverbs showed strong moral relevance. These adverbs co-occur with 1 to 5 moral types, with many primarily aligning with just one. The details are provided in Table 3.

The adverbs in the table predominantly align with specific moral types. For instance, "按期":

（12） 冬平很守信用，基本上能做到[**按期**]归还。
Dongping is reliable, usually repaying on time.

"按期" stresses timely actions, reflecting societal norms and order. Its moral significance is rooted in shared agreements, with phrases like "按期归还" (*àn qī guī huán*, return on time) and "按期纳税" (*àn qī nà shuì*, pay taxes on time) denoting contractual obligations. Thus, "按期" is linked to the moral type of "诚实守信," with clear semantics and a strong moral connection. The assessment identifies 37 adverbs with strong moral relevance, aligned with specific moral types across nine categories. Table 4 categorizes these adverbs and their associated moral types.

Table 3. Table of Adverbs Strongly Correlated with Moral Types

Number of Co-Occurring Moral Types	Number of Adverbs	Adverbs
1 type	19	按期(on schedule), 存心(deliberately), 如实(truthfully), 大声 (loudly), 无端(without reason), 厉声(sternly)……
2 types	7	随手(casually), 当众(in public), 私自 (privately), 借机 (opportunistically), 顺手(conveniently)……
3 types	5	公然 (openly), 成心 (intentionally), 按时 (on time), 如期 (as scheduled), 一同(together)
4 types	4	大肆 (recklessly), 随意 (casually), 私下 (privately), 瞎 (casually)
5 types	2	任意 (casually), 擅自 (without authorization)

The analysis shows that the rational meaning of the adverbs correlates with their moral implications. For example, "大肆(recklessly)" illustrates this connection:

（13）　儿童历来是种族主义分子[**大肆**]传播种族主义的主要对象。
Children are the main targets for racists to spread their ideology.

（14）　全国性[**大肆**]捕捞鳝、鳅，造成了灾难性剧减，甚至地域性濒于灭绝的严重状况。
Overfishing of eels and loaches has led to a catastrophic decline, with some regions near extinction.

The adverb "大肆" originated in verb phrases during the Warring States period and evolved into a standalone word through frequent use. Typically paired with negative verbs, it conveys actions done "without restraint," often implying violations of ethical and legal standards. Thus, it is linked to the moral type of [遵纪守法-]. In sentence (12), the verb "传播" takes on a negative moral dimension when modified by "大肆," indicating illegal actions. The corpus also shows that many verbs associated with "大肆" relate to environmentally harmful activities, as excessive actions can lead to ecological damage. For instance, in sentence (13), unchecked fishing results in environmental harm, further connecting "大肆" to the moral type of [保护环境-].

5.3 Analysis of Adverbs with Weak Correlation to Moral Types

The results reveal that 21 adverbs exhibited weak moral relevance. They were linked to 2 to 7 moral types, with most clustered around 2 to 3. Specific adverbs are provided in Table 5.

Table 4. Table of Adverbs with Strong Moral Type Relevance

Moral Type	Adverbs
遵纪守法 (law-abiding)	擅自 (without authorization), 私自 (privately), 任意 (casually), 大肆 (recklessly), 随意 (casually), 私下 (in private)
文明礼貌 (Civility)	大声 (loudly), 高声 (in a loud voice), 随手 (casually), 瞎 (randomly), 厉声 (sternly), 顺手 (conveniently), 硬 (firmly), 当众 (in public), 当面 (face-to-face)
自强 (Self-Reliance)	大力 (vigorously), 不断 (continuously), 稳步 (steadily), 潜心 (devotedly), 锐意 (resolutely), 一同 (together), 苦心 (painstakingly), 奋力 (strenuously)
诚实守信 (Integrity)	如实 (truthfully), 按时 (on time), 如数 (as much as needed), 按期 (on schedule), 如期 (as scheduled)
善良 (Kindness)	存心 (deliberately), 成心 (intentionally), 无端 (without reason)
正直 (Justice)	乘机 (taking advantage of an opportunity), 趁机 (seizing the opportunity), 公然 (openly), 借机 (taking advantage of a situation)
自律 (Self-discipline)	按时 (on time)
热情服务 (Enthusiastic service)	专程 (specially), 实地 (on-site)
保护环境 (Environmental)	大肆 (recklessly)

The moral types associated with these adverbs are varied, reflecting weaker moral relevance. For example, "相互":

（15）　大家都有刺怎么[**相互**]取暖呢？
How can people with thorns warm each other?

（16）　欧洲形成了两个[**相互**]对立的帝国主义集团。
Europe formed two opposing imperialist blocs.

（17）　往往是一种商品好销，各家便纷纷购进，内部之间[**相互**]压价。
When a product sells well, everyone buys in, leading to price competition.

The adverb "相互" has a colloquial tone, and its wide range of verb collocations in the corpus contributes to its association with multiple moral types.

In sentence (15), "取暖(qǔ nuǎn,to warm)" refers to physically gaining warmth from a heat source, but "相互" adds a social dimension, transforming the action into a metaphor for mutual support, reflecting community spirit during challenging times. In sentence (16), "对立"(duì lì, opposition) denotes conflict between two entities, and when modified by "相互," it emphasizes a sharp contrast, undermining the moral imperative

Table 5. Table of Adverbs with Weak Correlation to Moral Types

Number of Co-occurring Moral Types	Number of Adverbs	Adverbs
2 types	8	务必 (wù bì, must), 不大 (bù dà, not much), 日夜 (rìyè, day and night), 一心 (yìxīn, wholeheartedly)……
3 types	8	动辄 (dòngzhé, at any moment), 连声 (liánshēng, repeatedly), 常年 (chángnián, for years), 暗中 (ànzhōng, secretly)……
4 types	2	成天 (chéngtiān, all day), 悉心 (xīxīn, carefully)
5 types	1	互相 (hùxiāng, mutually)
6 types	1	相互 (xiānghù, mutually)
7 types	1	老是 (lǎoshì, always)

of peace. In sentence (17), "压价" (yā jià, price suppression) is a neutral commercial act, but "相互" introduces a competitive element, implying harmful business practices that violate the moral standards of compliance and legality in commerce.

This demonstrates that the moral significance of "相互" is inherently ambiguous, leading to its weaker moral relevance.

6   Conclusion

This study explores the moral semantics of adverbs and establishes an analytical framework for moral semantics. We analyzed a corpus of 10,313 adverb-verb phrases using a quantitative method to examine the moral tendencies of adverbs and their correlations with moral types.

The results of this study reveal that 73 adverbs exhibit distinct moral tendencies, with the majority displaying clear, low-abstraction semantics, while some are more ambiguous, characterized by weaker moral associations. A subset of 12 adverbs demonstrates strong moral inclinations, including eight with positive connotations (e.g., "奋力" [strenuously], "苦心" [painstakingly], "如实" [truthfully]) and four with negative connotations (e.g., "悍然" [recklessly], "大举" [on a large scale], "肆意" [wantonly]). Furthermore, 37 adverbs were found to be linked to nine specific moral types. For instance, the adverb "如期 (as scheduled)" is associated with the moral type "诚实守信 (integrity)", while "擅自 (without authorization)" correlates with "遵纪守法 (law-abiding)". This research enhances the understanding of adverb semantics and fills gaps in moral phrase data.

Acknowledgments. *This research is supported by the Major Project of the National Social Science Fund (17ZDA305) and the Special Fund for Basic Scientific Research Business Expenses of Central Universities (Wutong Innovation Platform, Beijing Language and Culture University, 21PT04).

References

1. Graham, J., Nosek, B.A., Haidt, J., et al.: Mapping the moral domain. Journal of Personality and Social Psychology **101**(2), 366–38 (2009)
2. Wang, H., Liu, C., Yu, D.: Research on the construction method of a Chinese moral dictionary for ethical computation in artificial intelligence. J. Chinese Info. Proc. **10**, 39–4 (2021)
3. Peng, S., Liu, C., Deng, Y., et al.: Morality between the lines: research on identification of chinese moral sentences. In: Li, S., Sun, M., Liu, Y., et al. (eds.) Proceedings of the 20th Chinese National Conference on Computational Linguistics, pp. 537-548. Hohhot, China: Chinese Information Processing Society of China (2021)
4. Shen, J.: The semantics and pragmatic explanation of the asymmetric use of "好不." Chinese Language **4**, 262–26 (1994)
5. Jia, Y.: Chinese Semantics, 2nd edn. Beijing Peking University Press, Beijing (1999)
6. Sun, D., Li, B.: A discussion on the changes in lexical semantics within combinatory structures. J. School of Chinese Lang. Literat. Nanjing Normal Univ. **04**, 163–16 (2011)
7. Zou, S.: Types and causes of semantics shifts in neutral words. Foreign Language Journal **06**, 61–6 (2007)
8. Zhang, Z.: Semantics shifts in neutral constructions in Chinese. Chinese Learning **03**, 48–5 (2008)
9. Chen, W.: The negative semantics shift of "有+N" - Taking "有问题" as an example. Journal of Xinjiang University (Philosophy and Humanities Edition) **47**(04), 144–15 (2019)
10. Zhang, J., Hou, M.: Research on negative forms in Chinese sentiment analysis. Linguistic Science **16**(3), 275–28 (2017)
11. Zhou, Z.: A discussion on the modifying role of adverbs in phrases. Shandong Foreign Language Teaching **02**, 20–2 (1987)
12. Zhu, Q.: Examining the semantics of the adverb "有点(儿)" from a systemic perspective. J. Xinjiang Univ. (Philosophy and Humanities Edition) **50**(01), 118–12 (2022)
13. Zhang, Y., Zou, H., Yang, B.: The pragmatic functions and selection differences of "总(是)" and "老(是)." Linguistic Science **1**, 31–3 (2005)
14. Zhang, G.: The expression mechanism and implementation conditions of subjective quantities in modern Chinese. World Chinese Teaching **36**(02), 211–22 (2022)
15. Wu, Z.: Moral evaluation and its rationality. Theory Journal **12**, 71–7 (2011)
16. Li, B., Chen, X.: The issue of positive and negative orientation of commendatory and derogatory words in Chinese. Lang. Charact. Appl. **03**, 136–14 (2009)
17. Dragut, E., Fellbaum, C.: The role of adverbs in sentiment analysis. In: Proceedings of Frame Semantics in NLP: A Workshop in Honor of Chuck Fillmore (1929-2014), pp. 38–41. Association for Computational Linguistics, Baltimore, MD, USA (2014)
18. Wang, H., Yu, D.: Construction of a fine-grained Chinese moral semantics knowledge base for machine moral judgment tasks. J. Chinese Info. Proc. **36**(7), 59–6 (2022)
19. Langacker, R.: Access, activation, and overlap: Focusing on the differential. J. Foreign Lang. **35**(1), 2–2 (2012)
20. Zhang, Y.: The nature, scope, and classification of adverbs in modern Chinese. Linguistic Research **01**, 51–6 (2000)
21. Xun, E., Rao, G., Xiao, X., Zang, J.: The development of the BCC corpus in the context of big data. Corpus Linguistics **3**(01), 93–109 + 11 (2016)

Research on the Distribution of Nouns and Verbs Based on Cognitive Expression

Wenjie Zhao[1]([⊠]) and Huizhou Zhao[2]

[1] Yangquan Techers College, Shanxi, China
zwjalbert@163.com
[2] Beijing Language and Culture University, Beijing, China

Abstract. Research on the distribution of parts of speech has found that the proportion of nouns in different languages is relatively stable at approximately 37%. This has been verified by a large amount of language data, but currently, there is a lack of explanation for this phenomenon. Starting from ontological philosophical thought, this study proposes a cognitive description framework for the world. Based on the descriptive framework with parameters, the distribution proportion of verbs in the text was 18.5% and the ratio of the proportion of nouns to that of verbs was close to 2:1. Experiments based on corpora verified that there should be a theoretical value for the proportion of nouns and verbs, which showed that the cognitive description framework proposed in this paper can explain the phenomenon of constant distribution of nouns and verbs to some extent. In addition, we found that the distribution of nouns and verbs was affected by text-genre factors. The ratio of the proportion of nouns to that of verbs can be used to distinguish between information-based and imaginative genres in Chinese and English.

Keywords: noun distribution · cognitive expression · verb distribution · semantic expression · text classification

1 Introduction

All the elements in a language can be divided into various categories. For example, phonemes are divided into vowels and consonants, and words can be classified into nouns, verbs, adjectives, and so on. Qualitative and quantitative research on the categories of language elements is an important way to deepen the understanding of language, especially the essential laws of language [1]. The distribution of parts of speech in a text is an important invariant in language, especially the distribution of nouns [2].

As Hudson said [3] (1994a: 338), there seem to be regularities in language, of which most of us have been completely unaware, which involves the statistical probability of randomly selected words belonging to a particular part of speech. The probability of nouns has caught scholars' attention and achieved certain results. Based on a study of the probability of nouns in the Brown and LOB corpora, Hudson concluded that nouns account for about 37% of English texts [3]. Based on the Chinese dependency treebank, Liu found that nouns account for approximately 41% of Chinese texts [4]. Liang and Liu

© The Author(s), under exclusive license to Springer Nature Singapore Pte Ltd. 2025
P. Jin et al. (Eds.): CLSW 2024, LNAI 15552, pp. 316–328, 2025.
https://doi.org/10.1007/978-981-96-3509-2_23

studied seven languages and obtained a noun probability of approximately 37% [5]. Yuan Li et al. studied the distribution of nouns in German [2], the result is about 38%. This strongly proves that the distribution of nouns is invariant in human language. Wenwen Li (2022) compared Chinese and English syntactic structures based on dependency grammar [6]. When analyzing the distribution of parts of speech in the self-built treebank, she raised the question "Is the proportion of parts of speech in a language within a certain range?" It can be said that people still have a deficiency in understanding parts of speech.

Regarding the essence of language, Wittgenstein pointed out that "the essence of language is precisely a picture of the essence of the world." [7] In his view on analyzing ordinary language, the essence of language corresponds to the essence of the world. Ontology is a philosophical theory that explores the origin or substrate of the world. In the field of computer science and technology, expression methods based on ontological philosophical thought are applied to construct a virtual world parallel to the real world. For example, ER diagrams and object-oriented methods are used for domain concept modeling, and knowledge graphs are used for knowledge modeling.

In conclusion, Hudson (1994) proposed that there may be a pattern in the distribution of nouns, but it is difficult to provide a clear explanation. Thus far, there is a lack of research on the "explanation" issue. Based on ontological philosophical thoughts and drawing on modeling expression methods in the field of computer science, this paper proposes a cognitive description theoretical framework for the world and uses this framework to explain the constancy of the distribution of nouns and verbs in human language.

2   Cognitive Description Theoretical Framework of the World

Language is a tool for human thinking and communication, but fundamentally, it is a tool that people use to cognize and describe the world. Regarding the world, Wittgenstein pointed out in "Tractatus Logico-Philosophicus" that "The world is the totality of facts, not of things", and "Facts are what is the case, and what is the case is the existence of states of affairs." [7] (Wittgenstein, Translated by Chen Qiwei, 2014). It is not difficult to find that in Wittgenstein's view, the world is composed of "occurrence" and "existence", that is, dynamic and static description. Since language is used to cognize and describe the world, the content of natural language consists of two aspects of "occurrence" and "existence".The common basic concepts of these expression methods, based on ontological philosophical thoughts, include entities, attributes, and relationships.

Based on the above analysis, we propose a cognitive description framework as shown in (Formula 1).

$$Expression = \{C, A\} \tag{1}$$

Expression is a set consisting of two sets of words. Among them, C is the core framework, which are composed of words corresponding to "entity, attribute, and relationship". A is the additional framework. The words in this set limitmodify those in the core framework and assist in describing the framework as a whole.

(Formula 2) is an expression about C. The two sets respectively correspond to the descriptions of "existence" and "occurrence". Where, e, e 1, and e 2 are entities, p is an attribute, is an entity relationship, and is an attribute relationship.

$$C = \{e, pr, p\} or \{e1, er, e2\} \tag{2}$$

(Formula 3) is an expression about A. This set is composed of several words that are not used to describe "entity, attribute, and relationship".

$$A = \{A_i | i = 1, 2, 3...n\} \tag{3}$$

Because there is an "or" relationship between the two sets in, there are two expressions. The former is used to describe "existence" and refers to the relationship between an entity and an attribute. An attribute is a certain characteristic of an entity and its extension is very rich. The most crucial attributes among them are time and space.

(1) Alice was born in 1994.
(2) Gary is in Washington.

In example (1), "1994" is a time attribute of the entity "Alice." Specifically, this is his birth time. Naturally, there were more time attributes. Example (2) is an instance of a space attribute. The cognitive result of the two example sentences is to describe a kind of "existence", that is, "Alice" is "Alice who was born in 1994", and "Gary" is "Gary who is in Washington".

The latter is used to describe "occurrence", referring to the relationship between entities.

(3) The earth revolves around the sun.

In example sentence (3), there are two entity concepts, "earth" and "sun". The entity relationship between the two is "the earth is rotating and the sun is the center of rotation". Of course, there will be some additional elements to standardize the expression, such as "around".

C is mainly composed of words that describe entities, attributes, and relationships. From the perspective of parts of speech, it is mainly composed of nouns and verbs. Nouns describe entities and attributes, and verbs describe relationships. As an additional framework, A is mainly composed of word classes such as adverbs, prepositions, numerals and auxiliary words.

In this way, we can use the element distribution proportion in the cognitive description framework proposed in this paper to predict the distribution of parts of speech in the text. For any *Expression* or sentence, the number of word elements card(Expression) = card(C) + card(A) = 3 + n, where n is the number of words in A. Noun word classes correspond to "entity" and "attribute" in C, , and the proportion is $2/(3 + n)$; verbal word classes correspond to "relationship", and the proportion is $1/(3 + n)$. In Li's (2022) research on Chinese-English dependency treebanks, the distribution of parts of speech conforms to Zipf's law. Nouns have the highest proportion, followed by verbs. Among them, the proportion of nouns in Chinese corpus was 31.65% (excluding pronouns), and the proportion of verbs was 16.62%. The proportion of nouns in English corpus was 28.15% (excluding pronouns), and the proportion of verbs was 15.43%. Generally, the ratio of the two is close to 2:1. Current research shows that the proportion of nouns in the text is close to a constant value, about 37%, that is, $2/(3 + n) = 37\%$, and thus n = 2.4.

This value corresponds to the average number of non-noun and non-verbal word classes corresponding to an "existence" expression or an "occurrence" expression in language.

By substituting the value of n = 2.4 into the cognitive description framework for calculation, we can obtain that the proportion of verbal words corresponding to "relationship" is 18.5%. This is the theoretical value of the proportion of verbs in the text. In the studies of Hudson [3], Best [9], and Guohui Liu [10], the proportions of verbs in the text can be calculated to be 18%, 18.2%, and 21%, which are close to our calculated theoretical value.

3 Verification of the Proportion of Verbs and Nouns Based on Treebanks

3.1 Introduction of Corpus

At present, the existing research on the proportion in text is mainly carried out based on solitary language, such as English [3], Chinese [4] [5], German [2] Portuguese [1], etc. Liang and Liu verified seven languages. "The laws discovered by linguists should more be the universal laws of human language" [6]. To verify whether a hypothesis can become a law requires empirical research based on data-driven. Corpus linguistics explores and discovers new language facts and features by using information technology based on large-scale real corpora [6]. At present, corpus-based linguistic research has become an important method in various fields of modern linguistic research. A treebank is a special kind of corpus, which annotated with syntactic information. According to different annotation systems, it can be divided into "phrase syntax treebank" and "dependency syntax treebank". A treebank contains more knowledge of language features and can provide higher value for language research.

The Universal Dependencies (UD) treebank is a cross-lingual grammatical annotation project. It has more than 500 contributors and has created more than 200 treebanks in over 100 languages. At the same time, UD is also a syntactic annotation framework. Any language learner can perform dependency syntactic annotation on languages according to this framework system. Currently, the treebank has been updated to version 2.13, including 148 languages and 259 treebanks.

For the verification work of this study, the UD treebank is selected. At the same time, it is carried out in combination with the Brown corpus, the Lancaster corpus, and the People's Daily annotated corpus from January to June 1998, which are corpora with part-of-speech annotations.

3.2 Distribution of Nouns and Verbs in Chinese and English Corpora

The Chinese corpora selected in this paper include the Lancaster corpus and the People's Daily annotated corpus. The English corpus is the Brown corpus. The part-of-speech annotation systems of the three corpora are not consistent. Table 1. Lists the total number of part-of-speech annotation symbols in the three corpora and the part-of-speech marking symbols related to nouns, verbs, and punctuation marks. Among them, the part-of-speech marks selection of the Brown corpus is a simplified version.

Table 1. Symbol markings for nouns, verbs, and punctuation in three corpora.

	Nouns Tag	Verbs Tag	Punctuation Tag
Lancaster	n,ns,nr,vn,ng,an,nz,nt,nx,r	v	w,ew
Brown	n,nt,nr,vn,ns,an,nz,ng,nx,r	v	w
People's Daily	NOUN,PRON,NUM	VERB	

Considering that in the studies of Hudson [3] and Haitao Liu [4], pronouns are regarded as a subclass of nouns. Therefore, we also adopt the same strategy here. Due to considerations of Chinese, a paratactic language, when judging nouns, more attention will be paid to functionality. Thus, phenomena such as the flexible use of part of speech like "vn" and "an" will also be regarded as nouns, because such words are equivalent to a noun in text. As pointed out by Yuan Li et al. [2], Hudson [3] did not include punctuation marks when calculating the distribution of nouns. Therefore, we will remove punctuation marks in our calculation process.

Table 2. Distribution proportions of nouns and verbs in three corpora

	Lancaster	People's Daily	Brown
Proportion of nouns	0.37	0.42	0.34
Proportion of verbs	0.21	0.19	0.18
PON/POV	1.76	2.21	1.88

According to the data in Table 2, the distribution of nouns is basically in line with the existing research conclusions, and the distribution of verbs is also relatively consistent with the theoretical values predicted by the cognitive description framework.

In the Brown Corpus, the distribution of nouns is 34%, slightly lower than the 37% of nouns in the Brown Corpus calculated by Hudson [3]. This is because the simplified part-of-speech-tagged Brown Corpus we adopted is different from Hudson's research. The distribution of nouns in People's Daily in 1998 is much higher than the predicted value, but it is consistent with the value of Haitao Liu [4]. In the tagging system of People's Daily in 1998, there is a situation of multiple tagging, that is, a phrase is marked with a part of speech, and each word in the phrase is also marked with a part of speech. When we count, all are included. If only the part of speech of phrases is counted, then the distribution of nouns in People's Daily in 1998 is 40% (the distribution of verbs is 19.6%). Coupled with the relatively single text type of People's Daily, which is almost all news reports. This text type emphasizes facts and emphasizes that certain things "happen". This also leads to an increase in the use of nouns in news texts. As a Chinese corpus, the LCMC corpus is a comprehensive corpus that includes many different types of texts. This dilutes the distribution of nouns to some extent. This difference in proportion caused by text types will be mentioned again later.

3.3   Distribution of Nouns and Verbs in the UD Treebank

As a standardized annotation framework, the part-of-speech system of more than 200 treebanks in the Universal Dependencies (UD) treebank is consistent. Table 3. Shows the part-of-speech symbols of the treebank, as well as the verb and noun symbols among them.

Table 3. Part-of-speech symbols in the UD treebank.

Nouns Tag	Verbs Tag	Punctuation Tag
NOUN、PRON、PROPN	VERB、AUX	PUNCT

The annotation files in the UD treebank are in *conllu* format. At the same time, each treebank file is accompanied by an *xml* file to show some annotation infomation about the treebank, including statistical information on the part-of-speech annotation of the corpus. As follows (Fig. 1).

Fig. 1. Part-of-speech statistical information in UD treebank files.

Using a Python script for statistical collation of data, we obtained the distribution of noun and verb proportions for 259 texts.(see in Fig. 2.)

Figure 2 Shows the distribution of noun and verb proportions in 259 files of the UD treebank. It can be seen that the fluctuation of data seems to change along a line. Through calculation, it can be obtained that the mean value of noun proportion in the entire treebank is 0.39, and the mean value of verb proportion is 0.2. The ratio of the two is 1.919, which is close to 2:1 obtained from the cognitive description framework.

Figure 3 uses box plots to show the overall distribution of noun and verb in the UD treebank. It can be seen from the figure that the two types of data are concentrated around 0.4 and 0.2 respectively, and on the whole, it presents a right-skewed distribution, indicating that the data is greatly affected by outliers. Most of the data is smaller than the mean value.

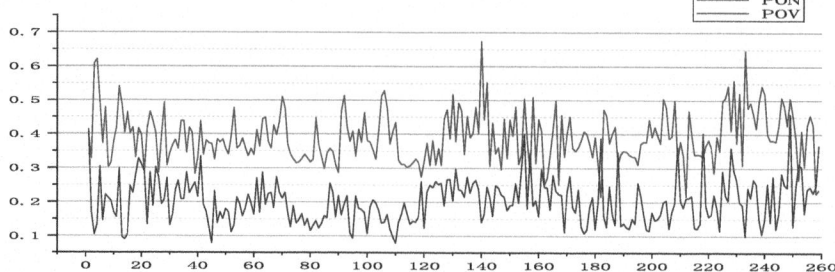

Fig. 2. Distribution of noun and verb proportions in the UD treebank. Here, the distribution is distinguished according to the texts in the treebank. For the same language, there will be many texts.

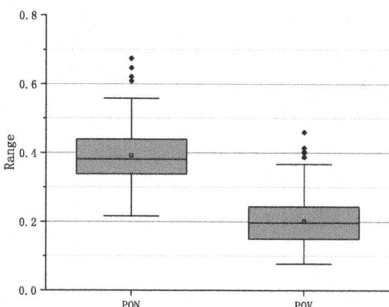

Fig. 3. Box plot of noun and verb proportions in the UD treebank.

The above statistical calculation is performed on the texts in the entire UD treebank. The results show that it generally conforms to the proportional distribution calculated by the cognitive description framework. There are only more than 100 languages in 259 files of the treebank. After summarization, 138 language samples are obtained. The following figure shows the ratio of noun and verb proportions in different languages.

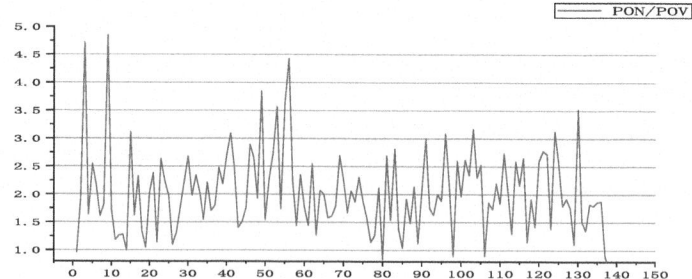

Fig. 4. Ratio of noun and verb proportions of 138 languages in the UD treebank.

Figure 4 shows the ratio of nouns to verbs in 138 languages in the UD treebank. It is not difficult to find that except for some extreme examples, most languages fluctuate around 2. Through calculation, it can be known that the mean value of the ratio is 2.03. This indicates that most languages have certain similarities and universality in the framework and part of speech chosen when cognitively describing the world. The box plot in Fig. 5. Showing the proportional distribution also corroborates this point. At the same time, the main body of the box plot of the noun proportion also falls within the interval of 37% − 45%, which is also in line with the conclusion in the study of Liang and Liu (2013).

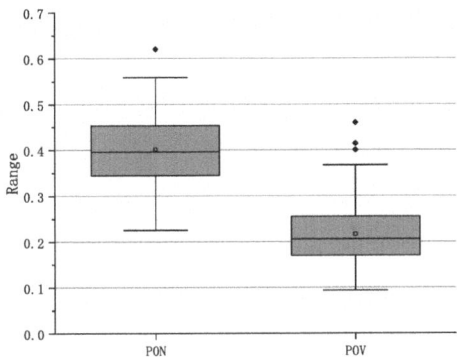

Fig. 5. Box plot of noun and verb proportions of 138 languages in the UD treebank.

3.4 Performance of Noun and Verb Distributions in Different Literary Styles

In the studies of Hudson and Yuan Li et al., it is all mentioned that stylistic classification will have an impact on the distribution of subcategories within nouns. Therefore, we calculated the distribution of nouns and verbs by distinguishing different literary styles.

Hudson [3] divided the literary styles in the Brown Corpus into two major categories: **informational literary style and imaginative literary style**. After counting the distribution of part of speech, it was found that "the average proportion of common nouns in informational literary styles is about 7 percentage higher than their proportion in imaginative literary styles. At the same time, the proportion of pronouns in informational literary styles is about 8 percentage lower than their proportion in imaginative literary styles" [2], thus obtaining a complementary relationship between common nouns and pronouns. We do not concern ourselves with the relationship between the subcategories within nouns. Instead, we want to find out whether the distribution of nouns and verbs will be different in different literary styles.

First, we presented the distribution of nouns and verbs in the 15 literary styles in the Lancaster Corpus and the Brown Corpus. At the same time, following Hudson's practice [3], we also divide the literary styles of the Lancaster Corpus into informational literary style and imaginative literary style.

Table 4. Proportions of nouns and verbs in 15 literary styles in the Lancaster Corpus and the Brown Corpus.

	Lancaster	PON	POV	PON/POV	Brown	PON	POV	PON/POV
imaginative literary	News report	0.38	0.19	2	news	0.40	0.16	2.5
	Editorial	0.36	0.21	1.7	belleslettres	0.32	0.17	1.9
	News commentary	0.39	0.20	1.95	editorial	0.33	0.18	1.8
	Religion	0.38	0.19	2	government	0.36	0.16	2.3
	Technology and commerce	0.34	0.23	1.5	hobbies	0.35	0.18	1.9
	Popular social life	0.35	0.22	1.6	learned	0.33	0.17	1.9
	Biography and essay	0.36	0.21	1.7	lore	0.33	0.17	1.9
	Others; reports and official documents, etc	0.45	0.19	2.4	religion	0.32	0.17	1.9
	Academic and scientific technology	0.39	0.19	2.1	reviews	0.35	0.15	2.3
informational literary	General fiction	0.33	0.24	1.4	adventure	0.33	0.21	1.6
	Detective fiction	0.35	0.23	1.5	fiction	0.32	0.21	1.5
	Science fiction	0.33	0.22	1.5	sciencection	0.31	0.21	1.5
	Martial arts fiction	0.35	0.24	1.5	mystery	0.32	0.22	1.5
	Romantic fiction	0.33	0.23	1.4	romance	0.32	0.22	1.5
	Humor	0.33	0.26	1.3	humor	0.32	0.19	1.7

Table 4 Shows the distribution of nouns and verbs in informational texts and imaginative texts as well as the ratio between the two that are calculated. Using SPSS, we calculated whether there is a significant difference between the two types of texts and obtained the following table.

Table 5. Independent sample t-test results of noun proportion, verb proportion, and ratio in 15 literary styles in the Lancaster Corpus and the Brown Corpus.

| | Literary style (mean ± sd) | | t | p |
	Informational	Imaginative		
PON	0.36 ± 0.03	0.33 ± 0.01	3.756	0.001
POV	0.19 ± 0.02	0.22 ± 0.02	−4.915	0.000
PON/POV	1.96 ± 0.27	1.49 ± 0.10	6.718	0.000

As can be seen from Table 5, different literary style samples show significance for noun proportion, verb proportion, and ratio ($p < 0.05$), which means that different literary style samples have differences in noun proportion, verb proportion, and ratio.

Specific analysis shows that:

- Literary style shows significance at the 0.01 level for noun proportion ($t = 3.756$, p = 0.001). From the specific comparison difference, it can be seen that the average value of informational texts (0.36) is significantly higher than that of imaginative texts (0.33).
- Literary style shows significance at the 0.01 level for verb proportion ($t = -4.915$, p = 0.000). From the specific comparison difference, it can be seen that the average value of informational texts (0.19) is significantly lower than that of imaginative texts (0.22).
- Literary style shows significance at the 0.01 level for ratio ($t = 6.718$, p = 0.000). From the specific comparison difference, it can be seen that the average value of informational texts (1.96) is significantly higher than that of imaginative texts (1.49).

The above results indicate that the distribution of nouns and verbs is indeed affected by different literary styles, and there are differences in the distribution of part of speech between imaginative literary styles and informational literary styles.

In language, nouns and verbs, as important content words, have important significance in the ratio of their distribution in linguistic typology. Seifart's study [11] found that languages with richer verb arguments have a smaller ratio of noun to verb proportions. Polisky's study [12] found that the ratio of noun to verb types is related to language centrality. Central preposed languages have a smaller ratio of noun to verb types than central postposed languages. According to the cognitive description framework in Sect. 2 of this paper, the theoretical value of the distribution of nouns and verbs is 2, but in different types of languages, this ratio will change, which is also a manifestation of language richness. Just like Chomsky's principle-parameter model, language "only has universal principles and a limited set of options (parameters) on how to apply universal principles."

In Table 4, the proportion of nouns in informational literary styles is approximately twice that of verbs, while in imaginative literary styles, this ratio is close to 1.5 times. By calculating the detailed data, we obtain that the distribution of nouns in contemporary German short essays measured by Best [9] is approximately 1.89 times that of verbs, falling between 1.5 and 2.0. The ratio of noun proportion to verb proportion in German letters measured by Wimmer and Altmann [1] is 2.1. From the perspective of literary style classification, both essays and letters can be classified as informational literary styles, and letters are more typical informational literary styles than essays. Thus, it can be seen that the ratio of nouns and verbs is affected by literary style, or such a ratio can be used as an indicator to distinguish Chinese and English informational literary styles from imaginative literary styles.

3.5 Summary

This section uses the Brown Corpus, the Lancaster Corpus, the annotated corpus in People's Daily in 1998, and more than 100 languages in the UD treebank to conduct data verification on the proposed cognitive description framework. The distribution of nouns and verbs in the entire corpus and in texts of 15 different literary styles are counted. The data proved the constant distribution of nouns in the text. At the same time, the theoretical value of the verb distribution proportion proposed in the framework is also verified. All these indicate that the cognitive description framework we propose can to a certain extent provide a cognitive explanation for the universal law of the constant distribution of nouns and verbs in human language.

4 Conclusion

The constant distribution of nouns in texts at around 37% is a universal law in language, and there must be a unified mechanism behind it. Starting from human cognition of the world and based on ontological philosophical thought, this paper constructs a cognitive language description framework. Using this theoretical framework, it provides a possible explanation for the constant proportion of nouns. And through this framework, it is predicted that the proportion of verbs in texts is also a constant value − around 18.5%. At the same time, the ratio of nouns and verbs in language is close to 2:1. In order to verify the applicability of the framework, multiple corpora such as the UD treebank are selected for empirical research. Firstly, the explanatory power of the language cognitive description framework is verified.

Secondly, an empirical study on the distribution of nouns and verbs in different literary styles is conducted, proving that different literary styles have significant differences in the proportions of nouns and verbs in texts. And the cognitive description framework proposed in this paper is used to explain the phenomenon of different proportions of nouns and verbs in informational and imaginative literary styles. We think that the distribution of nouns and verbs can be used to distinguish informational literary styles from imaginative literary styles. For Chinese and English corpora, the closer the ratio of nouns and verbs in a text is to 2, the stronger the informativeness of the literary style.

The cognitive language description framework we propose explains the constant law of the distribution of nouns and verbs in texts from the perspective of cognitive expression. This framework still has many parts that need to be refined. First, since this paper focuses on the problem of the constant law of the distribution of nouns and verbs, the components in the additional framework A are not subdivided, so a clear language implementation method cannot be given. The number of elements in A is only the average value calculated from the prior research results of nouns, and its detailed structure needs further study. Second, in terms of specific language implementation, we have adopted a simple approach. Just like "attribute concepts are not necessarily all realized as nouns", whether "entity" and "relationship" concepts directly correspond to nouns and verbs is also a question worth exploring. Third, the impact of different proportions of descriptions of "occurrence" and "existence" in texts on word category distribution also needs further detailed research.

The verification corpora in this paper mainly use Chinese and English as special cases to show. In terms of the cognitive structure of language, the implementation methods of these two languages are highly similar. According to the calculation data of Portuguese and German texts by Wimmer [1], on average, the proportion of nouns is basically around 37%, and the proportion of verbs is also around 18.5%. However, in some samples of Portuguese, the proportion of verbs is only about 9%. The data of the UD treebank also shows that there are more microscopic details in the distribution of nouns and verbs in language. Different languages have different influencing factors. Whether word category distribution can be used as a basis for linguistic typology judgment is still an in-depth direction for future research.

References

1. Wimmer, G., Altmann, G.: Some statistical investigations concerning word classes. Glotto-metrics **1**, 109 (2001)
2. Li, Y., Duan, T., Liu, H.: Is noun distribution an invariant of human language? –taking the distribution of nouns in written German as an example. J. Zhejiang Univ. (Humanit. Soc. Sci.) **49**(6), 39–48 (2019)
3. Hudson, R.: About 37% of word-tokens are nouns. Language **70**(2), 331–339 (1994)
4. Liu, H.: Theory and practice of dependency grammar. Science Press, Beijing (2009)
5. Liang, J., Liu, H.: Noun distribution in natural languages. Poznań Stud. Contemp. Linguist. **49**(4), 509–529 (2013)
6. Li, W.: Chinese-english syntactic contrast: a linguistic measurement study based on dependency treebanks. Social Sciences Academic Press, Beijing (2022)
7. Wittgenstein, L.: Tractatus logico-philosophicus and others. In: Translated by Qiwei, C. (ed.) The Commercial Press, Beijing, (2014)
8. Aristotle.: Metaphysics. In: Translated by Shoupeng, W. (ed.) The Commercial Press, Beijing, (1959)
9. Best, K.-H.: Word class frequencies in contemporary German short prose texts. J. Quant. Linguist. **1**(2), 144–147 (1994)
10. Liu, G.: An investigation of the frequency and stylistic distribution of english nominal elements based on corpus. Shandong Foreign Lang. Teach. (2016) 37(4)
11. Frank, S.: Cross-linguistic variation in the noun-to-verb ratio: The role of verb morphology and narrative strategies. In: Poster Presented at the Association for Linguistic Typology 9th Biennial Conference, University of Hong Kong, (2011)
12. Polinsky, M.: Headedness, again. UCLA Working Papers in Linguistics 17 (Theories of Everything) 348–359 (2012)
13. William, C.: Parts of speech as language universals and as language-particular categories. In: Vogel, P. M., Comrie, B. (eds.) Approaches to the Typology of Word Classes, pp. 65–102. De Gruyter Mouton (2000). https://doi.org/10.1515/9783110806120.65

14. Yin, B.: Quantitative research on chinese word categories. Stud. Chin. Lang. **6**, 428–436 (1986)
15. Zhang, X.: A Study on Chinese Factive Predicates. In: Fudan University Press, Shanghai, pp. 24–28 (2020)
16. Hao, Y., Wang, X., Bin, S., Liu, H.: A probability distribution of dependencies in interlanguage. Poznan Stud. Contemp. Linguist. **59**(1), 65–93 (2023)

The Evolution of Polysemy in Chinese Based on Conceptual Blending: The Cases of *Bì* and *Bì*

Shunmiao Li[✉]

Department of Applied Linguistics, School of Chinese Language and Literature, University of Chinese Academy of Social Sciences, Beijing, China
lishunmiao@gmail.com

Abstract. This paper examines the theory of conceptual blending from cognitive linguistics to reveal the process of semantic change and the cognitive mechanisms in polysemous words. In this study, quantitative and qualitative methods are combined to explore the lexical semantic evolution trends of these two words, based on linguistic evidence from corpora. It is revealed that 闭*bì* and 蔽*bì* demonstrate a dynamic process of fusion and divergence in the semantic construction through conceptual blending. In their semantic evolution, there is a phenomenon of semantic alternation, where complementing the contraction of the 'to conceal' meaning in 闭*bì* is the development of the 'to hide' meaning in 蔽*bì*. The pattern of sense distribution for these two words had primarily formed in the Modern Chinese period, yet instances of mixed usage still exist in some regions.

Keywords: Conceptual Blending · Semantic Evolution · Polysemy · Cognitive Linguistics

1 Introduction

The dynamic evolution of meanings in polysemous words has been widely discussed in linguistic research, particularly regarding the development and links between different senses. Polysemous words evolve from monosemous words that represent different semantic variants of a single lexeme, with the potential to develop into homophones whose meanings are entirely unrelated [1]. In Modern Chinese, 闭*bì* and 蔽*bì* are a pair of homophonic polysemous words that belong to distinct conceptual domains. It appears, however, that their meanings have overlapped during their evolution. Cognitive linguistics proposes that certain concepts from these two domains may intersect [2]. The word 蔽*bì* belongs to the conceptual domain of concealment, while 闭*bì* falls within the domain of opening and closing. When describing the seclusion or concealment of a person or object, the term '隐蔽' (*yǐn bì*, 'to conceal') is used in mainland China, whereas '隐闭' (*yǐn bì*, 'to hide') is commonly used in Hong Kong and Macau. This demonstrates that, synchronically, the two terms often exhibit lexical blending.

Previous research on the lexical semantics of terms like 闭*bì* and 蔽*bì* has primarily focused on the diachronic evolution of members within their respective conceptual domains [3, 4]. However, the relationship between their semantic developments has

P. Jin et al. (Eds.): CLSW 2024, LNAI 15552, pp. 329–339, 2025.
https://doi.org/10.1007/978-981-96-3509-2_24

received limited attention. Lexical meaning is constantly evolving, and its extensions have a relatively limitless potential [5]. Semantic change is a natural consequence of language use and is directly linked to cognitive processing. Cognitive linguistics emphasizes that the meanings of polysemous words are not only derived from the internal integration of their semantic structures, but also established through connections formed by a series of basic conceptual structures within people's world knowledge [6]. Therefore, it is necessary to make comparative analyses with other external vocabularies in order to deeply investigate the process and cognitive rationale for the extension of the meaning of polysemous words. This raises the following questions: How do the conceptual domains of 闭 *bì* and 蔽 *bì* establish connections in the construction of meaning? What are the patterns and trends in their semantic evolution? And what cognitive motivations drive these changes?

In this paper, we would like to explain the polysemy between the words 闭 *bì* and 蔽 *bì* in Chinese by utilizing dictionary and corpus data to trace the semantic changes of these terms. Drawing on conceptual blending theory from cognitive linguistics, we further explore how their meanings have evolved and become interconnected over time in their meaning construction. This study enriches cognitive research on the semantic evolution of polysemous words, establishes a cognitive model for polysemy research, and sheds light on the dynamic features and patterns of polysemous word development. Furthermore, it provides a theoretical foundation for lexicography, lexical research, and pedagogical practice.

2 Previous Studies on Meaning Construction Based on Conceptual Blending Theory

Polysemy reflects the changes and extensions of human cognition, with its occurrence depending on the speaker's psychological reality or awareness [7]. Lee [8] posits that lexical polysemy develops through the diachronic evolution of metaphors, suggesting that words used more frequently are more likely to evolve into polysemous terms. Fauconnier and Turner [9] point out that polysemy is an inevitable and conventional result of blending, reflecting the availability functions of certain frames shaped by contextual or cultural settings. In light of these perspectives, the semantic constructions derived from the core meanings of polysemous words, as well as the relationships between these meanings, can be explained through cognitive linguistics, particularly through conceptual blending theory.

Conceptual blending theory is a theoretical framework used to explore the integration of semantic construction and is understood as a dynamic cognitive process [10]. That is, it extends and develops mental space theory by revealing the cognitive processes and mechanisms behind the relationships between mental spaces, particularly in metaphors. This theory offers strong explanatory power for the dynamic construction of meaning.

Generally, conceptual blending theory proposes a four-space model, where conceptual blending occurs across four basic spaces: input space I, input space II, the generic space, and the blending space. Input space I and input space II provide extensive structural and relational information to the entire network, and partial correspondences exist between their structures. The generic space selectively represents common, abstract organizational structures shared by both input spaces, forming the foundation for the blending space. The blending space is a selective projection of the input spaces, reflecting relevant background features and cognitive experiences. The conceptual blending network consists of at least four mental spaces, an emergent structure, cross-space mappings, and selective projections. The mechanism of conceptual blending operates through three interrelated processes—composition, completion, and elaboration—to generate the emergent structure within the blending space.

Previous semantic research has not provided a detailed understanding of the relationship between the senses of polysemy, often placing excessive emphasis on the independence of their internal semantic structures while neglecting their connections to external contexts. In fact, the senses of polysemous words are not arbitrary or meaningless associations; rather, they are the results of cognitive processes and conceptual integration. Polysemy is a standard by-product of conceptual integration, but is only noticed in a small percentage of cases [9]. Current work in cognitive linguistics regarding polysemy predominantly relies on image schema theory to analyze the semantic relationships of polysemous words through their spatial structures [11, 12]. Additionally, some studies explore the semantic extensions of polysemous words through the lenses of metaphor, metonymy, and prototype categories [13, 14].

In this regard, this paper emphasizes the dynamic process of meaning construction and its connection to external meanings. Therefore, by employing conceptual blending theory to elucidate the cognitive processes underlying the semantic evolution of 闭 *bì* and 蔽 *bì*, this study will help clarify the distinctions and connections between their multiple senses, as well as their patterns of evolution and distribution.

3 Method

Employing both quantitative and qualitative research methods, this study attempts to collect the senses of 闭 *bì* and 蔽 *bì* from dictionaries such as '汉语大词典' (*Hànyǔ Dà Cídiǎn*, 'Comprehensive Chinese Dictionary') and '现代汉语词典' (*Xiàndài Hànyǔ Cídiǎn*, 'Modern Chinese Dictionary'), while utilizing the Ancient Chinese Corpus from the Chinese Language Knowledge Base '*Online Corpus*' to illustrate the usage and distribution of each sense.

First, example sentences containing 闭 *bì* and 蔽 *bì* are extracted from the corpus. Then, according to the dictionary definitions, the meanings of the target words used in these sentences are manually annotated and categorized. The usage frequency and distribution of each sense are analyzed, followed by a comparison of these results and a statistical assessment of the diachronic distribution of different senses over time.

By analyzing the relationships and evolutionary paths among the different senses of 闭 *bì* and 蔽 *bì*, this study aims to demonstrate the semantic change process of this pair of homophonic polysemous words and reveal their conceptual integration processes across various senses. As a result, this analysis will contribute to explaining the patterns and cognitive mechanisms underlying polysemy in Chinese.

4 The Diachronic Semantic Evolution of 闭*bì* and 蔽*bì* in Chinese

4.1 The Diachronic Semantic Evolution of 闭*bì*

Through the analysis of the corpus, this study has found that 闭*bì* appears 3,711 times in the Ancient Chinese Corpus [15]. It can be seen from the corpus that the active senses of 闭*bì* are predominantly of the verb, while the noun senses are relatively uncommon. Notably, during the Middle Chinese period, the statistics show that the meanings of 闭*bì* were most diverse; however, by the Modern Chinese period, they began to stabilize, retaining primarily the more commonly used core meanings, most of which are verb senses.

From a diachronic perspective, the data shows that the original meaning of the word 闭*bì* in ancient times referred to 'door bolt', and due to its phonetic similarity to '閟' (*bì*, 'to close the door'), it extended to indicate the action of 'closing the door'. This subsequently gave rise to the action sense of 'to close'. It is noted that its focus shifted from 'door bolt' to the action of 'to close'. Gradually, the meaning extended from the action itself to its purpose and result, conveying the sense of 'to obstruct' or 'to block'. These adjacent meanings reflect their close relationship and have evolved into commonly used senses.

It is observed that when 闭*bì* expresses its common verbal meaning of 'to close', it implicitly carries the attributive sense of 'to hide' or 'to conceal'. This indicates that the result of the action renders a person or object invisible or out of sight. At the same time, this action also creates an obstruction, thereby giving rise to the meaning of 'to defend'. In addition, the sense of the verb is also derived from the noun sense of 'beginning of autumn' or 'beginning of winter', which follow the law of nature's closure and have common features and elements with the sense of 'to hide'.

In the Middle Chinese period, the word 闭*bì* exhibited a significant diversity of meanings. Its senses of verbs and nouns exhibited varying levels of extension. On the one hand, based on the result of the action 'to obstruct', 闭*bì* developed meanings such as 'to imprison' and 'to terminate', which are closely tied to the political upheavals and military conflicts of this period. On the other hand, stemming from the sense of 'to hide', 闭*bì* derived meanings such as '遮蔽' (*zhē bì*, 'to obscure') and '隐覆' (*yǐn fù*, 'to cover'). Both of these paths represent extensions of their verbal meanings. Additionally, in terms of its sense of noun, the meanings derived from 闭*bì* are quite distant from its prototypical meaning. For example, the meanings of 'the beginning of autumn' and 'the beginning of winter' further gave rise to the sense of 'an alternate name for the twelfth lunar month'.

In the Modern Chinese period, it is apparent that a clear functional distinction has emerged among the various senses of 闭*bì*, with its less commonly used meanings noticeably declining. The verb senses formed a pattern centered around the primary meanings of 'to close', 'to block', 'to hide' and 'to stop', with an expanded range of collocational and modificational objects, extending from concrete nouns to abstract ones.

The above statistics show that the lexical semantics of 闭*bì* has changed over time. In terms of diachronic distribution, the various senses of 闭*bì* exhibit differing extents of activity across different periods, with the Middle Ages being the most active and containing the most number of senses. The increase in the number of senses resulted in an expansion of collocational patterns, moving from solid objects related to the original meanings to similar objects, and eventually to abstract concepts. Regarding the relationships between senses, verb senses and their derivatives demonstrate a degree of similarity, generally preserving features of the prototypical semantics, whereas noun senses tend to become increasingly marginalised from the prototypical meanings.

4.2   The Diachronic Semantic Evolution of 蔽*bì*

In this study, it is found that 蔽*bì* appears 2,678 times in the Ancient Chinese Corpus [15] in noun, verb, and adjective meanings, with the verb meaning being the most common. We can also conclude from the corpus that the frequency of meaning is highest in the Middle Chinese Period, and the number and types of terms are also more prosperous.

In the Ancient Chinese period, the original meaning of 蔽*bì* referred to 'the state of grass covering something', which was later extended to the verbal sense of 'to cover' or 'to block'. When used as a predicate, the word 蔽*bì* typically collocates with two types of nouns. The first type includes concrete nouns, such as body parts, celestial phenomena, or objects with covering properties, as seen in phrases like '蔽其面' (*bì qí miàn*, 'cover one's face') and '蔽日' (*bì rì*, 'cover the sky'). The second type consists of abstract nouns, such as '蔽贤' (*bì xián*, 'to conceal the virtuous'), expressing the meaning of 'to conceal'. It is clear that most of the objects in the sense of 'to cover' in this period are concrete nouns, which are closely related to the original meaning of 'grass cover'.

During the Middle Chinese Period, it was common for the word 蔽*bì* to have multiple meanings. The meaning of '遮挡' (*zhē dǎng*, 'to cover') was the most commonly used, with collocations increasingly involving concrete nouns, particularly celestial phenomena. Examples include '蔽风雨' (*bì fēng yǔ*, 'to shield from wind and rain'), '蔽风日' (*bì fēng rì*, 'to shield from wind and sun'), and '蔽风霜' (*bì fēng shuāng*, 'to shield from wind and frost'). When 蔽*bì* is used together with body part nouns, its meaning extends from 'to cover' to 'to protect'. It is noted that as 蔽*bì* shifts from modifying instrumental elements to describing human actions, it further develops senses such as 'to conceal', 'to obscure' and 'to cover up', with relatively active usage. Examples of parallel phrases include '隐蔽' (*yǐn bì*, 'to conceal') and '掩蔽' (*yǎn bì*, 'to hide'). Additionally, it is commonly observed that the meanings of '蒙蔽' (*méng bì*, 'to deceive') and '壅蔽' (*yōng bì*, 'to block' or 'to obscure') are actively used, typically appearing in the V + NP + O structure. Meanwhile, it is also evident that the nominal sense of 蔽*bì* has significantly diminished in usage, indicating a decline in its frequency.

In the Modern Chinese period, the meanings of 蔽*bì* largely inherited and developed from those established during the Middle Chinese period. The commonly used senses include 'to cover', 'to obscure', 'to conceal' and 'to protect'. It is evident that these meanings are primarily divided into two core concepts: 'to hide' and 'to cover'. At the same time, the use of 'to block' has decreased, while the senses related to 'to hide' and 'to obscure' have seen an increase.

Through the above analysis, from the Ancient Chinese period to the Modern Chinese period, the original meaning of 蔽*bì* has remained in use, though 'to cover' has become the more commonly used sense. These meanings have further extended into a series of active verbal senses, such as '隐藏' (*yǐn cáng*, 'to hide'), '壅蔽' (*yōng bì*, 'to obstruct'), and '掩护' (*yǎn hù*, 'to conceal' or 'to protect'). It is highlighted that most of the noun senses of 蔽*bì* are derived from its verbal senses, but as the verbal senses became more dominant, the usage of the noun senses gradually declined.

5 Cognitive Analysis on the Semantic Evolution of 闭*bì* and 蔽*bì*

5.1 Cognitive Analysis on the Semantic Evolution of 闭*bì*

By analysing the process of lexical evolution, it is found that 闭*bì* evolves from a noun in its original sense to a verb that activates the framework of the action of closing, including the semantic functions of the form, instrument and function of the action of closing.

A detailed analysis of the semantic construction from 闭*bì* [N] 'door bolt' to 闭*bì* [V] 'to close the door' (see Fig. 1) shows that input space I in the conceptual blending process is the mental space of concrete object concepts, specifically referring to the original meaning of the door bolt. Input space II is the action concept of closing in mental space. The generic space reflects the connection between the two input spaces in terms of function and result. That is, the basic function of the 'bolt' in input space I is to close the door to achieve the function of blocking; the act of closing in input space II also achieves the function of blocking and isolating, which is similar to input space I. These two input spaces are mapped and integrated to form the action situation of closing the door. Thus, it is concluded that the conceptual integration process from 闭*bì* as a noun to 闭*bì* as a verb reflects the expansion of this concept, from the physical object of a 'door bolt' to the associated functional action of closing.

In the construction of the meaning 'to block', the action object of 闭*bì* as a verb extends from 'door' to 'bridge', emphasizing the state of these objects being sealed or closed, thereby achieving the effect of preventing passage. It becomes evident that the object of the action further expands to abstract concepts as the context shifts, signifying the closure or blocking of information or distractions. At the same time, the verb 闭*bì* introduces the concept of obstructing vision, which connects to the effects of 'to hide' and 'to conceal'. It activates the notion that this effect can be achieved through means beyond just closing a door, thereby constructing the semantics of 'to hide' and 'to conceal' (Fig. 1).

5.2 Cognitive Analysis on the Semantic Evolution of 蔽*bì*

The polysemous development of 蔽*bì* also occurs through the creation of links with different morphemes, forming two input spaces. The common features are then projected into the generic space, forming an emergent structure through different integrative network concepts.

The development of the noun sense of 蔽*bì* from 'the state of grass covering' to 'curtains or protective gear' reflects a mirror network of conceptual integration. Input space I and input space II come from different domains: input space I refers to the natural covering or shading form of grass, while input space II involves curtains or protective gear. Both spaces share the function of covering or blocking, thus establishing a common framework of 'to cover'. This shared feature is placed in the generic space, where conceptual integration occurs in the blended space, forming a new emergent

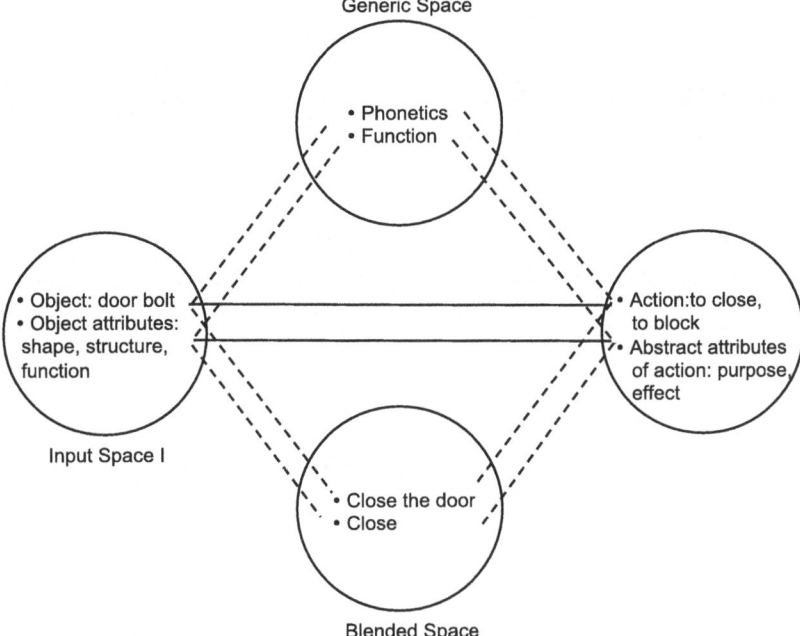

Fig. 1. Conceptual blending process from 闭*bì* [N] to 闭*bì* [V].

structure. Similarly, the noun sense of 蔽*bì* evolves from 'the state of grass covering' to 'barrier', integrating from a concrete physical state to a more abstract function of covering and symbolic significance, emphasizing the functional concept of barriers and obstacles.

Figure 2 illustrates the semantic construction process of 蔽*bì* from its noun sense 'the state of grass covering' to its verb sense 'to cover' and 'to block'. Input space I represent the source domain of physical concepts, describing the phenomenon of small grass covering something, while input space II contains the action concepts of 'to cover' and 'to block'. Through cognitive framework refinement and the elaboration of shared features, the sense of 蔽*bì* shifts from a material concept describing natural phenomena to an action concept. These verb senses integrate the original physical characteristics with the extended action concept, forming a semantic bridge between input space I and input space II, emphasizing the functional transition of the noun into its corresponding action. In various contexts, 蔽*bì* also extends from its prototypical meaning to peripheral senses through a semantic chain, where adjacent meanings are linked.

5.3 Cognitive Analysis of the Relationship Between the Semantic Construction of 闭*bì* and 蔽*bì*

The semantic evolution reveals that multiple semantic features of 闭*bì* and 蔽*bì* have been projected during their development. Although their core conceptual meanings differ significantly, some of their senses have established connections. The cognitive semantics

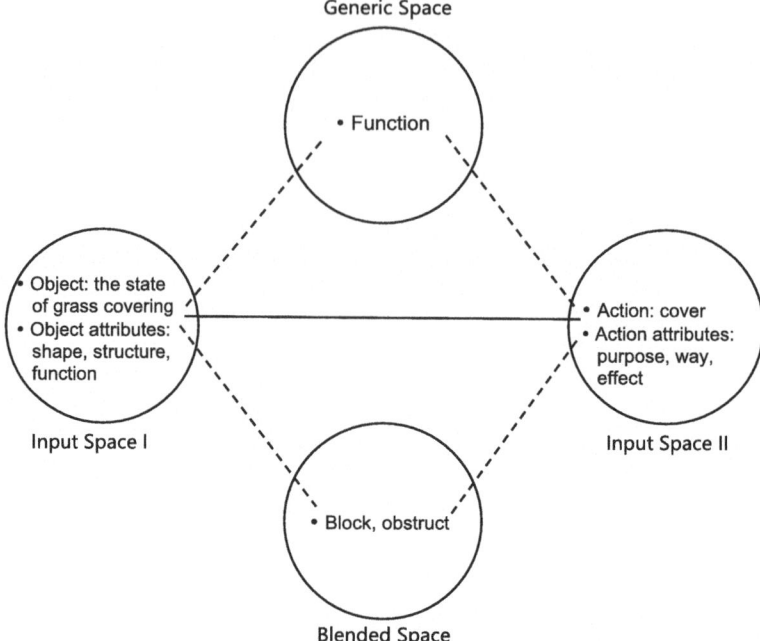

Fig. 2. Conceptual integration process from 蔽*bì* [N] to 蔽*bì* [V].

suggests that the integration space of one conceptual blending network can serve as the input space for another, forming a new blended space [16]. It is observed that through the reorganization of semantic motivation, several senses of 闭*bì* and 蔽*bì* have undergone integration, resulting in two different cognitive domains merging into a single sense. On the one hand, both 闭*bì* and 蔽*bì* share the characteristics of 'to hide' or 'to conceal' as the purpose and outcome of their actions, creating a relationship of synonymic aggregation between their senses. On the other hand, due to the partial similarity in the morphemes of 闭*bì* and 蔽*bì*, when the semantic assimilation of synonymous compound words occurs, the shared morphemes act as intermediaries, further strengthening the connection between their common senses.

Table 1 shows that the meanings of 'to block, to obstruct' are activated and constructed when 闭*bì* and 蔽*bì* are combined with '塞' (*sè*, 'plug'), forming the synonymous compound expressions '闭塞' (*bì sè*, 'to block') and '蔽塞' (*bì sè*, 'to obstruct'). The former expression 闭塞 *bì sè*, emphasizes the act of closing a passageway, while the latter 蔽塞 *bì sè*, highlights the act of covering or concealing an object to impede its passage. As a result, they are integrated into the broader semantic meaning of blocking or congestion.

In spite of this, the LIVAC synchronous Chinese corpus shows that the usage of '闭塞' (*bì sè*, 'to block') and '蔽塞' (*bì sè*, 'to obstruct') is different in scope. Specifically, 闭塞 *bì sè* is used across a relatively wide range of Chinese-speaking regions, including Taiwan, Singapore, and other global Chinese-speaking communities. As an adjective, it describes a state of blockage, referring not only to physical obstructions, such as blocked

Table 1. The Construction of the Overlapping Senses of 闭*bì* and 蔽*bì*

Meaning Construction	Input space I:闭*bì*	Input space II: 蔽*bì*	Generic space	Blended space
堵塞、壅塞 *dǔ sè, yōng sè* to block, to obstruct	To shut off an object through the action of closing or sealing	To prevent the passage of something by using an object as a barrier	To serve the function of creating some form of blockage or obstruction	To block at both physical and abstract levels
隐蔽、躲藏 *yǐn bì, duǒ cáng* to conceal, to hide	To cover or hide an object through the act of closing	To prevent an object from being noticed through the act of covering	To achieve the purpose of hiding and concealing	To prevent an object or event from being exposed

traffic routes, but also to non-physical barriers, including disruptions in information flow, social interaction, or other forms of isolation. When used as a noun, it typically denotes an abstract concept, signifying a state of obstruction or lack of flow. By comparison, 蔽塞 *bì sè* is only found in usage within Hong Kong. It is typically employed as an adjective to describe a state of physical obstruction, such as in the phrase '渠道蔽塞' (*qú dào bì sè*, 'blocked channel').

It is evident that although 闭塞 *bì sè* and 蔽塞 *bì sè* as synonymous compounds both carry the meaning of 'to block' or 'to obstruct', they have gradually developed distinct usage contexts and are now clearly differentiated in semantic domains.

In examining the semantic construction of 'to conceal' and 'to hide', it becomes clear that their meanings can be traced through the conceptual integration of 闭*bì* and 蔽*bì* with '隐' (*yǐn*, 'hide'). Diachronically, the use of '隐闭' (*yǐn bì*, 'to hide') has existed since the Han Dynasty, which demonstrates that it has traditionally been regarded as a semantic feature extending from the act of closure to avoidance, concealment, and non-interaction with the outside world. Synchronically, this expression is now retained only in Hong Kong, but its meaning has undergone a shift, focusing more on the concept of '隐' (*yǐn*, 'hide') to describe a state or location that is not easily detectable, such as ' 隐闭空间' (*yǐn bì kōng jiān*, 'hidden space'). In Hong Kong, '隐蔽' (*yǐn bì*, 'conceal') is often used in collocation with people, such as '隐蔽青年' (*yǐn bì qīng nián*, 'hidden youth'), which refers to self-contained youth who mostly stay at home and do not work.

Thus, it can be observed that '隐蔽' (*yǐn bì*, 'conceal'), both diachronically and synchronically, is used relatively widely across various regions. Describing physical spaces as '隐蔽' (*yǐn bì*, 'conceal') is a common usage in Chinese-speaking areas, where the word highlights elements such as scenes, locations, and events within the integration space.

In summary, the various senses of these polysemous words are not inherent properties of the words themselves, but rather byproducts of conceptual integration processes. They are also linguistic facts tied to the input spaces [17]. The polysemy of 闭*bì* and 蔽*bì* results from the spatial mapping process of selecting different elements of the input space and selectively projecting and refining them within the contextual knowledge framework. The polysemy of 闭*bì* and 蔽*bì* results from the selection of different input space elements during the process of spatial mapping, combined with background knowledge frameworks for selective projection and refinement. Then, conceptual integration combines the frameworks of 闭*bì* and 蔽*bì*, forming dynamically evolving mental spaces that enable ongoing meaning construction. This allows multiple senses to be differentiated, leading to the development of polysemy through integration.

6 Conclusion

This paper attempts to explain the phenomenon of polysemy in Chinese homophonous near-synonyms through conceptual blending theory. By employing corpus analysis, the study explores how polysemous words expand from one conceptual domain to another via conceptual blending, and investigates the relationships and evolutionary paths between their senses. The diachronic analysis reveals that the semantic evolution of the homophonous polysemous pair 闭*bì* and 蔽*bì* exhibits a hybrid developmental trend, combining both radial and chain-like patterns. It can be observed that several senses either increase, decrease, or shift based on the original meaning. In the process of evolution, polysemous words maintain stable core senses, and the increase in the frequency of sense usage drives the continual differentiation and development of senses during the process of evolution. It can also be concluded from the above analyses that the integration of concepts tends to facilitate the construction of meaning by means of in a systematic way that exhibits hierarchical characteristics. Through the activation of different cognitive background knowledge frameworks, polysemous words evolve from low-level integration of basic senses to high-level integration of extended senses. At the same time, connections are established both horizontally and vertically between the levels through related or similar semantics, mapping onto more abstract and broader dimensions. This creates a continuum in the semantic construction of polysemous words.

We found that in the process of semantic construction for 闭*bì* and 蔽*bì*, their overlapping senses exhibit a competitive relationship, with their aggregated senses coexisting over a certain period of time. The competition of the senses between 闭*bì* and 蔽*bì* in terms of the diachronic alternation was basically completed in the Modern Chinese period. In the process of evolution, their lexical alternation reflects the feature of increasingly clear functional divisions. Based on the principle of linguistic economy, similar senses between polysemous words are regulated and optimized through processes of transformation or reduction. This leads to the development of sense clusters that are associated with and similar to the core meaning of the word, ultimately maintaining a balance between words and senses within the lexical system.

Acknowledgments. This work was supported by the General Project of National Social Science Fund of China (23BYY19), and the Postgraduate Scientific Research and Innovation Program from University of Chinese Academy of Social Sciences (Graduate School of Chinese Academy of Social Sciences) (2024-KY-033).

References

1. Wu, Z.: Modern Russian vocabulary polysemy research. Commercial Press, Beijing (2007). (in Chinese)
2. Li, T.: Discourse coherence: a cognitive frame approach. National Defense Industry Press, Beijing (2013). (in Chinese)
3. Zhang, J.: A study on the evolution of Chinese concept domain members of 'opening and closing.' Zhejiang Normal University, Zhejiang (2021). (in Chinese)
4. Yue, X.: The diachronic alternations of basic words in covering semantic field. J. Tonghua Norm. Univ. **37**(3), 44–50 (2016). (in Chinese)
5. Feng, W.: Research on cognitive linguistics and Chinese vocabulary. World Book Publishing Company, Xi'an (2018). (in Chinese)
6. Lakoff, G.: Women, fire, and dangerous things: what categories revealed about the mind. The University of Chicago Press, Chicago (1987)
7. Anttila, R.: Historical and comparative linguistics. John Benjamins Publishing, Amsterdam (1989)
8. Lee, C.J.: Some hypotheses concerning the evolution of polysemous words. J. Psycholinguisic Res. **19**, 211–219 (1990)
9. Fauconnier, G., Turner, M.: Conceptual blending, form and meaning. Rech. En Commun. **19**, 57–86 (2003)
10. Fauconnier, G., Turner, M.: Blending as a central process of grammar: expanded version. In: Goldberg, A. (ed.) Conceptual Structure, Discourse, and Language, pp. 113–129. CSLI Publications, Stanford (1998)
11. Talmy, L.: Force dynamics in language and cognition. Cogn. Sci. **12**(1), 49–100 (1988)
12. Mori, S.: A cognitive analysis of the preposition over: image-schema transformations and metaphorical extensions. Canadian J. Linguist. Rev. Can. de Linguist. **64**(3), 444–474 (2019)
13. Tremblay, C., Macoir, J., Langlois, M., Monetta, L.: The role of polysemy on metaphor comprehension processing: The example of Parkinson's disease. J. Neurolinguistics **30**, 1–13 (2014)
14. Hsu, Tun-Yu., Hong, Jia-Fei.: Lexical semantic evolution of polysemous words in Ancient Chinese—Taking zǒu as an example. In: Liu, M., Kit, C., Qi, S. (eds.) Chinese Lexical Semantics. CLSW 2020, pp. 756–763. Springer International Publishing, Cham (2021). https://doi.org/10.1007/978-3-030-81197-6_62
15. Ancient Chinese Corpus. https://www.zhonghuayuwen.org/#/ylkzx/gdhyylk. Accessed 2 Nov 2024
16. Zawada, B.: Conceptual integration and intercategorial polysemy. Lang. Matters **38**(1), 150–175 (2007)
17. Fauconnier, G., Turner, M.: The way we think: conceptual blending and the minds hidden complexities. Basic Books, New York (2002)

Polarity Shift in the "*bù* 'not' + Adj./Verb" Construction

Nan Li[1,2,3](✉) 🄳 and Weidong Zhan[1,2]

[1] Department of Chinese Language and Literature, Peking University, Beijing, China
{linan2017,zwd}@pku.edu.cn
[2] Center for Chinese Linguistics, Peking University, Beijing, China
[3] Department of Information and Computing Sciences, Utrecht University, Utrecht, The Netherlands

Abstract. This paper examines polarity shift in the "不 *bù* 'not' + adj./verb" construction in Chinese. Through quantitative analysis, we demonstrate the widespread occurrence of this phenomenon. By categorizing and analyzing gradable adjectives and psychological verbs, we identify four key conditions for polarity shift within this construction: (1) the adjective or verb belongs to a pair of words with opposing polarities ("adj. - ~adj."/"verb - ~verb"); (2) the meaning of "不 *bù* 'not' + adj./verb" is equivalent to its antonymic counterpart, "~adj."/"~verb"; (3) the adjective or verb exhibits subjective emotional bias; and (4) an intermediate zone exists between "adj."/"verb" and "~adj."/"~verb". We conclude by discussing potential explanations for this phenomenon, including challenges in applying degree semantics to account for polarity shift.

Keywords: Gradable adjectives · Psychological verbs · Negation · Polarity · Degree semantics

1 Introduction

From a logical standpoint, negation implies a binary, contradictory relation, meaning that for a proposition p and its negation $\neg p$, there is no intermediate state between p and $\neg p$. However, in Chinese, when the negation adverb 不 *bù* "not" combines with certain predicates P, the semantic relations between the entire phrase and the predicate vary.

In examples (1), (2), and (3)[1], the bolded segments represent "不 'not' + adj." constructions which respectively negate the propositions "the food is clean", "the step is high", and "the crow is black". In examples (4) and (5), the bolded segments are "不 'not' + verb" constructions that negate the propositions "they like Neo-Confucianists" and "I advocate promoting propaganda".

---

[1] Due to length constraints, we have shortened example sentences in this paper. Complete sentences are available in the CLSW 2024 proceedings (Chinese version), sourced from the PKU CCL Corpus [1].

P. Jin et al. (Eds.): CLSW 2024, LNAI 15552, pp. 340–354, 2025.
https://doi.org/10.1007/978-981-96-3509-2_25

While these expressions negate specific propositions, rewriting them in semantically equivalent affirmative forms reveals varied semantic relations between these affirmative expressions and their negative counterparts. For example, in example (1), the "不 'not' + adj./verb" construction conveys "the food is dirty or problematic"; in example (2), "the step is low or neither high nor low"; in example (3), "the crow is white, gray, or another possible color"; in example (4), "they hate Neo-Confucianists"; and in example (5), "I oppose or neither advocate nor oppose promoting propaganda".

(1)   少年　儿童 应该　不 吃 不　干净　食物。
       young child should not eat **not clean** food
       "Children should not eat **unclean** food."

(2)   门前　　　　　　台阶 不　高。
       in_front_of_door step **not high**
       "The step in front of the door is **not high**."

(3)   我们 遇到　　一 只　不　黑　　的 乌鸦。
       we   encounter one CLF **not black** DE crow
       "We encountered a crow that was **not black**."

(4)   他们 不　喜欢 理学家。
       they **not like** Neo-Confucianists
       "They **do not like** Neo-Confucianists."

(5)   对 搞　宣传，　　我 既　　不 反对，　也　不　提倡。
       for doing propaganda, I　**neither not oppose**, also not advocate
       "For promoting propaganda, I **neither oppose** it nor advocate for it."

It is relatively straightforward to explain color adjectives like 黑 "black", 白 "white", and 灰 "gray" because they represent a range of colors rather than opposites. However, for pairs such as 干净-脏 "clean-dirty"[2], 高-矮 "high-low", 喜欢-讨厌 "like-hate", and 提倡-反对 "advocate-oppose", which express opposite concepts, the semantic relations are more nuanced. For instance, 不干净 "not + clean" is equivalent to 脏 "dirty", and 不喜欢 "not + like" is equivalent to 讨厌 "hate". In contrast, 不高 "not + high" implies "neither high nor low" combined with 矮 "low", while 不提倡 "not + advocate" suggests "neither advocate nor oppose" along with 反对 "oppose". Thus, for adjectives like 干净 "clean" and verbs like 喜欢 "like", the negation introduced by "不 'not' + adj./verb" does not follow binary logic but instead introduces polarity opposition. Table 1 contrasts

---

[2] We propose that there is an intermediate zone between 干净 "clean" and 脏 "dirty" regarding cleanliness, indicating a level of "not quite clean, but not dirty either". An example from the CCL Corpus supports this point: 白花花的水，哪能就这么浪费呀！裤头袜子有什么要紧啊！都是贴身穿的，又不脏。 "Such clean water, how can we just waste it? What's the big deal about not washing underwear and socks? They are worn close to the skin, and they're not dirty." Here, the speaker persuades someone to conserve water by saying that the worn underwear and socks are not dirty, while worn clothes are certainly not clean either.

the logical and actual interpretations of adjectives and verbs in the "不 'not' + adj./verb" construction on a scale of degrees.

Table 1. Degrees of "adj."/"verb" and "不 'not' + adj./verb" from Example (1)-(5)

Category	adj./verb	Logical and Actual Degrees On a Scale
Cleanliness	干净 "clean"	*clean* - **not quite clean but not dirty -** dirty
Height	高 "high"	*high* - medium (neither high nor low) - low
Liking	喜欢 "like"	*like* - neither like nor dislike - **dislike**
Advocacy	提倡 "advocate"	*advocate* - neither advocate nor oppose - oppose

* The italicized segments are degrees of "adj./verb". The bolded and highlighted segments are logical and actual degrees of "不 'not' + adj./verb", respectively.

Examples (1) and (4) highlight a phenomenon where, negation in the "不 'not' + adj./verb" construction does not introduce binary contradiction but rather polarity opposition. We refer to this as **Polarity Shift**, as the negation causes **a semantic shift** toward **the opposite polarity** of what the adjective or verb initially indicates on the scale (from logical to actual degrees, as shown in Table 1). For example, 不干净 "not + clean" shifts in meaning from "not quite clean but not dirty - dirty" to simply "dirty", aligning with 脏 "dirty".

Table 2. 100 Instances of the "不 'not' + adj." Construction in Shuo Wang's Novels

	Percentage
Exhibiting Polarity Shift	40%
Not Exhibiting Polarity Shift	60%

Table 3. Details of Instances Exhibiting Polarity Shift in Table 2

"不 'not' + adj."	Count	"不 'not' + adj."	Count	"不 'not' + adj."	Count
不好 "not + good"	26	不容易 "not + easy"	6	不高兴 "not + happy"	2
不严谨 "not + rigorous"	1	不客气 "not + polite"	1	不明白 "not + clear"	1
不真实 "not + truthful"	1	不真诚 "not + sincere"	1	不自由 "not + free"	1
		Total	**40**		

A quantitative analysis reveals that adjectives frequently exhibit polarity shift. Using a tokenization and POS-tagging tool [2], we extracted and analyzed the first 100 instances of gradable adjectives in the "不 'not' + adj." construction from 王朔 *Shuo Wang*'s novels 顽主 "The Troubleshooters" and 一点正经没有 "No Seriousness at All"[3]. Of these instances, 40% demonstrate polarity shift, with 26 occurrences of 不好 "not + good". Further details are provided in Table 2 and 3.

This paper explores the features of adjectives and verbs that trigger polarity shift, identifies the conditions under which polarity shift occurs, and proposes a potential explanation for this phenomenon.

2   The Selectivity for Adjectives in Polarity Shift

2.1   Previous Research

The syntactic distribution and semantic features of adjectives in Modern Chinese have been extensively studied [3–7]. A widely accepted view is that Chinese adjectives indicate the properties or states of objects. Zhu argued that adjectives can be classified based on structural complexity into simple forms and complex forms, which correspond to his later termed "gradable adjectives" and "non-gradable adjectives" [3,4][4]. Non-gradable adjectives are primarily descriptive, generally cannot be modified by degree adverbs or 不 "not", do not occur in pairs, and do not exhibit polarity. Therefore, they do not trigger polarity shift in the "不 'not' + adj." construction. This study focuses primarily on gradable adjectives.

Gradable adjectives, which denote properties of objects [3,6], can be further subdivided based on syntactic distribution and semantic features. [11] identified a series of gradable adjectives that appear in pairs, such as 大-小 "big-small" and 长-短 "long-short", based on their ability to occur in the "adj. + 了 (*le*) + quantifier" construction. [8] classified adjectives according to their scalar features into three types: 干净 "clean"-type words, 大小 "big-small"-type words, and

---

[3] 王朔 *Shuo Wang* is a contemporary Chinese novelist whose works are widely regarded as representative of Modern Chinese and are thus frequently used in linguistic analyses.

[4] Zhu classified adjectives in Modern Chinese into two types, 性质形容词 "property adjectives" and 状态形容词 "state adjectives", which respectively indicate the properties and states of objects. "Property adjectives" include monosyllabic adjectives (e.g., 大 "big", 红 "red", 多 "many") and some bisyllabic adjectives (e.g., 干净 "clean", 大方 "generous", 规矩 "proper"). "State adjectives", on the other hand, include reduplicative forms (e.g., 老老实实 "honest", 黑乎乎 "darkish"), adjectives with postmodifiers (e.g., 黑乎乎 "darkish", 黑咕隆咚 "pitch-black"), 煞白 "deathly pale"-type words, "很/挺 'very' + adj. + 的 *de*" construction (e.g., 挺好的 "pretty good"), and compounds with internal parallel structures (e.g., 又高又大 "tall and big"). Although this classification is widely recognized among Chinese linguists, it lacks direct counterparts in English linguistics. From the perspective of degree semantics, "property adjectives" can be seen as "gradable adjectives" and "state adjectives" as "non-gradable adjectives". In this paper we use the terms gradable and non-gradable adjectives to refer to these two types.

冷热 "cold-hot"-type words. [9] categorized adjectives into four types based on their quantitative features: rank-order adjectives, percentage adjectives, extreme adjectives, and positive/negative value adjectives. [6] divided adjectives into quantitative and non-quantitative categories based on their ability to be modified by degree markers. [16] classified adjectives into relative and absolute ones based on the presence of an upper or lower bound in their scalar structure, and into gradable and non-gradable adjectives based on their degree of gradability. [10] categorized adjectives into seven types based on their gradable structures: nominal adjectives, totally open ordinal adjectives, lower closed interval adjectives, upper closed interval adjectives, totally closed interval adjectives, totally open interval adjectives, and lower closed ratio adjectives.

Most research has centered on the gradability, scalar structure, and quantitative features of gradable adjectives, laying a foundation for discussing polarity in this section. However, existing studies have rarely examined the semantic features of the "不 'not' + adj." structure, especially in relation to polarity shift. Previous discussions mainly address when 不 "not" can modify adjectives and the its relation to degree semantics. For example, [9] noted that "any adjective that can be modified by the sequence 有点儿-很-最 'a little-very-most' can also be negated by 不 'not' ", and that the "不 'not' + adj." construction denotes a lower scalar degree. Some issues, like category overlaps, remain unresolved.

This section provides a detailed classification and analysis of gradable adjectives and examines the selectivity for adjectives in the "不 'not' + adj." construction that triggers polarity shift.

2.2 Classification of Adjectives

For a "不 'not' + adj." construction to trigger polarity shift, the adjective must belong to a pair of adjectives denoting opposing polarities. Thus, each category comprises pairs of gradable adjectives with opposite polarities.

高-低 "High-Low" Category. The 高-低 "high-low" category includes adjectives that describe the degree to which an object exhibits specific physical properties or dimensions. For example, 桌子很长/短 "the table is very long/short" refers to the table's position along the dimension of length. Between these polarities, there is often an intermediate zone, such as 高-中-低 "high-**middle**-low" or 早-**准时**-晚 "early-**on time**-late". Even without an explicit linguistic form for "middle/medium", phrases like 不胖不瘦 "not fat + not thin", 不浓不淡 "not thick + not light", and 不远不近 "not far + not near" reflect a cognitive recognition of this intermediate zone. These adjectives convey objective attributes and people generally show no subjective emotional preference for either polarity. This category aligns closely with the 量度形容词 "scalar adjectives" as defined in [11].

(6)   俺的 脚   不   重。
　　　 my   foot **not heavy**
　　　 "My foot is **not heavy**."

(7)   隔   条   不 窄   　的 胡同 就是 中队部。
　　　 across CLF **not narrow** DE alley is   squad-headquarters
　　　 "The squad headquarters is right across a **not narrow** alley."

Adjectives in the 高-低 "high-low" category do not trigger polarity shift. Each word in a pair from this category can occur in the "不 'not' + adj." construction, but this creates binary contradiction rather than polarity opposition. Whether negating the positive or negative polarity, "不 'not' + adj." semantically corresponds to "~adj."[5] in combination with the intermediate zone between "adj." and "~adj.", as seen in examples (2), (6), and (7). For instance, "The foot is not heavy" in example (6) is equivalent to "The foot is light" ∨ "The foot is neither heavy nor light." Similarly, "The alley is not narrow" in example (7) equals "The alley is wide" ∨ "The alley is neither wide nor narrow."

干-湿 "Dry-Wet" Category. This category also describes objective properties. For example, 这抹布是干/湿的 "the rag is dry/wet" refers to the moisture level of the rag. Similar to 高-低 "high-low", the 干-湿 "dry-wet" category includes two opposing polarities and people show no subjective emotional bias toward either polarity. However, unlike the 高-低 "high-low" category, 干-湿 "dry-wet" lacks an intermediate zone. For instance, an object is "dry" only when all moisture is completely removed and the humidity is reduced to zero, whereas any non-zero humidity is considered "wet". Due to this feature, polarity opposition aligns with contradictory opposition here: 不干 "not dry" = 湿 "wet", and 不湿 "not wet" = 干 "dry". Thus, polarity shift does not occur in this category.

(8)   什么 东西 掉进 水里 也   打 不 湿?
　　　 what thing falls into water also **not wet**
　　　 "What could fall into the water but **not get wet?**"

(9)   人们 在 研究   不 纯   的 气体。
　　　 people are studying **not pure** DE gases
　　　 "People are studying **impure** gases."

Currently, only two pairs fall into this category: 干-湿 "dry-wet" and 纯-杂 "pure-impure", as illustrated in examples (8) and (9).

诚实-虚伪 "Honest-Deceitful" Category. This category describes subjective qualities related to emotions, character, or evaluations. People generally have strong preferences for the positive polarity, such as 诚实 "honesty", 安全 "safe",

---

[5] In this paper, we use "~adj." and "~verb" to refer to the antonymic counterparts of "adj." and "verb", respectively.

and 公平 "fair", while rejecting the negative polarity, such as 虚伪 "deceitful", 危险 "danger", and 偏心 "biased".

For adjectives in this category, the "不 'not' + adj." construction is semantically equivalent to the antonymic adjective "~adj.", regardless of whether it denotes a positive or negative polarity. For example, 不明确 "not + clear" in example (10) means "vague"/"chaotic", while example (11) demonstrates that 不安全 "not + safe" conveys 安全的反义词 "the antonym of security". Like 干-湿 "dry-wet", this category lacks an intermediate zone, with no cognitive state between polarities such as "neither clear nor vague", "neither tidy nor messy", or "neither safe nor dangerous". Therefore, polarity shift does not occur in this category either.

(10)   目的 不 **明确** 的 管理,   必然   是 混乱   的。
        goal **not clear** DE management, inevitably is chaotic DE
        "Management with **unclear goals** will inevitably be chaotic."

(11)   金融   安全   的 反义词 是 金融   不 安全,   但 绝对
        financial security DE antonym is finance **not secure**, but absolutely
        不是 危机 爆发。
        not   crisis outbreak
        "The antonym of financial security is **financial insecurity**, but it is certainly not crisis outbreak."

积极-消极 "Positive-Negative" Category. This category also describes subjective qualities, particularly psychological traits or evaluations, and is influenced by cultural factors and personal experiences. People often favor positive adjectives like 开心 "happy", 幸运 "lucky", and 成熟 "mature", while disfavoring negative ones like 伤心 "sad", 倒霉 "unlucky", and 幼稚 "childish".

An intermediate zone occurs between in this category. For instance, between 熟悉 "familiar" and 陌生 "unfamiliar", there is a state like "normal friend", and between 详细 "detailed" and 简略 "concise", there is 详略得当 "detailed and brief appropriately".

The intermediate zone allows for polarity shift, but only for the positive ends of these pairs. In contexts like 情绪不稳定 "emotion + unstable" in example (12), 必然出大乱子 "inevitably cause big trouble" in example (13), and the magazine title 小流氓 "little rascal" in example (14), expressions such as 不坚强 "not + strong", "不镇静" "not + calm", and 不文雅 "not + refined" exhibit negative polarities, which oppose the polarities indicated by 坚强 "strong", 镇静 "calm", and 文雅 "refined".

(12)   总   有人   情绪   不 稳定、理智 不   坚强。
        always someone emotions not stable, sense **not strong**
        "There are always people who have unstable emotions, and **weak** senses."

(13)   事   到   临头 不   镇静，必然   出   大乱子。
        matter arrive hushy **not calm**, inevitably cause big-trouble
        'When it comes to a critical moment, if one is **not calm**, it will inevitably
        lead to major trouble."

(14)   他 将   不 文雅   的 《小流氓》   刊名   改 为
        he changed **not refined** DE "Little-Rascals" magazine-title to be
        《龙虎门》。
        "Dragon-Tiger-Gate"
        "He changed the **unrefined** magazine title 'Little Rascals' to 'Dragon
        Tiger Gate.'"

However, the negative ends in the 积极-消极 "positive-negative" category do
not trigger polarity shift in the "不 'not' + adj." construction. As seen in examples (15) and (16), the negation in these cases introduces contradictory relation
rather than polarity shift, so 不消极 "not negative" ≠ "positive" and 不保守 "not
conservative" ≠ "avant-garde".

(15)   我 希望 一切 问题   都 以 不 **消极**   的 方式   解决。
        I hope all   problems all with **not negative** DE manner resolve
        "I hope all problems are resolved in a **non-negative** manner."

(16)   这个 计划 既 不 保守，   也 不 前卫。
        this plan both **not conservative**, also not avant-garde.
        "This plan is **neither conservative** nor avant-garde."

2.3 Summary

Based on the previous discussion, the conditions required for polarity shift in
the "不 'not' + adj." construction can be summarized as follows:

  (I) The "adj." belongs to a pair of words with opposing polarities ("adj. -
      ~adj.");
 (II) The meaning of "不 'not' + adj." is equivalent to "~adj.";
(III) The "adj." exhibits subjective emotional biases;
(IV) An intermediate zone exists between "adj." and "~adj.".

Table 4 shows the distribution of these conditions and the occurrence of polarity shift across the adjective classifications discussed in this section. We observe
a continuum-like distribution across Conditions I, II, III, and IV from the top
to the bottom of the table, with one exception in Condition IV, where the first
and fourth categories contrast with the second and third. Polarity shift occurs
only in the 积极-消极 "positive-negative" category, with an asymmetry between
the positive and negative ends.

Table 4. Conditions for Polarity Shift based on Classification of Adjectives

Category		Cond. I	Cond. II	Cond. III	Cond. IV	Polarity Shift
高-低 "high-low"	positive	+	-	-	+	-
	negative	+	-	-	+	-
干-湿 "dry-wet"	positive	+	+	-	-	-
	negative	+	+	-	-	-
诚实-虚伪 "honest-deceitful"	positive	+	+	+	-	-
	negative	+	+	+	-	-
积极-消极 "positive-negative"	positive	+	+	+	+	+
	negative	+	-	+	+	-

*"+/−" indicates whether the condition or conclusion holds.

Condition II aligns closely with the definition of polarity shift, but lacks the concept of "shift". Notably, Conditions II and IV are intrinsically connected: if Condition IV does not hold-meaning no intermediate zone exists between the two polarities-then Condition II must hold, implying that negating one polarity inevitably points to the opposite polarity. Only when Condition IV holds can contradictory and polarity oppositions along the scale diverge, allowing polarity opposition to replace the contradictory opposition and enabling polarity shift along the scale.

3   The Selectivity for Verbs in Polarity Shift

3.1   Insights from the Classification of Adjectives

Following a similar approach as in the previous section, polarity shift in the "不 'not' + verb" construction theoretically requires the verb to exhibit polarity, meaning it must possess degree semantics, allowing modification by negation adverbs like 不 "not" and degree adverbs like 很 "very", 有点 "kind of", or 最 "most". A notable class of verbs with these features is psychological verbs.

Psychological verbs in Chinese have received relatively little attention in existing research, especially concerning degree semantics. [12] noted that psychological verbs semantically describe mental activities and can be syntactically identified by their appearance in the "Subject (a person) + 很 'very' + verb + Object" construction. The consistent modifiability of psychological verbs by 很 "very" sets them apart from other verbs, making them similar to adjectives. For this reason, [12] suggested classifying them as "adjectival verbs". Subsequent research has largely confirmed that the ability to combine with 很 "very" is a distinguishing feature of psychological verbs and explored this syntactic phenomenon from various perspectives [13,14].

In addition to their degree semantics, psychological verbs inherently carry subjective emotional bias, aligning with the conclusions drawn in the previous section. This section categorizes psychological verbs to examine their ability to exhibit polarity shift in the "不 'not' + verb" construction[6].

3.2 Classification of Psychological Verbs

爱-恨 "Love-Hate" Category. This category of psychological verbs has emotional polarities on a scale, such as 爱-恨 "love-hate", with an intermediate zone between these polarities. For instance, in example (17), the elderly woman 不爱 "not + love" drinking water, but this does not imply that she hates it-there is a neutral state where one feels neither joy nor aversion. For both positive and negative verbs in pairs of this category, the "不 'not' + verb" construction does not trigger polarity shift, as shown in examples (18) and (19). Tokyo residents 不欣赏 "not + appreciate" large courtyards, but this does not mean they 嫉妒 "envy" them. Similarly, 不嫉妒 "not + envy" others does not mean 羡慕 "admire" them.

(17)　老年　妇女　往往 不　爱　喝　水。
　　　 elderly women often **not love** drink water
　　　 "Elderly women often **does not love** to drink water."

(18)　东京　居民　　不　欣赏　　　深宅 大院。
　　　 Tokyo residents **not appreciate** large courtyards
　　　 "Tokyo residents **do not appreciate** large courtyards."

(19)　画师们　不　嫉妒 他人。
　　　 painters **not envy** others
　　　 "Painters **do not envy** others."

明白-纳闷 "Understand-Be Puzzled" Category. This category, silimar to the 干-湿 "dry-wet" category of adjectives, has no intermediate zone between polarities. Here, "不 'not' + verb" is semantically equivalent to the antonymic verb "~verb", and polarity shift does not occur. For example, in example (20), 不明白 "not + understand" means 纳闷 "being puzzled". Currently, the only pair of verbs identified in this category is 明白-纳闷 "understand-be puzzled".

(20)　自己 不　明白　　　该　　向　　哪个　方向　　努力。
　　　 self **not understand** should towards which direction strive
　　　 "One **does not understand** in which direction to strive."

喜欢-讨厌 "Like-Dislike" Category. This category also includes emotional polarities but with an intermediate zone. For instance, between "喜欢" "like" and 讨厌 "dislike", there exists a state of "not yet liking, but also not disliking".

---

[6] Some common psychological verbs, such as 感谢 "appreciate", 怀念 "miss", 强调 "emphasize", and 后悔 "regret", are not included in this discussion because they lack corresponding opposites in terms of polarity.

Similarly, between 信任 "trust" and 怀疑 "doubt", there is a state where one "has not yet established trust, but also does not suspect". For positive verbs in this category, occurring in the "不 'not' + verb" construction results in polarity shift. For example, in example (21), 不关心民间疾苦 "not + care about + the people's suffering" implies "ignore the people's suffering", and in example (22), 不满意 "not + be satisfied" means 失望 "be disappointed".

(21)   要   改正   不 关心 民众 疾苦   的 作风。
        must correct **not care** public hardships DE workstyle
        "The workstyle of **not caring** about the public's hardships must be corrected."

(22)   你 如果 不 **满意**,   可以 改   到   你 满意   为止。
        you if   **not satisfied**, can change until you satisfied end

Negative ends in this category, similar to those in the 积极-消极 "positive-negative" category of adjectives, do not trigger polarity opposition. For instance, in examples (23) and (24), 不忽视 "not + ignore" and 不失望 "not + be disappointed" do not imply 重视 "value" or 满意 "be satisfied". Therefore, polarity shift doesn't occur in these cases.

(23)   杰斐逊 并 不   忽视   财产权。
        Jefferson **not ignore** property rights
        "Jefferson **did not ignore** property rights."

(24)   他 不 让人   失望。
        he **not** let people **down**
        "He **do not let** people **down**."

To better showcase the characteristics of adjectives and verbs across categories and support future research, we provide additional examples in Tables 6 and 7 in the appendix. Due to space constraints, only Chinese terms are provided.

3.3 Summary

The conditions required for polarity shift in the "不 'not' + verb" construction can be summarized as follows. Table 5 demonstrates the distribution of these conditions and the occurrence of polarity shift across the (psychological) verb classifications.

(I) The "verb" belongs to a pair of words with opposing polarities ("verb - ~verb");
(II) The meaning of "不 'not' + verb" is equivalent to "~verb";
(III) The "verb" exhibits subjective emotional biases;
(IV) An intermediate zone exists between "verb" and "~verb".

The conditions above are parallel to those for the "不 'not' + adj." construction, as discussed in Sect. 2.3. Therefore, the conditions for polarity shift in the "不 'not' + adj./verb" construction can be uniformly presented as follows:

Table 5. Conditions for Polarity Shift based on Classification of Verbs

Category		Cond. I	Cond. II	Cond. III	Cond. IV	Polarity Shift
爱-恨 "love-hate"	positive	+	-	+	+	-
	negative	+	-	+	+	-
明白-纳闷 "understand-be puzzled"	positive	+	+	+	-	-
	negative	+	+	+	-	-
喜欢-讨厌 "like-dislike"	positive	+	+	+	+	+
	negative	+	-	+	+	-

*"+/−" indicates whether the condition or conclusion holds.

  (I) The "adj."/"verb" belongs to a pair of words with opposing polarities ("adj. - ~adj."/"verb - ~verb");

 (II) The meaning of "不 'not' + adj./verb" is equivalent to "~adj."/"~verb";

(III) The "adj."/"verb" exhibits subjective emotional biases;

(IV) An intermediate zone exists between "adj."/"verb" and "~adj."/"~verb".

4 Discussion

The analyses in the previous sections reveal that the occurrence of polarity shift in the "不 'not' + adj./verb" construction is closely related to the scalar properties of adjectives and verbs. This phenomenon occurs only when there is an intermediate zone between two polarities, allowing the meaning of the entire phase to shift from a combination of the intermediate zone and one polarity to the other polarity on a scale. Furthermore, our discussion indicates that, beyond the other three prerequisites-(1) the adjective or verb must have polarity, (2) the meaning of "不 'not' + adj./verb" must be equivalent to "~adj."/"~verb", and (3) an intermediate zone must exist between "adj."/"verb" and "~adj."/"~verb"-the subjective emotional bias of "adj."/"verb" also plays a critical role in exhibiting polarity shift.

Degree semantics introduces "degree" as a key element in semantics, suggesting that gradability in natural language is tied to scalar structures [7,15–17]. For adjectives, degree semantics formalizes their function as mapping an individual x to a specific value (or range) y on a relevant scale axis.

[7,17] each proposed models of scalar structure for positive and negative adjectives in Chinese (see Fig. 1). [17] argued that positive and negative adjectives map to complementary intervals: positive adjectives relate to a range from zero to a positive value $[0, n]$, which is always positive and monotonically increasing with a minimun value 0, while negative adjectives project onto a range from a positive value down to negative infinity $[-\infty, n]$, with no minimum value or objective zero point. [7] proposed that the positive range extends from a standard point $(N - p)$ upwards to infinity $[N - p, +\infty]$, while the negative range extends from a negative standard point $(N - n)$ down to the base of the scale (namely 0) $[0, N - n]$, with a 中庸区间 "medium zone" between the two standard points $[N - n, N - p]$. Both models claim that they can explain the asymmetric

syntactic distribution in antonymous adjective pairs, such as the phenomenon that only positive adjectives can combine with the degree marker 度 "degree" to form metonymic expressions and the relation between presupposed degrees of adjectives and their compatibility with the "X (an object) + 有多 'how much' + adj.?" construction.

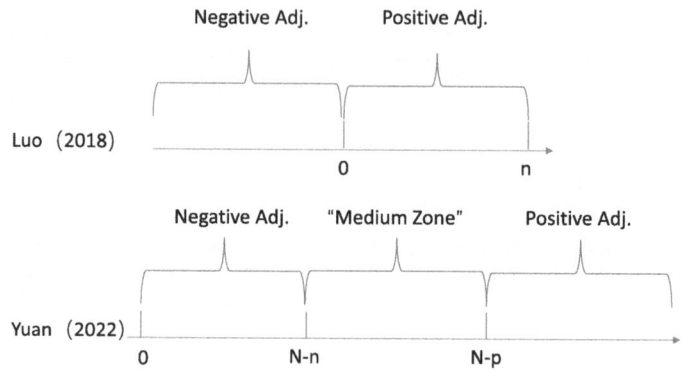

Fig. 1. Scalar Structures of Adjectives [7,17]

This paper does not intend to examine the syntactic and semantic details of gradable adjectives fully, nor to judge the superiority of these two scalar models. However, based on previous discussions, [17]'s model does not account for the intermediate zone between polarities, as observed in categories like 高-低 "high-low", 积极-消极 "positive-negative", 爱-恨 "love-hate", and 喜欢-讨厌 "like-dislike". Furthermore, neither model offers an potential explanation for polarity shift. They do not address the coexistence and distinction between contradictory and polarity opposition on a scale. An open question remained: could subjective emotional bias, as highlighted in Condition IV, pose challenges to modeling scalar structure?

Pragmatic analysis might offer new insights. [18] applied game theory to analyze the use of euphemistic expressions to express negative meanings (e.g., 不太聪明 "not + very + smart" as a euphemism for "stupid"). He observed that (1) euphemistic expressions are particularly effective in softening a speaker's tone, making the language more appropriate for some situational context, and (2) once these euphemistic expressions with negative meanings become conventionalized and grammaticalized, they develop into a communicative strategy that serves both speaker and listener. This convention makes speakers more likely to adopt euphemistic expressions in such cases.

In polarity shift, subjective preferences for positive terms in pairs from categories like 积极-消极 "positive-negative" or 喜欢-讨厌 "like-dislike" influence the pragmatic and emotional nuances of these words, affecting their frequency and distribution. People often combine positive words with negation to express negative meanings rather than using inherently negative words. Over time, this usage pattern can shift the opposition type in "不 'not' + adj./verb" construcions, reinterpreting contradictory opposition as polarity opposition and giving rise to polarity shift.

We recommend further research on incorporating subjective emotional bias into degree semantics and scalar structure to explain the coexistence of contradictory and polarity opposition on scales. Additionally, the impact of emotional bias on the syntax and semantics of relevant adjectives and verbs, as well as the psychological basis for intermediate zones between polarities, merits deeper investigation.

Acknowledgments. This research was conducted while the first author was affiliated with Peking University. This work was supported by the Major Project of the Ministry of Education, China, titled "Comprehensive Language Knowledge Base Research for Machine Language Capability Evaluation" (Project No. 22JJD740004). We would also like to thank the anonymous reviewers for their valuable feedback.

Disclosure of Interests. The authors have no competing interests to declare that are relevant to the content of this article.

Appendix

Table 6. Example Adjective Pairs by Category

Category	Examples
高-低 "high-low"	高-低(矮) 大-小 长-短 宽-窄 厚-薄 粗-细 深-浅 重-轻 远-近 快-慢 多-少 贵-便宜 早-晚 老-少 胖-瘦 硬-软 密-疏 稠-稀 浓-淡 清-浊 热-冷 满-空 好-坏(差)
干-湿 "dry-wet"	干-湿 纯-杂
诚实-虚伪 "honest-deceitful"	诚实-虚伪 安全-危险 公平-偏心 踏实-担心 自然-牵强 明确-含糊 清楚-模糊 整齐-杂乱
积极-消极 "positive-negative"	积极-消极 干净-脏 好-坏 好看-难看 灵活-死板 熟练-生疏 深刻-肤浅 高兴-难过 开心-伤心 细心-粗心 镇静-慌张 干脆-拖拉 坚强-软弱 详细-简略 光荣-可耻 严格-宽松 聪明-笨 清醒-糊涂 果断-犹豫 开明-保守 节俭-浪费 舒服-难受 幸福-痛苦 安静-吵闹 民主-专制 大方-小气 文雅-粗俗 熟悉-陌生 幸运-倒霉 主动-被动 热心-冷淡 认真-马虎 简单(容易)-困难 成熟-幼稚 宽裕-拮据 常见-罕见 善良-邪恶

Table 7. Example Verb Pairs by Category

Category	Examples
爱-恨 "love-hate"	爱-恨 欢迎-讨厌 提倡-反对 欣赏(羡慕)-嫉妒 惦记-忘记
明白-纳闷 "understand-be puzzled"	明白-纳闷
喜欢-讨厌 "like-dislike"	喜欢-讨厌 赞同(同意)-反对 关心-忽视 信任-怀疑 理解-误解 满意-失望 重视-轻视 尊重-轻慢

References

1. Zhan, W., Guo, R., Chang, B., Chen, Y., Chen, L.: The building of the CCL Corpus: its design and implementation. Corpus Linguist. **1**, 71–86 (2019). (in Chinese)
2. Luo, R., Xu, J., Zhang, Y., Zhang, Z., Ren, X., Sun, X.: PKUSEG: a toolkit for multi-domain Chinese word segmentation. arXiv preprint arXiv:1906.11455v3 (2019)
3. Zhu, D.: Xiàndài hànyu xíngróngcí yánjiū "A study of modern Chinese adjectives". Yuyán yánjiū "Linguistic Studies" **1**(1), 1–3 (1956). (in Chinese)
4. Zhu, D.: Yufǎ jiǎngyì "Lecture Notes on Grammar," 1st edn. The Commercial Press, Beijing (1982). (in Chinese)
5. Shen, J.: Shuō "youjiè" yu "wújiè" "On 'boundedness' and 'unboundedness' ' ". Stud. Chin. Lang. **5**, 367–380 (1995). (in Chinese)
6. Zhang, G.: A Study of the Function and Cognition of Modern Chinese Adjectives, 1st edn. The Commercial Press, Beijing (2006). (in Chinese)
7. Yuan, Y.: The polar degree of adjectives and their sentence-completing restrictions. Stud. Chin. Lang. **2**, 131–144 (2022). (in Chinese)
8. Huang, G., Shi, Y.: Hányu xíngróngcí de you biāojì hé wú biāojì xiànxiàng "The marked and unmarked phenomena of Chinese adjectives". Stud. Chin. Lang. **6**, 401–409 (1993). (in Chinese)
9. Shi, Y.: The effect of the quantity properties of adjectives on their syntactic behaviors. Chin. Teach. World **2**, 13–26 (2003). (in Chinese)
10. Chen, Y.: Constraints of scale structures on Chinese adjectives' syntactic behaviors. Master's thesis, Hunan University (2019). (in Chinese)
11. Lu, J.: Shuō liàngdù xíngróngcí "On gradable adjectives". Lang. Teach. Linguist. Stud. **3**, 46–59 (1989). (in Chinese)
12. Zhou, Y., Shao, J.: Hànyu xīnlǐ dòngcí jíqí jùxíng "Chinese psych-verb and its sentence patterns". Yuwén yánjiū "Chin. Lang. Stud." **3**, 32–48 (1993). (in Chinese)
13. Yang, H.: Shìlùn xīnlǐ zhuàngtài dòngcí jíqí bīnyu de lèixíng "A study on psych-verb and its object types". Chin. Lang. Learn. **3**, 33–36 (1994). (in Chinese)
14. Zhang, Y.: The extent of stative psychological verbs. Master's thesis, Jilin University (2009). (in Chinese)
15. Luo, Q.: Degree, scale and the semantics of Zhen and Jia. Stud. Lang. Linguist. **2**, 94–100 (2016). (in Chinese)
16. Luo, Q.: Gradability, scale structure and classification of simple adjectives in Chinese. Chin. Lang. Learn. **1**, 27–38 (2018). (in Chinese)
17. Luo, Q.: Scale structure and the polarity opposition of adjectives in Chinese. Stud. Lang. Linguist. **2**, 24–31 (2018). (in Chinese)
18. Jiang, Y.: A game-theoretical interpretation of the pragmatic felicity of NPIs of litotes. Contemp. Rhetoric **4**, 32–47 (2019). (in Chinese)

A Diachronic Account of the Semantic Variation of *Sān* ("three") and Its Combining Forms

Zimeng Mou[✉]

Beijing Foreign Studies University, Beijing, China
`mouzimen@163.com`

Abstract. With a particular focus on the combining forms and productivity, this paper traces the history of 三 *sān* ("three") used as cardinal numbers and examines the semantic variation of 三 *sān* ("three") in its indefinite meaning. Two levels of productivity are utilized in the current study. One is productivity at the lexical level, which indicates the ability for a simple word like 三 *sān* ("three") to make compounds or phrases, a phenomenon really prevalent in Chinese. The other is productivity at the semantic level, which evaluates the productivity of a certain meaning of one word. The results observe a decrease in the indefinite usage of 三 *sān* ("three") and its combining forms as well as some mechanisms of semantic change concerning metonymy, analogy, heterosemy, and metaphor.

Keywords: Productivity · Semantic variation · 三 *sān* ("three")

1 Introduction

In Chinese, apart from the denotation of an exact number, some numerals like 一 *yī* ("one"[1]), 二 *èr* or 两 *liǎng* ("two"), 三 *sān* ("three"), 九 *jiǔ* ("nine") and 百 *bǎi* ("hundred") can be used to indicate indefinite numbers. Those numerals can be roughly divided into two groups. While numerals like 一 *yī* ("one") sometimes suggest "a little", the meanings of 三 *sān* ("three") and some others are similar to "several" or "many" in some contexts. In the latter group, 三 *sān* ("three") is assumed to be the one that has the longest history in use and possibly derives most other indefinite numerals [1]. A probe into it can thus be of great significance to explorations of the rich phenomena of indefinite numbers in Chinese. In the meantime, this study is also an attempt to evaluate the semantic and lexical productivity of a word, in which little research has been done yet.

The paper is structured as follows. A clarification of related concepts and an outline of existing studies are presented in Sect. 2. Section 3 addresses the research questions and method of the study. In Sect. 4, the form and productivity of 三 *sān* ("three") as an unreliable numeral in the history of Chinese are examined. Section 5 concludes with major implications and limitations.

---

[1] In the brackets are literal meanings of the Chinese texts.

P. Jin et al. (Eds.): CLSW 2024, LNAI 15552, pp. 355–367, 2025.
https://doi.org/10.1007/978-981-96-3509-2_26

2 Literature Review

2.1 Conceptualization and Classification of Numerals in Chinese

In English, the notion of the "word" is comparatively salient and intuitive. One particularly easy and common way to recognize one unit as a word is to see whether it is bounded by spaces on both sides in its written form, which is termed as an orthographic word in morphology. However, this definition is not that practical and intuitive in Chinese since there is no evident sign of word boundaries in writing. In Chinese language and culture, the more clear-cut and sociologically recognized independent unit is the Chinese character named as 字 zì [2]. Over decades, scholars have enrolled in heated debates concerning the relationship between the concept of 字 zì ("Chinese character") in Chinese and the more universal notion of the "word". To date, a general consensus has not been reached yet, which results in the disagreement about exactly how to define numerals in Chinese.

Earlier studies like Ma Jianzhong's [3] and Li Jinxi's [4] regard numerals as a subtype of adjectives. Wang Li [5] was the first to establish numerals as a part of speech independent of others like adjectives. Most subsequent researchers like Ding Sheng Shu et al.'s [6] followed his assertion. Still, they admitted that numerals share some attributes of adjectives.

Opinions also diverge on which number should be classified as words and which should be considered as phrases. Wang Xia [7] synthesized previous research and listed five existing criteria for classification. The first kind of classification is based on the semantic criterion (e.g. [8, 9]). It argues that numerals refer to all those that indicate numbers. And to further distinguish numbers like one hundred and fifty-five with digit numbers like five, the concept of "compound numeral" is proposed. The second is a phonological criterion [10, 11]. It divides numbers with one or two syllables into words and numbers with three or more syllables into two or more words; for example, 三 sān ("three") and 十三 shí-sān ("thirteen") have one and two syllables respectively and are defined as one word; 一千三百三十三 yī-qiān-sān-bǎi-sān-shí-sān ("one thousand three hundred and thirty-three") has seven syllables and thus four words. This criterion is a bit artificial and rigid since no convincing explanation is provided for the reason why a word should have exactly one or two syllables. The third criterion draws upon the notion of digit numbers from zero to nine and median numbers like ten, hundred, etc. [12]. It categorizes numbers into four types including simplex numerals, compound numerals, numeral phrases and strings of numbers. Simplex numerals refer to digit numbers. Compound numerals are made up of digit numbers and median numbers, like 三十 sān-shí ("thirty"). Numeral phrases are the combination of simplex numerals and compound numerals, such as 三十三 sān-shí-sān ("thirty-three"). Strings of numbers are the combination of numbers without median numbers, like 三五 sān-wǔ ("three to five") and 二三 èr-sān ("two or three"). The fourth criterion defines words as those whose components cannot be used independently without changing their meanings [13]. Guided by this principle, 十三 shí-sān ("thirteen") and 三十 sān-shí ("thirty") belong to phrases and words respectively, since 十 shí ("ten") and 三 sān ("three") remain their original meaning in the former unit but not in the latter one. In the fifth criterion, only digit numbers and median numbers are numerals because they are the smallest independently useable units in Chinese (e.g. [14, 15]). Other numbers composed of those words are thus numeral phrases. This criterion ignores the possibility of compounds in numerals which is a really common phenomenon in other parts of speech.

Among the five criteria, the second one has little to do with meanings of the numbers and will not be considered here. All the other four criteria treat the digit number 三 *sān* ("three") as the simplex of numerals. The disagreement between them mainly lies in the categorization of numbers like 十三 *shí-sān* ("thirteen"), 三十 *sān-shí* ("thirty") and 三十一 *sān-shí-yī* ("thirty-one"), that is, whether they are compounds or phrases. This study adopts a refined version of the fourth criterion, which contends that the difference between compounds and phrases is whether meanings of the numbers are predictable from the individual lexemes and their construction. Based on this definition, numbers like 十三 *shí-sān* ("thirteen"), 三十 *sān-shí* ("thirty") and 三十一 *sān-shí-yī* ("thirty-one") are all phrases since their interpretations follow corresponding constructions.

The typology of numerals also varies in terms of their meanings and functions. Li Jinxi [4] and Yang Bojun [16] divided numerals into definite numerals and indefinite numerals. Shao Jingmin [17] and Huang Borong etc. [9] developed a dichotomy of cardinal numbers and ordinal numbers. Cardinal numbers are divided into digit numbers and median numbers in this structure. Focus of this study will be on the indefinite usage of a cardinal number 三 *sān* ("three"). Besides, although the majority of studies take indefinite numbers as a whole, some scholars make a further distinction between two types of indefinite numbers. Zhou Bingjun [18] may be the first to do such a job. He asserts that approximate numerals (约数 *yuē-shù* or 概数 *gài-shù* in later studies) are usually around the exact number being referred to while unreliable numerals (虚数 *xū-shù*) are of little relevance to what the number exactly denotes. Recent researchers like Zhou Shengya [19] had a similar statement. Approximate numerals are those indefinite in form, like 二三 *èr-sān* ("two or three"); unreliable numerals is the usage of a definite number like 三 *sān* ("three") to indicate "several" or "many". The current study will analyze 三 *sān* ("three") and its combining forms used as unreliable numerals.

2.2 Research on Unreliable Numerals in Chinese

Earlier research on unreliable numerals in Chinese scattered around the literature. Its originator may be Wang Zhong in the Qing Dynasty [20], who pointed out in his essay *On "sān" and "jiǔ"* that 三 *sān* ("three") and 九 *jiǔ* ("nine") can be understood as "many" in certain contexts. Another typical research is Kang Su and Song Guangtian's [21] classification of unreliable numerals in terms of their frequency, form and meaning. These studies mainly adopt the descriptive approach and are supported by self-selected examples of personal preference. In other words, their investigations are primarily based on their own observation and lack empirical evidence. Systematic studies using quantitative or qualitative methods are required to confirm their findings.

Some studies examined the phenomenon of unreliable numerals in specific texts including *The Analects of Confucius* [22], Du Fu's Poems [23], *Water Margin* [24], etc. Zhou Xiao Qing [22] suggested a trend of 三 *sān* ("three") becoming more indefinite in *The Analects of Confucius*. Lei Xingqiang [24] and Wang Ningning [23] concluded the various forms of unreliable numerals and revealed their stylistic and rhetorical effects on the texts. Still, restricted to a single text, these studies cannot fully depict the general usage of unreliable numerals in Chinese. Besides, those studies have their main focus on the synchronic variation of meanings conveyed by those numerals. Little research has been conducted on how people's use of the numerals may vary across different time periods. Given that, a diachronic investigation on those numerals with vague meanings using a wider range of data is needed to help fill the gap.

3 Research Method

3.1 Research Questions

This paper is designed to answer two questions: 1) What are the diachronic changes of the unreliable numeral 三 *sān* ("three") and its combining forms? 2) How does the productivity of 三 *sān* ("three") as an indefinite numerals vary in the history of Chinese?

3.2 Data Collection

Data used in this paper is extracted from the searchable Internet version of the CCL (Center for Chinese Linguistics) Chinese Corpora developed by Peking University [25]. The CCL Corpora are composed of a Classical Chinese corpus and a Modern Chinese corpus, the classification of which will facilitate this diachronic study.

The Classical Chinese Corpus consists of texts in 15 dynasties or periods from the West Zhou Dynasty to the middle of the Republic of China (1930). 13 dynasties or periods except the Sui Dynasty and the Republic of China are concerned in this study. The Sui Dynasty is left out in this paper due to a lack of entries containing 三 *sān* ("three"). The Republic of China is also excluded, since all the texts selected in this period are novels and the majority of them, such as 《上古秘史》 ("*A Secret History of the Distant Past*") and 《两晋演义》 ("*The Romance of the Two Jin Dynasties*"), describe or adapt stories in previous dynasties, which I believe are not representative of language usage in the period under examination. For the other 13 dynasties or periods, the character 三 *sān* ("three") is searched and the first 50 entries of each dynasty or period where *san* is used as a cardinal number are retrieved for analysis. The usage of 三 *sān* ("three") as ordinal numbers (e.g. 永初三年五月 ("May in the third year of Yongchu")) or names (e.g. 吴三桂) is not of this paper's interest. Moreover, following Sun Chaofen's [26] categorization, the 13 dynasties or periods are further classified into three phases as follows: Old Chinese (771 BCE to 220 CE, from the Zhou Dynasty to the East Han Dynasty), Middle Chinese (220 CE to 960 CE, from the Six Dynasties to the Five Dynasties), and Early Modern Chinese (960CE to 1900CE, from the Song Dynasty to the Qing Dynasty). One thing to be noted here is that the West Zhou Dynasty which is not included in Sun's categorization will be added to the Old Chinese phase in this study.

The Modern Chinese Corpus has two sub-corpora, a Modern Chinese sub-corpus (before 1949) and a Contemporary Chinese sub-corpus (after 1949). The first 200 instances of 三 *sān* ("three") used as a cardinal number in each sub-corpus are selected as the data.

3.3 Data Analysis

The first step is to calculate the number of 三 *sān* ("three") that signifies an unreliable numeral in each dynasty and phase, and then get a percentage of these unreliable numerals among all instances of 三 *sān* ("three") used as a cardinal number within that dynasty or phase. In this procedure, context serves as the major resource to decide whether 三 *sān* refers to an exact or an indefinite number, since most of the words or phrases that 三 *sān* composes are polysemous and may have different denotations in varied contexts; for instance, the phrase 三岁 *sān-suì* in 三岁贯女, 莫我肯顾 ("Many years have we had to do with you, And you have not been willing to show any regard for us"[2]). and 伏戎于莽, 升其高陵, 三岁不兴 ("([S]hows its subject) with his arms hidden in the thick grass, and at the top of a high mound. (But) for many years he makes no demonstration"[3]) is equivalent to "many years", in which 三 *sān* denotes "many", while 三岁 *sān-suì* in 今将军为秦将三岁矣 ("Now you have been a general in Qin for three years") and 不过三岁, 塞下之粟必多矣 ("In less than three years, there will surely be an abundance of grain in the border regions") refers to the exact number of three years. In addition, most approximate numerals will not be counted here as unreliable numerals for the reason that though the expression indicates a range, the number itself denotes a definite number; for example, 二三 *èr-sān* in which 三 *sān* denotes the exact number of three is not an unreliable numeral. An expression like 不过一二人, 二三人 ("no more than one to two people, or two to three people") usually will not be used when there are four or more people. Still, there are exceptions. 二三 *èr-sān* in some fixed expressions like 二三子 *èrsānzǐ* does not convey the meaning of exactly two or three people; for example, in 二三子何患无君 ("My children, why should you be troubled about having no prince?"[4]), 二三子 is an address for the hearers who can be several or many people. In such instances, 三 *sān* in 二三子 *èrsānzǐ* will be treated as unreliable numerals. Another coder will be invited to ensure inter-coder reliability and objectivity of this process. Disagreement emerged in the coding will be searched in reference books and sufficiently discussed to reach a consensus between researchers.

Next is to categorize different forms spotted in the data. In the current study, to avoid too many categories, only the component adjacent to 三 *sān* ("three") in a compound or phrase will be used for the division; for example, the structure exists in 腾骧磊落三万匹 ("tens of thousands of fine horses leaping with vigor") will be a combination of numerals concerning 三 *sān* ("three") instead of 三 *sān* ("three") + quantifier, since 万 *wàn* ("ten thousand") is the one nearest to 三 *sān* ("three"). And for 三 *sān* ("three") that does not form a compound or phrase, 三 *sān* ("three") itself will be treated as an independent unit, such as the one in 摽有梅, 其实三兮 ("Dropping are the fruits from

---

[2] Adapted from James Legge's translation, retrieved from https://ctext.org/pre-qin-and-han?searchu=%E4%B8%89%E5%B2%81%E8%B4%AF.

[3] Adapted from James Legge's translation, retrieved from https://ctext.org/pre-qin-and-han?searchu=%E5%8D%87%E5%85%B6%E9%AB%98%E9%99%B5.

[4] Translated by James Legge in *The Works of Mencius* (1970).

the plum-tree; There are [but] three [tenths] of them left!"[5]) where 三 *sān* independently suggests three-tenths.

In response to the second research question, the productivity of the indefinite meaning of 三 *sān* ("three") will also be evaluated and compared. It may be considered as a lexical or semantic counterpart of morphological productivity conducted from the users' perspective. It is an indicator suggesting users' awareness of 三 *sān* ("three") being an unreliable numeral and their ability to use it. This productivity will be measured by type frequency of the unreliable numeral 三 *sān* ("three").

Still, this measure has one particular problem for diachronic studies, as proposed by Cowie and Dalton-Puffer [27], that many types could indicate past rather than present productivity, since some words or phrases may have existed in the language for centuries. To minimize such an effect, the current study will exclude established words or idioms since people may take it as a whole and not care about the particular meaning of 三 *sān* ("three") while using it. To achieve this purpose, in current study, established words or idioms mainly refer to those appearing for more than one time with a consistent meaning about 三 *sān* ("three") throughout the data of the phase concerned. Take 三千 *sān-qiān* ("three thousand") and 三句话不离本行 ("stick to one's trade in talking") as an example. 三千 *sān-qiān* has two interpretations in the data. One means the definite number of three thousand, such as in the sentence 丞相陈平, 灌将军婴邑各三千户 ("Prime minister Chen Ping and General Guan Ying were each awarded three thousand families as their fiefs"); the other indicates an indefinite number of several thousand, as suggested by 礼仪三百, 威仪三千 ("It embraces hundreds of rules of ceremony, and thousands of rules of demeanor"[6]). In contrast, 三句话不离本行 ("stick to one's trade in talking") is a well-established idiom in which 三 *sān* is equivalent to "several". No instance with such an expression has been observed in the corpus that treats 三 *sān* as a concrete number. Accordingly, 三句话不离本行 ("stick to one's trade in talking") is considered to have been established while 三千 *sān-qiān* is not. Another thing to be noted is that the same expression used by two different authors will be counted as twice, since they represent two individuals' use of 三 *sān* ("three") as an indefinite numeral.

4 Results and Discussions

4.1 Distribution of the Unreliable Numeral 三 *sān*, ("three") and Its Combining Forms

Altogether four types of structures concerning 三 *sān* ("three") as an unreliable numeral are observed in the data. Table 1 illustrates the distribution of the structures in different phases.

The form of 三 *sān* ("three") followed by a quantifier, which is a most common structure for numerals in Modern and Contemporary Chinese, is also prevalent in Old

---

[5] Translated by James Legge, retrieved from https://ctext.org/pre-qin-and-han?searchu=%E6%91%BD%E6%9C%89%E6%A2%85%EF%BC%8C%E5%85%B6%E5%AE%9E%E4%B8%89%E5%85%AE.

[6] Adapted from James Legge's translation, retrieved from https://ctext.org/pre-qin-and-han?searchu=%E7%A4%BC%E4%BB%AA%E4%B8%89%E7%99%BE.

Table 1. Distribution of Structure Types of 三 *sān* ("three") as an Unreliable Numeral in Five Phases

	Old Chinese	Middle Chinese	Early Modern Chinese
三 *sān* ("three") + quantifier	30.8%	10.5%	35.6%
Combining numbers	48.7%	78.9%	62.2%
三 *sān* ("three") + noun	17.9%	10.5%	2.2%
三 *sān* ("three") used independently	2.6%	0	0
	Modern Chinese	Contemporary Chinese	
三 *sān* ("three") + quantifier	100%	50%	
Combining numbers	0	25%	
三 *sān* ("three") + noun	0	12.5%	
三 *sān* ("three") used independently	0	12.5%	

Chinese and Early Modern Chinese, accounting respectively for 30.8% and 35.6% of all identified unreliable expressions in each phase. In Old Chinese, 三 *sān* ("three") with temporal quantifiers take up the majority of 三 *sān* ("three") + quantifiers expressions. There are altogether 7 out of 13 such phrases, including 三年 *sān-nián* (e.g. 三年不目月, 精必矇 ("Not looking at the moon for several years will inevitably lead to blindness") in which 三年 *sān-nián* means several years), 三岁 *sān-suì* (e.g. 三岁为妇, 靡室劳矣 ("For many years I was your wife, And thought nothing of my toil in your house"[7]) in which 三岁 *sān-suì* means many years), and 三月 *sān-yuè* (e.g. 修橹轒辒, 具器械, 三月而后 成 ("The preparation of mantlets, movable shelters, and various implements of war, will take up several whole months"[8]) in which 三月 *sān-yuè* means several months), with 三 岁 *sān-suì* being the most frequently used one. 三年 *sān-nián* and 三月 *sān-yuè* reappear in Early Modern Chinese and occupy a relatively large proportion (8 out of 21). Some other quantifiers that are frequently used in modern times also show their appearance in the data, such as the expression 三杯 *sān-bēi* (e.g. 三杯竹叶穿心过, 两朵桃花上 脸来 (literally "Three cups of green bamboo leaves down the throat, Two pink peach blossoms on the cheeks"[9]) in which 三杯 *sān-bēi* actually indicates several cups) which appears nine times in different dynasties. It may be due to the more oral-like literary genres like 词 *cí* and 曲 *qǔ*. Besides, the 三 *sān* ("three") + quantifier expression is often

---

[7] Adapted from James Legge's translation, retrieved from https://ctext.org/pre-qin-and-han?sea rchu=%E4%B8%89%E5%B2%81%E4%B8%BA%E5%A6%87%EF%BC%8C%20%E9% 9D%A1%E5%AE%A4%E5%8A%B3%E7%9F%A3.

[8] Adapted from Lionel Giles's translation, retrieved from https://ctext.org/pre-qin-and-han?sea rchu=%E4%BF%AE%E6%A9%B9%E8%BD%92%E8%BD%80%E3%80%81%E5%85% B7%E5%99%A8%E6%A2%B0%E3%80%81%E4%B8%89%E6%9C%88%E8%80%8C% E5%90%8E%E6%88%90.

[9] Translated by Yang Shuhui and Yang Yunqin in *Stories to Caution the World* (2005).

observed to co-occur with a similar expression containing another unreliable numeral in Early Modern Chinese and Modern Chinese, such as 三 *sān* ("three") and 两 *liǎng* ("two") in 三杯 *sān-bēi* and 两朵 *liǎng-duǒ* in the previous example 三杯竹叶穿心过, 两朵桃花上脸来, as well as in 三年 *sān-nián* and 两头 *liǎng-tóu* in 三年两头 ("over the course of several years"). In contrast, 三 *sān* ("three") + quantifier takes a large proportion in Modern and Contemporary Chinese, but one thing to be noted here is that most of the usage appears in established words or idioms like 垂涎三尺 (literally "one's mouth waters several feet") in Modern Chinese and 三岁之魂, 百岁之才 (literally "The soul of a three-year-old, the talent of a centenarian") in Contemporary Chinese, which is different from Classical Chinese. Generally speaking, 三 *sān* ("three") remains at a lower level of usage in Classical Chinese compared to Modern and Contemporary Chinese, which is in line with the traditional claim that quantifiers are less used in Classical time than in Modern time.

The overwhelming majority of structure types in Classical Chinese belong to the combination of two numerals which accounts for 48.7%, 78.9%, and 62.2% respectively in Old Chinese, Middle Chinese and Early Modern Chinese. This form can be further divided into two kinds.

One is the combination of digit numerals and median numerals, including 三十 *sān-shí* ("thirty") (e.g. 孔子观于吕梁,悬水三十仞,流沫三十里 ("Confucius observed the waterfall at Luliang; it plunged down from a height of tens of *ren*, and the spray extended tens of *li*"), in which 三十 *sān-shí* indicates "tens of"), 三十六 *sān-shí-liù* ("thirty-six") (e.g. 水底鸳鸯三十六 (literally "thirty-six mandarin ducks underwater") where 三十六 *sān-shí-liù* sounds good but does not indicates an exact number of thirty-six), 三百 *sān-bǎi* ("three hundred") (e.g. 镜湖三百里, 菡萏发荷花 ("The Jinghu Lake stretches hundreds of *li*, where lotus blossoms bloom") in which 三百 *sān-bǎi* is equal to "hundreds of"), 三千 *sān-qiān* ("three thousand") (e.g. 法鼓震三千, 如何不得闻 ("The dharma drum reverberates through thousands of worlds; how could one not hear it?") where 三千 *sān-qiān* denotes "thousands of worlds"), 三万 *sān-wàn* ("thirty thousand") (e.g. 腾骧磊落三万匹, 皆与此图筋骨同 ("Tens of thousands of horses, galloping with vigor and grace, all share the same spirit and sinew as depicted in this painting") where 三万 *sān-wàn* is used to indicate a large number), and 三百亿 *sān-bǎi-yì* ("thirty billion") (e.g. 不稼不穑, 胡取禾三百亿兮 ("You sow not nor reap; How do you get your several millions of sheaves?"[10]) in which 三百亿 indicates an immeasurable number). Feng Youlan [1] once made an assumption about the origin of various multiples of 三 *sān* ("three") in Chinese denoting indefinite numbers. He contends that the multiple of 三 *sān* ("three") indicating a bigger number stems from that denoting a smaller number; for instance, 二十四 *èr-shí-sì* ("twenty-four") or 三十六 *sān-shí-liù* ("thirty-six") will be adopted to show the large number of something when the author thinks 十二 *shí-èr* ("twelve") is not enough, and the same applies to 三百 *sān-bǎi* ("three hundred"), 三千 *sān-qiān* ("three thousand"), and 三万 *sān-wàn* ("thirty thousand"). Though these words are not definite numerals here, the big number they denote has a potential influence on people's conception of those numerals when they are used as unreliable numerals. The example

---

[10] Adapted from James Legge's translation, retrieved from https://ctext.org/pre-qin-and-han?sea rchu=%E4%B8%8D%E7%A8%BC%E4%B8%8D%E7%A9%91%EF%BC%8C%E8%83%A1%E5%8F%96%E7%A6%BE%E4%B8%89%E7%99%BE%E4%BA%BF%E5%85%AE.

优优大哉, 礼仪三百, 威仪三千 (literally "All-complete is its greatness! It embraces the three hundred rules of ceremony, and the three thousand rules of demeanor"[11]) can also serve as an evidence for Feng Youlan's opinion. By contrast between 三百 *sān-bǎi* ("three hundred") and 三千 *sān-qiān* ("three thousand"), it suggests that the number of 威仪 *wēiyí* ("demeanor") is larger than 礼仪 *lǐyí* ("ceremony"). Here 三千 *sān-qiān* ("three thousand") is used since the author intends to indicate a larger number than 三百 *sān-bǎi* ("three hundred").

The other is the combination of two digit numerals without median numerals, the form of which is shared with approximate numerals as mentioned in the previous section, such as 三四 *sān-sì* ("three or four") (e.g. 池上碧苔三四点 ("There are several spots of green moss on the pond") where 三四 *sān-sì* means "several" instead of an exact number of three or four), 三五 *sān-wǔ* ("three to five") (e.g. 古来三五个英雄 ("Throughout history, there have been only a handful of heroes") in which 三五 *sān-wǔ* means "a small number of"), 两三 *liǎng-sān* ("two or three") (e.g. 两三点雨山前 (literally "Before the hills two to three raindrops sprinkle"[12]) where 两三 *liǎng-sān* actually suggests "a little"), 二三 *èr-sān* ("two or three") (e.g. 劝二三君子必先导焉 ("(King's uncle Chen Sheng) urges all of you to speak well of him"), in which 二三君子 refers to all the addressees and 二三 *èr-sān* can be "several" or "many" depending on the number of people present;), and 再三 *zài-sān* ("two or three") (e.g. 一弹再三叹, 慷慨有余哀 ("With each note played, there were accompanying sighs, and even after the music ceased, the sorrow lingered on") in which 再三 *zài-sān* means many times). Among them, 再三 *zài-sān* is used most frequently. It consists of 再 *zài* which is a variant of 二 *èr* ("two") as well as the numeral 三 *sān* ("three"). In sentences like 一弹再三叹, 慷慨有余哀 and 再三苦留 ("repeatedly and earnestly urge someone to stay"), the combination of 再 *zài* and 三 *sān* indicates "many". And as commented by Zhang Qiyun and Xie Juntao [28], 再三 *zài-sān* followed by adjectives in expressions like 求名责实, 再三乖谬 ("To seek the substance based on its name is exceedingly absurd") and 又与这村郎再三害怕 ("And (I) was extremely frightened by this rough man") are used to describe the extent rather than the exact number of times of 乖谬 ("absurdity") and 害怕 ("fear") and can be interpreted as "extremely". This kind of semantic transition based on similarity between meanings may be triggered by humans' ability to make metaphors.

Still, in spite of the popularity of the two kinds of expressions in Modern and Contemporary Chinese, neither kind is observed to serve as unreliable numerals in the data. The combinations of digit numerals and median numerals are used to indicate a definite number; for instance, 三十 *sān-shí* ("thirty") in 你爸爸作中人借来的三十块钱 ("thirty *yuan* borrowed from others with your father being the middleman") indicates the exact number of thirty, while the combination of two digit numerals without median numerals are employed as approximate numerals; for example, four or five children will not be very appropriate for a setting described as 一条瘦狗, 三两个蓬头赤脚的乡下孩子 ("a skinny dog, and two or three shabby, barefoot country boys") and thus 三两 *sān-liǎng* ("three or two") here will be categorized into approximate numerals and not considered as an unreliable numeral.

---

[11] Translated by James Legge, retrieved from https://ctext.org/pre-qin-and-han?searchu=%E7%A4%BC%E4%BB%AA%E4%B8%89%E7%99%BE.

[12] Translated by Xu Yuan Chong in *300 Song Lyrics Translated by Xu Yuan Chong* (2011).

The third kind of structure is 三 *sān* ("three") and the noun 三 *sān* ("three") modifies. The noun in this structure also includes verbs used as nouns. Most expressions in this kind appear only once or twice in our data since they are highly context-dependent. Also, it may serve as a good indicator for the productivity of 三 *sān* ("three") being an unreliable numeral since most of them are created by the author himself rather than fixed expressions inherited from previous generations, like 三请 *sān-qǐng* ("request for several times") in 三请, 宓子弗听 ("(He) requested for several times, but Mizi did not take his advice"), and 三槐 *sān-huái* ("several locust trees") in 三槐九棘位中居 ("occupy the position amidst several locust trees and wild jujubes"). As Table 1 has shown, there is an evident decrease from Old Chinese to Modern Chinese in the proportion 三 *sān* ("three") + noun takes in all structure types, which may be due to the gradual development of quantifiers in the history of Chinese. Additionally, since it is highly influenced by the productivity of the meaning of 三 *sān* ("three"), decrease of the productivity in late periods may also be one influencing factor. Contemporary Chinese sees an increase in the proportion, which is contributed by 三涨 *sān-zhǎng* ("several rises") in the idiom 一日三涨 ("Rise several times a day").This suggests that some 三 *sān* ("three") + noun expressions indicating indefinite numerals have been preserved in established words or phrases.

The last type of structure where 三 *sān* ("three") is used independently is relatively rare in our sample. Altogether there are two such expressions. One is 三 *sān* ("three") in 摽有梅, 其实三兮 ("Dropping are the fruits from the plum-tree; There are [but] three [tenths] of them left!"[13]) observed in the data of the Zhou Dynasty. Here 三 *sān* ("three") is a fraction to mean there is only a small portion left. The other is 三 *sān* ("three") being a noun in the idiom 举一反三 ("infer other things from one instance"). It comes from the saying 举一隅不以三隅反 ("When I have presented one corner of a subject to any one, and he cannot from it learn the other"[14]) in the Spring and Autumn Period where 三 *sān* ("three") is a numeral modifying 隅 ("example"). This kind of change may be termed as heterosemy, which in Zhan Fangqiong's [29] interpretation refers to the phenomenon that various meanings of a word pertaining to different grammatical categories. In general, the number of this structure is too small to suggest a possible changing pattern and will not be given much attention here.

4.2 Frequency and Productivity of the Unreliable Numeral 三 (*sān*, "three")

Table 2 shows the frequency the indefinite meaning of 三 *sān* ("three") is used in the data and the productivity of the unreliable numeral 三 *sān* ("three") to form compound words or phrases.

As manifested by Table 2, changes on the frequency and productivity of 三 *sān* ("three") suggest a similar trend through the history and thus will be analyzed together. While there is not much difference on the frequency and productivity between phases within the Classical or Modern period, the percentage does diverge greatly between

---

[13] See footnote 5.

[14] Adapted from James Legge's translation, retrieved from https://ctext.org/pre-qin-and-han?sea rchu=%E4%B8%BE%E4%B8%80%E9%9A%85%E4%B8%8D%E4%BB%A5%E4%B8%89%E9%9A%85%E5%8F%8D.

Table 2. Frequency and Productivity of 三 *sān* ("three") Being an Unreliable Numeral

	Old Chinese	Middle Chinese	Early Modern Chinese
Frequency	15.6%	12.7%	18.0%
Productivity	12.0%	8.0%	15.2%

	Modern Chinese	Contemporary Chinese
Frequency	1.0%	5.0%
Productivity	0	0

the two major periods --- the frequency and productivity of 三 *sān* ("three") being an unreliable numeral are much lower in Modern and Contemporary Chinese than their Classical counterpart. This phenomenon suggests that the meaning of 三 *sān* ("three") to mean "several" or "many" is much less used by moderners and new words or phrases containing 三 *sān* ("three") with such a meaning are more hardly to be coined now than in history. In particular, zero of the productivity in Modern and Contemporary Chinese indicates that almost all current words or phrases except those established ones that have been excluded from the evaluation of productivity adopts 三 *sān* ("three") as a definite number. Additionally, the structure of combining numbers shares a similar changing patterns with the simple word 三 *sān* ("three"), the reason for which may be analogy. Since 三 *sān* ("three") and a combination of numbers like 三千 *sān-qiān* ("three thousand") are formally and semantically related, the changes on one form may be easily modelled and analogized to the other.

Moreover, for the two meanings of 三 *sān* ("three") as ordinal numerals, while the employment of 三 *sān* ("three") as an unreliable numeral diminishes in Modern and Contemporary Chinese, its development at an early stage is not observed in the data, since it has already been used frequently and maturely in the Zhou Dynasty, but according to some scholars' statement, 三 *sān* ("three") indicating "several" or "many" is an extension of its basic meaning of "three", for "three" in many occasions can be described as "many" (e.g. [1, 20]). In this sense, the derivation of the indefinite meaning of 三 *sān* ("three") seems to be based on contiguity and thus regarded as a kind of metonymy. Then the decrease in the frequency and productivity of 三 *sān*'s ("three") indefinite meaning observed in this investigation may be considered as a process of "de-metonymization" where 三 *sān* ("three") gradually abandons its metonymical interpretation and returns to its basic meaning of an exact number.

5   Conclusion

As a diachronic study on the meanings of 三 *sān* ("three"), this paper proves the decrease in the indefinite usage of 三 *sān* ("three") and its combining forms in the history of Chinese. Some mechanisms of semantic change concerning metonymy, analogy, heterosemy, and metaphor are also spotted in the process. Besides, this study demonstrates how the productivity of a certain meaning may be evaluated with type frequency. Also,

Chinese characters or words are rich in their ability to make compounds or phrases, which may give rise to a new kind of productivity at the lexical level which is less concerned in studies on English. The current study is an attempt to combine and utilize these two kinds of productivity and evaluate the semantic variation of 三 sān ("three") in its indefinite meaning.

Still, this paper has some limitations. One lies in the number of samples taken for research. Only 50 entries of each dynasty or period in the Classical Chinese Corpora and 200 of that in the Modern Chinese Corpora are selected as the data, which is not sufficient to represent the usage of 三 sān ("three") throughout the history of Chinese. A more comprehensive study with a larger scale is expected. Besides, the genres of the text which also have an effect in the distribution are not strictly controlled here. As observed in the study, there is a discrepancy on the frequency 三 sān ("three") appears as an unreliable numeral in different genres. It is more likely for 三 sān ("three") to indicate an indefinite number in poems than in other informative or argumentative texts, which may influence the accuracy of this study. Additionally, other numerals like 两 liǎng ("two"), and 九 jiǔ ("nine") can also be used as indefinite numerals. A comparison may be made to find out the commonalities and differences between them. Furthermore, apart from frequency, distributional information is also believed to be an important indicator of semantic change [30]. Future research may also take context information into consideration by applying distribution-based paradigms like static neural embeddings, which has been tested as effective in Chinese [31], to detect changes in numeral meanings.

References

1. Feng, Y.L.: On "seventy-two". In: A Collection of Essays of Nandu, pp. 238–242. The Oriental Publishing Center, Shanghai (2017). (in Chinese)
2. Packard, J.L.: The Morphology of Chinese: A Linguistic and Cognitive Approach. Cambridge University Press, Cambridge (2004)
3. Ma, J.Z.: Ma's Grammar Book. The Commercial Press, Shanghai (1898). (in Chinese)
4. Li, J.X.: The New Chinese Grammar. The Commercial Press, Beijing (1924/1992). (in Chinese)
5. Wang, L.: Modern Grammar of Chinese. The Commercial Press, Shanghai (1944). (in Chinese)
6. Ding, S.S., et al.: Talks on Modern Grammar of Chinese. The Commercial Press, Beijing (1961). (in Chinese)
7. Wang, X.: Research on Chinese Ordinal Category. Social Sciences Academic Press, Beijing (2017). (in Chinese)
8. Zhang, Z.G., et al.: Modern Chinese. People's Education Press, Beijing (1982). (in Chinese)
9. Huang, B.R., Liao, X.D., et al.: Modern Chinese, 3rd edn. Higher Education Press, Beijing (2002). (in Chinese)
10. Hu, F.: Numerals and Quantifiers. Shanghai Educational Publishing House, Shanghai (1984). (in Chinese)
11. Lv, J.P.: Basics of Chinese Grammar. The Commercial Press, Beijing (2000). (in Chinese)
12. Zhang, W.G.: On numerals. In: Hu, M.Y. (ed.) A Sequel to Research on Parts of Speech, pp. 178–198. Beijing Language and Culture University Press, Beijing (2004). (in Chinese)
13. Lu, Z.W., et al.: Chinese Word Formation. Science Press, Beijing (1964). (in Chinese)
14. Fang, X.J.: Content Words in Modern Chinese. East China Normal University Press, Shanghai (2000). (in Chinese)

15. Guo, R.: Research on Parts of Speech in Modern Chinese. The Commercial Press, Beijing (2002). (in Chinese)
16. Yang, B.J.: A Comprehensive Guide on Chinese Grammar. The Commercial Press, Beijing (1955). (in Chinese)
17. Shao, J.M. (ed.): A General Course on Modern Chinese. Shanghai Educational Publishing House, Shanghai (2001). (in Chinese)
18. Zhou, B.J.: An Outline on Ancient Chinese. Hunan Education Publishing House, Changsha (1981). (in Chinese)
19. Zhou, S.Y.: A Draft History of Parts of Speech in Chinese. China Renmin University Press, Beijing (2018). (in Chinese)
20. Chen, Y.J.: On "three": also a comment on Wang Zhong's "interpretation of numerals 'three' and 'nine'". J. Xiangtan Normal Univ. (Soc. Sci. Ed.) (02), 3–12 (1987). (in Chinese)
21. Kang, S., Song, G.T.: On "unreliable numerals" in literary language. J. Shandong Normal Univ. (Soc. Sci.) (04), 93–94+92 (1984). (in Chinese)
22. Zhou, X.Q.: The exact and vague usage of the numeral "three": taking the analects of Confucius as an example. Central China Hum. (04), 210–215 (2019). (in Chinese)
23. Wang, N.N.: Cultural and Aesthetic Implications of Numbers in Du Fu's Poems. Unpublished Master's Thesis, Shaanxi Normal University (2021). (in Chinese)
24. Lei, X.Q.: Meaningful Numbers and Components of Characters in Water Margin. Unpublished Master's Thesis, Hubei Normal University (2013). (in Chinese)
25. Zhan, W.D., Guo, R., Chang, B.B., Shen, Y.R., Chen, L.: The building of the CCL corpus: its design and implementation. Corpus Linguist. (01), 71–86+116 (2019). (in Chinese)
26. Sun, C.: Word-Order Change and Grammaticalization in the History of Chinese. Stanford University Press, California (1996)
27. Cowie, C., Dalton-Puffer, C.: Diachronic word-formation and studying changes in productivity over time: theoretical and methodological considerations. In: Diaz Vera, J.E. (ed.) A Changing World of Words: Studies in English Historical Lexicography, Lexicology and Semantics, pp. 410–437. Rodopi, Amsterdam, New York (2002)
28. Zhang, Q.Y., Xie, J.T.: On Er, Liang, Lia and Zai in Chinese. J. Nanyang Normal Univ. (08), 23–27 (2008). (in Chinese)
29. Zhan, F.: A constructional account of the development of the Chinese stance discourse marker běnlái. J. Hist. Pragmat.Pragmat. **23**(2), 245–284 (2022)
30. Harris, Z.S.: Distributional structure. Word **10**(2–3), 146–162 (1954)
31. Chen, J., Peng, B., Huang, C.R.: Tracing lexical semantic change with distributional semantics: change and stability. In: Su, Q., Xu, G., Yang, X. (eds.) Chinese Lexical Semantics. CLSW 2022, pp. 244–252. Springer, Cham (2023)

The Relationship Between Lexical Attributes and Word Order and the Principle of Cognitive Load Balance

An Li[(⊠)] [iD] and Yuxuan Fan

College of International Education, Shandong University, Jinan 250100, China
lian@sdu.edu.cn

Abstract. This study employs a large-scale corpus to statistically analyze the attributes of lexical items in terms of frequency, average number of strokes per character, number of senses, and semantic features at different positions in sentence sequences. The study examines the relationship between various features and cognitive processing difficulty, revealing a balanced relationship between lexical attributes and cognitive load intensity in linear positions, both in terms of form and semantic aspects. Lexical attributes occurring at the beginning of sentences with a high cognitive load are advantageous in reducing cognitive processing difficulty, and vice versa. Building upon this analysis, the study proposes the principle of cognitive load balance, which influences lexical system attribute features. It is argued that this principle manifests the principle of least effort in the linear sequence processing of sentences in the human brain, supplementing the traditional linear correlation based on frequency among lexical attributes.

Keywords: Word Order · Word Frequency · Number of Senses · Number of Strokes · Cognitive Load

1 Introduction

The attributes of elements are universally connected, reflecting the fundamental tenet of structuralism regarding the systematicity of language. The research conducted at the lexical level in quantitative linguistics provides sophisticated, easily tested and cross-linguistically comparable mathematical models for lexical systematic depictions. In the 1920s, Zipf conducted pioneering research into the mathematical model of the relationship between word frequency and rank order. The development of quantitative linguistics has led to a broader examination of lexical attributes, encompassing various dimensions such as length, constituent complexity, polysemy, contextual connection, and frequency of use [1]. With regard to the Chinese language, a series of studies have been conducted by Wang [2], Deng & Feng [3], Zhang & Ma [4] which have employed quantitative analysis to investigate the relationships among lexical attributes in Chinese. These studies

Funding. General Project of the National Social Science Fund of China (Construction and Research of Academic Chinese Corpus and Language Knowledge Base for Second Language Learners) (24BYY049).

have included the number of senses and sense classes within their scope of investigation, thereby providing cross-linguistic evidence for synergistic relationships between lexical elements and expanding the horizon of attention to the synergistic elements at the lexical level.

At the level of lexical metrics, the most profound significance of the research is to reveal the cognitive motivations behind the non-randomness of the lexical system. Zipf's Law reveals the principle of Least Effort, and Köhler [5] further summaries the principles at the phonemic and morphemic levels as minimization of memory load, minimization of speech production load, and minimization of comprehension and decoding load. These principles, to a certain extent, reveal some basic features of human cognitive activities, indicating the value of this research path.

It is notable that existing studies have predominantly analyzed the relationships between lexical attributes (such as word frequency and word length) from the perspective of the static lexicon, with less emphasis placed on the distributional characteristics of lexical items in speech activities. The extant theories likewise fail to account for all lexical phenomena. For instance, pronouns such as *you, me and him* exhibit high-frequency features. In accordance with the overarching principle of Least Effort, these pronouns should manifest a high degree of polysemy, given their high-frequency characteristics. However, empirical evidence suggests that such words tend to have relatively few senses. This observation calls for an examination of potential constraint mechanisms in the construction of the lexical system.

This paper will examine the distribution characteristics of various lexical attributes, including frequency, average number of strokes per character, number of senses, and semantic features, within a linear sequence of sentences. It will also analyze the mechanisms by which lexical attributes are adapted to cognitive load on sentence sequences. The fundamental theoretical assumption is that vocabulary is employed in speech activities, which are themselves cognitive activities. It follows that the attribute system of the lexicon will be subject to adaptation in accordance with the cognitive processing activities of human beings in relation to speech sequences. Specifically, the objective is to ascertain whether word order is non-random. In general, each word type has a syntactic position that is characteristic of its function, particularly in the case of function words. The objective here is to examine the distribution probability of words with similar syntactic attributes. In the statistical analysis of phrases, a common phenomenon of high frequency preceding has been identified [6]. Nevertheless, there is a paucity of quantitative analysis at the sentence level. Barlow [7] conducted a statistical analysis of the relationship between word frequency and word order at the sentence level, focusing on the English language. The analysis yielded the conclusion that high-frequency words tend to precede other words in sentences. This provides evidence of a non-random distribution of vocabulary in speech sequences. However, further research is required to address some outstanding issues. Firstly, comparative analysis in languages other than English is necessary to prove the universality of this phenomenon. Barlow [7] highlighted that studies in a single language are insufficient to make this claim, and research in languages such as Chinese is essential. Secondly, research on speech sequence features is limited to word frequency. To link this feature with cognitive processing, evidence from other aspects of lexical attributes is required.

In light of the aforementioned analysis, this article will concentrate on two particular issues. Firstly, the objective is to examine whether the lexical-attribute system related to cognitive processing in sentences is non-random in linear sequence, and whether the attributes include both formal and semantic aspects. The formal attributes include word frequency, average number of strokes per character and the number of senses; the semantic aspects pertain to the semantic features. Secondly, if the distribution is non-random, an investigation will be conducted into whether the distribution can be explained from the perspective of the cognitive load. Furthermore, the effect of this mechanism on the lexical system will be analyzed.

2   Research Design

2.1   Corpus and Processing Platform

The corpus is derived from the *Shandong University Modern Chinese Corpus (SduMc)*, comprising approximately 800 million characters spanning the period from 1900 to 2022. It encompasses a diverse range of textual genres, including literature, news, magazines, blogs, comprehensive websites, textbooks, and others. The corpus has been divided into segments using the *pkuseg*(Version 0.0.25), which was developed by Peking University.

2.2   The Selection of Sentence and Sentence Length Type

The basis for division of sentences is established by the use of punctuation marks, namely the full stop, question mark and exclamation mark. Furthermore, restrictions were imposed in two ways. Initially, the complexity of sentences was regulated by selecting only sentences devoid of mid-sentence punctuation (e.g., commas, etc.), thereby concentrating the analyzed material on sentences exhibiting a single topical and focal structure. Secondly, sentences comprising letters, numbers, and other non-Chinese symbols were excluded from the analysis.

Sentence length was calculated as the number of words contained within the sentence. The lengths of all sentences within the study corpus were counted, and the median sentence length was found to be 8.0 words, with an average of 8.44, a plurality of 6, a skewness of 1.24, and a kurtosis of 10.21. The distribution of sentence lengths exhibited a notable leftward skew. Within a range of 5 words on either side of the median of 8, i.e., 3 to 13 words, more than 80% (83.2%) of the sentences are covered, and within the range of 3 to 24 words, more than 95% (95.33%) of the sentences are covered. Therefore, the study will focus on the range of 3 to 24 words.

2.3   Framework and Resources of Lexical Attribute Analysis

In regard to the data sources, the word frequency data is derived directly from the statistics of *SduMc*, which is consistent with the methodology employed by Barlow [7]. The number of senses is calculated in accordance with the methodology outlined in *The Contemporary Chinese Dictionary (5th Edition)*, which excludes the names of individuals and geographical locations.

The semantic features are based on *A Thesaurus of Modern Chinese (TMC)* [8], which divides the modern Chinese lexicon into five levels and nine classes. The classification of semantic types considers both semantic characteristics and grammatical attributes, enabling a comprehensive examination from both semantic and syntactic standpoints.

2.4 Stop Words

The lexicon can be categorized into two main groups: content words and function words. Our current study primarily concerns itself with content words. Function words, being predominantly closed-class words, exhibit a high frequency of usage. When counted alongside content words, this frequency can obscure the distinctive distribution patterns of the latter. This effect is particularly evident in studies of frozen expressions in English. For instance, when examining the frequency distribution of the phrase *knife and fork*, the inclusion of *and* would only lead to conclusions regarding the high frequency of this connector, which lacks substantive linguistic meaning.

TMC provides specific instructions for the exclusion of certain auxiliary word classes, including prepositions, conjunctions, particles, and modal particles.

3   Word Order and Formal Features of Lexicon

In the course of statistical analysis, the initial step is to categorize sentences based on their length, forming sentence length groups. Subsequently, the average word frequency, the average number of strokes per character and the average number of senses are calculated for each position.

3.1 Word Frequency and Word Order

The data indicates that, for each sentence length group, the distribution of average word frequency in word order position is highly consistent, generally exhibiting a trend of high frequency at the beginning and low frequency at the ending. In particular, the word frequency is highest at the beginning of sentences, and exhibits a significant decline for the first three words, the relative stability in the middle, and then the sharply drop for the last three words, reaching its lowest frequency at the ending of the sentence. Figure 1 illustrates the distribution of average word frequency in 12-word sentences as an example. Sentences of other length group are the same.

To assess the stability of word frequency distribution patterns, the rank-order statistical method is employed. The notation R_i is employed to represent the rank order of the frequency of a given word at position i within a given sentence. The average frequency of each word at each position is calculated for sentences of the same length. Subsequently, the evaluated frequencies are sorted in descending order, with the position number after sorting representing the rank order. In this context, the subscript i represents the word order. For a sentence of length n, the range of values for both rank order and word order is [1, n]. To facilitate differentiation, the maximum value is represented by n for word order and N for rank order when applicable.

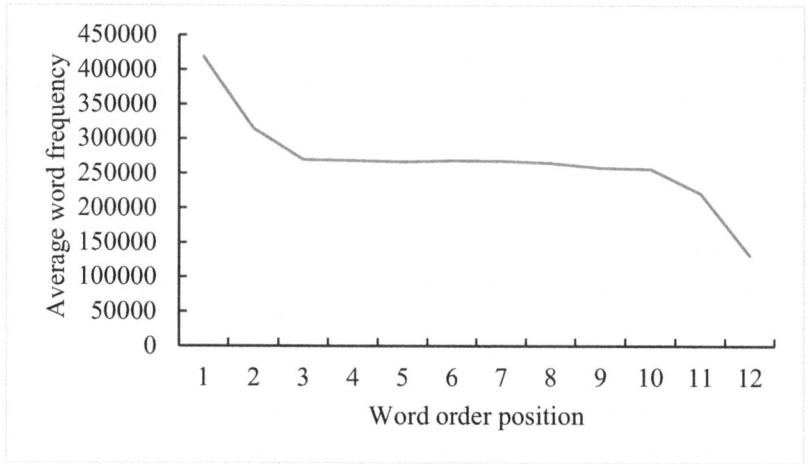

Fig. 1. The distribution of average word frequency across word order of 12-word sentences.

Table 1. The rank order of the beginning and ending words of sentences.

Order Type	Percentage of Type	Exception
$R_1 = 1$	100%	None
$R_2 = 2$	95.45%	$R_2 = 3$ when the sentence length is 24
$R_3 > R_2 > R_1$	100%	None
$R_n > R_{n-1} > R_{n-2}$	100%	None
$R_{n-1} = N - 1$	95.45%	$R_{23} = N - 2$ when the sentence length is 24
$R_n = N$	100%	None

Table 1 illustrates the statistical characteristics of rank order at the beginning and ending of the sentence. The first three rows of Table 1 present the statistical analysis of the beginning words of sentences, while the last three rows pertain to the ending words. The regular model can be described as follows: (1) For all sentence length groups, $R_1 = 1$ and $R_n = N$ are both present, indicating that the average frequency of words at the beginning of sentences is highest and lowest at the ending of sentences; (2) Except for 24-word sentences, all other sentence length groups have $R_2 = 2$, $R_{n-1} = N - 1$. The distribution of sentence lengths indicates that there are few, if any, 24-word sentences, which suggests that the data set is not representative. Even when outliers are present, $R_2 = 3$, $R_{23} = N - 2$ is in close alignment with the characteristics observed in other sentence length groups. (3) For all sentence length groups, $R_3 > R_2 > R_1$ and $R_n > R_{n-1} > R_{n-2}$ are both present, indicating a consistent decreasing trend in word frequency for the first three words and last three words of sentences.

The aforementioned statistical conclusions are in alignment with Barlow's analysis of English [7], thereby substantiating the same high-frequency-first pattern in Chinese sentences. This provides novel evidence for the theory of a high-frequency-first pattern in all languages.

3.2 Average Number of Strokes and Word Order

The complexity of writing a word is reflected in the average number of strokes per character. To conduct a similar approach to that employed for word frequency, a statistical analysis of the average number of strokes per character reveals a non-random distribution, and the trends are contrary to the observed trends in word frequency. Figure 2 illustrates the distribution of the average number of strokes for 12-word sentences, demonstrating a reduction in strokes at the sentence's beginning and an increase towards its ending. The central portion of the data set exhibits slight fluctuations that are analogous to the patterns observed in other sentence lengths.

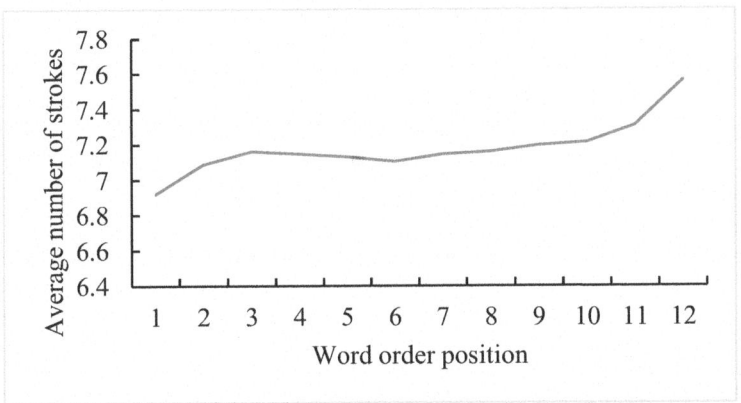

Fig. 2. Relationship between average number of strokes and word order in 12-word sentences.

The order of the number of strokes was analyzed using a similar approach to that employed for word frequency, whereby the average number of strokes was arranged and numbered in descending order to calculate rank orders.

As illustrated in Table 2, the pattern of fewer strokes at the beginning of sentences and more strokes at the ending is clearly discernible, with only the first two rows exhibiting exceptions, which occur in longer sentences. Nevertheless, the discrepancies between $R_1 = N - 1$, $R_2 = N - 2$, $N - 3$, and the overall regularity are not substantial. At the ending of sentences, all sentence length groups exhibit $R_n = 1$, $R_{n-1} > 2$ and $R_{n-1} > R_{n-2}$. The comprehensive analysis indicates that the average number of strokes in the word order sequence also exhibits a non-random distribution.

Table 2. The rank order and proportion of average number of strokes at the beginning and ending of sentences.

Order Type	Percentage of types	Exception
$R_1 = N$	95.45%	$R_1 = N - 1$ when sentence length is 24
$R_2 = N - 1$	90.91%	$R_2 = N - 2$ when sentence length is 21, $R_2 = N - 3$ when sentence length is 24
$R_3 < R_2$	100%	None
$R_{n-1} > R_{n-2}$	100%	None
$R_{n-1} > 2$	100%	None
$R_n = 1$	100%	None

3.3   Average Number of Senses and Word Order

A method similar to that used for word frequency was employed to analyze the average number of senses. The data demonstrates a general tendency for the number of senses to decrease at the beginning and ending of sentences, while exhibiting a higher and relatively consistent frequency in the middle of sentences. Figure 3 illustrates the distribution of numbers of senses for 12-word sentences, with comparable trends observed in sentences of varying lengths.

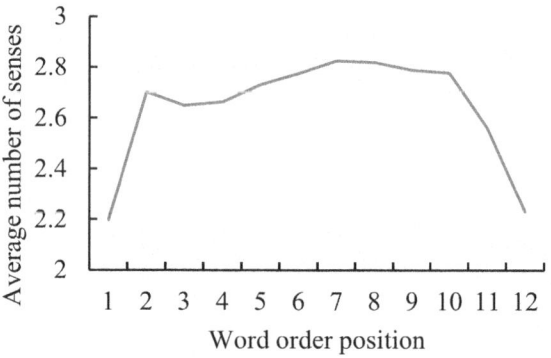

Fig. 3. The relationship between the average number of senses and word order in 12-word sentences.

A rank-order analysis was employed to examine the stability of the distribution of the average number of senses (see Table 3). The average number of senses was then arranged and numbered in descending order to calculate rank orders. Furthermore, patterns with strong regularities can be identified for all sentence lengths. These include: (1) the rank orders with the lowest average number of senses are distributed at the beginning or ending of sentences; (2) the second-to-last position has an average word frequency ranking at the 3rd or 4th.

Table 3. The type and proportion of rank orders of average number of senses at the beginning and ending of sentences.

Order Type	Percentage of types	Exception
$R_1 = 1$ or $R_1 = 2$	100%	None
$R_2 > R_1$	100%	None
$R_3 < R_2$	95.45%	$N = 5$
$R_{n-2} > R_{n-1}$	100%	None
$R_n = 1$ or $R_n = 2$	100%	None
$R_{n-1} = 3$ or $R_{n-1} = 4$	95.45%	$R_{n-1} = 5$ for $N = 24$

In conclusion, the three lexical attributes included in the statistical analysis demonstrate a discernible pattern of distribution across a wide range of sentence lengths. The corroboration of multiple attributes lends further support to the hypothesis that the distribution of lexical attributes in word order positions is not random.

4   Word Order and Semantic Features of Lexicon

In accordance with the tenets set forth in *TMC*, we undertake an in-depth examination of the semantic features inherent to linear sequences of sentences. Our analysis is particularly attentive to the presence of significant semantic features at the beginning and the ending of sentences in question. Thereafter, we proceed to investigate the intricate mechanisms underlying the mutual adaptation between linear sequences and semantic features of words.

4.1   The Trend of Change in the Proportional Difference of Semantic Classes in Adjacent Positions

By examining the trend of change in the proportional difference of semantic classes in adjacent positions, it is possible to ascertain whether there is a significant difference in the distribution of semantic classes at each position. In the computation, we let i represent the position number, s represent the semantic class code, S represent the total number of five-level semantic classes in *TMC*, $p_{i,s}$ represent the proportion of the s-*th* semantic class word at the i-*th* position, and use $D_{(i,i+1),s}$ to represent the proportional difference of semantic class s in adjacent positions.

$$D_{(i,i+1),s} = |p_{i+1,s} - p_{i,s}| \tag{1}$$

For $s \in S$, the total, the average, the maximum, and the standard deviation of $D_{(i,\,i+1)}$ can be calculated in order to reflect the difference in semantic content between positions i and $i + 1$ from a variety of perspectives. To illustrate, we utilize 8-word sentences (see Table 4) as a case study.

Table 4 presents the total number of D, which reflects the overall difference of semantic classes in adjacent positions of sentences. The average value of D reflects

Table 4. Statistical analysis of semantic class differences in adjacent positions in 8-word sentences.

Range	D in Total	D in Average	D in Max	D in Standard Deviation
1–2	67.147	0.140	11.143	0.759
2–3	21.730	0.045	2.262	0.172
3–4	12.842	0.027	0.935	0.080
4–5	9.983	0.021	0.475	0.043
5–6	13.223	0.028	0.604	0.066
6–7	19.652	0.041	1.375	0.120
7–8	57.110	0.119	3.291	0.293

the average difference, while the maximum value of D indicates whether there is a particularly large proportional difference of semantic classes in adjacent positions. The standard deviation of D, in turn, reflects the degree of dispersion of the proportional difference of each semantic class. A synthesis of the aforementioned data reveals a pattern whereby the values of D are largest in proximity to the sentence's extremities and diminish towards the sentence's midpoint. This trend is particularly evident in the semantic attribute, which exhibits pronounced fluctuations at the beginning and the ending of sentences.

To ascertain the universality of changes in semantic features at the beginning and ending of sentences, the rank-order analysis method is employed to statistically analyze all sentence lengths. Within each group of sentence lengths, the total D is arranged in descending order and its number is assigned as the rank order. For sentences of length n, there are $n - 1$ adjacent sequences, we use $R_{i,(i+1)}$ to representing the rank order of the i-th to $(i + 1)$-th position, where $R_{i,(i+1)} \in [1, N - 1]$.

Table 5. Distribution types and proportions of semantic classes at the beginning and the ending of sentences.

Order Type	Type Percentage	Sentence Length Type
$R_{1,2} = 1, R_{n-1,n} = 2$	50%	4–14
$R_{n-1,n} = 1, R_{1,2} = 2$	50%	3,15–24

Table 5 presents the statistical analysis of the distribution of semantic classes across different rank order types. The data reveals a 50% likelihood of either the beginning or ending of the sentence exhibiting the greatest difference in the proportion of semantic classes between the first two words.

In sum, the findings indicate that for all sentence length groups examined in this study, the semantic features at the beginning and ending of sentences exhibit the greatest variation. This indicates a statistical regularity in the semantic features at the beginning and the ending of sentences, thereby providing a foundation for conducting a specific semantic attribute analysis.

4.2 Differences in the Main Semantic Classes at the Beginning and Ending of Sentences

In accordance with the data presented in Table 5, we identify the five semantic classes exhibiting the most significant discrepancies in representation at the beginning and ending of sentences. Subsequently, we undertake a comparative analysis to ascertain the semantic features of words situated at the beginning and ending positions.

Table 6. Preferred semantic classes at the beginning of sentences.

Class (Level Three)	Class Proportion Difference
Creature-Human Nature-General Term	10.918%
Specific Object-Collective Noun-Thing Pronoun	7.831%
Time and Space-Time-Day and Night	3.632%
Abstract Object-Quantity-Quantity	1.824%
Abstract Object-Politics-Administration	1.482%

Table 7. Preferred semantic classes at the ending of sentences.

Class (Level Three)	Class Proportion Difference
Abstract Object-Events-Events	2.404%
Abstract Object-Events-Situations	2.162%
Abstract Object-Attributes-Factors	1.434%
Abstract Object-Events-Processes	1.300%
Abstract Object-Science and Education-Education	0.738%

Table 6 and Table 7, respectively, represent the top five dominant semantic classes at the beginning and the ending of sentences. The dominant words at the beginning of sentences can be classified into two categories: (a) *Creature-Human Nature-General Term, Specific Object-Collective Noun-Thing Pronoun* and *Abstract Object-Quantity-Quantity* classes, and (b) *Time and Space-Time-Day and Night, Abstract Object-Politics-Administration* classes. The dominant words at the ending of sentences are primarily situated within the (c)*abstract object* class.

Category (b) mainly includes temporal and numerical terms. In Chinese, time words often lead sentences, and numeral words commonly modify subjects, also appearing at the beginning of sentences. Thus, placing these words at the sentence's beginning is advantageous, partly due to syntactic preferences.

From the perspective of semantic features, it is noteworthy that the (a) and (c) categories show an opposition to each other. Firstly, both (a) and (c) words are nominal, and they are more likely to function as subjects and objects at the beginning and ending of sentences. Therefore, the distinction between (a) and (c) primarily reflects the differences in the semantic features of sentence subjects and objects. Secondly, in category (a), *living beings-humans-generic terms* and *specific objects-generic terms-object terms* are primarily pronouns referring to people and objects. The *abstract objects-political-Administration* class is classified as abstract objects in dictionaries, but its meanings often point to tangible buildings or personnel. To illustrate, in the sentence *How can I get to the embassy? embassy* refers to a specific building, with its abstract nature being considerably less pronounced than that of category(c). It functions more akin to category (a) in terms of reference. In contrast, category (c) is typically characterized by the predominance of nouns denoting abstract concepts.

5 Sentence Cognitive Load Balancing Mechanisms and Lexical Attributes

In order to analyze the mechanism of systematic interaction between word order and lexical attributes, it is necessary to adopt a cognitive processing perspective. The relationship between various lexical attributes and the difficulty of cognitive processing has been extensively investigated through experimental methods in the field of cognitive psychology. Some of the more established findings from this research can be utilized as a foundation for analysis.

5.1 Lexical Attributes and Cognitive Processing Difficulty

In terms of lexical cognitive processing, there is evidence of a word frequency effect, whereby the more frequently a word is used in everyday life, the more readily it is processed. This effect has been confirmed in a variety of lexical cognitive tasks, including lexical judgment, matching, naming, syntactic and semantic decisions [9]. The readability of reading materials has also been found to be affected by the use of commonly used words in readability studies.

With regard to morphological complexity, a fundamental conclusion has been reached, namely that the greater the complexity of a given form, the more challenging it is for the cognitive system to process it. In languages like English, the primary factor influencing writing complexity is word length. In contrast, Chinese characters exhibit a stroke effect at the character level, with characters having fewer strokes being more readily recognized [10, 11].

With regard to polysemy, research has revealed a prevalent ambiguity effect in the context of lexical cognitive processing. It is noteworthy that both superiority effects and inferiority effects have been documented in diverse experimental settings. In general, superiority effects are observed in lexical decision tasks and lexical naming tasks. This indicates that participants process polysemous words more rapidly and with greater accuracy in related experiments. However, in more complex tasks, such as word sense classification, the results are contrary to those observed for superiority effects of polysemous words. For example, Palmer & MacGregor et al. [12] observed that participants exhibited significantly slower and more error-prone processing of polysemous words in tasks requiring the distinction between specific and abstract meanings. Piercey & Joordens [13] observed that readers tend to linger longer on ambiguous words within coherent texts. This suggests that when readers do not require the precise determination of a word's meaning, words with multiple meanings may facilitate the expedited activation of the semantic network associated with the word, consequently accelerating recognition. However, when participants are required to determine the specific meanings of ambiguous words, competition among multiple semantic representations results in the consumption of greater resources and time, which in turn leads to inferior processing. Pexman & Hino et al. [14] proposed that the processing inferiority observed in semantic tasks is not solely attributable to the challenge of meaning activation. It may also be influenced by the additional time and cognitive resources required to make decisions among multiple meanings. This article addresses the phenomenon of polysemy in real-world speech. In actual reading or speech communication activities, it is not only necessary to identify words, but also to recognize the meanings of those words in context. Although this process is not directly comparable to ambiguity effect experiments, it is more akin to word sense classification tasks in cognitive processing, which also demonstrate inferiority effects.

In light of the characteristics of semantic classes in question, it can be surmised that the cognitive processing of both dominant words at the beginning and at the ending of sentences is relatively challenging. However, the underlying mechanisms appear to be distinct. The dominant words at the ending of sentences are primarily associated with the semantic class of *abstract object*. According to the specificity effect of vocabulary, the cognitive processing of vocabulary reveals that abstract words require a longer processing time and exhibit a lower accuracy rate than specific words. Dominant words at the beginning of sentences are predominantly pronouns, which aligns with the general rule of known information first, new information last [15, 16]. Typically, Chinese sentences follow the S-V-O structure. The statistical feature of advantageous noun vocabulary at the beginning and the ending of sentences reflects the vocabulary characteristics of the subject and object of the sentence. The preponderance of pronouns at the beginning is consistent with their function of expressing known information. This initial segment actually pertains to the object of the sentence, that is, the topic of the sentence [16]. This also indicates that although the isolated recognition of pronouns is not complex in terms of vocabulary meaning, their main function in language activities is referring and connecting, rather than representing the conceptual meaning of the vocabulary itself. In discourse, they play a mainly connecting role. While it is challenging to directly compare the processing difficulty of pronouns and abstract words, it is evident that their processing depends on longer contexts, involves a multitude of influencing factors, and is a more complex process.

Table 8 provides a summary of the attributes and relative processing difficulty of words at the beginning and ending of sentences. In terms of formal analysis, the frequency, average number of strokes per character, and number of senses associated with beginning words all indicate a relatively low level of cognitive processing difficulty. The frequency and stroke count of ending words indicate a high level of cognitive processing difficulty, whereas the number of senses indicates a low level of processing difficulty.

Table 8. Summary of the attributes of the beginning and ending words of sentences and their cognitive processing difficulty.

Lexical attributes	Beginning word		Ending word	
	Characteristics	Processing difficult	Characteristics	Processing difficult
Word frequency	High	Low	Low	High
Number of strokes	Few	Low	Many	High
Number of senses	Few	Low	Few	Low
Semantic attribute	Pronoun dominating	*High	Abstract word dominating	High

With regard to the semantic features of sentences, both the beginning and the ending words are balancing by a high level of cognitive processing difficulty. Table 8 includes an asterisk next to the processing difficulty of semantic features, as this difficulty is derived from their referential and cohesive functions, rather than the conceptual meaning itself.

5.2   The Principle of Cognitive Load Balance

The distribution of lexical attributes has been demonstrated to exert a moderating influence on the cognitive processing difficulty of a linear sequence of sentences. It has been demonstrated that the natural distribution of cognitive costs on the linear sequence of sentences is not uniform. The semantic scope of components situated closer to the beginning of a sequence is more extensive, resulting in elevated cognitive costs [6, 17, 18]. One significant factor in this discussion is that the components closer to the beginning of the sequence have fewer contextual cues to constrain and facilitate comprehension of word meanings. Conversely, the structure of the known information at the beginning also contributes to the imbalance in the cognitive load. As evidenced by the data presented in this article, the known information in the sentence is not explicitly stated, but rather conveyed through pronoun-dominated words whose actual referents are distributed across a longer context. In the cognitive processing of language, the establishment of connections between pronouns and their referents represents a significant cognitive challenge. The mechanism that adapts the lexical attribute system to the cognitive load of sentence linear sequences is manifested primarily as follows: Firstly, from the perspective of the cognitive load, the main formal features of the beginning words of sentences point to low cognitive processing difficulty, and the cognitive processing difficulty of the ending words of sentences is high in terms of word frequency, writing form, etc., which can form a certain balance with the cognitive load of the linear sequence of sentences; secondly, from the perspective of matching the form with the meaning, the beginning words of sentences represented by pronouns do not express complex conceptual meaning. The simple and easy-to-process form can make the human brain mainly process the substantive content pointed to by pronouns when processing sentences, while the ending words of sentences have to express the new information in sentences and bring new knowledge, thus focusing on their lexical meaning connotation, and the complexity of the form of the vocabulary writing is matched with it.

5.3 Cognitive Load Balancing Complements Linear Relationships for Lexical Attributes

The field of quantitative linguistics typically posits a linear relationship between a number of significant attributes associated with vocabulary. In his research on Chinese vocabulary, Wang [2] found that the higher the word frequency is, the greater the number of senses a word can be said to have, and the shorter the word length shall be. Conversely, the lower the word frequency is, the fewer senses a word can be said to have, and the longer the word length shall be. These findings suggest that word frequency plays a central role in determining the number of senses a word can be said to have. A review of the literature on vocabulary in other languages reveals a similar pattern of findings. The underlying rationale for this characteristic of vocabulary is elucidated by the principle of least effort, which postulates that the vocabulary system tends to utilize a symbol system that is as concise and accessible as possible to convey as many meanings as feasible. This principle is consistent with the general laws governing animal behavior and is therefore highly reliable.

The linear relationship between lexical attributes inevitably results in a high number of senses for words with a high frequency and a low number of strokes. This ensures that the least number of symbols are used to represent as many senses as possible, thereby ensuring efficiency. This is at odds with the feature identified in this study, whereby words at the beginning of sentences exhibit high frequency, a reduced number of strokes, and a concomitant reduction in the number of senses. This represents an additional perspective on the linear balance principle in the relationship between lexical attributes. In other words, the lexical system is, on the whole, concise. However, in some words that display special distributional or functional characteristics, modifications will be made to the attributes in order to adapt to the intensity of their cognitive load. In essence, the principle of cognitive balance is also consistent with *principle of least effort*, which occurs in the cognitive processing of sentences in the human brain.

6 Conclusion

Following the characterization of the distribution of lexical attributes in word order position, we put forward the hypothesis of cognitive load balance. It should be noted that this hypothesis is only supported by data at the statistical level. In this paper, we have counted a number of aspects, such as frequency, average number of strokes per character, number of senses and semantic features, which can be supported by each other from different data. Nevertheless, it remains challenging to conclude that lexical sequence position has been a primary driver in the evolution of lexical attributes, solely based on statistical methods. The Chinese lexical system has undergone an extended evolutionary process, during which a multitude of factors have exerted influence. Further investigation is required to gain a deeper understanding of this phenomenon, particularly with regard to the evolution of the lexical system over time and the psychological factors involved.

References

1. Liu, H.: An Introduction to Quantitative Linguistics. The Commercial Press, Beijing (2017). (in Chinese)
2. Wang, H.: Polysemous words: meaning length and frequency. Stud. Chin. Lang. **2**, 120–130 (2009). (in Chinese)
3. Deng, Y., Feng, Z.: A quantitative linguistic study on the relationship between word length and word frequency. J. Foreign Lang. **36**(3), 29–39 (2013). (in Chinese)
4. Zhang, P., Ma, J.: Semantic distribution of high frequency verbs in modern Chinese and the correlation between word frequency and word length. Appl. Linguist. **2**, 52–61 (2018). (in Chinese). https://doi.org/10.16499/j.cnki.1003-5397.2018.02.006
5. Köhler, R.: Zur linguistischen Synergetik: Struktur und Dynamik der Lexik. Bochum. N. Brockmeyer (1986)
6. Fenk-oczlon, G.: Word frequency and word order in freezes. Linguistics **27**(3), 517–556 (1989). https://doi.org/10.1515/ling.1989.27.3.517
7. Barlow, M.: Sequence and word frequency. Cogn. Linguist. Stud. **7**(2), 284–306 (2020). https://doi.org/10.1075/cogls.00058.bar
8. Su, X.: A Thesaurus of Modern Chinese. The Commercial Press, Beijing (2013). (in Chinese)
9. Zhang, B.: Psychology of Reading. Beijing Normal University Publishing Group, Beijing (2004)
10. Peng, D., Wang, C.: Basic processing unit of Chinese character recognition: evidence from stroke number effect and radical number effect. Acta Psychol. Sin. **1**, 9–17 (1997). (in Chinese)
11. Zhang, J.: On the stroke effect, word frequency effect and morpheme frequency effect in the recognition of Chinese one-character word by foreign student. TCSOL Stud. **1**, 22–29 (2008). (in Chinese). https://doi.org/10.16131/j.cnki.cn44-1669/g4.2008.01.006
12. Palmer, S.D., MacGregor, L.J., Havelka, J.: Concreteness effects in single-meaning, multi-meaning and newly acquired words. Brain Res. **1538**, 135–150 (2013). https://doi.org/10.1016/j.brainres.2013.09.015
13. Piercey, C.D., Joordens, S.: Turning an advantage into a disadvantage: ambiguity effects in lexical decision versus reading tasks. Mem. Cognit. **28**(4), 657–666 (2000). https://doi.org/10.3758/BF03201255
14. Pexman, P.M., Hino, Y., Lupker, S.J.: Semantic ambiguity and the process of generating meaning from print. J. Exp. Psychol. Learn. Mem. Cogn. **30**(6), 1252–1270 (2004). https://doi.org/10.1037/0278-7393.30.6.1252
15. Fang, M.: The syntactic performance practices of contrastive focus in Chinese. Stud. Chin. Lang. **4**, 279–288 (1995). (in Chinese)
16. Xie, H., Shi, F.: Prosodic encoding of the information structure of Chinese sentence in speech. J. Tianjin Univ. (Soc. Sci.) **21**(4), 301–309 (2019). (in Chinese)

17. Bolinger, D.L.: Linear modification. PMLA/Publ. Mod. Lang. Assoc. Am. **67**(7), 1117–1144 (1952). https://doi.org/10.1632/459963
18. Fenk-Oczlon, G.: Familiarity, information flow, and linguistic form. In: Bybee, J., Hopper, P. (eds.) Frequency and the Emergence of Linguistic Structure, pp. 431–448. John Benjamins Publishing Company (2001). https://doi.org/10.1075/tsl.45.22fen

A Typological Study on the Chinese Metaphorical and Metonymic Idioms Based on the Spreading-Activation Model

Yangyang Xi[✉]

School of Chinese Language and Literature, Wuhan University, Wuhan, China
2021101110005@whu.edu.cn

Abstract. In the Chinese lexical system, idioms constitute a crucial component. The study of idioms is extensive and longstanding, yet it often adheres to conventional perspectives, lacking in substantive innovation. This paper focuses on the application of the "Spreading-Activation Theory Model in the Understanding of Metaphorical and Metonymic Idioms in Chinese". Firstly, it clarifies the application and analysis of cognitive metaphor models in current idiom research, emphasizing three features of the source domain within idioms: (1) the relationship between the source and target domains, (2) the number of source domains within idioms, and (3) the inherent characteristics of the source domain. Drawing upon the Spreading-Activation Model, this study breaks free from existing theoretical frameworks, explores novel perspectives, and establishes a new classification system for metaphorical and metonymic idioms in Chinese. These idioms are classified into four categories: (1) Directional activation Idioms, (2) Cooperative activation Idioms, (3) Spreading activation Idioms, and (4) Superimposed activation Idioms. Through theoretical analysis, it derives a continuum of cognitive difficulty for these four idiom categories. This classification system broadens our understanding of idioms within ontological research, expands the typology of the Spreading-Activation Theory, and simultaneously contributes to idiom translation and teaching research.

Keywords: Chinese Metaphorical and Metonymic Idioms · Spreading-Activation Model · Idiom Categories

1 Introduction

In the Chinese language system, idioms constitute a highly significant component. Within the realm of teaching Chinese as a foreign language, idiom instruction is indispensable. In the field of teaching Chinese as a foreign language, there exist two widely acknowledged contradictions: one concerns the importance placed on idioms but the lack of emphasis, and the other relates to students' interest in idioms versus the difficulties they encounter. These two sets of contradictions represent pressing issues in the domain of teaching Chinese idioms to foreign learners.

P. Jin et al. (Eds.): CLSW 2024, LNAI 15552, pp. 384–401, 2025.
https://doi.org/10.1007/978-981-96-3509-2_28

Historically, discussions about idioms have predominantly occurred at the linguistic level, with limited attention to cognitive aspects. However, with the rise of cognitive linguistics and the development of cognitive metaphor theories, scholars are increasingly able to elucidate idiom content from fresh perspectives. However, Currently, there is still limited research focusing on idioms from the perspective of cognitive metaphor, and the semantic generation patterns of such idioms have received scant attention.

Given this context, this paper revolves around the core theme of "An Attempted Application of Activation Theory in the Teaching of Metaphorical and Metonymic Idioms". In the course of this specific study, it first clarifies the application and analysis of cognitive metaphor models in current idiom research, with a focus on three features of the source domain within idioms: (1) the relationship between the source and target domains, (2) the number of source domains, and (3) the inherent characteristics of the source domain. Combining the Spreading-Activation Theory, this study breaks away from existing theoretical frameworks, commencing from the initial stages of cognition, and constructs a novel classification system. Consequently, metaphorical and metonymic idioms are classified into four categories: (1) Directional Activation Idioms (where the source and target domains coexist), (2) Cooperative Activation Idioms (where only source domains are present, and multiple source domains exist), (3) Spreading Activation Idioms (where only source domains exist, and there is a single generic source domain), and (4) Superimposed Activation Idioms (where only source domains exist, and there is a single allusive or fable-like source domain).

This paper employs idioms found in the six volumes of *Developing Chinese* as corpus for classification. Based on this, it posits a hypothesis regarding the difficulty of acquiring idioms of different categories (with decreasing difficulty from left to right): Superimposed Activation Idioms > Spreading Activation Idioms > Cooperative Activation Idioms > Directional Activation Idioms.

2 Literature Review

Research on Chinese idioms from a cognitive perspective has long been a hot topic in academia, characterized by a substantial volume of studies, a wide array of types, and enduring interest. This study, using "idioms" and "cognition" as keywords, conducted a literature analysis using the CiteSpace tool on the CNKI database for the past 20 years. It is found out that this topic consistently produces research papers each year, showing no signs of interruption. Moreover, the yearly publication amount remains steady, indicating the sustained high interest and vitality of this research topic. (Hereafter, unless otherwise noted, "Chinese idioms" will be referred to as "idioms").

Research on the cognition of Chinese idioms primarily falls within the domains of linguistics and psychology, with differences in both methodology and perspective between these two fields. Psychology tends to employ empirical research methods and has enhanced its experimental techniques with technological advancements. For instance, Zhong [1] relied on the priming effect in his research, primarily based on subjective textual feedback and with relatively modest technological involvement. Wang [2] pioneered the use of eye-tracking and event-related potential techniques in this field. Su [3] employed functional magnetic resonance imaging (fMRI) to investigate brain activation during the comprehension of action idioms, while Ke [4] employed virtual reality technology to construct an Idiom Riddle Cultural Park, embracing a high level of technological sophistication.

In the realm of psychology, Chinese idioms are treated as experimental material to assess or verify specific theories or phenomena. For instance, Ke [4] employed Chinese idiom riddles as experimental material to conduct a scenario assessment of holistic thinking among the Chinese population. Song [5], Su [3], and Ye [6] used various categories of Chinese idioms to validate embodied effects in different scenarios. Yang [7] used idiom riddles as experimental material for meta-cognitive monitoring.

Linguistic research, on the other hand, exhibits a trend shifting from "theory" to "theory + empirical" studies. Idioms are established as the core object of study.

In the field of linguistics, research on this topic can be categorized into three main directions: translation studies, (Chinese as a foreign language) teaching research, and ontological research. Translation studies exhibit a rich array of methodologies and diverse research targets. Concerning methods for translating idioms, Song [8] observed the dynamic cognitive context through a pragmatic intervention perspective for idiom translation. Mo [9] employed the relevance theory to guide idiom translation, while Cen [10] examined homonymous-heterogeneous types of idioms in Vietnamese and Chinese, using the cultural affinity between the two languages as a translation strategy. Research in this area covers both sign language and foreign language translation. In sign language translation, scholars like Fu [11] explored the paths of idiom sign language translation from the perspective of cognitive metaphor. Foreign language translation encompasses specialized books, country-specific translations, and individual case studies. Wang [12], inspired by the concept of embodied cognition, analyzed 300 idioms from *Dream of the Red Chamber* in three English versions from the aspects of "reality-cognition-language". Cen [10] focused on the homonymous-heterogeneous aspects of Chinese-Vietnamese idioms, while Song [8] delved into novel English translation approaches for the idiom "望子成龙" (wàng zǐ chéng long, hope for one's child to succeed). Translation involves two languages, expressing the meaning of one language in another. Wu [13] posits that bilinguals, during lexical processing, only need to access one language, and lexical candidates from both languages are automatically activated. The common consensus in the above-mentioned literature is twofold: firstly, idioms are inherently metaphorical, a shared core in various research methods; secondly, translating idioms is challenging, regardless of whether it is sign language or foreign language translation. Wang [12] pointed out that the current challenges in idiom translation research stem from lack of in-depth cognitive analysis.

Research on idiom teaching primarily focuses on textbook compilation, learning methods, and error analysis. Hu [14] analyzed pragmatic errors in idioms like "炙手可热" (zhì shǒu kě rè, very influential or powerful) and continued discussions on their dictionary definitions. Huang [15] investigated learning methods for idioms in informal learning environments. Liu [16] proposed vocabulary consolidation strategies based on a comparison of Chinese-English textbooks from both China and abroad. The afore-mentioned studies reflect difficulties in three aspects: challenging textbook compilation, teaching complexities for instructors, and learning difficulties for students.

This article posits out that, whether in idiom translation studies or idiom teaching research, it is imperative to begin with the ontology, i.e., the idioms themselves. Subsequently, one must define categories, aiming to subdivide subtypes. Building on this foundation and incorporating various characteristics of idioms, a suitable entry point for in-depth analysis can be found, resulting in comprehensive and cognitively clear viewpoints. Investigating specific types, objects, or methods alone represents a misguided approach, diverting attention from the fundamental issues.

The subsequent focus is on ontological research within the field of linguistics. This type of research exhibits an overwhelming quantity, abounding both in absolute numbers and relative proportions. These research findings possess distinctive features: innovative theoretical perspectives, extensive coverage of materials, diverse research methodologies, and robust argumentation. They propel idiom research towards a path of theoretical, systematic, and scientific inquiry, offering novel dimensions, expanded perspectives, and new insights into the mechanisms of idioms, contributing significantly to the field. In general, these discussions share two points of consensus: the recognition of idioms as inherently metaphorical, a premise underlying virtually all idiom studies, and the acknowledgment of pervasive shortcomings, primarily related to the lack of a comprehensive approach and the inadequacy of methodologies. A significant aspect of idioms' metaphorical nature is the lack of alignment between their literal and practical meanings, a widely acknowledged premise in idiom research.

Addressing the issue, the concept of pervasive shortcomings pertains to the narrow scope of many studies, which tend to focus solely on local features and specific types of idioms. Research on idiomatic local features encompasses areas such as semantic similarity (Hu, [17, 18]; Jiang, [19, 20]), phonological complexity (Liu, [21]), semantic regularities (Hu, [22]), and interpretations based on literal readings (Wu, [23]). Research into specific types of idioms includes investigations into their internal structural types, similar idioms, idiom variations, and individual case studies. For instance, Wen [24] and Chen [25] examined symmetrical Chinese idioms as their research subjects. Wei [26] and Zhang [27] explored patterns of recognition in parallel structure idioms and double object structure idioms, respectively. Wang [28] investigated mixed Chinese-English idioms, and Zhang [29] focused on four-character phrases that are not considered idioms. Wei [30] concentrated on idioms containing the character "一" (yī) denoting "one" or "first". Both research on idiomatic local features and specific types represent facets or aspects of idiom studies, with the former emphasizing connotations and the latter highlighting extension. In essence, they represent two sides of the same coin. The features of idioms can serve as the basis for their classification, just as specific idiom types can reveal their common attributes. However, such an approach inherently limits the scope of inquiry and can lead to a failure to see the forest for the trees. The analysis of specific categories must always take into account the whole, or it risks making sweeping generalizations based on a partial perspective.

The issue of inadequate methodologies is mainly reflected in two aspects: excessive and inappropriate methods. Zhang [27], for instance, employed three distinct methods - the composite field mirror model, prism model, and term activation model - in investigating idiom semantics. One key insight here is that the value of research methods lies in precision, not quantity.

This article posits out that the two most significant breakthroughs in idiom research are the introduction of the Activation Theory and the utilization of new technologies. Notably, these two breakthroughs are converging. It is worth mentioning that Zhang [29] incorporated Chinese idioms into the cognitive framework of the Idiomatic Activation Set proposed by Langlotz [32], providing a reasonable explanation. Wang [31] constructed the "Hierarchical Progressive Model of Metaphorical Cognitive Processing", where "convention" represents the degree of conventionality. These two works represent two processes of understanding idioms. The structural perspective focuses on the internal compositional relationships within idioms, while the conventional perspective emphasizes the degree of association between literal and metaphorical meanings. Regrettably, there still exists a gap between theoretical self-consistency and specific practical applications. The structural perspective can naturally be divided into three categories in theory, but in corpus processing, there may be situations where classification is unclear. Assigning all idioms to a highly conventional metaphorical type lacks justification. Metaphorical idioms are just one type within idioms, and there are subcategories within them as well. It is inappropriate to consider the entire set as a single point without distinguishing the unresolved points, and this practice is not advisable.

Drawing lessons from the above, this study first clarifies the application analysis of cognitive metaphor models in current idiom research. It focuses on three characteristics of source domains within idioms: (1) the relationship between source and target domains, (2) the number of source domains within idioms, and (3) the specific attributes of source domains. Using this as a starting point and integrating the Spreading-Activation Theory model breaks through the existing theoretical framework and finds a new perspective. It conducts a systematic examination of idioms from a macroscopic viewpoint and proposes a new idiom classification model from a microscopic perspective.

3   Theoretical Perspective

The Spreading-Activation Model (hereafter referred to as SA) was proposed by Collins and Loftus [33]. Spreading-Activation is the recursive spreading process of initial stimulation. This model posits that when a concept is stimulated, it initiates an activation process, and its effects spread in all directions, propagating to other connected concepts. However, the energy of activation diminishes with increasing distance, meaning that closely related concepts are more likely to be activated than those farther away. From the operational perspective, the SA model functions as an organizational method of human memory. It asserts that memory organization resembles a complex network of connections, where specific memories diffuse among relevant concepts. In the Spreading-Activation Model, the strength of connections between concepts is represented by the links between nodes. The shorter the link, the stronger the connection, and conversely, the longer the link, the weaker the Connection (See Fig. 1).

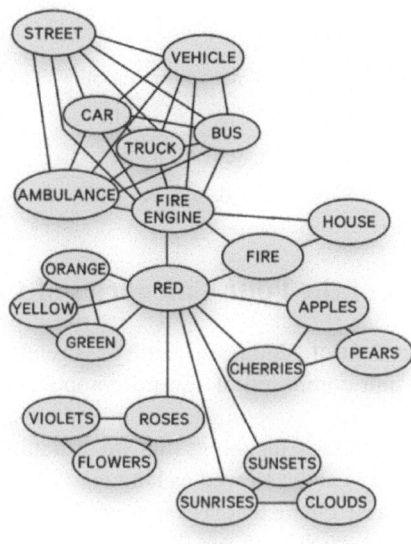

Fig. 1. The spreading activation model

4   Data and Analysis

The idiomatic data selected for this study are exclusively sourced from the six-volume series *Developing Chinese*. Based on the theoretical framework established in this paper, the idioms appearing in the *Developing Chinese* textbooks (all six volumes) were classified. According to the statistics, a total of 476 idioms are found throughout the six volumes. Among these, 310 idioms belong to the category of metaphorical idioms, accounting for approximately 65.1%, while 166 idioms fall into the non-metaphorical category, constituting approximately 34.9%. It is evident that the majority of the idioms selected in the Chinese language teaching materials fall under the category of metaphorical idioms. Assuming that this selection reflects a representative sampling, the distribution of idioms in actual language materials would likely follow a similar pattern, with a substantial proportion consisting of metaphorical idioms.

This paper conducted a classification and statistical analysis of idiom categories across all six volumes of *Developing Chinese*, as shown in Table 1.

Among these, there are 56 directional activation idioms, accounting for 18.1%, 113 cooperative activation idioms, making up 36.4%, 120 spreading activation idioms, representing 38.7%, and 21 superimposed activation idioms, constituting 6.8%.

Table 1. Statistical analysis of idiom types in Developing Chinese

Total Class	Subclass	Quantity	Percentage
Metaphorical and Metonymic Idioms	Directional activation idioms	56	18.1%
	Cooperative activation idioms	113	36.4%
	Spreading Activation idioms	120	38.7%
	Superimposed Activation idioms	21	6.8%

5   The Interpretation of the Four Categories of Chinese Idioms

In semantic studies, the concept of "compositionality" is related to the organization of meaning. For a linguistic unit composed of several components, its inherent meaning depends on the semantics of these components and how they are combined. Idioms, as members of fixed phrases, often have meanings that are difficult to derive using ordinary word formation rules, and they can be viewed as language structures with compositionality, consisting of four Chinese characters. These four characters can individually represent conceptual components, such as in "衣食住行" where each character represents an independent conceptual component, semantically distinct. They can also combine in pairs to form conceptual components, as in "鸡毛蒜皮" (jī máo suàn pí, trivial matters), where "鸡" and "毛" combine to form "鸡毛", and "蒜" and "皮" combine to form "蒜皮" To facilitate the understanding of the compositionality of idioms, refer to Fig. 2.

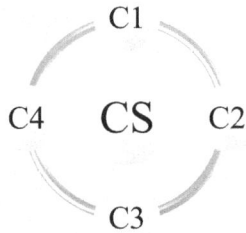

Fig. 2. Composite structure satellite image

In Fig. 2, the central element is the composite structure, which is composed of four components. According to Langlotz's model [32], there exist syntagmatic integration relationships between the components, while there are compositional relationships between the composite structure and the components.

The compositionality hypothesis in idiom processing posits that there exists a metaphorical or figurative relationship, rather than an arbitrary one, between the overall figurative meaning of idioms and the constituent elements of idioms (Xiao, [34]; Zhang, [35]; Yang & Zhang, [36]; Xi [37]). Wen [40] conducted a statistical analysis of VO idioms, concluding that when the object imposes strict constraints on the verb, it is more likely to form an idiom; otherwise, it is less likely. This finding indirectly confirms the interaction and influence between components in compositional structures. Such constraints align with a strong limitation on semantic, leading to unique forms and fixed meanings.

Idioms possess a metaphorical nature, and research on metaphorical idioms can be further subdivided into two categories: metonymy and metaphor. Metonymy is based on the mapping between the source and target domains within a domain, while metaphor is based on the mapping between the source and target domains. The former involves referential relationships, while the latter deals with analogical relationships. (Lakoff and Johnson, [38]; Croft and Cruse, [39]) Both metonymy and metaphor, however, share a common mechanism—namely, mapping. Therefore, this paper integrates the concepts of metonymy and metaphor into a unified category and results in the integrated category of "metaphorical and metonymic idioms". This integration inadvertently resolves certain issues related to the difficulty of determining whether an idiom belongs to metonymy or metaphor, as well as situations where an idiom can belong to both categories simultaneously. The need to categorize and identify such idioms within this framework becomes unnecessary and complex, whereas within this framework, these issues are no longer problematic (See Fig. 3).

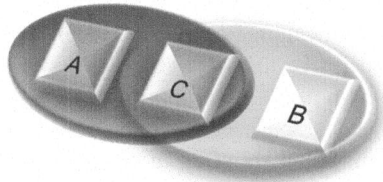

Fig. 3. Integration of metonymy and metaphor categories of idioms

A: Metaphorical Idioms
B: Metonymic Idioms
C: Idioms that are challenging to classify as belonging to either metonymy or metaphor

Zhang and Ji [27] classified idioms into three categories: highly compositional idioms, moderately compositional idioms, and lowly compositional idioms, based on the varying contributions of individual Chinese characters within idioms to their compositional meaning. This classification serves as a significant bridge between the literal and compositional meanings of idioms and holds great importance in the study of Chinese idioms. However, this classification does not delve into the interactions between individual Chinese characters within Chinese idioms, which is an indispensable aspect for understanding idiom meanings. This paper aims to approach this aspect by combining the Spreading-Activation model to analyze the semantic activation patterns of Chinese idioms.

Within the existing framework, there are three relevant concepts concerning metaphorical idioms: the source domain (the metaphorical concept), the metaphorical word, and the target domain (the intended meaning). Among these, the source domain is a mandatory element within idioms. This paper employs the source domain as the starting point and, considering several characteristics of the source domain, such as its co-occurrence with the target domain, the number of source domains involved, and whether the source domain possesses an allegorical nature, classifies metaphorical idioms into four categories: 1. Source-Target Co-occurrence Category; 2. Multi-Source Category; 3. Single Source Category; 4. Allegorical Category.

5.1 Directional Activation Idioms

Idioms in which both the source domain and the target domain co-occur exhibit a unique activation pattern, termed directional activation. Therefore, these idioms are referred to as directional activation idioms. Take the idiom "暴跳如雷" (bàotiào rú lé, fly into a rage), found in *Developing Chinese*, as an example. The source domain is "雷" (léi), meaning "thunder," and the target domain is "暴跳" (bàotiào), meaning "jumping furiously". When the concept of "雷" (thunder) enters the brain, it forms a Spreading-Activation map. From a sound perspective, thunder is loud and deafening; from a tangible perspective, thunder is a natural phenomenon, naturally associated with weather phenomena such as rain, snow, storms, and hail; from a mystical perspective, thunder signifies the wrath of celestial deities, foretelling ominous signs. However, "暴跳" (jumping furiously) provides direction to the meaning of "雷" (thunder). In this idiom, "雷" (thunder) refers to a furious anger, much like that of a celestial deity. The source domain "雷" (thunder) and the target domain "暴跳" (jumping furiously) collectively establish the meaning of an emotional state characterized by anger. *The Dictionary of Chinese Idioms* defines this phrase as "Jumping and shouting in anger, just like thunder, describing a furious and loud outburst".

Such idioms are not uncommon, with a total of 56 appearing in *Developing Chinese*, accounting for 18.1%. Examples include "受宠若惊" (shòu chǒng ruò jīng, to be flattered but also anxious), "聪明绝顶" (cōngmíng jué dǐng, extremely clever), "小心翼翼" (xiǎoxīn yìyì, extremely cautious), "门庭若市" (méntíng ruòshì, thronging with visitors), and "含情脉脉" (hánqíng mò mò, with affectionate looks). In the idiom "受宠若惊" (flattered but also anxious), the source domain "惊" (jīng, anxious) points to the target domain "受宠" (shòu chǒng, being flattered), conveying the idea of being pleased by favor but also feeling uneasy. In "聪明绝顶" (extremely clever), the source domain "绝顶" (jué dǐng, utmost) directs to the target domain "聪明" (cōngmíng, clever), describing extreme intelligence beyond comparison. In "小心翼翼" (extremely cautious), the source domain "翼翼" (yìyì, cautiously) points to the target domain "小心" (xiǎoxīn, careful), illustrating great care and caution. In "含情脉脉" (with affectionate looks), the source domain "脉脉" (mò mò, affectionate) is associated with the target domain "含情" (hánqíng, affectionate), often used to describe a young woman's slightly shy yet deeply caring expression.

These idioms are constrained by the target domain, and the activation direction from the source domain is unidirectional and fixed. This activation pattern can be likened to an arrow shot from a source domain (SD) toward a target domain (TD), mediated or directly focusing the spreading energy, thus highlighting the semantic essence of the idiom.

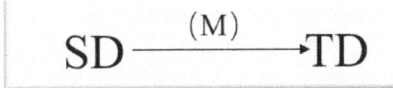

Fig. 4. Directional activation model

Figure 4 illustrates the directional activation model, with "SD" representing the source domain, "TD" representing the target domain, and "M" representing the metaphorical word. Parentheses indicate optional status of this component.

5.2 Cooperative Activation Idioms

Multiple-source category idioms fall into the category of cooperative activation exhibiting a distinct activation pattern. They have two prominent characteristics: firstly, only the source domain is explicitly present, and secondly, there are two or more source domains simultaneously at play. Due to the constraints of idiom length, such idioms typically involve two source domains, with a maximum of four. Through corpus analysis, it has been observed that these idioms predominantly feature either two-source or four-source domains.

Let us first examine the case of two-source domains with the idiom "鸡毛蒜皮" (jīmáo suànpí, trivial matters). "鸡毛" (jīmáo) refers to the feathers of a chicken, a material used to make shuttlecocks, arrows, feather fans, and similar items. From a tangible perspective, chicken feathers are useful. However, when describing a person, "鸡毛" signifies a serious or meticulous attitude, typically indicating determination and persistence in achieving a goal. Yet, in the idiom "拿着鸡毛当令箭" (názhe jīmáo dāng lìngjiàn, abusing authority with flimsy justification), "鸡毛" refers to trivial or extremely generalized words. In the film "鸡毛信" (jīmáo xìn, important message), chicken feathers represent urgent and important labels. In a "鸡毛店" (jīmáo diàn, small insignificant store), "鸡毛" indicates the establishment's shabby nature. Similarly, "蒜皮" (suànpí) can create a semantic network through Spreading-Activation, but we won't elaborate it here due to its little direct relevance to the topic at issue. In the idiom "鸡毛蒜皮" (jī máo suàn pí, trivial matters), the two source domains, when activated, intersect in a specific overlapping area, cooperatively generating the meaning of trivial and unimportant matters. This overlapping area signifies "trivial and unimportant", and their cooperation results in the idiomatic meaning of insignificant matters.

Now, let us consider idioms with four source domains, taking "衣食住行" (yī shí zhù xíng, basic necessities of life) as an example. The four source domains, "衣" (yī, clothing), "食" (shí, food), "住" (zhù, shelter), and "行" (xíng, transportation), individually form independent semantic networks. However, within this idiom, these four source domains share a semantic overlap area since they collectively represent the fundamental necessities of human life. This shared semantic territory constitutes the ultimate meaning of the idiom.

There are a total of 113 cooperative activation idioms in the six volumes of *Developing Chinese*, accounting for 36.4%. Examples of idioms with two source domains include "白马王子" (báimǎ wángzǐ, Prince Charming), "鼻青脸肿" (bíqīng liǎnzhuàng, black and blue), "垂头丧气" (chuítóu sàngqì, dejected), and others. Idioms featuring four source domains include "油盐酱醋" (yóu yán jiàng cù, oil, salt, soy sauce, vinegar), "生老病死" (shēng lǎo bìng sǐ, birth, aging, illness, death), "琴棋书画" (qín qí shū huà, music, chess, calligraphy, painting), and "酸甜苦辣" (suān tián kǔ là, sour, sweet, bitter, spicy).

In these idioms, multiple source domains are activated simultaneously, and different source domains, through common or similar semantic ranges, create an overlapping region. This overlapping region, facilitated by cooperative activation, directs the idiomatic meaning toward the target domain. This activation pattern is referred to as cooperative activation.

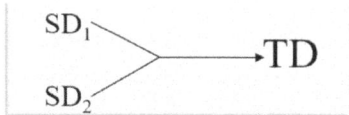

Fig. 5. Cooperative activation model

Figure 5 illustrates the cooperative activation model, with "SD1" representing Source Domain 1, "SD2" representing Source Domain 2, and "TD" representing the target domain. Source domains SD1 and SD2 simultaneously undergo Spreading-Activation, generating an overlapping area, and together, they cooperatively activate the target domain TD, resulting in the idiom's meaning. (...) indicates the more source domain(s) may be involved.

5.3 Spreading-Activation Idioms

Single Source Category idioms fall into the category of Spreading Activation, corresponding to a specific activation pattern. The only source domains, depending on their nature, are further categorized into two types. The first type consists of idioms with a single ordinary source domain. The second type comprises idioms with a single source domain rooted in folklore. Let us consider the first type with the idiom "鹤立鸡群" (hè lì jī qún, stand out from the crowd) as an example. This idiom itself represents a singular source domain. Once activated, it establishes a semantic network with multiple pathways, but only one of these pathways represents the actual meaning of the idiom. According to *The Dictionary of Idioms*, it means "standing out like a crane among chickens", metaphorically describing someone with exceptional appearance or talent.

This category of idioms is the most numerous, totaling 120 in the six volumes of *Developing Chinese*, making up the largest proportion at 38.7%. Examples include "滚瓜烂熟" (gǔn guā làn shú, well-versed), "九牛一毛" (jiǔ niú yī máo, a drop in the bucket), "浪子回头" (làngzǐ huítóu, prodigal son returns), among others. These idioms lack directed target domains or cooperative source domains, and their meanings exhibit spreading and uncertainty. In their semantic networks, one particular path, for uncertain reasons, is repeatedly strengthened and highlighted, forming the ultimate meaning. This activation pattern is referred to as Spreading-Activation.

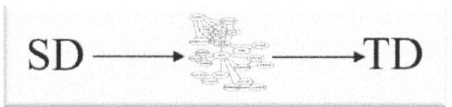

Fig. 6. Spreading activation model

Figure 6 illustrates the Spreading Activation model, with "SD" representing the source domain, "TD" representing the target domain, and a Spreading-Activation graph in between (see Table 1). Source domain SD undergoes Spreading-Activation, and activation energy reaches target domain TD within specific interpretations, ultimately yielding the meaning of the idiom.

5.4 Superimposed Activation Idioms

Idioms with allegorical status are categorized as Superimposed Activation idioms, corresponding to a specific activation pattern, referring to the latter of the two types mentioned in 7.3. In contrast to idioms with only one ordinary source domain, these idioms incorporate a folklore-based source domain that serves as the key to correctly understanding the idiom's meaning. Consider the idiom "塞翁失马" (sài wēng shī mǎ) as an example. This idiom activates a story taken from the "Huainanzi" as its sole source domain. The story goes as follows:

original text: 近塞上之人, 有善术者, 马无故亡而入胡. 人皆吊之, 其父曰: "此何遽不为福乎?"居数月, 其马将胡骏马而归. 人皆贺之, 其父曰: "此何遽不能为祸乎?" 家富良马, 其子好骑, 堕而折其髀. 人皆吊之, 其父曰: "此何遽不为福乎?" 居一年, 胡人大入塞, 丁壮者引弦而战. 近塞之人, 死者十九. 此独以跛之故, 父子相保.

translated text: Near the frontier, there was a person skilled in divination whose horse unexpectedly ran away into the land of the barbarians. Everyone consoled him, but his father said, "Who knows if this might not be a blessing?" Several months later, the horse returned, bringing along a fine steed from the barbarian lands. Everyone congratulated him, but his father said, "Who knows if this might not turn into a misfortune?" The family became rich in fine horses, and his son loved riding. One day, he fell off a horse and broke his leg. Everyone consoled him, but his father said, "Who knows if this might not be a blessing?" A year later, the barbarians invaded the frontier in great numbers, requiring all able-bodied men to take up arms and fight. Among the frontier people, nine out of ten were killed. However, due to the son's lameness, father and son were spared and survived together.

The moral of this story implies, "Good fortune may turn into misfortune, and misfortune may turn into good fortune. The transformation is limitless and profound." In other words, "An event that appears to be bad may, under certain conditions, turn out to be good," or "Misfortune can sometimes lead to good fortune." This category of idioms is the least numerous among the six volumes of *Developing Chinese*, comprising only 21 idioms, and representing the smallest proportion at 6.8%. Unlike idioms with a single ordinary source domain, these idioms operate through two activations, one from idiom to folklore and the other from folklore to meaning, using the folklore as a bridge. This activation pattern is referred to as Superimposed Activation.

$$SD_a \text{———} SD_b \text{———}\rightarrow TD$$

Fig. 7. Superimposed activation model

Figure 7 illustrates the Superimposed Activation model, with "SD_a" representing the initial source domain, "SD_b" as the bridge source domain, and "TD" as the target domain. In this framework, SD_a represents the initial source domain, SD_b serves as the bridge source domain, and TD denotes the target domain. SD_a initially activates SD_b, which in turn activates TD through the bridge source domain, ultimately achieving the expression of the idiomatic meaning.

5.5 Cognitive Difficulty Analysis of Four Categories of Idioms

These four distinct categories of idioms are characterized each by unique activation patterns that correspond to varying degrees of cognitive difficulty. In this section, we assess cognitive difficulty by analyzing three key factors: activation frequency, presence of assistance, and the nature of assistance. We establish a continuous gradient of cognitive difficulty and recognize that the complexity of idiom comprehension is contingent upon the intricacies of their activation patterns. To rephrase our objective, evaluating the cognitive difficulty of four categories of idioms is equivalent to determining the complexity of their respective activation patterns. Consequently, this section is primarily concerned with evaluating the complexity of these activation patterns.

Firstly, in terms of activation frequency, except for superimposed activation, directional activation, cooperative activation, and spreading activation each involve a single activation event. Therefore, these three activation types are simpler compared to superimposed activation, which necessitates two activation events.

Secondly, concerning the presence of assistance, directional and cooperative activation types benefit from assistance, while spreading and superimposed activation types do not. Consequently, the latter two are more complex in comparison to the former two.

Lastly, we examine the nature of assistance, focusing on directional and cooperative activation. For directional activation, the assistance involves targeting the activating object, namely the source domain, and defining a clear objective. Specifically, this entails establishing a meaningful target for the source domain. After activation, the activation energy is directed toward the target domain, providing a definite direction for activation. In such a scenario, activation is unidirectional and deterministic. In contrast, cooperative activation relies on semantic cooperation, also known as collision activation. In this mode, different source domains radiate their respective semantic networks, and these distinct semantic networks converge within an overlapping interval, collectively conveying the true meaning of the idiom. Clearly, from the perspective of the nature of assistance,

Table 2. Cognitive difficulty assessment of four types of idiomatic expression

Chinese Idioms	Activation Frenquency	Assistance Required	Nature of Assistance
Directional Activation	1	+(Yes)	Specify Objective
Cooperative Activation	1	+(Yes)	Semantic Cooperation
Spreading Activation	1	−(No)	/
Superimposed Activation	2	−(No)	/

cooperative activation is simpler than directional activation. The summarized analysis is presented in the Table 2.

It is important to note that superimposed activation relies on a bridge source domain for its dual activation process. Failure to clearly understand the context of this source domain can lead to misinterpretations, significantly increasing the complexity of this activation pattern.

Based on the above analysis, the varying complexities of different activation patterns are evident. The order from most complex to simplest is as follows: superimposed activation > spreading activation > cooperative activation > directional activation. Correspondingly, the continuum of cognitive difficulty for the four categories of idioms is as follows: idioms based on superimposed activation > idioms based on spreading activation > idioms based on cooperative activation > idioms based on directional activation.

6   Major Findings

In the preceding text, the core feature of idioms, the source domain, was utilized, and the Spreading-Activation model was adopted as the theoretical framework to delineate four activation patterns for Chinese idioms: Directional activation, cooperative activation, Spreading activation, and Superimposed activation. Subsequently, these activation patterns served as criteria for classifying Chinese idioms into four categories (See Fig. 8).

This figure is divided into two sections, with a satellite ring connecting the four categories. Let's first examine the satellite ring, where the core is a composite structure consisting of four components. According to the model proposed by Langlotz [30], there are syntagmatic integration relationships between components, and there are compositional relationships between the composite structure and components. The satellite ring connects to the four categories: Directional activation, Cooperative activation, Spreading activation, and Superimposed activation, each of which is depicted graphically.

This article combines the four inherent activation patterns within Chinese idioms with their external manifest features, specifically referring to the characteristics of the source domain. The source domain, as a necessary component of idiomatic expressions, serves as a tangible basis for distinguishing different types of idioms.

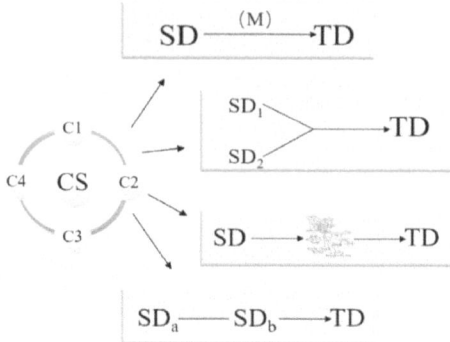

Fig. 8. Four categories of idioms with four activation patterns

To elaborate further, when both the source domain and the target domain coexist, the corresponding activation relationship is termed "Directional Activation." In this scenario, the target domain functions as the focal point, and the semantics emanating from the source domain are directed toward it. Examples of such idioms include "暴跳如雷" (bàotiào rú léi, fly into a rage), "受宠若惊" (shòu chǒng ruò jīng, overwhelmed by unexpected favor), "聪明绝顶" (cōng míng jué dǐng, extremely intelligent).

In cases where there is only a source domain, and multiple source domains coexist within a single idiom, the corresponding activation relationship is termed "Cooperative-Activation". In this scenario, different source domains within the same idiom reach a consensus of meaning within an overlapping semantic region, collectively conveying the ultimate meaning of the idiom. Based on the number of source domains, these idioms can be categorized into two types: those with two source domains, such as "鸡毛蒜皮" (jī máo suàn pí, trivial matters), and those with four source domains, such as "衣食住行" (yī shí zhù xíng, basic necessities of life).

In scenarios where there is only a source domain and a single, common-type source domain, the corresponding activation pattern is "Spreading-Activation" which fully conforms to the diffusion model of complete activation. Examples include "鹤立鸡群" (hè lì jī qún, stand out from the crowd), "滚瓜烂熟" (gǔn guā làn shú, well-versed), "九牛一毛" (jiǔ niú yī máo, a drop in the bucket).

In situations where there is only a source domain and a source domain with a reference to a story or fable, the corresponding activation pattern is "Superimposed Activation". This pattern involves activating the idiom through the activation of its underlying narrative, followed by the activation of the intended meaning of the idiom. Examples include "初出茅庐" (chū chū máo lú, just starting out), "塞翁失马" (sài wēng shī mǎ, a blessing in disguise) and others.

Through logical analysis, a continuum of varying cognitive difficulty for the four idiom categories has been established as follows: Superimposed activation idioms > Spreading activation idioms > Cooperative activation idioms > Directional activation idioms.

7 Conclusion

This study delves into Chinese metaphorical and metonymic Chinese idioms through the Spreading-Activation model, providing a comprehensive treatment of metaphorical and metonymic idioms based on the common mechanism of mapping. It examines the correspondence between the literal and conventional meanings of idioms and the pre-activation mechanisms among their components, focusing on the essential component "source domain". The study identifies four distinct activation modes and their corresponding idiom categories, and conducts a logical analysis to establish a cognitive difficulty continuum among these categories: Superimposed activation idioms > Spreading-activation idioms > Cooperative activation idioms > Directional activation idioms.

However, the study is subject to certain limitations: Firstly, the scope of the corpus is relatively narrow, necessitating the incorporation of larger-scale corpora in further research to validate and expand existing idiom classifications. Secondly, the analysis of cognitive difficulty gradient among the four idiom categories relies on logical analysis, which requires empirical research for verification. The use of implicit Markov models employing transition probabilities and emission probabilities can be considered to substantiate these conclusions. Thirdly, the empirical aspect of the study calls for complex ERP experiments to provide support.

References

1. Zhong, Y.P., Yang, Z.L.: A study on priming effect of impression formation in implicit social cognition. Acta Psychol. Sin. **30**(01), 21–26 (1998)
2. Wang, Y.W., et al.: Interpreting other minds and interactive minds in idioms: evidence from eye movements and ERPs. Acta Psychol. Sin. **44**(1), 100–111 (2012)
3. Su, D.Q., et al.: Brain regions activated during the semantic comprehension of Chinese action idioms and their embodiment effects: evidence from fMRI. Acta Psychol. Sin. **45**(11), 1187–1199 (2013)
4. Ke, X.X., et al.: A contextual assessment method and its application to the holistic thinking characteristics of Chinese people. Acta Psychol. Sin. **53**(12), 1299–1309 (2021)
5. Song, D.Q., et al.: The influence of 'cold' idiom semantic processing depth on temperature embodiment secondary effects. Stud. Psychol. Behav. **13**(4), 466–471 (2015)
6. Ye, H.S., et al.: Embodiment of mind: evidence from different disciplines. J. Soc. Sci. **5**, 117–128 (2013)
7. Yang, W.J., et al.: The Influence of cues on metacognitive monitoring processes in the riddle solving process. Psychol. Explor. **33**(1), 28–33 (2013)
8. Song, D.S.: Old tune, new interpretation: a new consideration of the English translation of '望子成龙.' Chin. Translators J. **4**, 29–31 (2000)
9. Mo, L.H., Ge, L.L.: Chinese idiom translation from the perspective of relevance translation theory. Soc. Sci. Hunan **2**, 189–191 (2012)
10. Cen, X.M.: A cultural analysis of homonymous and heteronymous meanings in Vietnamese and Chinese idioms and proverbs. J. Guangxi Minzu Univ. (Philosophy and Soc. Sci. Ed.) **38**(3), 161–164 (2016)
11. Fu, M.: Exploring the translation teaching of chinese idioms from the perspective of cognitive metaphor. Chin. J. Spec. Educ. **1**, 48–52+79 (2017)

12. Wang, Y.: The English translation of Chinese idioms from the perspective of embodied linguistics: a comparative study based on three English versions of '红楼梦'. Chin. Translators J. **40**(4), 156–164+190 (2019)

13. Wu, Y.J., Thierry, G.: Investigating bilingual processing: the neglected role of language processing contexts. Front. Psychol. **1**, 178 (2010). https://doi.org/10.3389/fpsyg.2010.00178

14. Hu, B.B.: Pragmatic deviation and dictionary definitions of '炙手可热'-type idioms. Lexicographical Stud. **4**, 40–48 (2009). https://doi.org/10.16134/j.cnki.cn31-1997/g2.2009.04.011

15. Huang, L.X.: Research on mobile language learning in informal learning environments: an analysis of Singaporean students' extracurricular Chinese idiom learning and creative activities. Mod. Dist. Educ. Res. **2**, 67–73 (2012)

16. Liu, Y.: The application of vocabulary consolidation strategies in elementary Chinese teaching materials: a comparison with overseas English teaching materials. TCSOL Stud. **4**, 52–61 (2012). https://doi.org/10.16131/j.cnki.cn44-1669/g4.2012.04.005

17. Hu, M., Li, F.X.: The cultural interpretation of the sequence-similarity principle in idioms. Dongyue Trib. **36**(10), 180–183 (2015). https://doi.org/10.15981/j.cnki.dongyueluncong.2015.10.029

18. Hu, M.: Reconstructing internal syntactic relations in idioms from syntactic similarity. Dongyue Trib. **35**(11), 178–181 (2014). https://doi.org/10.15981/j.cnki.dongyueluncong.2014.11.032

19. Jiang, C.S., Liao, D.Z.: The manifestation of analogy in idioms. Foreign Lang. Educ. **30**(6), 14–16+23 (2009). https://doi.org/10.16362/j.cnki.cn61-1023/h.2009.06.009

20. Jiang, C.S., Liang, J.X.: On imagery representation in idioms. Foreign Lang. Res. **4**, 52–54 (2007). https://doi.org/10.16263/j.cnki.23-1071/h.2007.04.017

21. Liu, Z.Q., et al.: Phonological symmetry and cognition of four-character idioms. Lang. Teach. Linguist. Stud. **3**, 48–57 (2003)

22. Hu, X.C., Wu, C.A.: On the evolution of the semantic tone of Chinese idioms. Chin. Lang. Learn. **5**, 65–76 (2016)

23. Wu, J.: On the cognitive model of 'interpreting idioms from context' and its dictionary compilation. Seeker **12**, 172–173+48 (2013). https://doi.org/10.16059/j.cnki.cn43-1008/c.2013.12.016

24. Wen, X., Ding, F.F.: Analysis of autonomous/dependent frame semantic models for symmetrical Chinese idioms. Foreign Lang. Teach. **3**, 30–41+52+147 (2017). https://doi.org/10.13458/j.cnki.flatt.004357

25. Chen, J.: Conceptual integration mechanism of structurally symmetrical four-character idioms in Chinese. Soc. Sci. Guangxi **10**, 132–135 (2010)

26. Wei, Z.J.: A study on the metaphorical mechanism of Chinese idioms from the perspective of embodied linguistics. Foreign Lang. China **16**(6), 26–33 (2019). https://doi.org/10.13564/j.cnki.issn.1672-9382.2019.06.005

27. Zhang, H., Ji, F.: Exploration of the semantic structure interpretation model of familiar phrases. Foreign Lang. Teach. **9**, 1–7 (2008)

28. Wang, S.H., Peng, Y.X.: Hybrid, integration, and empathy: a study on the cognitive pragmatic mechanism of mixed Chinese-English homophonic idioms in network humor. J. Xi'an Int. Stud. Univ. **30**(4), 1–6 (2022). https://doi.org/10.16362/j.cnki.cn61-1457/h.2022.04.018

29. Zhang, H., Sun, H.T., Gu, J.X.: ERP study on the interaction of rhythm and syntax in the processing of non-idiomatic four-character word groups: the sixth study of cognitive research on familiar phrase representation and understanding. Foreign Lang. Teach. **6**, 6–11 (2012). https://doi.org/10.13458/j.cnki.flatt.003840

30. Wei, Z.J.: Cognitive construction evidence for the polarity idioms with '一' in Chinese. Foreign Lang. China **12**(3), 50–56 (2015). https://doi.org/10.13564/j.cnki.issn.1672-9382.2015.03.007

31. Wang, X., Wang, Y.: The 'hierarchical progression model' of non-literal language cognitive processing in Chinese. J. Zhejiang Univ. Humanit. Soc. Sci. Ed. **50**(04), 176–188 (2020)
32. Langlotz, A.: Idiomatic Creativity. John Benjamins Publishing Company, Amsterdam (2006)
33. Collins, A.M., Loftus, E.F.: A spreading-activation theory of semantic processing. Psychol. Rev. **82**, 407–428 (1975)
34. Xiao, F.S.: A new exploration of the meaning of English idioms. Foreign Lang. Teach. **21**(2), 39–46 (2000)
35. Zhang, H.: Idioms: conventionalization and psychological representation - a cognitive study of idioms part one. Mod. Foreign Lang. **26**(3), 249–258, 250 (2003)
36. Yang, B., Zhang, H.: Cross-sensory perception and the study of synesthetic adjectives. Foreign Lang. Teach. **28**(1), 16–21 (2007). https://doi.org/10.16362/j.cnki.cn61-1023/h.2007.01.013
37. Xi, Y.: A research report on a novel typological study of the Chinese metaphorical and metonymic idioms. Front. Psychol. **15**, 1321778 (2024). https://doi.org/10.3389/fpsyg.2024.1321778
38. Lakoff, G., Johnson, M.: Metaphors We Live By. The University of Chicago Press, Chicago (1980)
39. Croft, W., Johnson, M.: Cognitive Linguistics. Cambridge University Press, Cambridge (2004)
40. Wen, X., Li, Y., Zhao, Y., Xu, H.: A study of identification of Chinese VO idioms with statistical measures. In: Dong, M., Gu, Y., Hong, J.F., Lin, J.X., Jin, P. (eds.) Chinese Lexical Semantics (CLSW 2023). LNCS. Springer, Cham (2024)

A Study on the Mapping Model of the Mid-Ancient Chinese Lexical Synaesthesia Metaphors—On the Differences in Synaesthesia Between Chinese Literature and Chinese Sutras

Bihai Wang[✉]

Tsinghua University, Beijing 10084, China
17888844811@163.com

Abstract. This paper systematically investigates synaesthetic metaphors in Mid-Ancient Chinese using a combined approach of quantitative and qualitative analysis. In addition to the previously generalized mapping model, the study identifies several key findings. Notably, vision-related synaesthetic metaphors appear fully developed, while those involving taste and touch remain underdeveloped. Furthermore, no evidence of reverse mappings exists between auditory and olfactory senses. The synaesthetic metaphors in Buddhist sutras are shaped by a negative perception of unclean touch and an emphasis on the dissemination of "vocal education", leading to an avoidance of tactile imagery. Additionally, auditory perception in these metaphors is characterized by a diverse range of sources and pathways. Regarding production patterns, the dominant form involves two identical sensory combinations being mapped to other senses. These three features reveal significant differences from those found in Chinese literary works.

Keywords: Synaesthetic Metaphor · Map Mode · the Mid-Ancient Chinese · Sensory Adjective

1 Introduction

Synaesthetic metaphors in language refer to the phenomenon where perception in one sensory domain is described using concepts from another sensory domain (Ullmann [1]; Williams [2]). Concerning the directionality of synaesthetic mapping, previous studies have developed models of metaphorical mapping across sensory words in various languages, grounded in the cognitive characteristics of those languages. Research in China has primarily focused on examining the metaphorical mechanisms and semantic evolution of specific sensory cases within synaesthetic metaphors, often drawing on corpus-based evidence. For example, studies by Wang Shaohua [3], Peng Yi and Bai Jiehong [4], and Wang Yuhong [5] among others, have investigated these phenomena. Additionally, the works of Xiong and Huang [6], Xiong and Huang [7], and Liu Hongchao et al. [8] have systematically explored synesthetic mapping rules in modern Chinese.

P. Jin et al. (Eds.): CLSW 2024, LNAI 15552, pp. 402–415, 2025.
https://doi.org/10.1007/978-981-96-3509-2_29

Zhao and Huang [9] suggested that synaesthetic metaphors in Chinese represent both a diachronic mechanism of change and a synchronic linguistic feature that persist across different stages of the language. In the Mid-Ancient Chinese, the interaction between Chinese and Sanskrit languages played a significant role, with the translation of Buddhist sutras serving as a major conduit. Thus the linguistic forms of synaesthetic metaphors in Buddhist texts differ from those found in Chinese literature.

Several scholars have already recognized this distinction and conducted case studies on the subject. For instance, Xiong and Huang[10] found that the gustatory term 味 (wèi, "taste") in Chinese Buddhist sutras extended beyond its literal meaning to function as a general sensory term. Hao Jing[11] observed that terms such as 痛 (tòng, "pain") and 痛痒 (tòng-yǎng, "pain and itch") in Buddhist sutras encompass broader sensory meanings, including "feeling" and "sensation".

Thus a thorough exploration of the distinct characteristics of Chinese literature and Buddhist sutras can offer valuable insights, particularly in understanding the evolution of complex synaesthetic phenomena in Chinese. In light of this, the present study aims to systematically investigate the phenomenon of synaesthesia in Middle Chinese and to compare the metaphorical mapping patterns observed in Chinese Buddhist sutras and Chinese literature using corpus-based empirical methodologies.

2 Selection and Tagging of the Corpus

According to the theory of synesthetic metaphors, the source domain corresponds to the category from which the basic meaning of a sensory word originates, while the target domain pertains to the category of the extended meaning of the sensory word applies. The sensory classification system introduced by Aristotle based on sensory organs, parallels with it found in Buddhism, which encompasses the senses of 色 (sè, "vision"), 声 (shēng, "sound"), 香 (xiāng, "smell"), 味 (wèi, "taste"), and 触 (chù, "touch"). Building upon this foundation, this study integrates Zhao's [13] expanded framework, which further divides sensory concepts into 11 sub-domains, reflecting the cognitive attributes of human perception. Touch includs hardness, strength, humidity, temperature, smoothness, sharpness, and pain level. Vision including color, light, dimension, and visual condition.

In this study, the classification of sensory adjective morphemes is based on the following principles:The primary reference is *Shuō Wén Jiě Zì*. If the term is not included, its meaning is assessed according to *The Grand Chinese Dictionary (Second Edition)*. For example, both dictionaries define the term 滑 (huá, "slippery") as "unhindered". Thus, it is classified under the tactile category of "smoothness".

A total of 179 sensory morphemes are extracted from Middle Chinese adjectives, including 45 touch morphemes, 13 taste morphemes, 6 smell morphemes, 7 sound morphemes and 108 vision morphemes. See Appendix A for detailed information.

The paper determines whether to include the disyllabic adjective word by taking into account the following references[1]: 1) the definition and history of it in *The Grand Chinese Dictionary*; 2) the allocation of the it within Academia Sinica Tagged Corpus

---

[1] All the example sentences utilized in this article are sourced from the Great Chinese Dictionary (Second Edition) and Academia Sinica Tagged Corpus of Middle Chinese.

of Middle Chinese; 3) the distribution of it's morpheme meaning and word meaning in the ancient Chinese documents.

When selecting a disyllabic adjective, the following criteria must be met: (1) it must be listed in *The Great Chinese Dictionary*, and by querying the corpus, it has been used in specialized Middle Chinese literature; (2) the original meanings of both morphemes composing the word must pertain to a specific sensory domain; (3) the overall meaning of the word must align with a particular sensory experience; (4) the meaning of one of the morphemes must differ from the complete meaning of the word, as discussed in Zhao Qingqing's [14] work[2].

For instance, the morphemes "短" (*duǎn*, "short") and "浅" (*qiǎn*, "shallow") in "短浅" (duǎn-qiǎn, "narrow and shallow") represent visual conditions. However, the whole meaning conveys a sense of limited knowledge and experience, failing to meet condition 3. The term "和柔" (*hé-róu*, "gentle") refers to a gentle tactile sensation, however "和" (hé, "gentle") represents a sense of mildness without any direct sensory expression, hence not meeting condition 2.

The whole meaning of "软滑" (*ruǎn-huá*, "soft and smooth") refers to a sensation aligning with the physical properties of the morphemes, yet fails to meet condition 4.The term "柔软" (*róu-ruǎn*, "soft") as applied in expressions like "其音柔软清净" (*qí-yīn-róu-ruǎn-qīng-jìng*, "the voice of the Buddha is soft and clear") meets all criteria.

Through labeling, it has been confirmed that there are 63 adjectives in Middle Chinese that contribute to synesthetic metaphorical mappings. The collection includes 12 visual adjectives, 7 tactile adjectives, 26 auditory adjectives, 12 taste adjectives, and 6 olfactory adjectives. For more detailed information, please refer to Appendix B.

3 Synesthetic Metaphorical Mapping of Adjectives in Middle Chinese

This paper identifies the sensations of compound morphemes as the basis for mapping, while the sensation conveyed by the word's meaning is designated as the target. This article refers to the classification of adjective synaesthesia mapping types in Wen Han [12], as follows:

Type1: morpheme A $_{(sensation\ A)}$ + morpheme B $_{(sensation\ B)}$ → Compound word $_{(sensation\ A/B)}$.

Type2: morpheme A $_{(sensation\ A)}$ + morpheme A $_{(sensation\ A)}$ → Compound word $_{(sensation\ B)}$.

Type3: morpheme A $_{(sensation\ A)}$ + morpheme B $_{(sensation\ B)}$ → Compound word $_{(sensation\ C)}$.

For instance, the term 光润 (*guāng-rùn*, "smooth and moisturizing") can be classified as Vision-visual condition + Touch-humidity → Vision, conforming to Type (1). The term 柔软 (*róu-ruǎn*, "soft") can be classified as Touch-strength + Touch-hardness → Sound, adhering to Type (2). 清凉 (*qīng-liáng*, "cool and refreshing") conveys a serene

---

[2] The directionality of sensory mapping in adjective synaesthetic metaphors exists when a specific morpheme within an adjective conveys a sensation that differs from the overall meaning conveyed by the word.

auditory sensation, so it's classified as Vision-visual condition + Touch-temperature → Sound, corresponding to Type (3). After statistical analysis, the following table can be obtained (Table 1).

Table 1. Sensation mapping and being mapped frequency table

The frequency of sensory mapping and its frequency of being mapped					
	TOUCH	VISION	TASTE	SOUND	SMELL
frequency of mapping	19	41	5	0	0
frequency of being mapped	7	12	12	26	6

It is evident that distinct tendencies exist among various sensations concerning their roles in mapping and being mapped. The frequency with which tactile and visual senses serve as the sources for mapping is significantly higher than when they act as the target. Taste, sound, and smell are more often mapped as targets than as sources. Therefore, there are two-way mappings[3] exist between touch, vision, and taste, whereas sound and smell predominantly exhibit one-way mappings.

The following sections categorize these sensations and provide a comprehensive overview of the associated phenomena and underlying patterns.

3.1 Tangible Tends to Function as a Mapping Source

This article identifies touch, as a mapping source, being capable of mapping onto vision, sound, and taste. A total of 9 words map from touch to vision, including 光润 (*guāng-rùn*, "glossy"), 麤大 (*cū-dà*, "large"), 润泽 (*rùn-zé*, "glossy"), 硬实 (*yìng-shí*, "sturdy"), 肥腻 (*féi-nì*, "greasy"), 轻利 (*qīng-lì*, "light-footed"), 重浊 (*zhòng-zhuó*, "dense and turbid"), 麤疏 (*cū-shū*, "rough"), and 干枯 (*gān-kū*, "shriveled").

1) 饭已, 面色润泽有威神。(《大楼炭经》) (触觉-湿度 + 触觉-湿度 → 视觉-视觉情状).

   *fàn yǐ, miàn sè **rùn-zé** yǒu wēi shén.*
   dining already face complexion glossy have prestige spirit.
   After dining, his complexion turned glossy, exuding dignity and spirit. (《*Da Lou Tan Jing*》) (Touch - humidity + Touch - humidity → Vision - visual condition).

   There are 6 words that map from touch to sound, including 软美 (*ruǎn-měi*, "gentle"), 轻重 (*qīng-zhòng*, "loud or light"), 清凉 (*qīng-liáng*, "cool"), 柔软 (*róu-ruǎn*, "soft"), 重浊 (*zhòng-zhuó*, "guttural"), 润泽 (*rùn-zé*, "melodious").

2) 所谓实语, 不虚发言用真正言。出清亮声, 润泽之声, 妙声, 喜声。(《佛本行集经》)(触觉-湿度 + 触觉-湿度 → 听觉).

---

[3] One-way mapping refers to adjectives that appear only when transferring from one sensory class to another, without reciprocal mapping, as described by Zhao Qingqing (2018). Two-way mapping applies to adjectives that reflect a bidirectional relationship between two sensations.

suǒ wèi shí yǔ bù xū fā yán yòng zhēn-zhèng AUX say true word NEG spurious speak word use real.

*yán chū qīng-liàng shēng **rùn-zé** zhī shēng miào shēng xǐ shēng*

word emit clear voice melodious DE voice wonderful voice happy voice

the true words are not false ones, but those based on sincerity, the emitted sound is clear, melodious, wonderful, and joyful.(《*Abhiniskramana-sutra*》)

(Touch - humidity + Touch - humidity → Sound)

There are 3 words that map to taste, including 甘脆 (*gān-cuì*, "sweet and crisp"), 甜滑 (*tiān-huá*, "sweet and glossy"), 甘润 (*gān-rùn*, "sweet and luscious").

3) 四时常有花, 可食, <u>甜滑</u>, 无子。(《齐民要术》)(味觉 + 触觉-平滑度 → 味觉)

*sì shí cháng yǒu huā kě shí, **tiān-huá** wú zǐ*

four seasons always have flowers can eat sweet and smooth NEG seeds

Flowers bloom all year round, are edible, possess a sweet and velvety taste, and do not produce seeds.(《*Qi Min Yao Shu*》)(Sound + Touch - smoothness → Taste)

There are 7 words that establish mappings from vision to touch, including 轻薄 (*qīng-báo*, "thin"), 轻微 (*qīng-wēi*, "slight"), 轻细 (*qīng-xì*, "light and fine"), 清冷 (*qīng-lěn*, "chilly"), 清凉 (*qīng-liáng*, "cool and refreshing"), 隆炽 (*lóng-chì*, "extremely hot"), 坚实 (*jiān-shí*, "hard"), all be found in Buddhist sutras.

4) 说于一切有处, 皆悉无常, 如芭蕉茎, 无有<u>坚实</u>。(《佛本行集经》)

(触觉-硬度 + 视觉-视觉情状 → 触觉-硬度)

shuō yú yī-qiè yǒu chù jiē xī wú-cháng rú bā-jiāo jīng

say at all have place all entire impermanence like plantain stem

*wú yǒu **jiān-shí***

NEG have rigidity

Everything in the world is constantly changing and flowing, just like the stem of a plantain, devoid of any rigidity. (《*Abhiniskramana-sutra*》)

(Touch - hardness + Vision - visual condition → Touch - hardness)

The analysis indicates that touch serves as the primary source, both one-way and two-way mappings. One-way synaesthesia includes mappings from touch to vision, sound, and taste. The combinations of vision and touch, however, can map to vision, touch, taste, and sound, making it the most prevalent form of synaesthetic mappings.

3.2 Vision Tends to Function as a Mapping Source

Vision serves as a mapping source for four senses: touch, sound, taste, and smell. 41 words utilize vision as the mapping source, while 12 words mapped to vision.

Vision-to-sound mappings occur most frequently, with a total of 17. Among these, 清凉 (*qīng-liáng*, "cool"), 清净 (*qīng-jìng*, "clean"), 软美 (*ruǎn-měi*, "soft and gentle"), 幽静 (*yōu-jìng*, "quiet"), 微妙 (*wēi-miào*, "subtle"), 微细 (*wēi-xì*, "tiny and light"), 润泽 (*rùn-zé*, "melodious"), 深远 (*shēn-yuǎn*, "deep and profound"), and 美妙 (*měi-miào*, "wonderful") found in Chinese Buddhist sutras.

5) 光而七尺, 色若如金, 其音甚大, 声而<u>清净</u>, 于人之上是则为尊。(《如来三昧经》)(视觉-视觉情状 + 视觉-视觉情状 → 听觉)

guāng ér qī chǐ sè ruò rú jīn qí yīn shèn dà shēng

light be seven feet color if like gold its sound very big sound

*ér **qīng-jìng** yú rén zhī shàng shì zé wéi zūn*

but clean at people DE above be then for Venerable

The light extends seven feet in length, its color just like gold, emitting a loud and clean sound. Above mankind stands the venerable one. (《*Tathagata Samadhi Sutra*》)

(Vision - visual condition + Vision - visual condition → Sound)

丽妙(*lì-miào*, "wonderful"), 深烈 (*shēn-liè*, "deep and intense"), 重浊 (*zhòng-zhuó*, "low and guttural"), 朗畅 (*lǎng-chàng*, "loud and smooth"), 清浊 (*qīng-zhuó*, "voiceless and voiced"), 清高 (*qīng-gāo*, "clear and melodious"), 清澈(*qīng-chè*, "clear and loud"), 清朗 (*qīng-lǎng*, "loud and vivid") indicate auditory sensations, which can be found in Chinese literature.

6) 善与人言, 音声丽妙, 如妇人好女。(郦道元《水经注》)

    (视觉-视觉情状 + 视觉-视觉情状 → 听觉)

*shàn yǔ rén yán yīn-shēng **lì-miào** rú fù-rén hǎ nǚ*

be good at with person specak sound wonderful like woman good girl

(orangutan) are very good at chatting with people, with beautiful voices like beautiful women. (*Li Daoyuan*《*Notes on Book of Waterways*》)

(Vision - visual condition + Vision - visual condition → Sound)

There are 9 words that map from vision to taste, including 醇厚(*chún-hòu*, "mellow"), 肥美 (*féi-měi*, "delicious"), 肥浓 (*féi-nóng*, "fat concentrated"), 肥鲜(*féi-xiān*, "be fresh and tender"), 厚薄 (*hòu-báo*, "thick and thin"), 肥腻 (*féi-nì*, "greasy"), 清净 (*qīng-jìng*, "clean and pure"), 焦苦 (*jiāo-kǔ*, "charred and bitter"), 微妙 (*wēi-miào*, "subtle").

7) 甥又觉之, 兼猥酿酒, 特令醇厚诣守备者, 微而酤之。(《生经》)(味觉 + 视觉-维度 → 味觉)

shēng yòu jué zhī jiān wěi niàng jiǔ tè lìng

nephew and insight it concurrently together brew wine specially make

***chún-hòu** yì shǒu bèi zhě wēi ér gū zhī*

mellow visit guard fielding person slight but sell it

As nephew gained some understanding, he began brewing wine, deliberately aiming for a rich and mellow taste. He intended to present it to the guards, and only sold a small portion to them. (《*Book of Sheng*》) (Taste + Vision - dimension → Taste)

There are 5 words map from vision to smell, including 焦臭 (*jiāo-chòu*, "burnt odor"), 清香 (*qīng-xiāng*, "fragrant aroma"), 妙香 (*miào-xiāng*, "wonderful aroma"), 臭烂 (*chòu-làn*, "stench") and微妙 (*wēi-miào*, "subtle").

In Middle Chinese, using vision as the mapping source, its mapping targets can be touch and taste. There are 3 words that map from taste to vision: 甘美 (*gān-měi*, "beautiful"), 肥浓 (*féi-nón*, "vigorous and thrive"), and 辛苦 (*xīn-kǔ*, "hard").

8) 一切丛林, 一切树木, 一切药草, 一切时苗, 皆悉肥浓, 长养滋茂。(《佛本行集经》)(视觉-视觉情状 + 味觉 → 视觉-视觉情状)

yī-qiè cóng-lín yí-qiè shù-mù yí-qiè yào cǎo yí-qiè shí miáo

all jungle all tree all medicine herbs all current seedling

jiē xī féi-nóng zhǎng yǎng zī mào
every entail vigorous and thrive grow generate multiply lush
All forests, trees, medicinal herbs and seedlings of agricultural crops grow robustly
and luxuriantly (《*Abhiniskramana-sutra*》)
(Vision - visual condition + Taste → Vision - visual condition)
Based on the above, visual perception tends to act as the mapping source and
exhibit one-way and two-way synaesthesia mappings.The combinations of two visual
morphemes can map to sound or taste.

3.3 Taste, Smell, and Sound Tend to Be the Mapping Sources

Taste serves as a mapping source to three senses: vision, sound and smell, with a total
of five words involved. Additionally, 12 other sensory words map to taste. The word
mapping from taste to sound is 甘美 (*gān-měi*, "sweet and luscious")[4] in the phrase "
辞为甘美内如剑戟" (*cí-wéi-gān-měi-nèi-rú-jiàn-jǐ*, "the words are sweet and alluring,
yet beneath their facade lie sharp swords and spears") in *Chu Yao Jing*.

Taste generally acts as the mapping source and engages in both one-way and two-
way synaesthetic mappings. One-way mappings occur from taste to smell and sound,
while two-way mappings happen between taste and vision.

Smell predominantly functions as the mapping target in one-way mappings, with six
words mapping to smell. Vision and taste can map to smell, but smell does not map to
other senses. Sound primarily serves as a mapping target, while touch, vision, and taste
can all map to sound. However, sound does not map to other senses.

3.4 Analysis of the Mapping Model of Synaesthesia Metaphors in Middle Chinese

The analysis suggests that Middle Chinese adjectives exhibit a hierarchical mapping
system for synaesthesia mappings and sensory accessibility. In terms of mapping types,
different feelings result in different types when they act as the mapping targets (Tables 2
and 3).

Table 2. The quantity of mapping types of different sensory as mapping source or target

Mapping types of different sensory words as mapping source				
Mapping types	Touch	Vision	Taste	Sum
Type1 quantity	10	21	2	33
Type2 quantity	5	18	2	25
Type3 quantity	3	2	1	6

As shown above, different sensations generate varying mapping types when serving
as the targets. It's evident that when touch, vision, and taste are used as mapping sources,

---

[4] Refer to the similar expression of "A honey tongue, a heart of gall", 美 (*měi*, "beautiful") is
treated as a taste sensation that is closer to the overall auditory meaning.

Table 3. The quantity of mapping types of different sensory as mapping target

Mapping types of different sensory words as mapping target						
Mapping types	Touch	Vision	Taste	Sound	Smell	Sum
Type1 quantity	7	9	8	5	4	33
Type2 quantity	0	3	3	18	1	25
Type3 quantity	0	0	1	4	1	6

Type (1) is most frequently preferred, followed by Type (2). Notably,vision shows the highest tendency to involve Type (2).When different sensations are used as mapping sources, touch, vision, taste, and smell are predominantly associated with Type (1). Touch originates exclusively from Type (1) and is produced solely through the mapping combinations of touch and vision.

Sound occurs in various forms, but it is predominantly generated through Type (2). Combinations such as touch + touch, vision + vision and taste + taste can map onto sound, with vision + vision being the most frequent. In Type (3), visual mapping does not exist. This means that combinations of two non-visual sensations cannot map to vision; visual morphemes must be involved in the formation of such words.

Although touch and vision, as well as taste and vision, can map onto each other, the probability of synaesthesia occurring from touch to vision or from taste to vision are significantly higher than the reverse. There are 9 mappings from taste to vision, accounting for 50% of the total. While there are 7 mappings in the opposite direction, accounting for 17.5%. The former occurs more than twice as frequently as the latter. The same goes for taste and vision, mappings from taste to vision accounts for 60%, while reverse accounts for 22.5%.

Synaesthetic mappings across different sensations reveal an asymmetric pattern. Touch, vision, and taste can function as mapping sources, and there is a degree of two-way mappings between them, placing them in the first level. In contrast, sound, and smell only serve as mapping targets and lack two-way mapping, placing them in the second level. The hierarchical structure and mapping model referenced here align with the work by Han Wen [12]. Building on this, the synaesthetic metaphor mapping model for adjectives in Middle Chinese is depicted in Fig. 1.

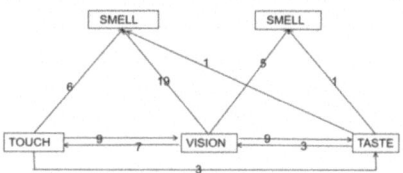

Fig. 1. The Mapping Model of the Mid-Ancient Chinese Lexical Synaesthesia Metaphor (The numbers on the model in the figure correspond to the number of sensory adjectives in Middle-ancient Chinese that represent feeling from one sensation to another).

This article summarizes the following rules of sensory mappings in the synaesthetic metaphors mappings. First, the synaesthetic metaphor system exhibits a hierarchical structure, which can be divided into two levels. Second, the system predominantly follows a one-way mapping pattern from lower to higher level. Third, while the first level allows two-way mappings, the primary direction is upward toward the second level, with pairwise combinations also possible for upward mappings.

4 Differences in Synesthesia Between Chinese Literature and Sutra

As a mechanism of diachronic evolution, synaesthetic metaphors manifest in various forms across different historical periods, with sensory mappings occurring at different stages. Compared with the modern Chinese synaesthetic metaphor mapping model Zhao and Huang [14] proposed. It reveals that the visual mappings have already formed and stabilized during the Middle Chinese period and continued into Modern Chinese. Touch and taste mappings are still in development, and the mapping from taste to touch have not yet been established.

Additionally, the mappings from touch to smell have not yet emerged, nor have the reverse mappings from sound to vision. And vision is the first to mature, followed by taste and touch, with sound development occurring later and at a slower pace.

Chinese Buddhist sutras are influenced by the original language and theoretical concepts of Buddhist scriptures, its metaphorical expression of adjective synaesthesia differs from that found in Chinese literature.

There are 7 words[5] in the Chinese Buddhist sutras that map from touch, with the targets being sound and vision, but none mapping back to touch. Furthermore, no other sensory domains map to touch in the sutras. In contrast, Chinese literature contains 11 words that map from touch, four of which map to touch itself, accounting for 36.36%. The absence of tactile terminology in the Chinese Buddhist sutras is thus a significant phenomenon.

Metaphorical mappings involving other senses do not map to touch, indicating a distinct tendency in the Chinese Buddhist sutras to avoid tactile expressions, likely due to underlying Buddhist beliefs. Wang Yunlu [15] observed that the Buddhist concept of "touching impure things and self-polluting" has contributed to the association of "impurity" with the act of touch. According to *Ding Fubao's Dictionary of Buddhism*, the term "touching filth" refers to the act of contacting unclean objects and thereby polluting oneself, thus leading to the interpretation of "touching" as "pollution". This perception is often viewed negatively, carrying a derogatory emotional undertone. As a result, users tend to favor words with positive emotional connotations and tactile perception is largely avoided in Buddhist sutra.

Significant differences exist between Chinese literature and Chinese Buddhist sutras in the way auditory perception is mapped. The formation and perception of sound in Chinese Buddhist sutras are expressed through three sensory categories: vision, touch, and taste, encompassing eight sensory sub-domains and nine mapping modes in 9 words.

---

[5] Words that are used simultaneously in both and express the same feeling will be excluded, and the calculation will not be repeated. The specific words that express touch and sound in different texts have been explained in the previous sections, see Sect. 3.1 and 3.2.

In comparison, Chinese literature employs two sensory categories, three specific subdomains and four mapping modes in 8 words, indicating that Buddhist sutras offer a more refined and complex approach to auditory expression and formation.

Adjectives describing sound in Chinese Buddhist sutras also appear in Chinese literature but map to different sensory domains, referring to the Table 4. Chinese literature favors mapping Type (1) and tends to prioritize the sensory categories conveyed by the source morphemes. In contrast, Buddhist sutras are inclined toward mapping Type (2), favoring transitions from one sensory domain to another.

Table 4. The generation modes of auditory mapping in Buddhist sutra and Chinese literature

Example of adjectives	Morpheme composition of mapping source	Sensation in Chinese Literature	Sensation in Buddhist sutra
柔软 (róu-ruǎn, "soft")	Touch-strength + Touch-hardness	Touch	Sound,Touch
甘美 (gān-měi, "sweet and luscious")	Taste + Taste	Taste	Sound
深远 (shēn-yuǎn, "deep and profound")	Vision-dimension + Vision-dimension	Vision	Sound

Buddhist sutras provide a richer and more nuanced depiction of auditory perception, offering a diverse range of sources for auditory expression. This emphasis may stem from the way Buddhism is traditionally disseminated. For example, in the Shurangama Sutra, it is said that the five Bhikkhus attained enlightenment upon hearing the Buddha's teaching in the Deer Park. Enlightenment via sound plays a crucial role in both the practice and transmission of Buddhism. Chanting and praising are integral daily practices in Buddhist temples and form the foundation of many Buddhist rituals, commonly referred to as "vocal education".

The classification and interpretation of sound in Buddhist sutras are highly detailed. The Brahma Sutra specifies that the Buddha uses eight types of voices when enlightening people, including the best voice, the gentle voice, and others. Individuals with different spiritual capacities perceive these voices in unique ways. Early Buddhism relies primarily on oral transmission, which underscores the central role of sound in spreading Buddhist teaching. This reliance on oral methods contributed to the development of the rich and diverse sonic culture within Buddhism.

5   Conclusion

This article systematically examines synaesthetic metaphors in adjectives from Mid-ancient Chinese. By combining corpus annotation with quantitative and qualitative analyses, a comprehensive mapping model for synaesthetic metaphors in Mid-ancient Chinese adjectives is developed. A comparison with the synaesthetic metaphors mapping model in modern Chinese adjectives reveals the developmental stages of synaesthesia in Middle Chinese. Vision-based synaesthesia have already formed and stabilized, while touch and taste are still in development. Certain metaphorical mappings have not yet emerged and auditory development at the second level occurred later and at a slower pace, with reverse mappings not yet present.

A comparison of synaesthetic metaphorical mappings between Chinese Buddhist sutra and literature reveals three key differences: (1) Chinese sutras avoid tactile sensation as a mapping target, likely due to Buddhist beliefs associating touch with impurity; (2) Chinese Buddhist sutras prefer Type (2), while Type (1) is more common in Chinese literature; (3) the metaphorical mappings of sound in Chinese Buddhist sutras exhibit greater variety and abundance than in Chinese literature, which may be related to the emphasis on sound in Buddhism and its role in vocal education. Whether the distinctive synaesthetic expressions found in Chinese Buddhist sutras influenced the use of synaesthetic language remains a subject for further exploration.

Funding. The research described in our paper was supported by the following funding: [National Social Science Fund Project]: [23VJXG058]. [Projects of Bases Sponsored by the Ministry of Education]: [22JJD740001].

Appendix A

(See Table 5)

Table 5. The Classification of Sensation of Morphemes in Mid-ancient Chinese

Sensation	Example							Quantity
TOUCH	冷	寒	轻	湿	凉	温	热	45
	暖	润	黏	冻	腻	硬	涩	
	柔	脆	刚	固	痛	软	韧	
	尖	锐	燥	炎	坚	炽	紧	
	强	弱	干	粗	烈	钝	滑	
	沉	麤	胀	利	疼	冽	重	
	喧	泽	牢					
TASTE	咸	美	甜	苦	淡	酸	醇	13
	鲜	浓	淳	辣	辛	甘		

(*continued*)

Appendix B

(See Table 6)

Table 5. (*continued*)

Sensation	Example							Quantity
SMELL	香	臊	焦	臭	腥	馨		6
SOUND	吵	喧	闹	寂	静	响	默	7
VISION	白	黑	亮	清	混	空	僵	108
	高	低	大	小	宽	烂	满	
	窄	狭	长	矮	短	丽	盈	
	细	方	圆	厚	红	妙	澈	
	杂	暗	幽	明	朗	冥	乱	
	枯	爽	壮	繁	扁	秀	昏	
	薄	艳	浑	深	浅	旷	阔	
	隐	隆	鲜	微	老	嫩	峭	
	眇	耀	疏	焦	缺	近	远	
	涨	张	畅	丑	博	浊	精	
	密	光	实	盛	纤	闇	虚	
	弘	蓬	华	平	赫	昂	澄	
	峻	卷	直	促	茂	纯	碎	
	美	丰	肥	瘦	稠	净	玄	
	阴	皓	素	黯	广	洁	密	
	散	灼	绵					

Table 6. Examples of Synaesthetic Metaphor in Mid-ancient Chinese

SOURCE	TARGET	EXAMPLE					QUANTITY	TOTAL
TOUCH	VISION	光润	润泽	干枯	硬实	麤疏	9	18
		重浊	麤大	轻利	肥腻			
	SOUND	软美	润泽	轻重	清凉	柔软	6	
		重浊						
	TASTE	甘润	甘脆	甜滑			3	
VISION	TOUCH	轻薄	清冷	清凉	隆炽	轻微	7	40
		轻细	坚实					

(continued)

References

1. Ullmann, S.: The Principles of Semantics, p. 266. Blackwell, Oxford (1957)
2. Willam, J.: Synaesthetic adjectives: a possible law of semantic change. Language **52**(2), 461–478 (1976)

Table 6. (*continued*)

SOURCE	TARGET	EXAMPLE					QUANTITY	TOTAL
	SOUND	清凉	丽妙	深烈	重浊	朗畅	19	
		微细	清静	软美	清浊	美妙		
		清高	清净	深远	幽静	清朗		
		微妙	隐隐	清亮	清澈			
	TASTE	醇厚	肥美	肥浓	肥鲜	微妙	9	
		厚薄	肥腻	清净	焦苦			
	SMELL	焦臭	清香	妙香	臭烂	微妙	5	
TASTE	VISION	甘美	肥浓	辛苦			3	5
	SMELL	甘润					1	
	SOUND	甘美					1	
SUM (11 words involve two synaesthetic mappings)								63

3. Wang, S.: Synaesthesia, Associations, Cognition Modern Foreigner Languages (02), 188–194+187 (2002). (in Chinese)
4. Peng, Y., Bai, J.: Cognitive linguistic perspective on synaesthetic. Foreign Lang. Their Teach. (01), 14–17 (2008). (in Chinese)
5. Wang, Y.: The cognitive mechanism of synaesthetic metaphor and its philosophical significance. Foreign Lang. Their Teach. (04), 13–16 (2008). (in Chinese)
6. Xiong J., Huang, C.-R.: The synaesthetic and metaphorical uses of 味 wei 'taset' in Chinese Buddist texts. In: Proceedings of 30th Pacific Asia Conference on Language, Information and Computation (PACLIC30), pp. 485–492 (2015)
7. Xiong, J., Huang, C.-R.: Being assiduous: do we have BITTERNESS or PAIN? The synaesthetics and conceptual metaphors of BITTERNESS and PAIN in Chinese and English. In: Lu, Q., Gao, H.H. (eds.) Chinese Lexical Semantics. LNAI, vol. 9332, pp. 15–23. Springer, Gewerbestrasse (2015)
8. Liu, H., Striklievers, F., Huang, C.: Automatic extraction and mapping directionality of synaesthetic sentences of modern Chinese. Comput. Eng. Sci. **37**(12), 2294–2299 (2015). (in Chinese)
9. Zhao, Q., Xiong, J., Huang, C.-R.: Linguistic synaesthesia, metaphor and cognition: the systematicity and significance of linguistic synaesthesia in Chinese. Stud. Chin. Lang. (02), 240–253+256 (2019). (in Chinese)
10. Xiong, J., Huang, C.-R.: The synaesthetic and metaphorical uses of 味 wei 'taste' in Chinese Buddhist Suttas. In: Pacific Asia Conference on Language, Information and Computation, pp. 485–492 (2016)
11. Hao, J.: A study on "痛" and "痛痒" having a meaning of feeling and its origin in the Chinese Buddhist Scriptures. Han Yu Shi Xue Bao (02), 53–64 (2022). (in Chinese)
12. Wen, H., Zheng, S.: A study of adding psychological feeling into the model of synaesthesia at the morpheme level in modern Chinese. In: Dong, M., et al. (eds.) CLSW 2023. LNAI, vol. 14514, pp. 400–414. Springer, Cham (2023). https://doi.org/10.1007/978-981-97-0583-2_31
13. Zhao, Q.: Embodied conceptualization or neural realization: a corpus-driven study of Mandarin Synaesthesia adjectives. Springer, Singapore (2020)

14. Zhao, Q., Huang, C.-R.: Mapping models and underlying mechanisms of synaesthetic metaphors in Mandarin. Lang. Teach. Linguist. Stud. (01), 44–55 (2018). (in Chinese)
15. Wang, Y., Le, Y.: The impacts of translation of Buddhist sutras to Chinese language—from the perspective of the word "Chu (触)" "Wochuo (龌龊)" having the lexical meaning of dirty. Zhejiang Soc. Sci. (12), 118–127+159 (2021). (in Chinese)

On the Interpretation of Numerals in Mandarin: A Closer Look at the Effects of Modals

Wei-Chen Chang[ID] and Huichen S. Hsiao[(✉)][ID]

Department of Chinese As a Second Language, National Taiwan Normal University, Taipei, Taiwan
{weichen.chang,huichen.hsiao}@ntnu.edu.tw

Abstract. *"Exactly n"*, *"at least n"* and *"at most n"* are three interpretations that will be derived when reading numerals in context. Testifying the previous claims [7, 9], this study aims to reveal how the interpretation of numerals is influenced by co-occurring modals through empirical study. Our preliminary results indicate that the universal modal *bixu* (be required to) triggers listeners' preferences for *"at least n"* reading, while the existential modal *keyi* (be allowed to) gives rise to *"at most n"*. Furthermore, based on the results of the self-paced reading task, the processing of interpreting numerals aligns more closely with the claims of the grammatical theory (cf. Chierchia et al. [7]; Spector [13]) than with the theory proposed by Kennedy [9]. This finding implies that the two-sided bounded interpretation of numerals is derived through the pragmatic mechanism—scalar implicature.

Keywords: numeral · modal · scalar implicature · grammatical theory

1 Introduction

There is a thriving interest in the interpretation of scalar terms, the expressions that entail the meaning of degree, scale, or quantity, in semantic research, including studies in Mandarin linguistics (e.g., Lin [1]; Hsiao et al. [2]). "Scalar Implicature (SI)" is a crucial topic in the field of scalar semantics. When listeners are presented with a sentence like (1), they will not interpret *some* as its basic semantic reading (*some and possibly all*). Instead, they negate the stronger alternative and infer a strengthening meaning (*some but not all*) with the assumption that speakers should provide sufficient information to avoid inaccuracies in their statements. The theory above is based on the Maxim of Quantity of Cooperative Principle proposed by Grice [3].

(1) I ate some of the cookies.

Numerals, as members of scalar terms, also raise similar discussion, but in a much more complicated way. The most notable difference between general scalar terms and numerals is that people have a stronger preference for enriched readings when encountering numerals compared to other scalar expressions. In high memory load conditions, where listeners are inclined to avoid computing scalar implicature to reduce processing costs, listeners prefer two-sided bounded readings of numerals (Marty et al. [4]). The priming task in Meye and Feiman [5] showed that participants produced more enriched readings in *numeral* trials than in *some* trials. They explained this phenomenon with the assumption that, unlike *some*, strong alternatives of numerals are stored in their basic semantics and do not need to be generated online. The lower processing cost of numerals allowed people to derive enriched readings more frequently. Zhao et al. [6] claimed that children acquire two-sided bounded interpretations of numerals much earlier, as demonstrated in their experiment with native Mandarin-speaking children.

In addition, even when embedded in downward entailing environments, where scalar implicature seems not to be computed due to the opposite direction of entailment relations between weak terms and stronger alternatives, numerals tend to be interpreted as two-sided bounded. No *metalinguistic negation*, conducted by adding strong intonational prominence to scalar terms (Chierchia et al. [7]; Fox & Spector [8]), is needed (Kennedy [9]). To explain the distinctions between general scalar terms and numerals, some researchers and experts have proposed various approaches. For example, the "under-specification" proposed by Carston[1] [10], the exact-based semantics view claimed by Breheny[2] [11] and the polysemy account favored by Guert[3] [12].

In this paper, we aim to test the following two core theories. Despite the belief in two-sided bounded interpretations as basic meanings, the account proposed by Kennedy [9] suggests that upper/lower bounded interpretations of numerals arise through scopal interaction between numerals and modals, constituting a matter of semantic content. According to this account, scope-taking is used to explain the shifts between different interpretations of numerals. Based on Kennedy [9], sentence like (2), which contain a universal modal, can be interpreted in two ways: either the numeral is inside the scope of the universal modal or the universal modal is inside the scope of the numeral. The former version evokes the two-sided bounded reading of the numeral, whereas the latter raises a lower bounded reading. Turning to the case of existential modals, as seen in (3), we can find similar scopal relations between the numeral and the modal. While the numeral is inside the scope of the existential modal, a two-sided bounded reading is derived. On the contrary, when the existential modal is within the scope of the numeral, the numeral will be interpreted as an upper bounded reading (*at most n*).

(2) Kim *is required to* take three classes.[4]

---

[1] Carston [10] claimed that "*exactly n*", "*at least n*" and "*at most n*" are all semantics of numerals, which means they are parallel to each other, with the view of *explicature*. Listeners select the best interpretation based on the current context and the background knowledge of the speaker and listener.

[2] Breheny [11] proposed that Numerically Quantified Noun Phrases (NQNPs) encode two-sided bounded readings as their basic semantics, with the lower bounded readings derived pragmatically.

[3] Guert [12] posited that the basic semantics of numerals are two-sided bounded readings. The underlying mechanism for shifting between two-sided bounded readings and lower bounded readings is determined by a semantic content referred to as *type shift*. It needs to be noted that, according to Guert [12], upper bounded readings (*at most n*) can only be derived through pragmatic reasoning.

[4] Examples (2) and (3) are cited from Kennedy [9]. The phrase 'be required to' denotes a universal modal, while 'be allowed to' denotes an existential modal.

(3) Kim *is allowed to* take three classes.

In contrast to Kennedy's claim, the grammatical theory maintains the pragmatic view on scalar terms of neo-Gricean that the basic semantics of scalar terms are lower bounded and upper boundedness arises through pragmatic reasoning. Nevertheless, the process of scalar implicature constitutes an *exhaustification*, which is conducted by inserting a covert exhaustivity operator *O*, modeled on *only*, into the sentences (Chierchia et al. [7]). The operator *O* can be inserted into any position within the sentence, which allows scalar implicature to be computed globally and locally. Therefore, the impacts from the other compositions in the sentence on the interpretation of the scalar term are explicable.

Spector [13] posited that in a sentence containing universal modal and numeral simultaneously, such as (2), both the numeral and the universal modal are within the scope of the operator *O* (e.g., (4)), resulting in the derivation of the lower bounded reading. The entire sentence can be inferred as follow: "Kim is required to take at least three classes, and he is not required to take at least four classes."

(4) *O* (Kim is required to take three classes)

The interaction between numerals and existential modals is not directly discussed by the grammatical account. Here, we attempt to expand on the concept of *free choice inference* proposed by Fox [14] and Chierchia et al. [7], which originally focused on disjunctive sentences with *or*. We can envision that a sentence like (3) is uttered by an authority and pertains to rules or regulations (Fox [14]). A listener infers that Kim is allowed to make a choice freely regarding the number of classes, and then yields at least three inferences "Kim is allowed to take one class.", "Kim is allowed to take two classes", and "Kim is allowed to take three classes". The researchers suggested that such free choice inference proceeds through a two-stage exhaustification, which includes the negation of the stronger alternative, as in (5a), and the negation of the strengthened readings of inferences like (5b).

(5) *OO* (Kim is allowed to take three classes.)
   a. ¬ (Kim is allowed to take four classes)
   b. ¬ (Kim is allowed to take one class, and he is not allowed to take two or three classes), ¬ (Kim is allowed to take two classes, and he is not allowed to take one or three classes), and ¬ (Kim is allowed to take three classes, and he is not allowed to take one or two classes)

So far, we have reviewed two different approaches to explain sentences containing numerals and modals. Both theories make similar predictions regarding the interpretations of numerals but differ in their explanations of the underlying mechanisms.

The present paper mainly aims to investigate the influence of modals on the interpretations of numerals. Which readings are produced when numerals interact with different kinds of modals? Will it follow the proposals of Kennedy [9] or the grammatical account that universal modals give rise to the preference for lower bounded readings (*at least n*) and existential modals lead to the rise of upper bounded readings (*at most n*)? Which account, scope-taking (Kennedy [9]) and *exhaustification* (Chierchia et al. [7]), successfully predicts the process of interpreting sentences containing modals and bare numerals?

Therefore, we conducted two experiments: an offline judgment task and an online self-paced reading task. The former was used to investigate the interpreting preference of the "modal + numeral" pattern. Additionally, it served to validate the effectiveness of the selected materials; if successful, these materials could be employed in the subsequent experiment. The latter was designed to testify the previous claims, particularly Kennedy [9] and grammatical theories (Fox [14]; Chierchia et al. [7]), which proposed distinct hypotheses concerning the underlying mechanisms of numeral interpretation.

2 Experiment 1: An Offline Judgment Task

2.1 Method

The first experiment was designed to investigate the effects of modals and also to validate the effectiveness of the materials we selected.

In this experiment, "*bixu* (必須)", which is equivalent to "be required to", represented a universal modal in Mandarin, while "*keyi* (可以)", indicating to "be allowed to", represented an existential one. We developed a questionnaire comprising 35 two-alternative forced-choice questions. Participants were asked to choose the better interpretation after reading the sentence containing a numeral and a modal, along with the prompt. (Check Fig. 1 for a more specific illustration.)

(6) 哥哥--/必須/可以拿五塊餅乾給妹妹

   Gēge --/bixu/kěyǐ ná wǔkuài bǐnggān gěi mèimei.

   (The brother --/is required to/is allowed to give five cookies to the younger sister.)

To compare the effects of different modal verbs, three modal conditions were established: with *bixu*, with *keyi*, and without any modal. In each context, a numeral is alternately paired with all three modal conditions, just as demonstrated in (6). In addition, to gather participants' instinctive responses and minimize overthinking, the questions were designed as a two-alternative forced choice rather than presenting all potential interpretations of the numerals. There were three control variables included: *context* (five different contexts), *modal* (*with bixu, with keyi, without modal*), and *alternative sets* (*lower × upper, two-sided × lower, two-sided × upper*), summing a total of 45 critical items. These 45 critical items were divided into three lists. Each list contains 15 critical items and 20 fillers.

A total of 113 native Mandarin speakers were recruited, with 37 for list A, 39 for list B, and 37 for list C. All of them had no prior exposure to formal linguistics and reached the threshold of accuracy in answering the filtering questions.

2.2 Results and Discussion

Table 1 presents the responses from participants in different conditions, and subsequent analysis will be carried out sequentially according to alternative settings.

In the *lower × upper* condition, significant effects of *modal* ($X^2(2) = 112.904$, $p < 0.05$) and *context* ($X^2(4) = 14.136$, $p < 0.05$) were found. When co-occurring with *bixu*, numerals tended to be interpreted as lower bounded readings, accounting for

「哥哥可以拿五塊餅乾給妹妹」
Gēge kěyǐ ná wǔkuài bǐnggān gěi mèimei.
(The brother is allowed to give five cookies to the younger sister.)

根據上面的句子，你覺得哥哥最後拿了幾塊餅乾給妹妹？
Gēnjù shàngmiàn de jùzi, nǐ juéde gēge zuìhòu ná le jǐkuài bǐnggān gěi mèimei?
(According to the sentence above, how many cookies do you think the brother gave to the younger sister eventually.)

a.哥哥拿了三塊餅乾給妹妹
  Gēge ná le sānkuài bǐnggān gěi mèimei.
  (The brother gave three cookies to the younger sister.)
b.哥哥拿了七塊餅乾給妹妹
  Gēge ná le qīkuài bǐnggān gěi mèimei.
  (The brother gave seven cookies to the younger sister.)

Fig. 1. Illustration of the sample question in Experiment 1

Table 1. Result of participants' answers in experiment 1

		lower × upper		*two-sided × lower*		*two-sided × upper*	
		lower	*upper*	*lower*	*two-sided*	*upper*	*two-sided*
without modal	*context 1*	59.46%	40.54%	0.00%	100.00%	5.41%	94.59%
	context 2	86.39%	13.51%	0.00%	100.00%	2.70%	97.30%
	context 3	79.49%	27.03%	8.11%	91.89%	0.00%	100.00%
	context 4	84.62%	15.38%	5.41%	94.59%	0.00%	100.00%
	context 5	67.57%	32.43%	0.00%	100.00%	2.56%	97.44%
with bixu	*context 1*	94.87%	5.13%	27.03%	72.97%	2.70%	97.30%
	context 2	94.87%	5.13%	27.03%	72.97%	5.41%	94.59%
	context 3	72.97%	27.03%	8.11%	91.89%	2.56%	97.44%
	context 4	89.19%	10.81%	10.81%	89.19%	0.00%	100.00%
	context 5	86.49%	13.51%	25.64%	74.36%	5.41%	94.59%
with keyi	*context 1*	**59.46%**	40.54%	**27.03%**	72.97%	**43.59%**	56.41%
	context 2	**54.05%**	45.95%	**35.14%**	64.86%	**51.28%**	48.72%
	context 3	32.43%	67.57%	**30.77%**	69.23%	27.03%	72.97%
	context 4	27.03%	72.97%	**20.51%**	79.49%	21.62%	78.38%
	context 5	20.51%	79.49%	**32.43%**	67.57%	**48.65%**	51.35%

87.83% of the responses. When *bixu* was replaced with *keyi*, the preference of interpreting numerals shifted toward upper bounded readings (61.50%). Although the result was generally in line with the prediction, the effect of context made it slightly complicated. While presenting in *context 1* and *context 2*, numerals co-occurring with *keyi* gained an increasing preference for lower bounded interpretations, which contradicted the initial expectation.

In the *two-sided* × *lower* condition, only the effect of *modal* was found to be significant ($X^2(2) = 47.855, p < 0.05$), while *context* was not ($X^2(4) = 3.186, p = 0.527$). Surprisingly, items containing *keyi* and numerals got more lower bounded readings (e.g., "at least n") than items containing *bixu* and numerals.

In the *two-sided* × *upper* condition, we observed significant effects of both *modal* ($X^2(2) = 129.896, p < 0.05$) and *context* ($X^2(4) = 12.513, p < 0.05$). When responding to items without modal and with *bixu*, participants consistently showed a strong preference for two-sided bounded readings. However, the presence of the existential modal *keyi* successfully induced the upper bounded readings. Additionally, *contexts 1, 2*, and *3* notably elicited more "*at most n*" interpretations.

In summary, the modals selected to represent the universal modal (*bixu*) and the existential modal (*keyi*) in Mandarin performed as expected. The universal modal led to the interpretation of numerals as lower bounded, while the existential modal elicited upper bounded readings on numerals. Secondly, we observed that *keyi* could evoke not only upper bounded interpretations but also lower bounded ones, potentially stemming from the polysemy of *keyi*. In semantics, *keyi* can convey both the meanings of [permission] and [ability]. The latter refers to the subject possessing specific skills or reaching a threshold, thus becoming capable of doing something. This aspect appears to be closely linked to lower boundedness (Peng [15]). Thirdly, when co-occurring with *keyi*, the preference for two-sided bounded readings was lower than when co-occurring with *bixu*. This phenomenon reflected the obligatory meaning of *bixu*, which required the subject to follow the rule without any exceptions.

At last, we also found that *keyi* was more likely to evoke lower bounded readings in several contexts. Most of these contexts were associated with demands or regulations related to numbers in daily life; for instance, applying for subsidies (*context 1*) and taking credits (*context 2*).

3   Experiment 2: An Online Self-Paced Reading Task

The primary objective of this experiment was to validate which theoretical approach the experts adopted to explain the interaction between numerals and modals is more reliable. Therefore, we developed a self-paced reading task with PsychoPy to investigate the online processing of native Mandarin speakers' interpretation of numerals.

3.1   Participants

A total of 114 participants were recruited and randomly assigned to three lists. Anyone scoring below 80% on filtering questions and not meeting the requirements (e.g., being a native Mandarin speaker, having no prior exposure to formal linguistics, and having no reading disorder) was excluded. Additionally, participants whose average reading times for all critical items exceeded the mean plus one standard deviation over all participants were also excluded. The final 96 participants were included in the analysis.

3.2 Procedure

The entire experiment took about 30 min and included five parts: an instruction, four practical trials, the first subpart of the main experiment, the second subpart of the main experiment, and a post-test. The main experiment was conducted using a Dell Inspiron 14 7000 laptop, which features a 14-inch monitor for running the PsychoPy program. The dimensions of the pictures were consistently 1920 * 1080 pixels with a white background, and the critical text was presented in black with a font size of 60 points.

In the experiment, participants were told to read a paragraph consisting of three sentences silently and naturally, neither too fast nor too slow. The paradigm of a complete question is shown in Fig. 2, and (7) provides the translation of all the sentences presented in the figure. The first picture that participants saw was a fixation lasting 600 ms, featuring only a cross in the center, which disappeared automatically. Then, all the sentences were displayed individually and in sequence. Participants were instructed to control their reading pace by using the spacebar on the keyboard. More specifically, as illustrated in Fig. 2, the first sentence (e.g., (7a)) appeared immediately after the fixation disappeared. Once participants finished reading and pressed the spacebar, the display switched to the second sentence (e.g., (7b)). Participants then pressed the spacebar again after completing the second sentence, at which point the third sentence (e.g., (7c)) was presented alongside the second sentence. After reading the entire paragraph, participants were required to answer a comprehension question about the context (e.g., (7d)) by pressing "*shì* (J)" for yes and "*fǒu* (F)" for no.

(7) a. 小星在和媽媽討論超市購物清單
    Xiǎoxīng zài hé māma tǎolùn chāoshì gòuwù qīngdān.
    (Xiǎoxīng is discussing the supermarket shopping list with his mom.)
   b. 小星買五個可頌當早餐,
    Xiǎoxīng mǎi wǔge kěsòng dāng zǎocān,
    (Xiǎoxīng bought five croissants for breakfast,)
   c. 他還買第六個當點心.
    tā hái mǎi dìliùge dāng diǎnxīn.
    (and he also bought a sixth one for dessert.)
   d. 小星買了五個可頌當早餐.
    Xiǎoxīng mǎi le wǔge kěsòng dāng zǎocān.
    (Xiǎoxīng bought five croissants for breakfast).

3.3 Materials

The design of our self-paced reading experiment was inspired by Panizza and Chierchia[5] [16], but we made some adjustments to investigate the effects of modals.

Each sentence in a paragraph served a distinct purpose. The first sentence provided background knowledge for the following sentences, but its data would not be analyzed. The second sentence featured a numeral and a modal (hereafter, it's termed *critical*

---

[5] Panizza and Chierchia [16] applied an eye-tracking experiment to investigate the influence of entailment on numerals interpretation.

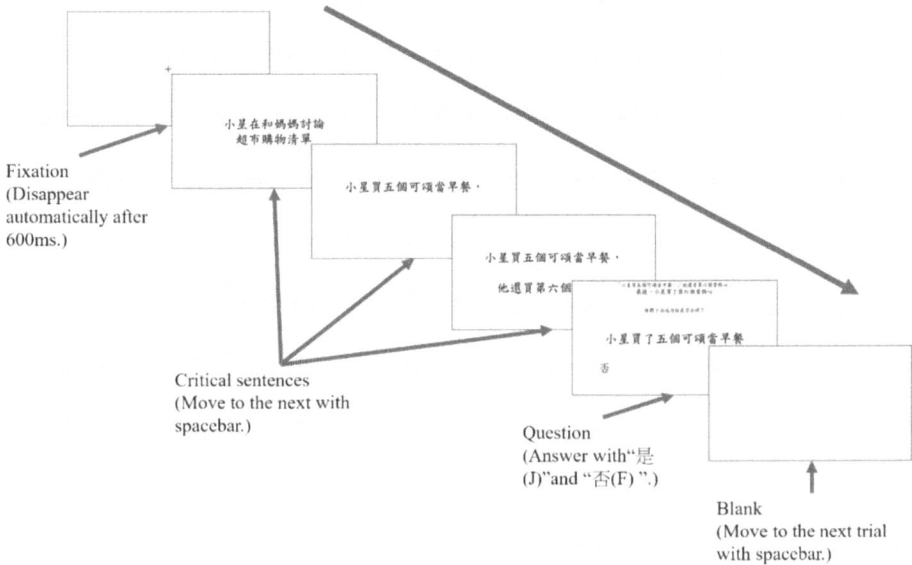

Fig. 2. The procedure of a sample of the trial

sentence in the paper), which was our critical sentence to reflect the online processing of numerals. The third sentence, aka. The continuation of the critical sentence, was used to verify the interpretation of numerals (hereafter, it's termed *continuation* in the paper). There were two types of continuations: the positive continuation (e.g., (8a)) and the neutral continuation (e.g., (8b)). The information conveyed by the positive continuation compelled the numeral in the second line to be derived as two-sided bounded, whereas the neutral one did not serve same function. If there were requirements for rereading numerals, we anticipated that positive continuations would necessitate more reading time.

(8) a. 小星必須/可以買五個可頌當早餐,他還買三明治當點心。

     Xiǎoxīng bìxū/kěyǐ mǎi wǔge kěsòng dāng zǎocān, tā hái mǎi sānmíngzhì dāng diǎnxīn.

     (Xiaoxing is required to/is allowed to buy five croissants for breakfast, and he also bought a sandwich for dessert.)

  b. 小星必須/可以買五個可頌當早餐, 他還買第六個當點心。

     Xiǎoxīng bìxū/kěyǐ mǎi wǔge kěsòng dāng zǎocān, tā hái mǎi dìliùge dāng diǎnxīn.

     (Xiaoxing is required to/is allowed to buy five croissants for breakfast, and he also bought a sixth one for dessert).

Four control variables were manipulated: *entailment* (2 conditions), *modal* (3 conditions), *continuation* (2 conditions), and *context* (4 conditions). A total of 48 critical items were included and distributed across three lists, each containing 16 critical items and 16 fillers. It should be noted in advance that we would skip the analysis and discussion on *entailment* because of its irrelevance to the topic of the present paper.

There were two different modules for predictions. Following the approach of Kennedy, the necessity for readers to decide between one-sided bounded and two-sided bounded interpretation led to slightly more reading time for the critical sentences containing modals than for those without. However, no distinction was predicted between *bixu* and *keyi* conditions due to the same underlying mechanisms.

Based on the approach of grammatical account, we anticipated that the sequence of critical sentence conditions would be as follows based on the length of time: *with keyi* > *with bixu* ≥ *without modal*. It depended on the position the operator *O* and the quantity of the operators. The free choice reference required a two-stage exhaustification, introducing additional processing load. Although reading sentences containing *bixu* necessitated re-consideration of the operator's position, both *with bixu* and *without* required only one exhaustification processing, and thus there might be no significant distinction between these two conditions.

3.4   Results and Discussion

Table 2 displays the average reading time under different conditions. The Ordering of different conditions based on the time taken to read the critical sentences was as follows: *with keyi* > *with bixu* > *without modal*. A two-way ANOVA was performed to analyze the effect of *modal* and *context* on reading time. A two-way ANOVA revealed that there was a statistically significant interaction between the effects of *modal* and *context* ($F(6, 756) = 4.165$, $p < 0.05$). Simple main effects analysis showed that *modal* did have a statistically significant effect on reading time ($p < 0.05$). Tukey's HSD analysis showed that there was a significant difference between the means of *with keyi* and *without modal*($p < 0.05$), but no significant difference between the means of *with keyi* and *with bixu* ($p = 0.096$) or between the means of *with bixu* and *without modal* ($p = 0.380$). However, a simple main effect analysis showed that *context* did not have a statistically significant effect on reading time ($p = 0.214$).

Based on the observation of the first experiment, it appeared that contexts strongly linked to regulations about numbers might impact the effect of *keyi*. In these scenarios, numerals combined with *keyi* were interpreted as lower bounded readings, deviating from the initially expected upper bounded readings. Similar contexts were also used in the second experiment, such as the context of courses taken. Consequently, we temporarily excluded data associated with these types of contexts and focused on data from relatively neutral contexts. A one-way ANOVA revealed that there was a significant effect of *modal* ($F(2, 381) = 12.342$, $p < 0.05$) (*with keyi* > *with bixu* > *without modal*: 2350ms > 1821ms > 1668ms). Tukey's HSD analysis found that there was a significant difference between the means of *with keyi* and *without modal*($p < 0.05$) or between the means of *with keyi* and *with bixu* ($p < 0.05$), but no significant difference between the means of *with bixu* and *without modal* ($p = 0.829$).

Regarding the analysis in the continuations, A two-way ANOVA revealed that there was no significant interaction of *modal* and *type of continuation* ($F(5,762) = 0.464$, $p = 0.629$), but simple main effects analysis showed there was a significant main effect of *modal* ($p < 0.05$) and *type of continuation* ($p < 0.05$). No significant main effect of *context* was observed ($F(3,764) = 0.751$, $p = 0.522$). Reading neutral continuations required more time than reading positive continuations. Besides, the positive continuations with *keyi* in the former sentences required the most reading time.

Table 2. Result of Experiment 2

mean RT for the critical sentences (ms)	without modal		with bixu		with keyi	
	1727		1891		2100	
	positive	neutral	positive	neutral	positive	neutral
mean RT for the continuations (ms)	1848	2229	2037	2525	2281	2537

In conclusion, our findings indicate that sentence containing the existential modal *keyi* and a numeral required significantly more time for readers to interpret, particularly when we excluded data from the contexts that *keyi* might unexpectedly evoke the lower bounded readings of numerals. This observation evidently aligns with the approach suggested by the grammatical account.

Furthermore, the results of continuations (the third sentence) highlight an anticipated phenomenon where neutral continuations take more time to read, as the information they convey is almost entirely new for participants. In contrast, positive continuations contain partially old information, such as the information about numbers that had been processed when reading preceding sentences.

At last, the positive continuations following sentences containing *keyi* required more reading time, which confirming that *keyi* elicits readers' upper bounded readings on numerals. When readers interpreted numerals in the sentences as "*at most n*", they encountered a contradiction when reading "a sixth one" and thus spent more time on processing. The reason why readers didn't meet the same problem in the *bixu* trials is that people have a strong preference for two-sided bounded readings on numerals combined with universal modal *bixu*. Similar results were found in the post-test, where participants had to choose the most suitable interpretations of numerals. When numerals co-occurred with *bixu*, participants reported 52.08% of two-sided bounded readings, 46.88% of lower bounded readings, and only 1.04% of upper bounded readings.

4 Conclusions

The empirical results of this study are inspiring and help us have a profound discussion on the interpretation of numerals in Mandarin from the perspective of the interactions between numerals and different modals. The findings validate the effects of universal modal and existential modal, where the former elicits lower bounded readings of numerals, and the latter evokes upper bounded interpretations. Moreover, the mechanism of processing numerals aligns more closely with the grammatical theory's approach, suggesting that the upper boundedness is related to the insertion of the exhaustivity operator *O*. However, a further question remains to be answered: why does the effect of existential modal *keyi* change depending on the context? It warrants further research.

Acknowledgments. This research was supported by National Science and Technology Council research grants (NSTC 111-2410-H-003-085-).

References

1. Lin, J.-W.: Issues in Chinese adjectival and nominal predicates: Semantic analyses and the teaching of Chinese [Xingrongci weiyuju ji mingci weiyuju de yixie wenti: tan yuyi fenxi yu huayu jiaoxue]. Chuugoku Gogaku [Zhongguo Yuxue] **267**, 1–23 (2020). (in Chinese)
2. Hsiao, H.S., Wang, Y., Yu, A.: A study on native mandarin speakers' homogeneity of degree adverbs and adjectives. In: Dong, M., Hong, J.-F., Lin, J., Jin, P. (eds.) CLSW 2023. LNCS, vol. 15414, pp. 3–10. Springer, Heidelberg (2024)
3. Grice, H.P.: Logic and conversation. In: Cole, P., Morgran, J. (eds.) Syntax and Semantics 3: Speech Acts, pp. 41–58. Academic Press, Cambridge (1975)
4. Marty, P., Chemla, E., Spector, B.: Interpreting numerals and scalar items under memory load. Lingua **133**, 152–163 (2013)
5. Meyer, M.C., Feiman, R.: Priming reveals similarities and differences between three purported cases of implicature: Some, number and free choice disjunctions. J. Mem. Lang. **120**, 104206 (2021). https://doi.org/10.1016/j.jml.2020.104206
6. Zhao, S., Ren, J., Frank, M.C., Zhou, P.: The development of quantity implicatures in Mandarin-speaking children. Lang. Learn. Dev. **17**(4), 343–365 (2021)
7. Chierchia, G., Fox, D., Spector, B.: The grammatical view of scalar implicatures and the relationship between semantics and pragmatics. Semant.: int. Handb. Nat. Lang. Mean. **3**, 2297–2332 (2012)
8. Fox, D., Spector, B.: Economy and embedded exhaustification. Nat. Lang. Semant. **26**(1), 1–50 (2018)
9. Kennedy, C.: A scalar semantics for scalar readings of number words. In: Caponigro, I., Cecchetto, C. (eds.) From Grammar to Meaning: The Spontaneous Logicality of Language, pp. 172–200. Cambridge University Press, Cambridge (2013)
10. Carston, R.: Informativeness, relevance and scalar implicature. In: Carston, R., Uchida, S. (eds.) Relevance Theory: Applications and Implications, pp. 179–236. John Benjamins, Amsterdam (1998)
11. Breheny, R.: A new look at the semantics and pragmatics of numerically quantified noun phrases. J. Semant. **25**(2), 93–139 (2008)
12. Geurts, B.: Take "five": the meaning and use of a number word. In: Liliane, T., Vogeleer, S. (eds.) Non-definiteness and Plurality, pp. 311–329. John Benjamins, Amsterdam (2006)
13. Spector, B.: Bare numerals and scalar implicatures. Lang. Linguist. Compass **7**(5), 273–294 (2013)
14. Fox, D.: Free choice and the theory of scalar implicatures. In: Sauerland, U., Stateva, P. (eds.) Presupposition and Implicature in Compositional Semantics, pp. 71–120. Palgrave Macmillan, London (2007)
15. Peng, L.-Z.: On modality of Modern Chinese [Xiandai Hanyu Qingtai Yanjiu]. Doctoral dissertation, Fudan University, Shanghai (2005). (in Chinese)
16. Panizza, D., Chierchia, G.: Numerals and scalar implicatures. In: Meibauer, J., Steinbach, M. (eds.) Experimental Pragmatics/Semantics, pp. 129–150. John Benjamins, Amsterdam (2011)

Toward a Lexicalization Continuum Approach to Intransitive Resultatives with Objects

Lulu Wang[1]([✉]) [iD] and Meng Wang[2] [iD]

[1] Communication University of China, Dingfuzhuang Eaststr. 1, Beijing 100024, China
lulu.wang@cuc.edu.cn
[2] Jiangnan University, Lihudadao 1800, Wuxi 214122, China

Abstract. This paper examines intransitive resultatives with objects in Chinese, focusing on three typical expressions such as 'hēzuì jiǔ,' 'chībǎo fàn,' and 'shuìxǐng jiào.' Contrary to the traditional views that intransitive resultatives do not take objects, empirical data from the corpus reveal varied frequencies of object candidates, suggesting that these constructions can co-occur with objects under specific conditions. The paper describes the syntactic and semantic features of these constructions and suggests that the objects in question may not function as typical objects but rather as idiomatic ones involving different degrees in lexicalization. We believe that the causative relation between the events is the core factor in the process of event integration. And thus, a lexicalization continuum is proposed to capture the degree of the lexicalized process of these intransitive resultatives with objects. This continuum provides a unified model to illustrate the variations between lexical semantics and syntactic configurations.

Keywords: Intransitive Resultatives · Lexicalization · Continuum · Objects

1 Introduction

In general, intransitive resultatives refer to the resultative constructions without objects. If the adjective complements denote to the agent of the verbal predicates, then the whole resultative constructions do not take objects [1][1].

---

[1] PRF, CLF, INDF, ART, and DEF are abbreviations for perfect, classifier, indefinite, article and definite, which are defined in the *Leipziq Glossing Rule*.

P. Jin et al. (Eds.): CLSW 2024, LNAI 15552, pp. 427–439, 2025.
https://doi.org/10.1007/978-981-96-3509-2_31

(1) a. 他   喝醉   了
      Tā   hēzuì   le
      he   drink-drunk PRF
      'He got drunk by drinking.'

    b. 你们   吃饱   了
      Nǐmen chībǎo   le
      you   eat-full   PRF
      'You got full by eating.'

    c. 我   睡醒   了
      Wǒ   shuìxǐng   le
      I   sleep-awake PRF
      'I was awake after sleeping.'

    d. 他   记错   了
      Tā   jìcuò   le
      he   remember-wrong   PRF
      'He was mistaken. '

However, there are some resultatives that appear transitive. The sentences with resultative complements have subjects and objects. And in some sentences, the complements are predicated of the subjects [2].

(2) a. 送   他   去   警察局   他   喝醉   了   酒。
      Sòng tā   qù   jǐngchájú,   tā   hēzuì   le   jiǔ (Flying Clouds)
      send him go   police-station he   drink-drunk PRF   wine
      'Send him to the police station, as he was drunk.'

    b. 你们   吃饱   了   饭   管   啥   闲   事。
      Nǐmen chībǎo le   fàn guǎn shá xián   shì (Fujian Daily)
      you   eat-full PRF rice care what leisure business
      'You are full and leave alone.'

    c. 这 个   时候   我   已经   睡醒   了   一   觉。
      Zhè gè shíhòu wǒ yǐjīng shuìxǐng le   yī   jiào
      this CLF time I   already sleep-awake PRF INDF.ART sleep
      'I have slept and now I am awake.'

    d. 他记错   了   门牌   号码。
      Tā jìcuò   le   ménpái hàomà
      he remember-wrong   PRF door   number
      'He remembered the door number wrong.'

At first sight, the above examples in (1) and (2) are mutually contradictory, in that the resultatives could be with or without objects, where the complements are predicated of the subjects. To illustrate the above examples, some consider that the examples in (2) are exceptions, especially with 'chībǎo fàn' and 'hēzuì jiǔ'. It is believed that these collocations could not be combined freely, and thus should be seen as idioms [3]. Others suggest that these examples are variations of separable verbs with the inserting complements, such as 'zuì' in 'hēzuì le jiǔ' [4]. In contrast with these explanations, some scholars believe the objects could be derived in the surface structure, if the verbal predicates are transitive, and the arguments of the verbal predicates and the complements are co-indexed [5, 6]. But some assume that the objects in example (2) are dummy objects [7]. That is, if we remove the objects, the sentences are still grammatical. There are assumptions that the objects are not free objects in the general sense, and they should be seen as shadow arguments [8]. It is also argued that such differences could be explained in the concept structuring theory, where the complements are treated as the main event and the verbal predicates are analyzed as the co-event. Therefore, the following objects of the verbal predicates could be in a less prominent position [9].

Previous studies have spotted the oddness of the objecthood co-occurred with the so-called intransitive resultatives in that such objects could not be used as freely as the regular objects. However, as we delve into the real data, we discover that present studies do not cover the data thoroughly and lack a deeper investigation into the differences within these intransitive resultatives with objects. For example, it is discovered that 'chībǎo fàn' and 'hēzuì jiǔ' are not the only exceptions, and there are other verbs and nouns that could be replaced on the V and N positions [10]. Considering these ideas, we have suspicions about the objecthood that occurred with the intransitive resultatives and hence propose the following questions. What are the real distributions of the intransitive resultatives with objects based on the co-occurrence frequencies? Do the intransitive resultatives with objects belong to the idiomatic expressions? Do they correspond to a lexicalization pattern or a constructional pattern? If we could answer the latter question, we could not only explain the phenomena, but also make predictions.

In the following sections, we firstly make a detailed examination on the co-occurrences of the intransitive resultatives and the following objects. Based on the empirical observation, we speculate on the syntactic and semantic features of such constructions, especially on the status of the objecthood and the causation motivation. Then we try to explain the differences between these constructions with the lexicalization pattern that they suit.

2   The Co-occurrences of Intransitive Resultatives with Objects: Case Studies of 'hēzuì', 'chībǎo', and 'shuìxǐng'

In this part, we choose 'hēzuì' 'chībǎo' 'shuìxǐng' as the research objects, which is due to the following considerations. Firstly, the most discussed exceptional collocations are those with 'hēzuì' and 'chībǎo,' and thus we treat these two as the main research objects. Secondly, there are discussions of 'shuìxǐng' in some literature, which reveal significant differences with the above two. So, we take it as a comparison. Lastly, examples like 'jìcuò' in (1d) and (2d) are transitive, and thus we exclude such tokens.

To have a thorough understanding of the distribution of the three resultatives within the real data, we search the collocations of such resultatives within the BCC corpus[2] and the Baidu Search Engine. The following table shows that there are big differences between the co-occurrences of these tokens with and without objects.

---

[2] The BCC (BLCU Corpus Center) corpus is developed by Beijing Language and Culture University, and the website is http://bcc.blcu.edu.cn/.

Table 1. The search results of 'hēzuì le (jiǔ),' 'chībǎo le (fàn),' and 'shuìxǐng le (jiào).'

Search items	Results of BCC corpus	Results of Baidu
hēzuì le jiǔ	599	65,300,000
chībǎo le fàn	107	15,400,000
shuìxǐng le jiào	4	37,700
hēzuì le	4609	100,000,000

Table 2. The search results of 'hēzuì le (jiǔ)', 'chībǎo le (fàn)', and 'shuìxǐng le (jiào)' (continued).

Search items	Results of BCC corpus	Results of Baidu
chībǎo le	6364	100,000,000
shuìxǐng le	3740	100,000,000

As the results show, 'hēzuì le jiǔ' is the most popularly used collocations compared to 'chībǎo le fàn' and 'shuìxǐngle jiào.' The number of the token 'chībǎo le fàn' is one fifth of that of 'hēzuì le jiǔ', and the number of 'shuìxǐng le jiào' is less than one percent of that. Compared to this, these resultatives are more commonly used without objects. And we can see that, in the results of Baidu, all three tokens of 'hēzuì le', 'chībǎo le', 'shuìxǐng le' reach the largest number of 100,000,000.

Next, we investigate further the possible distributions of the objects, which are shown in the following tables.

Table 3. The search results of 'hēzuì le n'.

Search items	Results of BCC corpus
hēzuì le n	606(708)[3]
hēzuì le jiǔ(wine)	599
hēzuì le píjiǔ(beer)/xiāngbīnjiǔ(champagne)/pútaojiǔ(wine)	1/1/2
hēzuì le lǎozi(me)/tóu(head)/rén(people)	1/1/1

In the overall 606 tokens of 'hēzuì le n', there are 599 tokens of 'hēzuì le jiǔ'. The other options are rare, which could be classified into two subtypes. One type is the patient, and 'píjiǔ', 'xiāngbīnjiǔ' and 'pútaojiǔ' are subtypes of 'jiǔ'. The other type is the agent, and such agent objects are different from patient objects in the deep structure (Tables 4).

---

[3] We have 708 results in total, but only 606 tokens are the ones with objects. The numbers in the following two tables have the same patterns.

Table 4. The search results of 'chībǎo le n.'

Search items	Results of BCC
chībǎo le n	222(397)
chībǎole le fàn(rice)	107
chībǎo le fànshí(meals)/jiǔfàn/jiérì de fàncài/zhǔrénjiā de fàn	1/1/1/1
chībǎo le dùzi(belly)/dùpí	40/3
chībǎo le zǎofàn(breakfast)/zǎocān/wǔcān/wǎnfàn/xiāoyè/yèxiāo/xiàwǔchá	3/1/1/2/1/1/1
chībǎo le shāokǎo(barbecue)/shāoròu/shāguō záhuì/ròujiámó hé	1/2/1/1/
zhāngyúxiǎowánzi/yúntūn/huǒguō/dōngxi/shǒuzhuāròu hé	1/1/2/1/
zānbā/zānbā/yěwèi/miàn/KFC/lǎojiǔ	1/1/1/1
chībǎo le nǎi(milk)/mǐhú děng shípǐn	5/1
chībǎo le píba(loquat)/shuǐlí/jiāngguǒ	1/1/1
chībǎo le cǎo(grass)/tónglèi de ròu/xuě/mì/niǎodàn/yànmài/cǎoliào/bāomǐlìzi/yùmǐlì	5/1/3/1/1/3/1/1/1
chībǎo le fēng(wind)/shuǐ/rìguāng	15/2/1

Here, the objects that followed 'chībǎo le' are more complex than that of 'hēzuì le.' Out of the total number of 222 tokens of 'chībǎo le n', almost half are 'chībǎo le fàn'. And the other half have 44 different words or expressions. This could prove that the collocations with 'chībǎo' are more flexible since they have more candidates for the object position. These objects could also be classified into two types. One of them is patient-object, including 'fàn'(rice) and other expressions of meals and food. The other one is theme-object, including 'dùzi/dùpí'(belly). In the patient objects, the diverse types are related ontologically. For example, 'fàn' could be related to 'zǎofàn'(breakfast), 'wǔfàn'(lunch), and 'wǎnfàn'(supper), which are different types of meals. 'fàn' could also be related to various kinds of food, such as a dish or a kind of fruit. Besides the food for human, there is food for animals, such as 'cǎo'(grass). Also, there are anthropomorphic things, such as 'feng'(wind), which is consumed by 'fēngfān'(sail) (Table 5).

Table 5. The search results of 'shuìxǐng le n.'

Search items	Results of BCC corpus
shuìxǐng le n	9(176)
shuìxǐng le jiào(sleep)	4
shuìxǐng le wǔjiào(noon-sleep)	5

Here, 'shuìxǐng le n' only has 9 collocations, in which 'shuìxǐngle jiào' has four tokens. It is obvious that the options for the objects here are the most limited.

Summing up the above results, the intransitive usage of these three resultative constructions is quite common, while their usage with objects demonstrates differences. Among them, 'hēzuì' with 'jiǔ' as the object is more common since the vast majority are paired with 'jiǔ'. And 'chībǎo' has more candidates to fill in the object position. The biggest difference lies in 'shuìxǐng' where not having an object is more common, and the usage with objects is limited. Moreover, for 'hēzuì' and 'chībǎo', the objects they take can be divided into two situations: one is where the objects are the patient, such as 'hēzuì le jiǔ' and 'chībǎo le fàn'; the other is where the objects are the agent and theme separately, such as 'hē zuì le rén' and 'chībǎo le dùzi'. Although their semantic roles differ, their pairings with the verbal predicates are also relatively restricted. That is, the choice of words that can be paired in the object position is limited to a certain range. For example, the selection of some potential objects also depends on the subject, as in 'chībǎo le fēng' where the subject is 'fēngfān (sail)', not the usual agent of 'eating', namely 'rén (people)' This also illustrates that the co-occurrence of intransitive resultatives with objects is not completely fixed but has certain selection restrictions in the process of combining with other components, and their degree of 'exceptionality' varies as such. In the following sections, we will focus on analyzing the syntactic and semantic characteristics of the co-occurring constituents and their selection restrictions.

3 The Syntactic Status and Cognitive Motivation of Intransitive Resultatives with Objects

3.1 On the Predicate Types of the Resultatives

Generally, verbs are divided into transitive and intransitive verbs depending on their requirements on the objects. Transitive verbs require one or more objects, but intransitive verbs require none. As for Chinese resultatives, there are both intransitive and transitive types, which are illustrated in (1) and (2) separately. As the results in Table 1 shows, the intransitive usages of the three resultatives are more frequently used. Also, as the results in Table 2 and 3 show, the subjects of the intransitive usages could be agent (3a) or theme (3b).

(3) a. 他　　喝醉　　　　了
      Tā　　hēzuì　　　le
      he　　drink-drunk　PRF
      'He got drunk by drinking.'

    b. 酒　　喝醉　　　　了
      Jiǔ　　hēzuì　　　le
      wine　drink-drunk　PRF
      'Someone got drunk, because of the wine.'

Intransitive verbs could be differentiated into unergative and unaccusative verbs, both of which assign only one thematic role, but the former assigns an agent, as in 'he cried,' and the latter assigns a theme, as in 'the boat sank' [11]. Similarly, the above intransitive resultatives have both the unergative (3a) and unaccusative (3b) alternations.

Accordingly, four predicate types of resultatives are proposed: unergative, transitive, ergative and causative. Some resultative verbal compounds exhibit the unergative-transitive alternation, such as (4a-b) [12].

> (4)   a. 他 喝醉　　　 了
> 　　　　Tā hēzuì　　　 le
> 　　　　he drink-drunk　PRF
> 　　　　'He got drunk by drinking.'
> 　　　b. 他 喝醉　　　 了　 酒
> 　　　　Tā hēzuì　　　 le　 jiǔ
> 　　　　he drink-drunk　PRF wine
> 　　　　'He drank wine and got drunk.'
> 　　　c. 这　　 瓶　 酒　 喝醉　　　 了　　 他
> 　　　　Zhè　 píng jiǔ　hēzuì　　　 le　 tā
> 　　　　this　 CLF wine drink-drunk　PRF he
> 　　　　'This bottle of wine got him drunk (from drinking it).'

In (4a), the subject of the unergative resultative is the agent. In (4b), the subject of the transitive resultative is the agent and the object of that is the theme. While in (4c), the thematic roles of subject and object seemed inverse, as the object is the agent, and the subject is the theme. If so, this thematic structure violates the thematic hierarchy[4], where agent precedes theme in the hierarchy, and it is the agent that should be in the subject position. To solve this problem, a causative hierarchy is proposed to override the thematic hierarchy, where the subject receives a c-role of Cause, and the object receives a c-role of Affectee [14]. In this paper, we do not discuss such inverse resultatives, since they require a broader discussion on the constructional approach. Nonetheless, with these alternations, intransitive resultatives exhibit variations between lexical semantics and syntactic configurations.

3.2   On the Nature of the Objects

It has been suggested that differentiating between transitive and intransitive verbs lies not only in the objects, but also in the nature of the objects. Intransitives verbs could have cognate objects[5], but transitive verbs could have any kind of objects [15]. The resultative sentence in (4b) is analyzed as transitive [12]. But we have questions on the objecthood of 'jiǔ' in such resultatives. The objects in such a position could not be substituted or modified as freely as regular objects.

---

[4] The thematic hierarchy: agent > beneficiary > recipient / experiencer > instrument > theme/patient > location (> means precedes) [13].

[5] Cognate objects are etymologically related to the verb and are similar in morphological forms, such as 'sing a song,' 'live a life,' and 'laugh a laugh'.

(5) a. *他   喝醉   了   茅台
     *Tā   hēzuì   le   máotái
     he   drink-drunk PRF Maotai (a brand of white spirit)
  b. *他   喝醉   了   一/这/三   瓶   酒
     *Tā   hēzuì   le   yī/zhè/sān   píng   jiǔ
     he   drink-drunk PRF INDF.ART/this/three CLF   wine

The above ungrammatical sentences show that 'jiǔ' could not be substituted by other nominals, indefinite or definite noun phrases, or numeral phrases. Hence, the nominals in the object position should be non-referential and generic.

Further, if we apply the test of *bǎ/bèi* alternations, it also shows that the objects are different from regular objects, since they could not be fronted as in the *bǎ/bèi* sentences.

(6) a. *他   把   酒   喝醉   了
     *Tā   bǎ   jiǔ hēzuì   le
     he   BA   wine drink-drunk PRF
  a' *酒   被   他   喝醉   了
     *Jiǔ   bèi   tā   hēzuì   le
     wine BEI   he   drink-drunk PRF
  b. *他   把   饭   吃饱   了
     *Tā   bǎ   fàn chībǎo   le
     he   BA   rice eat-full   PRF
  b' *饭   被   他   吃饱   了
     *Fàn   bèi   tā   chībǎo   le
     rice BEI   he   eat-full   PRF
  c. *他   把   觉   睡醒   了
     *Tā   bǎ   jiào shuìxǐng   le
     he   BA   sleep sleep-awake PRF
  c' *觉   被   他   睡醒   了
     *Jiào bèi   tā   shuìxǐng   le
     sleep BEI he   sleep-awake PRF

Since the *bǎ/bèi* alternations are ungrammatical, 'tā hēzuì le jiǔ' is not strictly transitive. Then how should we define the objects like 'jiǔ' in the above sentences? Could they be analyzed as the cognate objects just as the case of intransitive verbs in English? The idea of the cognate object may not suit Chinese very well, since there are no morphological inflections in Chinese [8]. In addition, there is no etymological relation between 'hēzuì' and 'jiǔ.' However, there is a certain semantic relation between the two constituents, which is the causative relation within the construction.

If we substitute 'jiǔ (wine)' to other drinks, such as 'shuǐ (water),' we will have ungrammatical sentences.

(7) *他   喝醉   了   水/茶/可乐
    *Tā   hēzuì   le   shuǐ/chá/kělè
    he   drink-drunk PRF water/tea/Cola

It is easy to explain that drinking water is less likely to cause someone to get drunk. But drinking wine is much more likely to cause someone to get drunk. Such differences are clearer in the following negating tests.

(8) a. 他   喝   了   酒   但是   没   醉
      Tā   hē   le   jiǔ,   dànshì   méi   zuì
      he   drink   PRF   wine   but   not   drunk
      'He drank the wine, but not got drunk.'
    b.*他   喝   了   水，   但是   没   醉
      *tā   hē   le   shuǐ,   dànshì   méi   zuì
      He   drink   PRF   water   but   not   drunk

Comparing the grammatical sentence in (8a) and the ungrammatical one in (8b), we could tell that there is a causative inference in between the lexical semantics of 'hējiǔ' and 'zuì'. This is like the strong association that lies in 'sweep' and 'floors,' in that 'the strong association between sweeping and floors means that no particular context needs to be specified with intransitive sweep to ensure the appropriate interpretation of the unexpressed participant.' [16: 115] That is to say, when we look at sentence 'tā hēzuì le' as in (1a), we have an underspecified cognition of the unseen object, which is much likely to be 'jiǔ'(wine), not 'cha'(tea) or 'shui' (water).

This causative relation between the verbal predicates and the complements is also apparent in verb-copying alternations.

(9) a. 他   喝   酒   喝   醉   了
      Tā   hē   jiǔ   hē   zuì   le
      he   drink   wine   drink   drunk   PRF
      'He drank the wine, and then he got drunk.'
   b. 他   吃   饭   吃   饱   了
      Tā   chī   fàn   chī   bǎo   le
      he   eat   rice   eat   full   PRF
      'He ate the rice, and then he got full.'
   c. 他   睡   (了)   (一)   觉   睡   醒   了
      Tā   shuì   le   yī   jiào   shuì   xǐng   le
      he   sleep   PRF   INDF.ART   sleep   sleep   awake   PRF
      'He slept, and then he woke up.'

The sentences in (9a-c) are the alternations of (1a-c), where the main verb with the object precedes the copying verb with the complement in the surface structure. As the principle of temporal sequence defines, the relative word order between syntactic units is determined by the temporal order of the states they represent in the conceptual world [17]. Hence, the event of the first verb occurs before that of the copying verb, which naturally reveals a causation relationship between them as in (9a-b). The sentence in (9c) is different, there is no causative meaning, but rather a sequential meaning. Moreover, the first verbs in (9a-b) should be non-finite, and the following objects should also be generic. But it is not true in (9c), where the first verb 'shuì' could be followed by the past particle 'le' and the object 'jiào' could be modified by the numeral 'yī'. These facts show that we should treat the case of (9c) separately, where 'shuì-jiào' is a separable verb which has different syntactic distributions. As for (9a-b), they have similar distributions and the first verbs with objects are co-events, while the copying-verbs with complements are the main events. And thus, the objects are assumed to be less prominent since they appear in the co-events, rather than the main events [9: 60–61].

We believe that the nature of object in the above sentences involves a lexicalization pattern in describing such innate knowledge, which is also determined by the conceptual structure of the construction. In the next section, we analyze the intransitive resultatives in the figure-ground profiling theory, and then investigate the lexicalization degree of them in a continuum way.

4   The Lexicalization Continuum of Intransitive Resultatives with Objects

In concept structuring theory, a basic causative situation consists of two events where one event occurs as the result of the other. The former is the resulting event, and the latter is the causing event. In the Figure-Ground profiling theory, the resulting event functions as the Figure and the causing event functions as the Ground [18]. In (4b), 'he jiǔ' is the causing event and 'zui' is the resulting event. The semantic structure of this kind of causation can be illustrated as in (10).

(10) [tā   zuì   le]   **RESULTed FROM**   [tā   hē   jiǔ   le]
     he   drunk   PRF   he   drink wine   PRF

To note that, 'jiǔ' (wine) in (10) could not be substituted or omitted. This causative relation is rooted in the lexical semantics of the combination of 'he' and 'jiǔ.' We assume this causative usage is a lexicalization of the objects conflated into it. This could be proved by the frequency results in Table 2. 'hēzuì le jiǔ' has the highest frequencies. Also, it is emphasized that the meaning of the verbs must be revealed by the syntactic forms [19]. Thus, 'jiǔ' is a part of the lexicalization pattern of this type of intransitives surface structures.

In this sense, 'hēzuì jiǔ' is more like 'shuìxǐng jiào' in the degree of lexicalization. Since 'shuìjiào' is a separable word, one can insert numerals, resultatives in between. As the definition of separable words illustrates, they could be expanded in the phrasal level, but the meaning of the word is intact. It is suggested that separable words are syntactically flexible, but semantically decomposable expressions. They could be divided into four types based on the degree of decomposability of the verb-object words [20]. For example, 'hējiǔ,' 'chīfàn' and 'shuìjiào' are all decomposable but they have selection constraints. Further, only when the objects are interpreted as the parts of the lexical items, the resultatives could be regarded as intransitives. This is not to say that we assume the intransitive resultatives with objects as words. Rather, we think they are phrasal constructions with a certain degree of event integration, which is the reconceptualization process of conceptual integration or conflation of events [18]. The intransitives without objects in (1) and those with objects in (2) both undergo the process of event integration, but they have different degrees of lexicalization. To illustrate, 'jìcuò' in (1-2d) is used as freely as a transitive verb, while 'hēzuì' and 'chībǎo' in (1-2a) and (1-2b) are used with certain constraints, such as the generic usage of the objects and the causative inference relations between the events. As for 'shuìxǐng' in (1-2c), they are typical separable words which are already lexicalized but syntactically flexible.

Based on the empirical data from the corpus and the theoretical analysis above, we believe that intransitive resultatives with objects involve different degrees of lexicalization. We do not adopt the traditional method of categorial classification[6], rather, we prefer the prototype theory [22]. We suggest two prototypes of phrasal resultatives and lexicalized resultatives, and they lie in the two opposite points in the continuum of the degree of lexicalization as the following figure shows (Fig. 1).

phrasal	semi lexicalized		lexicalized
记错	吃饱	喝醉	睡醒
jì-cuò	chī-bǎo	hē-zuì	shuì-xǐng
remember-wrong	eat-full	drink-drunk	sleep-awake

Fig. 1. The lexicalization continuum of resultatives with objects.

Recalling the examples in (1), we now could represent their degree of lexicalization degree within the continuum. On the leftmost side of the continuum is 'jìcuò,' which means that these kinds of resultatives are more like phrasal ones. They are transitive and take regular objects. In the middle of the continuum are 'chībǎo' and 'hēzuì,' where 'chībǎo' is closer to the side of the phrasal side and 'hēzuì' is closer to the other way around. This could illustrate the fact that 'chībǎo' is more flexible in taking more object candidates than 'hēzuì.' On the rightmost side of the continuum is 'shuìxǐng,' which is a separable word, but shows phrasal variations. In this way, we could illustrate their differences in object taking possibilities and the lexicalization degrees. Moreover, this continuum could also be used to illustrate other intransitives with objects, such as the pattern of 'V-lèi le N' (Fig. 2).

phrasal			semi lexicalized			lexicalized		
伸累	了	舌头	写累	了	字	理累	了	发
shēn-lèi	le	shétou	xiě-lèi	le	zì	lǐ-lèi	le	fà
stretch-tired	PRF	tongue	write-tired	PRF	character	cut-tired	PRF	hair

Fig. 2. The lexicalization continuum of 'V-lei le N'.

---

[6] Categories are defined in terms of a conjunction of necessary and sufficient features [21: F29].

5 Concluding Remarks

This paper focuses on the intransitive resultatives with objects. To illustrate the intransitive nature of the resultatives, we first investigate the distribution in the real data and summarize the co-occurring candidates in the object position. Then we further discuss the syntactic status and the cognitive motivation of the construction. We believe that the causative relation between the causing event and the resulting event is the core factor in the event integration process of intransitive resultatives with objects. In the end, we propose a lexicalization continuum to illustrate the differences among the above resultatives, and this continuum could also be used to investigate the degree of lexicalization of other resultatives with objects.

Admittedly, the empirical evidence in this paper is limited. Although the typical cases of 'hēzuì,' 'chībǎo' and 'shuìxǐng' exhibit clearly the nature of the co-occurred objects as idiomatical objects with syntactic and semantic constraints, we need more data from the real corpus to support the conclusion. Besides, the data provided in this paper include colloquial texts such as Weibo and literal texts such as novels and newspapers. Yet, we did not discuss the differences between these styles, and we believe this is another promising issue to be discussed in the future.

Acknowledgments. This paper is supported by the National Social Science Foundation of China (20BYY158). We are also thankful to Professor Liu Meijun, Zhao Qingqing, and the anonymous reviewers of CLSW 2024 for their comments and suggestions.

References

1. Ma, Z., Lu, J.-M.: A Survey on the adjectives as complements (3rd). Chin. Lang. Learn. **6**, 7–9 (1997). (in Chinese)
2. Lü, S.-X.: The flexibility of mandarin syntax. Stud. Chin. Lang. **1**, 1–9 (1986). (in Chinese)
3. Shi, Y.-Z.: How to treat the exceptions of grammatical rules: from 'chībǎo fàn' and 'hēzuì jiǔ.' Chin. Lang. Learn. **6**, 29–30 (2000). (in Chinese)
4. Guo, R.: On the valency structure and constituents combination. In: Shen, Y., Zheng, D.-O. (eds.) Studies on the Valence Grammar of Mandarin Chinese, pp. 168–191. Peking University Press, Beijing (1995). (in Chinese)
5. Ren, Y.: An analysis on subject-object displacement sentences. Stud. Chin. Lang. **4**, 320–328+384 (2001). (in Chinese)
6. Yuan, Y.-L.: On the valence of verb-resultative constructions in mandarin: toward a top-down and bottom-up analysis. Stud. Chin. Lang. **5**, 1–9 (2001). (in Chinese)
7. Huang, X.-Q.: On the three kinds of objects of resultatives. Chin. Lang. Learn. **6**, 69–72 (2006). (in Chinese)
8. Shi, C.-H.: On the Syntactic and Semantic Studies on Chinese Resultatives. Beijing Language and Culture University Press, Beijing (2008). (in Chinese)
9. Song, W.-H.: On the Syntax of Modern Chinese V-R Compounds: A Study Based on Conceptual Structures. Peking University Press, Beijing (2007). (in Chinese)
10. Yang, X.: The distribution and generation of the chībǎo fàn/hēzuì jiǔ construction. Bull. Linguist. Stud. **2**, 102–114+390 (2021). (in Chinese)
11. Perlmutter, D.M.: Impersonal passives and unaccusative hypothesis. In: Proceedings of the 4th Annual Meeting of the Berkeley Linguistic Society, pp. 157–189 (1978)

12. Cheng, L., Huang, C.T.J.: On the Arguments Structure of Resultative Compounds. Pyramid Press (1994)
13. Bresnan, J., Kanerva, J.M.: Locative inversion in Chicheŵa: a case study of factorization in grammar. Linguist. Inq. **20**(1), 1–50 (1989)
14. Li, Y.-F.: The thematic hierarchy and causativity. Nat. Lang. Linguist. Theory **13**, 255–282 (1995)
15. Chao, Y.-R.: A Grammar of Spoken Chinese. University of California Press (1968)
16. Rappaport Hovav, M., Levin. B.: Building verb meanings. In Butt, M., Geuder, W. (eds.) The Projection of Arguments: Lexical and Compositional Factors. CSLI, Stanford, pp. 97–134 (1998)
17. Tai, J.H.-Y.: Temporal sequence and Chinese word order. In: Typological Studies in Language, vol. 6 (1985)
18. Talmy, L.: Toward a Cognitive Semantics, Vol. 2: Typology and Process in Concept Structuring. MIT Press, Cambridge (2000)
19. Liu, M.-J.: A frame-based morpho-constructional approach to chinese verb distinction and categorization. In: Kit, C.-Y., Liu, M.-J. (eds.) Frontiers of Empirical and Corpus Linguistics, pp. 163–197. China Social Sciences Press (2018). (in Chinese)
20. Wang, L.-L., Müller, S.: Regularity and idiomaticity in Chinese separable verbs. In: The Proceedings of the 14th Chinese Lexical Semantics Workshop. Springer, Heidelberg (2013)
21. Taylor, J.R.: Linguistic Categorization: Prototypes in Linguistic Theory. Oxford University Press, Oxford (2001)
22. Rosch, E.: Cognitive Reference Points. Cognitive Psychology. Wiley, New York (1975)

A Comparative Study of *V-Guòlái* and *V-Shànglái* in Chinese Expressing Approach-Motion

Ziyan Li[✉]

Hangzhou Dianzi University, Hangzhou, China
liziyan@hdu.edu.cn

Abstract. When expressing motion events in modern Chinese, both *V-guòlái* (过来) and *V-shànglái* (上来) can represent the movement of approaching, such as *zhuī guòlái* (追过来) and *zhuī guòlái* (追上来) 'catch up'. However, in certain cases, they cannot be interchanged, such as *jià guòlái* (嫁过来) and **jià shànglái* (嫁上来) 'marry up', *bān guòlái* (搬过来) and *bān shànglái* (搬上来) 'move up'. This study compares *V-guòlái* and *V-shànglái* from three perspectives: semantic composition, features of verbs and objects using corpus analysis based language component substitution and semantic analysis. The findings are as follows: First, the main semantic difference affects event outcome and semantic focus. In terms of the event outcome, *V-guòlái* emphasis the action process, while *V-shànglái* focuses on the action result. In terms of the semantic focus, *V-guòlái* focuses on *lái* and *V-shànglái* focuses on *shàng*, the semantic focus is not symmetric. Secondly, when they are used as the complements, whether *guòlái* and *shànglái* can be interchangeable depends on the semantic features of their corresponding main verbs. Finally, when a nominal object N is inserted to the sentence structure, it generally serves as the figure for the sentences like *V-guò-N-lái*, whereas for sentences like *V-shàng-N-lái*, N can either be the figure or the ground. In phrases such as *V-guòlái/shànglái-N*, N is generally used as a figure.

Keywords: Motion event · Verb-complement Construction · Directional Complement · *guòlái* · *shànglái*

1 Introduction

When expressing movement events in modern Chinese, both *V-guòlái* (过来) and *V-shànglái* (上来) can represent the movement of approaching as complement. The two have similar semantics under certain contextual conditions and can be used interchangeably. For example:

P. Jin et al. (Eds.): CLSW 2024, LNAI 15552, pp. 440–454, 2025.
https://doi.org/10.1007/978-981-96-3509-2_32

(1) a. 他蓦地一惊，以为是敌人**追过来**了，就停住脚步。

    *Tā mòde yī jīng, yǐwéi shì dírén **zhuī guòlái** le, jiù tíngzhù jiǎobù.*

    a'. 他蓦地一惊，以为是敌人**追上来**了，就停住脚步。

    *Tā mòde yī jīng, yǐwéi shì dírén **zhuī shànglái** le, jiù tíngzhù jiǎobù.*

    'He was startled and thought the enemy was **chasing after** him, so he stopped.'

    b. 秘书赶紧**追上来**, 一手打着伞给他遮雨, 一手搀扶住他.

    *Mìshū gǎnjǐn **zhuī shànglái**, yī shǒu dǎ zhe sǎn gěi tā zhē yǔ, yī shǒu chānfú zhù tā.*

    b'. 秘书赶紧**追过来**，一手打着伞给他遮雨，一手搀扶住他。

    *Mìshū gǎnjǐn **zhuī guòlái**, yī shǒu dǎ zhe sǎn gěi tā zhē yǔ, yī shǒu chānfú zhù tā.*

'The secretary quickly **caught up**, holding an umbrella in one hand to shelter him from the rain and supporting him with the other hand.'

(2) a. 那人边说边掏出一张名片朝暖暖**递过来**。

    *Nà rén biān shuō biān tāochū yī zhāng míngpiàn cháo Nuǎnnuǎn **dì guòlái**.*

    a'. 那人边说边掏出一张名片朝暖暖**递上来**。

    *Nà rén biān shuō biān tāochū yī zhāng míngpiàn cháo Nuǎnnuǎn **dì shànglái**.*

    'The person took out a business card and **handed it over to** Nuannuan while he was talking.'

    b. 当那张纸**递上来**时，林白霜瞥了一眼。

    *Dāng nà zhāng zhǐ **dì shànglái** shí, Lín Báishuāng piē le yī yǎn.*

    b'. 当那张纸**递过来**时，林白霜瞥了一眼。

    *Dāng nà zhāng zhǐ **dì guòlái** shí, Lín Báishuāng piē le yī yǎn.*

    'When the paper was **handed over**, Lin Baishuang glanced at it.'

In the sentence a′ and b′ of example (1) and (2), *guòlái* or *shànglái* are interchanged from sentence a and b, respectively. Example (1) demonstrates autonomous displacement event and example (2) demonstrates causing displacement events. From the comparison, the sentence (1a′), (1b′), (2a′), (2b′) are all grammatically valid, and they are schematically consistent. However, there are some scenarios when *guòlái* and *shànglái* cannot be interchanged, or the schematic is inconsistent after interchanging. For example:

(3) a. 她觉得她自从**嫁过来**就没有过过这样顺心的日子。

  *Tā juéde tā zìcóng **jià guòlái** jiù méiyǒu guòguo zhèyàng shùnxīn de rìzi.*

  'She felt that, she had never had such a smooth life since she **got married**. '

 a'. *她觉得她自从**嫁上来**就没有过过这样顺心的日子。

  Tā juéde tā zìcóng **jià shànglái jiù méiyǒu guòguo zhèyàng shùnxīn de rìzi.*

(4) a. 那就好好睡一觉，我明天帮你把东西**搬过来**。

  *Nà jiù hǎohǎo shuì yī jiào, wǒ míngtiān bāng nǐ bǎ dōngxi **bān guòlái**.*

  'Have a good sleep, I'll help you **move** your stuff **over** tomorrow.'

 a'. 那就好好睡一觉，我明天帮你把东西搬上来。

  *Nà jiù hǎohǎo shuì yī jiào, wǒ míngtiān bāng nǐ bǎ dōngxi **bān shànglái**.*

  'Have a good sleep, I'll help you **move** your things **over** tomorrow.'

  'Have a good sleep, I'll help you **move** your things **up** tomorrow.'

In the example (3a), *jià guòlái* cannot be interchanged by *jià shànglái*. In the example (4a), though the grammar still holds after interchange *bān guòlái* with *bān shànglái*, (4a') is understood as the upward movement of "moving things up (from downstairs)" in the general context.

Based on such linguistic phenomena, this work will compare *guòlái* and *shànglái* from both semantic and grammatical perspectives through the methods of language component replacement and semantic analysis. It should be noted that, researchers have different opinions on whether *guòlái* and *shànglái* are words or phrases, according to various starting points or perspectives. Chao [1] classified *guòlái* and *shànglái* as compound words with verb-complement structure. Zhu [2] classified *lái* as the complement of the tendency verbs *guò* and *shàng*. This work mainly focuses on the scenario where *guòlái* and *shànglái* are used as a whole as the compound complements. In order to facilitate the discussion, the later content treats *guòlái* and *shànglái* as verbs unless otherwise specified.

The second section analyzes the internal semantic composition of *guòlái* and *shànglái*; the third section analyzes the semantic characteristics of the main verbs that match *guòlái* and *shànglái* when they are used as complements; the fourth section discusses the semantic characteristics of the object combined with V-*guòlái* and V-*shànglái*; the last section briefly summarizes the main content of this article.

2 The Semantic Composition of *Guòlái* and *Shànglái*

Guòlái and *shànglái* can be used as the main verb of a sentence when expressing displacement, or they can be used as complements after other verbs. Regardless whether they serve as main verbs or complements, their semantics have certain correlation. [3, 4].

Lv [5] suggests the verb *guòlái* means an object is coming from another place to the speaker (or narrative object), the direction verb *guòlái* means people or things move from one place to another with action; the verb *shànglái* means an object is coming from low to high, from one place to another; and the trend verb *shànglái* means the people or object is moving from low to high with the action, and means that people or object is approaching somewhere with the action. Liu [6] also believes that the tendency meaning of *guòlái* includes: (1) It means that the person or object (passing a certain point in space) approaches the foothold through action; (2) It means that the person or object rotates in the direction of the foothold through action. The tendency meaning of *shànglái* includes: (1) It means to move a person or object from a lower place to a higher place through action, and the foothold is at a higher place; (2) It means moving a person or object closer to the target in front of you, with the foothold on the target. It can be seen that, *guòlái* and *shànglái* both have the semantic meaning of 'people or objects are approaching somewhere'. In order to clarify the semantic characteristics of the two, we still need to deeply study the internal semantic composition.

Before diving into the internal semantic composition of motion verb, we need to clarify the conceptual framework of motion events first. Different cognitive and linguistic theories describe the conceptual framework of motor events from different perspectives, among which the 'Source-Path-Goal' conceptual framework proposed by Fillmore [7] has the most profound influence. This conceptual framework believes that a motion event describes the process of a subject (Theme) starting from a certain source point, passing through a certain path and finally reaching the goal location. Therefore, a motion event consists of four essentials: source point, path, goal, and motion subject. Lakoff [8] believes that human being forms a certain image schema based on the physical experience and accordingly, forms a syntactic structure based on the image schema. One of the image schema of human kinesthesia is the 'Source-Path-Destination'. Talmy [9, 10] proposed the conceptual framework of 'Figure-Motion-Path-Ground', in which 'Figure' and 'Ground' refer to the motion subject and the subject that provides a positional reference for displacements, respectively. The 'Path' is the course that the motion subject follows when it is displaced relative to the reference ground. Although researchers have different opinions on the use of concepts, they all regard 'Path' as an important component of motion events, and *guòlái* and *shànglái* are linguistic components that encode path elements.

Many researchers have explored the grammatical structure of Chinese motion events[10–13]. Liu [14] discussed the semantic composition of the combination form of motion verb, analyzed the path elements in the semantic components of motion verb, and pointed out that the semantic components of *guò* are Route (R), *shàng* Including Direction (D) + Endpoint (E), *lái* means 'Deictic'. Based on this, the path meaning of *guòlái* is expressed as 'R + Deictic', and the meaning of *shànglái* is 'D + E + Deictic'. The main difference is that using *shànglái* to express displacement can describe the direction of movement, and can imply the result of movement (i.e. the 'end point' in the semantic component), which can be demonstrated in below example:

(5) a. 怎么办呢？他马上就要**追上来**了！雷楚一边狂奔，一边测度着身后威廉的距离，眼看两个人的距离越来越短，自己马上就要被追上了。

*Zěnme bàn ne? Tā mǎshàng jiù yào **zhuī shànglái** le! Léi Chǔ yī biān kuángbēn, yī biān cèduó zhe shēnhòu William de jùlí, yǎnkàn liǎng gè rén de jùlí yuèlái yuè duǎn, zìjǐ mǎshàng jiù yào bèi zhuīshàng le.*

'What shall I do? He's about to **catch up**! Lei Chu ran wildly while estimate the distance from William. Seeing that the distance between the two was getting closer, she was about to be caught up.'

a'. 怎么办呢？他马上就要**追过来**了！

Zěnme bàn ne? Tā mǎshàng jiù yào zhuī guòlái le!

'What shall I do? He's about to **catch up**! '

b. 他们⋯⋯"力争把落下的步子**追上来**"。

Tāmen... 'lìzhēng bǎ làxià de bùzi zhuī shànglái'.

'They "striving to **catch up with** the steps left behind". '

b'. *力争把落下的步子追过来。

*Lìzhēng bǎ làxià de bùzi zhuī guòlái.

c. 这都能**追上来**，"博尔特"果然名不虚传啊！

Zhè dōu néng zhuī shànglái, 'Bolt' guǒrán míngbùxūchuán a!

'Unbelievable that he **caught up**, "Bolt" deserves his reputation! '

c'. *这都能**追过来**，"博尔特"果然名不虚传啊！

*Zhè dōu néng zhuī guòlái, 'Bolt' guǒrán míngbùxūchuán a!

The four sentences in Example (5) all use *zhuī shànglái/guòlái* as the example. Among which, sentences a', b', and c' are obtained by replacing *guòlái* with *shànglái* in the original sentences a and b. Comparing sentences (5a) and (5a'), we can find that (5a') is grammatically valid. However, in terms of specific semantics, the *zhuī shànglái* in (5a) can express the result from far to near (i.e., "the distance is getting closer"), and the *zhuī guòlái* in (5a') can only mean that the pursuit action occurs but does not cover the result (i.e., "the pursuit is about to begin"). The *lìzhēng* in example (5b) and the *néng* in (5c) both require subsequent events to have a certain result, so even the main verbs in the two sentences are is *zhuī*, after replacing *shànglái* with *guòlái*, the sentence does not hold.

Therefore, we can make a schematic diagram of the conceptual meaning of *guòlái* and *shànglái*, as shown in Fig. 1 and Fig. 2:

Fig. 1. The conceptual meaning of *V-guòlái*   **Fig. 2.** The conceptual meaning of *V-shànglái*

Figure 1 demonstrates the conceptual meaning of *V-guòlái*, Fig. 2 demonstrates the conceptual meaning of *V-shànglái*. In the above figure, the circle represents the motion subject, the triangle represents the motion reference object (from the speaker's observation perspective, the reference object may not be the actual position of the speaker), and the arrow represents the motion action. The different positions of the arrow end points indicate that the *guòlái*, motion path may not include the end point, while the *shànglái* motion path may include the end point.

In addition to the consequentiality in the semantic components, there are also differences in the semantic focus of *guòlái* and *shànglái*. See the following two sets of example sentences.

(6) a. 用摄影记者才有的那种敏捷步伐**跑过来**！

     *Yòng shèyǐng jìzhě cái yǒu de nà zhǒng mǐnjié bùfá **pǎo guòlái**!*

  a'. 用摄影记者才有的那种敏捷步伐**跑来**！

     *Yòng shèyǐng jìzhě cái yǒu de nà zhǒng mǐnjié bùfá **pǎolái**!*

     '**Ran over** with the agile steps that only a photojournalists has!'

  b. 王小兰也将一只装得满满的袋子**递过来**。

     *Wáng Xiǎolán yě jiāng yī zhī Zhuāng de mǎnmǎn de dàizi **dì guòlái**.*

  b'. 王小兰也将一只装得满满的袋子递来。

     *Wáng Xiǎolán yě jiāng yī zhī Zhuāng de mǎnmǎn de dàizi **dìlái**.*

     'Wang Xiaolan also **handed over** a brimming bag. '

(7) a. 感到一股又闷热又潮湿的蒸气**扑上脸来**。

     *Gǎndào yī gǔ yòu mēnrè yòu cháoshī de zhēngqì **pūshàng liǎn lái**.*

     'Felt a hot and humid steam **rushing towards** the face. '

  a'. 感到一股又闷热又潮湿的蒸气**扑上脸**。

     *gǎndào yī gǔ yòu mēnrè yòu cháoshī de zhēngqì **pūshàng liǎn**.*

     'Felt a hot and humid steam **rushing onto** the face. '

  b. 家树……直走出亭子，**迎上大道来**……

     *Jiāshù... zhí zǒuchū tíngzi, **yíngshàng dàdào lái**......*

     'Jiashu walked out of the pavilion directly, and **come up to** the avenue.'

  b'. 家树……直走出亭子，**迎上大道**。

     *Jiāshù... zhí zǒuchū tíngzi, **yíngshàng dàdào**.*

     'Jiashu walked out of the pavilion directly, and **headed towards** the avenue. '

Guòlái can be interchanged with *lái* in many cases, as shown in example (6). By replacing *guòlái* with *lái* in the two examples (6a) and (6b), the basic meaning of the sentences does not change. The difference between *guòlái* and *lái* is that *guò* serves to highlight the motion process and must be used only when the motion process information cannot be omitted by default [15], while spatial information related to the specific positional relationship such as the direction, route, and end point of the object's motion is represented by *lái*. Therefore, we can conclude the semantic focus of *guòlái* is on *lái*.

On the other hand, both *shàng* and *lái* in *shànglái* have the function of expressing spatial information of displacement. Here *shàng* means 'attachment', indicating the position change between the motion subject and the reference object, and *lái* represents the change in position between the motion subject and the observer's perspective. *Shànglái* can be interchanged with *shàng* in certain contexts, especially when paired with an object. If we removed *lái* in (7a) and (7b), the sentence only loses the observer's perspective, that is, it cannot express the positional relationship between the motion subject and the speaker, but the sentence's expression of the positional changes on the motion subject is not affected. Therefore, we can conclude the semantic focus of *shànglái* is on *shàng*.

3 Verbs Paired with *Guòlái* and *Shànglái*

In the previous section, we analyzed the semantic composition of *guòlái* and *shànglái* and presented the differences in terms of consequentiality and semantic focus. However, when they are used as complements, we need to consider their own semantics, and the semantics of the main verb they are paired with. In the first section we concluded that, when used as complements, *lái* and *guòlái* can be interchanged in different contexts, but they cannot be interchanged in some other contexts. In examples (1) and (2), when the verbs are *zhuī* and *dì*, the complements can be replaced, but in examples (3) and (4), when the verbs are *jià* and *bān*, the complements cannot be replaced, the semantics is changed after interchange. In this section we will discuss the impact of the semantic characteristics of verbs on *guòlái* and *shànglái*.

Many researchers have discussed the classification of motion verbs from the semantic perspective. For example, Fang [16] classified motion verbs into 'state motion verbs' and 'directional motion verbs'. Shi [17] categorized modal verbs according to the way they encode paths as 'integrative verbs' that encode both modes and paths, and 'analytical verbs' that encode only one of the modes or paths. Zeng [18] divided motion verbs into 'spatial verbs' and 'non-spatial verbs' according to their semantic components. He also classified spatial verbs into 'non-motion verbs', 'subject motion verbs', 'object motion verbs' and 'accompanied motion verbs'. Li [19] classified motion verbs into 'motion verbs without paths', 'motion verbs with continuous paths', 'motion verbs with discrete paths', and 'indicative motion verbs' according to the characteristics of the path components in the place-moving words.

Based on the BCC corpus, we sorted out the corpus of the *V-guòlái/shànglái* structure, and summarized the verbs that can be paired with *guòlái/shànglái* and express physical motion events, excluding virtual motion events[1] such as orientation and extension, as is listed in Table 1.

Table 1. Verbs paired with *guòlái* and *shànglái*

Complement	Verbs
guòlái	*pǎo* 跑 'run'/*pū* 扑 'pounce'/*dì* 递 'hand over'/*chōng* 冲 'rush'/*lā* 拉 'pull'/*kāi* 开 'open'/*duó* 夺 'snatch'/*qiǎng* 抢 'rob'/*fēi* 飞 'fly'/*dǎ* 打 'beat'/*chuī* 吹 'blow'/*bān* 搬 'move'/*kào* 靠 'lean against'/*piāo* 飘 'float'/*qǐng* 请 'invite'/*bēn* 奔 'gallop'/*wéi* 围 'enclose'/*yào* 要 'ask for'...
shànglái	*duān* 端 'hold sth. Level with both hands'/*pá* 爬 'climb'/*zǒu* 走 'walk'/*yǒng* 涌 'gush'/*zhuī* 追 'chase'/*pū* 扑 'pounce'/*sòng* 送 'give'/*shēng* 升 'rise'/*yíng* 迎 'go to meet'/*wéi* 围 'enclose'/*fú* 浮 'float'/*lā* 拉 'pull'/*pǎo* 跑 'run'/*lāo* 捞 'dredge'/*còu* 凑 'collect'/*mào* 冒 'emit'...

As we have discussed in the previous section, not all verbs that can be paired with *guòlái*, can be paired with *shànglái*. In addition, Table 1 also indicates that some verbs

---

[1] References for 'virtual motion' can be found in: Talmy, L. Toward a Cognitive Semantics. Cambridge, MA: MTI Press, 2000.

can only express the upward movement after being combined with *shànglái*, these verbs cannot express the movement from far to near. Therefore, we classify the verbs in Table 1 into four groups based on two factors: 'whether they can be paired with *guòlái* or *shànglái*', and 'whether it indicates the movement from far to near when they paired with *shànglái*'. The classification results are shown in Table 2.

Table 2. The paired verbs with *guòlái/shànglái* and the classification of motion properties

Group	*V-guòlái*	*V- shànglái*	V-shànglái: far to near	Example
A	√	√	√	**Group A₁:** pǎo 跑 'run'/fēi 飞 'fly'/pū 扑 'pounce'/bēn 奔 'gallop'/pá 爬 'climb'/tiào 跳 'jump'… **Group A₂:** kào 靠 'lean against'/wéi 围 'enclose'/yíng 迎 'go to meet'/zhuī 追 'chase'/bī 逼 'press on towards'… **Group A₃:** dì 递 'hand over'/lā 拉 'pull'/dǎ 打 'beat'/duān 端 'hold sth. Level with both hands'/bān 搬 'move'…
B	√	√	×	duó 夺 'snatch'/qiǎng 抢 'rob'/qǔ 取 'take'/jì 寄 'send'/tiāo 挑 'choose'…
C	√	×	—	yào 要 'ask for'/jià 嫁 '(of a woman) marry'/qǔ 娶 'marry (a woman)'…
D	×	√	×	shēng 升 'rise'/fú 浮 'float'/mào 冒 'emit'/zhǎng 涨 'rise'/diào 吊 'hang'…

Sentences with four groups of motion verbs paired with *guòlái/shànglái* are represented in the examples (8) and (9).

(8) a. 把笑容合适的摆在脸上，他轻快的**跑过来**。

    *Bǎ xiàoróng héshì de bǎi zài liǎn shàng, tā qīngkuài de **pǎo guòlái**.*

    'Put a proper smile on his face, he **ran over** briskly. '

  a'. 赵大明…见徐秘书下车，迎面**跑上来**。

    *Zhào Dàmíng...jiàn Xú mìshu xià chē, yíng miàn **pǎo shànglái**.*

    'Zhao Daming saw Secretary Xu getting off the car, then **ran towards** him. '

  b. 他开始挣脱，她就把那张冰凉的脸紧**靠过来**。

    *Tā kāishǐ zhēngtuō, tā jiù bǎ nà zhāng bīngliáng de liǎn jǐn **kào guòlái**.*

    'He just start to pull away, and she **pressed** her cold face **against** him. '

  b'. 当我们不去注意她时，她又慢慢地**靠上来**。

    *Dāng wǒmen bù qù zhùyì tā shí, tā yòu mànmàn de **kào shànglái**.*

    'When we didn't pay attention to her, she **leans in** slowly. '

  c. 她深表赞同，给我**递过来**一杯鸡尾酒。

    *Tā shēnbiǎo zàntóng, gěi wǒ **dì guòlái** yī bēi jīwěi jiǔ.*

    'She strongly agreed and **handed** me a cocktail. '

  c'.每人都**递上来**一卷钞票。

    *Měi rén dōu **dì shànglái** yī juǎn chāopiào.*

    'Each one **handed over** a roll of banknotes. '

(9) a.把他面前那双筷子**取过来**，在茶杯里面洗了一洗……

    *Bǎ tā miàn qián nà shuāng kuàizi **qǔ guòlái**, zài chábēi lǐ miàn xǐ le yī xǐ......*

    'He **took over** the pair of chopsticks in front of him, washed them in the teacup…'

  a'.查看地质队从江底钻孔中**取上来**的岩芯。

    *Chákàn dìzhì duì cóng jiāng dǐ zuānkǒng zhōng **qǔ shànglái** de yánxīn.*

  'To inspect the rock cores **taken** by the geological team **from** the bottom of the river. '

  b. 队长向旁人**要过来**一把镰刀……

    *Duìzhǎng xiàng pángrén **yào guòlái** yī bǎ liándāo...*

    'The captain **asked for** a sickle from the others. '

  b'. *队长向旁人**要上来**一把镰刀。

    Duìzhǎng xiàng pángrén **yào shànglái yī bǎ liándāo.*

  c. *饭菜从 600 元一桌到 1000 元一桌，用了两年多才**涨过来**。

    Fàncài cóng 600 yuán yī zhuō dào 1000 yuán yī zhuō, yòng le liǎng nián duō cái **zhǎng guòlái.*

  c'. 饭菜从 600 元一桌到 1000 元一桌，用了两年多才**涨上来**。

    *Fàncài cóng 600 yuán yī zhuō dào 1000 yuán yī zhuō, yòng le liǎng nián duō cái **zhǎng shànglái**.*

    'The price of a table meal took more than two years to **increase** from 600 yuan **to** 1000 yuan.'

Among the four groups of motion verbs, only in group A, we can interchange *guòlái* and *shànglái* when motion verbs are paired, as is shown in (8). Group A verbs can be further divided into three subcategories as A1, A2, and A3. A1 and A2 describe voluntary displacement, and group A3 describes caused displacement. The difference between A1 and A2 is that: the verbs in group A1 only describe the state of motion and do not include the displacement path; the verbs in group A2 have a path that moves in the direction of the motion reference object (attached to the reference object). If the A2 group verb is paired with *shànglái*, it is more likely to be understood as a displacement from far to near, as is shown in (8b′). Whether the collocation of the verbs in groups A1 and A3 with *shànglái* indicates displacement from far to near dependents on the specific context, as is shown in (8a′) and (8c′). Group D verbs express upward displacement, so they generally cannot be paired with *guòlái*. For example, in example (9c′), if we replace *shànglái* with *shànglái* to form example (9c′), the semantic is not valid.

Groups B and C both belong to the situation where the complement is *guòlái*, and *guòlái* expresses movement from far to near, while the sentence is ungrammatical or the semantics changes if *guòlái* is replaced by *shànglái*, as is shown in (9a), (9a′), (9b) and (9b′). We can find that the common point between groups B and C is that the displacement they represent not only includes changes in the objective or physical position of the object, but also includes the transfer of ownership, which belongs to the phenomenon of virtual motion. Similar examples include:

(10) a. 雅禅的那把里倒许有子弹，**借过来**用用，好不好？

    *Yǎshàn de nà bǎ lǐ dào xǔ yǒu zǐdàn, **jiè guòlái** yòngyòng, hǎo bù hǎo?*

    'There may be bullets in Yashan's one, how about **borrow** it to use? '

  a′. *雅禅的那把里倒许有子弹，**借上来**用用，好不好？

    Yǎshàn de nà bǎ lǐ dào xǔ yǒu zǐdàn, **jiè shànglái yòngyòng, hǎo bù hǎo?*

  b. 她……甚至于向丈夫建议，把杨家住的房**买过来**。

    *Tā...shènzhì yú xiàng zhàngfu jiànyì, bǎ Yáng jiā zhù de fángzi **mǎi guòlái**.*

    'She even suggested to her husband to **buy** the house where the Yang family lives.'

  b′. *她甚至于向丈夫建议，把杨家住的房**买上来**。

    Tā shènzhì yú xiàng zhàngfu jiànyì, bǎ Yáng jiā zhù de fángzi **mǎi shànglái.*

  c. 下个月的房租已经**付过来**了。

    *Xià gè yuè de fángzū yǐjīng **fù guòlái** le.*

    'The rent for next month has already been **paid**. '

  c′. *下个月的房租已经**付上来**了。

    Xià gè yuè de fángzū yǐjīng **fù shànglái le.*

  d. 这个账号上的很多文章都是**转载过来**的。

    *Zhè gè zhànghào shàng de hěn duō wénzhāng dōu shì **zhuǎnzǎi guòlái** de.*

    'Many articles on this account are **reprinted**. '

  d′. *这个账号上的很多文章都是**转载上来**的。

    Zhè gè zhànghào shàng de hěn duō wénzhāng dōu shì **zhuǎnzǎi shànglái de.*

The events such as *jiè*, *mǎi*, *fù* and *zhuǎnzǎi* in the above example sentences all include changes in ownership. Many expressions describing virtual motion events show grammatical features that are different from objective physical motion events, such as *zhuǎnzǎi guòlái* to express a change in orientation, *kàn guòlái* to express a line of sight, and *míngbai guòlái* to express a change in state. In these examples, we cannot replace the complement with *shànglái*.

Zhong et al. [20] pointed out that from a cognitive perspective, real motion and virtual motion have different mental scanning methods when realizing scene perception. Real motion usually adopts the overall scanning method, while virtual motion tends to adopt the sequential scanning method. Since language form is mainly related to cognitive method, we speculate that the fact that *guòlái* paired with verbs B and C cannot be replaced by *shànglái* is related to the fact that it has the characteristics of virtual motion. There are still many issues that need to be discussed in depth about virtual motion, and we are not yet able to make a detailed analysis of them.

4   The Object Combined with *V-guòlái* and *V-shànglái*

We have discussed the characteristics of the verb V in *V-guòlái/shànglái* in the previous section. In this section we regard *V-guòlái/shànglái* as an overall structure and analyze its combinational relationship with the object.

Guòlái and *shànglái* are both compound trend verbs, and their components can be used as verbs to take objects independently. Therefore, the collocation of *V-guòlái/shànglái* and the object can be divided into two situations, *V-guò/shàng-N-lái* and *V-guòlái/shànglái-N*. To simplify the expression, we call the former situation as 'middle object' and the latter situation as 'post-object'.

When the nominal object N is a middle object, the examples of *V-guò/shàng-N-lái* are as shown in Examples (11) and (12):

(11) a. 从旁边**蹿过**<u>一个人</u>**来**。
　　　*Cóng pángbiān **cuānguò** <u>yī gè rén</u> **lái**.*
　　　'<u>A person</u> **jumped over** from the side. '
　　a'. 谁料迎面**跑上**<u>一个人</u>**来**。
　　　*Shuí liào yíng miàn **pǎoshàng** <u>yī gè rén</u> **lái**.*
　　　'Unexpectedly, <u>someone</u> **ran towards** them. '
　　b. 罗雪茵忽然**凑过**<u>脸</u>**来**……
　　　*Luó Xuěyīn hūrán **còuguò** <u>liǎn</u> **lái**...*
　　　'Luo Xueyin suddenly **leaned** <u>her face</u> **in**…'
　　b'. 他突然笑得有点奇怪，**凑上**<u>嘴</u>**来**…
　　　*Tā tūrán xiào de yǒu diǎn qíguài, **còushàng** <u>zuǐ</u> **lái**...*
　　　'He suddenly laughed a little weirdly, and **leaned in** with <u>his mouth</u>…'
　　c. 宜姑**端过**<u>茶</u>**来**……
　　　*Yígū **duānguò** <u>chá</u> **lái**...*
　　　'Yigu **brought over** <u>tea</u> …'
　　c'. 这当儿，寿儿已经**端上**<u>茶</u>**来**……
　　　*Zhè dāngr, Shòu'ér yǐjīng **duānshàng** <u>chá</u> **lái**...*
　　　'At that moment, Shou'er had already **brought** <u>tea</u>…'
　　d. "抽烟吗？"她**递过**<u>烟</u>**来**……
　　　*"Chōu yān ma? " Tā **dìguò** <u>yān</u> **lái**...*
　　　'"Do you want to smoke? "She **handed over** <u>cigarette</u>…'
　　d'. 一旁有人**递上**<u>钱</u>**来**……
　　　*Yī páng yǒu rén **dìshàng** <u>qián</u> **lái**...*
　　　'Someone **handed over** <u>money</u>…'

(12) a. 甚至当报录人**奔过**亭子**来**时……

　　*Shènzhì dāng bàolù rén **bēnguò** tíngzi **lái** shí...*

　　'Even when the reporter **ran over** the pavilion…'

　a'. 甚至当报录人**奔上**亭子**来**时……

　　*Shènzhì dāng bàolù rén **bēnshàng** tíngzi **lái** shí...*

　　'Even when the reporter **rushed up to** the pavilion…'

　b. 被轻风搀着**走过**河滩**来**时……

　　*Bèi qīngfēng chān zhe **zǒuguò** hētān **lái** shí...*

　　'When **carried across** the riverbank by the gentle breeze…'

　b'. 被轻风搀着**走上**河滩**来**时……

　　*Bèi qīngfēng chān zhe **zǒushàng** hētān **lái** shí...*

　　'When **carried up to** the riverbank by the gentle breeze…'

　c. *老者一阵沉默，悲哀慢慢**堆过**脸**来**。

　　Lǎozhě yī zhèn chénmò, bēiāi mànmàn **duīguò liǎn **lái**.*

　c'. 老者一阵沉默，悲哀慢慢**堆上**脸**来**。

　　*Lǎozhě yī zhèn chénmò, bēiāi mànmàn **duīshàng** liǎn **lái**.*

　　'The old man fell silent for a moment, and sadness slowly **piled up on** his face.'

The nominal object N in example (11) is the motion subject, among which a and a', b and b' are autonomous motion events, and c and c', d and d' are caused motion events. Observing the two sentences in Example (11), we can find that *rén, liǎn, zuǐ, chá, yān, qián*, etc. that represent the motion subject can both use *V-guò-N-lái* structure and *V-shàng-N-lái* structure. However if N is motion reference, then we can only use *V-shàng-N-lái* structure, as is demonstrated in Example (12) and example (7b). In examples (12) and (7b), when the middle object is a noun indicating a motion reference such as *tíngzi, hētān, liǎn, dàdào*, if we replace *shànglái* with *guòlái*, then the sentence is not valid. Examples (12a'), (12b') and the *guò* in *yíngguò dàdào* converted from (7b) all mean 'crossing' rather than a motion process.

When the nominal object N is a post-object, the example sentences of *V-guòlái/shànglái-N* are as shown in (13) and (14) respectively.

(13) a. 从暗影里摇摇晃晃**走过来**一个人。

　　　*Cóng ànyǐng lǐ yáoyáo-huànghuàng **zǒu guòlái** yī gè rén.*

　　　'A person **staggering over** from the shadows. '

　　a'. 这时从后边又**走上来**一个人。

　　　*Zhè shí cóng hòu biān yòu **zǒu shànglái** yī gè rén.*

　　　'At this moment, another person **walked up from** behind. '

　　b. 到了晚上……他才**端过来**一盏牛油灯。

　　　*Dào le wǎnshàng...tā cái **duān guòlái** yī zhǎn niúyóu dēng.*

　　　'At night... he **brought over** a bull oil lamp. '

　　b'. 但我**端上来**馒头，她倒自主地拿起就吃。

　　　*Dàn wǒ **duān shànglái** mántou, tā dào zìzhǔ de náqǐ jiù chī.*

　　　'But when I **brought up** Mantou, she took it and ate on her own. '

(14) a. *甚至当报录人**奔过来**<u>亭子</u>时……

　　　* *Shènzhì dāng bàolù rén **bēn guòlái** <u>tíngzi</u> shí...*

a'. *甚至当报录人**奔上来**<u>亭子</u>时……

　　　Shènzhì dāng bàolù rén **bēn shànglái <u>tíngzi</u> shí...*

b. *被轻风搽着**走过来**<u>河滩</u>时，快活的声音。

　　　Bèi qīngfēng chān zhe **zǒu guòlái <u>hētān</u> shí...*

b'. *被轻风搽着**走上来**<u>河滩</u>时，快活的声音。

　　　Bèi qīngfēng chān zhe **zǒu shànglái <u>hētān</u> shí...*

c. *老者一阵沉默，悲哀慢慢**堆过来**<u>脸</u>。

　　　Lǎozhě yī zhèn chénmò, bēiāi mànmàn **duī guòlái <u>liǎn</u>.*

c'. *老者一阵沉默，悲哀慢慢**堆上来**<u>脸</u>。

　　　Lǎozhě yī zhèn chénmò, bēiāi mànmàn **duī hànglái <u>liǎn</u>.*

The noun objects *rén*, *niúyóu dēng* and *mántou* in example (13) are all motion subjects, among which a and a′ are independent motion events, and b and b′ are caused motion events. Each example sentence in Example (14) is obtained by moving the mid-object to the post-object in the corresponding sentence of Example (12), and the object in each clause is still a motion reference. After sentence replacement, we can found the post-object cannot be combined with *V-guòlái* and *V-shànglái* if it is a motion reference. Therefore, unlike the case of mid-object, the post-object can only express the motion subject whether it is pared with *V-guòlái* or *V-shànglái*.

Based on the above analysis, we can summarize the corresponding relationship between the semantics represented by the nominal object N and *V-guòlái/shànglái* as Table 3. Combined with our analysis of the internal semantic composition of *guòlái/shànglái* in the Sect. 2, we speculate that, the semantics of objects entering different syntactic positions in *V-guòlái/shànglái* are related to the different semantic focus of *guòlái/shànglái*. That is, in motion events, the nominal object indicating the motion reference can only appear after the component of the path semantic focus, while the nominal object indicating the motion subject can either appear after the component of the path semantic focus, or after the components of the path without semantic focus.

Table 3. The semantics of the combination of the nominal object N and *V-guòlái/shànglái*

	V-guòlái	*V-shànglái*
middle object	subject	subject or object
post-object	subject	subject

5 Summary

Based on corpus and related cognitive linguistics research results, this article studies the difference and similarities of *V-guòlái* and *V-shànglái* in motion events from three perspectives: semantic composition, semantic characteristics of main verbs, and semantic characteristics of nominal objects. The conclusion is as follows:

First, in terms of semantic characteristics. The motion event represented by *shànglái* contains the result, while the motion event represented by *guòlái* is not required to contain the result. The semantic focus of *guòlái* is *lái*, while the semantic focus of *shànglái* is *shàng*.

Second, the semantic characteristics of the main verbs. Whether *guòlái* and *shànglái* as complements are interchangeable, is related to the semantic characteristics of the main verbs they paired with. In motion events, *guòlái* and *shànglái* are interchangeable with verbs expressing independent motion and caused motion. But only when the verb has a path of movement in the direction of the motion reference object, which is attached to the reference object, *V-shànglái* is more likely to be understood as a movement from far to near. If the verb only describes a state of movement or causes an action, then whether *V-shànglái* is a movement from far to near should be analyzed based on the specific context. Verbs describing virtual motion events involving the transfer of ownership can only be paired with *guòlái*. Among these verbs, some cannot be paired with *shànglái*, and others that are replaced *guòlái* with *shànglái*, can only express upward displacement, rather than displacement from far to near. When the verb has an upward directional path, it can only be paired with *shànglái*. In such situation, *shànglái* cannot be replaced by *guòlái*.

Third, the semantic characteristics of nominal objects. When the object is a mid-object, the object paired with *V-guòlái* can only represent the motion subject, while the object paired with *V-shànglái* can be either the motion subject or the motion reference object. When the object is a post-object, the object paired with *V-guòlái* and *V-shànglái* can only be the motion subject. Only in certain contexts, the post-object combined with *V-guòlái* can be motion reference. We speculate that the relationship between object position and semantics is related to the semantic focus of *guòlái/shànglái*.

The above conclusion has certain value for international Chinese teaching practice and subsequent research on Chinese motion events, especially for the construction of the overall grammatical framework of motion events. However, there still remains problems to be further analyzed. In the future work, we will focus on more detailed analysis of virtual motion events and try to find the grammatical interface between virtual motion and real motion.

References

1. Chao, Y.: A Grammar of Spoken Chinese (中國話的文法), 1st edn. The Chinese University Press, Hong Kong (1980). (in Chinese)
2. Zhu, D.: Chinese Language (语法讲义), 1st edn. The Commercial Press, Beijing (1982). (in Chinese)
3. Dictionary Editing Office of Institute of Linguistics: Modern Chinese dictionary (现代汉语词典). The Commercial Press, Beijing (2016). (in Chinese)

4. Liu, Y., Pan, W., Gu, W: Practical Modern Chinese Grammar (实用现代汉语语法). The Commercial Press, Beijing (2019). (in Chinese)
5. Lv, S.: Modern Chinese Eight Hundred Words (现代汉语八百词), 1st edn. The Commercial Press, Beijing (1980). (in Chinese)
6. Liu, Y.: Analysis of Directional Complement (趋向补语通释), 1st edn. Beijing Language and Culture University Press, Beijing (1998). (in Chinese)
7. Fillmore, C: The case for case. In: Bach, E., Harms, R. (eds.) Universalsin Linguistic Theory, pp. 1–88. Holt, Rinehart and Winston, University of Texas (1968)
8. Lakoff, G.: Women Fire and Dangerous Things: What Categories Reveal About the Mind. The University of Chicago Press, Chicago (1987)
9. Talmy, L: Lexicalization patterns: semantic structure in lexical forms. In: Shopen, T. (ed.) Language Typology and Syntactic Description, Vol. 3: Grammatical Categories and the Lexicon. Cambridge University Press (1985)
10. Talmy, L. Toward a Cognitive Semantics, Volume I: Concept Structuring Systems. MTI Press, Cambridge (2000)
11. Shen, J.: A typological investigation of "dynamic complement structure" in modern Chinese (现代汉语-动补结构的类型学考察). Chin. Teach. World **3**, 17–23 (2003). (in Chinese)
12. Li, X.: A critical review of researches on motion events typologies (移动事件类型学研究述评). Foreign Lang. Res. **4**, 1–9 (2012). (in Chinese)
13. Lamarre, C.: Motion-event of Chinese language (中国語の移動表現). In: Matsumoto, Y. (ed.) Typology of Motion-Event (移動表現の類型論). Kurosio Press, Tokyo (2017). (in Japanese)
14. Liu, M., Tsai, H., Hu, C., Chou, S.: The proto-motion event schema: integrating lexical semantics and morphological sequencing. J. Chin. Linguist. **43**(2), 503–547 (2015)
15. Li, Z.: Research on path components in Chinese Motion events (汉语位移表述中路径成分研究). Osaka University, Osaka (2022). (in Chinese)
16. Fang, M.: The "Motion Verb" and Spatial Representation: Syntactic Perspectives on Japanese and Chinese (『移動動詞』と空間表現—統語論的な視点から見た日本語と中国語). Hakuteisha Press, Tokyo (2004). (in Japanese)
17. Shi, W.: A diachronic Investigation of the Lexicalization Types of Chinese Motion Events (汉语运动事件词化类型的历时考察). The Commercial Press, Beijing (2014). (in Chinese)
18. Zeng, C.: A Cognitive Study of Motion Space in Modern Chinese (现代汉语位移空间的认知研究). The Commercial Press, Beijing (2014). (in Chinese)
19. Li, Z.: A comparative study of two motion verbs Lái and Guò lái. In: Dong, M., Gu, Y., Hong, J.: Chinese Lexical Semantics: 22nd Workshop, pp. 339–352. Springer, Heidelberg (2021)
20. Zhong, S., Zhao, J.: A contrastive study of the cognitive mechanisms between factual motion and fictive motion from the perspective of cognitive linguistics (真实位移与虚拟位移建构机制的认知对比研究). Foreign Lang. China (中国外语) **14**(1), 36–42 (2017). (in Chinese)

Research on the Semantic Map
of Multifunctional Morpheme Sui

Huijie Zhuang and Mo Li[✉]

School of Culture and Communication, Central University of Finance and Economics,
Beijing 100098, China
zhuanghuijie@cufe.edu.cn, limo0904@163.com

Abstract. In this paper, the multifunctional morpheme of Chinese word "Sui(随)" is comprehensively researched, and then the diachronic semantic evolution and synchronic distribution are combined to explore the historical hierarchy of the semantic evolution of "Sui(随)" by utilizing the semantic map method. It is pointed out that "Sui(随)" in some dialects is semantically discontinuous. But from a diachronic perspective, these semantic related functions can be discovered, which is the advantage of diachronic semantic map. Word meanings are not isolated and scattered, and the intrinsic meanings are systematic. The semantic evolution of "Sui(随)" has its own characteristics, but also has family characteristics of words with the conceptual field of "follow". Additionally, the semantic map method effectively demonstrates the semantic relationships and lexical co-lexicalization.

Keywords: Semantic Map · Semantic Evolution · Grammaticalization · Multifunctional Morpheme "Sui(随)"

1 Forward

Regarding the emergence of the preposition "Sui(随)", the academic community currently has a relatively consistent view, believing that "Sui(随)" already had the usage of a preposition in the Pre-Qin Period. In the book "Comprehensive Explanation of Function Words in Ancient Chinese (古代汉语虚词通释》)" 释 and "Dictionary of Function Words in Ancient Chinese (《古汉语虚词词典》)", it points out that the preposition "Sui(随)" is used to introduce the route and the object relied on when performing an action, that is, "along" and "according to", and the example "予乘四载，随山刊木" from《尚书·益稷》is cited as the earliest appearance of the preposition "Sui(随)". Beijia Ma [1] also regarded the "Sui(随)" in "随山刊木" as the critical point of the transformation from a verb to a preposition. Yumei Shi [2] analyzed the character "Sui(随)" in "随山濬川" from the perspective of the history of linguistics, and believed that "随山濬川" should be understood as "开山疏川". Bo Wu [3] pointed out that in Western Han Dynasty, there were only a few examples of "Sui(随)" used as prepositions. With the extensive use of the sentence pattern "随 N + VP", "Sui(随)" has been

P. Jin et al. (Eds.): CLSW 2024, LNAI 15552, pp. 455–469, 2025.
https://doi.org/10.1007/978-981-96-3509-2_33

gradually grammaticalized as a comitative preposition from a verb, and then further developed into a "via" preposition and a "according to" preposition. Fuxiang Wu [4] conducted research on the grammaticalization of Chinese comitative prepositions from a typological perspective, and pointed out that there is a pattern of grammaticalization from comitative verb to comitative preposition and subsequently to coordinate conjunction. Fei Yu [5] studied the frequently used words in the Han Dynasty, focusing on the evolution of "Sui(随)" and "Cong(从)", and pointed out that the status of "Cong(从)" and "Sui(随)" began to change from the Western Han Dynasty. Although "Sui(随)" emerged later, it developed rapidly, and in the Chinese Buddhist scriptures of the Eastern Han Dynasty, the frequency of "Sui(随)" significantly surpassed that of "Cong(从)".

In general, the existing studies focused on the grammaticalization of "Sui(随)", emphasized diachronic research, neglected the lexical semantic differences in the synchronic distribution, and conducted less systematic research on the meaning of "Sui(随)". Semantic map is an empirical method that intuitively shows the connections between the lexical semantic functions of different languages or the same language at different times. At present, there are few studies on the diachronic semantic map of Chinese. This paper uses the semantic map method to combine the diachronic evolution and the synchronic distribution of dialects of "Sui(随)", discusses the semantic implication and the mechanism of evolution in the diachronic evolution, and tries to explain the semantic distribution characteristics of "Sui(随)" in the synchronic distribution of modern Chinese by combining the diachronic evolution of the words in the "follow" conceptual field.

2　Semantic Function Entries of "Sui(随)"

On page 1252 of the 7th edition of "Modern Chinese Dictionary", the meanings of "Sui(随)" are: 1) verb, follow: "跟 随 gēn suí" 2) verb, obey: "随 顺 suí shùn" 3) verb, let: "随 意 suí yì" 4) conveniently: "随 手 suí shǒu" 5) <dialect> resemble: "他 长 得 随 他 父 亲 tā zhǎng dé suí tā fù qīn"; 6) (Suí) Surname.

On page 517 of "Modern Chinese Eight Hundred Words", the meanings of "Sui(随)" are: 1) verb, follow, it is often used with "Zhe(着)" and must be followed with a noun object: "随 着 经 济 建 设 高 潮 的 到 来 suí zhe jīng jì jiàn shè gāo cháo d e dào lái ……"; 2) let, allow, it must be followed with a noun object and mostly used in sentences without a subject, and the preceding part is often a verb or a clause: "去 不 去 随 你 qù bù qù suí nǐ".

Based on the existing research results and dialect surveys, in this paper ten semantic functions of "Sui(随)" are selected as follows: follow, obey, let, immediately, comitative, according to, via, human direction, human source, along. Referring to the existing research results, the semantic function of each entry with example sentences is explained as follows.

A. Follow, to walk or proceed in accordance with. (1) <ruby>小张随父亲回老家了<rt>xiǎozhāngsuífùqīnhuílǎojiāle</rt></ruby>。

B. Obey, to follow the commands or guidance of. (2) <ruby>找对象的事你就随我<rt>zhǎoduìxiàngdeshìnǐjiùsuíwǒ</rt></ruby>的<ruby>意吧<rt>deyìba</rt></ruby>。

C. Let, not to interfere the behavior and wishes of others and let them decide. (3) <ruby>去不<rt>qùbú</rt></ruby><ruby>去随你<rt>qùsuínǐ</rt></ruby>。

D. Immediately, adverb with meaning of "immediately, right away". (4) <ruby>随吃随做<rt>suíchīsuízuò</rt></ruby>。

E. Comitative. (5) <ruby>你随我一起去学校吧<rt>nǐsuíwǒyīqǐqùxuéxiàoba</rt></ruby>。

F. According to. (6) <ruby>随吃多少而做多少<rt>suíchīduōshǎoérzuòduōshǎo</rt></ruby>。(This sentence means "cook according to how much you eat" in Linwu dialect)

G. Via. (7) <ruby>伴在后进不见伴退<rt>bànzàihòujìnbújiànbàntuì</rt></ruby>，<ruby>畏盗贼便随邪径御车涉路<rt>wèidàozéibiànsuíxiéjìngyùchēshèlù</rt></ruby>。(《<ruby>出曜<rt>chūyào</rt></ruby><ruby>经<rt>jīng</rt></ruby>》<ruby>第六卷<rt>dìliùjuàn</rt></ruby>)

H. Human direction. (8) <ruby>证知诸法<rt>zhèngzhīzhūfǎ</rt></ruby>，<ruby>建立无畏<rt>jiànlìwúwèi</rt></ruby>，<ruby>度诸疑网<rt>dùzhūyíwǎng</rt></ruby>，<ruby>不随他语<rt>bùsuítāyǔ</rt></ruby>。(《<ruby>佛本行集经<rt>fóběnhángjíjīng</rt></ruby>》<ruby>第三十八卷<rt>dìsānshíbājuàn</rt></ruby>)

I. Human source. (9) <ruby>而今圣夫将我与彼行于世事<rt>érjīnshèngfūjiāngwǒyǔbǐhángyúshìshì</rt></ruby>，<ruby>从其随索多少钱物<rt>cóngqísuǒduōshǎoqiánwù</rt></ruby>，<ruby>得以而为彼大沙门作食布施<rt>déyǐérwéibǐdàshāménzuòshíbùshī</rt></ruby>。(《<ruby>佛本行集经<rt>fóběnhángjíjīng</rt></ruby>》<ruby>第四十卷<rt>dìsìshíjuàn</rt></ruby>))

J. Along. (10) <ruby>随水流向下找<rt>suíshuǐliúxiàngxiàzhǎo</rt></ruby>，<ruby>应该能找得到<rt>yīnggāinéngzhǎodedào</rt></ruby>。

Base on the above ten semantic functions, this paper investigates and sorts out the semantics and functions of "Sui(随)" in 43 dialect points in the "Modern Chinese Dialect Dictionary" edited by Li Rong and Mandarin. In these dialect points, 21 points has the words "Sui(随)" and the semantic functions of "Sui(随)" in different dialects are listed as follows.

In Yan'an dialects, it has six semantic functions: "follow", "obey", "let", "immediately", "comitative" and "along". In Baoding, it has five: "follow", "obey", "let", "immediately" and "along". In Linwu, it has five: "obey", "let", "immediately", "according to" and "along". In Rongcheng, it has four: "follow", "obey", "let" and "according to". In Xi'an, it has four: "obey", "immediately", "let" and "according to". In Jinan, it has three: "follow", "obey" and "let". In Yinchuan, it has three: "follow", "obey" and "immediately". In Danyang, it has three: "let", "immediately" and "comitative". In Nanchang, it has three: "obey", "let" and "immediately". In Urumqi, it has two: "follow" and "obey". In Chengdu, it has two: "let" and "comitative". In Yangzhou, it has two: "let" and "immediately". In Xuzhou, it has two: "obey" and "let". In Guiyang, Suzhou, Jinhua, Changsha, Fuzhou and Nanning, it has only one: "let". In Liuzhou and Pingxiang, it has only one: "comitative".

According to the dialect survey, "Sui(随)" has many semantic functions in different dialects, and the initial verb meaning has disappeared in many dialects, therefore, the relationships between the semantic functions of "Sui(随)" cannot be established from the actual usage in Chinese dialects. Based on the diachronic semantic investigation of "Sui(随)" and the grammaticalization and semantic evolution path, the connection of these semantic functions will be established from the diachronic perspective, then the synchronic semantic map will be drawn using the dialect data, and finally the diachronic conceptual space will be validated.

3 Diachronic Semantic Investigation of "Sui(随)"

3.1 Semantic Function of "Sui(随)" in Ancient Chinese

The original meaning of "Sui(随)" is "follow", as stated in 说文·辵部, "随, 从也". In the period of Ancient Chinese, the basic meaning of "Sui(随)" is "follow". In addition, "Sui(随)" also has the semantic functions of the verb "obey", the adverb "immediately", and the prepositions "according to, along". Regarding the emergence of the preposition "Sui(随)", the academic community generally believes that it already existed in the Pre-Qin period, as stated by Beijia Ma [1], Bo Wu [3] etc.

In the Ancient Chinese period, the examples of "Sui(随)" with the meaning of "follow" and "obey" are given as follows:

(11) 使者入, 及众介随入, 北面东上。(《仪礼·聘礼》) (follow)

(12) 十一月, 克减侯宣多, 而随蔡侯以朝于执事。(《左传·文公十七年》) (follow)

(13) 自吾执斧斤以随子, 未尝见材如此其美也。(《庄子·人间世》) (follow)

(14) 夫物有常容, 因乘以导之, 因随物之容。(《韩非子·喻老》) (obey)

From the above examples, it can be seen that "Sui(随)" was a notional verb with strong action in the Pre-Qin period, and its object was mostly a noun referring to a person. In (11), the sentence pattern is "NP$_1$ + V$_1$ (随) + NP$_2$ + 而/以 + V$_2$" or "NP$_1$ + V$_1$ (随) + NP$_2$ + V$_2$", the sememe of "Sui(随)" with the meaning "follow" is similar to that of "Cong(从)", and "Sui(随)" also contains [+follow after] [+do something together] (the relationship between NP$_1$ and NP$_2$ is a master-slave relationship) [+run] [+displacement]. In (12), "Sui(随)" has four sememes, so it is also regarded as a verb. In the middle of the sentence, there is a connection of "而/以", which does not meet the conditions of grammaticalization. In this ambiguous context, one can understand that the actions of V$_1$(随) and V$_2$ are continuous, and the other can understand that V$_1$ (随) is the premise or basis for the occurrence of the action of V$_2$. When the object after "Sui(随)" changes from a noun referring to a person to an inanimate thing, and the content becomes more abstract, the verb meaning of "Sui(随)" begins to be grammaticalized.

At the same time, "Sui(随)" also extended the concept of "obey" from the actual behavior of [+follow after] to the subjective willingness to "follow" the opinions of others to do something through metaphorical extension, as in (14). The detailed literature survey results in Ancient Chinese period are shown in Table 1.

During this period, the main prepositional function of "Sui(随)" is "according to", which means "in accordance with". The examples are as follows:

Table 1. The semantic functions of "Sui(随)" in Ancient Chinese period

Literaure	Verb		Adverb	Preposition		Literaure	Verb		Adverb	Preposition	
	follow	Obey	Immediately	According to	Along		follow	Obey	Immediately	According to	Along
尚书					2	韩诗外传	4	1			
诗经						吴子	1				
周易	7					尉缭	1				
仪礼	5		1	2		六韬	3				
周礼						司马法				1	
礼记	5		1			慎子					
春秋公羊传						通玄真经	7				
春秋谷梁传	2					关尹子	3	1			
左传	2					鹖冠子	4			3	
国语	5			1		邓析子	1				
战国策	25	1		1		孝经					
论语				1		素问	19				2
孟子						灵枢	16	2		7	1
墨子	7		1			孔子家语	5			3	
庄子	19					孔丛子	4	1			
荀子	4		1			史记	75	1	3	1	3
韩非子	25	2				新语	1			9	
吕氏春秋	10			10		春秋繁露	20	1		3	
老子	3			1		淮南	25	1		7	1
商君书	5					新序	12			12	1
管子	20	2		3	1	说苑	11			1	1
晏子	1			3		新书	4				
孙子	1			1		马王堆汉墓帛书	2		1		
大戴				1		合计	364	13	8	71	12

(15) 欲生而不事，……贵之而弗喜，随其天资而安之不极。（《淮南子》第七卷) (according to)

(16) 上多喜善赏，不随其功，则士不为用。（《管子·七臣七主》) (according to)

Initially, the object after "Sui(随)" was a specific person, and then in the serial verb structure, the object of "Sui(随)" expanded from the "Shi(时)", "Su(俗)" to the abstract concepts such as "Tianzi(天资)" and "Guiju(规矩)". "Suibian(随变)" and "Suishi(随时)" are further grammaticalized than "Suishan(随山)" and "Suizhi(随之)". However, this structure appears very rarely, and the verb characteristics of "Sui(随)" have not completely disappeared. In (15)(16), "Sui(随)" can be understood as a verb meaning "obey", or as a preposition meaning "according to".

From semantic evolution of "Sui(随)" in Ancient Chinese, "Sui(随)" extended from the original meaning of "follow" to the meaning of "obey", and from the meaning of "obey" to the meaning of "according to". This also verifies the hypothesis of the connection between "obey" and "according to" of "Cong(从)" mentioned above.

The function of the time adverb "immediately" of "Sui(随)" is derived from the meaning of the verb "follow", indicating the sequence of two events, emphasizing that the latter event occurs immediately after the former event. For example:

(17) 兼执足，左首，随入西上，参分庭一在南。(《仪礼·士昏礼》)(immediately)

(18) 父以足受，笑而去。良殊大惊，随目之。(《史记·留侯世家》) (immediately)

Therefore, the connection between "follow" and "immediately" is established.

When the object after "Sui(随)" is "water or river", it extends the meaning of the verb "along", and the common sentence pattern is $NP_1 + V_1$ (随) $+ NP_2 + V_2$, but at this time, "Sui(随)" is mostly understood as a verb. For example:

(19) 于是乃命西征，随流而攘，风之所被，罔不披靡。(《汉书·司马相如传》)(along)

The meaning of "along" contains the sememes [+run] [+displacement] [+path]. Bo Wu [3] pointed out that when following others, the follower must follow the path of the person being followed, so "follow" and "along" have something in common. When the object carried by "Sui(随)" becomes an object that does not have the ability to perform actions, the verb meaning of "follow" of "Sui(随)" completely disappears, and at this time, "Sui(随)" can only be understood as the preposition "via". The connection between "follow" and "along" can be established from the extension of meanings.

In the period of Ancient Chinese, the dominant word expressing the meaning of "follow" was "Cong(从)", and the usage of "Sui(随)" was relatively rare. At this time, the main usage of "Gen(跟)" was as the noun "heel", and it did not have the verb usage yet. In the Pre-Qin period, the types of objects that the verb "Cong(从)" took after it, continued to expand, from referring to human objects to object objects, location objects, time objects, and so on. The semantic functions of "Cong(从)" included "follow", "obey", "locative source", "range", "via", "time source", "state source", "according to", "human source", "along".

During this period, there were some examples of the continuous use of "Suicong(随从)", all expressing the meaning of the verb "follow". For example:

(20) 是故豪杰皆可变业，务学诗书，随从外权，上可以得显，下可以得官爵。(《商君书·农战》)(follow)

3.2 Semantic Function of "Sui(随)" in Middle Chinese

In the period of Middle Chinese, the usage examples of "Sui(随)" increased rapidly. In the conceptual field of the verb "follow", the literature examples of "Sui(随)" had exceeded those of "Cong(从)". For example:

(21) 公卿百僚，皆随其后，到河上，乃得还。(《搜神记》第六卷)(follow)

During this period, the examples of the adverbial meaning "immediately" of "Sui(随)" increased rapidly compared to before. For example:

(22) 因吟啸良久，随而下笔。(《世说新语·文学第四》)(immediately)

In Wei Jin Southern and Northern Dynasties Period, with the expansion of the objects that follow "Sui(随)", and the prepositional function of "Sui(随)" continued to strengthen and improve. During this period, the more frequently used prepositional function of "Sui(随)" was "according to", and the object after the "according to" function became more abstract. In addition to nouns that could be used as criteria, psychological verbs indicating preferences, intentions, and other factors that could be used as criteria were also added. For example:

(23) 自地兀后，但所耕地，随饷盖之。(《齐民要术·杂说》)(according to)
(24) 以狐血鹤血涂一丸，内爪中，以指万物，随口变化，即山行木徙，人皆见之。(《抱朴子·内篇》)(according to)

The detailed literature survey results in this period are shown in Table 2.

In the Middle Chinese period, the new functions of "Sui(随)" contain prepositional functions such as "along", "comitative", "via", "let", "human source", and "human direction". However, as can be seen from Table 2, the examples of these functions were not many.

First of all, the sememe "along" had been grammaticalized as a preposition during this period. For example:

(25) 以渍米汁随瓮边稍稍沃之，勿使曲发饭起。(《齐民要术》第八卷 (along)

Secondly, the semantic function of the object-path meaning of "Sui(随)" is further expanded, such as generating functions like "via" and "comitative".

In addition, "Sui(随)" also developed the prepositional function of "let" in the Middle Chinese period. "Let" developed from the meaning of the verb "obey". It means not interfering with the behavior and wishes of others and letting them decide, that is, it contains four sememes: [+obey] [+not interfere] [+speech] [+wish]. "Sui(随)" often appears in the sentence pattern of NP$_1$ + V$_1$ (随) + NP$_2$ + V$_2$. When the object after it expands to specific behaviors, it gradually evolves into the function of the preposition "let".

Table 2. The semantic functions of "Sui(随)" in Middle Chinese period

Literaure	Verb		Adverb	Preposition						
	follow	Obey	Immediately	Comitative	Via	According to	Let	Human direction	Human source	Along
抱朴子内篇	9	1	1							
世说新语	3		1			8				
搜神记	24	1	3	2		6				1
洛阳伽蓝记	5					2	1		2	
颜氏家训	6		3			4	2			
道行般若经	72	22	1	1		6		1		
佛说兜沙经						95				
阿门佛国经	1	1								
佛说遗日摩尼宝经	3	3				6				
佛说般舟三昧经	5	2				9				
般舟三昧经	14	4		1		2				
文殊师利问菩萨署经	4					9				
法镜经	1	2				5				
阿含口解十二因缘经	2					3				
中本起经	2	3				2	3			2
修行本起经	4	1	2			5				
梵摩渝经						4				
佛说义足经	5	4	1				2			1
大明度经	35	21	1			7		2		1
佛说菩萨本业经	1	1				31	2			
了本生死经		1				2				
佛说四愿经	5	1								
六度集经	14	3		2		1	2			
生经	18	3		1		8	2			2
佛说普曜经	11	1				19	1			1
光赞经	6	2				19				
大楼炭经	11	1	6			16	6			
阿育王传	8	4	2			1	5			
出曜经	70	14	2	1	2	9	30		1	6
大庄严论经	30	13	2	1		101	5	1	2	
妙法莲华经	13	5	1			22	8			
悲华经	10	5	2			31	17			
百喻经	1	3				35				
佛本行集经	119	29	9	1		2	84	4	2	4
佛说伅真陀罗所问如来三昧经	12	6	1			95				

(*continued*)

Table 2. (*continued*)

Literaure	Verb		Adverb	Preposition							
	follow	Obey	Immediately	Comitative	Via	According to	Let	Human direction	Human source	Along
佛说阿阇世王经	8	1				24				
齐民要术	11	4	5			8	6			1
Sum	543	162	43	10	2	597	176	8	7	19

(26) 唯道可贵，皆作沙门，随其教化。(《《六度集经》第八卷)(let)

Thus, the connection between "let" and "obey" can be established. Combining the above analysis, the connection in the conceptual space of "Sui(随)" in the Middle Chinese period is shown in Fig. 1 as follows.

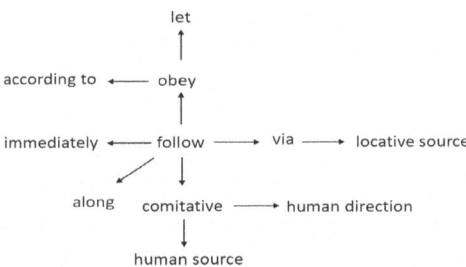

Fig. 1. The conceptual space of "Sui(随)"

In the Middle Chinese period, "Sui(随)" and "Cong(从)" engaged in fierce competition in expressing the meaning of "follow". Judging from the literature examples and combinatorial capabilities, "Sui(随)" defeated "Cong(从)" and became the dominant word in this conceptual field. "Gen(跟)" mainly meant "heel" and had no verb or prepositional usages yet.

During this period, there were a total of 38 cases of the continuous use of "Suicong(随从)", all expressing the meaning of the verb "follow". For example:

(27) 唯逆王边诸恶臣耳，供养恭敬随从入城。(《阿育王传》第一卷))(follow)

3.3 Semantic Function of "Sui(随)" in Early Modern Chinese

In the early modern Chinese period, the core usage of "Sui(随)" is the verb "follow". For example:

(28) 须达既蒙受请，更得圣者相随，……至舍卫之城。(《敦煌变文·降魔变文》)(follow)

Since the Tang and Song Dynasties, the common functions of "Sui(随)" also contain the prepositional function of "let" and the adverbial function of "immediately". For example:

(29) "　五娘说那里话 ！ 小的又不赖他 ， 有一句说一句 。 随爹怎的问 ，
也只是这等说。"(《金瓶梅》第二十五回)(let)

(30) 童奶奶绰了这个口气，随道：……(《醒世姻缘传》 第七十回))(immediately)

Compared with the Middle Chinese period, some prepositional functions began to shrink. For example, the usage examples of the prepositional function of "according to" decreased significantly. For example:

(31) 五湖四海随缘去，到处为家一不归。(《祖堂集·伏牛和尚》)(according to)

In this period, although the usage examples of the "comitative" function of "Sui(随)" increased compared to the previous period, the overall proportion of usage examples was still small. For example:

(32) 陵左手揽发，右手台刀，头随刃落，血洒流四方。(《敦煌变文集·汉将王
陵变》)(comitative)

In addition, "Sui(随)" also has some marginal functions with very few usage examples, such as "along". Due to semantic limitations, these functions did not develop in the later period. For example:

(33) 其僧问出山路，师指随流而去。其僧归到盐官处，具陈上事。(《祖堂
集·大梅和尚》)(along)

The detailed literature survey results in this period are shown in Table 3.

Generally speaking, in this period, the core meaning of "Sui(随)" is "follow". The prepositional functions of "Sui(随)" begin to decrease, and there are no examples of the meanings of "via", "human source" and "human direction". The adverbial functions of "Immediately" developed rapidly during the Yuan Ming and Qing dynasties. Since there is no new semantic function of "Sui(随)" in this period, the conceptual space is the same as that of the Middle Chinese period.

In the period of early modern Chinese, the new word "Gen(跟)" in the conceptual field of "follow" developed rapidly. "Gen(跟)" began to compete with "Sui(随)" from the Ming Dynasty, and it replaced "Sui(随)" as the dominant word in the conceptual field of "follow" in the Qing Dynasty. "Gen(跟)" extended the semantic meaning of "follow" in the Song Dynasty. Due to the influence of the family nature of the core word "Sui(随)" in the field, "Gen(跟)" quickly developed several prepositional functions on the basis of the meaning of "follow", such as functions of "comitative", "comparison",

Table 3. The semantic functions of "Sui(随)" in early modern Chinese period

Literaure	Verb		Adverb	Preposition			
	follow	Obey	Immediately	Comitative	According to	Let	Along
敦煌变文集	109	4	6	8		12	2
祖堂集	32	1		2	35	2	1
大唐三藏取经诗话					35		
新刊大宋宣和遗事	5		3	1			
五代史平话	9		1		4	1	
全相平话五种	53		4		1		1
关汉卿戏曲集	21	1		2	6	1	
元刊杂剧三十种	29	1		1			
老乞大谚解					7		
朴通事谚解			2				
永乐大典戏文三种	25	1					
水浒传	208	1	13	5	1	8	2
西游记	158	1	58	8	14	15	1
金瓶梅	44	1	17	4	23	122	8
平妖传	71		1		13	18	
醒世姻缘传	72		62	3	4	22	
儒林外史	12	1	24		10	12	
红楼梦	104	2	14	1	1	68	1
歧路灯	74	3	11	3	19	9	1
Sum	1026	17	216	38	173	290	17

"human direction", "association", and in the Ming Dynasty, the function of "coordinate" appeared. Although "Sui(随)" is no longer the dominant word in the conceptual field of "follow" in the later period, its core meaning is still the verb "follow". At the same time, the adverbial functions of "Sui(随)" are further developed, and examples of the prepositional function gradually decrease. In this period, the usage examples of the content word "Cong(从)" decrease, and its common functions are "locative source", "time source", "range", "via", etc.

According to our statistics, during the period of early modern Chinese, the combination of "Suicong(随从)" shows a total of 50 times. Among them, 16 cases are used as a noun to mean "people who follow", and 34 cases are used as the meaning of the verb "follow". The combination of "Gensui(跟随)" shows a total of 250 times, all of which express the meaning of the verb "follow". The combination of "Gencong(跟从)" shows a total of 21 times. Among them, only 1 case is used as a noun "people who follow", and the rest express the meaning of the verb "follow".

Finally, taking "follow" as the connection point, the conceptual spaces of "Sui(随)" in this paper, "Cong(从)" and "Gen(跟)" in Huijie Zhuang [6, 7] are integrated to obtain the conceptual space centered on the meaning of "follow", as shown in Fig. 2.

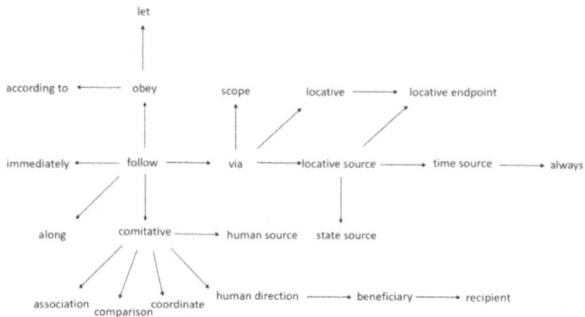

Fig. 2. The conceptual space of the meaning of "follow"

4   Synchronic Semantic Mapping of "Sui(随)"

In Mandarin Chinese, "Sui(随)" has five semantic functions: "let", "obey", "follow", "immediately" and "comitative". In Baoding dialect, it has six semantic functions: "according to", "let", "obey", "follow", "immediately" and "along". In Jinan, it has three: "let","obey" and "follow". In Linwu, it has five: "according to", "let", "obey", "immediately" and "along". In Chengdu, it has two: "let" and "comitative". The semantic maps of "Sui(随)" in the above dialects are shown in Fig. 3.

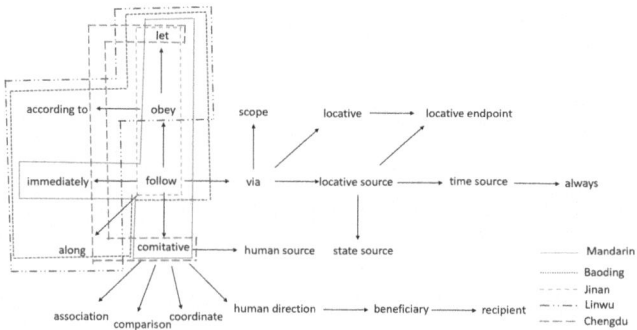

Fig. 3. The semantic maps of "Sui(随)"(1)

In Guiyang, Jinhua, Changsha, Fuzhou, and Nanning, it has one semantic function of "let". In Liuzhou and Pingxiang, it has one: "comitative". In Urumqi, it has two:

"obey" and "follow". In Yinchuan, it has three: "obey", "follow" and "immediately". In Yangzhou, it has two: "let" and "immediately". In Xuzhou, it has two: "let" and "obey". The semantic maps of "Sui(随)" in the above dialects are shown in Fig. 4.

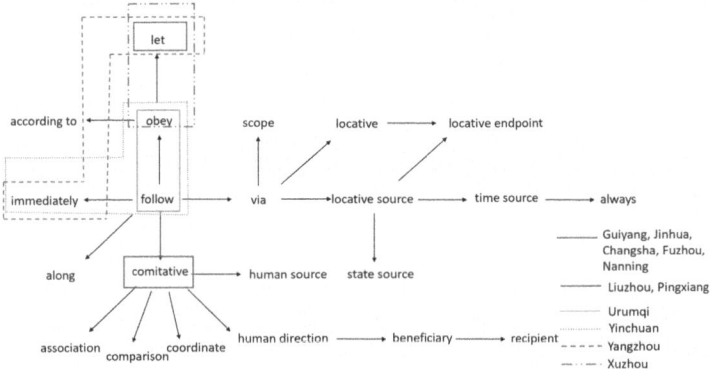

Fig. 4. The semantic maps of "Sui(随)"(2)

In Xi'an, it has four: "according to", "let", "obey" and "immediately". In Rongcheng, it has five: "according to", "let", "obey", "immediately" and "follow". In Danyang, it has three: "let", "immediately" and "comitative". In Yan'an, it has six: "obey", "follow", "according to", "let", "comitative" and "immediately". In Nanchang, it has three: "let", "obey" and "immediately". The semantic maps of "Sui(随)" in the above dialects are shown in Fig. 5.

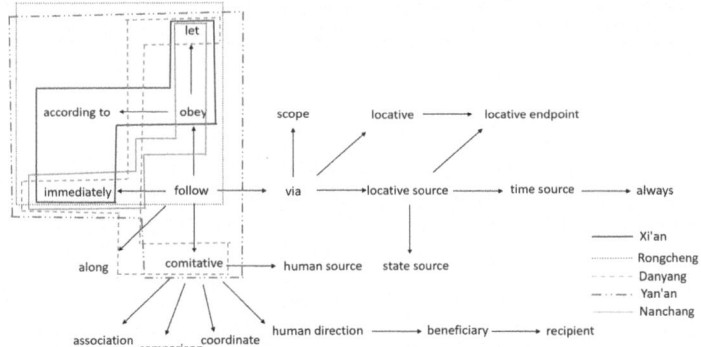

Fig. 5. The semantic maps of "Sui(随)"(3)

5   Conclusions

Based on the evolution of the semantic functions of "Sui(随)" in diachronic and synchronic planes and the construction of its semantic maps, the following conclusions can be drawn.

(1) "Sui(随)" was grammaticalized as a preposition during the Tang and Song dynasties. After the Yuan Dynasty, the usages of various prepositional functions gradually shrank, and its core meaning was still the verb "follow", but it is less used in spoken language. In the history of Chinese, the dominant word in the conceptual field of the verb "follow" has experienced historical evolution of "Cong(从)", "Sui(随)", and "Gen(跟)", and the evolution of the dominant word in this conceptual field is closely related to lexical grammaticalization. We speculate that the reason for "Sui(随)" in the Qing Dynasty withdrawing from the dominant position may be related to the rise of Beijing Mandarin in the Qing Dynasty.

(2) The synchronic state of language is the product of diachronic evolution, and the explanation of the synchronic pattern must have a diachronic viewpoint. For example, based on the research on the synchronic semantic functions of words with the meaning of "Sui(随)", it is impossible to establish the connections between various functional nodes from the actual usage of dialects. In the end, through the diachronic semantic function investigation of words with the meaning of "follow" in different periods, we can gradually establish the connections between various functional nodes based on diachronic language materials, and finally integrate the diachronic conceptual space.

(3) The functional distribution of "Sui(随)" in modern Chinese dialects often violates the adjacency requirement of semantic maps, and the same lexeme may have discontinuity of functional nodes in different dialect semantic maps. However, most of this discontinuity on semantic maps can find the basis for the implied or disappeared connections among various semantic function nodes in the history of language. The semantic functions of Chinese dialect are the precipitation of Chinese in different historical periods in different synchronic regions, and different regions have different selections and retentions of the same multifunctional morpheme, therefore, Chinese dialect vocabulary have both commonalities and their own unique systematicity. When conducting a synchronic investigation of multifunctional morphemes in Chinese dialects, it is very necessary to combine it with the study of diachronic semantic evolution, otherwise, it may be impossible to clarify the true connections among the various semantic functions of polysemous words.

(4) The semantic evolution of "Sui(随)" has semantic function evolution models of "follow-comitative", "comitative-coordinate" and "follow-obey-according to". And this is related to the semantic implication of the meaning of "follow". For example, the meaning of "follow" contains five semantic sememes: [+follow after], [+do something together], [+run], [+displacement] and [+path]. When some semantic sememes are highlighted and some are weakened, the semantic focus changes. After long-term or high-frequency usage and being taken for granted by people, new semantic functions are generated. The "comitative" function highlights the meaning of [+do something together], and weakens the semantic sememes of [+follow after], [+run], [+displacement] and [+path]. The "coordinate" function is based on the "comitative" function. The master-slave relationship between NP_1 and NP_2 connected disappears, and the syntactic structure of NP_2 moves up and is parallel to NP_1.

(5) In the diachronic evolution of vocabulary, syntactic positions provide possibilities for lexical grammaticalization and catalyze the process of grammaticalization. However, even if words in the same conceptual field are in the same syntactic position,

grammaticalization does not necessarily occur. For example, "Sui(随)" often appears in the sentence pattern of "$NP_1 + V_1$ (随) + $NP_2 + V_2$". When the object after "Sui(随)" expands to specific behaviors, "Sui(随)" gradually evolves into the function of the preposition "let".

From the perspective of the conceptual field of "follow", the evolution of word meanings has inter-connectivity. In the conceptual field of "follow", "Sui(随)" was influenced by "Cong(从)" and also developed functions such as "via", "human source" and "according to" in the Middle Chinese period. "Cong(从)" was in turn influenced by "Sui(随)" and developed the function of "immediately". This kind of influence is mutual and has a domino effect. The conceptual space (semantic network) behind vocabulary is an important manifestation of human thinking and cognition. It reveals how humans organize and understand the world through language. The conceptual space is a psychological representation that constructs a structured representation of knowledge through the relationships between words. This semantic network not only reflects the internal connections of language, but also reveals the complexity and dynamics of human cognitive processes.

Acknowledgments. This work is supported by the general project of the National Philosophy and Social Science Foundation of China "Research on Semantic Maps of Chinese Prepositions(23BYY041)" and the support program "New Seedling Scholars" of Central University of Finance and Economics.

References

1. Ma, B.: Modern Chinese Prepositions (in Chinese). Zhonghua Publishing House, Beijing (2002)
2. Shi, Y.: On the character Sui (随) in the phrase Sui Shan Jun Chuan(随山浚川). Stud. Lang. Linguist. **6**(2) (2005)
3. Wu, B.: Grammaticalization process of verb sui (随). J. Wenzhou Univ. **5**(4) (2012)
4. Wu, F.: A typological study of grammaticalization of the comitative preposition in Chinese language. Stud. Chin. Lang. (1), 43–58+96 (2003)
5. Yu, F.: Studies on commonil used words of Han Dynasty. Changchun: Jilin University Doctoral Dissertation (2008)
6. Zhuang, H.: Research on the diachronic semantic map of multifunctional morpheme gen (跟)—the diachronic evolution of words with the meaning of "follow". J. Chin. Charactor Stud. **10**(8) (2012)
7. Zhuang, H.: Research on the semantic map of multifunctional morpheme cong. In: Chinese Lexical Semantics 23rd Workshop, CLSW 2022,Virtual Event, 14–15 May 2022, Revised Selected Papers, vol. 04, pp. 186–207 (2023)

An Empirical Study on Approximators *jǐ* and *duō* in Mandarin

Yu-Jui Huang⬤, Yun-Han Wang⬤, and Huichen S. Hsiao(✉)⬤

Department of Chinese as a Second Language, National Taiwan Normal University, Taipei, Taiwan
{yujui.huang,yunhan.wang,huichen.hsiao}@ntnu.edu.tw

Abstract. This empirical study investigates Mandarin approximators that convey uncertain quantities, focusing on *jǐ* and *duō*, which both suggest "a few." We analyze the values—exact numbers given by participants in fill-in tasks—and the interval, which refers to the spans between the most commonly selected upper and lower boundaries by participants. Forty-nine native speakers completed fill-in tasks. The results suggest that *duō* has significantly higher upper and lower boundaries than *jǐ*. *Hǎo duō* "quite a few" has a higher upper boundary than *hǎo jǐ* (all *ps* < .05) since the meaning of *duō* initially implies "excess." By exploring the interval based on the mode, we discovered that the *jǐ* interval is 3 to 5, whereas *duō* ranges from 3 to 10. Additionally, the preferred values are 3, 5, and 10, corresponding to round numbers and the cultural implication in Chinese. Overall, findings on *jǐ* and *hǎo jǐ* partially support previous research, while the results suggest an alternative interval for *duō* and *hǎo duō*.

Keywords: Approximator · Approximate interval · Granularity · *jǐ* & *duō* "a few"

1 Introduction

Quantifier indeterminacy expresses an imprecision range of values and uncertain quantification [1, 2]. These vague expressions have been well recognized as derived from The Principle of Economy, which is used to reduce cognitive costs [3, 4]. Therefore, language users often use approximators and round numbers to indicate uncertain quantities instead of precise numerical expressions. Commonly seen Mandarin approximators[1] included *jǐ* "a few," *duō* "a few," *lái* "about/or so," and *shàngxià* "about," and *zuǒyòu* "around" [5] The current study focuses on the range value represented by the Mandarin approximator *jǐ* "a few" and *duō* "a few." Previously, scholars have analyzed the construction and meaning of the approximators. Lü [1] noted that *duō* "a few" is placed after quantifiers and is utilized to indicate the meaning of "excess." Zong and Zhang [6] suggested that

---

[1] Based on the similarity in Mandarin, each pair (*jǐ* and *duō*; *hǎo jǐ* and *hǎo duō*, and *shí jǐ* and *shí duō*) would be translated into the same term in English. Since the prediction and discussion may be affected, it is noted that they are temporary terms. The difference between our target approximators will be discussed in Sect. 3.4.

© The Author(s), under exclusive license to Springer Nature Singapore Pte Ltd. 2025
P. Jin et al. (Eds.): CLSW 2024, LNAI 15552, pp. 470–480, 2025.
https://doi.org/10.1007/978-981-96-3509-2_34

due to the harmony of meaning, *duō* "a few" is only compatible when there is space for further refinement. Luo [7] mentioned that when using a *duō* approximate construction (e.g., *shí duō ge xuéshēng* "more than 10 students"), the speaker is uncertain about the precise number. However, still, the range is between 10 and 20. Also, according to the position of *duō* "*a few*," although the surface syntax is similar, the phrase's meaning is slightly different. In subsequent work, Luo [8] suggested that the numeral within the construction, which is linked to granularity, also impacts the phrase's meaning. Wei's study [9] examined the collocation of measure words to gain insight into the syntax and semantics of *jǐ* "a few" and *duō* "a few." According to Wei, *jǐ* "a few" represents vagueness regarding a specific number, and *duō* "a few" refers to the excess of the average amount. Rui and Hong [10] discussed the difference between *jǐ* "a few" and *duō* "a few" in terms of construction. They claimed that both *jǐ* "a few" and *duō* "a few" are interchangeable in most constructions, but neither "*measure word + *jǐ*" nor "**duō* + numeral" is syntactically correct. In addition, studies have addressed the interval of these approximators from different perspectives. Li [11] proposed that the range of *jǐ* "a few" is below 10. Liu [12] investigated the value interval of the approximators *jǐ* "a few," *duō* "a few," and *lái* "about/or so." by survey with options for range delimited by round numbers 1, 3, 9, and 5 (e.g., 1 to 5). Liu's study adopted the concept of round numbers, which also serve as cognitive reference numbers, and this will be introduced below.

Based on the concepts of round numbers and granularity, Krifka [4] and Jansen and Pollmann [13] pointed out that some numbers are more frequent than others. In decimal number system languages, 10, 5 (halving of ten), and 2 (doubling of one) are the round numbers (i.e., cognitive reference points). It was hypothesized that there are cognitive number scales, with the numbers being the nodes. Furthermore, there are levels of granularity according to the distance between the nodes on the scales, including fine-grained and coarse-grained [4, 14]. In coarse-grained scales, fewer nodes with only cognitively salient numbers remained, and the distance between nodes was further. For example, a scale with only multiples of ten is one of the standard coarse-grained scales, which reflects the salience of 10. Thus, round numbers are frequently selected when expressing imprecise quantification. Liu [12] proposed that not only are numbers 2, 5, and 10 round numbers but number 3 is also a relatively cognitive reference point number in Chinese. As mentioned above, Liu [12] chose numbers 1, 3, 9, and 5 as the upper and lower boundaries of the interval options in the survey. The options, however, he designed were arbitrary instead. Specifically, his criteria for determining which number served as the upper/lower boundary is relatively subjective. This approach led to the ambiguity in the upper bound values for *duō* "a few" and *hǎo duō* "quite a few" in the research findings. Additionally, the interval could vary owing to social interaction, so the methods and results above may not accurately reflect the cognitive judgment of language users. Therefore, the current study aims to examine the results from previous studies by asking whether the interval of *jǐ* "a few" and *duō* "a few" are significantly different; what are the differences between the value interval of three patterns, including basic prototypes and those with different modifiers[2], *hǎo*-"quite" and *shí*- "ten." Moreover, we further

---

[2] Considering the regional usage differences and the focus of the current study, we investigated six approximators, leaving other unpaired usages for future research.

investigated whether the above-mentioned round numbers are preferred when specifying the approximator's interval by examining whether these are more frequently chosen.

To achieve the above goals, we survey with two fill-in tasks to probe the value interval of the approximator *jǐ* "a few" and *duō* "a few," including the interval when these morphemes are collocated with the degree adverb *hǎo* "quite," and the numeral *shí* "ten." In contrast to the design of Liu [12], we collected the value by asking participants to determine the upper and lower boundaries based on sentences with an approximator, aiming to gather data directly reflecting native speakers' intuition.

2   Materials and Method

The current study utilizes two fill-in tasks to inspect Mandarin native speakers' intuition of the value interval of the approximators *jǐ* "a few" and *duō* "a few." In Task 1, participants were asked to provide the upper and lower boundary values after reading sentences with an approximator. In Task 2, after reading sentences similar to those in Task 1, participants were asked to answer the interval with "numeral value (low) - numeral value (high)." Detailed information is provided as follows.

2.1   Participants

55 participants were recruited for the study. All were native Mandarin speakers living in Taiwan. After eliminating invalid responses[3], 49 participants' responses remained in the analysis[4].

2.2   Materials

The experimental materials of this study were designed to investigate the boundary and the interval of six approximators, including *jǐ* "a few" and *duō* "a few"; *hǎo jǐ* "quite a few" and *hǎo duō* "quite a few"; *shí jǐ* "more than ten" and *shí duō* "more than ten." In the sentences, verbs, measure words, and nouns with no numeral implicature were chosen to prevent the judgment from being disturbed (i.e., *mǎi* "buy," *kàn* "watch"; *biàndāng* "bento/ lunchbox"). Moreover, ten native speakers were recruited for the norming study. The purpose of the norming study is to confirm that the responses were made according to the approximators. The participants were initially requested to finish the survey, followed by an interview. During the interview, participants were asked if any of the verbs or NPs had numeral implicatures. All question sentences were modified and verified after the

---

[3] When eliminating invalid responses, there were two criteria: first, due to the concern that linguistic profession-related experience might disturb the responses. Suppose participants have linguistic-related experience, including linguistic profession, teaching Mandarin as a second language. Their responses would be eliminated. Second, if a participant answers over half of the certain filler questions incorrectly, they would be considered not taking the tasks seriously; their responses would not be included in the analysis.

[4] Six participants were eliminated due to illegible background or over the half wrong answers of fillers.

norming study, confirming that the verbs and NPs would not affect the value and interval responses.

The survey has two tasks: Task 1, upper and lower boundaries; Task 2, interval. The material for Task 1 included two practice questions, six target questions, and six filler questions. First, the participants read a sentence with an approximator (i.e., *Qīnqīn mǎi le duō jiàn yīfú*. "Qinqin bought a few clothes"), then two questions, one with *zuìduō* "at most" (i.e., *Qǐngwèn tā kěnéng zuìduō mǎi le jǐ jiàn yīfú?* "How many clothes did she possibly buy at most?") and another one with *zuìshǎo* "at least" (i.e., *Qǐngwèn tā kěnéng zuìshǎo mǎi le jǐ jiàn yīfú?* "How many clothes did she possibly buy at least?") which requested the lower boundary.

The practice questions were similar to the filler questions. The difference is that the sentences contain specific numbers instead of approximators. (e.g., *Cáocǎo yāoqǐng le 35 wèi xiǎopéngyǒu lái tāde pàiduì, yǐzhī zhìshǎo yǒu 2 wèi xiǎopéngyǒu shēngbìng wúfǎ cānjiā* "Caocao invited 35 children to his party, it is known that there are at least 2 children were sick so that they would not join.") The participants' responses to practice and filler questions were expected to be based on calculations, not on the language intuition of approximators.

Task 2 is designed to examine the interval of approximators. It consisted of two practice questions and six target questions. Participants also encountered sentences as in Task 1, then the question (i.e., *Qǐngwèn tā kěnéng mǎi le jǐ jiàn yīfú?* "How many clothes did she possibly buy?"). Overall, the questions in the two tasks were designed to elicit different perspectives on the value interval. Task 1 focused on the upper and lower boundaries (i.e., the endpoint of the interval), whereas Task 2 emphasized the interval (i.e., the range); we obtained the collective interval of the approximators.

2.3 Experimental Procedure

The fill-in tasks were formatted as a survey questionnaire via Survey Cake. As mentioned above, there were two fill-in tasks, with each question requesting information on both the upper/lower boundary and the interval. In Task 1, participants were presented with sentences containing either an approximator in Mandarin for target questions or precise numbers for filler questions. Then, they were asked to provide numeral values based on the upper and lower boundary questions. The sequence of asking upper and lower boundaries was counterbalanced. Task 2 followed a similar procedure, but participants would only see one question after reading the sentence and be instructed to respond with the format "numeral value (low) to numeral value (high)." Half of the participants were asked to indicate the upper/lower boundary first and then the interval, while the other half had the opposite sequence. Participants were also told not to move forward through the questionnaire without pausing or returning to the previous questions to avoid them from changing their responses.

2.4 Data Coding and Analysis

After collecting participants' responses, we split the interval of responses from Task 2 into two numeral values to merge responses from both tasks. Next, we separate the outliers based on the box plot of each approximator's responses and calculate the mean of each approximator's upper/lower boundary based on the data without outliers. It is worth noting that although the outliers may disturb the calculation of the means, these responses also mirrored participants' intuition so that the outliers would be discussed separately. Then, we conducted independent sample *t*-tests to examine the statistical difference of the boundaries between *jǐ* "a few" and *duō* "a few"; *hǎo jǐ* "quite a few" and *hǎo duō* "quite a few"; *shí jǐ* "more than ten" and *shí duō* "more than ten," respectively. Secondly, to compare with previous studies' results, we look at the mode[5] for the boundaries and the interval delimited by the mode of upper and lower boundaries. Considering the concepts of round numbers and granularity, we expected that the participants would respond with round numbers; additionally, we would obtain the upper boundary value of *hǎo duō* "quite a few," which was not provided in previous studies.

3 Results and Discussion

Section 3.1 presents the descriptive data collected via two fill-in tasks. It shows the average value (M), including the standard deviation (SD) and the mode given by the participants. Then, Sect. 3.2 describes the independent sample *t*-test results comparing the upper and lower bound of *jǐ* "a few" and *duō* "a few," *hǎo jǐ* "quite a few," and *hǎo duō* "quite a few"; *shí jǐ* "more than ten" and *shí duō* "more than ten." Sect. 3.3 outlines the outliers set apart from the rest of the data based on the box plot. Lastly, Sect. 3.4 will discuss the results of the current study related to the previous studies and why participants chose particular numbers.

3.1 Data Overview

Table 1 below shows the descriptive data collected from the participants for the two types of fill-in tasks collectively, including average scores, standard deviation, and mode. The mode presents the overall preferred values, which are used to compare with the results from previous studies.

As can be seen in Table 1, the means of the upper and lower boundary of *jǐ* "a few" were 2.49 and 7.33, respectively. The mode is 3 and 5, indicating that most participants prefer the interval for *jǐ* "a few" from 3 to 5. Regarding *duō* "a few," the means of the boundaries are 2.94 and 8.90. 3 and 10 are the mode which represents the most preferred interval boundaries. When integrated with the degree adverb morpheme *hǎo* "quite," *hǎo jǐ* "quite a few" has 3.44 and 9.34 as the means of the boundaries, and the mode are 3 and 10, displaying the preferred interval of *hǎo jǐ* "quite a few" is 3 to 10. The means of *hǎo duō*, "quite a few," are 3.72 and 11.35.

The mode of the lower boundary is 3, whereas both 9 and 10 are the mode of the upper boundary, suggesting that participants adopted 3 to 9 or 3 to 10 as the interval. Finally, incorporating the numeral morpheme *shí* "ten," *shí jǐ* "more than ten," exhibit 11 and 18.92 as the means of the upper and lower boundaries; the interval is from 11 to 19, as inferred from the mode. *Shí duō* "more than ten" has 11.00 and 19.00 as the means of the boundaries, and 11 and 19 are the upper and lower boundary mode. Since *shí duō*

---

[5] In this study, "mode" refers to each question's most frequently occurring values.

Table 1. Descriptive Statistics for all Approximators

approximator	Upper/lower bound	N	M (SD)	Mode (n)
jǐ "a few"	upper	64	7.33 (2.92)	5 (21)
	lower	71	2.49 (0.67)	3 (33)
duō "a few"	upper	58	8.90 (1.53)	10 (28)
	lower	72	2.94 (1.11)	3 (34)
hǎo jǐ "quite a few"	upper	53	9.34 (0.81)	10 (24)
	lower	80	3.44 (1.53)	3 (32)
hǎo duō "quite a few"	upper	65	11.35 (5.16)	9/10 (21)
	lower	76	3.72 (1.63)	3 (24)
shí jǐ "more than ten"	upper	72	18.92 (0.44)	19 (69)
	lower	61	11.00 (0.00)	11 (61)
shí duō "more than ten"	upper	72	19.00 (0.00)	19 (72)
	lower	63	11.00 (0.00)	11 (63)

"more than ten" has corresponding means and mode of the boundaries, it implies that participants adopted distinct intervals for *shí duō* "more than ten." The results suggest that *duō* "a few" imposes a higher upper boundary than *jǐ* "a few," similar to *hǎo duō* "quite a few" compared to *hǎo jǐ* "quite a few." Lastly, *shí jǐ* "more than ten" and *shí duō* "more than ten" show similar intervals.

3.2 Significance of Statistical Comparison Results

Table 2 below shows the results of *jǐ* "a few" comparing *duō* "a few"; *hǎo jǐ* "quite a few" comparing *hǎo duō* "quite a few," and *shí jǐ* "more than ten" versus *shí duō* "more than ten."

According to Table 2, *jǐ* "a few" and *duō* "a few" show significant differences in both the upper boundary (t (97.05) = -3.76, $p < .001$) and the lower boundary (t (141) = -2.93, $p = .004$), as *duō* "a few" has higher upper and lower boundary than *jǐ* "a few." When analyzing the difference between *hǎo jǐ* "quite a few" and *hǎo duō* "quite a few," the results show that *hǎo duō* "quite a few" is significantly higher than *hǎo jǐ* "quite a few" only in the upper boundary (t (67.82) = -3.10, $p = .003$). In contrast, the lower boundaries show no significant difference (t (154) = -1.13, $p = .260$). Regarding the lower boundary of *shí jǐ* "more than ten" and *shí duō* "more than ten," since both groups have standard deviations of zero, a *t*-test was not conducted. Moreover, there is no significant difference between the upper boundary of *shí jǐ* "more than ten" and *shí duō* "more than ten" (t (71.00) = -1.62, $p = .109$).

Overall, *duō* "a few" and *hǎo duō* "quite a few" have relatively higher boundaries, while *shí jǐ* "more than ten" and *shí duō* "more than ten" displayed similar intervals as 11 to 19. The *t*-test results correspond to the descriptive data, supporting the difference between *jǐ* "a few" and *duō* "a few"; *hǎo jǐ* "quite a few" and *hǎo duō* "quite a few,"

Table 2. *t-test* Results for *jǐ* "a few" and *duō* "a few"

Bound	Approximators	M (SD)	df	t-score	p-value
Upper	*jǐ* "a few"	7.33 (2.92)	97.05	−3.76	<.001***
	duō "a few"	8.90 (1.53)			
Lower	*jǐ* "a few"	2.49(0.67)	141	−2.93	.004*
	duō "a few"	2.94 (1.11)			
Upper	*hǎo jǐ* "quite a few"	9.34 (0.81)	67.82	-3.10	.003*
	hǎo duō "quite a few"	11.35 (5.16)			
Lower	*hǎo jǐ* "quite a few"	3.44 (1.53)	154	−1.13	.260
	hǎo duō "quite a few"	3.72 (1.63)			
Upper	*shí jǐ* "more than ten"	18.92 (0.43)	71.00	−1.62	.109
	shí duō "more than ten"	19.00 (0.00)			
Lower	*shí jǐ* "more than ten"	11.00 (0.00)	n/a[a]		
	shí duō "more than ten"	11.00 (0.00)			

[a]Since both groups' SDs are 0, the *t*-test was not applicable and thus not conducted.

whereas the similarity between *shí jǐ* "more than ten" and *shí duō* "more than ten." Next, Sect. 3.3 examines the outliers based on the number of responses and the value.

3.3 Outlier Analysis

Figure 1 shows that in the construction "(*hǎo* 'quite') + approximator + classifier/measure word," the upper bound had more outliers than the lower. Specifically, *hǎo duō* "quite a few" has the highest number of outlier responses, with 29 outliers in the upper and 2 in the lower bound. The standard deviation data from the descriptive analysis also support this distribution (upper bound: SD = 5.16).

While examining the responses' values, we found that multiples of five and ten were most preferred, even in outlier responses. As shown in Fig. 2, the numbers 20, 30, and 100 are preferred considering the upper bound, whereas 5 and 10 are commonly chosen as lower boundary responses.

Regarding the construction "*shí* + approximator," the results are shown in Fig. 3. Owing to the morpheme *shí* "ten," only a few participants responded with 15 or 17 as the upper boundary value. However, more participants responded outlier, choosing 10, 13, or 15. The numeral morpheme *shí* "ten" defined the upper bound as "no more than 20." On the other hand, there is no such fine cut for the lower bound, leading participants to judge subjectively and to contribute to a relatively discrete distribution. The results above present the boundary values of *jǐ* "a few" and *duō* "a few"; *hǎo jǐ* "quite a few" and *hǎo duō* "quite a few"; *shí jǐ* "more than ten" and *shí duō* "more than ten"; the interval according to the mode of the upper and lower boundaries, and the outliers. The section below discusses the results of the present study and those of previous studies.

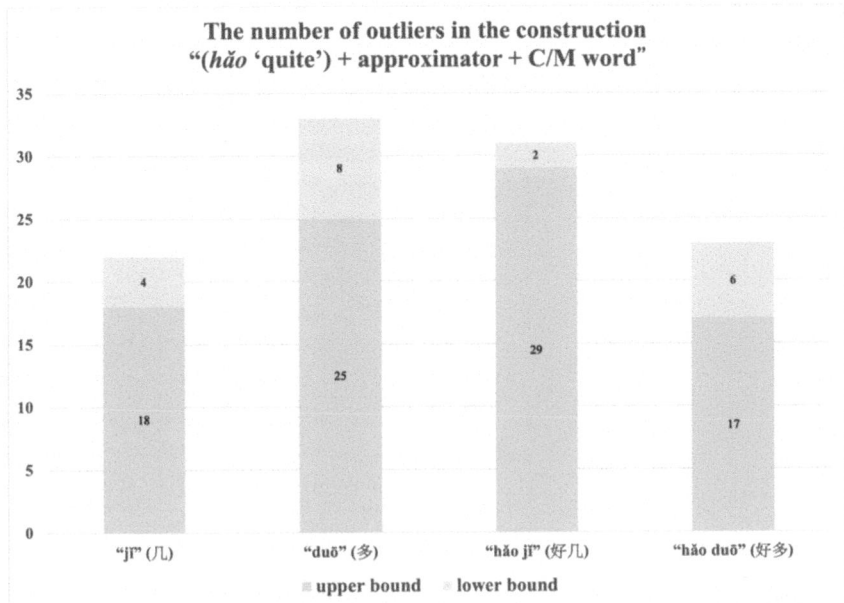

Fig. 1. The number of outliers in the construction "(*hǎo* 'quite') + approximator + C/M word"

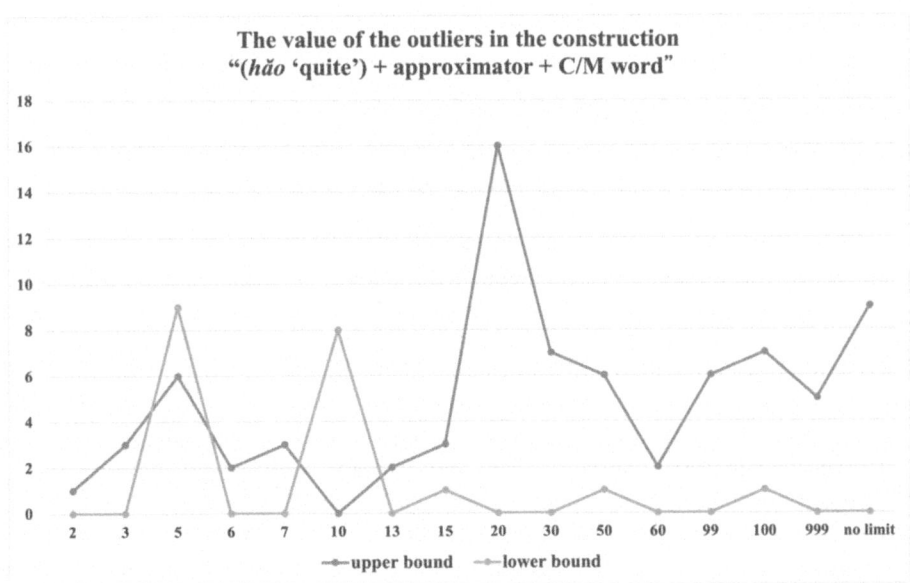

Fig. 2. The value of the outliers in the construction "(*hǎo* 'quite') + approximator + C/M word"

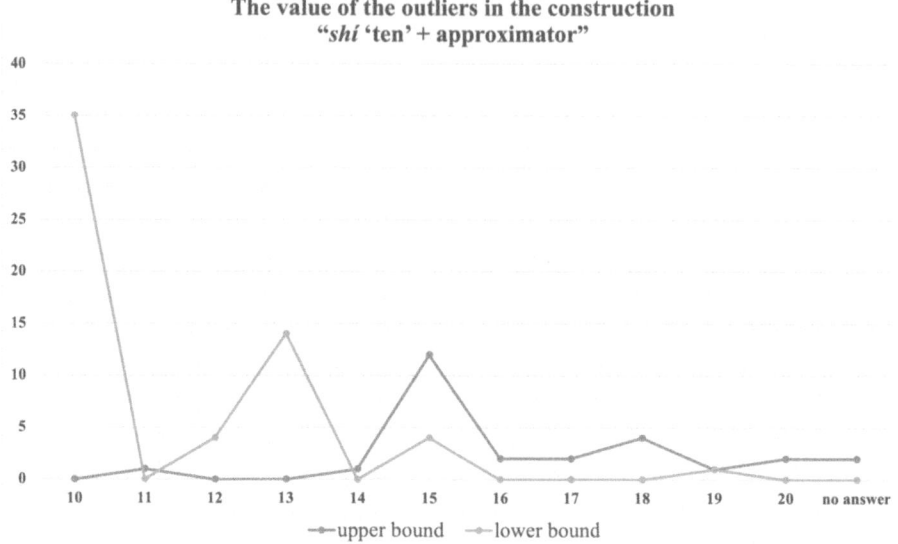

Fig. 3. The value of the outliers in the construction "*shí* 'ten' + approximator"

3.4 Discussion

According to the data above, our experimental results partially align with previous studies [11, 12]. First, concerning *jǐ* "a few" and *hǎo jǐ* "quite a few," our results were consistent with Li's [11] view, in which these approximators indicated values below 10. However, as Liu [12] proposed that *jǐ* "a few" was referred to as "1 to 5" and *hǎo jǐ* "quite a few" as "5 to 10," the present results only supported the upper boundaries, we found that both approximators took 3 as lower boundaries. Regarding *duō* "a few" and *hǎo duō* "quite a few," Liu [12] suggested *duō* "a few" represents the values beyond 3, and we found parallel results; furthermore, we supplemented the upper boundary as 10. Meanwhile, the current results indicated "3 to 9" or "3 to 10" as the interval of *hǎo duō* "quite a few," referring to a contrasting view from Liu [12] having "the values over 10" as the results. Concerning *shí jǐ* "more than ten" and *shí duō* "more than ten," we found that both of their intervals were "11 to 19," whereas scholars found "13 to 19" as the interval of *shí jǐ* "more than ten" and "11 to 15" or "11 to 19" for *shí duō* "more than ten."

The results suggested that *duō* "a few" and *hǎo duō* "quite a few" have relatively higher upper boundaries than *jǐ* "a few" and *hǎo jǐ* "quite a few" when comparing pair-wisely in the *T*-test (all *ps* < .05). We consider the difference owing to the original meaning of *duō* "a few" as "excess." Namely, the word's meaning affected the language users' judgments of the interval. On the other hand, the interval of *shí jǐ* "more than ten" and *shí duō* "more than ten" were limited to "11 to 19" due to the numeral morpheme *shí* "ten."

Regarding the overall frequency of numbers, the numbers 3, 5, and 10 had higher frequency than the others. Jansen and Pollmann [13] and Krifka [4] have suggested some possible reasons for the numbers 5 and 10, including the round numbers (i.e., cognitive reference point numbers), granularity, and number system. People tend to utilize round numbers when constructing cognitive number scales, including fine-grained and coarse-grained scales. Since coarse-grained scale requires less processing effort, they are generally preferred by language users. In decimal languages, the coarse-grained scales often consist of round numbers (e.g., 10, 5, and 2), implying these are cognitively salient numbers [13]. Consequently, 10 and 5 are commonly selected when expressing imprecise quantification. Meanwhile, the salience of 5 and 10 is also supported by observing the number frequency in the corpus of language adapting decimal systems, such as English [15]. Regarding the number 3, Liu [12] suggested its uniqueness in Chinese. Traditionally, the number 3 was referred to as "a few"; in addition, *Tao Te Ching* (also known as *Dao De Jing*) [16] mentioned, "The Tao gave birth to one, and one gave birth to two, and two gave birth to three. Three gave birth to everything." (*Dào shēng yī, yī shēng èr, èr shēng sān, sān shēng wànwù*), that is, the number 3 as a node and beyond that could be anything.

The findings not only support and further supplement the findings of previous studies [11, 12] but also indicate that Mandarin speakers tend to take both the original meaning of lexeme and round numbers as references. In referring to the interval of the approximator (e.g., *duō*), Mandarin speakers specifically and commonly select 3, 5, and 10 as reference points when delimiting the interval.

4   Conclusion

In conclusion, the present study focused on the value of the approximators *jǐ* "a few" and *duō* "a few" and their value when collocated with the degree adverb *hǎo* "quite" and the numeral *shí* "ten," respectively. Unlike Liu's [12] design, in the current survey, participants are asked to fill in values for the upper and lower bound to collect data in line with native Mandarin speakers' intuition. Two fill-in tasks were administered to investigate the value and the interval. It is found that participants judged according to semantic meaning properties, such as the literal meaning of *duō* "a few" and the restriction of numeral morpheme *shí* "ten"; therefore, *duō* "a few" and *hǎo duō* "quite a few" have relatively higher boundaries than *jǐ* "a few" and *hǎo jǐ* "quite a few." Both *shí jǐ* "more than ten," and *shí duō* "more than ten," are considered as the interval of 11 to 19. Additionally, the numbers 3, 5, and 10 were commonly chosen, supporting the round numbers and granularity proposed by previous studies [4, 12, 14]. The results provide pedagogical implications concerning relatively specific intervals to help CSL learners comprehend the approximators' meanings and usage.

Acknowledgments. This research was supported by National Science and Technology Council research grants (NSTC 111–2410-H-003–085-).

References

1. Lü, S.-X.: Zhongguo Wenfa Yaolue [Essentials of Chinese Grammar]. The Liber Arts Press, Taipei (1985). (in Chinese)

2. Iacona, A.: Vagueness and quantification. J. Philos. Log. **45**, 579–602 (2016)
3. Zipf, G.K.: Human Behavior and the Principle of Least Effort. Addison-Wesley Press, Boston (1949)
4. Krifka, M.: Approximate interpretation of number words. Philosophische Fakultät II Humboldt-Universität zu Berlin (2007)
5. Guo, D.-D., Song, J.-H., Peng, W.-M., Zhang, Y.-B.: Research on quantifier phrases based on the corpus of international chinese textbooks. In: Hong, J.-F, Zhang, Y.-S., Liu, P.-Y. (eds.) CLSW 2019, LNCS, vol. 11831, pp. 840–852. Springer, Heidelberg (2020)
6. Zong, S.-H., Zhang, L.-C.: Hanyu liang daici "duo" de yongfa ji qi jieshi [The usage and explanation of the Chinese quantity-representing pronoun duo]. Fore. Lang. Teach. Res. (bimonthly) **40**(4), 262–269 (2008). (in Chinese)
7. Luo, Q.-P.: Approximate constructions using duo "more" in Chinese. In: Wu, Y.-F., Hong, J.-F., Su, Q. (eds.) CLSW 2017, LNCS, vol. 10709, pp. 64–78. Springer, Heidelberg (2018)
8. Luo, Q.-P.: "Duo" zai shuliang jiegou zhong de fenbu yu yuyi jieshi — jian tan celiang de jizhi [The distribution and interpretation of "Duo" in quantity expressions and the grammar of measurement]. Linguist. Sci. **1**, 13–26 (2019). (in Chinese)
9. Wei, Y.-L.: Shuo gaishuci "duo" he "ji" [Chinese approximate word duo and ji]. Stud. Lang. Linguist. **38**(1), 50–53 (2018). (in Chinese)
10. Rui, J.-Y., Hong, J.-F.: Jinyi gaishuci "duo" he "ji" de jufa jiegou tanwei [Exploring the syntactic structures of synonymous quantifiers "duo" and "ji"]. Sinogram Cult. **9**, 30–22 (2022). (in Chinese)
11. Li, Y.-M.: Hanyu liang fanchou yanjiu [The Study of Quantification in Chinese], pp. 80–83. Central China Normal University Press, Hubei (2000). (in Chinese)
12. Liu, J.: "Ji, duo, lai" biao yueliang de caiyi yu jiaxue sikao [Difference comparison of "Ji, Duo, Lai" and reflections on teaching]. Chin. Lang. Learn. **2**, 57–66 (2022). (in Chinese)
13. Jansen, C.J., Pollmann, M.M.: On round numbers: pragmatic aspects of numerical expressions. J. Quant. Linguist. **8**(3), 187–201 (2001)
14. Solt, S., Cummins, C., Palmović, M.: The preference for approximation. Int. Rev. Pragmatics **9**(2), 248–268 (2017)
15. Coupland, N.: How frequent are numbers? Lang. Commun. **31**(1), 27–37 (2011)
16. Ching, T.T.: https://ctext.org/dao-de-jing/zh. Accessed 30 Oct 2024

Counter-Expectation Information Structure in Mandarin Chinese and its Cognitive-Pragmatic Mechanisms

Li Bai[1]([✉]) [iD] and Yongzhong Li[2]

[1] School of Liberal Arts, Jiangxi Normal University, Nanchang 330022, China
pearl1819@163.com
[2] School of International Education, Jiangxi Normal University, Nanchang 330022, China

Abstract. The paper digs into the counter-expectation information structure (CEIS) of discourses in Mandarin Chinese, involving the relationships between the information units, the variant models, and their cognitive-pragmatic mechanisms. The linguistic data from corpus and the statistics on CNKI lead to the key findings. First off, "condition", "expectation" and "counter-expectation" are the three main information units of the CEIS. The relationships between "conditions and expectations", "expectations and counter-expectations", and "conditions and counter-expectations" are "cause-and-effect and analogy", "negation", and "bridging" respectively, which abide by the principles of "proximity and similarity", "prominence" and "closure" in Gestalt Principles. Second, with the aid of VOSviewer, we discovered that "condition + counter-expectation" and "independent counter-expectation" are the two most frequently used variant models of the CEIS. The default of expectations in these models is due to the collaboration of mechanisms like stereotypical relations, metonymy, quantity iconicity and language economy. Finally, the study briefly explores the online information processing of counter-expectation based on the governing principles of typology, integration and unpacking.

Keywords: Mandarin Chinese · Counter-Expectation · Information Structure · Variant Models · Cognitive-Pragmatic Mechanisms

1 Introduction

Information structure is the organizational structure of information units (cf. Halliday [1]). Taking a functional approach, information units were typically discussed under the classical bipartite models, such as "theme-rheme", "given information-new information", "presupposition-focus" etc. (cf. Mathesius [2], Firbas [3], Halliday [1], Jackendoff [4]). Besides, Brown [5] and Chafe [6] proposed the tripartite model which took semi-active information into consideration in addition to the given and the new.

The counter-expectation information structure (CEIS), as the existence of the whole to the part, is the magnetic field that conveys information deviating from expectation. However, existing studies give more attention to counter-expectation markers which

P. Jin et al. (Eds.): CLSW 2024, LNAI 15552, pp. 481–501, 2025.
https://doi.org/10.1007/978-981-96-3509-2_35

range from adverbs, conjunctions to phrases and constructions (cf. Wu [7], Wang [8], Chen and Wang [9], Zeng and Yuan [10]), but pay far less attention to the information structure that includes these markers. In actual language use, giving up the more economical unmarked form and using a large number of pragmatic markers is precisely to better convey the counter-expectation information and achieve the best cognitive effect. And in order to clarify the transmission process of counter-expectation information, we should focus on the information structure in which it is located.

Information structure is a cognitive domain in nature (cf. Zimmermann and Fery [11]). At the same time, information structure possesses the significant property of pragmatics due to its emphasis on context (cf. Ward, Birner and Kaiser [12]). That is to say, it is necessary to grasp the CEIS in the connection between language use and human cognitive mechanism, and explore the mental representation of information structure in the interaction of information units (cf. Mazzone [13]). As such, we attempt to exploit the CEIS in Mandarin Chinese from the perspective of Cognitive Pragmatics.

2 Previous Relevant Studies

In this section, we first take a closer look at the previous studies on the five models of CEIS, including the bipartite model, dahl's tripartite model, the semantic context model, the pragmatic inference model, and the cognitive model. Based on these relevant models, the three key questions to be discussed in the paper are proposed.

2.1 Previous Models of the CEIS

The Bipartite Model: The bipartite model includes two kinds of information units: expectation and counter-expectation. In some way, the "expectation + counter-expectation" model resembles the given-new model or the topic-focus model when compared to the traditional information structures (cf. Lu [14]). Besides, Cuenca [15] and Volkova [16] found that counter-expectation markers can foreground their subsequent information, creating a "background-foreground" information structure.

Dahl's Tripartite Model: Grounding on the expectation of participants in speech events, Dahl [17] divided discourse information into expectation, neutral information and counter-expectation. Though neutral information is a part of the basic information of discourses, it has little to do with expectation and counter-expectation.

The Semantic Context Model: Ma [18] generalized the semantic context of 反而 *fǎn'ér* 'instead' into ABCD: (A) the phenomenon or situation A occurred; (B) it was said (based on common sense)/expected that the occurrence of A would cause the phenomenon or situation B; (C) in fact B did not occur; (D) instead, the phenomenon or situation C appeared, which is the opposite of B. For example:

(1)   (A)今天午后下了一场雷阵雨，(B)原以为天气可以凉快一些，
(C)可是并没有凉下来，(D)反而更闷热了。
(A) Jīntiān wǔhoù xià le yìchǎng léizhènyǔ, (B) yuányǐwéi tiānqì
    Today afternoon fall PRT a thunderstorm   thought weather
kěyǐ liángkuài yìxiē, (C) **kěshì** bìng méiyǒu liáng xiàlái, (D) **fǎn'ér** Gèng mēnrè le.[1]
could cool some   but and not cool down   instead more muggy PRT
'There was a thunderstorm this afternoon. I thought it would be cooler, but it didn't,
instead, it got more muggy.'

Yuan [19] pointed out that Ma's analysis of *fǎn'ér* presented a counter-expectation
scenario: typically, the condition event P would trigger the expected result Q; in reality,
not only did Q not appear, but also the result R was contrary to Q and even got higher
scale of counter-expectation than ~ Q appeared[1].

The Pragmatic Inference Model: Mou [20] proposed that the fundamental semantic
structure of *fǎn'ér* is "the fact + the expected result (inference) + negation of the
expected result + contrary to the expected result", and "the expected result" is usually
absent as default information.

Taking 还是*háishì* 'still' as an example, Li [21] conceptualized the structure "(虽
然*suīrán* 'al(though)') condition p, (但*dàn* 'but') háishì + result q" as follows: (a) real
world: condition p triggers result q; (b) mental world: only can ~ p trigger result q; (c)
contrasting results: whether p or ~ p occurs, it can trigger result q; (d) consequently,
(though) condition p, (but) still + result q.

The Cognitive Model: By examining the usage of 竟然*jìngrán* 'actually, unexpectedly' and 偏偏*piānpiān* 'just, deliberately', Chen and Wang [9] delineated the cognitive
model of expectation as a four-part pattern: the condition (i.e., prior knowledge state),
expectation, current information and the nature of the expectation (usually located at the
end of the clause, determining whether the overall discourse information is consistent
with expectation or not). For instance:

(2)   鸵鸟是鸟，（所以）应该会飞，可竟然不会飞。
Tuóniǎo shì niǎo, (suǒyǐ) yīnggāi huì fēi, **kě jìngrán** búhuì fēi.
Ostrich BE bird so should can fly but surprisingly cannot fly
'Ostriches are birds and (therefore) should be able to fly, but surprisingly it cannot.'
Condition: Ostriches are birds
Expectation: (therefore) should be able to fly
Current information: but surprisingly it cannot
The nature of the expectation: counter-expectation information

2.2 Research Space

Specifically, the aforementioned five models of the CEIS have the following implied
drawbacks:

---

[1] The examples in the paper are collected from CCL corpus (Center for Chinese Linguistics,
Peking University) and recorded daily discourses with some deletion and simplification. The
bold words in examples are the counter-expectation markers.

The bipartite model does not apply to the counter-expectation discourse information structure since it targets clausal information structures. Those classical information structures like the given-new model, the background-foreground model and the topic-focus model can aid in the overall configuration of the discourse when it comes to sentence groups. However, as the discourse moves forward, the new information and focus will change dynamically, making it difficult to anchor the information units.

Dahl's tripartite model regards interlocutors as its core, embodying the fundamental properties of counter-expectation information. Nevertheless, the concept of "neutral information" which is relatively vague and unrelated to expectation should not be appended to the CEIS.

The semantic context model presents a quite whole picture of the CEIS by starting from the using context of counter-expectation markers, but it does not specify the concrete and concise terms for the information units.

The pragmatic inference model and the cognitive model generally take into account the event fact, cognition, and semantic-pragmatic factors, but the concerned studies are exclusive models for certain adverbs or conjunctions (including those comparative studies like Shan [22]), which must be taken into consideration on a vast scale of discourse markers. Additionally, the inferential and cognitive analyses stay on the static level and almost ignore the dynamic integration process of the CEIS.

Almost no research to date have explored the pairwise relationship between the internal units of the CEIS in addition to discussing the relationship between expectations and counter-expectations. The relationship between the information units is crucial as it is the key to the transmission of counter-expectation information. Therefore, it is not only the so-called "new" information but the relationship between the given and the new that influences the discourse.

In short, there is still room for the study, including the relationships between the information units in the CEIS, the commonly used variant models and the integration process of counter-expectation information. As a result, the paper will focus on the following research questions through a cognitive-pragmatic window:

On the Static Dimension: RQ1: What are the core information units of the CEIS? What connections exist between these units?

RQ2: What are the typical variant models of the CEIS? And why expectations can usually be omitted from the standpoint of cognitive pragmatics?

On the Dynamic Dimension: RQ3: What cognitive-pragmatic principles that underline the online information processing of the CEIS?

The research below is organized in terms of these questions. Section 3 discusses the relationships between the information units of the CEIS. Section 4 introduces the typical variant models and the related cognitive-pragmatic motivations. Section 5 presents the cognitive-pragmatic principles guiding the online information processing. Section 6 draws a conclusion and gives suggestions for further studies.

3   The Relationships Between the Information Units of the CEIS

3.1   The Information Units of the CEIS

We draw from the pragmatic inference model and the cognitive model in the previous section, and clarify that "condition", "expectation" and "counter-expectation" are the core units of the CEIS based on the principles of simplicity, inclusiveness and consistency in description. The whole model can be summed up by the formula "A + B + ~ B + C": A (condition) —> B (expectation) —> ~ B (direct negation of the expectation) —> C (indirect negation of expectation), for counter-expectation information can negate expectation information directly as well as indirectly.

3.2   The Relationships Between the Information Units

The Relationship Between Conditions and Expectations: Cause-And-Effect and Analogical Relationship

Conditions in CEISs are the key to triggering expectations. They can generally be divided into particular states of affairs and generalized constants, with the latter mostly showing as epistemic modalities. When conditions are particular states of affairs, the relationship between conditions and expectations is direct or indirect cause-and-effect. For instance:

(3)   前几天刚修好的洗衣机，今天又坏了。
Qián jǐ tiān gāng xiū hǎo de xǐyī jī,
Before some day just repair good PRT washing machine
jīntiān **yòu** huài le.
today again break down PRT
'The washing machine which was repaired several days ago broke down again today.'

(4)   昨天我们队居然输了。
Zuótiān wǒmēn duì **jūrán** shū le.
Yesterday we team unexpectedly fail PRT
'Unexpectedly, our team lost the game yesterday.'

In example (3), the condition "the washing machine was repaired" can give rise to the regular expectation "the washing machine can function well at least for a while"; in this case, the condition and the expectation are in a direct cause-and-effect relationship. While in example (4), there is no direct link between the condition "yesterday we played in a game" and the expectation "our team would win", the former nonetheless provides an event frame for the occurrence of the latter. In this way, we see this unidirectional dependency as indirect cause-and-effect relationship in a broad sense.

The relationship between conditions and expectations is analogical when conditions are generalized constants. Analogies highlight the interconnection of all things in the world via the mode of thinking in which people understand the unfamiliar by means of the familiar. The analogical relationship can be illustrated by the following example:

(5)   她会开车，但是没有驾照。
Tā huì kāichē, **dànshì** méiyǒu jiàzhào.
She can drive but donot have driver's license
'She can drive but does not have a driver's license.'

Based on our common sense, anyone who can drive usually possesses a driver's license, hence the condition "She can drive" is likely to inspire the expectation "She has a driver's license". Another instance, similar to example (2), is when individuals perceive atypical members of the bird category, such as "ostriches", they frequently use prototypes like sparrows, swallows, robins as references. Analogically, they incline to generate the expectation that "ostriches should be able to fly". This suggests that analogy is the reasoning process that is prone to be over-generalized, especially when a scenario shifts from the general to the particular, or from the conventional to the unconventional.

The Relationship Between Expectations and Counter-Expectations: Negation Relationship

Counter-expectations are the direct and/ or indirect negation of expectations. The direct negation primarily displays as an oppositeness relationship, as seen in example (6); whereas the indirect negation mostly indicates as a deviation relationship brought on by variations in semantic-pragmatic scales, as shown in example (7).

(6)   这么大的超市**居然**卖假货！
         Zhème dà de chāoshì **jūrán** mài jiǎ huò!
         So big PRT supermarket surprisingly sell fake goods
         'How dare such a big supermarket sell counterfeit goods!'

(7)   说好的十点钟见面，谁知道他十一点**才**到。
         Shuōhǎo de shí diǎnzhōng jiànmiàn, **shéi zhīdào** tā shíyī diǎn cái dào.
         Agree PRT ten o'clock meet who know he eleven o'clock until arrive
         'We were supposed to meet at ten o'clock, but he didn't arrive until eleven o'clock.'

Here it is crucial to note that expectations and counter-expectations are asymmetrical negation relationships: from the perspective of information dependency, expectations can exist independently from counter-expectations, but this is not the case on the contrary, because the information boundaries of counter-expectations are made clear by expectations; from the perspective of linguistic encoding, counter-expectations must be explicitly expressed because they are always the information foci; while expectations often implicitly exist due to their lowest information value.

The Relationship Between Expectations and Counter-Expectations: Bridging Relationship

Conditions and counter-expectations are respectively located at the beginning and the end of the complete CEIS, and the coherence between them needs to be bridged by expectations. For example:

(8)   我批评了小李，还以为他会生气呢，**没想到**他还听大度的。
         Wǒ pīpíng le Xiǎo Lǐ, hái yǐwéi tā huì shēngqì ne,
         I criticize PRT Xiao Li still thought he would angry PRT
         méi xiǎngdào tā hái tǐng dàdù de.
         not expect he still broad-minded PRT
         'I criticized Xiao Li, and thought he would be angry, but he was quite broad-minded.'

(9)   讲了一上午课，嗓子**反而**不疼了。
         Jiǎng le yí shàngwǔ kè, sǎngzi **fǎndào** bù téng le.
         Speak PRT one morning lecture throat on the contrary not sore PRT
         '(To my surprise,) after a morning of lectures, my throat didn't feel sore any more.'

The inference from conditions to expectations is made clockwise when expectations are present (as in example (8)). However, expectations are always left out in real linguistic data. In example (9), the expectation "The throat would be sorer after a morning of lectures" has to be motivated for the coherence of the condition "a morning of lectures" and the counter-expectation "the throat didn't feel sore any more". That is to say, expectations always act as bridges between conditions and counter-expectations, regardless of whether they are coded explicitly or not.

3.3 Gestalt Principles and the Relationships Between the Information Units

Gestalt Principles, which have their roots in Gestalt Psychology, reflect the way in which people perceive the world through relationships between all the things such as proximity, similarity, inclusion and opposition. These principles play a prominent role in experiential processing and mental representation (cf. Evans and Green [23]). The relationships between the information units of the CEIS can be unified in the principles of Gestalt Psychology (see Table 1).

In detail, the cause-and-effect and analogical relationships between conditions and expectations correspond to the gestalt principles of proximity and similarity respectively. The principle of proximity describes the propensity to see objects that are close to each other in time and space as a whole, such as situations that consistently occur sequentially tend to be seen as causes and effects. For instance, "a thunderstorm" and "getting cooler", "sleepless all night" and "sleepy the next day" are two pairs of antecedent and consequent frequently occurring one after the other, and therefore they are in cause-and-effect relationship.

The principle of similarity refers to the fact that things that are akin in shape, size, appearance etc. can be grouped together. When conditions are assumed to be generalized constants, people tend to categorize a new particular individual situation into situations of a similar kind. The phenomenon contributes to analogical thinking which presumes that things are going as usual and is one of the fundamental heuristics to understand the current situation from a comparable one (cf. Brown and Yule [24]).

The principle of prominence is demonstrated by the negation relationship between expectations and counter-expectations. It is the principle that is closely related to figure-ground distribution, i.e. the more distinct the figures are from their backgrounds, the easier it is to tell them apart. In the CEIS, counter-expectations and expectations are conceptualized as figures and backgrounds respectively, making the former more salient than the latter. As shown in example (6), when the expectation "selling real goods" and the counter-expectation "selling fake goods" are complementary antonyms, the two share the same semantic field evenly, creating a "face-vase" effect: an almost 50/50 split between the figure and the ground. In another example like (7), taking the expectation "agreeing to meet at ten o'clock" as a reference, the addressee would naturally treat the counter-expectation "arriving at eleven o'clock" which surpluses the time scale of the expectation as the conspicuous figure.

The principle of closure is reflected in the bridging relationship between conditions and expectations. According to the principle of closure, even if some part of an object is missing, this will not affect its perception as a whole. Relevance Theory has a similar vein for it treats juxtaposed successive discourses as a whole, presuming that they are in optimal relevance on the communicative principle of relevance and supposing people tend to gear to the maximization of relevance on the cognitive principle of relevance (cf. Sperber and Wilson [25]). Therefore, even in the absence of expectations, the established relationship between conditions and counter-expectations can automatically set off bridging inference, yielding the best language use effect with minimal cognitive effort.

Table 1. The relationships between the information units and gestalt principles

Information units	Relationship	Gestalt principle
Conditions and expectations	Cause-and-effect relationship	The principle of proximity
	Analogical relationship	The principle of similarity
Expectations and counter-expectations	Negation relationship	The principle of prominence
Conditions and counter-expectations	Bridging relationship	The principle of closure

4   The Variant Models of the CEIS and Their Cognitive-Pragmatic Motivations

4.1   Data and Methodology

To summarize as accurately as possible the typical models of the CEIS, we make use of network statistics and the software VOSviewer1.6.19 to do a favor. First, we take "counter-expectation" as the keyword to search within the scope of "title, keyword and abstract"[2] in CNKI (China National Knowledge Infrastructure) and get 742 papers (2003–2023). After excluding the papers on ancient Chinese, dialects and other foreign languages, we find 663 papers that meet the requirements. Then, we upload the citation data ("Refworks") of these papers into VOSviewer and count the counter-expectation expressions that occur equal to and more than twice (≥ 2). The results and their co-occurrence distribution network with the main keywords are shown in Table 2 and Fig. 1.

---

[2] The other two relevant search options "topic" and "keyword" in CNKI have 804 papers and 272 papers respectively. The former involves several papers of very low relevance, and the total number of the latter is quite small, both of which are not conducive to VOSviewer to access the keywords.

Table 2. The forms of expression for counter-expectations

Label	Weight \<Links\>	Weight \<total link strength\>	Weight \<occurrences\>
还-*hái*-still	7	12	12
反倒-*fǎndào*-instead	6	7	4
什么-*shénme*-what	6	7	4
别看-*biékàn*-despite	7	7	3
x比y还w-*x bǐ y hái w* -x more y than w	5	7	4
x比y更w-*x bǐ y gèng w* -x more y than w	4	6	2
竟然-*jìngrán*-unexpectedly	5	6	4
其实-*qíshí*-actually	4	6	4
并-*bìng*-and	5	6	3
谁知-*shéizhī*-who knows	5	5	3
哪里是x-*nálǐ shì x* -it is not x	5	5	2
再x也y-*zài x yě y* -no matter how x still y	5	5	2
怎么-*zěnme*-how come	3	6	2
倒-*dào*-instead	4	4	2
偏(偏)-*piān(piān)*-just	4	4	2
万万-*wànwàn*-surprisingly	3	4	2
不料-*búliào*-unexpectedly	3	3	2
却-*què*-yet	3	3	2
反而-*fǎn'ér*-instead	2	3	2
不是-*búshì x*-not x	2	3	2
连……也/都 -*lián…yě/dōu*-even	2	2	2
还NP/ VP呢-*hái NP/ VP ne* -barely as NP/ VP	2	2	2
亏你x-*kuī nǐ x*-being x	2	2	2
原来-*yuánlái*-turn out that	2	2	2

Based on Table 2, we remove counter-expectation trigger words (such as *Kuī nǐ* VP, *hái* NP/ VP *ne*, *biékàn*), counter-expectation intensifiers (such as *wànwàn*), irrelevant items for contrast (like *x bǐ y gèng w*) and combine similar items (*nálǐ shì x* and *búshì x*), and add some highly prevalent counter-expectation markers (such as *tài*, *dànshì/kěshì*). In total, there are 20 counter-expectation markers. Taking these markers as keywords,

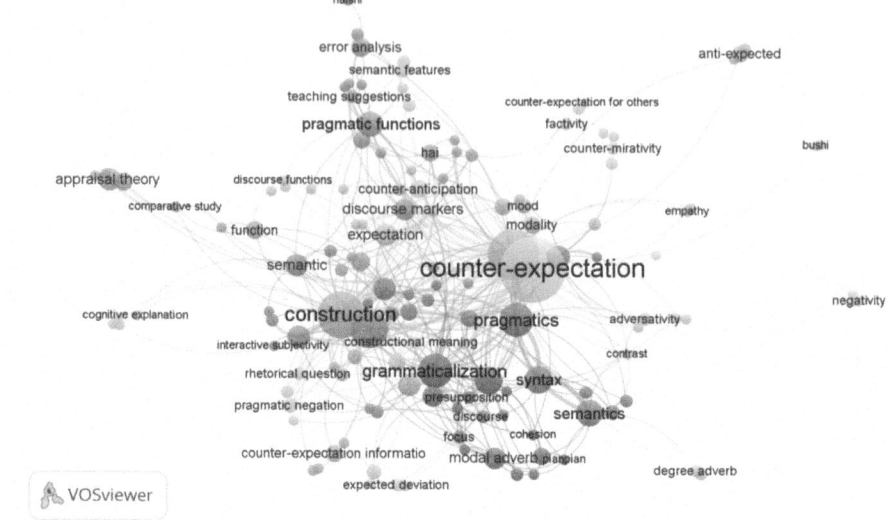

Fig. 1. The co-occurrence distribution network of counter-expectation expressions and other main keywords

we select 2000 pieces of relevant linguistic data (100 pieces for each marker) from the CCL corpus and then determine the main models of the CEIS. The models and their occurrences are illustrated in Table 3.

Table 3. The models of the CEIS and their occurrences

Type [a]	Counter-expectation markers	Condition + expectation + counter-expectation		Expectation + Counter-expectation[b]		Condition + Counter-expectation		Independent counter-expectation	
		A + B + B/C	A + B + B | C	B +~ B/C	B +~B + C	A +~B/C	A +~B + C	~B/C	~B + C
Mood	并-bìng-and					87		13	
	竟然/居然-jìngrán/jūrán -unexpectedly	2				54		44	
	偏(偏)-piān(piān)-just	3	1			71		25	
	倒-dào-instead	27	7		12	49	5		
	太-tài-too					16	3	68	13
	反而/反倒-fǎn'ér/fǎndào-instead	2	3			35	60		
	连……也/都-lián...yě/dōu-even			18		28		43	11

(*continued*)

Table 3. (*continued*)

Type [a]	Counter-expectation markers	Condition + expectation + counter-expectation		Expectation + Counter-expectation[b]		Condition + Counter-expectation		Independent counter-expectation	
		A + B + ~B/C	A + B + ~B + C	B +~ B/C	B +~B + C	A +~B/C	A +~B + C	~B/C	~B + C
	原来-*yuánlái*-turn out that			14	5	35		42	4
	x比y还w-*x bǐ y hái w* -x more y than w			15		26		59	
Adversative	但是/可是-*dànshì/kěshì*-but	17	2			63	18		
	然而-*rán'ér*-however	5		1		83	11		
	却-*què*-yet	13	9			46	32		
	其实/事实上-*qíshí/Shìshíshàng*-actually	26	1	22		51			
	再x也y-*zài x yě y* -no matter how x still y					89	11		
Negative	不料/未料-*búliào/wèiliào*-unexpectedly	8		17		75			
	没想到-*méixiǎngdào*-unexpectedly	14		21	4	35		17	9
	谁知-*shéizhī*-who knows	28		29		43			
	不是x/哪里是x-*búshì x/nálǐ shì x*-not x						93	7	
Interrogative	怎么-*zěnme*-how come	10		9		45		36	
	什么-*shénme*-what	15		29		56			
	Total/percentage	193/ 9.65%		196/9.8%		1220/61%		391/19.55%	

[a]Lu [14] first of all divides counter-expectation markers in Mandarin Chinese into interrogative and non-interrogative types based on their forms, and then divide the latter into negative and non-negative types based on their functions, in which the non-negative contains mood and adversative types.

[b]"Expectation+counter-expectation" model is usually caused by conventionalized collocations, such as "shuōhǎo dē..., zěnme...?" "hái yǐwéi...shéi zhī..." "zěnme...? hái yǐwéi...".

As illustrated in Table 3, the "condition + counter-expectation" model, which accounts for 61%, is the most common variant used in the vast majority of the counter-expectation markers. The independent counter-expectation model, which occupies approximately 20%, is much less prevalent than the "condition + counter-expectation" model, but still more common than the "condition + expectation + counter-expectation" model and "expectation + counter-expectation" model. Therefore, we will probe on the "condition + counter-expectation" model and the independent counter-expectation model, and make cognitive-pragmatic interpretations for the default of expectation in these two popular models.

4.2 The Typical Variant Models of the CEIS

"Condition+Counter-Expectation" Model: A+ ~B/C and A+~B+C

The "condition + counter-expectation" model can be represented as adversative type "A +~ B/C" and "adversative + negative" progressive type "A + B + C". The expectation B is optional, while the counter-expectation ~ B and C must appear for one or both. For instance:

(10)　　　A+(B)+~B+C: 马上就要考试了，（还以为你会好好复习，）
　　　　　　　　　　　　可是你并没有复习，反倒跑出去玩了。
　　　　　　　　　　　Mǎshàng jiùyào kǎoshì le, (hái yǐwéi nǐ huì hǎohǎo fùxí,)
　　　　　　　　　　　Soon will exam PRT thought you would good review
　　　　　　　　　　　kěshì nǐ bìng méiyǒu fùxí, **fǎndào** pǎo chūqù wán le.
　　　　　　　　　　　but you and did not review instead run out play PRT
　　　　　　　　　　　'The exam is coming soon, (I thought you would study hard,)
　　　　　　　　　　　(but) instead of studying, you hung out and played.'
　　　　　A+~B/ C: 马上就要考试了，可是你并没有复习。
　　　　　　　　　　　Mǎshàng jiùyào kǎoshì le, **kěshì** nǐ bìng méiyǒu fùxí.
　　　　　　　　　　　Soon will exam PRT but you and did not review
　　　　　　　　　　　'The exam is coming soon, but you did not study.'
　　　　　A+~B+C: 马上就要考试了，你反倒跑出去玩了。
　　　　　　　　　　　Mǎshàng jiùyào kǎoshì le, nǐ **fǎndào** pǎo chūqù wán le.
　　　　　　　　　　　Soon will exam PRT you instead run out play PRT
　　　　　　　　　　　'The exam is coming soon, but you hung out and played.'

In this model, conditions cannot be removed in most circumstances. On the one hand, conditions include the starting topic and its description of the whole discourse. In the discourses with a persistent topic, it would become confusing if conditions are left out. As shown in example (11), removing 仁海*rénhǎi* (the monk's name) which is the topic of the two coordinate clauses would make it unclear even ungrammatical. In the discourses with progressive topics, the description parts of conditions are the topics of subsequent information. In (12), the description "always speaks a bit bluntly" in the first clause is the topic of the next one, the discourse would become illogical if the condition is omitted.

(11)　　　仁海是和尚，**但是**有老婆。
　　　　　　Rénhǎi shì héshàng, **dànshì** yǒu lǎopó.
　　　　　　Rénhǎi is monk but have wife
　　　　　　'Rénhǎi is a monk, but he has a wife.'
(12)　　　小张说话有点冲，**可**他领导不觉得这是什么缺点。
　　　　　　Xiǎo Zhào shuōhuà yǒudiǎn chòng, **kě** tā lǐngdǎo bù juéde zhèshì shénme quēdiǎn.
　　　　　　Xiǎo Zhào speak a bit bluntly but he leader not think this what flaw
　　　　　　'Xiao Zhao always speaks a bit bluntly, but his leader does not see it as a flaw.'

On the other hand, whether conditions are particular states of affairs or generalized constants, they are not easily omitted. For example, if we overlap the condition of particular states of affairs in example (1) "There was a thunderstorm this afternoon", the hearer who forgot the rain would wonder "Why do you say it will be cooler today?" And if the condition of generalized constants is absent but the information is not shared by all the participants in speech events, then the counter-expectation information can not be transmitted smoothly.

Independent Counter-Expectation Model: ~B/C and ~B + C

The prerequisite for the feasibility of the independent counter-expectation model is that conditions must be concealable under given circumstances. Here are the cases:

First, counter-expectations can evoke the situations pertaining to conditions when expectations and counter-expectations are complementary in sense relations. For instance:

(13)　他**居然**没死。/还活着。
　　　Tā **jūrán** méi sǐ. / hái huózhē.
　　　He surprisingly not dead still alive
　　　'Surprisingly, he is not dead/ still alive.'

"Not dead" in example (13) can not only activate the expectation "dead", but imply that the condition relates to exceedingly dangerous events. In other words, it does provide the hearer with a basic idea of the condition so that the discourse comprehension is unaffected. Besides "dead and alive", "true and false", "present and absent", "man and woman", "odd and even" etc. are complementary antonyms, the sight of the one would naturally activate the other.

Second, conditions can be cut out when counter-expectations implicate specific semantic-pragmatic scales. In this case, counter-expectations are in the same direction as expectations, only higher or lower than expectations on measures including temporal, quantitative, spatial, momentum, degree, and psychological quantities, which are called over-expectations and below-expectations (cf. Qi and Hu [26]).

(14)　你**怎么就**来了？/**才**来？
　　　Nǐ **zěnme jiù** lái le?/ **cái** lái?
　　　You how come already come PRT/ just come
　　　'How come you come so early/ late?'

(15)　我**只/已经**吃了一块蛋糕。
　　　Wǒ **zhǐ/ yǐjīng** chī le yí kuài dàngāo.
　　　I only/already eat PRT one piece cake
　　　'I only/ already ate one piece of cake.'

(16)　这鞋子**太**小/大了。
　　　Zhè xiézǐ **tài** xiǎo/dà le.
　　　This shoes so small/big PRT
　　　'The shoes are too small/ big to wear.'

All of the aforementioned cases demonstrate the counter-expectations that are quantitatively lower or higher than expectations. Meanwhile, the existence of the progressive model "~B + C" is also because of semantic-pragmatic scales. For example:

(17)　他不但没赚钱，**还**亏本了。
　　　Tā bùdàn méi zhuàn qián, **hái** kuīběn le.
　　　He not only not earn money even lose money PRT
　　　'Not only did he not make money, but lost money.'

The progressive clause represents the increasing intensity of the counter-expectation meaning, since the fact "lost money" is much more negative than the fact "did not make money". Taking the possible situations into consideration, the utterance (17) can be a response to a neutral question "Did he make money from his business?", and can also be a negation to a hearsay or supposition "It is said/ seemed that he made plenty of money by doing business.". In both cases, the response represents that the speaker is confident enough to let the previous speaker know the fact. The confidence of speakers usually reflects a sense of superiority based on their social or intellectual advantage. However, there is a difference on the subject of counter-expectation. Under the former situation, the counter-expectation raising from the speaker's expectation "Doing business makes money.", pertains to self counter-expectation; while under the latter situation, the counter-expectation deviating from the previous speaker's expectation "He made plenty of money by doing business.", belongs to the other counter-expectation.

Third, when the participants in conversations do not share some information, or do not reach agreement on certain issue, the counter-expectations are often direct or indirect negations of the previous speakers' expectations. At this stage, the conditions are usually included in the previous speakers' utterances. For instance:

(18)	A: 你们比赛输了？
	B1: 我们才没输呢！
	B2: **怎么**可能！
	A: Nǐmen bǐsài shū le?
	    You game lose PRT
	    'You lost the game?'
	B1: Wǒmen cái méi shū ne!
	    We just not lose PRT
	    'We didn't!' (direct negation)
	B2: **Zěnme** kěnéng!
	    How possible
	    'How can that be!' (indirect negation)

(19)	A: 这件衣服不错。
	B1: 我觉得不怎么样。
	B2: 你要求**还**真低。
	A: Zhè jiàn yīfu búcuò.
	    This piece clothes not bad
	    'This piece of clothes is not bad.'
	B1: Wǒ juéde bú zěnmeyàng.
	    I think not good
	    'I don't think it's good.' (direct negation)
	B2: Nǐ yāoqiú **hái** zhēn dī.
	    You requirement still really low
	    'You're really asking for less.' (indirect negation)

In example (18), the information imbalance between A and B leads to different epistemic stances (cf. Heritage [27]). A is in an unknowing position, but his question is quite directional, which reveals his expectation "B's team lost the game". While B who is in a knowing position, is absolutely confident to negate the expectation. Here B's direct or indirect negation are quite strategic, namely, to counter A's expectation. In example (19), however, it is not a matter concerning information territory, but discrepancies on the views of aesthetics. In this regard, the intensity of the counter-expectation meaning in (19) is lower than (18).

Although conditions can be disregarded in the circumstances mentioned above, occasionally independent counter-expectations would approach or even be mistaken with some other similar concepts, like in (20) and (21):

(20)　你怎么来了？
Nǐ **zěnme** lái le?
You how come come PRT
'How come you come here?'

(21)　刚才差一点摔跤。
Gāngcái **chàyìdiǎn** shuāijiāo.
Just now almost fall
'I almost fell just now.'

The utterance (20) can be used under at least three circumstances: a) I did not think you would come; b) I did not let you to come; c) I never considered that you would come. Under circumstances a) and b), (20) can be identified as counter-expectation information, concerning with epistemic modality and deontic modality; while c) indicates that there was no expectation, and the speaker is just astonished. In this case, (20) should be regarded as "surprise" or "unpreparedness" within the semantic subcategories of mirativity (cf. Aikhenvald [28]). Besides, it is important to distinguish between "wishes/ hopes" and expectations, because the former is mostly positive, while the latter is much more neutral and based on conditions. In (21), the expectation is uncertain since the condition is absent, which leaves the appearance of the road remains unknown. If the speaker was walking on streets, then "to fall" is out of expectation; but if the speaker was climbing mountain stairs, then "to fall" is within expectation. Furthermore, "chayidian VP" is mostly a response to the speaker's personal and also the general desire of the listeners, since nobody wants to fall, whether the road is smooth or rugged. That is to say, "wishes/ hopes" are generally more subjective and affective than counter-expectations.

4.3　The Cognitive-Pragmatic Motivations for the Default of the Expectations in Typical Models

In the "condition + counter-expectation" model and the independent counter-expectation model, the absence of expectations is a common practice. According to cognitive pragmatics, the motivations are as follows:

First of all, it is the pervasiveness of stereotypical relations. When conditions motivate conventional frames, expectations are highly accessible and thus can be skipped. The condition of example (11) "Renhai is a monk" could activate the encyclopedic knowledge and cultural frame of Buddhist monks, including purging the world of mortals, ardently practicing meditation, being compassionate etc.. Therefore, the conventional expectation "Monks cannot have wives" is so well acknowledged that can be omitted. Another similar example like (13), the counter-expectation information "He is not dead/ alive" makes the opposite situation "He is dead/not alive" prominent in mental world, hence it can be concealed in expression. In conclusion, the expectations triggered by stereotypical relations have the characteristics of being conventional, universal and stable, and thus can be hidden in language.

Second, it is the mechanism of metonymy. Stereotypical relations are the practical ways of people perceiving the world and therefore prone to being over-generalized since they are summarized from multiple specific situations of the same kind. In this sense, stereotypical relations represent the metonymic relations between things (cf. Li [29]). As shown in example (2), the over-generalized expectation "ostriches should be able to fly" comes from the stereotype "Birds can fly", which is supported by the metonymic way of thinking "PART FOR WHOLE". What is more, the general principle of gestalt principles known as "the law Pragnanz" points out that people always tend to perceive things as complete and stable organizations. This indicates that gestalt and metonymy are interrelated cognitive mechanisms that aid the completion of the CEIS when expectations are absent.

Third, it is the coordinating force between quantity iconicity and language economy. Discourse length and information value are determined by the principle of quantity iconicity, i.e., the lower the information value of a unit, the more concise the linguistic form, and vice versa. Expectations possessing the lowest information value belong to unmarked content, while counter-expectations with the highest information value need to be marked as explicitly as possible. On the other hand, the default of expectations reflects the principle of language economy. The second maxim of the principle of quantity in the Cooperative Principle reveals that the contribution should not be more informative than is required. Expressions should be brief on the premise of understanding. The principle of speakers also points out a similar vein that what we need to say is the changed and the new, and what need not is the constant and the old (see Brown and Yule [24]). On the scale of information value, the principle of language economy is in competition with the principle of quantity iconicity on the expression of counter-expectation, but they reach a consensus on the default of expectations.

5 The Online Information Processing of the CEIS

In the nine principles of governing on online information processing (cf. Fauconnier and Turner [30]), what concerns the construal of counter-expectations the most are principles of topology, integration and unpacking. We will go through each one in detail.

5.1 Principle of Topology

The term "topology", which was originally used to explore physical spatial relationships, refers to the characteristics of an object that retains its homomorphism in deformation. For instance, the shape of a coil can be square or circular, large or small, but the shared topological feature with hollow holes remains constant. Like the physical world, the mind and language also have topological properties. While construing the counter-expectations in discourses, the principle of topology promotes the interaction between mental space and linguistic space through two characteristics:

One is topological constancy, which means that topological structures and relationships remain the same even if the input spaces have been selected, compassed and projected (cf. Fauconnier and Turner [30]). The cause-and-effect, analogical, negation and bridging relationships between the information units, and their manifestation in gestalt principles of proximity, similarity, salience and closure, are all topological relations inside the CEIS. Furthermore, the complete model of the CEIS which serves as an idealized reference for other variant models due to its great discriminability and prominence is similarly topologically invariant. In this sense, the CEIS is quite similar to schemata, idealized cognitive models (ICMs), frames etc. that are coded in our long-term memory, functioning as prototypes for their variants.

The other is topological connectivity, referring to the capability of information units to link and activate each other. Such kind of connectivity licenses associative processing and therefore related inferences (cf. Mazzone [13]). From a neurological perspective, Collins and Loftus's "Activation-Spreading Model" and Rumelhart, Hinton and McClelland's "Connectionist Model" propose that relevant information nodes are stored in the human brain as a network of neurons, and the presence of one node will activate other nodes adjacent to it (see Li [29]). Similarly, the presence of conditions and/ or counter-expectations will motivate expectations in a way of automatic heuristics, showing their property of topological connectivity.

5.2 Principle of Integration

Under the microscope of the principle of integration, information integration is a process from the surface to the inside, from sensibility to rationality. Specifically, information integration consists of three layers of escalating complexity in a mental chronology, and is represented by two input spaces, a generic space and a bending space on the types of mental space.

The first-order integration regards sentence groups as a one cohesive whole and helps to process basic cognitive domains by completing perception in terms of shapes, colors, odors and other sensory stimuli. The formation of input space in the first-order integration depends on background information, such as cognitive frames and stereotypical relations derived from perceptual experience and encyclopedic knowledge, in addition to the current discourse information (cf. Li and Bai [31]). The second-order integration moves towards schematization, reflecting the relationship between conceptual and linguistic structures and embodying the cognitive-semantic logic of the information clusters. In the second-order integration, the generic space abstracts the commonalities of the input spaces, eliminating the irrelevant while preserving the relevant. The third-order integration further organizes, improves and refines the information obtained from the integration of the first two orders in the blending space, and then generates the emergent meaning in the compression of concepts and the construction of information structures. For instance:

> (22) 他年纪轻轻的，**怎么**就驼背了？
> Tā niánjì qīngqing de, **zěnme** jiù tuóbèi le?
> He age young PRT how come already hunchbacked PRT
> 'Why is he hunchbacked at such a young age?'

In (22), the first-order integration mobilizes the unified sensory images of "young" and "hunchbacked", initially forming two input spaces. Then the second-order integration abstracts the shared structure of input spaces, i.e. the relationship between age and appearance. At last, the third-order integration organizes the information projected from the input spaces, activating the conventional expectation "young people are generally not hunchbacked" and thus understand the counter-expectation information "young but hunchbacked" (see Fig. 2).

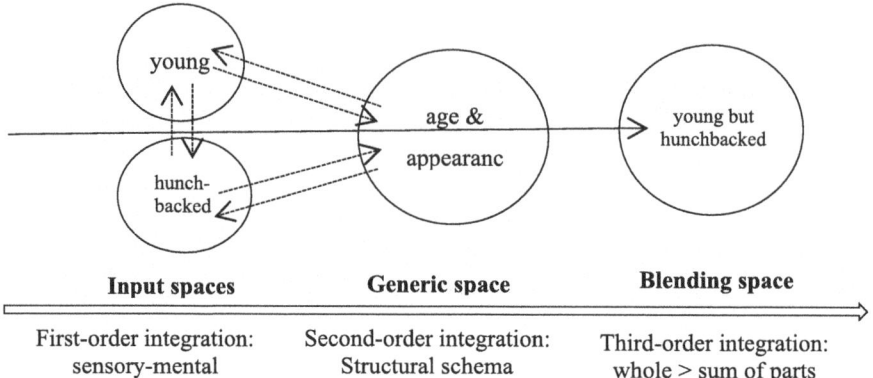

Fig. 2. The construal of counter-expectation information

5.3 Principle of Unpacking

Principle of unpacking works when different sources of information cannot be coordinated in the blending space, at this point, the information that is about to be integrated will be decomposed and returned to the input space for reconstruction (cf. Fauconnier and Turner [30]). Compared with the process of integration which is automatic, unconscious and on general-level in many cases, that of unpacking is quite controlled, conscious and on personal-level. Conscious attention can affect subsequent automatic processing of inputs (cf. Mazzone [13]). That is to say, the principle of unpacking and the principle of integration runs in opposing directions, which are somewhat in a competition with one another.

Under the instinct of cognitive labor saving, the human brain will automatically activate common sense and make judgments based on the default assignment and associated expectations supplied by conventional knowledge (cf. Ungerer and Schmid [32]). But when expectations originate from an unconventional context, the initial integration of the CEIS is prone to failure. If smooth automatic processing fails, then conscious controlled processing is usually required. The human brain will turn to explore contextual factors and processing therefore turns to specialized processes. Such kind of succession in information processing is the optimal process of integrating information of the mind. For example:

(23)　　(a) 今天下暴雨，他却出门了。
　　　　　Jīntiān xià bàoyǔ, tā **què** chūmén le.
　　　　　Today fall hard rain he but go out PRT
　　　　　'It was raining heavily today, but he went out.'
　　　　(b) 今天下暴雨，他却没出门。
　　　　　Jīntiān xià bàoyǔ, tā **què** méi chūmén.
　　　　　Today fall hard rain he but not go out
　　　　　'It was raining heavily today, but he did not go out.'

The condition "raining heavily today" usually triggers the conventional expectation "not went out", and therefore "he went out" can be understood as counter-expectation information naturally in (23a). But when it comes to (23b), the conventional expectation "not went out" changes into counter-expectation with the marker 却*què* 'but'. To make sense of it, the human brain would engage working memory, and use reductive inference to discern the cognitive-semantic logic between the condition and the counter-expectation, and then get the specialized expectation "He usually goes out when it rains hard." At this time, the listener needs to further figure out the appropriate cognitive context to rationalize the expectation, for example, "he" is an urban flood control worker, a railway security inspector, or an undercover agent who conceals his actions by taking advantage of rainstorms in film and TV works and the like. In short, the principle of unpacking ensures that the mental space is open to access information so that the contextual expectation can be activated after the conventional expectation fails to decode the counter-expectation information.

6　Conclusion

The complete CEIS in Mandarin Chinese consists of "condition", "expectation" and "counter-expectation". In terms of the connections between these information units, conditions and expectations are cause-and-effect and analogical relationships, expectations and counter-expectations are negation relationship, conditions and counter-expectations are bridging relationship, which are in correspondence with the gestalt principles of proximity and similarity, prominence, and closure.

The two common variant models of the CEIS are "condition + counter-expectation" and "independent counter-expectation". Both of these models have the capacity to omit expectations, primarily resulting from the collaborative operation of stereotypical relations, conceptual metonymy, quantity iconicity and the principle of language economy. And the online processing of the CEIS is guided mainly by the three principles of governing: the principles of topology, integration and unpacking.

The concerned issues on the CEIS in Mandarin Chinese are enormous and intricate, and what the research touches on is only a small portion. The discussion of the relationships between the information units and the variant models needs to be corroborated by a larger corpus analysis and compared with other languages. Besides, the online processing principles of the CEIS need to be further tested by brain-neural experiments.

Acknowledgments. This study was funded by the National Social Science Foundation Project titled *A Corpus-Based Study on the Variation of Chinese and English Idiomatic Constructions* *from the Perspective of Social-Cognition* (grant number: 24YBB081, PI: Yongzhong Li) and the Postgraduate Innovation Fund Project titled *The Study of Counter-Expectation Category in Contemporary Chinese and English from the perspective of Cognitive Pragmatics* (grant number: YC2022-B096, PI: Li Bai).

Disclosure of Interests.   The authors have no competing interests to declare that are relevant to the content of this article.

References

1. Halliday, M.A.K., Hasan, R.: Cohesion in English. Longman, London (1976)
2. Mathesius, V.: Functional linguistics. In: Vachek, J. (ed.) Praguiana: Some Basic and Less Well-known Aspects of the Prague Linguistics School, pp. 121–142. John Benjamins Publishing Company, Amsterdam (1929/1983)
3. Firbas, J.: On defining the theme in functional sentence perspective. Travaux Linguistiques de Prague **1**, 267–280 (1964)
4. Jackendoff, R.S.: Semantic Interpretation in Generative Grammar. MIT Press, Mass (1972)
5. Brown, G.: Prosodic structure and the given/new distinction. In: Cutler, A., et al. (eds.) Prosody: Models and Measurements, pp. 67–77. Springer-Verlag, Berlin (1983)
6. Chafe, W.: Discourse, Consciousness and Time: The Flow and Displacement of Conscious Experience in Speaking and Writing. Chicago University Press, Chicago (1994)
7. Wu, F.X.: On the pragmatic function of the construction *X bubi Y Z*. Stud. Chin. Lang. **3**, 222–231 (2004). (in Chinese)
8. Wang, Y.-F.: From lexical to pragmatic meaning: contrastive markers in spoken Chinese discourse. Text **25**(4), 469–518 (2005)
9. Chen, Z.Y., Wang, M.Y.: The cognitive model of expectations and the types: on a series of phenomena related to *jingran* and *pianpian*. Lang. Teach. Linguist. Stud. **5**, 48–63 (2021). (in Chinese)
10. Zeng, J.H., Yuan, Y.L: The semantic features and construal mechanisms of the expectational negative adverb *Kong* in Mandarin. In: Dong, M., Hong, JF., Lin, J., Jin, P. (eds.) CLSW 2023, LNCS, vol. 14514, pp. 101–115. Springer, Singapore (2024). https://doi.org/10.1007/978-981-97-0583-2_9
11. Zimmermann, M., Féry, C.: Information Structure: Theoretical, Typological, and Experimental Perspectives. Oxford University Press, Oxford (2010)
12. Ward, G., Birner, B., Kaiser, E.: Pragmatics and information structure. In: Huang, Y. (ed.) The Oxford Handbook of Pragmatics, pp. 567–589. Oxford University Press, Oxford (2017)
13. Mazzone, M.: Cognitive Pragmatics: Mindreading, Inferences, Consciousness. Walter de Gruyter GmbH & Co KG (2018)
14. Lu, F.Z.: A Study on Contemporary Chinese Counter-expectation Markers. China Social Sciences Press, Beijing (2017). (in Chinese)
15. Cuenca, M.-J.: Pragmatic markers in contrast: the case of *well*. J. Pragmat. **40**, 1373–1391 (2008)
16. Volkova, L.: Pragmatic markers in dialogical discourse. In: Lege Artis. Language Yesterday, Today, Tomorrow. De Gruyter Open, Warsaw, vol. II, no. 1, pp. 379–427 (2017)
17. Dahl, Ö.: Grammaticalization and the life cycles of constructions. RASK **14**, 91–133 (2001)
18. Ma, Z.: Say *fan'er*. Stud. Chin. Lang. **3**, 172–176 (1983). (in Chinese)
19. Yuan, Y.Y.: The Focus Structure and Semantic Interpretation of Chinese Sentences. The Commercial Press, Beijing (2012). (in Chinese)

20. Mou, S.R.: An investigation on international students' usage of *fan'er* and teaching strategies. Chin. Lang. Learn. **1**, 96–102 (2013). (in Chinese)
21. Li, S.S.: '*Haishi*' The source and emergence conditions of the modal meaning of *haishi*. Chin. Lang. Learn. **5**, 54–63 (2019). (in Chinese)
22. Shan, Q. C.: The semantic characteristics of the counter-expectation adverbs "Fǎn'ér" and "Ohiryo" in Chinese and Korean from the perspective of comparison. In: Dong, M., Hong, JF., Lin, J., Jin, P. (eds.) CLSW 2023, LNCS, vol. 14514, pp. 343–357. Springer, Singapore (2024). https://doi.org/10.1007/978-981-97-0583-2_27
23. Evans, V., Green, M.: Cognitive Linguistics: An Introduction. Edinburgh University Press, Edinburgh (2006)
24. Brown, G., Yule, G.: Discourse Analysis. Foreign Language Teaching and Research Press, Beijing (2000)
25. Sperber, D., Wilson, D.: Relevance: Communication and Cognition. Harvard University Press, Cambridge (1986)
26. Qi, H.Y., Hu, J.F.: On under-expectation information of the marked *X shi X* structure. Chin. Teach. World **2**, 31–39 (2006). (in Chinese)
27. Heritage, J.: The epistemic engine: sequence organization and territories of knowledge. Res. Lang. Soc. Interact. **45**(1), 30–52 (2012). https://doi.org/10.1080/08351813.2012.646685
28. Aikhenvald, A.Y.: The essence of mirativity. Linguist. Typol. **16**(3), 435–485 (2012). https://doi.org/10.1515/lity-2012-0017
29. Li, Y.Z.: Figurative Thinking in Discourse Narration. China Social Sciences Press, Beijing (2017). (in Chinese)
30. Fauconnier, G., Turner, M.: The Way We Think: Conceptual Blending and the Mind's Hidden Complexities. Basic Books, New York (2002)
31. Li, Y.Z., Bai, L.: The analysis of Chinese counter-expectation discourse for commonweal based on embodied-cognitive linguistics: exemplified by the discourses in "Xiao Lin's caricature." Shandong Fore. Lang. Teach. **5**, 141–146 (2022). (in Chinese)
32. Ungerer, F., Schmid, H.-J.: An Introduction to Cognitive Linguistics. Foreign Language Teaching and Research Press, Beijing (2006)

The Schematic Transformation Mechanism
of the Spatial Adverb *Lǐ*

Xiaotong Xu and Jie Zhou[(✉)]

University of Macau, Macau, China
`jiezh.1005@connect.um.edu.mo`

Abstract. Current discussions on the mechanism of the omission of locative words are limited by the nature of the noun head, failing to explain the omission of spatial words governed by the same type of noun head in different sentence patterns and address the underlying motivation for spatial words causing nouns to become locative. This paper used Distinctive Collexeme Analysis to examine the semantic distributions of the synonymous motion constructions "N1 + Vjìn + N2" and "N1 + Vjìn + N2 + lǐ". Based on their spatial roles, verbs were divided into two categories: $V_{\text{spatial relation}}$ and $V_{\text{spatial region}}$. The study showed that $V_{\text{spatial relation}}$ tended to co-occur with "N1 + Vjìn + N2"; $V_{\text{spatial region}}$ tended to co-occur with "N1 + Vjìn + N2 + lǐ". Thus, this paper constructed the interaction continuum of verb spatial roles and noun semantic roles, pointing out that the omission of *lǐ* is the interaction between verbs' spatial role and the location, with the cognitive motivation being the schema transformation mechanism of *lǐ*.

Keywords: Spatial Word · Spatial Role · Image Schema · Location

1 Introduction

Space and time are the two fundamental categories most concerned by cognitive linguistics. As the main means of expressing spatial relationships in Chinese, locative words have always received significant attention from academia. Scholars have conducted extensive and profound discussions from various perspectives, including the cognitive functions of locative words [1–4], the grammaticalization paths of locative words [5, 6], and the mechanisms of the omission of locative words [7–10]. These studies often considered locative words as the sole research object, aiming to describe their grammar, semantics, and cognitive functions. However, locative words exhibit different features in various contexts, as shown in (1):

© The Author(s), under exclusive license to Springer Nature Singapore Pte Ltd. 2025
P. Jin et al. (Eds.): CLSW 2024, LNAI 15552, pp. 502–515, 2025.
https://doi.org/10.1007/978-981-96-3509-2_36

(1) a. Mèimei zài tóngnián kǎojìn dàxué *lǐ.
   younger sister in same year test into university *inside
   "My younger sister was admitted to the university in the same year".
   b. Xuéshēng pǎo jìnle xuéxiào (lǐ).
   Student run into school (inside)
   "The student ran into the school".
   c. Xuéshēngmen dōu pǎo jìnle xuéxiào (*lǐ) zuòzhe děng lǎoshī.
   Students all run into school (*inside) sit wait teacher.
   "All the students ran into the school (*inside) and sat waiting for the teacher".

Previous research suggested that the function of locative words is to make categories locative, leading to two issues: first, it fails to explain the omission of *lǐ* "in" in institutional nouns within different contexts. Second, it does not address the motivation behind the locativization of noun components once they enter a sentence.

(1) illustrates that the influence of the nature of nouns on the omission of locative words can only reflect how isolated noun components transform from entities to locations, but fails to explain the omission of *lǐ* in higher-level constructions. Therefore, focusing solely on the interaction between locative words and nouns is insufficient to describe their function. Specific contexts are needed to focus on the interaction of the whole "N + lǐ" (into N) with other items in higher-level constructions.

This paper examines the motion construction "N1 + Vjìn + N2" (N1 + Vinto/in + N2) and investigates the distribution of its two lower-level constructions, C1 "N1 + Vjìn + N2" and C2 "N1 + Vjìn + N2 + lǐ" (hereafter referred to as C1 and C2). Using the collostructional analysis proposed by Gries & Stefanowitsch [11], it is shown that the co-occurrence tendencies of verbs that can appear in both constructions are not the same. Furthermore, based on these co-occurrence tendencies, the interaction continuum of verb spatial roles and noun semantic roles is constructed (as shown in Fig. 1), indicating that the appearance and disappearance of *lǐ* reflect the interaction pattern between the spatial roles of verbs and locations.

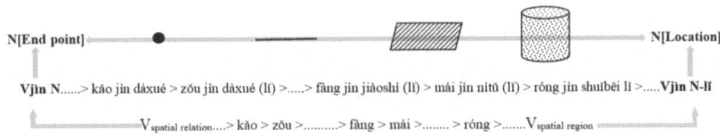

Fig. 1. The interaction continuum of verb spatial roles and noun semantic roles

On this basis, the research questions are refined as follows:

1. What are the differences in the co-occurrence tendencies of verbs with the constructions C1 and C2?
2. What are the semantic differences between the constructions?
3. How do the spatial roles of verbs interact with the arguments of the constructions?
4. What is the cognitive motivation behind the omission of locative words?

2   Co-occurrence Tendencies of Verbs Within C1 and C2

Construction grammar theory considers the internal structure of language as a dynamic system that continuously changes in language use, which is the "construction network" composed of constructions at various levels [12–17]. Langacker [14] points out that instance constructions are the most basic language structures, and to fully describe a language, one must first explain the syntactic distribution of instance constructions. An important principle supporting this assertion is the "Schematization Transparency Principle" [15]: the result of merging a schema with its instances is a unified concept equivalent to that instance. In short, the form-meaning pairing of instance constructions is essentially equivalent to the form-meaning pairing of higher-level schema constructions. Therefore, the clustering of multiple instance constructions is able to describe and generalize the core semantics of schema. The construction network perspective provides a new viewpoint for the study of synonymous constructions in Chinese.

C1 and C2 have similar meanings and can be interchangeable in specific contexts, such as:

> (2)   a. Yàoshi chā jìnle suǒyǎn.
> Key insert into lock hole
> "The key was inserted into the lock".
> b. Yàoshi chā jìnle suǒyǎn lǐ. (self-constructed)
> Key insert into lock hole in
> "The key was inserted into the keyhole".

This fits the definition of "alternation pairs" by Gries & Stefanowitsch [11]. We adopt Distinctive Collexeme Analysis to explore the semantic differences between the two constructions by examining their semantic clustering of verbs.

2.1   Data Collection

The multi-domain module of the BCC corpus was selected. Keywords "Vjìn + N" and "Vjìn + N + lǐ" were used for retrieval, and valid sentences were obtained through manual analysis. It should be noted that in "N1 + Vjìn + N2", N2 can be a locative noun that cannot co-occur with lǐ, which is not included in this section, for example:

(3)   Tāmen dǎsuàn bǎ měiguó de jíxiàn yùndòng dài jìn zhōngguó.
They plan BA American extreme sports bring to China
"They plan to introduce extreme sports from the United States into China".

Another type of N2 which cannot co-occur with lǐ due to its semantic restrictions is not included, such as:

> (4)   Xiǎo yànzi fēi jìn chuāngzi.
> Young swallow fly into window
> "Young swallows flew into the window".

To eliminate the influence of prosody, disyllabic "X lǐ" is not included, such as:

(5) Wǒmen dǎsuàn yījù gōng jìn shān lǐ.
Our reconnaissance comrade make the plan in one fell swoop attack into mountain
"Our reconnaissance comrades plan to launch an attack into the mountains".

After selection, a total of 16,237 instances of C1 were obtained, with 259 verbs; 11,378 instances of C2 were obtained, with 381 verbs. There are 188 verbs that can appear in both constructions.

To analyze the collocational strength between verbs and the specific synonymous interchangeable constructions using Distinctive Collexeme Analysis, four types of data are needed: 1) the frequency of V1 in C1; 2) the frequency of V1 in C2; 3) the frequency of other verbs in C1 excluding V1; 4) the frequency of other verbs in C2 excluding V1. Taking the verb *zhù* "live in" as an example, its data is organized into a 4×4 contingency table, as shown in Table 1.

Table 1. Frequency of the verb *zhù* (live in) in the verb slot of N and N lǐ

Construction	*zhù*	Other verbs	Total
C1 Vjìn + N	1392	19,991	21,383
C2 Vjìn + N + lǐ	52	13,262	13,314
Total	1444	33,253	34,697

2.2 Data Analysis

After obtaining the data for 188 verbs, the collocational strength between verbs and constructions was analyzed using Coll.analysis 4.0 in R. Results show that out of the 188 verbs, 96 verbs tend to co-occur with C1, and 92 tend to co-occur with C2. Table 2 reveals the top five verbs with the highest collocational strength for each construction.

Table 2. Comparison of significant co-occurring verbs in the verb slot of C1 and C2

C1 Vjìn + N (V in N) (N = 21383)		C2 Vjìn + N + lǐ (V into N) (N = 13314)	
Co-occuring verbs	Coll. Strength	Co-occuring verbs	Coll. Strength
zhù "live" (1392:52)	1.03E + 03	*fàng* "put" (957:1651)	7.17E + 02
chōng "rush" (1498:292)	4.37E + 02	*mái* "bury" (113:617)	6.76E + 02
kuà "cross" (695:43)	4.17E + 02	*shēn* "stretch" (397:903)	5.35E + 02
tà "tread" (787:77)	3.98E + 02	*diào* "fall" (261:610)	3.67E + 02
sòng "give" (1264:282)	3.00E + 02	*sāi* "stuff" (474:781)	3.02E + 02

As shown in Table 2, the top ten significant co-occurring verbs for C1 and C2 are different, indicating that the verbs of synonymous constructions differ in types and distributions. This raises two questions: first, previous research mostly recognizes the function of locative words as locative markers. Why, then, do nouns of the same type tend to become locative when paired with certain verbs (e.g., *mái* "bury" and *sāi* "stuff") but not with others (e.g., *chōng* "rush" and *kuà* "cross")? Second, do the semantic roles of N in the two constructions differ?

3   Semantic Differences Between C1 and C2

Goldberg [16] proposed the semantic coherence principle in construction grammar: the meaning of a construction tends to be consistent with the semantics of its typical co-occurring verbs. This principle provides an operational method for exploring the meaning of constructions, that is, to generalize the meaning of the construction by analyzing the semantics of significant co-occurring verbs. As shown in Table 2, the significant co-occurring verbs of C1 are mostly manner-of-motion verbs (e.g., *chōng* "rush", *kuà* "cross", and *pǎo* "run"), representing the manner of motion conceptualization. Thus, the construction means the subject moving into a location in a certain manner, which belongs to the path schema. The significant co-occurring verbs of C2 are mostly non-motion verbs with the meanings of filling or containing (e.g., *mái* "bury", *sāi* "stuff", and *xiàn* "sink"), meaning that the subject enters a location and is contained or partially contained by that location, which belongs to the container schema.

3.1   Opposition of Verbs' [±Direction]

The opposing vector and scalar of verbs refer to the opposition of verbs' directional meanings. Vector verbs are those with directional meanings, while scalar verbs are the opposite. The opposition of directional meanings is formally manifested in the spatial and temporal opposition of their subsequent directional complements.

The academia generally recognizes that the grammatical meanings of directional complements include directional meaning, result meaning, and state meaning [18, 19]. The correspondence between meaning and form is also investigated [20, 21]. The paper is inspired by Xu's [21] method of distinguishing the semantic types of directional complements through the *lái/qù* "come/go" test: if "Vjìn" can simultaneously add *lái/qù*, then "Vjìn" indicates spatial directional meaning, and "Vjìn + lái/qù" also indicates spatial directional meaning; otherwise, it indicates non-spatial result or state.

The significant co-occurring verbs of C1 can generally add *lái/qù* "come/go", as shown in Table 3.

In C1, "Vjìn" indicates a spatial directional meaning, where *jìn* represents the movement direction from outside to inside. In contrast, the significant co-occurring verbs in C2 mostly cannot simultaneously add *lái/qù* "come/go" (see Table 4). In C2, "Vjìn" indicates a non-spatial result meaning, where *jìn* represents the result of the action as displacement into a three-dimensional place.

3.2   Opposition of Verbs' [±Action] and [±Result]

Zhang and Tan [22] discussed the syntactic and semantic features of resultative verbs based on the causal concept framework. They pointed out that resultative verbs are non-volitional verbs that produce certain objective results under specific causes, such as *guā*

Table 3. Co-occurrence of significant co-occurring verbs of C1 with *lái/qù* "come/go"

Significant co-occuring verbs	*lái* "come"	*qù* "go"
zhù "live"	*zhù jìn lái* "live in"	*zhù jìn qù* "live in"
chōng "rush"	*chōng jìn lái* "rush in"	*chōng jìn qù* "rush in"
kuà "cross"	*kuà jìn lái* "cross in"	*kuà jìn qù* "cross in"
tà "tread"	*tà jìn lái* "tread in"	*tà jìn qù* "tread in"
sòng "give"	*sòng jìn lái* "give"	*sòng jìn qù* "give"

Table 4. Co-occurrence of significant verbs in C2 with *lái/qù* "come/go"

Significant co-occuring verbs	*lái* "come"	*qù* "go"
fàng "put"	*fàng jìn lái* "put"	*fàng jìn qù* "put"
mái "bury"	**mái jìn lái* "bury"	*mái jìn qù* "bury"
tūn "swallow"	**tūn jìn lái* "swallow"	*tūn jìn qù* "swallow"
xiàn "sink"	**xiàn jìn lái* "fall into"	*xiàn jìn qù* "fall into"
xī "inhale"	**xī jìn lái* "suck in"	*xī jìn qù* "suck in"

"scratch". Additionally, they constructed a syntactic-semantic continuum of resultative verbs based on the strength of their action and result meanings.

We found that the significant co-occurring verbs in C1 are mostly action verbs, such as *chōng* "rush" and *liū* "slip". In contrast, the significant co-occurring verbs in C2 are mostly resultative verbs, such as *zhā* "prick" and *juǎn* "roll". Differing from Zhang and Tan [22], this paper further refines the resultative meaning of verbs to those related to space category, i.e., the result of the action is the deformation of an entity.

The concept of deformation comes from Liang's discussion of the shape category in Chinese [23]. She pointed out that the shape category belongs to the subcategory of Talmy's spatial configuration, which, along with the spatial orientation category and the position change category, constitutes a complete spatial structure. Spatial deformation includes the deformation of the object itself (e.g., expansion, contraction) and the configuration of the object's movement path, such as the path "a circle" in "the car runs a circle around the sports field", which depicts the shape of the path as "circular". Liang also discussed the word classes in Chinese that express configurational meaning, including shape nouns (e.g., *gùn* "stick"); geometric adjectives (e.g., *fāng* "square"); dimensional adjectives (e.g., *gāo* "high"); container classifiers (e.g., *xiāng* "box"); shape classifiers (e.g., *kē* "grain"); spatial adverb (e.g., *lǐ* "in"); deformation transitive verbs (e.g., *lǒng* "gather"); and path deformation verbs (e.g., *gǔn* "roll").

Deformation verbs are verbs that can depict the shape change of an object under the action of force, and they can take shape nouns as their objects. For example:

(6) Wǔ gè nǚháizi zhèngzài duī xuě rén.
Five-CL girl build snowman
"Five girls were making a snowman".

(7) Hóngqí zài chuāng zhǐ shàng chuō le gè xiǎo kǒng
Hong Qi ZAI window paper poke-LE-CL small hole
"Hong Qi poked a small hole in the window paper".

Among the top ten significant co-occurring verbs in C2, three belong to this category (e.g., zhā "prick", xiàn "sink", and mái "bury"), and we found more verbs with these characteristics among the non-top ten co-occurring verbs (e.g., qiā "pinch", guā "scratch", chuō "poke", kè "carve", etc.). The significant co-occurring verbs in C1 are mostly action verbs, whose core semantics are action behavior, expressing the manner of the subject's displacement movement, without deformation.

4   The Interaction Pattern Between the Spatial Roles of Verbs and the Arguments of Constructions

Cognitive linguistics posits that noun categories have spatial properties, while verb categories have temporal properties. Typically, nouns can be modified by quantifiers, and verbs have tense and aspect features. The academia generally explores the spatiotemporal characteristics of Chinese through language comparison [24–28] or specific linguistic phenomena [29–32] in terms of the spatiotemporal properties of nouns and verbs.

The spatial roles of verbs discussed here differ from the general sense of spatiality. Spatiality is related to the spatial domain. Langacker [15] pointed out that material substances mainly appear in space, and nouns are exemplified in the spatial domain, highlighting a region within that cognitive domain. Correspondingly, verbs highlight processes and are exemplified in the temporal domain. Thus, nouns are considered to have spatial properties, while verbs have temporal properties.

The spatial roles of verbs do not conflict with their temporality. Spatial roles refer to participate roles within the semantic framework of verbs with spatial properties. Many studies related to verbs' thematic roles are concerned with the spatial meaning of verbs. These include the determination and description of locative objects [33] and lexicalization patterns of paths [34]. However, these studies are limited to single phenomena and lack systematic argumentation. Therefore, we attempted to incorporate locative and path roles of verbs into their spatial role frames, systematically describing and discussing the interaction pattern between the spatial roles of verbs and the argument roles of the motion construction "N1 + Vjìn + N2".

4.1   The Spatial Roles of Verbs

The spatial role frame of verbs is based on the cognition of space category in the real world. Space category includes two subcategories: spatial region and spatial relation [13, 35]. Thus, the spatial roles of verbs include spatial regions and spatial relations. Spatial regions refer to the locations and scenes related to the actions indicated by the verbs, which can be the places where the actions occur or the spaces shaped by the actions.

Formally, these are expressed as the thematic roles of the objects being locative (e.g., *zhù bīnguǎn* "live in a hotel") or results of deformation (e.g., *chuō yígè dòng* "poke a hole"). Spatial relations refer to the movement features of the actions indicated by the verbs, specifically the direction and shape of the movement path.

Based on the analysis of the spatial roles of verbs above, the semantic features of the co-occurring verbs discussed are reclassified as shown in Fig. 2: the vector verbs and action verbs are spatial relation verbs, represented as $V_{spatial\ relation}$; deformation verbs are spatial region verbs, represented as $V_{spatial\ region}$.

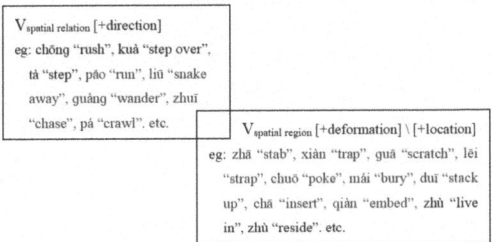

Fig. 2. Types of verbs' spatial roles

Based on the types of spatial roles of verbs, 188 co-occurring verbs were classified. The co-occuring tendencies of verbs with C1 and C2 are plotted by Chi.plot[1], based on the results from Coll.analysis 4.0, with X representing association strength (calculated by log odds ratio) and Y representing the logarithm of the co-occurring frequency of verbs in the two constructions.

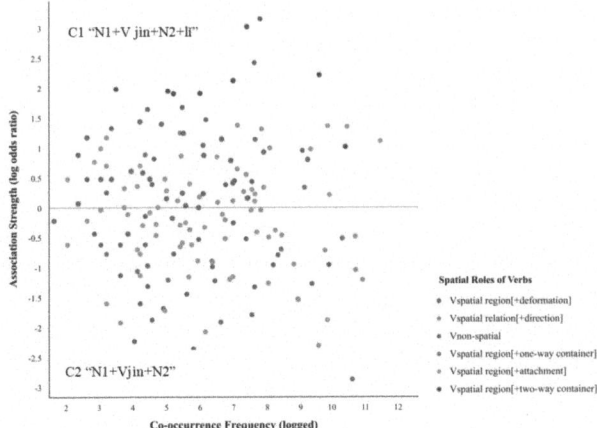

Fig. 3. The co-occuring tendencies of verbs with C1 and C2

---

[1] https:\\www.chiplot.online/.

According to Fig. 3, first, $V_{\text{spatial region}}$ [+deformation], $V_{\text{spatial region}}$ [+two-way container], and $V_{\text{spatial region}}$ [+attachment] tend to co-occur with C2. Second, $V_{\text{spatial relation}}$ [+direction] and $V_{\text{spatial region}}$ [+one-way container] tend to co-occur with C1. Third, verbs without spatial roles show randomness in their selection for the two constructions, with no obvious tendency.

The main difference between $V_{\text{spatial region}}$ [+one-way container] and $V_{\text{spatial region}}$ [+two-way container] is the possibility of the noun following the verb being construed as a container: $V_{\text{spatial region}}$ [+one-way container] indicates that the noun can only be construed as a container. $V_{\text{spatial region}}$ [+two-way container] indicates that the noun can be construed as either a container or a contained entity, such as the verb *róng* "dissolve".

If the container only serves as the object of the verb, the verb is a one-way container verb, such as *zhù* "live" and *duǒ* "hide". The container can be seen as the spatial region where the contained entity exists. The difference between $V_{\text{spatial region}}$ [+two-way container] and $V_{\text{spatial region}}$ [+one-way container] is reflected in the opposition between the spatiality and the entity nature of the object.

4.2   The Interaction Pattern Between Verbs and Constructions

It is demonstrated that there is a correlation between the spatial roles of verbs and the co-occurring constructions. However, how the spatial roles of verbs integrate with argument roles requires a comprehensive consideration of the differences in the construction' argument roles and the schematic features of *jìn*.

In C1, the semantic role of N is the endpoint, which relates to the path schema. The significant co-occurring items in C1 are mostly $V_{\text{spatial relation}}$ [+direction]. The directionality of the verb can activate the path schema, thus the spatial role of the verb integrates with the endpoint argument of C1, and N is naturally construed as the endpoint without the syntactic necessity of the locative word *lǐ*.

For another type of significant co-occurring verb in C1, $V_{\text{spatial region}}$ [+one-way container], when the action is placed in a movement scene, the spatial role [container] of the verb has conceptual similarity with the endpoint of the movement: the contained entity enters the container through actual movement. It can be said that the contained entity-container schema is a three-dimensional extension of the path-endpoint schema. In this case, the container can be metaphorically construed as the endpoint. Therefore, the spatial meaning related to unidirectional container verbs integrates with the endpoint argument of C1, and N is interpreted as the endpoint through conceptual metaphor, showing the non-syntactic necessity of the locative word *lǐ*. However, unlike $V_{\text{spatial relation}}$ [+direction], the metaphor is the cognitive basis for construing the container as the endpoint, thus emphasizing the similarity between the cognitive domains of the container and movement. Formally, this is reflected in the reduced actionality and increased continuity of $V_{\text{spatial region}}$ [+one-way container], mostly being durative verbs (e.g., *zhù* "live" and *cún* "store").

The essential feature of a locative is spatial containment, meaning that a locative, as a space, has the capacity to contain other entities [30]. In other words, the schema related to the locative role is the container schema.

It has been argued that the constructional meaning of C2 differs from C1 in that C2 emphasizes containment. Unlike C1, the semantic role of "N + lǐ" is not the endpoint but the locative. This seems consistent with previous research that the function of locative words is to spatialize categories. However, the function of *lǐ* here cannot be simply identified as spatialization. The spatialization theory attributes the use of *lǐ* to the nature of the noun head, but a significant drawback is that it cannot explain the selection tendency of verbs. Therefore, we point out that the omission of *lǐ* is driven by the different interaction patterns between the spatial roles of verbs and the locative role.

The first type of verbs tending to co-occur with C2 are $V_{\text{spatial region}}$ [+two-way container], which can activate the container schema but are bidirectional. Therefore, when interacting with the locative argument of C2, the word *lǐ* is needed to highlight the internal space of N, metonymically construing N as a container and thus as a locative.

The second type of verbs that tend to co-occur with C2 are $V_{\text{spatial region}}$ [+deformation]. Their most typical semantic feature is [+result], with participant roles being agent, patient, and its result. In combination with *jìn*, result is being contained by a space, and patient is the containing space. It can be seen that $V_{\text{spatial region}}$ [+deformation] itself cannot activate the container schema and requires a metaphor to link the result category with the spatial category to allow the patient to be interpreted as a locative. This cognitive process is formally expressed by the word *lǐ* which activates the container schema and establishes the association between result and containment to complete the metaphor.

The third type of verbs that tend to co-occur with C2 are $V_{\text{spatial region}}$ [+attachment]. According to Shao's definition of the spatial containment feature of locatives [30], attachment is a two-dimensional manifestation of spatial containment. The spatial role of $V_{\text{spatial region}}$ [+attachment] can integrate with the locative argument, formally expressed as an unmarked form, such as *shāfā fàng kètīng* "sofa placed in the living room". Therefore, the driving force for these verbs to co-occur with C2 is not spatialization but increasing the spatial dimension of N to meet the semantic requirements of *jìn*: *lǐ* transforms the spatial role of $V_{\text{spatial region}}$ [+attachment] from a two-dimensional plane into a three-dimensional container.

5 The Cognitive Motivation for the Omission of *Lǐ*: Transformation of Image Schemas

Based on the differences in the interaction patterns between *lǐ* and the spatial roles of verbs, *lǐ* has the function of cross-schema transformation. It is particularly noted that we are discussing tendencies. The path schema and *lǐ* are not mutually exclusive; under specific pragmatic forces, the path schema can also use *lǐ*. Therefore, what drives the co-occurrence of $V_{\text{spatial relation}}$ and "N + lǐ"?

When $V_{\text{spatial relation}}$ co-occurs with "N + lǐ", it indicates that the speaker conceptualizes the movement scene by shifting from a sequential scan of the movement path to an overall scan of the internal endpoint, transforming the scene's schema from a path to a container. This schema transformation is achieved by adding the explicit linguistic marker *lǐ* to profile the internal space of the endpoint, allowing the endpoint to be construed as a locative based on a part-whole metonymy. We refer to this as the cross-schema transformation function of *lǐ*.

For example, the former is a path schema (see Fig. 4a), and the latter combines path schema and container schema (see Fig. 4b).

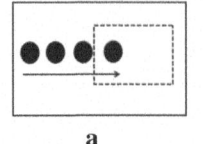   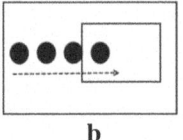

a   b

Fig. 4. a. The *zǒu jìn jiàoshì* schema; b. The *zǒu jìn jiàoshì lǐ* schema.

Figure 4a highlights the movement itself, which can be highly conceptualized to become a temporal reference point for another event, fitting into structures containing temporal reference points such as *as soon as* and *before*. Figure 4b highlights the position of the moving entity and cannot serve as a temporal reference point. For example:

(8) a.*Měidāng shàngkè de shíhou lǎoshī yī jìn zǒu jìn jiàoshì lǐ, tā jiù hǎn yī shēng "qǐlì".
    *Every time class DE time teacher one walk into classroom in he just shout one voice "stand up"
    "Every time when class is in session and the teacher walks into the classroom, he calls out 'stand up'."
    b. Měidāng shàngkè de shíhou lǎoshī yī jìn zǒu jìn jiàoshì, tā jiù hǎn yī shēng "qǐlì".
    Every time class DE time teacher one walk into classroom he just shout one voice "stand up"
    "Every time when class is in session and the teacher walks into the classroom, he calls out 'stand up'."

Additionally, in the path schema, *jiàoshì* "classroom" is abstracted as a point serving as the endpoint of the path, with its spatial containment attribute not highlighted. In some contexts, *jiàoshì* may not have any spatiality at all. However, the spatiality of *jiàoshì lǐ* "in the classroom" cannot be diminished. For example:

(9) a. *Ràng duōméitǐ jiàoxué zǒu jìn jiàoshì lǐ.
    *Let multimedia teaching walk into classroom in
    "Let multimedia teaching be integrated into the classroom."
    b. Ràng duōméitǐ jiàoxué zǒu jìn jiàoshì.
    Let multimedia teaching walk into classroom
    "Let multimedia teaching be integrated into the classroom."

In summary, when $V_{spatial\ relation}$ interacts with N, N is naturally construed as the endpoint, and the spatial containment feature of N is obscured. The speaker's attention is focused on the moving process, highlighting the path of movement. The path schema is further reinforced due to the strong directionality of $V_{spatial\ relation}$ and the feature of *jìn*. Therefore, the explicit marker *lǐ* is used to enhance the accessibility of the container schema, bringing the containment nature of N to the forefront and making it the focus of attention. At this point, the speaker's conceptualization process shifts from the path schema to the container schema.

6   Conclusion

Cognitive grammar posits that meaning is equivalent to the conceptual construal of objective scenes by cognitive subjects. Words are not merely bricks for building houses used only for combining or expressing complex meanings in constructions, but provide or activate channels to access related open knowledge domains [13].

Based on the classification of the spatial roles of co-occurring verbs discussed earlier, we identified two interaction patterns between verbs and C1 and C2. Pattern 1: When the spatial role of the verb is a spatial relation (i.e., $V_{spatial \; relation}$), the term can activate the path schema, tending to omit *lǐ*; Pattern 2: When the spatial role of the verb is a spatial region (i.e., $V_{spatial \; region}$), the term can activate the container schema, tending to highlight *lǐ*.

A particularly noteworthy issue is that, according to the basic viewpoint of cognitive grammar that terms can activate image schemas, theoretically, $V_{spatial \; region}$ should be able to activate the container schema without *lǐ* directly. However, the data shows a tendency for $V_{spatial \; region}$ to co-occur with *lǐ*, which we believe results from the dual schema characteristics of *jìn*.

Specifically, *jìn* itself can activate both path and container schema, leading to two results: First, the container activation ability of *jìn* makes N2 in both constructions have three-dimensional spatial characteristics. The difference between N2 and "N2 + lǐ" is that "N2 + lǐ" is a composite expression that enhances the prominence of N2 as a three-dimensional spatial locative [15]. Second, the constructional meaning of C1 is an entity displacement movement into space, with the movement direction specified as *jìn* (movement from outside to inside), and the semantic role of N2 is an endpoint. This indicates that the container schema of *jìn* is suppressed in C1; the constructional meaning of C2 is entity entering space and being contained by space, with "N2 + lǐ" being the spatial region where N1 is located after the movement ends, and its semantic role is locative. This indicates that the container schema of *jìn* is activated in C2.

Therefore, the co-occurring tendency of verbs results from the interaction between the spatial roles of verbs and the schemas of *jìn*. Specifically, when the spatial role of the verb is a spatial relation, it is easier to activate the path, which can integrate with the upper schema, completely suppressing the container schema of *jìn*. When the spatial role of the verb is a spatial region, it is easier to activate the container, conflicting with the upper schema. Using the container nature of *jìn*, N2 can be interpreted as a locative, but to counterbalance the stronger upper schema, the explicit container marker *lǐ* is added to strengthen the container schema. This interaction can be likened to a schema seesaw, where the path activated by the upper schema is the inherent weight, and to tilt the schema balance towards the container side, additional weight is added.

When the following N needs to be interpreted as a locative rather than an endpoint, it must rely on the explicit linguistic marker *lǐ*. When we replace *jìn* with *mǎn* "full", which cannot activate the path schema, we find that N2 strongly rejects the locative word, as in (10):

> (10) Mùliào duī mǎn le yuànzǐ *lǐ.
> Wood pile full LE courtyard *in
> "Wood is piled up all over the courtyard."

In summary, in the motion construction "Vjìn + N + (lǐ)", the conventional semantic role of N is the endpoint. Construing it as a locative is an unconventional marked expression. lǐ is the marker for converting the noun from an endpoint to a locative, and the cognitive basis for this conversion is the schema transformation mechanism of lǐ.

References

1. Qi, H.: The spatial system in Modern Chinese [现代汉语的空间系统]. Chin. Teach. World [世界汉语教学] **1**, 23–34 (1998). (In Chinese)
2. Fang, J.: Basic strategies in the cognitive process of spatial orientation reference in Chinese [论汉语空间方位参照认知过程中的基本策略]. Stud. Chin. Lang. [中国语文] **1**, 12–20 (1999). (In Chinese)
3. Guo, R.: The cognitive basis of Chinese local words "shang" "xia" and teaching Chinese language as a second language [方位词"上""下"的语义认知基础与对外汉语教学]. Appl. Linguist. [语言文字应用] **4**, 69–75 (2004). (In Chinese)
4. Tong, S.: The cognitive basis of "shang" as a noun of locality [也说方位词"上"的语义认知基础——兼与缑瑞隆先生商榷]. Appl. Linguist. [语言文字应用] **1**, 87–92 (2006). (In Chinese)
5. Fang, J.: Differentiation and grammaticalization of locative terms in modern Chinese [现代汉语方位成分的分化和语法化]. Chin. Teach. World [世界汉语教学] **2**, 5–15+2 (2004). (In Chinese)
6. Jiang, H.: Grammaticalization of "NP+shang" structure ["N+上"的语法化研究]. J. Guangxi Norm. Univ. (Philos. Soc. Sci. Ed.) [广西师范大学学报(哲学社会科学版)] **6**, 88–90 (2009). (In Chinese)
7. Chu, Z.: The omission of Chinese locatives in "zai (在) +locative phrases" [汉语"在+方位短语"里方位词的隐现机制]. Stud. Chin. Lang. [中国语文] **2**, 112–122+191 (2004). (In Chinese)
8. Wang, L.: A study on the omission rules of frame prepositions in Modern Chinese [现代汉语框式介词的隐现规律考察]. Ningxia Soc. Sci. [宁夏社会科学] **1**, 169–172 (2014). (In Chinese)
9. Luo, K.: Research on deletion of localizer in the structure "zai(在) + NP + localizer" in poetry [诗歌作品"在+N+方位词"中方位词删略现象研究]. TCSOL Stud. [华文教学与研究] **2**, 68–77 (2016). (In Chinese)
10. Yang, C.: The usage of localizers in Mandarin circumposition zai+NP+L [汉语框式介词"在+N+L"中方位词的隐现研究]. Foreign Lang. Res. [外文研究] **3**, 1–10+105 (2019). (In Chinese)
11. Gries, S., Stefanowitsch, A.: Extending collostructional analysis: a corpus-based perspective on "alternations." Int. J. Corpus Linguist. **9**(1), 97–129 (2004)
12. Lakoff, G.: Women, Fire, and Dangerous Things. The University of Chicago Press, Chicago (1987)
13. Langacker, R.W.: Foundations of Cognitive Grammar, vol. I. Theoretical Prerequisites. Stanford University Press, Stanford (1987)
14. Langacker, R.W.: Grammar and Conceptualization. Mouton de Gruyter, Berlin (1999)
15. Langacker, R.W.: Cognitive Grammar: A Basic Introduction. Oxford University Press, New York (2008)
16. Goldberg, A.E.: Constructions: A Construction Grammar Approach to Argument Structure. The University of Chicago Press, Chicago (1995)
17. Goldberg, A.E.: Constructions at Work: The Nature of Generalization in Language. Oxford University Press, Oxford (2006)

18. Chen, C.: Review on the nature of post-verb directional verbs [动后趋向动词性质研究述评]. Chin. Lang. Learn. [汉语学习] **2**, 41–43 (1994). (In Chinese)
19. Liu, Y.: A Comprehensive Explanation of Directional Complements [趋向补语通释]. Beijing Lang. Cult. Univ. Press, Beijing (1998). (In Chinese)
20. Fan, X.: A Grammar Perspective from Three Dimensions [三个平面的语法观]. Beijing Lang. Cult. Univ. Press, Beijing (1996). (In Chinese)
21. Xu, J.: Discussing the grammatical meaning of directional complements [也谈趋向补语的语法意义]. J. Ningxia Univ. (Human. Soc. Sci. Ed.) [宁夏大学学报(人文社会科学版)] (03), 62–65 (2011). (In Chinese)
22. Zhang, M., Tan, J.: The syntactic-semantic continuum and semantic change of result verbs [结果义动词的句法语义连续统及语义演变]. Chin. Lang. Learn. [汉语学习] 6, 41–48 (2022). (In Chinese)
23. Liang, Y., Sun, R.: A study on Chinese space category based on the space configuration theory [空间构形与汉语形状范畴]. Foreign Lang. Res. [外语学刊] **5**, 91–95 (2016). (In Chinese)
24. Wang, W.: On the trait of temporality in English and that of spatiality in Chinese [论英语的时间性特质与汉语的空间性特质]. Foreign Lang. Teach. Res. [外语教学与研究] **2**, 163–173+318 (2013). (In Chinese)
25. Zhang, Y.: The relationship between negation in thinking and temporal and spatial thinking in English and Chinese: evidences from English and Chinese negation words "not/no" and "bu/mei" [试论英汉否定思维与时空性思维的关系——来自英汉否定词"not/no"和"不/没"的证据]. J. Foreign Lang. [外国语(上海外国语大学学报)] **6**, 24–32 (2021). (In Chinese)
26. Sun, C., Zhang, H.: On the spatiotemporal idiosyncratic differences between English and Chinese [也谈英汉时空性特质差异]. Foreign Lang. Teach. [外语教学] 4, 14–19 (2021). (In Chinese)
27. Song, J., Wang, W.: Approaching the strong tendency to spatiality in Chinese classifiers from the perspective of classifier reduplication [论汉语量词重叠及其强空间性特征]. J. Shanghai Jiaotong Univ. (Philos. Soc. Sci. Ed.) [上海交通大学学报(哲学社会科学版)] **2**, 137–146 (2022). (In Chinese)
28. He, Q.: Progressive expression types in human languages and the discrepancies in temporality and spatiality [人类语言进行体表达式的类型及其时空性差异]. J. Foreign Lang. [外国语(上海外国语大学学报)] **46**, 2–16 (2023). (In Chinese)
29. Liu, S., Pan, W.: The influence of the syntactic location on the spatiality of nouns [句法位置对名词空间性的影响]. J. Huazhong Univ. Sci. Technol. (Soc. Sci. Ed.) [华中科技大学学报(社会科学版)] **1**, 38–43 (2007). (In Chinese)
30. Shao, J.: On categorization and the property of locative objects from a semantic and cognitive view [处所宾语的语义分类和认知属性]. Chin. Lang. Learn. [汉语学习] **5**, 104–112 (2012). (In Chinese)
31. Cao, Y., Tong, J.: Zero-verbal existential construction: Syntactic and semantic features and cognitive interpretation [零动词存在构式的句法语义特征及认知阐释]. Contem. Foreign Lang. Stud. [当代外语研究] **3**, 131–139 (2022). (In Chinese)
32. Yi, J., Qiu, B.: A cognitive semantic analysis of the spatial dimension adjective "Deep/Shallow" from the perspective of lexical typology. In: Dong, M., Hong, JF., Lin, J., Jin, P. (eds.) Chinese Lexical Semantics. CLSW 2023. Lecture Notes in Computer Science, vol. 14514. Springer, Singapore (2024). https://doi.org/10.1007/978-981-97-0583-2_24
33. Zhao, X.: Typical locative objects and atypical locative objects [典型处所宾语与非典型处所宾语]. Chin. Lang. Learn. [汉语学习] **3**, 103–112 (2013). (In Chinese)
34. Wu, J.: Reviewing the typological categorization of motion events in Chinese and English. [英汉运动事件的框架结构比较研究]. J. East China Univ. Sci. Technol. (Soc. Sci. Ed.) [华东理工大学学报(社会科学版)] (05), 103–109+116 (2015)
35. Talmy, L.: Toward a Cognitive Semantics. The MIT Press, Cambridge (2000)

Author Index

The manufacturer's authorised representative in the EU is Springer
Nature Customer Service Centre GmbH, Europaplatz 3, 69115 Heidelberg,
Germany. If you have any concerns regarding our products, please
contact ProductSafety@springernature.com

Printed and bound by CPI Group (UK) Ltd, Croydon, CR0 4YY

29/04/2026

02099551-0008